PERSONAL WRITINGS
BY WOMEN TO 1900

PERSONAL WRITINGS BY WOMEN TO 1900

A BIBLIOGRAPHY OF AMERICAN AND BRITISH WRITERS

COMPILED BY GWENN DAVIS AND BEVERLY A. JOYCE

UNIVERSITY OF OKLAHOMA PRESS : NORMAN

Library of Congress Catalog Card Number: 88-37865
ISBN: 0-8061-2206-4

Copyright © 1989 by Gwenn Davis and Beverly A. Joyce. Published in the
United States of America by the University of Oklahoma Press, Norman, Publishing
Division of the University. All rights reserved. Manufactured in Great Britain.
First University of Oklahoma Press edition, 1989.

First published in Great Britain by Mansell Publishing Limited, *A Cassell Imprint*, London.

CONTENTS

INTRODUCTION

Personal Writings by Women to 1900: A Bibliography of American and British Writers is designed to focus on American and British women's published accounts of their own experiences. This volume, the first of a series intended to make accessible a listing of literary works by women writers, well known and neglected, covers autobiographies, letters, diaries and travel literature. Later volumes will treat poetry, drama, short fiction, juvenile literature, and pseudonyms and alternative names. All have been developed from a complete reading of *The National Union Catalog, Pre-1956 Imprints* (NUC) and the catalog of the British Museum (now the British Library), Department of Printed Books, *General Catalogue of Printed Books* (BL), supplemented by the data base of the Online Computer Library Center (OCLC), other standard bibliographies and biographical dictionaries, and inspection of many of the works. The purpose of this series is to demonstrate something of the variety of women's literary activity before the twentieth century and to enable readers to find and rediscover their work. Each bibliography will present the writers in alphabetical order and an appendix will place them in order of publication date; it will also supply an index to types of works and topics appropriate to the genre under consideration. The individual volumes are intended to be useful on their own as guides to particular literary forms. Taken together as a series, they will permit their users to compare an individual author's work to others in a given genre as well as to see her full range of literary publications.

The total number of women's publications in NUC and BL is enormous. Romances, novels, and works on household management which are traditionally thought to constitute women's writings represent only a fraction of the works. Women wrote biographies and histories, joined nearly every religious and political controversy, published volumes of essays, and offered advice on spiritual and moral as well as domestic concerns. There is much more to be done in reestablishing a complete picture of women's publishing activity. This series, however, focuses on original, creative works in genres that have received little attention, literary forms that can begin to be addressed critically only after the extent of women's activity in them is known. Personal writing, as we define it here, covers a range of types and genres, from spiritual autobiographies to accounts of lawsuits, from explorations of the African continent to diaries of domestic life in villages. The main criteria are that these works represent women's accounts of their feelings and pursuits in their own words and that they appeared in printed books. These works are primary sources rather than critical or historical ones. We include autobiographies but not biographies, correspondence and travel letters but not epistles on moral or social issues, accounts of journeys but not guidebooks. The books cited here are often heterogeneous, but we believe that to be an accurate reflection of the ingenuity, diversity, and at times eccentricity of women's writings. The generic distinctions commonly used to describe male authors do not always encompass the variety of forms these women use, though some of these writings would qualify as autobiographies, memoirs or travel narratives as they are traditionally defined.

Autobiography as a form has received much recent attention, yet critics such as William C. Spengemann, James Olney, Susanna Egan and Janet Varner Gunn deal primarily with male writers. We hope this bibliography will expand the possibilities of research into women's autobiographical work. Women were not as a rule trained in classical rhetoric or schooled in traditional literary forms. As a result, their choices of genre are less bound by earlier models. Women's personal writings often have the texture, the range of tones of private conversations, and they combine different subjects in ways classically educated authors might not. While some of these writers were in public life and imagined for themselves a general audience, many more wrote for family and friends as if in confidence or at least in private. We list in the index two groups which do take conventional forms: spiritual autobiography which is confessional, private, and focused entirely on religious feelings; and autobiography which covers a greater variety of experiences, is usually narrative, retrospective, and intended for a particular audience. Frances Julia Pakenham's *Life lines; or, God's work in a human being* recounts the spiritual consolation she found in troubled times, while Mary Antoinette Doolittle's work covers her searchings and conversion to Shakerism. These, along with Minerva Hill's *Some of the most peculiar words which my holy Savior has said to me from time to time*, are quite distinct as a group. The autobiographies include such works as Frances Willard's *Glimpses of Fifty Years*, Matilda Betham-Edwards' *Reminiscences*, Emily Soldene's *My Theatrical and Musical Reminiscences* and Elizabeth (Grant) Smith's *Memoirs of a Highland Lady* which was written for her children.

These two classes have recognizable patterns and forms that can be set apart from the other personal writings, the more diffuse works that combine observations of historic events with comments on domestic arrangements or professions of religious faith with anecdotes of family history. Some works in this collection are quite straightforward, as Louisa Twining's *Recollections of Workhouse Visiting and Management during Twenty-five Years*; others are more fanciful, as Georgina Weldon's account of *The Ghastly Consequences of Living in Charles Dickens' House*. We have included these books as reflections on personal experience. Emily Lowe's *Unprotected Females in Norway*, for example, describes Scandinavian scenery and customs, supplies advice on budgets for the trip, and offers tart feminist commentary, "The only use of a gentleman in travelling is to look after the luggage, and we take care to have no luggage." Florence Marryat's *"Gup"* turns a satirist's eye on her compatriots' conduct in India, yet complains of feckless Indian servants. Some are moving accounts of a mother's or sister's last illness, others present harrowing stories of

shipwrecks, captivity among North American Indians, nursing wounded soldiers in Virginia or the Crimea; still others describe the quiet pleasures of people watching or nature study in rural settings. All of these works, whether traditional in form or not, represent women's own pictures of their lives.

In addition to works women writers saw through publication themselves, we have included memorial volumes. Collections of letters, diaries, etc. published after the author's death are listed so long as they incorporate a substantial amount of the woman's own writings and remarks. While many of these have been edited, especially the religious memoirs that reproduce excerpts of journals or memoranda as illustrations of the writer's devotion, they also present private reflections and personal statements. Memorial volumes comprise twelve percent of all the works here and cover the full range of personal writings. We have excluded biographies, those secondary materials which are interpretive and do not consist chiefly of the woman's own language and thoughts. We do include some family histories, such as Emily Pomeroy Dodge's *Anniversary Memorial*, a letter to her brothers recalling a family reunion and the deaths of their parents, and childhood memoirs which include stories told by other family members, but we exclude genealogies and histories of the author's birthplace or lineage. Similarly, we exclude purely didactic or pragmatic works such as Emily Peart's *A Book for Governesses by One of Them*. Letters of advice to young gentlewomen (or men), servants, etc. on manners and moral conduct, pamphlets on religious controversies or debates on doctrinal issues, and essays of an instructive character are not listed.

Travel literature is, however, an important form of personal writing, and may at times be a type of autobiography. Margaret Galletti di Cadhilac's *Our Home By The Adriatic* is the record of twelve years of her marriage to an Italian Count; Lady Charlotte Pepys' *A Journey on a Plank From Kiev to Eaux-Bonnes* deals as much with the discomforts of her invalid's coach as it does with the scenery of Russia. As with the other forms of personal writing, we exclude works of a purely scholarly or instructive nature, surveys of the topography, history or institutions of a country or region, for example, as well as guidebooks to towns, cathedrals, etc. which do not include accounts of personal travel. Close to half the works in this volume give some account of journeys, but less than twenty percent are strictly on tourism. The travel works, like the other autobiographical writings, often combine a variety of forms in one book reflecting the special character of the women's interests. They come from women who are now obscure as well as from the celebrated.

There are famous women here: the explorers Isabella Bird Bishop and Mary Kingsley; the American Civil War nurse and orator Mary Livermore; Catherine Parr, widow of Henry VIII; Jane Austen and Elizabeth Barrett Browning; Sarah Wakefield, a captive of the Sioux; Anna Leonowens, whose work became a Broadway musical; and Mary Anne Clarke, whose liaison with the Duke of York caused a political crisis. The majority, however, were not heroines, poets, victims, adventurers or wives of great men. Just as their individual works often combine travel to exotic places with domestic instruction or piety with gossip, their persona' writings considered together give a sense of the complexity of women's lives. Many were little known in their own day, and their experiences, had they not shared them in print, would have attracted no attention. Reading their work now gives a fresh image of people who were not the stereotypical angels in the house, chastened Cressidas or gentle tamers. Their works are rich in two ways: in the range of experiences they cover and in the variety of forms they take.

Most were solidly middle class. Only four percent were titled or lived in the highest social, diplomatic or political circles, while less than three percent were farm women, factory workers, servants and slaves. Black and native Americans, the working poor of London or Liverpool are sparsely represented. Of that great middle group, over half had the means to travel and to manage households with at least one in domestic help. The colonists, settlers and military wives generally had more servants and enjoyed a higher standard of living, if not of comfort, than they would have had at home. Missionaries, five percent of all listed here, had more prestige than their income would normally suggest. Nuns and governesses, about one percent, were of course less affluent than others of similar birth or upbringing. As a group, though, the majority are representative of the book buying public. They wrote for themselves, for their friends, their patrons, their grandchildren. Their readers would have found them much like their own circle of intimates.

Women's personal writings recreate in another way the history and development of commercial publication. Very few of these books, only one percent, appeared before 1700. The earliest works are predominately religious, spiritual autobiographies like Barbara Blaugdone's or advice like *The Countess of Lincoln's Nurserie*. The authors published modest but passionate testimony on their own behalf; editors and family members issued accounts of exemplary lives. About five percent belong to the eighteenth century. The majority of these works are journals and letters; many were edited and published by others. The correspondence between Sarah (Hagar) Osborn and Susanna Anthony, early American Quakers, and their diaries were issued after their deaths. Margaret Fox, wife of George Fox, appears in a memorial volume of her correspondence. Mary [Bosanquet] Fletcher, widow of a Methodist clergyman, published brief letters on her marriage and her faith, but most of her private writings, including her diary, were brought out in the early nineteenth century. A fairly small number of women actually saw their own works through the press in this period. Many more, women who had attained some reputation in their own circles, were commemorated by their ministers, friends or descendents.

Eighteenth century women left a more varied collection of works than their predecessors, and travel literature really begins with them though some of these accounts were not published at the time. Celia Fiennes, whose *Through England on a Side Saddle in the Time of William and Mary* is still well known, was not published until 1888, but Lady Mary Wortley Montagu's travel letters appeared in 1763, the year after her death. Sarah (Maese) Murray Aust published her travels in Scotland and the Lake district as a guide for others. Helen Maria Williams presented a political and social commentary with her tour to Switzerland; Emily Brittle, a young girl, saw publication of her travel notes in verse, *The India Guide*. Baroness Craven, later Margravine of Brandenburg, Anspach and Bayreuth, not only issued in 1789 the letters she wrote to her second husband while on a tour through the Crimea to Constantinople, but also wrote her own memoirs in 1826.

Personal writings in the eighteenth century range from well developed descriptions of the author's life and acquaintance to accounts of lawsuits and appeals for justice. Colley Cibber's daughter, Charlotte Charke, described her life in theatrical society. Elizabeth Cairns' memoir is a spiritual autobiography as is Elizabeth Wast's. Deborah (Sampson) Gannett, who served in the Continental Army disguised as a man, told her story in a speech to patriotic Americans and also in a memoir. Margaret Coghlan's recollections on the Revolutionary War, perhaps in some ways an answer to Gannett's, are "dedicated to the British nation." Mary Tonkin, an espionage agent of the British government, gives her account of spying on France in an indignant public appeal for the financial recognition she never received. Although their numbers are still relatively small, women who published personal accounts in the eighteenth century come from more diverse backgrounds. They demonstrate both an increasing consciousness of the power of the printed word and a greater awareness of their readers' interests.

The nineteenth century works, over ninety percent of this volume, encompass all the major forms of personal writing. Letters, journals, autobiography and travel literature occur throughout the period, though of course the volume of publication increases with time. Certain great historical events such as the American Civil War and the Sepoy Rebellion do inspire eyewitness accounts. Sarah Palmer nursed Union soldiers in Virginia, Elizabeth Collins spent the war on a Southern plantation; her fellow Confederate sympathizer, Sarah Giddings, found herself *In the Enemies' Land.* Perhaps the most moving account of the Indian Mutiny is the memorial volume of Rose Monckton's letters home. She remained at her husband's fort in Futtehgurh while foreseeing her final danger. Occasional writings comprise less than one percent of the total; though, of course, many other writers refer to important events in their journals and autobiographies. Towards the end of the nineteenth century, as transportation became more available and tourism assumed its modern importance as recreation and as a symbol of

prosperity, accounts of world tours, pilgrimages to the old country, and visits to the festivals of Bayreuth and Oberammergau increase. Despite these two trends, to occasional works and to tourists' diaries, there is no part of the age that does not offer a full range of personal writing.

Two groups of writers produced more works than might be expected given their numbers in the general population: missionaries and members of the Society of Friends. Quaker tradition emphasizes individual expression and from its inception has given women an equal place as ministers. Friends' meetings encourage public sharing of spiritual and social concerns, which probably accounts for the number of printed books by Quaker women. Missionary writing shows a strong sense of audience. From their posts in India, China, Africa, Samoa and other parts of the world remote to British and American parishioners, these women sent profiles of their converts and detailed accounts of the difficulties of maintaining familiar styles of domestic life. Missionary correspondents wrote to inspire larger donations and to reassure those at home of the worth of their undertakings. As a result, many of these works are less intimate than other kinds of personal writings.

Members of the aristocracy and wives of statesmen seldom published their own writings. The Marchioness of Dufferin and Ava recalled her experiences in Canada, and her two volume journal, *Our Viceregal Life in India*, gives, as the title suggests, a semi-official account. The Duchesses of Devonshire, Georgiana and Elizabeth, on the other hand, are represented in family papers collected a half century after Elizabeth's death. Two American Presidents' wives, Abigail Adams and Dolly Madison, appear in memorial collections of their papers. A few acquaintances of famous figures did record their own memories. Elizabeth Keckey, born a slave, later dressmaker and confidant to Mary Todd Lincoln, wrote an account soon after the American Civil War that remains an important historical source. Excerpts of correspondence of royal ladies from Elizabeth I to Princess Charlotte may be found here, but until Queen Victoria became an author, lending the highest respectability to travel and personal writings, few women of great position published. Below stairs exposés, glimpses of famous women by ordinary people which are now so common, are also relatively rare.

Other public women, actresses, concert artists, even well known writers also published personal material less extensively than they do today. Fanny Burney's memoirs are exceptional. Women writers in the great tradition, Jane Austen and George Eliot, are the subjects of carefully censored memorial volumes. Others, the prolific popular writers Sara Jane (Clarke) Lippincott and Florence Marryat, quite famous in their own time, wrote sketches of life abroad or reminiscences of specific periods in their lives rather than full scale autobiographies. Members of literary circles are remembered for their connections to literary men. The Countess of Blessington held conversations with Lord Byron; Thomas Carlyle prepared his wife Jane's papers for publication. Celebrity autobiographies, gossip or anecdotes of well known people do not appear in great numbers until the twentieth century. The audience may well have been there for books about the famous, but earlier standards of privacy and reticence prevented their appearance.

The act of publication in the nineteenth century shows some daring, some unconventionality, yet the women in this collection are not simply eccentrics. Some do use the power of the press to seek remedies. Elizabeth Packard wrote four strident protests at her confinement in an insane asylum and condemnations of the institution of marriage. But if she exemplifies one extreme, Maria Theresa Longworth is a more complicated case. Jilted by William Yelverton, heir to the Viscount Avonmore, she published their correspondence in her outrage at his betrayal. She also wrote three accounts of her travels to America and around the world which show her to be every bit as indefatigable a tourist and sharp a social critic as Frances Trollope. Martha Morgan indicts the Mormons for their treatment of women and gives one of the most important accounts of the trek West.

Ideal wives and mothers, angels in the house, appear in memorial volumes, yet not all compilers sought to present types of virtue. Mary Frampton's diary, edited by her niece, preserves comments on the great events of the day as well as on rural life. The collected papers of Mary Lyon, founder of Mount Holyoke College, show a tough minded advocate for the advancement of women. Stories of affliction, insanity and physical handicaps overcome by inner strength fascinated the Victorians as much as they do modern audiences. Ann Leak, born without arms, includes her trips to Australia and America in her autobiography. Her patience in suffering, stamina and curiosity make her a strong model.

Repentant prostitutes and convicts, traditional counterparts to the legends of good women and staple characters of the chapbooks, are here in very small numbers, less than one percent of the whole. One prostitute, Anon., bequeathed her cautionary tale to Thomas Skinner. Julia Johnstone, however, proudly defends herself against her rival Harriette Wilson. Margaret Leeson, another great courtesan, writes one of those rare gossipy autobiographies. Criminals, such as Ann Carson the bigamist, Bridget Dergan the murderer, and Mary Goodenough, executed in 1692, serve as warnings. Zilla Fitz-James, "the female bandit of the South West," offers a bit of adventure with her last words. These confessions, like the captivity narratives, the most sensational works in this volume, are most likely to be fictionalized. Katherine Evans and Sarah Cheevers sent their families authentic horrifying accounts of their persecution. On the other hand, Lucy (Brewer) West, who, having been seduced and abandoned, disguised herself as a man and served as a marine, cannot be reliably identified. Her story, versions of which were published as Louise Baker, Lucy Brewer and Eliza Webb, seems to contain an element of truth, but shows that the closer to conventional images of wicked women or female victims the account, the more likely it is to be fabricated or altered.

Pioneer women and settlers in all parts of the world illustrate the hardships of the frontier. Harriet Daly writes of "Digging, squatting, and pioneering" in Australia, Sarah Heckford of being "A lady trader in the Transvaal" and Annie Martin of ostrich farming in South Africa. Lois Lovina Murray combines her story of pioneer life in Kansas with sketches of the territory, its leading citizens, and notes on her favorite cause, the Temperance Movement. Miriam Colt found nothing worthy of such civic pride in that "fairyland" on the plains. Mrs. Edward Millet adds a guide for tourists and settlers to her story of five years as a chaplain's wife in Western Australia. Perhaps the most experienced settler was Mary Anne (Stewart) Broome whose books on sheep station life in New Zealand were succeeded by *A Year's Housekeeping in South Africa* and nine years later by an account of Australia. Most of the private journals of frontier women rediscovered in the past twenty years were not available to the writers' contemporaries. Those diaries, kept on isolated homesteads, have been preserved in family archives. The published volumes combine domestic detail with advice for prospective settlers, further demonstrating the increasing audience for these books.

Personal writings in the nineteenth century both contradict and confirm traditional views of womens' lives. Virtuous housewives, dedicated governesses and intrepid homesteaders are all here. Women who were moral leaders, keepers of community and domestic order, and advocates of the great causes of abolition, temperance and suffrage are here in force: Amelia Bloomer, Josephine Butler, Frances (Wright) D'Arusmont, Elizabeth Fry, Elizabeth (Cady) Stanton, Sojourner Truth, Angelina (Grimke) Weld, Frances Willard, Mary Wollstonecraft. Others, less well known, took their causes to new territory. The abolitionist and suffragist, Jane Swisshelm, was one of the early settlers of St. Cloud, Minnesota. Laura Haviland maintained a station on the Underground Railroad near the Canadian border. Others made fact finding tours, as Asenath (Hatch) Nicholson did to Ireland "for the purpose of personally investigating the condition of the poor." Some of the early nurses served at Gettysburg, Balaclava and Mashonaland; Dr. Elizabeth Blackwell opened the medical profession to women. Clergymen's wives combined community service with domestic duty. Women were leading Theosophists and Spiritualists. The Evangelists include Quaker ministers like Lydia Barclay and itinerant preachers like Jennie Smith. Hannah and Martha More took tracts to working class homes; Mary Merryweather set up a school in a silk mill.

As the educators and hospital workers demonstrate, not all the social activists were unpaid volunteers, ladies of leisure. Similarly, governesses and seamstresses were not the only women to earn their own livings. Louisa May Alcott and Charlotte Yonge supported their families by writing and were influential spokeswomen for moral causes and arbiters of literature for young minds. Emily Faithful was a publisher, Annie Dumond a book agent, and Eloise Abbott a bookseller as well as a teacher. Elizabeth Cochrane, better known as Nellie Bly, pioneered investigative journalism. These early career women combined social concern with employment.

Other women shared the nineteenth century interest in the natural world and the new disciplines of geography and sociology. Elizabeth Agassiz accompanied her husband to Brazil, Caroline David followed hers to the South Pacific, and Sarah (Wallis) Bowdich Lee finished her first husband's work on Madeira after his death. Emily Gosse studied the sea coast of southern England; Jane Mary Hayward observed the birds in her own country retreat. Still others analyzed the social customs of other cultures. Jane Smart's remarks on the Moors in India were published in 1743. Nearly every traveler who gained access to the harems of Arab countries wrote about them, and most writers comment on the condition of women in the places they visited. These writers were very much involved in the world around them as observers, commentators, and often as reformers.

The women who published personal writings were explorers, contemplatives, naturalists, preachers, nurses, musicians, housewives, poets, orators, teachers. While they held no elective posts and few were hereditary leaders, they witnessed, influenced and spoke out on the issues of their times. They visited every continent and informed their readers on the manners and conditions they found. For the most part, they were women of some privilege though most were not wealthy. As time went on the number of women who published their memoirs, diaries and travel experiences increased as did their sense of the requirements and interests of their audience.

The entries for this series of bibliographies were first developed by a complete reading of NUC and BL because they represent the most complete collections of works in English by American and British authors, and they offer the further advantage of guiding the reader to locations where the works may be seen. OCLC and other standard bibliographical and biographical sources were used to establish the most complete list possible. We have used other general sources, a selected list of which is supplied, to help in identifying and characterizing the works and to supply biographical background for the authors. In some cases the older sources, written before the canons of literature were established, have been most helpful because they treat authors who have since been forgotten. In other cases, more recent scholarship has supplied information not available in the earlier reference works. We also consulted more specialized sources for autobiographical and travel literature, a selected bibliography of which is included below. We plan a similar bibliography of specialized sources for each volume of this series. We have found, however, only a handful of personal works listed in sources such as Kaplan or Matthews that are not in NUC, BL or OCLC. We have cited in the entries standard, widely available bibliographies which readers may wish to consult, and a list of the abbreviations for them is given. Finally, we saw about half the works included here in order to be sure they fit the parameters of this volume, and we examined others that we excluded.

In reading the catalogs to develop the materials for this series we established only a few guidelines for exclusion. We chose to end our collection with the nineteenth century, as more work has been done and more resources are available for twentieth century writers. We realize that some works by earlier writers were not published until the twentieth century, but the volume of information we had was so large, that we chose to confine ourselves to works that were available to readers before 1900. We looked for original literary works, not scholarly works or practical works such as Elstob's Anglo-Saxon grammars or Mrs. Beeton's cookbooks. We excluded materials in translation, periodical publications unless they were later collected in a book, and manuscripts. Having collected this information, we separated it by genre in several ways. We used reference works such as the ones listed in our bibliography, library classifications, publishers' descriptions and advertisements, biographies and literary criticism. We also read a large number of the works themselves. In preparing this volume we further applied the guidelines listed above. NUC, BL and OCLC doubtless do

not hold every book ever printed and tired eyes have undoubtedly missed some works, but we hope we have provided as full a listing within these guidelines as possible. This is not intended to be an analytic or descriptive bibliography. The scope of the entire series is too great to permit full annotation of each entry. We provide instead brief notes intended to clarify the character of the work if that is not made evident by its full title and subtitle.

The entries in *Personal Writings* supply for each author the following information: her name, following the way it is listed in NUC; her husband's name; nationality; birth and death dates where known; alternative forms of her legal name under which she published or was known; and pseudonyms under which she published personal writings. Birth names are placed in parentheses. Where a birth name is known and the husband's name is not, the title, Mrs., is omitted. Where the birth name is not clear, we do supply the title Mrs. In cases where the woman is identified only by initials which may be either hers or her husband's, we also place the title, Mrs., after the proper name. We list all known forms of a woman's legal name(s) as alternative names. For example, Florence (Marryat) Church Lean, who published under her birth name and both married names, is listed as:

LEAN, Florence (Marryat) Church, Mrs. Francis Lean [Br. 1837–1899] ALT: Church, Mrs. Ross; Marryat, Florence

She is cross-referenced under both Church and Marryat. Complete cross listings are also given for all forms of an author's real name. Pseudonyms used in other literary genres are not listed in this volume. So, for example, Anna Cummings Johnson, who published travel literature under the pseudonym, A Lady, and essays and poetry under the pseudonym, Minnie Myrtle, is identified as:

JOHNSON, Anna Cummings, Miss [Am. 1818–1892] PSEUD: Lady, A.

In the later volume of poetry she will be identified and cross-indexed as: Minnie Myrtle, pseud. and in the dictionary of pseudonyms and alternative names will be listed both ways. We have followed

NUC for the form of proper names except for a few cases where BL has more complete information. So, for example, Lady Eastlake is listed as: Eastlake, Elizabeth (Rigby), Lady and is cross-indexed under Rigby where she appears in BL. Janetta (Hughan) Manners, Duchess of Rutland, is listed as Rutland, Janet (Hughan) Manners, Duchess of, and cross-referenced as Manners, following NUC rather than BL style. Editors and compilers are also cross-referenced to their subjects.

Memorial volumes are listed under the subject's name as the primary entry even though they may appear under the editor or compiler's name in NUC and BL. So, although BL lists Margaret Newlin's biography of Mary Ann Longstreth under Newlin, in our bibliography it appears as:

LONGSTRETH, Mary Ann [Am. 1811–1884]
Memoir of Mary Ann Longstreth by an old pupil, Margaret Newlin
Philadelphia: J. B. Lippincott co., 1886. 224p.
BL NUC OCLC
[Includes excerpts from journals; trip to Europe in 1853]

A cross-reference from Newlin will direct the reader to Longstreth. We have reversed the practice of the catalogs in order to provide an alphabetical listing of the women whose personal writings are the subject of this volume. In the case of multiple authorship, works are listed under the name of the woman who appears first on the title page of the book and cross-references are given from all known forms of the names of the co-authors.

For each work we list the title, the name or pseudonym under which it was written where this differs from the author entry, co-authors, place, publisher, date of first publication, page numbers, and catalog(s) in which it was found. Information from multiple sources is merged to form the most complete entry possible. Lean's two travel works appear as:

"Gup." Sketches of Anglo-Indian life and character. Pub. as: Mrs. Ross Church
L: Richard Bentley, 1868. 284p. NUC BL OCLC
[Seven years' experiences as Army wife]

– – – – – Tom Tiddler's ground.
L: S. Sonnenschein, Lowrey & co., 1886. 212p.
NUC BL OCLC
[Travel: U.S. & Canada]

The second work was published as Lean, while the first appeared under Church.

We try whenever we can to present the information in its fullest possible form. Any omissions within the entries indicate that the information was unavailable. We print, in most cases, the full title, as this often gives the character and flavor of the work. We do omit information not relevant to the primary work, as, for example, lists of appendices. We list compilers and editors, but not illustrators. Cross-references are also supplied from all known forms of the legal name for all co-authors, editors, and compilers. Wherever possible we give full names rather than initials in both entries and cross-references. We do use a few standard abbreviations (L for London, NY for New York, and U.S. for United States) within the entries. We also supply standard abbreviations of U.S. states as part of the place of publication, except for cities (Philadelphia or Chicago, for example) whose location is well known.

The appendix is a chronological listing and sets the writers into their appropriate general time frame. The list is divided by century to 1700, by half century for the eighteenth and by quarter century for the nineteenth century. Because a number of works were published long after the woman's death, we place names in parentheses to indicate posthumous publication. Writers who were not published during the time period that includes their date of death are listed there with an asterisk preceding their names as well as in parentheses in the time period of publication. So, Maria Edgeworth, who died in 1849, is entered as: *Edgeworth in the period 1826–1850 and as (Edgeworth) in the periods 1851–1875 and 1876–1899 when her personal writings were issued. The appendix is simply intended as a guide to life span and dates of publication. As we use the date of death in assigning a writer to a given period, some women may appear in a period later than their time of greatest activity. So, Elizabeth I, who died in 1603, is listed under the period 1600–1699 even though she is generally regarded as a sixteenth century figure.

Exact dates of publication and precise dates of birth and death where known may be found in the main entries.

The index is intended to refer readers to general topics and types of works. We have used entry numbers, as many writers' work takes a variety of forms and deals with several topics. We have tried to group works rather than to enumerate every possible subject or class. For example, governesses, school teachers, and founders of educational institutions are listed as Educators; opera singers and concert pianists are classed as Musicians. We cover five broad types of common themes or subjects: occupations (Musicians, Educators, Social workers); geographic locations (Scotland, India, Africa); personal convictions (Spiritualists, Social reformers); types of experiences (Captivity narratives, Illnesses, World tours); and types of works (Spiritual autobiographies, Childhood reminiscences, Memorial volumes). Cross-references will direct the reader from particular categories to the general ones, as from "Actresses" to "Theatres and theatrical life" or from "Abolitionists" to "Social reformers."

Individual works may be listed in several categories. "Gup," for instance, is cited both as "Military life" and under "India." We have tried to avoid duplication of places, however. A grand tour of the European continent will be cited under "Europe," while a trip to Switzerland appears under "Switzerland" but not again under "Europe." In order to provide an overview of the types and formats of the works in this volume, we have provided some general classifications. Many works might be designated as letters, but we have distinguished between "Correspondence" (familiar letters between family members, friends or literary acquaintances) and letters of travel which appear only under the geographical designation and/or types of experiences. So, *Letters from Oberammergau* would be cited under "Germany" and "Festivals and fairs" but not under "Correspondence." Similarly, "Spiritual autobiographies" are not listed again under "Autobiographies;" posthumous collections of letters edited by others would be listed under "Memorial volumes" and "Correspondence."

We have not tried to indicate in this volume all the other literary activities of these writers. Florence Lean's plays and fiction which she published under her birth name, Marryat, will appear in the appropriate volumes, and the dictionary of pseudonyms and alternative names will direct readers to each genre. We hope this first volume will stand on its own as a resource for the study of women's personal writings and that later, taken together with the other volumes, it will give readers an overview of individual women's creative work.

Finally, we would like to thank some people whose help has been invaluable, chief among them Wayne Joyce. Judith Coker, Daryl Morrison and Kristy Wallisch gave able research assistance, and Sheila Leppert entered the entire volume on a data base. We would also like to thank Professor George Economou, Dean Kenneth Hoving and the Faculty Research Council of the University of Oklahoma for financial support crucial to completing this volume, and the National Endowment for the Humanities for A Travel to Collections grant.

The librarians and staff of the Library of Congress and the British Library have been models of patience and resourcefulness. We would also like to thank for their special assistance the librarians of: Boston Public Library, Buffalo and Erie County Public Library, Case Western Reserve University Library, Chicago Historical Society, Cornell University, Duke University, Friends Historical Library of Swarthmore College, John Hay Library, Brown University, The Houghton, Law School and Harvard College Libraries of Harvard University, Huntington Library, Library Company of Philadelphia, Newberry Library, New York Public Library, Pitt's Theology Library, Emory University, Princeton University Library, Rutgers University Library, University of British Columbia Library, University of Kansas Libraries, University of Oregon Library, University of Pennsylvania Library, University of Virginia Library and Yale University Library.

SELECTED SOURCES

GENERAL

Adams, Oscar. *A Dictionary of American Authors*. 6th ed. Boston: Houghton, 1904. Repr. Detroit, MI: Gale, 1969.

Adburgham, Alison. *Women in Print: Writing Women and Women's Magazines from the Restoration to the Accession of Victoria*. London: Allen, 1972.

Adelman, Joseph. *Famous Women*. New York: Lonow, 1926.

Alexander, William. *The History of Women from the Earliest Antiquity: Giving Some Account of Almost Every Interesting Particular Concerning That Sex, Among All Nations Ancient and Modern*. 2 vols. London: Strahan, 1779.

Allibone, S. Austin. *A Critical Dictionary of English Literature and British Authors*. 3 vols. Philadelphia: Lippincott, 1889.

American Authors 1600–1900. Ed. Stanley J. Kunitz and Howard Haycraft. New York: Wilson, 1938.

American Women Writers: Bibliographical Essays. Ed. Maurice Duke, Jackson R. Bryer, and M. Thomas Inge. Westport, CT: Greenwood, 1983.

American Women Writers: A Critical Reference Guide from Colonial Times to the Present. 4 vols. Ed. Lina Mainiero. New York: Ungar, 1979.

American Writers Before 1800: A Biographical and Critical Dictionary. Ed. James A. Levernier and Douglas R. Wilmes. Westport, CT: Greenwood, 1983.

Amory, Thomas. *Memoirs of Several Ladies of Great Britain*. 2 vols. London: Noon, 1775.

Authors of the Nineteenth Century. Ed. Stanley J. Kunitz and Howard Haycraft. New York: Wilson, 1936.

Baker, Ray Palmer. *History of English-Canadian Literature to the Confederation. Its Relation to the Literature of Great Britain and the United States*. New York: Russell, 1920.

Bald, Marjory A. *Woman Writers of the Nineteenth Century*. Cambridge: Cambridge UP, 1928.

Ballard, George. *Memoirs of British Ladies, Who Have Been Celebrated for Their Writings or Skill in the Learned Languages, Arts and Sciences*. London: Evans, 1775.

Baskervill, William Malone. *Southern Writers: Biographical and Critical Studies*. Nashville, TN: M. E. Church, South. 1902–1903.

Betham, Mary Matilda. *A Biographical Dictionary of the Celebrated Women of Every Age and Country*. London: Crosby, 1804.

The Biographical Cyclopaedia of American Women. Comp. Mabel Ward Cameron and Erma Conckling Lee. New York: Halvord, 1924. Repr. Detroit, MI: Gale, 1974.

Biographium Femineum. The Female Worthies: or, Memoirs of the Most Illustrious Ladies of All Ages and Nations. 2 vols. London: S. Crowder, 1766.

Black, Helen C. *Notable Women Authors of the Day*. Glasgow: Bryce, 1893.

Blanck, Jacob N. *National Bibliography of American Literature*. New Haven, CT: Yale UP, 1955.

Boase, Frederic. *Modern English Biography, containing . . . many concise memoirs of persons who have died since . . . the year 1850 . . . with an index of the most interesting matter*. 6 vols. Truro: Netherton, 1892–1921.

British Authors Before 1800: A Biographical Dictionary. Ed. Stanley J. Kunitz and Howard Haycraft. New York: Wilson, 1952.

British Museum. Department of Printed Books. *General Catalogue of Printed Books*. Photolithographic edition to 1955. London: Trustees, 1959–66.

The Cambridge History of American Literature. Ed. William Peterfield Trent et al. New York: Macmillan, 1944.

The Cambridge History of English Literature. Ed. A. W. Ward and A. R. Waller. New York: Putnam's, 1907–17.

Casey, Elizabeth. *Illustrious Irishwomen*. 2 vols. London: Tinsley, 1887.

Chambers, Robert. *A Biographical Dictionary of Eminent Scotsmen*. New ed. Rev. by Thomas Tomson. 3 vols. London: Blackie, 1870.

Costello, Louisa Stuart. *Memoirs of Eminent Englishwomen*. 4 vols. London: Bentley, 1844.

Crone, John S. *A Concise Dictionary of Irish Biography*. Dublin: Talbot, 1928.

Davidson, James Wood. *The Living Writers of the South*. New York: Carleton, 1869.

Derby, J. C. *Fifty Years Among Authors*. Hartford, CT: Winter, 1886.

Dictionary of American Biography. Ed. Allen Johnson et al. 11 vols. New York: Scribner, 1946–58.

Dictionary of National Biography. Ed. Sir Leslie Stephen and Sir Sidney Lee. 22 vols. London: Oxford UP, 1921–22.

Dictionary of Welsh Biography Down to 1940. London: Honourable Society of Cymmrodorian, 1959.

Duyckinck, Evert Augustus and George Long. *Cyclopedia of American Literature*. 2 vols. New York: Scribner, 1835.

The Europa Biographical Dictionary of British Women. Ed. Anne Crawford et al. Detroit, MI: Gale Research Co., 1983.

Fullerton, Bradford Morton. *Selective Bibliography of American Literature 1775–1900*. New York: Payson, 1932.

The General Biographical Dictionary. . . . Ed. Alexander Chalmers. 32 vols. London: Nichols, 1912–17.

Griswold, Rufus Wilmot. *The Prose Writers of America 1815–1857*. Philadelphia: Coates, 1870.

Hale, Sarah Josepha Buell. *Woman's Record; or Sketches of All Distinguished Women from "The Beginning," till A.D. 1850*. New York: Harper, 1853.

Hamilton, Catherine. *Women Writers: Their Works and Their Ways*. 1st Ser. Freeport, NY: Books for Libraries, 1971.

Hart, John Seely. *Female Prose Writers in America*. Philadelphia: Butler, 1851.

Hays, Mary. *Female Biography; or Memoirs of Illustrious and Celebrated Women of All Ages and Countries*. 3 vols. London: Phillips, 1803.

Higginson, Thomas Wentworth. *Contemporaries*. Boston: Houghton, 1900.

Highfill, Philip H., Sr., Kalman A. Burnim and Edward A. Langhans. *A Biographical Dictionary of Actors, Actresses, Musicians, Dancers, Managers and other Stage Personnel in London 1660–1800*. 4 vols. Carbondale, IL: Southern Illinois UP, 1973.

Hill, Georgiana. *Women in English Life*. 2 vols. London: Bentley and Son, 1896.

Hogrefe, Pearl. *Tudor Women: Commoners and Queens*. Ames, IA: Iowa State UP, 1975.

The International Dictionary of Women's Biography. Comp. and ed. Jennifer S. Uglow. New York: Continum, 1982.

James, Edward T., et al. *Notable American Women: A Biographical Dictionary*. 3 vols. Cambridge, MA: Belknap Press of Harvard UP, 1971.

Johnstone, Grace. *Leading Women of the Restoration*. London: Digby, 1892.

Kavanagh, Julia. *English Women of Letters*. 2 vols. London: Hurst, 1863.

Lauterbach, Edward S. and W. Eugene Davis. *The Transitional Age: British Literature 1880–1920*. Troy, NY: Whitston, 1973.

Lee, Anna Maria. *Memoirs of Eminent Female Writers*. Philadelphia: Desilver, 1827.

Meyer, G. D. *The Scientific Lady in England 1650–1760*. Berkeley, CA: U of California P, 1955.

Miller, Elizabeth W. *The Negro in America: A Bibliography Compiled by Elizabeth W. Miller for the American Academy of Arts and Sciences*. Cambridge, MA: Harvard UP, 1966.

Moers, Ellen. *Literary Women: The Great Writers*. Garden City, NY: Doubleday, 1976.

Moore, Virginia. *Distinguished Women Writers*. New York: Dutton, 1934.

National Union Catalog. Pre-1956 Imprints. London: Mansell, 1968–81.

OCLC (Online Computer Library Center). Dublin, OH: 1967–.

The Oxford History of English Literature. Ed. T. P. Welson and Bonamy Dobrée. Oxford: Oxford UP, 1944–.

Reynolds, Myra. *The Learned Lady in England*. Boston: Houghton, 1920.

Ross, Ishbel. *Ladies of the Press; the Story of Women in Journalism by an Insider, Ishbel Ross*. New York: Harper Brothers, 1936.

Rothstein, Pauline Marcus. "Women: A Selected Bibliography of Books." *Bulletin of Bibliography* 32 (1975): 45–54.

Rowbotham, Sheila. *Hidden From History: Rediscovering Women in History from the 17th Century to the Present*. New York: Pantheon, 1973.

Shirley, J. *The Illustrious History of Women*. London: Harris, 1686, 1702.

Showalter, Elaine. *A Literature of Their Own*. Princeton, NJ: Princeton UP, 1977.

Sims, Janet. *The Progress of Afro-American Women: A Selected Bibliography and Resource Guide*. Westport, CT: Greenwood, 1980.

Spacks, Patricia Meyer. *The Female Imagination*. New York: Knopf, 1975.

Stonehill, Charles A. and Helen W. *Bibliographies of Modern Authors*. 2nd ser. London: Castle, 1972.

Tobin, James E. *Eighteenth Century English Literature and Its Cultural Background*. New York: Fordham UP, 1939.

Todd, Janet, ed. *A Dictionary of British and American Women Writers 1660–1800*. Totowa, NJ: Rowman, 1986.

Wages, Jack D. *Seventy-four Writers of the Colonial South*. Boston: Hall, 1979.

Wallas, Ada. *Before the Bluestockings*. New York: Lane, 1910.

Watson, George. *The New Cambridge Bibliography of English Literature*. 3 vols. Cambridge: Cambridge UP, 1969.

Wheeler, Ethel Rolt. *Famous Blue Stockings*. New York: Lane, 1910.

Whiting, Lilian. *Women Who Have Ennobled Life*. Philadelphia: Union, 1915.

Williams, Ora. *American Black Women in the Arts and Social Sciences: A Bibliographic Survey*. Rev. and expanded ed. Metuchen, NJ: Scarecrow, 1978.

Wright, Richardson L. *Forgotten Ladies*. Philadelphia: Lippincott, 1928.

Wright, Thomas. *Womankind in Western Europe*. London: Groombridge, 1869.

SPECIALIZED

American Social History As Recorded by British Travellers. Comp. and ed. Alan Nevins. New York: Holt, 1931.

Arksey, Laura, Nancy Pries and Marcia Reed. *An Annotated Bibliography of Published American Diaries and Journals*. Detroit, MI: Gale, 1983.

Bates, Ernest Stuart. *Inside Out: An Introduction to Autobiography*. 1st Am. ed. New York: Sheridan, 1937.

Beard, Mary R. *America Through Women's Eyes*. New York: Macmillan, 1934.

Blasing, Mutlu Konuk. *The Art of Life: Studies in American Autobiographical Literature*. Austin, TX: U of Texas P, 1977.

Brignano, Russell C. *Black Americans in Autobiography: An Annotated Bibliography of Autobiographies and Autobiographical Books Written Since the Civil War*. Durham, NC: Duke UP, 1974.

Brockett, L. P., M.D. and Mrs. Mary C. Vaughan. *Woman's Work in the Civil War: A Record of Heroism, Patriotism and Patience*. Philadelphia: Zeigler, 1867.

Brooks, John Graham. *As Others See Us: A Study of Progress in the United States*. New York: Macmillan, 1910.

Bruss, Elizabeth W. *Autobiographical Arts: The Changing Situation of a Literary Genre*. Baltimore, MD: John Hopkins UP, 1976.

Burr, Anna R. *The Autobiography: A Critical and Comparative Study*. Boston: Houghton, 1909.

Butterfield, Stephen. *Black Autobiography in America*. Amherst, MA: U of Massachusetts P, 1974.

Clark, Arthur Melville. *Autobiography: Its Genesis and Phases*. Edinburgh: Oliver, 1935.

Clark, Thomas D., ed. *Travels in the New South: A Bibliography*. 2 vols. Norman, OK: U of Oklahoma P, 1962.

Clark, Thomas D., ed. *Travels in the Old South: A Bibliography*. 3 vols. Norman, OK: U of Oklahoma P, 1956.

Cockshut, A. O. J. *The Art of Autobiography in Nineteenth and Twentieth Century England*. New Haven, CT: Yale UP, 1984.

Cooley, Thomas. *Educated Lives: The Rise of Modern Autobiography in America*. Columbus, OH: Ohio State UP, 1976.

Coulter, E. Merton. *Travels in the Confederate States: A Bibliography*. Norman, OK: U of Oklahoma P, 1948.

Couser, G. Thomas. *American Autobiography: The Prophetic Mode*. Amherst, MA: U of Massachusetts P, 1979.

Delany, Paul. *British Autobiography in the Seventeenth Century*. London: Routledge, 1969.

The Discoverers: An Encyclopedia of Explorers and Exploration. Ed. Helen Delpar. New York: McGraw, 1980.

Egan, Susanna. *Patterns of Experience in Autobiography*. Chapel Hill, NC: U of North Carolina P, 1984.

Faragher, John Mack. *Women and Men on the Overland Trail*. New Haven, CT: Yale UP, 1979.

The Female Autograph. New York Literary Forum, Ed. Donna C. Stanton and Jeanine Parisier. Vols. 12–13. New York: New York Literary Forum, 1984.

Forbes, Harriette Merrifield. *New England Diaries 1602–1800: A Descriptive Catalogue of Diaries, Orderly Books and Sea Journals*. Topham, MA: priv. pr., 1923.

Gunn, Janet Varner. *Autobiography: Toward a Poetics of Experience*. Philadelphia: U of Pennsylvania P, 1982.

Jeffrey, Julie Roy. *Frontier Women: The Trans-Mississippi West 1840–1880*. New York: Hill, 1979.

Jelinek, Estelle C., ed. *Women's Autobiography: Essays in Criticism*. Bloomington, IN: Indiana UP, 1980.

Kaplan, Louis, et al, comps. *A Bibliography of*

American Autobiographies. Madison, WI: U of Wisconsin P, 1961.

Lee, L. L. and Merrill Lewis, eds. *Women, Women Writers, and the West*. Troy, NY: Whitston, 1980.

Matthews, William, comp. *American Diaries: An Annotated Bibliography of American Diaries Written Prior to the Year 1861*. Berkeley, CA: U of California P, 1945.

Matthews, William, comp. *British Autobiographies: An Annotated Bibliography of British Autobiographies Published or Written Before 1951*. Berkeley, CA: U of California P, 1955.

Matthews, William, comp. *British Diaries: An Annotated Bibliography of British Diaries Written Between 1442 and 1942*. Berkeley, CA: U of California P, 1950.

Matthews, William, comp. *Canadian Diaries and Autobiographies*. Berkeley, CA: U of California P, 1950

Matthews, William. "Seventeenth Century Autobiography." *Autobiography, Biography and the Novel*. Papers read at a Clark Library Seminar, May 13, 1972. Berkeley, CA: U of California P, 1973.

Mehlman, Jeffrey. *A Structural Study of Autobiography*. Ithaca, NY: Cornell UP, 1955.

Mesick, Jane Louise. *The English Traveller in America 1785–1835*. New York: Columbia UP, 1922.

Middleton, Dorothy. *Victorian Lady Travellers*. New York: E. P. Dutton, 1965.

Morris, John N. *Versions of the Self*. New York: Basic, 1966.

Nevins, Allan, ed. *America Through British Eyes*. Rev. ed. New York: Oxford UP, 1948.

Nineteenth-Century Theatrical Memoirs. Comp. Claudia D. Johnson and Vernon E. Johnson. Westport, CT: Greenwood, 1982.

Olney, James, ed. *Autobiography: Essays Theoretical and Critical*. Princeton, NJ: Princeton UP, 1980.

Olney, James. *Metaphors of Self: The Meaning of Autobiography*. Princeton, NJ: Princeton UP, 1972.

O'Neill, Edward. *Biography by Americans 1658–1936. A Subject Bibliography*. Boston: Gregg, 1972.

Peterson, Linda H. *Victorian Autobiography: The Tradition of Self-Interpretation*. New Haven, CT: Yale UP, 1986.

Pilling, John. *Autobiography and Imagination: Studies in Self-Scrutiny*. London: Routledge, 1981.

Pinto, Vivian A. Da Solo. *Introduction to English Biography in the Seventeenth Century*. London: Harrap, 1951.

Ponsonby, Arthur, comp. *English Diaries*. London: Methuen, 1922.

Ponsonby, Arthur, comp. *More English Diaries*. London: Methuen, 1927.

Ponsonby, Arthur, comp. *Scottish and Irish Diaries*. London: Methuen, 1927.

Reed, Joseph W., Jr. *English Biography in the Early Nineteenth Century 1801–1838*. New Haven, CT: Yale UP, 1966.

Shea, Daniel B. *Spiritual Autobiography in Early America*. Princeton, NJ: Princeton UP, 1968.

Shumaker, Wayne. *English Autobiography: Its Emergence, Materials, and Form*. Berkeley, CA: U of California P, 1954.

Smith, D. Nichol. *Characters from the Histories and Memoirs of the Seventeenth Century*. Oxford: Clarendon, 1918.

Spacks, Patricia Ann Meyer. *Imagining a Self: Autobiography and Novel in Eighteenth Century England*. Cambridge, MA: Harvard UP, 1972.

Spengemann, William C. *The Forms of Autobiography: Episodes in the History of a Literary Genre*. New Haven, CT: Yale UP, 1972.

Stauffer, D. A. *English Biography Before 1700*. Cambridge, MA: Harvard UP, 1930.

Stevenson, Catherine Barnes. *Victorian Women Travel Writers in Africa*. Twayne's English Authors Series. Boston: Twayne, 1982.

Stull, Heidi L. *The Evolution of the Autobiography from 1770–1850: A Comparative Study and Analysis*. American University Studies, Series III: Comparative Literature, Vol. II. New York: Lang, 1985.

Tuckerman, Henry T. *America and Her Commentators. With a Critical Sketch of Travel in the United States*. New York: Antiquarian, 1961.

Wright, Luella M. *The Literary Life of the Early Friends 1650–1725*. New York: Columbia UP, 1932.

SELECTED ABBREVIATIONS

BL	British Museum. Department of Printed Books. *General Catalogue of Printed Books.*
C	Coulter, E. Merton. *Travels in the Confederate States: A Bibliography.*
K	Kaplan, Louis, et al, comps. *A Bibliography of American Autobiographies.*
MAD	Matthews, William, comp. *American Diaries: An Annotated Bibliography of American Diaries Written Prior to the Year 1861.*
MB	Matthews, William, comp. *British Autobiographies: An Annotated Bibliography of British Autobiographies Published or Written Before 1951.*
MBD	Matthews, William, comp. *British Diaries: An Annotated Bibliography of British Diaries Written Between 1442 and 1942.*
MC	Matthews, William, comp. *Canadian Diaries and Autobiographies.*
N	Nevins, Allan, ed. *America Through British Eyes.*
NUC	*National Union Catalog. Pre-1956 Imprints.*
OCLC	Online Computer Library Center.
PD	Ponsonby, Arthur, comp. *English Diaries.*
PMD	Ponsonby, Arthur, comp. *More English Diaries.*
PSI	Ponsonby, Arthur, comp. *Scottish and Irish Diaries.*

THE BIBLIOGRAPHY

1. A., E. <u>see</u> CONNER, Eliza Archard

2. A., E. S., pseud. <u>see</u> STONE, Letitia Willgoss

3. A., L. M. <u>see</u> ALDRICH, Louisa M.

4. A., R. F. <u>see</u> LEE, Rachel Fanny Antonina

5. A--N, Miss <u>see</u> ANDERSON, Bessie

6. A--S, Mrs. <u>see</u> ALTHANS, Margaret Magdalen (Jasper)

7. ABBOTT, Eloise (Miles) [Am. b. 1821]
Personal sketches and recollections: in a series of familiar letters to a friend, and miscellaneous essays.
Boston: Abel Tompkins, 1861. 359p. NUC K OCLC
[Bookseller & teacher]

8. ABBOTT, Emma [Am. 1850-1891]
The life and professional career of Emma Abbott. [Comp.] Sadie E. Martin.
Minneapolis, MN: L. Kimball pr. co., 1891. 192p. NUC K OCLC
[Includes autobiography; opera singer]

9. ABBOTT, Frances E., ed. <u>see</u> HALL, Arethusa

10. ABBOTT, Katherine Mixer [Am. b. 1865]
South shore trolley trips.
Boston: Heintzemann, 1898. 108p. NUC OCLC
[Massachusetts]

11. -----Trolley trips on a bay state triangle for sixty sunny days.
Lowell, MA: Thompson & Hill, 1897. 86p. NUC

12. -----Trolley trips, the historic New England coast. Long Island shore, Connecticut valley, Narragansett Bay, Buzzards Bay and Massachusetts.
Boston: Heintzemann, 1899. 123p. NUC OCLC

13. ABELL, Lucia Elizabeth (Balcombe) [Br. d. 1871]
Recollections of the Emperor Napoleon, during the first three years of his captivity on the Island of St. Helena.
L: John Murray, 1844. 251p. NUC BL OCLC
[His residence at her father's house]

14. ABERDEEN and TEMAIR, Ishbel Maria (Marjoribanks) Gordon, Marchioness of [Br. b. 1857] ALT: Gordon, Ishbel Maria (Marjoribanks), Marchioness of Aberdeen and Temair
Through Canada with a kodak.
Edinburgh: W. H. White & co., 1893. 249p. NUC BL OCLC

15. ABINGTON, Frances (Barton) [Br. 1737-1815] ALT: Barton, Frances
The life of Mrs. Abington--formerly Miss Barton--celebrated comic actress. ... Including ... notes upon the history of the Irish stage.
L: Reader, 1888. 124p. BL OCLC
[Includes her letters to David Garrick]

16. ACKERMANN, Jessie A. [Am. 19/20c]
The world through a woman's eyes.
Chicago: priv. pr., 1896. 325p. NUC OCLC
[Travel: Alaska, South Pacific, Asia, India, Africa]

17. ACKLOM, Gertrude Mary [Br. 19c]
"Clear Shining." A memoir of Gertrude Mary Acklom, etc. By her mother, [Mary Acklom].
L: W. Hunt & co., 1864. 74p. BL
[May contain original material]

18. ACKLOM, Mary, comp. <u>see</u> ACKLOM, Gertrude Mary

19. ACTRESS, pseud. <u>see</u> ELLERSLIE, Alma

20. ADAMS, Abigail <u>see</u> SMITH, Abigail (Adams)

21. ADAMS, Abigail (Smith), Mrs. John Adams [Am. 1744-1818] Familiar letters of John Adams and his wife during the Revolution. With a memoir of Mrs. Adams. [Comp.] Charles Francis Adams.
Boston: Houghton Mifflin, c1875; NY: Hurd & Houghton, 1876. NUC BL OCLC

22. -----Letters of Mrs. Adams, the wife of John Adams. With an introductory memoir by her grandson, Charles Francis Adams.
Boston: C. C. Little & J. Brown, 1840-41. 2v. NUC BL OCLC
[Letters date from 1761 to 1816.]

23. ADAMS, Ann see ADAMS, Barbara Ann (Shadecker)

24. ADAMS, Barbara Ann (Shadecker) [Am. b. 1810] ALT: Adams, Ann
Early days at Red River settlement and Fort Snelling. Reminiscences of Mrs. Ann Adams, 1821-29.
n.p.: n.p., 1891. NUC OCLC
[Repub. later in Collections of the Minnesota Historical Society, 1894]

25. ADAMS, Charles Francis, comp. see ADAMS, Abigail (Smith)

26. ADAMS, Emma Hildreth [Am. 1827-1900?]
Among the northern icebergs.
Oakland, CA: Pacific Press pub. co., 1890. 158p. NUC OCLC

27. -----Jottings from the Pacific; life and incidents in the Fijian and Samoan islands.
Oakland, CA: Pacific Press pub. co., 1890. 160p. NUC BL OCLC

28. -----Jottings from the Pacific, no. 2. The Tonga Islands and other groups.
Oakland, CA; San Francisco; NY & L: Pacific Press pub. co., 1891. 160p. NUC

29. -----To and fro, up and down in southern California, Oregon and Washington territory, with sketches in Arizona, New Mexico and British Columbia.
San Francisco: Hunt & Eaton, 1888. 608p. NUC OCLC

30. -----To and fro in southern California, with sketches in Arizona and New Mexico.
Cincinnati, OH: W. M. B. C. Press, 1887. 288p. NUC OCLC

31. -----Two cannibal archipelagoes, New Hebrides and Solomon groups.
Oakland, CA: Pacific press pub. co., 1890. 157p. NUC
[Jottings from the Pacific, no. 3.]

32. ADAMS, Hannah [Am. 1755-1832] A memoir of Miss Hannah Adams, written by herself. With additional notices by a friend [Hannah Farnham (Sawyer) Lee].
Boston: Gray & Bowen, 1832. 110p. NUC BL K OCLC
[43 pages of autobiography followed by biography.]

33. ADAMS, Harriet L., ed. see VICTOR, Sarah Maria

34. ADAMS, John, co-author see ADAMS, Abigail (Smith)

35. ADAMS, Mrs. John see ADAMS, Abigail (Smith)

36. ADAMS, Mary Rose Columba [Br. 1832-1891]
Memoir of Mother Mary Rose Columba, first prioress of St. Dominic's convent. [Comp.] Rev. William Robert Barnard Brownlow.
L: Burns & Oates, 1895. 384p. NUC BL OCLC
[Includes letters, diaries, & travel to Australia]

37. ADAMS, Mary (Still) [Am. b. 1839]
Autobiography, or, "In God we trust".
Los Angeles: Buckingham bros., pr., 1893. 288p. NUC K OCLC
[Wife of Methodist clergyman]

38. ADDERLEY, C. F. [Br. 19c]
ALT: Fitzatherley, Mrs. PSEUD:
Reedpen, Peregrine
Our town; or, rough sketches of
character, manners, etc. Pub. as:
Peregrine Reedpen
L: R. Bentley, 1834. 2v. NUC

39. ADDISON, Daniel D., ed. <u>see</u>
LARCOM, Lucy

40. ADEANE, Jane Henrietta, ed.
<u>see</u> STANLEY, Maria Josepha
(Holroyd), Baroness Stanley of
Alderley

41. ADELAIDE, Queen Consort of
William IV, King of Great Britain
and Ireland [Br. 1792-1849]
Queen Adelaide.
L: Wertheim & Macintosh, 1851.
40p. BL
[May contain personal material]

42. AGASSIZ, Elizabeth Cabot
(Cary), Mrs. Louis Jean Rodolphe
Agassiz [Am. 1822-1907]
A journey in Brazil. With Louis
Jean Agassiz.
Boston: James R. Osgood & co.;
Boston & NY: Houghton Mifflin,
1867. 540p. NUC BL OCLC

43. AGASSIZ, Louis Jean Rodolphe,
co-author <u>see</u> AGASSIZ, Elizabeth
Cabot (Cary)

44. AGASSIZ, Mrs. Louis Jean
Rodolphe <u>see</u> AGASSIZ, Elizabeth
Cabot (Cary)

45. AGGS, Mary, comp. <u>see</u> PEASE,
Martha Lucy (Aggs)

46. AGNEW, Anna, Mrs. [Am. 19c]
From under the cloud; or,
personal reminiscences of
insanity.
Cincinnati, OH: R. Clark & co.,
1886. 196p. NUC K OCLC
[Indianapolis, Ind. hospital for
insane.]

47. AGNEW, Margaret [Am. 19c]
The conspiracy explained and
defended, in a letter to the Rev.
William W. Phillips, D.D.
NY: n.p., 1832. 30p. NUC
[Probably religious controversy]

48. AGUILAR, Grace [Br. 1816-
1847]
Memoirs of Grace Aguilar.
NY: Appleton, 1847. NUC

49. AIKEN, Aunt Lizzie <u>see</u> AIKEN,
Eliza N. Atherton

50. AIKEN, Eliza N. Atherton [Am.
1817-1906] ALT: Aiken, Aunt
Lizzie
The story of Aunt Lizzie Aiken.
[Comp.] Mary Eleanor (Roberts)
Anderson, Mrs. Galusha Anderson.
Chicago: Jansen, McClurg & co.,
1880. 226p. NUC BL OCLC
[Includes excerpts of her diary
and letters. Pioneer settler in
Illinois, Union nurse, missionary
in Chicago.]

51. AIKIN, Anna Letitia <u>see</u>
BARBAULD, Anna Letitia (Aikin)

52. AIKIN, Anna Letitia, comp.
<u>see</u> BARBAULD, Anna Letitia
(Aikin)

53. AIKIN, Lucy [Br. 1781-1864]
Correspondence of William Ellery
Channing, D.D. and Lucy Aikin,
from 1826-1842. Ed. Anna Letitia
(Aikin) LeBreton.
L: Williams & Norgate; Boston:
Roberts, 1874. 426p. NUC BL OCLC

54. -----Memoirs, miscellanies
and letters of the late Lucy
Aikin; including those addressed
to the Rev. Dr. [William Ellery]
Channing from 1826 to 1842. Ed.
Philip Hemery Le Breton.
L: Longman & co., 1864. 440p. NUC
BL OCLC

55. AIKIN, Lucy, comp. <u>see</u>
BARBAULD, Anna Letitia (Aikin)

56. AITKEN, Cora Kennedy [Br.
19c]
Legends and memories of Scotland.
L: Hodder & Stoughton, 1874.
155p. NUC BL OCLC
[In verse]

57. ALB, pseud. <u>see</u> WHITEING,
Helen

58. ALBY, Ann [OCLC: Anne] Eliza
(Dow) [Am. b. 1790] ALT: Dow, Ann
Eliza
The life and adventures of Ann
Eliza Dow: being a true narrative
written by herself.
Burlington, VT: the author, 1845.
24p. NUC K OCLC

59. ALCOTT, Louisa May [Am. 1832-
1888]
Hospital sketches.
Boston: James Redpath, 1863.
102p. NUC BL OCLC
[Personal experiences in Civil
War, pro-Union]

60. -----Louisa May Alcott, her
life, letters, and journals. Ed.
Ednah Dow (Littlehale) Cheney.
Boston: Roberts bros., 1884.
404p. NUC BL MAD OCLC

61. ALDEN, Cynthia May
(Westover), co-author see OBER,
Corolyn Faville

62. ALDERSON, Mary Anne, Lady,
comp. see BARNWELL, Anne

63. ALDRICH, Louisa M., Mrs. [Am.
19c] ALT: A., L. M.
Six weeks in old France; or, Dr.
Thom's holiday by L. M. A.
Letters from Château de
Montagland.
Albany, NY: American Bureau of
Foreign Travel, 1887. 317p. NUC
OCLC
[Travel: Touraine]

64. ALEXANDER, Mrs., comp. see
ALEXANDER, Priscilla

65. ALEXANDER, Esther Frances
[Br. 1837-1917] ALT: Alexander,
Francesca; Francesca
Christ's folk in the Apennine.
Remi- niscences of her friends
among the Tuscan peasantry. Ed.
John Ruskin.
Orpington: George Allen, 1887.
2v. NUC BL OCLC

66. ALEXANDER, Evelyn Ferguson
[Br. 19c]
Five years in a south London
parish. A memorial of E. F.
Alexander.
L: priv. pr., 1888. 182p. BL
[May contain personal material.]

67. ALEXANDER, Francesca see
ALEXANDER, Esther Frances

68. ALEXANDER, Mary [Br. 1760-
1809]
Some account of the life and
religious experience of M.
Alexander, late of Needham
Market.
York: W. Alexander, 1811. 210p.
NUC BL MB OCLC
[Autobiography, member of the
Society of Friends]

69. ALEXANDER, Priscilla [Br. d.
1864]
Memorial of a beloved child, by
her mother, [Mrs. Alexander].
L: pr. for priv. circ. by A. W.
Bennett, 1865. 56p. NUC
[Biography with quotes of child's
conversations]

70. ALEXANDER, Sophia, Mrs.
William Henry Alexander [Br. 19c]
Memorials of William Henry
Alexander and Sophia Alexander.
L: F. B. Kitto, 1867. 165p. BL
MBD
[Members of Society of Friends;
her diary (1826-1865) is
included]

71. ALEXANDER, William Henry, co-
author see ALEXANDER, Sophia

72. ALEXANDER, Mrs. William Henry
see ALEXANDER, Sophia

73. ALFORD, Fanny see ALFORD,
Frances Oke

74. ALFORD, Frances Oke, Mrs.
Henry Alford [Br. d. 1878] ALT:
Alford, Fanny
Reminiscences of a clergyman's
wife. Ed. the Dean of Canterbury
[Henry Alford].
L: n.p., 1860. 195p. BL MB

75. ALFORD, Henry, ed. see
Alford, Frances Oke

76. ALFORD, Mrs. Henry see
ALFORD, Frances Oke

77. ALICE MAUD MARY, Consort of Louis IV, Grand Duke of Hesse Dormstadt [Br. 1843-1878]
The Alice Birthday Book ... . Selections from the letters of ... Princess Alice. [Comp.] Charlotte Elizabeth Ferguson-Davie.
L: Hatchards, 1885. 277p. BL

78. ALLAN-OLNEY, Mary [Am. 19c]
The new Virginians.
Edinburgh: Blackwood, 1880. 2v. NUC OCLC
[Account of the experiences of an English family in Virginia after the Civil War. NUC also lists under Emily Marion Harris as supposed author.]

79. ALLEMAN, Tillie (Pierce) [Am. 19c]
At Gettysburg; or, what a girl saw and heard of the battle. A true narrative.
NY: W. L. Borland, 1889. 118p. NUC OCLC

80. ALLEN, Elizabeth, Miss [Am. 19c]
Sketches of Green Mountain life; with an autobiography of the author.
Lowell, MA: N. L. Dayton, 1846. 160p. NUC K OCLC
[Brief autobiography including travel in N.Y. state; short stories]

81. ALLEN, Hannah [Br. 17c] ALT: Watt, Hannah (Allen)
Satan his methods and malice baffled. A narrative of God's gracious dealings with that choice Christian Hannah Allen, afterwards married to Mr. Watt.
L: John Wallis, 1683. 79p. BL
[Autobiography]

82. ALLEN, Hannah Hunton Stafford [Br. 19c]
A beloved mother. Life of Hannah S. Allen. [Comp.] her daughter, J. B. [Jane Budge].
L: S. Harris & co., 1884. 188p. NUC BL MBD
[Quaker diary 1835-1849]

83. ALLEN, Harriet Trowbridge, Mrs. [Am. d. 1877]
Travels in Europe and the East: during the years 1858-59 and 1863-64.
New Haven, CT: Tuttle, Morehouse & Taylor, pr., 1879. 506p. NUC OCLC

84. ALLEN, Mary S. [Am. 19c]
From west to east; or, the old world as I saw it: being a journey from California to the Holy Land and Egypt, by way of England, France, Switzerland, and Italy.
Chicago: Free Methodist pub. house, 1898. 114p. NUC

85. ALLEN, Rose [Br. 19c]
The autobiography of Rose Allen. Ed. a lady.
L: Longman & co., 1849. 162p. BL MB
[Experiences in domestic service]

86. ALLEN, Sarah [Am. 19c]
A narrative of the shipwreck and unparalleled sufferings of Mrs. Sarah Allen (late of Boston) on her passage in May last from New York to New Orleans. Being the substance of a letter from the unfortunate Mrs. Allen to her sister in Boston.
2d ed. Boston: Pr. for M. Brewster, 1816. 24p. NUC OCLC
[Author shipwrecked on coast of Florida]

87. ALLEY, Rev. G., ed. see HUNTER, Grace

88. ALLEY, Sarah [Am. 18c]
An account of a trance or vision ... 1798 ... taken of her own mouth.
Poughkeepsie, NY: Nicholas Powers, 1798. 11p. NUC

89. ALLIBONE, Susan [Am. 1813-1854]
A life hid with Christ in God. Being a memoir of Susan Allibone. Chiefly compiled from her diary and letters. By Alfred Lee, Bishop of the Protestant Episcopal church in Delaware.
Philadelphia: J. B. Lippincott, 1856. 592p. NUC BL OCLC

90.   ALSOP, Christine R.
(Majolier), Mrs. Robert Alsop
[Br. 1805-1879] ALT: Majolier,
Christine R.
Memorials of Christine Majolier
Alsop. Comp. Martha Braithwaite.
L: Samuel Harris & co., 1881;
Philadelphia: H. Longstreth,
1882. 248p. NUC BL MB OCLC
[Includes autobiography, journal,
letters; travel: France &
England; member of Society of
Friends]

91. ALSOP, Mrs. Robert see ALSOP,
Christine E. (Majolier)

92. ALTHANS, Mrs. Frederick
Charles see ALTHANS, Margaret
Magdalen (Jasper)

93. ALTHANS [NUC: ALTHENS],
Margaret Magdalen (Jasper), Mrs.
Frederick Charles Althans [Br.
1752-1789]
The Christian character
exemplified from the papers of
Mrs. Frederick Charles A--s, of
Goodman's Fields.
n.p.: n.p., 1791. NUC BL
[Religious in tone. Includes
personal reminiscences.]

94. -----Letters by ... the late
Mrs. A--s.
n.p.: n.p., 1796. BL

95. ALTHENS, Margaret Magdalen
(Jasper) see ALTHANS, Margaret
Magdalen (Jasper)

96. AMBROSI, Marietta [Am.
19/20c]
Italian child-life; or,
Marietta's good times.
Boston: D. Lothrop, c1892. 182p.
NUC

97. AMBROSS, Miss, comp. see
CATLEY, Ann

98. AMERICAN LADY, AN, pseud. see
GRIFFIN, Mary (Sands)

99. AMERICAN LADY, AN, pseud. see
WILLARD, Mrs. F. J.

100. AMES, Julia A. [Am. 1860-
1891)
A young woman journalist: a
memorial tribute to Julia A.
Ames.
Chicago: The Women's Temperance
Pub. Assn. The Temple, 1892.
240p. NUC OCLC
[Includes journal of a tour of
Europe]

101. AMES, Mary E. (Clemmer) [Am.
1839-1884] ALT: Clemmer, Mary;
Hudson, Mary E. (Clemmer) Ames
Ten years in Washington. Life and
scenes in the national capitol,
as a woman sees them.
Hartford, CT: A. G. Worthington &
co., 1860. 587p. NUC

102. ANDERSON, Bessie [Br. 19c]
ALT: A--n, Miss
The morning of life: a memoir of
Miss A--n, who was educated for a
nun with many interesting
particulars and original letters
of Dr. Doyle, late Roman Catholic
Bishop of Caslow. By M.M.C.M.
[Mary M. C. Methuen].
Bath: Burns & Goodwin, 1851.
157p; L: n.p., 1851. BL
[Return to Protestantism, based
on her own account.

103. ANDERSON, Mrs. Galusha see
ANDERSON, Mary Eleanor (Roberts)

104. ANDERSON, Mrs. Galusha,
comp. see AIKEN, Eliza N.
Atherton

105. ANDERSON, Mary see DE
NAVARRO, Mary (Anderson)

106. ANDERSON, Mary Eleanor
(Roberts), Mrs. Galusha Anderson
[Am. 1840-1916] ALT: Roberts,
Mary Eleanor
Scenes in the Hawaiian Islands
and California.
Boston: Am. Tract Society, 1865.
238p. NUC OCLC
[NUC attr. Mary Evarts (Anderson)
Street, Am. 1838-1905.]

107. ANDERSON, Mary Eleanor
(Roberts), comp. see AIKEN, Eliza
N. Atherton

108. ANDERSON, Mary Evarts aee
ANDERSON, Mary Eleanor (Roberts)

109. ANDREW, Agnes [Br. 19c]
The triumph of faith in humble
life; or, a memoir of Mrs.
Andrew, of Paisley.
L: Religious Tract Society, 1853.
54p. BL
[May contain personal material.]

110. ANDREW, Jane [Br. 19c]
Recorded mercies: being the
autobiography of Jane Andrew ...
also, reminiscences of her valued
friend, the late Mrs. Daniel
Smart. Comp. her younger daughter
[A. Smart].
L: E. Wilmshurst, 1890. 51p. BL
MB

111. ANDREWES, Margaret (Hamer)
[Br. 19/20c] ALT: Hamer, Margaret
PSEUD: Browne, Maggie
Chats about Germany. Pub. as:
Maggie Browne.
L: Cassell & co., 1884. 222p. NUC
BL OCLC

112. ANNESLEY, Miss M., ed. see
BOCKING, Hannah (Dakin)

113. ANON [Br. 19c]
Another voice from the grave ...
exemplified in the dying
confession and exercises of an
unfortunate female. Written down
by Thomas H. Skinner.
Philadelphia: Religious Tract
Society of Philadelphia, 1819.
24p. NUC K OCLC
[Prostitute; OCLC says it is
fiction]

114. ANON [Br. 19c]
Recollections of a beloved
sister, interspersed with
reflections addressed to her own
children. By Mrs. Wayland.
2d ed. Derby: H. Mozley & son,
1830. 152p. BL

115. ANSELL, Mrs. [Br. 19c]
My reminiscences of colonial
life.
Boston: J. Warren, 1882. 107p. BL

116. ANSPACH, H. S. H., the
Margravine of see CRAVEN,
Elizabeth (Berkeley), Baroness
Craven

117. ANTHONY, Susanna [Am. 1726-
1791]
The life and character of Miss
Susanna Anthony ... consisting
chiefly in extracts from her
writings. Ed. Samuel Hopkins.
Worcester, MA: Pr. Leonard
Worcester, 1796. 193p. NUC BL MAD
OCLC
[Chiefly from religious diary;
member of Society of Friends]

118. ANTHONY, Susanna, co-author
see OSBORN, Sarah (Haggar)

119. ANTIN, Mary [Am. 1881-1949]
From Plotzk to Boston.
Boston: W. B. Clarke & co., 1899.
80p. NUC K OCLC
[Jewish life; immigration to
U.S.]

120. APPERSON, M. M. see
PHILLIPS, Minnie Mary (Apperson)

121. ARBLAY, Frances (Burney) d'
[Br. 1752-1840] ALT: Burney,
Fanny; D'Arblay, Frances (Burney)
The diary and letters of Madame
D'Arblay (1798-1840). Ed. her
niece, Charlotte Frances Barrett.
L: Bickers & son; L: Henry
Colburn, 1842-46. 7v. NUC BL MBD
OCLC

122. -----The early diary of
Frances Burney, 1768-1778. With a
selection from her correspondence
and from the journals of her
sisters, Susan and Charlotte
Burney. Ed. Annie Raine Ellis.
L: G. Bell & sons, 1889. 2v. NUC
BL OCLC

123. -----Memoirs of Madame
d'Arblay ... compiled from her
voluminous diaries and letters,
and from other sources. By Helen
Berkeley, pseud. [Anna Cora
(Ogden) Mowatt Ritchie].
NY: J. Mowatt & co., 1844. 2v. BL
OCLC

124. ARCHER, Ann Sheldon see
SHELDON, Ann

125. ARCHER, Ruby [Am. 19c]
Notes and poems in Europe.
Kansas City, MO: n.p., 1896. 101
numb. lines. NUC
[Journal of Cunard voyage;
Descriptions, poems, character
sketches, etc.]

126. ARMOUR, Mary Susan [Br. 19c]
Recollections of Miss Mary S.
Armour.
Edinburgh: pr. for priv. circ.,
1858. 60p. BL
[May contain personal material]

127. ARMS, Mary L. (Day) [Am. b.
1836] ALT: DAY, Mary L.
Incidents in the life of a blind
girl, Mary L. Day, a graduate of
the Maryland Institution for the
Blind.
5th ed. Baltimore, MD: James
Young, 1859. 206p. NUC K OCLC

128. -----The world as I have
found it. Sequel to Incidents in
the life of a blind girl.
Baltimore, MD: James Young, 1878.
312p. NUC K OCLC

129. ARMSTRONG, Clarissa Chapman
[Am. 1805-1890]
C. C. A. May 15 ... 1885.
Celebration of the 80th birthday
of Mrs. Clarissa Chapman
Armstrong.
Hampton: Normal School Steam
Press, 1885. 32p. OCLC

130. -----Reminiscences of a
missionary chair.
San Francisco: C. A. Murdock &
co., 1886. 18p. NUC
[Missionary in Hawaii]

131. ARMSTRONG, Isabel Julien
[Br. 19c]
Two roving Englishwomen in
Greece.
L: Sampson Low, Marston & co.,
1893. 300p. NUC BL OCLC

132. ARMSTRONG, Robert G., comp.
see HOBBIE, Hannah

133. ARNOLD, Eunice C. Sprague
[Am. 19c]
Maple leaves and myrtle wreaths.
Being a collection of short poems
and essays, many of which were
written in youth. Including
"Scraps from a schoolgirl's
portfolio," and "Incidents of the
war".
Charlotte, MI: J. Saunders & co.,
1872. 124p. NUC OCLC

134. ARRINGTON, Pattie D. B.,
Mrs. [Am. 19c]
Is justice a farce?: a true story
of love, marriage, separation,
and divorce: property in
litigation for years and justice
is not known in the case: how it
began but has never ended.
Raleigh, NC: n.p., 1893. 31p. NUC
OCLC

135. ARRIVÉ, Elizabeth, Mrs. [Br.
19c]
Memoirs of the late Mrs.
Elizabeth Arrivé of Guernsey.
[Comp.] William Toase.
Guernsey: H. Broward, 1818. 98p.
BL

136. ARUNDELL, Mary Ann, Baroness
Arundell of Wardour [Br. 19c]
Memoir and letters of Lady Mary
Arundell. [Comp.] Joseph Hirst.
Leicester: n.p., 1894. 152p. BL

137. ASHBRIDGE, Elizabeth
(Sampson) [Am. 1713-1755]
Some account of the early part of
the life of Elizabeth Ashbridge
... written by herself.
Philadelphia: H. & T. Kite, 1807.
60p. NUC BL K MB OCLC
[Member of Society of Friends]

138. ASHFORD, Mary Ann [Br. 19c]
Life of a licensed victualler's
daughter. Written by herself.
L: Saunders & Otley, 1844. 91p.
BL MB

139. ASHMORE, Harriette [Br. 19c]
Narrative of a three months'
march in India; and a residence
in the Dooab.
L: R. Hastings, 1841. 354p. NUC
BL OCLC

140. ASKEWE, Anne [Br. 1521-1546]
ALT: Kyme, Anne (Askewe)
The account of the sufferings of
Anne Askewe, for opposing the
gross fiction of
transubstantiation ... . Written
by herself, and reprinted by a
Catholic.
L: F. & J. Rivington, 1849. 52p.
BL
[Martyred at Smithfield]

141. ASPINALL, Clara [Br. 19c]
Three years in Melbourne.
L: L. Booth, 1862. 299p. BL OCLC

142. ATKINS, Josiah, ed. see
HOUSE, Abigail (Clark)

143. ATKINS, Rebecca (Crittenden)
[Am. b. 1829]
"Truth stranger than fiction."
Book of fate. Autobiography of
Rebecca Atkins. Her life of fate.
Lincoln, NB: n.p., 1896. 184p.
NUC K

144. ATKINSON, Lucy, Mrs. T. W.
Atkinson [Br. 19c]
Recollections of Tartar steppes
and their inhabitants.
L: John Murray, 1863. 351p. NUC
BL OCLC

145. ATKINSON, Lulu (Hurst) [Am.
b. 1869] ALT: HURST, Lulu
Lulu Hurst, (the Georgia wonder),
writes her autobiography, and for
the first time explains and
demonstrates the great secret of
her marvelous power.
Rome, GA: Lulu Hurst book co.,
1897. 267p. NUC K
[Spiritualist]

146. ATKINSON, Mrs. T. W. see
ATKINSON, Lucy

147. ATMORE, Charles, comp. see
ATMORE, Eliza

148. ATMORE, Eliza [Br. 18c]
A short account of Eliza Atmore
... . To which are subjoined some
of her letters. Comp. Charles
Atmore.
York: Wilson & co., 1794. 36p. BL

149. AUFFRAY, Edith (O'Gormon)
see O'GORMON, Edith

150. AUNT BECKY, pseud. see
PALMER, Sarah A.

151. AUNT BETTY see VENEY,
Bethany

152. AUST, Sarah (Maese) Murray,
Mrs. [Br. 1744-1811] ALT: Murray,
Hon. Mrs. Sarah
A companion, and useful guide to
the beauties of Scotland, to the
lakes of Westmoreland,
Cumberland, and Lancashire, and
to the curiosities in the
district of Craven in the west
riding of Yorkshire. To which is
added, a more particular
description of Scotland,
especially that part of it,
called the Highlands. By the
Honorable Mrs. Murray, of
Kensington.
L: pr. for author, sold by G.
Nichol, 1799. 35p. NUC BL OCLC
[Author guides travelers by her
own journeys to the Lakes in 1790
and to the Highlands in 1796.]

153. AUSTEN, Jane [Br. 1775-1817]
Letters of Jane Austen. Ed.
Edward, Lord Brabourne.
L: R. Bentley & sons, 1884. 2v.
BL OCLC
[Chiefly letters to her sister
Cassandra, 1773-1845]

154. AUSTIN, Emily M. [Am. 19c]
Mormonism; or life among the
Mormons, by Emily M. Austin,
being an autobiographical sketch;
including an experience of
fourteen years of Mormon life.
Madison, WI: M. J. Cantwell,
1882. 253p. NUC K OCLC

155. AUSTIN, Jane (Goodwin) [Am.
1831-1894]
Nantucket scraps: being the
experiences of an off-islander,
in season and out of season,
among a passing people.
Boston & NY: Houghton Mifflin &
co., 1882. 354p. NUC BL OCLC

156. AUSTIN, Sarah (Taylor), co-
author see TAYLOR, Susannah
(Cook)

157. AUSTIN, Sarah (Taylor), ed.
see GORDON, Lucie (Austin) Duff

158. AUTY, Annie [Br. b. 1830]
ALT: Tolson, Annie
Annie, the drunkard's daughter
... a faithful account of the
life, experience, and labours of
Annie Auty, formerly Mrs. Tolson,
the Yorkshire and Lancashire
revivalist. Written by herself.
L: C. W. Banks, 1867. 112p. NUC
BL

159. AVELING, Thomas W. B., ed.
see GLENORCHY, Willielma
(Maxwell) Campbell, Viscountess

160. AVERY, Mary H. [Br. 19c]
"Up in the clouds;" or,
Darjeeling and its surroundings,
historical and descriptive.
Calcutta: W. Newman & co., 1898.
125p. BL

161. AVONMORE, Maria Theresa
(Longworth) Yelverton,
Viscountess see LONGWORTH, Maria
Theresa

162. AYLMER, Louisa Anne,
Baroness [Br. 19c]
Narrative of the passage of the
Pique across the Atlantic.
L: J. Hatchard & son, 1837. 82p.
NUC BL
[Shipwreck of the Pique, a
frigate]

163. AYNSLEY, Harriet Georgiana
Maria Murray [Manners-Sutton] see
MURRAY-AYNSLEY, Harriet Georgiana
Maria [Manners-Sutton]

164. B., A. see BAYMAN, A. Phelps

165. B., A. see BRASSEY, Annie
(Allnut), Baroness

166. B., A. F., Miss see BARLOW,
Adela F.

167. B., J., comp. see ALLEN,
Hannah Hunton Stafford

168. B., L. see BENTON, Lucy

169. B., M. E. see BLAKE, Mary
Elizabeth (McGrath)

170. B., M. E. P. see BOULINGNY,
Mary E. (Parker)

171. B., R., ed. see WIGHT, Sarah

172. B., R. L., pseud. see
DOUTNEY, Harriet G. (Storer)

173. B., S., comp. see BROWN,
Sarah

174. B., W., co-author see BRAIN,
Ada B.

175. BACKHOUSE, Anna (Gurney)
[Am. 1820-1848]
A brief sketch of the life of
Anna Backhouse by one who knew
her well, loved her much, and was
often instructed by her.
Burlington, NJ: J. Rodgers, 1852.
201p. NUC MBD OCLC
[Member of Society of Friends;
includes diary, travel in
France.]

176. BACKHOUSE, Deborah [Br.
1793-1827]
A memoir of Deborah Backhouse of
York.
York: Tract Association of the
Society of Friends, pr. W.
Alexander & son, Castlegate,
1828. BL
[Member of Society of Friends;
includes correspondence]

177. BACKHOUSE, Hannah Chapman
(Gurney) [Br. 1787-1850]
Extracts from the journal and
letters of H. C. Backhouse. Ed.
Jane Gurney Fox.
L: R. Barrett, 1858. 291p. NUC BL
MBD OCLC
[Includes travel in England &
U.S.]

178. BACKHOUSE, Katharine
(Capper), ed. see CAPPER, Mary

179. BACON, Anne (Coke), Lady
[Br. 1528-1610]
The works of Francis Bacon. ...
Coll. & ed. James Spedding ... R.
L. Ellis ... & D. D. Heath.

L: Longman & co., 1857-74. 14v.
BL OCLC
[Volume 8, 1857, includes her letters]

180. BACON, Charles W., co-author see NICHOLS, Alice S.

181. BACON, Francis, co-author see BACON, Anne (Coke), Lady

182. BACON, Georgeanna Muirson (Woolsey) [Am. 1833-1906]
Letters of a family during the War for the Union 1861-1865. With [co-author and joint editor] Eliza Newton (Woolsey) Howland.
New Haven, CT: Tuttle, Morehouse & Taylor, 1899. 2v. NUC OCLC
[Letters of pro-Union family; primarily of Bacon & Howland.]

183. -----Three weeks at Gettysburg.
NY: A. D. F. Randolph, 1863. 24p.
NUC OCLC
[On hospital work; also pub. as: What we did at Gettysburg]

184. BACON, Jane (Meautys) Cornwallis, Lady [Br. c1581-1659]
ALT: Cornwallis, Jane (Meautys), Lady
The private correspondence of Jane, Lady Cornwallis; 1613-1644.
Ed. Lord Braybrooke.
L: pr. S. & J. Bentley, Wilson & Fley, 1842. 314p. NUC BL OCLC

185. BACON, Lydia B. (Stetson) [Am. 1786-1853]
Biography of Mrs. Lydia B. Bacon.
Boston: Mass. Sabbath School Soc., 1856. 348p. NUC OCLC
[Incl. journal during War of 1812; she and husband were prisoners of British in Detroit. Traveled home to New England via Niagara Falls. Mostly her letters.]

186. BADDELEY, Sophia see STEELE, Elizabeth

187. BADGER, Catherine Naomi, ed. see WHITING, Martha

188. BAGOT, Daniel, ed. see HATTON, Augusta

189. BAGSHAWE, Catherine, Mrs. [Br. 1760-1818]
The Bagshawes of Ford: A biographical pedigree. By William Henry Greaves Bagshawe.
L: Mitchell & Hughes, 1886. 610p.
BL MBD
[Includes her diary]

190. BAGSHAWE, William Henry Greaves, comp. see BAGSHAWE, Catherine

191. BAGSHAWE, William Henry Greaves, comp. see MURRAY, Mary

192. BAILEY, Abigail (Abbot), Mrs. Asa Bailey [Am. 1746-1815]
Memoirs of Abigail Bailey who had been the wife of Major Asa Bailey, formerly of Landaff, (N. H.), written by herself... . Ed. Ethan Smith.
Boston: S. J. Armstrong, 1815. 275p. NUC K OCLC
[Her memoirs, sufferings from husband's cruelty, spiritual reflections.]

193. BAILEY, Abigail, Mrs. [Am. 1746-1815] ALT: Bayley, Abigail
Memoirs of Mrs. Abigail Bailey.
Boston: Samuel T. Armstrong, 1815. 275p. NUC MAD
[Includes diary, 1767-1792]

194. BAILEY, Mrs. Asa see BAILEY, Abigail (Abbot)

195. BAILEY, Florence Augusta (Merriam) [Am. 1863-1948] ALT: Merriam, Florence Augusta
My summer in a Mormon village.
Boston & NY: Houghton Mifflin & co., 1894. 171p. NUC BL OCLC

196. BAILEY, Margaret Jewett (Smith) [Am. 19c] PSEUD: Rover, Ruth
The grains, or, passage in the life of Ruth Rover with occasional pictures of Oregon, natural and moral.
Portland, OR: pr., Carter & Austin, 1854. NUC K
[Originally pub. in monthly numbers; fictionalized autobiography; mission life]

197. BAILLIE, E. C. C., Mrs. [Br. 19c]
A sail to Smyrna: or, an Englishwoman's journal; including impressions of Constantinople, a visit to a Turkish harem, and a railway journey to Ephesus.
L: Longmans, Green & co., 1873. 253p. NUC BL

198. BAILLIE, Lady Grisell (Hume) [Br. 1665-1746]
Memoirs of the lives and characters of the Right Honourable George Baillie of Jerviswood and of Lady Grisell Baillie. By their daughter, Grisell, Lady Murray of Stanhope.
Edinburgh: priv. pr., 1822. 170p. BL

199. BAILLIE, Marianne [Br. 1795?-1825]
First impressions on a tour upon the continent in the summer of 1818, through parts of France, Italy, Switzerland, the borders of Germany, and a part of French Flanders.
L: J. Murray, 1819. 375p. NUC BL OCLC

200. -----Lisbon in the years 1821, 1822 and 1823.
L: J. Murray, 1824. 2v. NUC BL OCLC
[In the form of letters]

201. BAILY, Mrs. L. A. see GARDNER, Mary

202. BAINBRIDGE, Lucy (Seaman) [Am. 1842-1928]
Round the world letters.
Providence, RI: n.p., 1881; NY: R. P. Blackall, 1882. 542p. NUC OCLC
[Two years' tour around the world]

203. BAIRD, Elizabeth Thérèse (Fisher), Mrs. H. S. Baird [Am. 1810-1890]
Indian customs and early recollections. By Mrs. H. S. Baird. In State Historical Society, Report and collections ... 1880-82.
Madison, WI: State Hist. Soc. of Wisconsin, 1882. 326p. NUC OCLC
[Pioneer life in old Northwest]

204. -----Reminiscences of early days on Mackinac Island [Wisconsin].
Madison, WI: State Hist. Soc. of Wisconsin, 1898. 64p. NUC OCLC

205. BAIRD, Mrs. H. S. see BAIRD, Elizabeth Thérèse (Fisher)

206. BAKER, Charlotte Alice [Am. 1833-1909]
A summer in the Azores, with a glimpse of Madeira.
Boston: Lee & Shepard, 1882. 174p. NUC OCLC

207. BAKER, Frances J. [Am. 19c]
A trip tb China.
Petersburg, MI: A. P. Faling, pr., 1897. 28p. NUC OCLC

208. BAKER, G., Mrs. [Br. 19c]
Fraud, fancy, fact: which is it? An inquiry into the mystery of spiritualism, with a narrative of personal experience.
L: pr. for the authoress, 1862. 16p. BL

209. BAKER, Harriette Newell (Woods) [Am. 1815-1893]
The autobiography of a remarkable woman. Ed. Walter Baker.
L: A. T. Roberts son & co., 1894. 243p. BL

210. BAKER, Louisa see WEST, Lucy (Brewer)

211. BAKER, Walter, ed. see BAKER, Harriette Newell

212. BALCOMB, Amelia [Br. 19c]
Glances of Brighton: past and present.
L: Whitbread, 1856. 70p. BL

213. -----Rambles in the realms of thought.
L: Whitbread, 1855. 70p. BL
[History of Brighton, description of scenery & sites, with moral observations in verse.]

214. BALDWIN, Mary Briscoe [Am. 1811-1877]
Mission life in Greece and Palestine. Memorials of Mary Briscoe Baldwin, missionary to Athens and Joppa. [Comp.] Emma Raymond Pitman.

L: Cassell, Pettery Galpin & co., 1881?. 360p. NUC BL OCLC
[Large extracts from her "diary letters"]

215. BALFOUR, Alice Blanche [Br. 19c]
Twelve hundred miles in a waggon.
L & NY: Edward Arnold, 1895. 265p. NUC BL OCLC
[Travel: S. & E. Africa]

216. BALL, Hannah [Br. 1733-1792]
Memoirs of Miss Hannah Ball ... extracted from her diary of thirty years' experience. By Joseph Cole.
York: pr. for her sister by Wilson, Spence & Mawman, 1796. 71p. NUC BL MBD OCLC
[Religious diary 1767-1792, Methodist Sunday school movement]

217. -----Memoir of Miss Hannah Ball. With extracts from her diary and correspondence. Revised & enlarged. By John Parker.
L: J. Mason, 1839. NUC BL

218. BALLIN, Ada S. [Br. 19c]
Holiday resorts on the east coast. Notes of a visit to Yarmouth, Lowestoft, Cromer.
2d ed. L: n.p., 1892. 32p. NUC

219. BANBURY, Countess of see BANBURY, Elizabeth Price

220. BANBURY, Elizabeth Price [Br. 17c] ALT: Banbury, Elizabeth, Countess of; Price, Elizabeth
The true Countess of Banbury's case, relating to her marriage, rightly stated. In a letter to the Lord Banbury.
L: n.p., 1696. 34p. NUC BL OCLC

221. BANCROFT, Marie Effie (Wilton), Lady [Br. 1839-1921]
Mr. and Mrs. Bancroft on and off the stage. Written by themselves. [With Sir Squire Bancroft Bancroft].
L: Richard Bentley & son, 1888. 2v. NUC BL OCLC

222. BANCROFT, Sir Squire Bancroft, co-author see BANCROFT, Marie Effie

223. BANIM, Mary [Br. 19c]
Here and there through Ireland.
Dublin: Freeman's Journal, pr., 2 pts. 1891,92. 1st part 308p. NUC BL OCLC
[Includes some history and anecdotes of old Ireland collected by the traveling author. Repr. from the "Weekly Freeman"]

224. BANKS, Martha Burr [Am. 19/20c]
Heroes of the South seas.
NY: American Tract Soc.; Young People's Missionary Movement, 1896. 220p. NUC OCLC
[Travel & missionary work]

225. BARBAULD, Anna Letitia (Aikin) [Br. 1743-1825] ALT: Aikin, Anna Letitia
Memoir, letters, and a selection from the poetry and prose writings of Anna Letitia Barbauld. Comp. Grace A. Ellis.
Boston: J. R. Osgood & co., 1874. 2v. BL OCLC

226. -----Memoir of Mrs. Barbauld, including letters and notices of her family and friends. [Comp.] her great niece, Anna Letitia (Aikin) (LeBreton).
L: G. Bell & sons, 1874. 236p. BL OCLC

227. -----The works of Anna Letitia Barbauld. Memoir by Lucy Aikin.
L: Longman, Hurst, Rees, Orme, Brown & Green, 1825. 2v. NUC BL OCLC
[v.1: poetry; v.2: correspondence and miscellaneous pieces incl. prose essays and two dialogues]

228. BARBER, Agnes Schultz [Am. 19c]
History of our own times.
n.p.: n.p., 1867. NUC
[On Civil War]

229. BARBER, Julia Langdon, Mrs. [Am. 19c]
Mediterranean mosaics; or, the cruise of the yacht Sapphire, 1893-1894.
NY: priv. pr., c1895. 283p. NUC OCLC

230. BARBER, Mary [Am. b. 1848]
The true narrative of the five
years' suffering and perilous
adventures, by Miss Barber, wife
of "Squatting Bear," a celebrated
Sioux chief.
Philadelphia: Barclay, c1873.
108p. NUC K OCLC

231. BARBER, Mary Ann Serrett
[Br. d. 1864]
Bread-winning; or, the ledger and
the lute. An autobiography.
L: William Macintosh, 1865. 125p.
BL

232. -----Oshielle: or, village
life in the Yoruba country; from
the journals and letters of a
catechist there ... .
L: James Nisbet & co., 1857.
222p. NUC OCLC
[Protestant missionary]

233. BARBOUR, Margaret Frazer,
comp. see SANDEMAN, Mrs. Stewart

234. BARCLAY, Lydia Ann [Br.
1799-1862]
A selection from the letters of
Lydia Ann Barclay, a minister of
the Gospel.
Manchester: George Harrison,
1862. 462p. NUC BL OCLC
[Member of the Society of
Friends]

235. BARFIELD, Mary [Br. 19c]
Memoirs of the late Mrs. M.
Barfield ... with extracts from
her correspondence. Ed. Samuel
Summers.
L: n.p., 1821. BL

236. BARKER, Lady, ed. see
BRASSEY, Annie (Allnutt),
Baroness

237. BARKER, Mary Anne (Stewart),
Lady see BROOME, Mary Anne
(Stewart) Barker

238. BARKLY, Fanny Alexandra,
Mrs. [Br. 19c]
Among Boers and Basutos and with
Barkly's horse, the story of our
life on the frontier.
Extended & rev. ed. L: Roxburghe
Press, 1896. 257p. NUC BL OCLC
[Basutoland]

239. BARLOW, Adela F. [Br. 19c]
ALT: B., A. F., Miss
Convent experiences. Pub. as:
Miss A. F. B.
L: Thomas Scott, 1875. 44p. BL
[Autobiography]

240. BARLOW, Anna see BARLOW,
Debbie

241. BARLOW, Debbie [Am. 19c]
The young converts: or, memoirs
of the three sisters, Debbie,
Helen and Anna Barlow. Comp. by a
lady [Julia C. (Marvin) Smalley,
Mrs. B. H. Smalley]. Ed. the Rev.
I. T. Hecker.
NY: P. O'Shea, 1861. 263p. NUC
OCLC
[Excerpts from Debbie's letters,
describing the girls' conversion
after attending convent school.]

242. BARLOW, Helen see BARLOW,
Debbie

243. BARNARD, Lady Anne (Lindsay)
[Br. 1750-1825] ALT: Lindsay,
Lady Anne
Extracts from the journal of a
residence at the Cape of Good
Hope, and of a short tour to the
interior. In Lives of the
Lindsays; or, a memoir of the
Houses of Crawford and
Balcarres.... [Comp.] Alexander
William Crawford Lindsay, Earl of
Crawford and Balcarres.
Wigan: priv. pr., 1840. 4v. NUC
BL OCLC

244. BARNARD, Sophia [Br. 19c]
Travels in Algiers, Spain, etc.
with a faithful and interesting
account of the Algerines, etc.
L: Goyder, 1820. 140p. NUC BL
OCLC

245. BARNEY, A. M., Miss [Br.
19c]
The star in the East. An account
of the Church Missionary
Society's work in North India;
with sketches of the country and
people.
L: J. F. Shaw & co., 1860. 224p.
BL

246. BARNS, Lucy [Am. 1780-1809]
The female Christian: containing
a selection from the writings of
Miss Lucy Barns; who departed
this life Aug. 27, 1809.
Portland, ME: Francis Douglas,
pr., 1809. 71p. NUC BL OCLC

247. BARNWELL, Anne [Br. 19c]
The records of a humble life.
[Comp.] Mary Anne, Lady Alderson.
Ed. Beata Francis.
L: Strahan & co., 1881. 66p. BL

248. BARRETT, Rev. Alfred, comp.
see CRYER, Mary (Burton)

249. BARRETT, Charlotte Frances,
ed. see ARBLAY, Frances (Burney)
d'

250. BARRETT, Elizabeth see
BROWNING, Elizabeth (Barrett)

251. BARRINGTON, Jane Elizabeth
(Liddell), Viscountess, co-author
see NORMANBY, Maria (Liddell)
Phipps, Marchioness of

252. BARROT, Georgiana M. [19c]
Account of a voyage to Manilla,
in a series of letters from the
lady of the Consul-General of
France to all India, M. Adolphe
Barrot, to her uncle.
Yarmouth: for priv. circ., 1842.
58p. BL

253. BARRY, Octavia, comp. see
WELLESLEY, Lady Victoria Tylney
Long

254. BARTER, Charlotte [Br. 19c]
PSEUD: Plain Woman, A
Alone among the Zulus. By a plain
woman.
L: Society for Promoting
Christian Knowledge, 1866. 104p.
NUC BL

255. -----Home in South Africa.
By a plain woman.
L: Society for Promoting
Christian Knowledge, 1867. 158p.
BL

256. BARTLETT, Amelia, Mrs.
Thomas Bartlett [Br. 19c]

Memorials of Amelia, wife of Mr.
Thomas Bartlett ... consisting of
extracts from her devotional
papers and familiar
correspondence.
L: Burton, Clay & Smith, 1821.
192p. BL

257. BARTLETT, Mrs. Thomas see
BARTLETT, Amelia

258. BARTON, Frances see
ABINGTON, Frances (Barton)

259. BARTRAM, Lady Alfred [Br.
19c] PSEUD: Lady, A
Recollections of seven years
residence at the Mauritius, or
the Isle of France, by a lady.
L: J. Cawthorn, 1830. 208p. NUC
BL MB OCLC

260. BARTRUM, Katherine Mary [Br.
19c]
A widow's reminiscences of the
siege of Lucknow.
L: J. Nisbet & co., 1858. 102p.
NUC BL OCLC
[Sepoy Rebellion, 1857-58.]

261. BASKIN, Mary [Br. 19c]
PSEUD: Sweet Briar
Only a life: an autobiographical
story. By Sweet Briar.
L: F. E. Longley, 1874. 182p. BL

262. BASSETT, Hannah [Am. 1815-
1855]
Memoir of Hannah Bassett, with
extracts from her diary.
Lynn, MA: W. W. Kellogg, pr.,
1860. 72p. NUC OCLC

263. BATEHAM, Minerva Dayton [Am.
1856-1885] ALT: Bateham, Minnie
D.
The invalid singer; life and
writings of Minnie D. Bateham.
[Ed.] her mother, J[osephine]
P[enfield] C[ushman].
Boston: James H. Earle, 1895.
125p. NUC OCLC

264. BATEHAM, Minnie D. see
BATEHAM, Minerva Dayton

265. BATEMAN, Major C. A., ed.
see HARRIS, Louisa

266. BATES, Mrs. D. B. [Am. 19c]
Incidents on land and water; or,
four years on the Pacific Coast
... being the narrative of the
burning of the ships Nonantum,
Humayoon and Fanchon, together
with many startling adventures on
sea and land.
Boston: James French; Libby,
1857. 336p. NUC BL K OCLC

267. BATES, Elizabeth Mary, Mrs.
Ely Bates [Br. 19c]
Selections from the
correspondence of Mrs. Ely Bates
and incidents of her early life.
By Mrs. T. G. Tyndale.
Oxford: Henry Alden, 1872-73. 2v.
BL

268. BATES, Mrs. Ely see BATES,
Elizabeth Mary

269. BATES, Emily Catherine see
BATES, Emily Katherine

270. BATES, Emily Katharine [Br.
19/20c] ALT: BATES, Emily
Catherine
Kaleidoscope: shifting scenes
from East to West.
L: Ward & Downey, 1889. 275p. NUC
BL
[Travel: Oceanica, Japan, Alaska]

271. -----A year in the great
republic.
L: Ward & Downey, 1887. 2v. NUC
BL N OCLC
[Travel: U.S. & Canada]

272. BATES, Walter, ed. see
FROST, Sarah (Schofield)

273. BATHGATE, Janet [Br. 19c]
Aunt Janet's legacy to her
nieces. Recollections of humble
life in Yarrow in the beginning
of the century.
Selkirk: G. Lewis & co., 1894.
198p. NUC BL MB OCLC

274. BAUCUS, Georgiana, comp. see
NIND, Mary C.

275. BAXTER, Katherine Schuyler
[Am. b. 1845]
A godchild of Washington, a
picture of the past.
L & NY: F. T. Neely, c1897. 651p.
NUC BL OCLC

[Includes sketches of notable New
Yorkers]

276. -----In beautiful Japan; a
story of bamboo lands.
L & NY: F. T. Neely; NY: Merriam
Co., c1895-6. 381p. NUC BL OCLC
[Also pub. as: In bamboo lands]

277. BAXTER, Lucy E. (Barnes)
[Br. 1837-1902] PSEUD: Scott,
Leader
A nook in the Appenines; or, a
summer beneath the chestnuts.
L: C. Kegan Paul, 1879. 285p. NUC
OCLC
[Diary of a vacation in Tuscany.]

278. -----Tuscan studies and
sketches.
L: T. Fisher Unwin; NY: Scribner
& Welford, 1887. 329p. NUC BL
OCLC

279. BAYARD, Martha (Pintard)
[Am. 18c]
The journal of Martha Pintard
Bayard: London, 1794-1797. Ed.
Samuel Bayard Dod.
NY: Dodd, Mead & co., 1894. 141p.
NUC BL OCLC

280. BAYDEN, Anna L., ed. see
POMROY, Rebecca Rossignol
(Holliday)

281. BAYLEY, Abigail see BAILEY,
Abigail

282. BAYLEY, Annie Margaret Clive
[Br. b. 1852]
Vignettes from Finland; or,
Twelve months in strawberry land.
L: S. Low, Marston & co., 1895.
301p. NUC BL OCLC

283. BAYLY, Mrs., comp. see
SEWELL, Mary (Wright)

284. BAYLY, Mary, Mrs., comp. see
SEWELL, Mary (Wright)

285. BAYMAN, A. Phelps, Mrs. [Br.
19c] ALT: B., A. PSEUD: English
Lady, An
Notes and letters on the American
war. By an English lady.
L: William Ridgway, 1864. 82p.
NUC BL OCLC
[Letters 1862-64. Civil War.
Foreign public opinion.]

286. BEALE, Catherine Hutton, ed.
see HUTTON, Catherine

287. BEAMISH, Esther Matilda
Grace [Br. d. 1882]
"A voice that is still."
Memorials of Esther Beamish.
[Comp.] her sister, Frances L. M.
Beamish.
L: J. F. Shaw & co., 1885. 357p.
NUC BL
[May contain original material]

288. BEAMISH, Frances L. M.,
comp. see BEAMISH, Esther Matilda
Grace

289. BEAUCHAMP, Ann (Cook) [Am.
d. 1826] ALT: Cook, Ann
Letters of Ann Cook, late Mrs.
Beauchamp, to her friend in
Maryland.
Washington: n.p., 1826. 91p. NUC

290. BEAUCLERK, Lady Diana de
Vere see HUDDLESTON, Lady Diana
de Vere (Beauclerk)

291. BEAUFORT, Charlotte Sophie
(Leveson Gower) Somerset, Duchess
of [Br. 1771-1854] ALT: Somerset,
Charlotte Sophie (Leveson Gower),
Duchess of Beaufort
A sketch of the character of a
beloved mother, with extracts
from her correspondence during
the last forty years of her life.
[Comp.] Lady Louisa Elizabeth
(Somerset) Finch.
Oxford: Oxford Chronicle co.,
1861. 2v. NUC BL

292. BEAUFORT, Emily Anne see
STRANGFORD, Emily Anne
(Beaufort), Smythe, Viscountess

293. BEAUMONT, Agnes see STORY,
Agnes (Beaumont)

294. BEAUMONT, Betty (Bentley)
[Am. b. 1828]
A business woman's journal. A
sequel to "Twelve years of my
life".
Philadelphia: T. B. Peterson &
bros., c1888. 362p. NUC K OCLC

295. -----Twelve years of my
life. An autobiography.
Philadelphia: B. Peterson, c1887.
366p. NUC K OCLC

296. BEAVAN, Mrs. F. [19C]
Sketches and tales.
L: n.p., 1845. MC
[Reminiscences of 7 yrs. in
backwoods of New Brunswick in
1820s & 30s; settlers' customs
and manners.]

297. BECK, Mary Elizabeth [Br.
19c]
East and West.
L: R. Clay, sons, & Taylor, 1872.
220p. NUC OCLC
[Travel: Egypt, Palestine,
U.S.A.; Society of Friends]

298. BECKETT, Catherine Stella
(Campbell) [Am. 1852-1888]
In memoriam: Catherine S.
Campbell Beckett. Ed. Rev. Levi
Jenkins Coppin.
n.p.: n.p., 1888. 109p. NUC OCLC

299. BEDINGFIELD, Charlotte,
Lady, co-author see JERNINGHAM,
Hon. Frances, Lady

300. BEECHER, Catherine Esther
[Am. 1800-1878]
Educational reminiscences and
suggestions.
NY: J. B. Ford & co., 1874. 276p.
NUC K OCLC
[Recollections of own education
and attempts to develop girls'
school.]

301. BEECHER, Eunice White
(Bullard), Mrs. Henry Ward
Beecher [Am. 1813-1897]
Letters from Florida.
NY: D. Appleton & co., 1879. 85p.
NUC BL OCLC

302. BEECHER, Mrs. Henry Ward see
BEECHER, Eunice White (Bullard)

303. BEERS, Fannie A., Mrs. [Am.
19c]
Memories. A record of personal
experiences and adventure during
four years of war.
Philadelphia: J. B. Lippincott,
1888. 336p. NUC C K OCLC
[Hospital work in the South]

304. BEESLEY, Sarah [Br. 19c]
My life.
Banbury?: priv. pr., 1892. 259p.
BL

305. BEKE, Emily (Alston) [Br.
19c]
Jacob's flight; or, a pilgrimage
to Harran, and thence in the
patriarch's footsteps to the
promised land.
L: Longman, Green, Longman,
Roberts & Green, 1865. 360p. NUC
BL OCLC
[Travel: Syria]

306. BELL, Deborah [Br. 1688/9-
1738]
A short journal of the labours
and travels in the work of the
ministry, of that faithful
servant of Christ, Deborah Bell.
L: pr. Luke Hinde, 1762. 71p. NUC
BL MBD OCLC
[Member of Society of Friends;
travel in England]

307. BELL, Frances Augusta [Br.
19c]
A memoir of Miss F. A. Bell ...
with specimens of her
compositions, in prose and verse.
Ed. Rev. Grant Johnson.
L: Hatchard & son, 1827. 175p.
NUC BL

308. BELL, Gertrude Margaret
Lowthian [Br. 1868-1926]
Safar Nameh. Persian pictures. A
book of travel.
L: R. Bentley & son, 1894. 294p.
NUC BL

309. BELLAIRS, Nona Maria
Stevenson [Br. 19c]
Going abroad; or, glimpses of art
and character in France and
Italy.
L: Charles J. Skeet, 1857. 293p.
NUC BL

310. BELLAMY, George Anne [Br.
1731?-1788]
An apology for the life of George
Anne Bellamy, late of Covent
Garden. Written by herself. To
which is annexed her original
letter to John Calcraft, Esq.,
etc. Ed. Alexander Bicknell.
L: for the author, 1785. 5v. NUC
BL OCLC

311. BELLOC, Bessie Rayner
(Parkes) [Br. 1829-1925] ALT:
Parkes, Bessie Rayner
La belle France.

L: Strahan & co., 1868. 320p. NUC
BL OCLC

312. -----Summer sketches and
other poems.
L: John Chapman, 1854. BL
[Travel letters and poems on
places visited.]

313. BENGER, Elizabeth Ogilvy,
ed. see HAMILTON, Elizabeth

314. BENJAMIN, Mary Gladding
(Wheeler) see EVERETT, Seraphina
Haynes

315. BENNET, Grace, Mrs. John
Bennet [Br. 19c] ALT: Murray,
Grace, Mrs.
Memoirs of Mrs. Grace Bennett,
lately deceased; relict of the
Rev. John Bennet. ... To which
are subjoined extracts from her
diary. [Comp.] William Bennet.
Macclesfield: E. Bayley; L: T.
Conder, 1803. 87p. BL OCLC
[Mrs. Bennet was formerly Mrs.
Grace Murray to whom John Wesley
was at one time engaged.]

316. BENNET, Mrs. John see
BENNET, Grace

317. BENNET, William, comp. see
BENNET, Grace

318. BENNETT, Anna R. (Gladstone)
[Am. 19c] ALT: Bennett-Gladstone,
Anna R.
Einsiedeln in the dark wood, or,
Our Lady of the hermits. The
story of an Alpine sanctuary.
NY: C. N. Benziger; L: Burns &
Oates, 1883. 206p. NUC OCLC
[Travel: Switzerland]

319. BENNETT, George Bright,
comp. see BENNETT, Sarah

320. BENNETT, Sarah [Br. 19c]
The Christian governess: a memoir
and a selection from the
correspondence of Miss S.
Bennett. Comp. George Bright
Bennett.
L: J. Nisbet & co., 1862. 292p.
BL

321. BENNETT-GLADSTONE, Anna R.
see BENNETT, Anna R. (Gladstone)

322. BENSLY, Agnes Dorothee (von Blomberg), Mrs. R. L. Bensly [Br. 19c]
Our journey to Sinai. A visit to the convent of St. Catarina.
L: Religious Tract Society, 1896. 185p. BL OCLC

323. BENSLY, Mrs. R. L. see BENSLY, Agnes Dorothee (von Blomberg)

324. BENSON, Mary Eleanor [Br. 1863-1890]
The story of Russia.
L: Rivingtons, 1885. 268p. NUC BL

325. BENSON, P., Mrs. [Br. 19c]
Footsteps of mercy. An account of some of the Lord's dealings with P. Benson.
L: Alfred Gadsby, 1873. 64p. BL
[Spiritual autobiography, 1837-1867]

326. BENTLEY, Eliza [Am. 19c]
Precious stones for Zion's walls. A record of personal experience in things connected with the Kingdom of God on earth.
Toronto: W. Briggs, 1897. 403p. NUC BL

327. BENTON, Lucy [Br. 19c] ALT: B., L.
Recollections of New Street, Birmingham in the year 1817.
n.p.: n.p., 1877. 10p. BL

328. BENTON, Rhoda Angeline [Am. b. 1819]
"Beautiful thoughts." Compiled by Alice Bragg Sturdy from the writings of Rhoda Angeline Benton.
Los Angeles: The Medium, 1899. 40p. NUC OCLC

329. BERGER, Florence K. [Br. 19c]
A winter in the city of pleasure; or, life on the lower Danube.
L: R. Bentley & son, 1877. 294p. NUC BL OCLC
[Travel: Bucharest, Gipsies; legends]

330. BERKELEY, Hon. George, co-author see SUFFOLK, Henrietta (Hobart) Howard, Countess of

331. BERKELEY, Mrs. George see SUFFOLK, Henrietta (Hobart) Howard, Countess of

332. BERKELEY, HELEN, pseud., comp. see ARBLAY, Frances (Burney) d'

333. BERLYN, Annie, Mrs. Alfred Berlyn [Br. 19c]
Sunrise-land. Rambles in eastern England.
L: Jarrold & sons, 1894. 346p. NUC BL OCLC

334. BERLYN, Mrs. Alfred see BERLYN, Annie

335. BERRY, Mary [Br. 1763-1852]
Extracts of the journals and correspondence of Miss Berry from the year 1783 to 1852. Ed. Lady Maria Theresa (Villiers) Lister Lewis.
L: Longmans, Green, & co., 1865. 3v. NUC BL PD OCLC

336. BERRY, Mary, comp. see RUSSELL, Rachel (Wriothesley) Vaughn, Baroness Russell

337. BESANT, Annie (Wood) [Br. 1847-1933]
Annie Besant: An autobiography.
L: T. Fisher Unwin; Philadelphia: H. Altemus, 1893. 368p. NUC BL MB OCLC

338. -----Autobiographical sketches.
L: Freethought pub. co., 1885. 169p. BL OCLC
[Theosophist; correspondence, reminiscences, etc.]

339. BEST, M. C., Mrs. [BL: Best, M. C.] [Br. 19c]
Abroad: and how to live there. A narrative of three years' residence in Germany and Switzerland. By Mrs. Best.
L: Seeley, Jackson and Halliday, 1860. 345p. NUC
[The English Christian abroad; new ed., L: 1864]

340. BETANCOURT COSIO Y CISNEROS, Evangelina see CISNEROS, Evangelina

341. BETHAM-EDWARDS, Matilda
Barbara <u>see</u> EDWARDS, Matilda
Barbara Betham-

342. BETHUNE, Divie, comp. <u>see</u>
GRAHAM, Isabella (Marshall)

343. BETHUNE, George Washington,
comp. <u>see</u> BETHUNE, Joanna
(Graham)

344. BETHUNE, Joanna (Graham)
[Am. 1770-1849]
Memoirs of Mrs. Joanna Bethune.
Comp. her son, the Rev. George
Washington Bethune.
NY: Harper & bros., 1863. 250p.
NUC MAD OCLC
[Includes diary]

345. BETHUNE, Joanna (Graham),
ed. <u>see</u> GOODALE, Anna

346. BETHUNE, Joanna (Graham),
comp. <u>see</u> GRAHAM, Isabella
(Marshall)

347. BETTLE, Jane [Am. 1773-1840]
Extracts from the memorandums of
Jane Bettle, with a short memoir
respecting her.
2d ed. Philadelphia: J. & W.
Kite, 1843. 116p. NUC BL MAD OCLC
[Journal, 1832-1840; Society of
Friends]

348. BETTS, Rachel [Br. d. 1831]
A short account of the last
illness and death of Rachel
Betts. To which are added some
extracts from her letters and
from a diary, found after her
decease.
L: J. Betts, 1831. 64p. NUC BL
OCLC

349. BEVAN, Ada Frances [Br. 19c]
Reminiscences of Ada Frances
Bevan. By her mother [Emma
Frances Bevan, Mrs. Francis A.
Bevan].
L: pr. for priv. circ., 1861.
63p. BL

350. BEVAN, Emma Frances, comp.
<u>see</u> BEVAN, Ada Frances

351. BEVAN, Frances, comp. <u>see</u>
BEVAN, Ada Frances

352. BEVAN, Mrs. Francis A.,
comp. <u>see</u> BEVAN, Ada Frances

353. BEWICKE, Alice E. Neva <u>see</u>
LITTLE, Alice Helen Neva
(Bewicke)

354. BEWICKE, Alice Helen Neva
<u>see</u> LITTLE, Alicia Helen Neva
(Bewicke)

355. BIANCIARDI, Elizabeth
Dickinson (Rice) [Am. 1833-1885]
At home in Italy.
NY & Boston: Houghton, Mifflin &
co., 1884. 300p. NUC BL OCLC

356. BICKERDYKE, Mary Ann (Bull)
[Am. 1817-1901]
Mary A. Bickerdyke, "Mother,"
(Written by Julia A. (Houghton)
Chase). The life story of one
who, as wife, mother, army nurse,
prison agent and city missionary,
has touched the heights and
depths of human life.
Lawrence, KS: Women's relief
corps, 1896. 145p. NUC K OCLC
[Based on letters and
conversations with Bickerdyke]

357. BICKERSTETH, Charlotte,
comp. <u>see</u> BICKERSTETH, Elizabeth

358. BICKERSTETH, Elizabeth [Br.
19c] ALT: Birks, Elizabeth
(Bickersteth)
Doing and suffering: memorials of
Elizabeth and Frances, daughters
of the late Rev. E. Bickersteth,
by their sister [Charlotte
(Bickersteth) Ward].
L: Seeley, Jackson & Halliday,
1852. 221p. NUC BL

359. BICKERSTETH, Frances <u>see</u>
BICKERSTETH, Elizabeth

360. BICKERSTETH, Mary Jane [Br.
19c]
Japan as we saw it.
L: S. Low, Marston & co.; NY: C.
Scribner's sons, 1893. 354p. NUC
BL

361. BICKFORD, James, comp. <u>see</u>
BICKFORD, Mary Ann (Dunn)

362. BICKFORD, Mary Ann (Dunn)
[Am. 1824-1845]

The authentic life of Mrs. Mary Ann Bickford, who was murdered in the city of Boston, on the 27th of October, 1845. Comprising a large number of her original letters and correspondence never before published. Comp. James Bickford.
Boston: the compiler, 1846. 48p. NUC OCLC

363. BICKNELL, Alexander, ed. <u>see</u> BELLAMY, George Anne

364. BICKNELL, Alexander <u>see</u> STEELE, Elizabeth

365. BIDDLE, Henry D., ed. <u>see</u> DRINKER, Elizabeth (Sandwith)

366. BILLER, Sarah (Kilham), ed. <u>see</u> KILHAM, Hannah (Spurr)

367. BILLINGTON, Elizabeth (Weichsel) [Br. 1768-1818]
Memoirs of Mrs. Billington, from her birth ... with copies of several original letters ... written by Mrs. Billington, to her mother, the late Mrs. Weichsel.
L: James Ridgway, 1792. 78p. NUC BL OCLC

368. BINGHAM, Mary Helen [Br. 1808-1825]
A memoir of Miss Mary Helen Bingham, who died in the seventeenth year of her age. By John Bustard.
L: pr. for the author, 1827. 208p. NUC BL MBD
[Methodist; based on her diary & letters; Rev. ed.: NY: T. Mason & G. Lane, 1837.]

369. BINGLEY, W., ed. <u>see</u> SOMERSET, Frances (Thynne) Seymour, Duchess of

370. BIRCH, John William Newell, ed. <u>see</u> BIRCH, Mary (Newell)

371. BIRCH, Mary (Newell) [Br. d. 1837]
Letters written by the late Mrs. Birch ... in the ninety-ninth and hundredth year of her age. Ed. John William Newell Birch.
L: pr. by A. Spottiswoode, 1837?. 152p. NUC BL OCLC

372. BIRD, ·Isabella <u>see</u> BISHOP, Isabella Louisa (Bird)

373. BIRKS, Elizabeth (Bickersteth) <u>see</u> BICKERSTETH, Elizabeth

374. BIRRELL, Rev. Charles Morton, ed. <u>see</u> GREY, Mrs. Henry

375. BIRT, Anna [Br. 19c]
A narrative of recent occurences in Posen. Accompanied by letters from an English lady resident in Posen.
n.p.: n.p., 1848. BL

376. BISHOP, Harriet E. [Am. 1817-1883] ALT: Macconkey, Harriet E. (Bishop)
Dakota war-whoop; or, Indian massacres and war in Minnesota.
St. Paul, MN: D. D. Merrill, 1863. 304p. NUC BL OCLC

377. -----Floral home; or, first years of Minnesota.
NY: Sheldon, Blakeman & co., 1857. 342p. NUC BL OCLC
[School teacher; travel in Minn., information on Indian tribes.]

378. -----Minnesota; then and now.
St. Paul, MN: D. D. Merrill, Randall & co., 1869. 100p. NUC OCLC
[Descriptive & historical verse]

379. BISHOP, Isabella Louisa (Bird), Mrs. J. F. Bishop [Br. 1831-1904] ALT: Bird, Isabella; Bishop, Isabella Lucy (Bird)
Among the Tibetans.
NY: Revell; L: The Religious Tract Soc., 1894. 159p. NUC BL OCLC

380. -----The Englishwoman in America.
L: J. Murray, 1856. 464p. NUC BL OCLC

381. -----The golden Chersonese and the way thither.
L: J. Murray, 1883. 384p.; NY: G. P. Putnam's sons, 1883. 483p. NUC BL OCLC
[Travel: China & the Malay peninsula]

382. -----The Hawaiian archipelago. Six months among the palm groves, coral reefs and volcanoes of the Sandwich Islands.
2d ed. L: J. Murray, 1872. 318p. NUC OCLC

383. -----Journeys in Persia and Kurdistan, including a summer in the Upper Karun region and a visit to the Nestorian rayahs.
L: J. Murray; NY: G. P. Putnam's sons, 1891. 2v.   NUC OCLC

384. -----Korea and her neighbors; a narrative of travel, with an account of the recent vicissitudes and present position of the country.
3d ed. NY & Chicago: F. H. Revell, c1897. 488p. NUC OCLC

385. -----A lady's life in the Rocky Mountains.
L & NY: J. Murray, 1879. 296p. NUC BL N OCLC
[Estes Park, Colo.]

386. -----Notes on Old Edinburgh.
Edinburgh: Edmonston & Douglas, 1869. 32p. NUC BL

387. -----Unbeaten tracks in Japan.
NY: G. P. Putnam; L: J. Murray, 1880. 2v.   NUC BL OCLC

388. -----The Yangtze Valley and beyond; an account of journeys in China, chiefly in the province of Sze Chuan and among the Man-tze of the Somo territory.
L: J. Murray, 1899. 558p. NUC BL OCLC

389. BISHOP, Isabella Lucy (Bird) see BISHOP, Isabella Louisa (Bird)

390. BISHOP, Mrs. J. F. see BISHOP, Isabella Louisa (Bird)

391. BISHOP, Maria Catherine, comp. see CRAVEN, Pauline Marie Armande Algaé (Ferron de Ferronnays)

392. BISHOP, Maria Catherine, comp. see URQUHART, Harriet Angelina (Fortesque)

393. BISHOP, Sydney Olive [Br. 19c]
Sketches in Assam.
Calcutta: T. S. Smith, 1885. 257p. BL

394. BISLAND, Elizabeth see WETMORE, Elizabeth (Bisland)

395. BIXBY, Olive Jennie [Am. 19c]
My child-life in Burmah; or, recollections and incidents.
Boston: W. G. Corthell; Providence, RI: M. H. Bixby, c1880. 172p.   NUC BL OCLC
[Missions: Burma]

396. BLACK, Sophia C., Mrs. [Am. 19c]
Brief narrative of the wreck of the schooner "Minerva" in the gulf stream, Sept., 1849.
Baltimore, MD: n.p., 1851. 12p. NUC

397. BLACKALL, Emily (Lucas) [Am. 19c]
Two weeks among Indians, and glimpses of work in their behalf.
Chicago: Women's Baptist Home Mission Society, 1882. 15p. NUC OCLC
[Missionary; Five civilized tribes]

398. BLACKFORD, Charles Minor, co-author see BLACKFORD, Susan Leigh (Colston)

399. BLACKFORD, Mrs. Charles Minor see BLACKFORD, Susan Leigh (Colston)

400. BLACKFORD, Susan Leigh (Colston), Mrs. Charles Minor Blackford [Am. 1835-1916]
Memoirs of life in and out of the army in Virginia during the War Between the States. Comp. Susan Leigh Blackford. Annotated and ed. her husband, Charles Minor Blackford.
Lynchburg, VA: J. P. Bell co., pr., 1894-96. 2v. NUC BL C OCLC

401. BLACKWELL, Caroline S. [Br. 19c]
A living epistle, or, gathered fragments from the correspondence of the late C. S. Blackwell.

L: J. F. Shaw & co., 1874. 380p.
BL

402. BLACKWELL, Elizabeth, Dr.
[Am. 1821-1910]
Pioneer work in opening the
medical profession to women;
autobiograph-ical sketches.
n.p.: n.p., 1893. 265p. NUC BL K
MB OCLC
[L & NY: Longmans, Green & co.;
Hastings: K. Barry, 1895. 265p.]

403. BLACKWOOD, Lady Alicia [Br.
19c]
Narrative of personal experiences
and impressions during a
residence on the Bosphorus
throughout the Crimean War.
L: Hatchard, 1881. 318p. NUC BL
MB OCLC

404. -----Scutari, the Bosphorus
and the Crimea. Twenty-four
sketches.
Ventnor, Isle of Wight: J.
Lavers, 1857. 2v in 1. NUC

405. BLACKWOOD, Hariot Georgina
see DUFFERIN AND AVA, Hariot
Georgina (Hamilton) Hamilton-
Temple-Blackwood, Marchioness of

406. BLAKE, Edith (Osborne) see
OSBORNE, Edith

407. BLAKE, Margaret Jane [Am.
1811-1880]
Memoirs of Margaret Jane Blake of
Baltimore, MD, and selections in
prose and verse by Sarah R.
Levering.
Philadelphia: Press of Innes &
son, 1897. 48p. NUC
[Blake was a slave in Baltimore
before the Civil War.]

408. BLAKE, Mary E. [19c]
A Mexican holiday.
n.p.: n.p., 1885?. 30p. OCLC

409. BLAKE, Mary Elizabeth
(McGrath) [Am. 1840-1907] ALT:
B., M. E.
An epic of travel; gotten up
without regard to cost, sense, or
meter; in eight cantos; dedicated
to the third Raymond California
party of 1822. By M. E. B.
Boston: n.p., 1884. 12p. NUC

410. -----Mexico: picturesque,
political, progressive. With
Margaret Frances Sullivan.
Boston: Lee & Shepard; NY: C. T.
Dillingham, 1888. 228p.   NUC OCLC
[Pt 1. Picturesque Mexico by
Blake; Pt 2. Political and
progressive Mexico by Sullivan]

411. -----On the wing; rambling
notes of a trip to the Pacific.
Boston: Lee & Shepard, 1883.
235p. NUC OCLC

412. -----A summer holiday in
Europe.
Boston: Lee & Shepard; L: S.
Bagster; NY: C. T. Dillingham;
Dublin: Eason & son, 1890. 203p.
NUC BL OCLC

413. BLAKENEY, Mary Aspinall [Br.
19c]
Souvenirs of travel in and around
the Mediterranean, 1893-4.
Ramsgate: pr. for priv. circ.,
1895. 86p. BL

414. BLAND, Samuel K., comp. see
BLAND, Sarah Nash

415. BLAND, Mrs. Samuel K. see
BLAND, Sarah Nash

416. BLAND, Sarah Nash, Mrs.
Samuel K. Bland [Br. 19c]
The field and the garner: being
the living and dying memorials of
a quiet Christian. Compiled from
the diary, correspondence, etc.
of Mrs. S. K. Bland. Comp. her
husband, Samuel K. Bland.
L: Partridge, Oakey & co., 1854.
117p. BL MB

417. BLANDY, Mary [Br. 1720-1752]
Miss Mary Blandy's own account of
the affair between her and Mr.
Cranstoun, from the commencement
of their acquaintance ... to the
death of her father ... to which
is added an appendix containing
copies of some original letters
... together with an exact
relation of her behaviour whilst
under sentence.
L: A. Millar, 1752. 64p. NUC BL
OCLC

418. BLANKENSHIP, Mattie A., Mrs.
[Am. 19c]

A statistical and descriptive
poem of Texas.
Dallas, TX: J. M. Colville, 1892.
23p. NUC OCLC

419. BLAUGDONE, Barbara [Br. 17c]
An account of the travelings,
sufferings, and persecutions of
Barbara Blaugdone. Given forth as
a testimony to the Lord's power,
and for the encouragement of
friends.
L: T. S. [Tace Sowle], 1691. 38p.
BL
[Member of Society of Friends]

420. BLAZE DE BURY, Marie Pauline
Rose (Stewart), Baroness [Br.
19c]
Germania; its courts, camps, and
people.
L: Henry Colburn, 1850. 2v. NUC
BL OCLC

421. BLAZE DE BURY, Marie Pauline
Rose (Stewart), Baroness, ed. see
ELIZABETH, Princess Palatine,
Abbess of Herford

422. BLEECKER, Sophia [Am. 19c]
Lays of a lifetime. The record of
one departed. By Mary Noel
(Bleecker) Macdonald Meigs.
NY: Dana & co.; L: S. Low & son &
co., 1857. 157p. NUC
[A memoir of Sophia, Meigs'
sister, whose poems, under the
pseudonyms Katy-did and Katy-
didn't, are included.]

423. BLENCOWE, Robert Willis, ed.
see FIENNES, Celia

424. BLENNERHASSETT, Rose [Br.
19c]
Adventures in Mashonaland. By two
hospital nurses. With Lucy
Sleeman.
L & NY: Macmillan & co., 1893.
340p. NUC BL OCLC

425. BLESSINGTON, Marguerite
(Power) Farmer Gardiner, Countess
of [Br. 1789-1849] ALT: Gardiner,
Marguerite (Power) Farmer,
Countess of Blessington
The Blessington papers.
L: pr. for priv. circ., 1895.
234p. NUC OCLC

[Collection of autograph letters
and historical documents, chiefly
letters written to Lady
Blessington.]

426. -----Conversations of Lord
Byron with the Countess of
Blessington.
L: Henry Colburn, 1834. 412p. NUC
BL OCLC

427. -----The idler in France.
L: H. Colburn; Philadelphia:
Carey & Hart, 1841. 2v. NUC BL OCLC

428. -----The idler in Italy.
L: H. Colburn, 1839. 3v. NUC BL
OCLC

429. -----Journal of a tour
through the Netherlands to Paris,
in 1821.
L: Longman, Hurst, Rees, Orme, &
Brown, 1822. 171p. NUC BL OCLC

430. -----The literary life and
correspondence of the Countess of
Blessington.
L; Woking [pr.]: n.p., 1855. BL

431. BLOOD, Gertrude Elizabeth
see CAMPBELL, Gertrude Elizabeth
(Blood)

432. BLOOMER, Amelia (Jenks) [Am.
1818-1894]
Life and writings of Amelia
Bloomer. Comp. Dexter C. Bloomer.
Boston: Arena Pub. co., 1895.
387p. NUC BL OCLC

433. BLOOMER, Dexter C., comp.
see BLOOMER, Amelia (Jenks)

434. BLOOMFIELD, Georgiana
(Liddell), Baroness [Br. 1822-
1905]
Reminiscences of court and
diplomatic life.
L: Kegan Paul, Trench; Leipzig:
B. Tauchnitz, 1883. 2v. NUC BL MB
OCLC

435. BLOOMFIELD, Georgiana
(Liddell), Baroness, comp. see
NORMANBY, Maria (Liddell) Phipps,
Marchioness of

436. BLUNDELL, Isabella Frances
[Br. 19c] ALT: Copland, Isabella
Frances (Blundell)
Gamle Norge, Old Norway; or, our
holiday in Scandinavia.
L: Hamilton, Adams & co., 1862.
312p. BL

437. BLUNDEN, Constance Jane [Br.
19c]
Fragrant memories of Constance
Jane Blunden.
L: E. Wilmshurst, 1896. 79p. BL
[Includes letters & journal]

438. BLUNT, Lady Anne Isabella
Noel, Baroness Wentworth [Br.
1837-1917]
A pilgrimage to Nejd, the cradle
of the Arab race. A visit to the
court of the Arab emir, and "Our
Persian Campaign". Ed. Wilfred
Scawen Blunt.
L: J. Murray, 1881. 2v. NUC BL
OCLC

439. BLUNT, Fanny Janet
(Sandison) [Br. b. 1840] ALT:
Blunt, Mrs. John E. PSEUD:
Consul's daughter and wife, A
The people of Turkey: twenty
years residence among Bulgarians,
Greeks, Albanians, Turks and
Armenians. By a consul's daughter
and wife. Ed. Stanley Lane Poole.
L: n.p., 1878. 2v. BL MB

440. BLUNT, Mrs. John E. see
BLUNT, Fanny Janet (Sandison),
Lady

441. BLUNT, Wilfred Scawen, ed.
see BLUNT, Lady Anne Isabella
Noel, Baroness Wentworth

442. BLY, NELLIE, pseud. see
COCHRANE, Elizabeth

443. BOADEN, James, ed. see
INCHBALD, Elizabeth (Simpson)

444. BOADEN, James, ed. see
JORDAN, Dorothy (Bland)

445. BOCKING, Hannah (Dakin) [Am.
1760-1855]
Light in the valley; or, the life
and letters of Mrs. Hannah
Bocking. Ed. Miss M. Annesley.
NY: Carlton & Porter, 1860. NUC

446. BODDINGTON, Mary, Mrs. [Br.
19c]
Sketches in the Pyrenees, with
some remarks on Languedoc,
Provence, and the Cornice.
L: Longman, Rees, Orme, Brown,
Green & Longman, 1837. 2v. NUC BL
OCLC

447. -----Slight reminiscences of
the Rhine, Switzerland, and a
corner of Italy.
L: Longman, Rees, Orme, Brown,
Green, & Longman, 1834. 2v. NUC
BL OCLC

448. BOEHM, Anthony William, co-
author see WEBB, Elizabeth

449. BOGUE, David, comp. see
TURNER, Joanna

450. BOLAINE, Betty [Br. 19c]
Life and history of Betty
Bolaine, late of Canterbury, a
well known character for
parsimony and vice. ...
Interspersed with original
poetry. By Elizabeth Burgess.
Canterbury: H. Ward, 1832. 40p.
NUC BL

451. BOLTON, Abby [Am. 1827-1849]
The lighted valley; or, the
closing scenes in the life of a
beloved sister. [Comp.] Rhoda
Bolton.
NY: Robert Carter & bros., 1850.
236p.; L: Hamilton, Adams & co.,
1850. 194p. NUC BL OCLC
[Includes letters; travel in
England.]

452. BOLTON, Rhoda, comp. see
BOLTON, Abby

453. BOND, Catherine [Br. 19c]
Goldfields and chrysanthemums.
Notes of travel in Australia and
Japan.
L: Simpkin, Marshall, 1898. 270p.
NUC BL

454. BONAR, J. J., ed. see GOW,
Elizabeth

455. BOND, Elizabeth [Br. 19c]
Letters of a village governess;
descriptive of rural scenery and
manners.

L: pr. for author by E. Blackader, 1814. 2v. NUC BL OCLC

456. BONER, Charles, co-author see MITFORD, Mary Russell

457. BOOBBYER, Anna [Br. b. 1828]
Broken purposes, but answered prayers: a record of Jehovah's loving kindness.
L: Marshall bros., 1896. 334p. BL
[Religious autobiography]

458. BOONE, Martha (Rees) [Br. 1778-1816]
Selections from the papers of Martha Boone, late of Birmingham, found after her decease; to which is prefixed a brief memoir.
L: Bensley & son, 1817. 39p. NUC

459. BOOTH, Elizabeth [Am. 19c]
Reminiscences by Elizabeth Booth of New Castle, Delaware.
New Castle, DL: Del. Print. priv., 1884. 202p. NUC OCLC

460. BOOTH, John, ed. see EATON, Charlotte Anne (Waldie)

461. BOSANQUET, Mary see FLETCHER, Mary (Bosanquet)

462. BOSWELL, James, ed. see DOUGLAS, Lady Jane

463. BOTHMER, Marie, Graffin von see BOTHMER, Mary von, Countess

464. BOTHMER, Mary von, Countess [Br. 1845-1921] ALT: Bothmer, Marie, Graffin von
German home life.
2d ed. NY: D. Appleton, 1876. 312p. NUC BL OCLC

465. BOTTA, Anne Charlotte (Lynch) [Am. 1815-1891] ALT: Lynch, Anne Charlotte
Memoirs of Anne C. L. Botta, written by her friends. With selections from her correspondence and from her writings in prose and poetry. Ed. Vincenzo Botta.
NY: J. S. Tait & sons, 1894. 459p. NUC BL OCLC

466. BOTTA, Vincenzo, ed. see BOTTA, Anne Charlotte (Lynch)

467. BOTTOME, Margaret (McDonald) [1827-1906]
A sunshine trip: glimpses of the Orient. Extracts from letters.
NY & L: Edward Arnold, 1897. 215p. NUC BL OCLC

468. BOULINGNY, Mary E. (Parker) [Am. 19c] ALT: B., M. E. P.
Bubbles and ballast. Being a description of life in Paris during the brilliant days of the empire; a tour through Belgium and Holland, and a sojourn in London.
Baltimore, MD: Kelly, Piet and co., 1871. 372p. NUC BL OCLC

469. BOURNE, Jane [Br. 19c]
Northern reminiscences.
Whitehaven: J. Robinson, 1832. 145p. BL
[Tour of New England where she grew up. Poetry and prose.]

470. BOUTELLE, Ann L. [Am. 1819-1835]
Biographical sketch of Ann L. Boutelle.
Boston: Benjamin H. Greene, 1836. 35p. NUC
[Focuses on days preceding her death; incl. poems.]

471. BOWDICH, Sarah (Wallis) see LEE, Sarah (Wallis) Bowdich

472. BOWDICH, Thomas Edward, co-author see LEE, Sarah (Wallis) Bowdich

473. BOWDICH, Mrs. Thomas Edward see LEE, Sarah (Wallis) Bowdich

474. BOWDLER, Henrietta Maria, ed. see SMITH, Elizabeth

475. BOWEN, Harriet M. (Gardiner) [Am. 1832-1852]
A brief memoir of Harriet, with some of her essays in prose and verse. By her mother, Mrs. William [Marilla (Dunton)] Gardiner.
Oberlin, OH: J. M. Fitch, 1855. 129p. NUC OCLC
[OCLC lists Bowen as Brown]

476. BOWERS, Bathsheba [Am. 1672-1718]

An alarm sounded to prepare the inhabitants of the world to meet the Lord in the way of his judgments.
NY: n.p., 1709. NUC
[Religious autobiography]

477. BOWLES, Caroline see SOUTHEY, Caroline Anne (Bowles)

478. BOWMAN, Henrietta [Br. 1838-1872] ALT: Bowman, Hetty
Speaking yet: or remains in prose and verse of the late Hetty Bowman. Ed. M. M. Gordon.
L: Book society; Bristol: W. Mack, 1874. 157p. BL
[Includes poetry]

479. BOWMAN, Hetty see BOWMAN, Henrietta

480. BOWNAS, Samuel C. see HANSON, Elizabeth

481. BOWNE, Eliza (Southgate) [Am. 1783-1809]
A girl's life eighty years ago. Selections from the letters of E. S. Bowne.
NY: Scribner's sons, 1887. 239p.
NUC BL OCLC

482. BOWYER, Edith M. (Nicholl) [Am. 19c] ALT: Nicholl, Edith M.
Observations of a ranch woman in New Mexico.
L & NY: Macmillan, 1898. 271p.
NUC K OCLC
[Farm life in New Mexico]

483. BOYD, Belle [Am. 1843/4-1900] ALT: Hardinge, Belle (Boyd)
Belle Boyd, in camp and prison.
L: Saunders, Otley & co., 1865.
2v. NUC BL K OCLC
[Personal account of Civil War, pro-South]

484. BOYD, Mrs. Orsemus Bronson [Am. 19c]
Cavalry life in tent and field.
NY: J. Selwin Tait, 1894. 376p.
NUC BL K OCLC

485. BOYDEN, Anna L., comp. see POMROY, Rebecca Rossignol (Holliday)

486. BOYKIN, Laurette Nisbet, Mrs. S. Boykin [Am. 1866-1894]
The annals of an invertebrate.
Nashville, TN: Press of Brandon prtg. co., 1895. 109p. NUC OCLC
[Autobiographical account of consumption.]

487. BOYKIN, Mrs. S. see BOYKIN, Laurette Nisbet

488. BRABOURNE, Edward, Lord, ed. see AUSTEN, Jane

489. BRADLEY, Eliza, Mrs. James Bradley [Br. b. 1783]
An authentic narrative of the shipwreck and sufferings of Mrs. E. Bradley.... Written by herself.
Boston: James Walden, 1820. 108p.
NUC BL MB OCLC

490. BRADLEY, Emily Tennyson, ed. see STUART, Lady Arabella

491. BRADLEY, Mrs. James see BRADLEY, Eliza

492. BRAGG, Alice, comp. see BENTON, Rhoda Angeline

493. BRAIN, Ada B. [Br. 19c]
"Our pilgrimage." In Notes of a voyage in the Orient Steamship Company's S. S. "Garonne" in the early part of the year 1891. By W[illiam] B[utler].
Bristol: Allen, Davies & co., 1892. 109p. BL
[pp. 63-109 are by her]

494. BRAITHWAITE, Martha [Br. 1823-1895]
Loving service. A record of the life of Martha Braithwaite, by her daughter [Elizabeth (Braithwaite) Emmott].
L: Headley bros., 1896. 296p. NUC BL MBD OCLC
[Member of Society of Friends; includes diary.]

495. BRAITHWAITE, Martha, comp. see ALSOP, Christine R. (Majolier

496. BRANDRETH, Mrs. Henry Rowland see BRANDRETH, Mary Elizabeth (Shepherd)

497. BRANDRETH, Mary Elizabeth (Shepherd), Mrs. Henry Rowland Brandreth [Br. b. 1808]
Some family and friendly recollections of 70 years, of Mary Elizabeth Brandreth, widow of Henry Rowland Brandreth ... and daughter of Henry John Shepherd, Q. C., and Lady Mary Shepherd.
[Westerham, Eng.: C. Hooker, 1886?]. 188p. NUC
[A family chronicle including personal anecdotes and letters.]

498. BRASSEY, Annie (Allnutt), Baroness [Br. 1839-1887] ALT: B., A.
A cruise in the "Eöthen".
L: pr. for priv. circ., 1873. 166p. NUC MC OCLC
[Travel: Canada & U.S. Atlantic Coast]

499. -----In the trades, the tropics and the roaring forties.
L: Longmans, Green, & co., 1885 [1884]. 532p.; Leipzig: B. Tauchnitz, 1885. 2v. NUC BL OCLC
[Travel: British West Indies]

500. -----The last voyage ... 1887. Ed. Lady Barker [Mary Ann (Stewart) Barker Broome].
L & NY: Longmans, Green & co., 1889. 490p. NUC BL OCLC
[Travel: India & Australia]

501. -----Sunshine and storm in the East; or, cruises to Cyprus and Constantinople.
L: Longmans & co., 1880 [1879]. 448p; Leipzig: B. Tauchnitz, 1880. 302p. NUC BL OCLC

502. -----A voyage in the "Sunbeam." Our home on the ocean for eleven months [1876-77].
L: Longmans, Green & co., 1878. 504p. NUC BL OCLC
[Also pub. in 1878 under title: Around the world in the yacht "Sunbeam."]

503. BRAY, Anna Eliza (Kempe) Stothard, Mrs. Edwin Atkyns Bray [Br. 1790-1883] ALT: Stothard, Anna Eliza; Stothard, Mrs. Charles Alfred
Autobiography of A. E. Bray. Ed. John A. Kempe.

L: Chapman and Hall ltd., 1884. 356p. NUC BL MB OCLC

504. -----A description of that part of Devonshire bordering on the Tamar and the Tavy ... in a series of letters to the late Robert Southey, Esq., by Mrs. Bray.
L: J. Murray, 1836. 3v. NUC BL OCLC
[Later pub. as: The borders of the Tamar and the Tavy.]

505. -----Letters written during a tour through Normandy, Brittany, and other parts of France in 1818.
L: Longman, Hurst, Rees, Orme and Brown, 1820. 322p. NUC BL OCLC

506. -----Memoirs, including original journals, letters papers, and antiquarian tracts of the late Charles Alfred Stothard and some accounts of a journey in the Netherlands. By Mrs. Charles Stothard.
L: pr. for Longman, Hurst, Rees, Orme, & Brown, 1823. 497p. NUC BL MB OCLC

507. -----The mountains and lakes of Switzerland: with descriptive sketches of other parts of the continent.
L: n.p., 1841. 3v. BL

508. BRAY, Mrs. Edwin Atkyns see BRAY, Anna Eliza (Kempe) Stothard

509. BRAYBROOKE, Lord, ed. see BACON, Jane (Meautys) Cornwallis, Lady

510. BRAYTON, Patience (Greene) [Am. 1733-1794]
A short account of the life and religious labours of Patience Brayton ... of Massachusetts. Mostly selected from her own minutes.
New Bedford, MA: pr. by A. Shearman, 1801. 142p.; NY: Isaac Collins & son, 1801. 135p. NUC OCLC
[Member of the Society of Friends.]

511. BREMNER, Christina Sinclair [Br. 19/20c]

A month in a Dandi; a woman's wanderings in Northern India.
L: Simpkin, Marshall, Hamilton, Kent & co., 1891?. 214p. NUC OCLC

512. BRENGLE, Annie M. see KLOCK, Annie Maria (Brengle)

513. BRENT, Linda see JACOBS, Harriet (Brent)

514. BRERETON, Jane [Br. 1685-1740]
Poems on several occasions, with letters to her friends and an account of her life.
L: Edward Cave, 1744. 303p. NUC BL

515. BREWER, Lucy see WEST, Lucy (Brewer)

516. BREWSTER, Margaret Maria see GORDON, Margaret Maria (Brewster)

517. BRIDGES, Charles, ed. see GRAHAM, Mary Jane

518. BRIDGES, F. D. [Br. 19c]
Journal of a lady's travels round the world.
L: J. Murray, 1883. 413p. NUC BL OCLC

519. BRIDGMAN, Eliza Jane (Gillett) [Am. 19c]
Daughters of China; or, sketches of domestic life in the celestial empire.
NY: R. Carter & bros., c1852. 234p. NUC BL K OCLC

520. BRIGGS, Caroline (Clapp) [Am. 1822-1895]
Reminiscences and letters of Caroline C. Briggs. Ed. George S. Merriam.
Boston & NY: Houghton Mifflin, 1897. 445p. NUC BL K OCLC

521. BRIGHTWELL, Cecelia Lucy, ed. see OPIE, Amelia (Alderson)

522. BRINE, Anne [Br. 18c]
Some account of the choice experience of Mrs. Anne Brine, as written by herself and collected out of her letters. [Ed.] John Brine.
L: John Ward & John Eynon, 1750. 54p. NUC BL

523. BRINE, John, ed. see BRINE, Anne

524. BRISTOL, Elizabeth Chudleigh Hervey, Countess of see HERVEY, Elizabeth Chudleigh

525. BRITTAN, Harriett G. [BL Harriette] [Am. 1823-1897]
Scenes and incidents of every-day life in Africa.
2d ed. NY: Pudney & Russell, 1860. 353p. NUC BL OCLC
[Liberia; Missions]

526. -----A woman's talks about India.
Philadelphia: American Sunday School Union, 1880. 214p. NUC BL OCLC

527. BRITTAN, Harriette see BRITTON, Harriet G.

528. BRITTLE, Emily [Br. 18c]
The India guide; or, journal of a voyage to the East Indies in the year MDCCLXXX in a poetical epistle to her mother.
Calcutta: pr., George Gordon, 1785. 1v. NUC BL OCLC
[Includes two letters and other poems]

529. BROADBELT, Ann, Mrs. [Br. 1786-1838]
Memoirs of Mrs. Ann Broadbelt, of Killinghall, Yorkshire. [Comp.] Samuel Thompson.
L: n.p., 1838. 426p. NUC BL MBD OCLC
[Methodist; diary 1809-1837.]

530. BROMLEY, Clara Fitzroy (Kelly) [Br. 19c]
A woman's wanderings in the western world. A series of letters, etc.
L: Saunders, Otley & co., 1861. 299p. NUC BL OCLC
[Travel: U.S.]

531. BROOK, Mrs. Charles John [Br. 19c]
Six weeks in Egypt. Fugitive sketches of Eastern travel.
L: Simpkin & Marshall, 1893. 238p. NUC BL

532. BROOKE, C., Mrs. [Br. 19c]
A dialogue between a lady and her
pupils, describing a journey
through England and Wales. 3d ed.
considerably enlarged. By the
Rev. John Evans.
L: Sherwood, Neely & Jones, 1812.
323p. BL

533. BROOKE, Tina [Br. 19c]
A trip to Skye. By Bell Munro and
T. Brooke.
Lockerbie: priv. pr. by James
Halliday, 1873. 92p. BL
[Travel story in third person
about two cousins, Tina & Bell]

534. BROOKER, Charles, ed. see
BROOKER, Elizabeth

535. BROOKER, Elizabeth [Br. 19c]
The fallacy of infidelity and the
veracity of the scriptures,
demonstrated in the death of the
Christian. Memoirs of Mrs. E.
Brooker to which are added brief
extracts from her diary. Ed.
Charles Brooker.
L: Francis Westley, 1822. 128p.
BL

536. BROOKHOUSE, Ann [Br. 19c]
A narrative of the seizure and
confinement of Ann Brookhouse,
who was assaulted in one of the
streets of London and carried off
... as related by herself.
Written by a friend.
L: pr. for author & sold by C.
Rivingtons & J. Johnson, 1798?.
116p. NUC BL

537. BROOKS, Abbie M. [Am. 19c]
PSEUD: Sunshine, Silvia
Petals plucked from sunny climes.
By Silvia Sunshine.
Nashville, TN: So. Methodist pub.
house, c1879. 495p. NUC OCLC
[Early settlement of Florida;
travel in Florida and Cuba]

538. BROOKS, Sarah Merriam, Mrs.
[Am. 19c]
Across the Isthmus to California
in '52.
San Francisco: C. A. Murdock &
co., 1894. 79p. NUC OCLC

539. BROOME, John H., ed. see
STONE, Letitia Willgoes

540. BROOME, Mary Anne (Stewart)
Barker [Br. 1831-1911] ALT:
Barker, Mary Anne (Stewart), Lady
Letters to Guy.
L: Macmillan, 1885. 227p. NUC BL
OCLC
[Life in Australia]

541. -----Station amusements in
New Zealand.
L: W. Hunt, 1873. 278p. NUC BL
OCLC

542. -----Station life in New
Zealand.
L: MacMillan & co., 1870. 238p.
NUC BL OCLC
[Experiences as wife of a sheep
farmer.]

543. -----Travelling about over
new and old ground.
L & NY: G. Routledge & sons,
1872. 353p. BL OCLC
[Australia, N. America, S.
America, Africa, Asia]

544. -----A year's housekeeping
in South Africa.
L: MacMillan & co., 1877. 332p.
NUC BL MB OCLC
[Pub. in U.S. under titles:
Letters from South Africa and
Life in South Africa]

545. BROOME, Mary Anne (Stewart)
Barker, ed. see BRASSEY, Annie
(Allnutt), Baroness

546. BROUGHALL, Mary [Br. 19c]
Our home in Aveyron, with studies
of peasant life and customs in
Aveyron and the Lot. With George
Christopher Davies.
Edinburgh & L: W. Blackwood &
sons, 1890. 283p. BL OCLC
[Travel: France]

547. BROUGHTON, Mrs. Vernon
Delves, ed. see PAPENDIEK,
Charlotte Louise Henrietta
(Albert)

548. BROWN, Miss [Br. 19c]
The foreign tour of the Misses
Brown, Jones and Robinson being
the history of what they saw and
did at Biarritz and in the
Pyrenees. By Miss Brown.
L: Bickers & co., 1878. NUC

549. BROWN, Mrs. Charles John, comp. see BROWN, Kate

550. BROWN, Elizabeth (Silcock) [Br. 1791-1821]
Fragments, letters, &c, &c, the endeared memorials of a beloved wife. Ed. Henry Brown.
Thetford: J. Rogers, pr., 1822. 87p. NUC

551. BROWN, Harriet M. (Gardiner) see BOWEN, Harriet M. (Gardiner)

552. BROWN, Helen E., Mrs. [Am. 19c]
Abroad; or, Lilian's new school. Sketches of travel in Europe.
Boston: Am. Tract Soc., c1870. 389p. NUC

553. BROWN, Henry, ed. see BROWN, Elizabeth (Silcock)

554. BROWN, Jane, Mrs. [Br. 19c]
Memorial sketch of a beloved daughter. By Mrs. F. E. Gordon.
L: pr. for priv. circ., 1872. 51p. BL
[May contain personal material.]

555. BROWN, Kate [Br. 19c]
Recollections of the last days of a daughter beloved. [Comp.] Mrs. Charles John Brown.
L: J. Nisbet & co., 1863. 64p. BL
[May contain personal material]

556. BROWN, Kate (Montrose) Eldon [Am. 19c] ALT: Montrose, Kate
Kate Montrose; an autobiography.
Sacramento, CA: Russell & Winterburn, prs., 1866. 24p. NUC K OCLC

557. BROWN, Louisa, Mrs. [Am. 1812-1886]
Reminiscences.
Nevada, IA: Representative pr., 1898. 60p. K

558. BROWN, Mary [Br. 19c]
Lines on the trip promoted by members of the Littleborough and Smallbridge Reform Clubs ... 1888, to Chester and Hawarden, the residence of the Right Hon. W. E. Gladstone, MP.
Littleborough: Wm. Brown, 1888. BL

559. -----A pleasant remembrance of my visit to the Manchester Royal Jubilee Exhibition of 1887 in 52 verses.
Littleborough: Wm. Brown, 1888. 11p. BL

560. BROWN, Sarah [Br. 1810-1827]
PSEUD: Sunday School Teacher, A
Memoirs and letters, or the effects of religious instruction exemplified in the life, writings, and triumphant death of Miss Sarah Brown of Deptford. By a Sunday School teacher [Preface signed S.B.].
Deptford: William Brown, 1827. 51p. BL
[Includes letters]

561. BROWN, Sarah [Br. 1802-1821]
A short account of Sarah Brown. 1821. By William Brown.
York: W. Alexander & sons, 1821. 35p. BL
[Written by her father, who repeats her conversations & prayers.]

562. BROWN, Sara Hall, ed. see WHITTEN, Mary Delano

563. BROWN, Thomas, ed. see PHILIPS, Katherine (Fowler)

564. BROWN, William, comp. see BROWN, Sarah

565. BROWNE, Felicia Dorothea see HEMANS, Felicia Dorothea (Browne)

566. BROWNE, MAGGIE, pseud. see ANDREWES, Margaret (Hamer)

567. BROWNING, Elizabeth (Barrett), Mrs. Robert Browning [Br. 1806-1861] ALT: Barrett, Elizabeth
The letters of Elizabeth Barrett Browning. Ed. Frederic G. Kenyon.
L: Smith, Elder & co., 1897. 2v. BL OCLC

568. -----Letters of Elizabeth Barrett Browning addressed to Richard Hengist Horne. Ed. S. R. T. Mayer.
L: R. Bentley & son, 1877. 2v. NUC BL OCLC

569. -----The letters of Robert Browning and Elizabeth Barrett Browning, 1845-1846. Ed. Robert Wiedeman Barrett Browning.
L: Smith, Elder & co., 1899. 2v. BL OCLC

570. -----Mrs. E. B. Browning's letters and essays, with a memoir.
NY: J. Miller, 1877. 2v. NUC

571. BROWNING, H. Ellen [Br. 19c]
A girl's wanderings in Hungary.
L & NY: Longmans, Green & co., 1896. 332p. NUC BL OCLC

572. BROWNING, Robert, co-author see BROWNING, Elizabeth (Barrett)

573. BROWNING, Mrs. Robert see BROWNING, Elizabeth (Barrett)

574. BROWNING, Robert Wiedeman Barrett, ed. see BROWNING, Elizabeth (Barrett)

575. BROWNLOW, Emma Sophia (Edgcumbe) Cust, Countess [Br. 1791-1872] ALT: Cust, Emma Sophia (Edgcumbe), Countess Brownlow
Slight reminiscences of a septuagenarian from 1802 to 1815.
L: John Murray, 1866. 199p. NUC BL MB OCLC

576. BROWNLOW, Rev. William Robert Barnard, comp. see ADAMS, Mary Rose Columba

577. BRUCE, John, ed. see ELIZABETH, Queen of England

578. BRYAN, Hugh, co-author see HUTSON, Mary

579. BRYAN, Ruth [Br. 19c]
Handfuls of purpose; or, gleanings from the inner life of R. Bryan.
L: W. H. Collingridge, 1862. 460p. BL
[Extracts from her diary]

580. -----Letters of Ruth Bryan.
L: J. Nisbet & co., 1865. 358p. BL

581. BRYCE, Campbell, Mrs. [Am. 19c]

The personal experiences of Mrs. Campbell Bryce during the burning of Columbia, South Carolina by General W. T. Sherman's Army, February 17, 1865.
Philadelphia: Lippincott press, 1899. 53p. NUC OCLC

582. -----Reminiscences of the hospitals of Columbia, S.C., during the four years of the Civil War.
Philadelphia: Lippincott, 1897. 31p. NUC OCLC

583. BRYDGES, Sir Egerton, ed. see NEWCASTLE, Margaret (Lucas) Cavendish, Duchess of

584. BUCHAN, Elspeth Simpson [Br. 18c] ALT: Simpson, Elspeth
Eight letters between the people called Buchanites and a teacher near Edinburgh ... one by Mrs Buchan ... together with two from Mrs. Buchan ... to a clergyman in England.
L: n.p., 1785. BL

585. BUCK, Lillie Brown (West) [Am. 1860-1939] PSEUD: Leslie, Amy
Amy Leslie at the fair.
Chicago: W. B. Conkey co., 1893. 263p. NUC OCLC
[Personal recollections of the World's Columbian Exposition in Chicago.]

586. BUCKHOUT, B. M., Mrs. [Am. 19c]
Aftermath from city and country, berg and thal. Gathered and garnered by Mrs. B. M. Buckhout.
NY: W. B. Smith & co., 1882. 265p. NUC OCLC

587. BUCKINGHAM, Rev. Mr., co-author see KNIGHT, Sarah (Kemble)

588. BUCKINGHAM AND CHANDOS, Alice Anne (Montgomery) Temple-Nugent Brydges-Chandos, Duchess of see EGERTON OF TATTON, Alice Anne (Montgomery) Temple-Nugent Brydges-Chandos Grenville, Countess

589. BUCKLAND, Anne Walbank [Br. 19c]

The world beyond the Esterelles.
L: Remington & co., 1884. 2v. NUC
BL OCLC
[Travel: Italy]

590. BUDGE, Jane, comp. see
ALLEN, Hannah Hunton Stafford

591. BUDGETT, Sarah, Mrs. [Br.
1783-1839]
A memoir of the late Mrs. Sarah
Budgett ... extracts from her
letters and journals. By John
Gaskin.
L: n.p., 1840. BL MBD
[Methodist; diary 1806-1818]

592. BULFINCH, Charles, co-author
see BULFINCH, Hannah

593. BULFINCH, Ellen Susan, ed.
see BULFINCH, Hannah

594. BULFINCH, Hannah [Am. 1768-
1841]
Life and letters of Charles
Bulfinch, with other family
papers. Ed. his granddaughter,
Ellen Susan Bulfinch.
Boston & NY: Houghton Mifflin,
1896. 323p. NUC MAD OCLC
[Includes extracts from her
diary]

595. BULLARD, Anne Tuttle Jones,
Mrs. [Am. 19c]
Sights and scenes in Europe: a
series of letters from England,
France, Germany, Switzerland, and
Italy, in 1850.
St. Louis, MO: Chambers & Knapp,
1852. 255p. NUC BL OCLC

596. BULMER, Agnes (Collinson)
[Br. 1775-1836]
Memoir of Mrs. Agnes Bulmer ... .
To which is subjoined, Mrs.
Bulmer's last poem, Man the
offspring of divine benevolence.
By Anne Ross Collinson.
L: J. G. & F. Rivington, 1837.
NUC BL

597. -----Select letters ... .
[Ed.] the Rev. William M.
Bunting.
L: Simpkin & Marshall, 1842.
299p. NUC BL

598. BULMER, Agnes (Collison),
ed. see MORTIMER, Elizabeth
(Ritchie)

599. BULWER, Edward George Earle
Lytton, Baron Lytton, co-author
see LYTTON, Rosina Anne Doyle
(Wheeler) Bulwer-Lytton, Baroness

600. BULWER, Rosina Anne Doyle
(Wheeler) Baroness Lytton see
LYTTON, Rosina Doyle (Wheeler)
Bulwer-Lytton, Baroness

601. BUMPASS, Eugenia H., comp.
see BUMPASS, Frances Moore Webb

602. BUMPASS, Frances Moore Webb,
Mrs. [Am. 1819-1898]
Autobiography and journal. Comp.
Eugenia H. Bumpass. Ed. Mrs. F.
A. Butler.
Nashville, TN: Publishing house
of the M. E. Church, South, 1899.
82p. K OCLC

603. BUNBURY, Selina [Br. 1802-
1882]
Lady Flora, or the events of a
winter in Sweden and a summer in
Rome in the years 1846 and 1847.
L: T. Cautley Newby, 1870. 2v.
NUC OCLC
[Fictionalized account]

604. -----Life in Sweden; with
excursions in Norway and Denmark.
L: Hurst & Blackett, 1853. 2v.
NUC BL OCLC

605. -----My first travels:
including rides in the Pyrenees,
scenes during an inundation at
Avignon, sketches in France and
Savoy, visits to convents and
houses of charity.
L: T. Cautley Newby, 1859. 24p.
BL OCLC

606. -----Rides in the Pyrenees.
L: T. C. Newby, 1844. 2v. NUC BL
OCLC

607. -----Russia after the war.
The narrative of a visit to that
country.
L: Hurst & Blackett, 1857. 2v.
NUC BL

608. -----A summer in northern Europe including sketches in Sweden, Norway, Finland, the Aland Islands, Gothland, etc.
L: Hurst & Blackett, 1856, 2v. NUC BL OCLC

609. -----A visit to my birthplace.
Boston: J. Loring's Sabbath school bookstore, 1828. 137p. NUC OCLC
{This is Am. ed., rev. & improved}

610. -----A visit to the catacombs, or first Christian cemeteries at Rome; and a midnight visit to Mount Veseuvius.
L: W. W. Robinson, 1849, 35p. BL OCLC

611. BUNKLEY, Josephine M. [Am. 19c]
[BL: Miss Bunkley's Book.]   The testimony of an escaped novice from the Sisterhood of St. Joseph, Emmetsburg, Maryland, the Mother-house of the Sisters of Charity in the United States.
NY: Harper & bros., 1855, 338p. NUC BL K OCLC
[Also pub. as: The escaped nun: or, Disclosures of convent life; and The confessions of a sister of charity. NY: DeWitt & Davenport, 1855. 344p.]

612. BUNSEN, Frances (Waddington) Von, Baroness [Br. 1791-1876]
The life and letters of Frances, Baroness Bunsen. [Comp.] Augustus John Cuthbert Hare.
L: Daldy, Isbister & co. NY: G. Routledge & sons, 1879.   NUC BL OCLC

613. BUNTING, Hannah Syng [Am. 1801-1832]
Memoir, diary and letters of Miss Hannah Syng Bunting, of Philadelphia, who departed this life May 25, 1832, in the thirty-first year of her age. Ed. Rev. Timothy Merritt.
NY: Waugh, 1833. 2v. in 1. NUC OCLC

614. BUNTING, Rev. William M. see BULMER, Agnes (Collinson)

615. BUNYON, Charles John, ed. see MC DOUGALL, Harriette (Bunyon)

616. BURDETTE, Mary G. {Am. 19c}
A trip through the Indian country.
Philadelphia: Women's Baptist Home Mission Union, 1899?. 18p. NUC

617. BURDETTE, Mary G., ed. see CRAWFORD, Isabel Alice Hartley

618. BURGESS, Elisa [Am. b. 1801?]
Life thoughts and memorials of Mrs. Elisa Burgess.
Brooklyn, NY: Press of Rogers & Sherwood, 1878. 91p. NUC OCLC
{Poetry and prose}

619. BURGESS, Elizabeth see BOLAINE, Betty

620. BURGESS, Marianna [Am. 19c]
PSEUD: Embe
Stiya, a Carlisle Indian girl at home; founded on the author's actual observations. By Embe.
Cambridge, MA: Riverside Press, 1891. 115p. NUC OCLC

621. BURGHESH, Priscilla Anne (Wellesley Pole) Fane, Lady see WESTMOTRLAND, Priscilla Anne (Wellesley Pole) Fane, Countess of

622. BURK, Martha Jane (Canary) see CANARY, Martha Jane

623. BURKE, Emily P. [Am. 19c]
Reminscences of Georgia.
Oberlin, OH: J. M. Fitch, 1850. 252p. NUC OCLC
[Northern schoolteacher who taught in Atlanta}

624. BURLEND, Edward, comp. see BURLEND, Rebecca

625. BURLEND, Rebecca [Am. 1793-1872]
A true picture of emigration; or fourteen years in the interior of North America; being a full and impartial account of the various difficulties and ultimate success of an English family who emigrated from Barwick-in-Elmet, near Leeds, in the year 1831. Comp. Edward Burlend.
L: G. Berger, 1848. 62p. NUC OCLC
[Pike County, IL pioneers]

626. BURN, Edward, comp. see HUTCHINSON, Elizabeth

627. BURNABY, Elizabeth Alice Frances (Hawkins-Whitshed) see LE BLOND, Elizabeth Alice Frances (Hawkins-Whitshed) Burnaby Main

628. BURNABY, Mrs. Frederick Gustavus see LE BLOND, Elizabeth Alice Frances (Hawkins-Whitshed) Burnaby Main

629. BURNET, Lady Margaret (Kennedy) [Br. 1630?-1685?] ALT: Kennedy, Lady Margaret
Letters from the Lady Margaret Kennedy, to John, Duke of Lauderdale.
Edinburgh: n.p., 1828. 107p. NUC BL

630. BURNEY, Charlotte, co-author see ARBLAY, Frances (Burney) d'

631. BURNEY, Fanny see ARBLAY, Frances (Burney) d'

632. BURNEY, Susan, co-author see ARBLAY, Frances (Burney) d'

633. BURNHAM, Sarah Maria [Am. 1818-1901]
Pleasant memories of foreign travel.
Boston: B. Whidden, 1896. 240p. NUC OCLC
[Travel: Europe]

634. BURNS, Mary E., Mrs. [Am. 19c]
A vision and a voice from two worlds; being the experience of Mary E. Burns, as related by herself.
Brooklyn, NY: Collins & Day, 1895. 31p. NUC

635. BURNS, Robert, co-author see DUNLOP, Frances Anne (Wallace)

636. BURNS, Robert, co-author see M'LEHOSE, Agnes (Craig)

637. BURRELL, W. S., co-author see CUTHELL, Edith E.

638. BURTON, Isabel (Arundell), Lady [Br. 1831-1896]
AEI. Arabia, Egypt, India. A narrative of travel.
L & Belfast: W. Mullan & son, 1879. 488p. NUC BL OCLC

639. -----The inner life of Syria, Palestine, and the Holy Land. From my private journal, by I. Burton.
L: H. S. King & co., 1875. 2v. NUC BL OCLC

640. -----The romance of Isabel, Lady Burton. The story of her life. Told in part by herself and in part, by W. H. Wilkins.
L: Hutchinson & co.; NY: Dodd, Mead & co., 1897. 2v.   NUC BL OCLC

641. BURTON, Mary see CRYER, Mary (Burton)

642. BURTON, Phillipina see HILL, Phillipina (Burton)

643. BURWELL, Letitia M. [Am. 19c] PSEUD: Thacker, Page
A girl's life in Virginia before the war.
NY: F. A. Stokes co., 1895. 209p. NUC BL OCLC

644. -----Plantation reminiscences, by Page Thacker.
Owensboro, KY?: n.p., 1878. 69p. NUC OCLC
[Virginia]

645. BURY, Lady Charlotte Susan Maria (Campbell) [Br. 1775-1861] ALT: Campbell, Lady Charlotte Susan Maria
Diary illustrative of the times of George the Fourth interspersed with original letters from ... Queen Caroline [Amelie Elizabeth, consort of George IV].
L: H. Colburn, 1838. 2v. NUC BL MBD OCLC

[Includes travel: Italy, France, Switzerland]

646. BURY, Elizabeth (Lawrence) [Br. 1644-1720]
An account of the life and death of Mrs. Elizabeth Bury ... chiefly collected out of her own diary ... . Comp. Samuel Bury.
Bristol: J. Penn, 1720. 244p. NUC BL MBD OCLC
[Includes letters and diary]

647. BURY, Samuel, comp. see BURY, Elizabeth (Lawrence)

648. BURY PALLISER, Mrs. see PALLISER, Fanny (Marryat) Bury

649. BUSH, Eliza C. [Br. 19c]
My pilgrimage to eastern shrines.
L: Hurst & Blackett, 1867. 317p. NUC BL OCLC
[Travel: Levant]

650. BUSH, Phillipa Call, comp. see EVERETT, Anne Gorham

651. BUSH, Rachel Harriette [Br. 1831-1907]
The valleys of Tirol, their traditions and customs and how to visit them.
L: Longmans, Green & co., 1874. 453p. NUC

652. BUSSING, Ann (Van Nest) [Am. b. 1809?]
Reminiscences of the Van Nest homestead.
NY: Pr. for priv. circ., 1897. 16p. NUC
[May contain personal material.]

653. BUSTARD, John, comp. see BINGHAM, Mary Helen

654. BUTLER, Annie Robina [Br. 19c]
Glimpses of Maori-land.
NY: Am. Tract Society, 1886. 318p.; L: Religious Tract Society, 1886. 260p. NUC BL OCLC

655. BUTLER, Mrs. F. A., ed. see BUMPASS, Frances Moore Webb

656. BUTLER, Frances Anne (Kemble) see KEMBLE, Frances Anne

657. BUTLER, Jessee H. [Am. 19c]
Twelve years in California. Its climate; its soil; its past; its present and future.
n.p.: n.p., 1883. NUC

658. BUTLER, Josephine Elizabeth (Grey) [Br. 1828-1906]
Personal reminiscences of a great crusade for the abolition of state regulation of vice.
L: H. Marshall & son, 1896. 409p. NUC BL MB OCLC

659. BUTLER, Perdue, co-author see HASTINGS, Rosetta (Butler)

660. BUTLER, William, co-author see BRAIN, Ada B.

661. BUTT, Mary Martha see SHERWOOD, Mary Martha (Butt)

662. BUXTON, Clare Emily [Br. 19c]
On either side of the Red Sea. With Hannah Maude Buxton [b. 1872] and Theresa Buxton. Ed. Edward North Buxton.
L: Edward Stanford, 1895. 163p. NUC BL OCLC

663. BUXTON, Edward North, ed. see BUXTON, Clare Emily

664. BUXTON, Hannah (Gurney), Lady [Br. 1783-1872]
Memorials of Hannah Lady Buxton. From papers collected by her granddaughters.
L: Baker & son, 1883. 258p. NUC BL
[Member of Society of Friends; includes journal & letters]

665. BUXTON, Hannah Maude, co-author see BUXTON, Clare Emily

666. BUXTON, Theresa, co-author see BUXTON, Clare Emily

667. BYRD, Ann [Am. 1798-1831]
Narratives, pious meditations, and religious exercises, of Ann Byrd, late of the city of New York, deceased.
Philadelphia: J. Richards, 1843. 127p. NUC K OCLC
[Member of Society of Friends]

668. BYRNE, Julia Clara (Bush), Mrs. W. Pitt Byrne [Br. 1819-1894]
The Beggynhoff, or, the city of the single.
L: Chapman & Hall, 1869. 176p. NUC BL OCLC

669. -----Cosas de España, illustrative of Spain and the Spainiards as they are.
L & NY: A. Strahan, 1866. 2v. NUC BL OCLC

670. -----Flemish interiors.
L: Longman & co., 1856. 359p. NUC BL

671. -----Gheel, the city of the simple.
L: Chapman & Hall, 1869. 195p. NUC BL OCLC

672. -----Gossip of the century; personal and traditional memories-- social, literary, artistic, etc.
L: Ward & Downey, 1892. 2v. NUC BL OCLC

673. BYRNE, Mrs. W. Pitt see BYRNE, Julia Clara (Bush)

674. BYROM, Beppy see BYROM, Elizabeth

675. BYROM, Elizabeth [Br. 1722-1801] ALT: BYROM, Beppy
The journal of Elizabeth Byrom in 1745. Ed. Richard Parkinson. Repr. from: The private journal and literary remains of John Byrom, v2, pt 2; Manchester: Chatham Society, pr. C. Simms & co., 1857. 32p. NUC BL P
[Account of Bonnie Prince Charlie's visit to Manchester and other events August 14, 1746-January 22, 1746.]

676. BYRON, George Gordon Noel, Baron Byron, co-author see LAMB, Lady Caroline (Ponsonby)

677. BYRON, George Gordon Noel, Baron Byron, co-author see PIGOT, Elizabeth Bridget

678. C., E. B. see CHASE, Eliza Brown

679. C., H. G. see CREAMER, Hannah Gardner

680. C., J. P., ed. see BATEHAM, Minerva Dayton

681. C., M. I. see CARRINGTON, Margaret Irvin (Sullivant)

682. C., Mary F. see CARR, Mary Frances

683. CADDY, Florence, Mrs. [Br. b. 1837]
Footsteps of Jeanne d'Arc. A pilgrimage.
L: Hurst & Blackett, 1886. 375p. NUC BL OCLC

684. -----To Siam and Malaya in the Duke of Sutherland's yacht, 'Sans Peur'.
L: Hurst & Blackett, ltd., 1889. 362p. NUC BL OCLC

685. CADHILAC, Margaret Isabella (Collier) Galletti d', Countess see GALLETTI DI CADHILAC, Margaret Isabella (Collier), Countess

686. CAHOONE, Sarah S. [Am. 19c]
Visit to Grand-papa; or a week at Newport.
NY: Taylor & Dodd, 1840. 213p. NUC BL OCLC
[Also pub. 1842 as: Sketches of Newport and its vicinity ... .]

687. CAIRNS, Elizabeth [Br. 1685-1741]
Memoirs of the life of Elizabeth Cairns ... written by herself some years before her death. Ed. John Greig.
Glasgow: John Brown, 1762. 228p. NUC BL MB
[Spiritual autobiography]

688. CAKE, Susan (McDonough) [Am. 1816-1896]
Aunt Susan's own story of her life. With additional incidents, her favorite hymns and quaint sayings. Comp. William U. Cake.
Philadelphia: John J. Hood, c1897. 70p. NUC OCLC
[Includes poetry]

689. CAKE, William U., comp. <u>see</u> CAKE, Susan (McDonough)

690. CALAMITY JANE, pseud. <u>see</u> CANARY, Martha Jane

691. CALDERON DE LA BARCA, Frances Erskine (Inglis), Marchioness [Br. 1804-1882]
Life in Mexico, during a residence of two years in that country.
Boston: C. C. Little & J. Brown, 1842. 2v. NUC BL OCLC

692. CALDERWOOD, Margaret (Stewart) [Br. 1715-1774]
Letters and journals of Margaret Calderwood from England, Holland and the Low Countries in 1756.
Ed. Alexander Fergusson.
Edinburgh: D. Douglas, 1884. 386p. NUC BL MBD OCLC

693. CALDWELL, Nancy, Mrs. [Am. 1781-1865]
Walking with God; leaves from the journal of Mrs. Nancy Caldwell.
Ed. James O. Thompson.
Keyser, WV: Mountain Echo Office, 1886. 199p. NUC

694. CALHOUN, John S. <u>see</u> HOW, Mary Jane (Gordon)

695. CALLCOTT, Maria (Dundas) Graham, Lady [Br. 1785-1842] ALT: Graham, Maria (Dundas)
Journal of a residence in Chile, during the year 1822; and a voyage from Chile to Brazil, in 1823.
L: Longman et al & John Murray, 1824. 512p. NUC BL MB OCLC

696. -----Journal of a residence in India.
Edinburgh: Archibald Constable, 1812. 211p. NUC BL MB OCLC

697. -----Journal of a voyage to Brazil, and residence there during part of the years 1821, 1822, 1824.
L: Longman, Hurst, Rees, Orme, & Brown, 1824. 335p. NUC BL OCLC

698. -----Letters on India.
L: Longman, Hurst, Rees, Orme & Brown, 1814. 382p. NUC BL MB OCLC

699. -----Three months passed in the mountains east of Rome, during the year 1819.
L: Longman, Hurst, Rees, Orme and Brown, 1820. 305p. NUC BL OCLC

700. CAMERON, Charles, ed. <u>see</u> CAMERON, Lucy Lyttleton (Butt)

701. CAMERON, Jane <u>see</u> MAWSON, Jane (Cameron)

702. CAMERON, Lucy Lyttleton (Butt) [Br. 1781-1858]
The life of Mrs. Cameron: partly an autobiography, and from her private journals... . Ed. her oldest son, Charles Cameron.
L: Darton & co., 1861. NUC BL MB OCLC

703. CAMPBELL, Mrs. A. <u>see</u> CAMPBELL, Isabella

704. CAMPBELL, Lady Charlotte Susan Maria <u>see</u> BURY, Lady Charlotte Susan Maria (Campbell)

705. CAMPBELL, Lady Colin <u>see</u> CAMPBELL, Gertrude Elizabeth (Blood)

706. CAMPBELL, Gertrude Elizabeth (Blood), Lady Colin Campbell [Br. d. 1911] ALT: Blood, Gertrude Elizabeth
Salsomaggiore and its surroundings.
L: M. Ward & co., 18--?. 22p. NUC

707. CAMPBELL, Henrietta Ann, Mrs. [Br. 19c]
Sacred recollections of a beloved daughter who "is not dead but sleepeth".
Liverpool: G. Smith, Watts & co., 1854. 97p. NUC
[Also contains tribute by the author to her mother]

708. CAMPBELL, Isabella [Br. 19c]
Letters, extracted from the memoir of Isabella Campbell.
Greenock: R. B. Lusk, 1829. 12p. NUC BL

709. -----Peace in believing: a memoir of Isabella Campbell of Fernicarry. By Robert Stones.
Greenock: n.p., 1829. BL
[Includes letters]

710. CAMPBELL, Isabella, Mrs. A. Campbell [Br. 1830-1887]
Rough and smooth: or Ho! for an Australian gold field. By Mrs. A. Campbell.
Quebec: Hunter, Rose & co., 1865. 138p. NUC OCLC

711. CAMPBELL, Thomasina M. A. E. [Br. 19c]
Notes on the Island of Corsica in 1868.
L: Hatchard & co., 1868. 160p. NUC BL OCLC
[Cover title: Southward ho! Corsica 1868]

712. CAMPBELL, Willielma (Maxwell), Viscountess Glenorchy see GLENORCHY, Willielma (Maxwell) Campbell, Viscountess

713. CAMPLIN, Sarah, Mrs. [Br. 19c]
Memorial of Mrs. [Sarah] Camplin. Ed. Eliza Talitha Tooth.
L: N. Archer, 1833. 60p. BL
[May contain personal material.]

714. CANARY, Martha Jane [Am. 1852-1903] ALT: Burk, Martha Jane (Canary) PSEUD: Calamity Jane
Life and adventures of Calamity Jane, by herself.
Billings, MT: n.p., 1895?. 7p. NUC K

715. CANTERBURY, The Dean of, ed. see ALFORD, Frances Oke

716. CAPPE, Catharine (Harrison) [Br. 1744-1821]
Memoirs of the life of the late Mrs. Catharine Cappe written by herself. Ed. Mary Cappe.
L: Longman, Hurst, Rees, Orme & Brown, 1822. 467p. NUC BL OCLC

717. CAPPE, Mary, ed. see CAPPE, Catherine (Harrison)

718. CAPPER, Katharine, ed. see CAPPER, Mary

719. CAPPER, Mary [Br. 1755-1845]
A memoir of Mary Capper, late of Birmingham, a minister of the Society of Friends. Ed. Katharine Capper Backhouse.

L: Charles Gilpin; York: J. L. Linney, 1847. 426p. NUC BL MBD OCLC

720. CARBUTT, Mrs. Edward Hamer see CARBUTT, Mary (Rhodes)

721. CARBUTT, Mary (Rhodes) Lady, Mrs. Edward Hamer Carbutt [Br. 19c]
Five months' fine weather in Canada, western U.S., and Mexico.
L: S. Low, Marston, Searle & Rivington, ltd., 1889. 243p. NUC BL OCLC

722. CARDWELL, Lucy [Am. 19c]
Some account of Lucy Cardwell, a woman of colour, who departed this life on the 25th of the 3rd month, 1824--aged 39 years. [Comp.] Elizabeth Ladd.
Philadelphia: pr. for B. & T. Kite, 182-?. 4p. NUC
[Last words of a Quaker woman; biographical details by E. Ladd.]

723. CAREY, Amelia (Fitz Clarence), Viscountess Falkland see FALKLAND, Amelia (Fitz Clarence) Carey, Viscountess

724. CAREY, Frances Jane [Br. 19c]
Journal of a tour in France in the years 1816 and 1817.
L: Taylor & Hessey, 1823. 502p. NUC BL OCLC

725. CARLETON, Mrs. John see CARLETON, Mary (Moders)

726. CARLETON, Mary (Moders), Mrs. John Carleton [Br. 1642?-1673] ALT: The German Princess; Moders, Mary; Stedman, Mary
An historical narrative of the German Princess. ... Written by herself.
L: for Charles Moulton, 1663. 23p. NUC BL OCLC
[Numerous editions; apologia by false German princess.]

727. CARLILE, James, ed. see SWINTON, Jane

728. CARLYLE, Jane Baillie (Welsh), Mrs. Thomas Carlyle [Br. 1801-1866]

Early letters of Jane Welsh Carlyle, together with a few of later years and some of Thomas Carlyle, all hitherto unpublished. Ed. David G. Ritchie.
L: S. Sonnenschein & co., 1889. 332p. NUC BL OCLC

729. -----Letters and memorials of Jane Welsh Carlyle ... prepared for publication by Thomas Carlyle. Ed. James Anthony Froude.
NY: C. Scribner's sons; L: Longmans & co., 1883. 2v. NUC BL MBD OCLC P

730. CARLYLE, Jane Welsh, co-author see SMITH, Mary

731. CARLYLE, Thomas, co-author see SMITH, Mary

732. CARLYLE, Mrs. Thomas see CARLYLE, Jane Baillie (Welsh)

733. CARMICHAEL, A. C., Mrs. [Br. 19c]
Domestic manners and social condition of the white, coloured, and negro population of the West Indies.
L: Whittaker, Treacher & co., 1833. 2v. NUC BL OCLC

734. CARNE, Elizabeth Catherine Thomas [Br. 1817-1873] PSEUD: Wittitterly, John Altrayd
Three months rest at Pau, in the winter and spring of 1859. By John Altrayd Wittitterly.
L: Bell & Daldy, 1860. 267p. NUC

735. CARNES, Hannah [Br. 19c]
The life of Hannah Carnes. Compiled from her own papers.
Weymouth: B. Benson, 1838. 60p. BL
[Spiritual autobiography; includes poems]

736. CAROLINE AMELIE ELIZABETH, Queen Consort of George IV, King of Great Britain and Ireland, co-author see BURY, Lady Charlotte Susan Maria (Campbell)

737. CAROLINE AMELIE ELIZABETH, Queen Consort of George IV, King of Great Britain and Ireland, co-author see CHARLOTTE AUGUSTA OF WALES

738. CARPENTER, Mary [Br. 1807-1877]
Six months in India.
L: Longmans, Green & co., 1868. 2v. NUC BL OCLC

739. CARPENTER, Mary Thorn [Am. 19c]
A girl's winter in India.
NY: A. D. F. Randolph & co., c1892. 240p. NUC OCLC

740. -----In Cairo and Jerusalem. An eastern note-book.
NY: A. D. F. Randolph & co., c1894. 222p. NUC OCLC

741. CARR, Alice Vansittart (Strettell), Mrs. J. W. Comyns Carr [Br. b. 1850]
North Italian folk. Sketches of country and town life.
L: Chatto & Windus, 1878. 282p. NUC BL OCLC

742. CARR, Mrs. J. W. Comyns see CARR, Alice Vansittart (Strettell)

743. CARR, Mary Frances [Am. 19c]
ALT: C., Mary F.
Shakers: a correspondence between Mary F. C. of Mount Holly City and a Shaker sister, Sarah L[ucas] of Union Village. Ed. R. W. Pelham.
Union Village, OH: n.p., 1868. 24p. NUC BL OCLC

744. CARRINGTON, Mrs. Henry Beebee see CARRINGTON, Margaret Irvin (Sullivant)

745. CARRINGTON, Margaret Irvin (Sullivant), Mrs. Henry Beebee Carrington [Am. 1831-1870] ALT: C., M. I.
Ab-sa-ra-ka, home of the Crows: being the experience of an officer's wife on the Plains and marking the vicissitudes of peril and pleasure during the occupation of the new route to Virginia City, Montana 1866-7.

Philadelphia: n.p., 1860. NUC BL
OCLC
[Describes 1866 massacre at Fort
Philip Kearney, Wyoming, by Crow
Indians.]

746. -----Ocean to ocean. Pacific
Railroad and adjoining
territories, with distances and
fares of travel from American
cities.
Philadelphia: J. B. Lippincott &
co., 1869. 31p. NUC OCLC
[Her husband, Henry Beebee
Carrington, claimed authorship in
1903 letter.]

747. CARROLL, W. R., ed. see
GREEN, Rachel W. (Cope)

748. CARROTHERS, Julia D. [Am.
19/20c]
Kesa and Saijiro; or, lights and
shades of life in Japan.
NY: American Tract Society,
c1888. NUC OCLC

749. -----Lights and shades of
missionary life.
Omaha, NE: Presbyterian pub. co.,
1884. 18p. NUC OCLC

750. -----The sunrise kingdom;
or, life and scenes in Japan, and
woman's work for women there.
Philadelphia: Presbyterian Board
of Pub., c1879. 408p. NUC OCLC

751. CARSON, Ann (Baker), Mrs.
John Carson [Am. 19c] ALT: Smyth,
Ann; Smyth, Mrs. Richard
The history of the celebrated and
beautiful Mrs. Ann Carson, widow
of the late unfortunate
Lieutenant Richard Smyth with a
circumstantial account of her
conspiracy against the late
Governor of Pennsylvania, Simon
Snyder; and of her sufferings in
the several prisons of that
state.
Philadelphia: the author, 1822.
315p. NUC K
[Bigamist; accused of murder of
Capt. John Carson]

752. -----The memoirs of the
celebrated and beautiful Mrs. Ann
Carson, daughter of an officer of
the U.S. Navy, and wife of
another, whose life terminated in
the Philadelphia prison. 2d ed.
rev., enl. and cont. till her
death, by Mrs. M[ary] Clarke.
Philadelphia & NY: n.p., 1838.
2v. NUC OCLC

753. CARSON, Mrs. John see
CARSON, Anne (Baker)

754. CARTER, Anna Maria [Br. 18c]
Selections from the letters &c.
of the late Miss Carter. Ed.
William Palmer.
Exeter: R. Trewman & son, 1793.
53p. BL

755. CARTER, Anne [Br. 19c]
PSEUD: Lady, A
Letters from a lady to her sister
during a tour to Paris in the
months of April and May, 1814.
L: Longman, Hurst, Rees, etc.,
1814. 170p. BL OCLC

756. CARTER, Elizabeth, Mrs. [Br.
1717-1806]
Letters from Mrs. Elizabeth
Carter to Mrs. Montagu between
the years 1755 and 1800. Ed.
Montagu Pennington.
L: F. C. & J. Rivington, 1817.
3v. NUC BL OCLC

757. -----A series of letters
between Mrs. Elizabeth Carter and
Miss Catherine Talbot from the
year 1741 to 1770. To which are
added letters from Mrs. Carter to
Mrs. [Elizabeth] Vesey between
the years 1763 and 1787.
L: F. C. & J. Rivington, 1808.
2v. NUC BL OCLC

758. CARTER, Mary, Mrs. [Br. 19c]
Mrs. Mary Carter's letters.
L: Clayton & co., 1860?. 37p. BL

759. CARTER, Melissa (Booth),
Mrs. [Am. b. 1845]
Beulah land. An autobiography.
Boston: J. H. Earle, 1888. 258p.
NUC K OCLC

760. CARY, Anne M. [Am. 19c]
Cary letters. Ed. Caroline
Gardiner (Cary) Curtis.
Cambridge, MA: Riverside press,
1891. 335p. NUC MAD OCLC
[Includes travel: Canada and
Northern U.S.]

761. CARY, Catherine E. [Br. 19c]
Memoirs of Miss C. E. Cary
written by herself.
L: T. Traveller, 1825. 3v. NUC BL
MB
[Lady in waiting to Queen
Charlotte]

762. -----Sequel to the memoirs
of Miss E. Cary.
L: the authoress, 1826. 54p. NUC
BL

763. CARY, Margaret, Mrs. [Am.
1719-1760]
Cary letters. Ed. Caroline
Gardiner (Cary) Curtis.
Cambridge, MA: Riverside press,
1891. 335p. NUC K OCLC
[Includes extracts from her
diary.]

764. CASE, Adelaide, Mrs. [Br.
19c]
Day by day at Lucknow. A journal
of the seige of Lucknow.
L: R. Bentley, 1858. 348p. NUC BL
MB OCLC

765. CASTLE, Egerton, ed. see
JERNINGHAM, Hon. Frances, Lady

766. CASWELL, Harriett S. (Clark)
[Am. b. 1834]
Our life among the Iroquois
Indians.
Boston & Chicago: Congregational
Pub. Soc., 1892. 321p. NUC BL K
OCLC

767. CATHARINE, Queen of England
[Br. 1512-1548] ALT: Parr,
Catharine
The lamentacion of a synner, made
by the moste vertuous lady Quene
Caterine, bewailying the
ignoraunces of her blind life ...
.
L: Edwards Whitchurche, 1548. NUC
BL
[Spiritual autobiography]

768. CATLEY, Ann [Br. 1745-1789]
ALT: Lascelles, Ann Catley
The life and memoirs of the late
Miss Ann Catley, the celebrated
actress: with biographical
sketches of Sir F. B. Delaval and
the Hon. Isabella Pawlet. By Miss
Ambross.
L: J. Bird, 1790?. 56p. BL
[Actress and courtesan]

769. -----The life of Miss Anne
Catley, celebrated singing
performer of the last century,
including an account of her
introduction to public life, her
professional engagements in
London and Dublin, and her
various adventures and intrigues
... . Carefully comp. and ed.
from the best and most authentic
records extant.
L: n.p., 1888. 78p. NUC BL OCLC

770. CATLOW, Agnes [Br. 1807?-
1889]
Sketching rambles; or, nature in
the Alps and Alpennines. With
Maria E. Catlow.
L: J. Hogg & sons, 1861. 2v. NUC
BL
[Travel: Switzerland and Italy]

771. CATLOW, Maria E., co-author
see CATLOW, Agnes

772. CAVENDISH, Elizabeth
Christiana (Hervey) Foster,
Duchess of Devonshire see
DEVONSHIRE, Elizabeth (Hervey)
Foster Cavendish, Duchess of

773. CAVENDISH, Georgiana
(Spencer), Duchess of Devonshire
see DEVONSHIRE, Georgiana
(Spencer) Cavendish, Duchess of

774. CAVENDISH, Margaret (Lucas),
Duchess of Newcastle see
NEWCASTLE, Margaret (Lucas)
Cavendish, Duchess of

775. CAZNEAU, Jane Maria
(McManus), Mrs. William Leslie
Cazneau [Am. 1807-1878] PSEUD:
Montgomery, Cora; Montgomery,
Corinne

Eagle Pass: or, life on the
border. Pub. as: Corinne
Montgomery
NY: G. P. Putnam, 1852. 188p. NUC
BL OCLC
[Life in Texas]

776. -----In the tropics, by a
settler in Santo Domingo.
2d ed. NY: Carleton, 1863. 306p.
NUC OCLC
[Travel: Dominican Republic]

777. -----The king of rivers,
with a chart of our slave and
free soil territory.
NY: C. Wood, 1850. 19p. NUC
[Mississippi River]

778. -----Our times. By Cora
Montgomery.
NY: n.p., 1852. NUC

779. -----Our winter Eden: pen
pictures of the tropics.
NY: Authors' pub. co., 1878.
130p. NUC OCLC
[Dominican Republic]

780. -----The queen of islands
and the king of rivers. By Cora
Montgomery.
NY: C. Wood, 1850. 50p. NUC OCLC
[Cuba and Mississippi River]

781. CAZNEAU, Mrs. William Leslie
see CAZNEAU, Jane Maria (McManus)

782. CECIL, Catherine, ed. see
HAWKES, Sarah (Eden)

783. CECIL, Rev. Richard, co-
author see HAWKES, Sarah (Eden)

784. CEDARHOLM, Caroline, Mrs.
[Am. 19c]
A narrative of the dangerous
journey of Mrs. Caroline
Cedarholm, the Norwegian
missionary, across the desert to
Arizona.
n.p.: n.p., 187?. 59p. NUC OCLC

785. CELLIER, Elizabeth, Mrs.
[Br. 17c]
Malice defeated.
L: pr. for Elizabeth Cellier,
1680. 46p. NUC BL OCLC
[Autobiographical account of
false imprisonment for treason in
Popish plot, 1678.]

786. CHACE, Elizabeth (Buffum)
[Am. 1806-1899]
Anti-slavery reminiscences.
Central Falls, RI: E. J. Freeman
& son, 1891. 47p. NUC K OCLC

787. CHADWICK, John White, ed.
see HOLLEY, Sallie

788. CHALLICE, Annie Emma
(Armstrong) [Br. 1821-1875]
Memories of French palaces.
L: Bradbury, Evans & co., 1871.
352p. NUC BL OCLC

789. CHAMBERS, Charlotte see
RISKE, Charlotte (Chambers)
Ludlow

790. CHAMBERS, Fanny see
INGLEHART, Fanny (Chambers) Gooch

791. CHAMPNEY, Elizabeth
(Williams) [Am. 1850-1922] ALT:
Champney, Lizzie W.
Three Vassar girls abroad. By
Lizzie W. Champney.
Boston: Estes and Lauriat, c1882.
236p. NUC BL OCLC
[France and Spain]

792. -----Three Vassar girls at
home.
Boston: Estes and Lauriat, c1887.
233p. NUC BL OCLC
[Southwestern States and Western
U.S.]

793. -----Three Vassar girls in
England.
Boston: Estes and Lauriat, c1883.
238p. NUC BL OCLC

794. -----Three Vassar girls in
France; A story of the siege of
Paris.
Boston: Estes and Lauriat, c1888.
240p. NUC BL OCLC

795. -----Three Vassar girls in
Italy.
Boston: Estes and Lauriat, 1885.
240p. NUC BL OCLC

796. -----Three Vassar girls in
Russia and Turkey.
Boston: Estes and Lauriat, c1889.
240p. NUC BL OCLC

797. -----Three Vassar girls in
South America.
Boston: Estes and Lauriat, c1884.
239p. NUC OCLC
[Travel: Andes, Amazon, Panama.
This volume and her series,
"Witch Winnie", are intended for
younger readers.]

798. -----Three Vassar girls in
Switzerland.
Boston: Estes and Lauriat, c1890.
239p. NUC OCLC

799. -----Three Vassar girls in
the Holy Land.
Boston: Estes and Lauriat, c1892.
272p. NUC OCLC

800. -----Three Vassar girls in
the Tyrol.
Boston: Estes and Lauriat, 1887
[1886]. 235p. NUC OCLC

801. -----Three Vassar girls on
the Rhine.
Boston: Estes and Lauriat, 1887
[1886]. 235p. NUC OCLC

802. CHAMPNEY, Lizzie W. see
CHAMPNEY, Elizabeth (Williams)

803. CHANDLER, Ellen Louise see
MOULTON, Ellen Louise (Chandler)

804. CHANDLER, Mary [Br. 1687-
1745]
The description of Bath. A poem.
L: n.p., 1733; 3d ed. L: James
Leake, 1736. 77p. BL NUC OCLC

805. CHANNING, Barbara H. [Am.
19c]
The sisters abroad; or, an
Italian journey.
Boston: Whittemore et al, 1857.
267p. NUC OCLC

806. -----Sunny skies; or,
adventures in Italy.
Boston: D. Lothrop & co., 1869.
261p. NUC

807. CHANNING, William Ellery,
co-author see AIKEN, Lucy

808. CHANTAL, Sister Teresa de
see O'GORMAN, Edith

809. CHAPIN, Elisabeth Leonard
[Am. 19c]
Experiences of a little traveler
... extracts from the
correspondence of Elisabeth
Leonard Chapin. Ed. her sister,
Mary Louise Marshall.
Chicago: G. E. Marshall, 1898.
248p. NUC OCLC
[Voyages]

810. CHAPLIN, Holroyd, ed. see
CHAPLIN, Matilda Adriana

811. CHAPLIN, Matilda Adriana
[Br. 19c]
Memoir of Mrs. Matilda Adriana
Chaplin. Ed. Holroyd Chaplin.
L: n.p., 1899. 32p. BL

812. CHAPMAN, M. Louise, Mrs.
[Am. 19c]
How a baby crossed a mountain.
New Haven, CT: Tuttle, Morehouse
& Taylor, 1881. 16 l. NUC
[Travel: Switzerland]

813. CHAPMAN, Maria Weston, ed.
see MARTINEAU, Harriet

814. CHAPONE, Hester (Mulso) [Br.
1727-1801]
The posthumous works of Mrs.
Chapone, containing her
correspondence with Mr. [Samuel]
Richardson, a series of letters
to Mrs. Elizabeth Carter, and
some fugitive pieces.
L: J. Murray; Edinburgh: A.
Constable & co., 1807. 2v. NUC
BL OCLC

815. CHARKE, Charlotte (Cibber)
[Br. d. 1760?]
A narrative of the life of Mrs.
Charlotte Charke, youngest
daughter of Colley Cibber, Esq.
Written by herself.
L: W. Reeve, etc., 1755. 277p.
NUC BL MB OCLC
[Theater, society life]

816. CHARLES, Elizabeth (Rundle)
[Br. 1828-1896] ALT: Charles,
Mrs. Rundle
Our seven homes; autobiographical
reminiscences of Mrs. Rundle
Charles. Ed. Mary Davidson.
L: J. Murray, 1896. 236p. NUC BL
OCLC

817. -----Wanderings over Bible
lands and seas.
n.p.: n.p., 1862. 317p.; L & NY:
T. Nelson & sons, 1866. 301p. NUC
BL OCLC
[Malta, Holy Land, Tyre and Coast
of Asia Minor.]

818. CHARLES, Mrs. Rundle <u>see</u>
CHARLES, Elizabeth (Rundle)

819. CHARLOTTE AUGUSTA OF WALES,
Consort of Prince Leopold of
Saxe-Coburg [Br. 1796-1817] ALT:
Wales, Charlotte Augusta,
Princess of
A brief memoir of the Princess
Charlotte. By Lady Rose Sophia
Mary (Fane) Weigall.
L: J. Murray, 1874. 169p. NUC BL
OCLC
[Includes letters]

820. -----Letters from the
Princess Charlotte.
n.p.: n.p., 1839. 4v. BL

821. -----Lines written by ...
Princess Charlotte, a few weeks
previous to her death.
L: D. Cox, 1817.

822. -----Royal correspondence:
or, letters, between her late
Royal Highness, the Princess
Charlotte and her royal mothre
[sic], Queen Caroline of England,
during the exile of the latter,
etc.
L: Jones & co., 1822. 118p. NUC
BL

823. -----The very affectionate
and last letter of the late
Princess Charlotte of Wales, to
her beloved mother, the present
Queen of England.
L: J. Turner, etc., 1817?. 7p.;
Aylesbury: pr. by W. Woodman for
D. Williams, 1817. 8p.; L: D.
Cox, 1817. 7p. BL

824. CHARLOTTE ELIZABETH <u>see</u>
TONNA, Charlotte Elizabeth
(Browne)

825. CHARLTON, Mary [Br. c1794-
1830]
The life, adventures, and
vicissitudes of Mary Charlton,
the Welch orphan. Written by
herself.
Rochester: pr., W. Epps for
Langley, 1810?. 35p. NUC

826. CHASE, Eliza Brown [Am.
19/20c] ALT: C., E. B.
Over the border: Acadia, the home
of "Evangeline". By E. B. C.
Boston: J. R. Osgood & co., 1884.
215p. NUC
[Nova Scotia]

827. CHASE, Julia A. (Houghton),
ed. <u>see</u> BICKERDYKE, Mary Ann
(Ball)

828. CHATTERTON, Georgiana, Lady
<u>see</u> CHATTERTON, Henrietta
Georgiana Marcia Lascelles
(Iremonger), Lady

829. CHATTERTON, Georgiana, Lady,
comp. <u>see</u> FEATHERSTONHAUGH, Lady

830. CHATTERTON, Henrietta
Georgiana Marcia Lascelles
(Iremonger), Lady [Br. 1806-1876]
ALT: Chatterton, Georgiana, Lady
Home sketches and foreign
recollections.
L: Saunders & Otley, 1841. 3v.
NUC BL OCLC

831. -----Memoirs of Georgiana,
Lady Chatterton. With some
passages from her diary. [Ed.]
Edward Heneage Dering.
L: Hurst and Blackett, 1878.
309p. NUC BL MBD OCLC
[Social life in England and
France]

832. -----The Pyrenees, with
excursions into Spain.
L: Saunders & Otley, 1843. 2v.
NUC BL

833. -----Rambles in the south of
Ireland during the year 1838.
L: Saunders & Otley, 1839. 2v.
NUC BL OCLC

834. CHATTERTON, Henrietta
Georgiana Marcia Lascelles
(Iremonger), Lady, comp. <u>see</u>
FEATHERSTONHAUGH, Lady

835. CHEEVER, Elizabeth Hopkin
see CHEEVER, Elizabeth Hoppin
Wetmore

836. CHEEVER, Elizabeth Hoppin
[BL: Hopkin] Wetmore, Mrs. George
Barrell Cheever [Am. 1814-1886]
Memorabilia of George Barrell
Cheever, D. D. late pastor of the
Church of the Puritans ... and of
his wife Elizabeth Wetmore
Cheever.
NY: J. Wiley & sons; Fleming H.
Revell, 1890. NUC BL OCLC
[Includes her poems and letters.]

837. CHEEVER, George Barrell, co-
author see CHEEVER, Elizabeth
Hoppin Wetmore

838. CHEEVER, Mrs. George Barrell
see CHEEVER, Elizabeth Hoppin
Wetmore

839. CHEEVERS, Sarah, co-author
see EVANS, Katherine

840. CHENEY, Ednah Dow
(Littlehale), ed. see ALCOTT,
Louisa May

841. CHENNELLS, Ellen [Br. 19c]
PSEUD: English Governess
Recollections of an Egyptian
princess by her English governess
... . Being a record of five
years' residence at the court of
Ismael Pasha, khédive.
Edinburgh & L: W. Blackwood &
sons, 1893. 2v. NUC BL OCLC

842. CHESTER, Madam see CHESTER,
Mary

843. CHESTER, Mary [Br. 19c] ALT:
Chester, Madam
Memoirs of Madam Chester of
Manchester; by herself.
L: pr. for the authoress, 1868.
177p. NUC BL

844. CHICKERING, Hannah B. [Am.
1817-1879]
Recollections of Hannah B.
Chickering. [Comp.] Sarah E.
Dexter.
Cambridge, MA: Riverside press,
1881. 50p. NUC OCLC

845. CHILD, F., Miss [Br. 19c]
An historical appendix to the
spinster at home in the close of
Salisbury.
Salisbury: Frederic A. Blake,
1852.
[Historical notes]

846. -----The Salisbury
exhibition. A poem.
2d ed. Salisbury: F. A. Blake,
1852. 24p. BL

847. -----The Salisbury Jubilee
for the Peace of 1856. A poem.
Salisbury: F. A. Blake, 1856
20p. BL
[Poem on Salisbury places &
legends.]

848. -----The spinster at home,
in the close of Salisbury. No
fable. Together with tales and
ballads.
Salisbury: W. B. Brodie, 1844.
395p. BL

849. -----A visit to Swanage,
Dorset, in the month of May.
Salisbury: James Bennett, pr.,
1853. 15p. BL

850. CHILD, L. Maria, ed. see
JACOBS, Harriet (Brent)

851. CHILD, Lydia Maria (Francis)
[Am. 1802-1880] ALT: Francis,
Lydia Maria
Letters from New York.
1st series L: R. Bentley; NY: C.
S. Francis; Boston: J. Munro,
1843. 310p. NUC BL OCLC

852. -----Letters from New York.
2d series NY: C. S. Francis &
co.; Boston: J. H. Francis, 1845.
287p. NUC BL OCLC

853. -----The letters of Lydia
Maria Child. Ed. John Greenleaf
Whittier.
Boston & NY: Houghton, Mifflin &
co., 1883. 280p. NUC BL OCLC

854. CHILD, Lydia Maria
(Francis), ed. see JACOBS,
Harriet (Brent)

855. CHORLEY, Henry, ed. see
HEMANS, Felicia Dorothea (Browne)

856. CHORLEY, Henry, ed. <u>see</u> MITFORD, Mary Russell

857. CHRISTEEN <u>see</u> GEIER, Christeen

858. CHRONIQUEUSE, pseud. <u>see</u> LOGAN, Olive (Logan)

859. CHUBBUCK, Emily E. <u>see</u> JUDSON, Emily E. (Chubbuck)

860. CHUBBUCK, Harriet [Am. 19c]
My two sisters: a sketch from memory. [Harriet and Lavinia Chubbuck]. [By Emily E. (Chubbuck) Judson]
Boston: Ticknor, Reed & Fields, 1854. 112p. NUC BL OCLC
[Includes poetry by Lavinia]

861. CHUBBUCK, Lavinia <u>see</u> CHUBBUCK, Harriet

862. CHUDLEIGH, Elizabeth <u>see</u> HERVEY, Elizabeth Chudleigh

863. CHURCH, Rev. Henry L., comp. <u>see</u> COUSINS, Emma (Barber)

864. CHURCH, Mary [Br. 19c]
Sierra Leone: or, the liberated Africans in a series of letters from a young lady to her sister in 1833 and 34.
L: Longmans, 1835. 49p. NUC BL

865. CHURCH, Mrs. Ross <u>see</u> LEAN, Florence (Marryat) Church

866. CHURCHILL, Caroline M. (Nichols) [Am. 1833-1926]
Little sheaves gathered while gleaning after reapers. Being letters of travel commencing in 1870 and ending in 1873.
San Francisco: n.p., 1874. 99p. NUC
[Travel: California and Nevada]

867. -----Over the purple hills; or, sketches of travel in California.
Chicago: Hazlitt & Reed, pr., 1877. 256p. NUC OCLC

868. CHURCHILL, Elizabeth Kittredge, Mrs. [Am. 1829-1881]
Bethlehem [NH], and its surroundings.
Providence, RI: S. S. Rider, 1876. 57p. NUC OCLC
[New Hampshire travel]

869. CISH, Jane [Am. 18c]
The vision and wonderful experience of Jane Cish, shewing how she was converted, and how she fell into a trance ... being a copy from her own mouth.
Philadelphia: pub. at the request of several of her friends, 1793. 16p. NUC

870. CISNEROS, Evangelina Betancourt Cosio y [Am. 19c] ALT: Betancourt, Evangelina
The story of Evangelina Cisneros. Her rescue by Karl Decker, told by herself.
NY: Continental pub. co., 1891. 257p. NUC BL K OCLC

871. CLACY, Mrs. Charles <u>see</u> CLACY, Ellen

872. CLACY, Ellen, Mrs. Charles Clacy [Br. 19c]
A lady's visit to the gold diggings of Australia in 1852-53.
L: Hurst & Blackett, 1853. 302p. NUC BL

873. CLAFLIN, Agnes Elizabeth [Am. 1849-1869]
From shore to shore. A journey of nineteen years.
Cambridge, MA: Riverside, 1873. 383p. NUC OCLC
[Letters from Europe]

874. CLAGHORN, Mrs. James L. [Am. 19c]
Letters written to my son, during my two years' travel in Europe, 1865-1867.
Philadelphia: Henry B. Ashmead, 1873. 326p. NUC OCLC

875. CLANWILLIAM, Elizabeth Meade, Countess of <u>see</u> MURRAY, Lady

876. CLAPP, Eliza Thayer [Am. 1811-1888]
Essays, letters, and poems.
Boston: priv. pr., 1888. 200p. NUC
[Unitarian]

877. CLARE, Josephine, Mrs. [Am. 19c]
Narrative of the adventures and experiences of Mrs. Josephine Clare, a resident of the South at the breaking out of the rebellion, her final escape from Natchitoches, La., and safe arrival at home, in Marietta, Pa.
Lancaster, PA: Pearson & Geise, 1865. 36p. NUC C OCLC

878. CLARINDA, pseud. see M'LEHOSE, Agnes (Craig)

879. CLARK, Alice Georgina Caroline (Strong), ed. see STUART, Lady Louisa

880. CLARK, Francis E., ed. see CLARK, Lydia Fletcher (Symmes)

881. CLARK, Mrs. Godfrey, ed. see STUART, Lady Louisa

882. CLARK, Lydia Fletcher (Symmes) [Am. 1814-1859] ALT: Symmes, Lydia Fletcher
My mother's journal. Ed. her son, Francis E. Clark.
n.p.: pr. for priv. circ., c1900. 60p. NUC OCLC

883. CLARK, Susie Champney [Am. b. 1856]
The round trip from the hub to the Golden Gate.
Boston: Lee & Shepard; NY: C. T. Dillingham, 1890. 193p. NUC OCLC

884. CLARKE, Adam, comp. see COOPER, Mary (Hanson)

885. CLARKE, Mrs. Adam see CLARKE, Mary (Cooke)

886. CLARKE, Mary, ed. see CARSON, Ann (Baker)

887. CLARKE, Mary Anne (Thompson) [Br. 1776-1852]
Authentic memoirs of Mrs. Clarke, in which is portrayed the secret history and intrigues of many characters in the first circles of fashion and high life. Ed. Elizabeth Taylor.
L: T. Tegg, 1800. 212p. NUC BL OCLC
[Mistress of the Duke of York; includes letters]

888. -----The rival princes; or, a faithful narrative of facts relating to Mrs. M. A. Clarke's political acquaintance with Colonel Wardle, Major Dodd, etc., etc., etc., who were concerned in the charges against the Duke of York, etc.
L: pr. for the author & pub. by C. Chapple; NY: David Longworth, 1810. 2v. NUC BL OCLC

889. CLARKE, Mary (Cooke), Mrs. Adam Clarke [Br. 1760-1836]
Mrs. Adam Clarke; her character and correspondence. [Comp.] her daughter [Mary Ann (Clarke) Smith, Mrs. Richard Smith].
L: Partridge & Oakey, 1851. 244p. NUC

890. CLARKE, Mary Cowden see CLARKE, Mary Victoria (Novello) Cowden

891. CLARKE, Mary E. B. [Br. 19c]
Sketches of my childhood.
Edinburgh: W. Oliphant & co., 1874. 64p. BL MB
[Possibly fiction]

892. CLARKE, Mary Victoria (Novello) Cowden [Br. 1809-1898] ALT: Clarke, Mary Cowden
My long life. An autobiographic sketch.
L: T. Fisher Unwin, 1896. 260p. NUC BL OCLC

893. CLARKE, Olive Cleaveland, Mrs. [Am. b. 1785]
Things that I remember at ninety-five.
n.p.: n.p., 1881. 14p. NUC K OCLC
[Reminiscences of life in Hampshire County, Mass.]

894. CLARKE, Olive (Rand) see RAND, Olive

895. CLARKE, Sara Jane see LIPPINCOTT, Sara Jane (Clarke)

896. CLARKE, Mrs. Stanley [Br. 19c]
From the deck of a yacht.
L: Remington & co., 1882. 134p. NUC BL
[Travel: Levant]

897. CLAVERS, MARY, MRS., pseud.
see KIRKLAND, Caroline Matilda
(Stansbury)

898. CLEMANS, Mrs. F. M. see
CLEMANS, Sarah Isabella

899. CLEMANS, Rev. F. M., comp.
see CLEMANS, Sarah Isabella

900. CLEMANS, Sarah Isabella,
Mrs. F. M. Clemans [Am. 19c]
Flowers from the pathway of a
consecrated life. Comp. her
husband, Rev. F. M. Clemans.
Columbus, OH: William G. Hubbard,
1836. 296p. NUC

901. CLEMENS, Louisa Perina
Courtauld [Br. 19c]
Narrative of a pilgrim and
sojourner on earth, from 1791 to
the present year 1870.
Edinburgh: H. Armour & co., 1870.
BL MB
[Religious journal; travel:
Netherlands, Scotland, Ireland
and U.S.]

902. CLEMENT, Clara (Erskine) see
WATERS, Clara (Erskine) Clement

903. CLEMMER, Mary see AMES, Mary
E. (Clemmer)

904. CLEMONS, Mrs. [Br. 19c] ALT:
Clemons, Mrs. Major
The manners and customs of
society in India; including
scenes in the Mofussil stations.
By Mrs. Major Clemons.
L: Smith, Elder & co., 1841.
369p. NUC BL OCLC

905. CLEMONS, Mrs. Major see
CLEMONS, Mrs.

906. CLERGYMAN, A, pseud., comp.
see WESTON, Ann

907. CLERGYMAN OF THE CHURCH OF
SCOTLAND, A, pseud., comp. see
WOODBURY, Fanny

908. CLERGYMAN'S DAUGHTER, A,
pseud. see SIMPSON, Mary Emily

909. CLERK, Alice M. (Frere),
Mrs. Godfrey Clerk [Br. 19c] ALT:
Frere, Alice M.

The antipodes and round the
world; or, travels in Australia,
New Zealand, Ceylon, China,
Japan, and California.
L: Hatchards, 1870. 633p. 2v. in
1. NUC BL OCLC

910. CLERK, Mrs. Godfrey see
CLERK, Alice M. (Frere)

911. CLEVELAND, Cecelia Pauline
[Am. b. 1850]
The story of a summer, or,
journal leaves from Chappaqua.
NY: G. W. Carleton & co., 1874.
274p. NUC BL OCLC

912. CLIMERSON, Emily Jane, ed.
see POWYS, Caroline (Girle)

913. CLINTON, Elizabeth
(Knevitt), Countess of Lincoln
see LINCOLN, Elizabeth
(Knevitt), Countess of

914. CLOUGH, Anne Jemima [Br.
19c]
A memoir of Anne Jemima Clough.
By her niece, Blanche Athena
Clough.
L & NY: E. Arnold, 1897. 348p.
NUC BL OCLC
[Principal of Newnham College;
includes excerpts from
autobiography.]

915. CLOUGH, Blanche Athena,
comp. see CLOUGH, Anne Jemima

916. CLOUGH, Margaret Morley,
Mrs. [Br. 1803-1827]
Extracts from the journal and
correspondence of the late Mrs.
M. M. Clough.
L: J. Mason, 1829. 174p. NUC BL
MB
[Missionary diary; travel:
Ceylon]

917. COATES, Ellen see FREEMAN,
Ellen (Coates)

918. COBB, Mrs. Henry P. see
COBB, Phoebe H. (Sayre)

919. COBB, Mary (Blackburn) [Br.
1773-1802]
Extracts from the diary and
letters of Mrs. Mary Cobb.

L: pr. by C. & R. Baldwin, 1805.
324p. NUC BL MBD OCLC
[Baptist; diary 1792-1802]

920. COBB, Phoebe H. (Sayre),
Mrs. Henry P. Cobb [Am. 19c]
Sketches.
Detroit, MI: Win & Hammond, 1893.
NUC
[Journal of travel to Chicago, N.
California, Pennsylvania, New
York, New England States,
Washington D. C. in 1892.]

921. COBBE, Frances Power [Br.
1822-1904]
Life of Frances Power Cobbe, by
herself.
Boston & NY: Houghton Mifflin; L:
R. Bentley & son, 1894. 2v.   BL
MB OCLC

922. COCHNOWER, Florence Octie
Courtney, Mrs. [Am. 19c]
Recollections awakened by the
unveiling of the Thomas statue!
By the Army of the Cumberland.
Crawfordsville, IN: n.p., 1879.
7p. NUC

923. COCHRANE, Elizabeth [Am.
1867-1922] ALT: Seaman, Elizabeth
(Cochrane) PSEUD: Bly, Nellie
Nellie Bly's book. Around the
world in seventy-two days.
NY: The Pictorial Weeklies co.,
1890. 286p. NUC OCLC

924. -----Six months in Mexico.
NY: Am. Publishers co.; J. W.
Lovell, 1888. 205p. NUC OCLC

925. -----Ten days in a mad-
house; or, Nellie Bly's
experiences on Blackwell's Island
feigning insanity in order to
reveal asylum horrors.
NY: N. L. Munro, c1887. 120p. NUC
OCLC

926. CODMAN, John, ed. <u>see</u>
TUCKER, Susannah Humphrey (Clapp)

927. COGHILL, Mrs. Harry, ed. <u>see</u>
OLIPHANT, Margaret Oliphant
(Wilson)

928. COGHLAN, Mrs. John <u>see</u>
COGHLAN, Margaret (Moncrieffe)

929. COGHLAN, Margaret
(Moncrieffe), Mrs. John Coghlan
[Br. 18c]
Memoirs of Mrs. Coghlan, daughter
of the late Major Moncrieffe,
written by herself, and dedicated
to the British nation; being
interspersed with anecdotes of
the late American and present
French war.
L: pr. for the author; J. Lane;
Dublin: Z. Jackson, 1794. 2v. NUC
BL MB OCLC

930. COHEN, S. Jane (Picken) [Am.
19c]
Henry Luria; or, the little
Jewish convert, 1824-1832.
NY: J. F. Trow, pr., 1860. 215p.
NUC K OCLC
[On mixed marriage between
Christian woman and son of Jewish
rabbi. Incl. original poems.]

931. COIT, Martha <u>see</u> GREENE,
Martha (Coit) Hubbard

932. COIT, Mehetabel (Chandler)
[Am. 1673-1758]
Mehetabel Chandler Coit; her
book, 1714. Comp. & ed. by Marie
Petit Gilman, Emily Serena
Gilman, and L. G. Lane,
grandchildren of Daniel Lathrop
Coit.
Norwich, CT: Bulletin pr., 1895.
19p. NUC MAD OCLC
[Diary 1673-1758; commonplace
book & family notes.]

933. COKE, Lady Jane (Wharton)
Holt [Br. 1706-1761]
Letters from Lady Jane Coke to
her friend Mrs. Eyre at Derby
1747-1758. Ed. Florence A. Monica
Rathbone, Mrs. Ambrose Rathbone.
L: S. Sonnenschien, 1899. 169p.
NUC BL OCLC

934. COKE, Lady Mary [Br. 1726-
1811]
The letters and journals of Lady
Mary Coke. Ed. J. A. Home.
Edinburgh: David Douglas, 1889-
96. 4v. NUC BL MBD OCLC

935. COKER, Hannah Lide, Mrs.
[Am. 19c]
A story of the late war.
Charleston, SC: Walker, Evans &
Cogswell, 1887. 47p. NUC K OCLC

936. COLE, Emma see HANSON, Emma (Cole)

937. COLE, Mrs. Henry Warwick [Br. 19c]
A lady's tour round Monte Rosa, with visits to the Italian valleys ... in a series of excursions in the years 1850-56-58.
L: Longman, Brown, Green, Longmans and Roberts, 1859. 402p. NUC BL OCLC

938. COLE, Joseph, comp. see BALL, Hannah

939. COLE, Rebecca, Mrs. Tollmache Cole [Br. 19c]
Letters written by the late Mrs. Tollmache Cole, of Woodbright, to her six orphan children.
Woodbridge: J. Loder, 1817. 8p. BL

940. COLE, Mrs. Tollmache see COLE, Rebecca

941. COLENSO, Frances Ellen [Br. 19c]
My chief and I; or, six months in Natal after the Langalibalele outbreaks.
L: Chapman & Hall, 1880. 327p. NUC

942. COLES, Rev. George, ed. see REYNOLDS, Catherine

943. COLES, Rev. George, ed. see LOWE, Ann

944. COLESON, Ann [Am. 19c]
Miss Coleson's narrative of her captivity among the Sioux Indians.
Philadelphia: Barclay & co., [c1864]. 70p. NUC OCLC

945. COLLIER, Mrs. [Br. 19c]
Autobiography of Mrs. Collier, a Bible woman. Ed. E. Nightingale.
L: n.p., c1880. BL MB

946. COLLINS, Elizabeth [Br. 19c]
Memories of the southern states.
Taunton: J. Barnicott, pr., 1865. 116p. NUC BL C
[Southern sympathizer; plantation life, 1859-1863]

947. COLLINS, Elizabeth (Ballinger) Mason [Am. 1755-1831]
Memoirs of Elizabeth Collins, of Upper Evesham, New Jersey, a minister of the gospel of Christ, in the Society of Friends.
Philadelphia: Nathan Kite, 1833. 144p. NUC K OCLC

948. COLLINS, Elizabeth M. (Smith), Mrs. Nat Collins [Am. b. 1844] ALT: Collins, Libby (Smith)
The cattle queen of Montana ... a story of the personal experiences of Mrs. Nat Collins ... . Comp. Charles Wallace.
Spokane, WA: Dyer pr. co., n.d. 260p.; St. James, MN: C. W. Foote, 1894. 249p. NUC K OCLC

949. COLLINS, Laura G. (Case) [Am. 1826-1912]
By-gone tourist days; letters of travel.
Cincinnati, OH: R. Clarke co., c1899. 326p. NUC
[Travel: Europe]

950. COLLINS, Libby (Smith) see COLLINS, Elizabeth M. (Smith)

951. COLLINS, N. J. H., Mrs. [Am. 19c] PSEUD: Janet
Reminiscences; or, a few glimpses from over the sea. By Janet.
Philadelphia: Collins & co., 1891. 303p. NUC OCLC
[Travel: Great Britain]

952. COLLINS, Mrs. Nat see COLLINS, Elizabeth M. (Smith)

953. COLLINSON, Anne Ross, comp. see BULMER, Agnes (Collinson)

954. COLLIS, Mrs. Charles H. T. see COLLIS, Septima Maria (Levy)

955. COLLIS, Septima Maria (Levy), Mrs. Charles H. T. Collis [Am. 1842-1917]
A woman's trip to Alaska.
NY: Cassell Pub. co., c1890. 194p. NUC OCLC

956. -----A woman's war record, 1861-1865.
L & NY: Putnam, 1889. 78p. NUC K OCLC
[Companion of her husband at the front]

957. COLMAN, Lucy Newhall (Danforth) [Am. 1871-1906]
Reminiscences.
Buffalo, NY: H. L. Green, 1891. 86p. NUC BL K

958. COLQUHOUN, Lady Janet Sinclair [Br. 1781-1846]
A memoir of Lady Janet Colquhoun. [Comp.] James Hamilton.
L: J. Nisbet, 1849. 285p. NUC BL MBD OCLC
[Based on her diary 1805-1844; chiefly religious]

959. COLT, Miriam (Davis) [Am. b. 1817]
Went to Kansas; being a thrilling account of an ill-fated expedition to that fairy land, and its sad results; together with a sketch of the life of the author.
Watertown, NY: L. Ingalls, 1862. 294p. NUC BL MAD OCLC

960. COLVILE, Zélie Isabelle (Richaud de Préville) Lady [Br. 19c]
Round the black man's garden.
Edinburgh & L: W. Blackwood & sons, 1893. 344p. NUC BL OCLC
[Travel: Africa]

961. COLVILLE, Elizabeth (Melvill), Lady Colville of Culross [Br. fl. 1603] ALT: Culross, Lady; Melvill, Elizabeth
Select biographies. By William King Tweedie.
Edinburgh: Wodrow Society, 1845-1847. NUC BL OCLC
[v.1 contains her letters.]

962. COMERFORD, Bridget Mary Teresa see COMERFORD, Rev. Mother Mary Teresa

963. COMERFORD, Rev. Mother Mary Teresa [Am. 1821-1881] ALT: Comerford, Bridget Mary Teresa
Memoir of Rev. Mother Mary Teresa Comerford. By Josephine Hagerty.
San Francisco: P. J. Thomas, 1882. 120p. NUC OCLC
[Contains extracts of letters]

964. COMLY, John, co-author see COMLY, Rebecca

965. COMLY, Mrs. John see COMLY, Rebecca

966. COMLY, Rebecca, Mrs. John Comly [Am. b. 1773]
Journal of the life and religious labours of John Comly, late of Byberry, Pennsylvania.
Philadelphia: T. E. Chapman, 1853. 645p. NUC MAD OCLC
[Includes extracts from her journal and letters.]

967. COMSTOCK, Elizabeth L. (Rous) Wright [Br. 1815-1891]
Life and letters of Elizabeth L. Comstock. Comp. her sister, C. Hare.
L: Headley bros.; Philadelphia: J. C. Winston, 1895. 511p. NUC BL OCLC

968. CONE, Mary [Br. 19c]
Two years in California.
Chicago: S. C. Griggs & co., 1876. 238p. NUC BL OCLC

969. CONINGSBY, Margaret (Coningsby) Newton, Countess of [Br. 1709?-1761]
Letters of Margaret, Countess of Coningsby from France in 1737-8.
Middle Hill: C. Gilmour, 1842. 45p. NUC BL OCLC

970. CONNER, Eliza Archard [Am. 19c] ALT: A., E.
"E.A." abroad, a summer in Europe.
Cincinnati, OH: W. E. Dibble & co., 1883. 372p. NUC OCLC

971. CONSTABLE, A., ed. see SEWARD, Anna

972. CONSTAPLE, Hope [Br. 19c]
London after dark; or, rambles by night.
L: H. Clements, 1894. 80p. BL
[Walking tour of the evils of London.]

973. CONSUL'S DAUGHTER AND WIFE, A, pseud. see BLUNT, Fanny Janet (Sandison) Lady

974. CONTEMPORARY, A, pseud. see RENNIE, Eliza

975. CONWAY, Katherine Eleanor
[Am. 1853-1927]
New footsteps in well-trodden
ways.
Boston: The Pilot pub. co., 1899.
252p. NUC OCLC
[Travel: primarily Italy]

976. COOK, Ann see BEAUCHAMP, Ann
(Cook)

977. COOK, Frances [Br. 17c]
Mris [Mistress] Cookes
meditations: being an humble
thanksgiving to her Heavenly
Father for granting her a new
life, having concluded her selfe
dead ... in that great storme,
Jan. the 5th, 1649. Composed by
her selfe at her unexpected safe
arrival at Corke.
L: Reprinted by C. S.; Sold by
Thomas Brewster & Gregory Mould,
1650. 16p. BL OCLC

978. COOKE, Bella (Beeton) [Br.
1821-1908]
Light on the weary path. A
continuation of "Rifted clouds".
Ed. Rev. Joseph Pullman.
L: Hodder & Stoughton, 1898.
292p. BL

979. -----Rifted clouds; or, the
life story of Bella Cooke. A
record of loving kindness and
tender mercies. Written by
herself. Ed. Rev. Joseph Pullman.
L: Hodder & Stoughton, 1886.
360p.; NY: Palmer & Hughes; B.
Cooke, 1884. 448p. NUC BL MB OCLC
[Autobiography & diary;
Methodist.]

980. COOKE, Emily Sarah [Br. 19c]
Letters from a sister. Ed. George
Cooke.
Doncaster: n.p., 1841. 51p. BL

981. COOKE, George, ed. see
COOKE, Emily Sarah

982. COOKE, Harriet B., Mrs. [Am.
b. 1786?]
Memories of my life work. The
autobiography of Harriet B.
Cooke.
NY: Robert Carter, 1858. 356p.
NUC K OCLC

983. COOKE, Sophia [Br. 19c]
Memoir of Mrs. Sophia Cooke, late
of Stalham, Norfolk. Compiled
chiefly from her own manuscripts.
Norwich: Fletcher & Alexander,
1857. 237p. BL

984. COOKE, Sophia [Br. 1814-
1895]
Sophia Cooke; or, forty-two years
work in Singapore. By Mrs. Eliza
Ann Walker.
L: Elliot Stock, 1899. 91p. BL
[Includes some of her letters]

985. COOPER, Anna Julia (Haywood)
[Am. b. 1869]
A voice from the South, by a
black woman of the South.
Xenia, OH: Aldine, 1892. 304p.
NUC OCLC
[Essays and reflections on status
of Blacks and women.]

986. COOPER, Elizabeth, comp. see
STUART, Lady Arabella

987. COOPER, Jane [Br. 1738-1762]
Letters wrote by Jane Cooper; to
which is prefixt some account of
her life and death.
2d ed. Bristol: William Pine,
1764. 40p. NUC BL OCLC

988. COOPER, Maria Susanna, Mrs.
[Br. 18c]
Letters between Emilia and
Harriet. [By Maria Susanna
Cooper]
L: R. & J. Dodsley, 1762. 175p.;
Dublin: Peter Wilson, 1762. 180p.
NUC BL

989. COOPER, Mary (Hanson) [Br.
1786-1812]
Memoirs of the late Mrs. Mary
Cooper. [Comp.] Adam Clarke.
L: J. Butterworth & son, 1814.
211p.; NY: J. Soule & T. Mason,
1816. 161p. NUC BL MBD OCLC
[Methodist; includes letters &
diary.]

990. COOPER, Mary Sarson
(Winfield) [Br. 1813-1851]
Memorials of Mrs. Mary Sarson
Cooper, late of Dunstable,
compiled from her diary and
correspondence by Henry Fish.
L: For the author, 1855. 195p.
NUC BL

991. COOPLAND, Mrs. R. M. [Br. 19c]
A lady's escape from Gwalior and life in the fort of Agra, during the mutinies of 1857.
L: Smith, Elder & co., 1859 316p. NUC BL MB OCLC
[Sepoy Rebellion, 1857-58]

992. COPE, Susannah [Br. 19c]
The life and extraordinary adventures of Susannah Cope, the British female soldier.
Banbury: Cheney, 1810. 8p. BL

993. COPELAND, Isabella Frances (Blundell) see BLUNDELL, Isabella Frances

994. COPLESTON, Mrs. Edward Arthur [Br. 19c]
Canada; why we live in it, and why we like it.
L: Parker, son, & Bourn, 1861. 121p. NUC BL MC OCLC

995. COPPIN, Rev. Levi Jenkins, ed. see BECKETT, Catherine Stella (Campbell)

996. CORBET, M. E. see CORBET, Mary Elizabeth

997. CORBET, Mary Elizabeth [Br. 19c] ALT: Corbet, M. E.
A pleasure trip to India, during the visit of H. R. H. the Prince of Wales. Afterwards to Ceylon.
L: W. H. Allen & co., 1880. 231p. NUC BL

998. CORDER, Susanna, ed. see FRY, Elizabeth (Gurney)

999. CORF, Eliza [Br. 19c]
Moral and religious essays, poems, anecdotes, and extracts from my diary.
L: Simpkin Marshall & co., 1852. 2v. BL OCLC

1000. CORINNA, pseud. see THOMAS, Elizabeth

1001. CORNABY, Hannah (Last) [Hollingsworth K] [Am. b. 1822]
Autobiography and poems.
Salt Lake City, UT: pr. J. C. Graham & co., 1881. 158p. NUC K OCLC

[Englishwoman who became Mormon. Frontier and pioneer life.]

1002. CORNER, Caroline [Br. 19c]
My visit to Styria.
L: J. Burns, 1882. 32p. BL

1003. -----Rhineland.
L: J. Burns, 1884. 80p. BL

1004. CORNISHWOMAN, A, pseud. see ELLIS, Elizabeth Furss

1005. CORNWALLIS, Caroline Francis [Br. 1786-1858]
Selections from the letters of Caroline Frances Cornwallis ... also some unpublished poems.
L: Trübner & co., 1864. 482p. NUC BL OCLC

1006. CORNWALLIS, Jane (Meautys), Lady see Bacon, Jane (Meautys) Cornwallis, Lady

1007. CORT, Mary Lovina [Br. 19c]
Siam: or, the heart of farther India.
NY: Anson D. F. Randolph & co., 1886. 399p. NUC BL OCLC

1008. COSMOPOLITAN, A, pseud. see VELDE, M. S. Van de, Mme.

1009. COSTELLO, Louisa Stuart [Br. 1799-1870]
Béarn and the Pyrenees. A legendary tour to the country of Henri Quatre.
L: Richard Bentley, 1844. 2v. NUC BL OCLC

1010. -----The falls, lakes and mountains of North Wales.
L: Longman, Brown, Green & Longmans, 1845. 221p. NUC BL OCLC

1011. -----A pilgrimage to Auvergne, from Picardy to Le Velay.
L: Richard Bentley, 1842. 2v. NUC BL OCLC

1012. -----A summer amongst the Bocages and the vines.
L: Richard Bentley, 1840. 2v. NUC BL OCLC

1013. -----A tour to and from Venice by the Vaudois and the Tyrol.
L: John Ollivier, 1846. 435p. NUC BL

1014. COSTON, Martha Jay (Scott) [Am. b. 1828]
A signal success. The work and travels of Mrs. Martha J. Coston. An autobiography.
Philadelphia: J. B. Lippincott, 1886. 333p. NUC BL K OCLC

1015. COTTERELL, Sir Charles, co-author see PHILIPS, Katherine (Fowler)

1016. COTTERELL, Constance [Br. 19/20c]
Summer holidays in northeast England.
L: Walter Scott, 1895. 143p. NUC BL OCLC

1017. COTTON, Elizabeth Reid see DENNEY, Elizabeth Reid (Cotton) Hope

1018. COULOMB, Emma [Br. 19c]
Some account of my intercourse with Madame Blavatsky from 1872 to 1884; with a number of additional letters and a full explanation of the most marvellous theosophical phenomena.
L: Elliot Stock, 1885. 112p. NUC BL

1019. COULTHARD, Clara [Br. 19c]
ALT: Tanner, Clara (Coulthard)
One witness more.
Warminster: R. E. Vardy, 1845. 51p. BL
[Account of her religious experience.]

1020. COURTENAY, Thomas Peregrine, comp. see TEMPLE, Dorothy (Osborne), Lady

1021. COUSIN MARY, pseud. see HUSTON, Mary E.

1022. COUSINS, Emma (Barber) [Br. 1826-1866]
The Christian sufferer. Memorials ... chiefly compiled from her papers and letters by the Rev. Henry L. Church.
L: J. Neal, 1868. 100p. NUC

1023. COWELL, Christiana B. (Coffin), Mrs. D. B. Cowell [Am. 1821-1862]
Life and writings of Mrs. Christiana B. Cowell, consort of Rev. D. B. Cowell, who died in Lebanon, Maine, Oct. 8, 1862, aged 41 years.
Biddeford, ME: J. E. Butler & co., 1872. 296p. NUC OCLC
[Includes poetry and a hymn.]

1024. COWELL, Mrs. D. B. see COWELL, Christiana B. (Coffin)

1025. COWELL, Elizabeth Susan [Br. 19c]
Leaves of memory.
L: Seeley & co., 1892. 89p. BL MB
[Includes poetry, travel in France, Italy & India.]

1026. COWLES, Helen Maria [Am. 1831-1851]
Grace victorious; or, the memoir of Helen M. Cowles. [Comp.] Henry Cowles.
Oberlin, OH: J. M. Fitch, 1856. 230p. NUC MAD OCLC

1027. COWLES, Henry, comp. see COWLES, Helen Maria

1028. COWPER, Hon. Charles Spencer, ed. see COWPER, Mary (Clavering), Countess

1029. COWPER, Katrine Cecilia (Compton), Countess [Br. 1845-1913]
A month in Palestine.
L: J. Bumpus, 1889. 116p. NUC OCLC

1030. COWPER, Mary (Clavering), Countess [Br. 1685-1724]
Diary of Mary, Countess Cowper, lady of the bedchamber to the Princess of Wales, 1714-1720. Ed. Hon. Charles Spencer Cowper.
L: J. Murray, 1864. 207p. NUC BL MBD

1031. COWPER, William, co-author
see HESKETH, Harriet (Cowper),
Lady

1032. COX, Francis Augustus,
comp. see TOMES, Ann

1033. COX, Lydia (Noyes) [Am.
1814-1844]
Recollections and gathered
fragments of Mrs. L. N. C. of
Williamsburg, L.I. Ed. Mrs.
Phoebe Palmer.
NY: Piercy & Reed, pr., 1845.
231p. NUC OCLC
[Methodist]

1034. CRAFTS, James Monroe, ed.
see HEATH, Betsey

1035. CRAFTS, William F. see
HEATH, Betsey

1036. CRAIK, Dinah Maria (Mulock)
[Br. 1826-1887] ALT: Mulock,
Dinah Maria
Fair France: Impressions of a
traveller.
L: Hurst & Blackett, 1871. 313p.;
NY: Harper & bros., 1871. 238p.
NUC BL OCLC

1037. -----An unknown country.
L: Macmillan & co., 1887. 187p.;
NY: Harper & bros., 1887. 238p.
NUC BL OCLC
[Travel: Northern Ireland]

1038. -----An unsentimental
journey through Cornwall.
L: Macmillan & co., 1884. 144p.
NUC BL OCLC

1039. CRANE, Bathsheba H. (Morse)
[Am. b. 1811]
Life, letters, and wayside
gleanings, for the folks at home.
Boston: J. H. Earle, 1880. 480p.
NUC OCLC
[Minister's wife in various
parishes: Vermont, Boston, etc.]

1040. CRANE, Jane Miriam
(Havergal), ed. see HAVERGAL,
Frances Ridley

1041. CRANE, Jane Miriam
(Havergal) see HAVERGAL, Maria
Vernon Graham

1042. CRAVEN, Mrs. Augustus see
CRAVEN, Pauline Marie Armande
Algaé (Ferron de la Ferronays)

1043. CRAVEN, Elizabeth
(Berkeley) Baroness Craven [Br.
1750-1828] ALT: Brandenburg,
Anspach and Bayreuth, H. S. H.
the Margravine of
A journey through the Crimea to
Constantinople in a series of
letters ... to His Serene
Highness, the Margrave of
Ansbach, and Bayreuth.
L: G. G. J. & J. Robinson, 1789.
415p. NUC BL OCLC

1044. -----Memoirs of the
Margravine of Anspach, written by
herself.
L: Henry Colburn, 1826. 2v. NUC
BL MB OCLC

1045. CRAVEN, Pauline Marie
Armande Algaé (Ferron de la
Ferronnays), Mrs. Augustus Craven
[Br. 1808-1891]
A memoir of Mrs. Augustus Craven.
With extracts from her diaries
and correspondence. By Maria
Catherine Bishop.
L: R. Bentley & sons, 1894. 2v.
NUC BL OCLC

1046. CRAWFORD AND BALCARRES,
Alexander William Crawford
Lindsay, Earl of, comp. see
BARNARD, Lady Anne (Lindsay)

1047. CRAWFORD, Cora Hayward [Am.
19c]
The land of the Montezumas.
2d ed. NY: J. B. Alden, 1889.
311p. NUC OCLC

1048. CRAWFORD, Isabel Alice
Hartley [Am. b. 1865]
The heroine of Saddle Mountain.
Ed. Mary G. Burdette.
Chicago: R. R. Donnelly, 1897.
52p. NUC OCLC
[Missionary to Oklahoma
Territory, Kiowas. Incl. excerpts
from her diaries. In series:
"Young women among blanket
Indians."]

1049. CRAWFORD, Lavinia [Am. 1830-1882]
The life of Lavinia Crawford, thirty years missionary in India, written mostly by herself in journals and letters.
Boston: F. B. pr. estab., 1886. 192p. NUC OCLC

1050. CRAWFORD, Mabel Sharman [Br. 19c]
Life in Tuscany.
L: Smith, Elder & co., 1859. 337p. NUC BL OCLC

1051. -----Through Algeria.
L: R. Bentley, 1863. 362p. NUC BL OCLC

1052. CREAMER, Hannah Gardner [Am. 19c] ALT: C., H. G.
Gift for young students. By H. G. C.
Salem, MA: George Creamer, 1848. 258p. NUC OCLC
[Autobiography of a governess; reminiscences of school life.]

1053. CRESSWELL, Mrs. Francis, ed. see FRY, Elizabeth (Gurney)

1054. CRESSWELL, Rachel Elizabeth (Fry), ed. see FRY, Elizabeth (Gurney)

1055. CRICHTON, Kate [Br. 19c]
Six years in Italy.
L: C. J. Skeet, 1861. 2v. NUC BL MB OCLC

1056. CROCKER, Maria, co-author see CROCKER, Sophia

1057. CROCKER, Sophia [Am. 1794-1822]
The twins: or, an account of the happy lives and triumphant deaths of Sophia Crocker, who died May 13th, 1822, and her sister Maria, who died Nov. 3d, 1823.
Norwich, CT: pr. at Courier office, 1828. 44p. NUC OCLC
[Comp. largely from diaries of the authors.]

1058. CROFT, James, ed. see HESKETH, Harriet (Cowper), Lady

1059. CROGGON, Lucy (Emra) [Br. 19c] ALT: Emra, Lucy
Onward and upward.
Sittingbourne: n.p., 1853. BL

1060. -----Things new and old; or, recollections by a district visitor in prose and verse. Pub. as: Lucy Emra
L: Hamilton, Adams & co., 1839. BL

1061. -----Things seen and known: or, a book of remembrance.
L: Hamilton, Adams & co., 1844. BL
[Poetry & prose.]

1062. -----Transcripts from my tablets. By a lover of nature.
Dublin: n.p., 1849. NUC BL

1063. CROKER, the Rt. Hon. John Wilson, ed. see HERVEY, Mary (Lepell) Hervey, Baroness

1064. CROKER, Thomas Crofton, ed. see WARWICK, Mary (Boyle) Rich, Countess of

1065. CROMMELIN, Maria Henrietta de la Cherois [Br. 19/29c] ALT: Crommelin, May
Over the Andes from the Argentine to Chili and Peru.
L: Richard Bentley & son, 1896. 387p. NUC BL OCLC

1066. CROMMELIN, May see CROMMELIN, Maria Henrietta de la Cherois

1067. CROSBY, Medora Robbins [Am. 19/20c]
The ancients in London, June 29 to July 31, 1896.
Boston: Ellis, 1890. 44p. NUC
[London visit of the Ancient and Honorable Artillery Company of Boston]

1068. CROSLAND, Camilla Dufour (Toulmin), Mrs. Newton Crosland [Br. 1812-1895] ALT: Toulmin, Camilla Dufour
Landmarks of a literary life, 1820-1892.
L: S. Low Marston & co.; NY: Charles Scribner's sons, 1893. 298p. NUC BL MB OCLC

1069. -----Light in the valley. My experiences of spiritualism. L & NY: G. Routledge & co., 1857. 228p. NUC BL OCLC

1070. CROSLAND, Mrs. Newton see CROSLAND, Camilla Dufour (Toulmin)

1071. CROSS, John Walter, ed. see EVANS, Marian

1072. CROSS, Marian (Evans) see EVANS, Marian

1073. CROSSE, Mrs. Andrew see CROSSE, Cornelia A. H.

1074. CROSSE, Cornelia A. H., Mrs. Andrew Crosse [Br. 19c] Red letter days of my life. L: Richard Bentley & son, 1892. 2v. NUC BL OCLC [Memoirs of the 1850s & 60s.]

1075. CROUCH, Louisa J., comp. see NORTH, Mary E.

1076. CROWLEY, Ann [Br. 1766-1826] Some account of the religious experiences of Ann Crowley. Lindfield: W. Eade, 1842. 50p. NUC BL [Autobiography]

1077. CROWLEY, Ann [Br. 1757-1774] Some expressions of Ann Crowley ... during her last illness. L: Mary Hinde, 1774. 16p. NUC BL

1078. CROWLEY, Julia M. (Corbitt), Mrs. Richard Crowley [Am. 19c] Echoes from Niagara; historical, political, personal. Buffalo, NY: C. W. Moulton, 1890. 413p. NUC OCLC [Wife of N.Y. State Senator 1865-69]

1079. CROWLEY, Mrs. Richard see CROWLEY, Julia M. (Corbitt)

1080. CRUTE, Sallie Spotswood, Mrs. [Am. 19c] Buds from memory's wreath.

Philadelphia: Claxton, Remsen & Haffelfinger, 1873. 180p. NUC OCLC [Verse & prose]

1081. CRYER, Mary (Burton) [Br. 1811-1843] ALT: Burton, Mary The devotional remains of Mrs. Cryer. L: Hamilton, Adams & co., 1854. 270p. BL OCLC [Methodist; later pub. as: Rooted and grounded in love: journals and letters of Mrs. Mary Cryer.]

1082. -----Holy living exemplified in the life of Mrs. Mary Cryer. [Comp.] Rev. Alfred Barrett. L: J. Mason, 1845. 326p. NUC BL OCLC [Includes letters]

1083. CULBERTSON, Rosamond [Am. b. 1803] Rosamond: or, a narrative of the captivity and suffering of an American female under the popish priests, in the island of Cuba ... NY: Leavitt, Lord & co.; Boston: Crocker & Brewster, 1836. 292p. NUC BL OCLC

1084. CULROSS, Lady see COLVILLE, Elizabeth (Melvill), Lady Colville of Culross

1085. CUMBERLAND, Henry Frederick, Duke of, co-author see GROSVENOR, Henrietta (Vernon) Grosvenor, Countess

1086. CUMMING, Constance Frederica Gordon see GORDON-CUMMING, Constance Frederica

1087. CUMMING, Kate [Am. 1835-1909] Gleanings from Southland; sketches of life and manners of the people of the South before, during and after the war of secession, with extracts from the author's journal ... . Birmingham, AL: Roberts & son, 1895. 277p. NUC OCLC

1088. -----A journal of hospital life in the Confederate army of Tennessee.
Louisville, KY: J. P. Morton & co; New Orleans, LA: W. Evelyn, [1866]. 199p. NUC OCLC
[Most of this material, revised and rewritten, appeared in "Gleanings from Southland."]

1089. CUMMINS, George David, comp. see HOFFMAN, Virginia Haviside

1090. CUMMINS, Margaret [Am. 19c]
Leaves from my portfolio, original and selected, together with a religious narrative.
St. Louis, MO: William E. Foote, pr., 1860. 181p. NUC K OCLC

1091. CUNLIFFE, Mary [Br. 19c]
Letters from abroad.
L: Army & Navy Coop. Soc., 1875. 51p. BL
[Travel: Palestine, U.S., Russia]

1092. CURNOCK, Nehemiah, ed. see HURD, Mary Fanny (Bickford)

1093. CURRIE, Helen (Alexander) [Br. 1654-1729]
Passages in the lives of Helen Alexander and James Currie of Pentland.
Belfast: M. Ward & co., 1869. 78p. NUC
[The account of Helen Alexander was written from her dictation in 1729.]

1094. CURTIS, Caroline Gardiner (Cary), ed. see OTIS, Harriet

1095. CURTIS, Caroline Gardiner (Cary), ed. see CARY, Anne M.

1096. CURTIS, Caroline Gardiner (Cary), ed. see CARY, Margaret

1097. CURWEN, Alice [Br. d. 1679]
A relation of the labour, travail and suffering of that faithful servant of the Lord, Alice Curwen, who departed this life the 7th day of the 6th month 1679 and resteth in peace with the Lord. [Comp.] Anne Martindell.
L: n.p., 1680. 55p. NUC
[Member of Society of Friends; contains her letters.]

1098. CUSACK, May Frances Clare [Br. 1830-1899]
Nun of Kenmare; an autobiography.
Boston: Ticknor; L: Josiah Child, 1888. 558p. NUC BL K MB

1099. CUSHING, Mrs. Caleb see CUSHING, Caroline Elizabeth (Wilde)

1100. CUSHING, Caroline Elizabeth (Wilde), Mrs. Caleb Cushing [Am. d. 1832]
Letters descriptive of public monuments, scenery, and manners in France and Spain.
Newburyport, MA: E. W. Allen & co., 1832. 2v. NUC BL OCLC

1101. CUSHMAN, Charlotte Saunders [Am. 1816-1876]
Charlotte Cushman: her letters and memories of her life. Ed. Emma Stebbins.
Boston: Houghton, Osgood & co., 1878. 308p. NUC BL OCLC

1102. CUSHMAN, Josephine Penfield, ed. see BATEHAM, Minerva Dayton

1103. CUSHMAN, Pauline [Am. 1833-1893]
Life of Pauline Cushman, the celebrated spy and scout. By F. L. Sarmiento.
Philadelphia: J. E. Potter, 1865. 374p. NUC K OCLC
[Based on her notes and memoranda. Two versions of her story were pub. 1864 as: "An inside view of the Army police ..."; Cincinnati, OH: Rickey & Carroll; 50p. and "The romance of the great rebellion;" NY: Wynkoop & Hollenbeck; 32p.]

1104. CUST, Emma Sophia (Edgcumbe), Countess Brownlow see BROWNLOW, Emma Sophia (Edgcumbe) Cust, Countess

1105. CUSTER, Elizabeth (Bacon), Mrs. George Armstrong Custer [Am. 1842-1933]
"Boots and saddles," or, life in Dakota with General Custer.
NY: Harper, 1885. 312p. NUC BL K OCLC

1106. -----Following the Guidon.
NY: Harper & bros, 1890. 341p.
NUC BL OCLC

1107. -----Tenting on the plains;
or, Gen. Custer in Kansas and
Texas.
NY: C. L. Webster, 1887. 702p.
NUC BL K OCLC

1108. CUSTER, Mrs. George
Armstrong see CUSTER, Elizabeth
(Bacon)

1109. CUTHELL, Edith E. [Br. 19c]
Indian memories. By W. S. Burrell
and E. E. Cuthell.
L: R. Bentley & son, 1893. 304p.
NUC BL OCLC
[Travel: India]

1110. CUTLER, Esther [Am. 1775-
1809]
A short view of the life of
Esther Cutler. Collected from her
own writings by Elijah R. Sabin.
Providence, RI: David Heaton;
Jonathan Cutler, 1810. 48p. NUC
BL

1111. CUTLER, Helen R. [Am. 19c]
Jottings from life, or, passages
from the diary of an itinerant's
wife.
Cincinnati, OH: Poe & Hitchcock,
1864. 282p. NUC BL K OCLC

1112. CUTTS, Lucia Beverley, ed.
see MADISON, Dorothy (Payne)
Todd

1113. D., A. see DUTTON, Amy

1114. D., A. see DUTTON, Anne

1115. D'A., Anna see D'ALMEIDA,
Anna

1116. D., A. G., Mrs. [Am. 19c]
Writings of Mrs. A. G. D. with a
sketch of her character.
Newburyport, MA: Charles Norris &
co., 1810. 72p. NUC

1117. D., C., pseud. see
DeMORGAN, Sophia Elizabeth
(Frend)

1118. D., E., Mrs. see Dornford,
Eleanor, Mrs.

1119. D., M., co-author see KERR,
M., Mrs.

1120. D., M., pseud. see DOUGLAS,
M., Mrs.

1121. D., M. B. M. see DUNCAN,
Mary Balfour Manson

1122. D., M. F. see DICKSON,
Maria Frances

1123. D., M. J. M. see DUNBAR,
Margaret Juliana Maria

1124. D., P. see DOW, Peggy

1125. D., S. see DOHERTY, Sarah

1126. DABNEY, Roxana Lewis [Am.
19c]
Annals of the Dabney family in
Fayal.
Boston: Pr. Alfred Mudge & son
for priv. circ., 1806-1871?. 3v.
NUC
[Family letters 1785-1871; life
in Fayal, Portugal.]

1127. DAHLGREN, Madeline (Vinton)
see DAHLGREN, Sarah Madeline
(Vinton) Goddard

1128. DAHLGREN, Sarah Madeline
(Vinton) Goddard [Am. 1825-1898]
ALT: Dahlgren, Madeline (Vinton);
Goddard, Sarah Madeline (Vinton)
South Sea sketches. A narrative.
Boston: J. R. Osgood & co.;
Baltimore: J. Murphy, 1881. 238p.
BL NUC OCLC
[Travel: Peru & Chile]

1129. DALL, Caroline Wells Healey
[Am. 1822-1912]
My first holiday; or, letters
from Colorado, Utah and
California.
Boston: Roberts bros, 1881. 430p.
NUC OCLC

1130. DALLAS, Maria [Am.]
Auto-biographical memoir.
n.p.: n.p., n.d. 9p. NUC

1131. D'ALMEIDA, Anna [Br. 19c]
ALT: D'A., Anna
A lady's visit to Manilla and
Japan. By Anna D'A.
L: Hurst & Blackett, 1863. 297p.
NUC BL OCLC

1132. DALRYMPLE, Kate, Mrs. [Br.
17/18c]
The diary of Mrs. Kate Dalrymple
1685-1735.
Edinburgh: n.p., 1856. BL

1133. DALY, Harriet W. [Br. 19c]
Digging, squatting and pioneering
life in the northern territory of
South Australia.
L: S. Low, Marston, Searle &
Livingston, 1887. 368p. NUC BL
OCLC

1134. DALY, Mary Anne [Br. 19c]
A retrospect: being memorials of
some who have long since departed
this life.
Dublin: George Herbert, 1882.
175p. NUC
[Includes letters and poems.]

1135. DALY, Rev. Robert, ed. <u>see</u>
POWERSCOURT, Theodosia A.
(Howard) Wingfield, Viscountess

1136. DAMER, Hon. Mary Georgina
Emma (Seymour) Dawson [Br. d.
1848]
Diary of a tour in Greece,
Turkey, Egypt and the Holy Land.
L: H. Colburn, 1841. 2v. NUC BL
MBD OCLC

1137. DANA, Mary S. B. <u>see</u>
SHINDLER, Mary Stanley Bunce
(Palmer) Dana

1138. D'ARBLAY, Frances (Burney)
<u>see</u> ARBLAY, Frances (Burney) d'

1139. DARBY, Eleanor [Br. 19c]
The sweet South; or, a month at
Algiers. With a few short lyrics.
L: Hope, 1854. 120p. NUC BL

1140. DARLING, Flora Adams [Am.
1840-1910]
Mrs. Darling's letters, or,
memories of the Civil War.
NY: J. W. Lovell co., 1884. 238p.
NUC BL OCLC

1141. DARLING, Grace Horsley [Br.
1815-1842]
Grace Darling; her true story
from unpublished papers in
possession of her family.
L: Hamilton, Adams & co., 1880.
BL
[Based on family records,
primarily biography.]

1142. D'ARUSMONT, Frances
(Wright) [Br. 1795-1852] ALT:
Wright, Francis PSEUD:
Englishwoman, An
Biography, notes, and political
letters of Frances Wright
D'Arusmont.
Dundee: J. Myles; Boston: J. P.
Merdum, 1844. 48p.; NY: J. Windt,
1844. 2v. NUC BL OCLC

1143. -----Fanny Wright unmasked
by her own pen.
NY: pr. for the purchasers, 1830.
16p. NUC BL OCLC
[Explanatory notes on the
institution of Nashoba and her
letter to Robert L. Jennings,
advising him to leave his wife
and family, and follow her
destinies.]

1144. -----Views of society and
manners in America: in a series
of letters from that country to a
friend in England, during the
years 1818, 1819 and 1820. By an
Englishwoman.
L: Longman, Hurst, Rees, Orme &
Brown, 1821. 523p. NUC BL N OCLC
[Abolitionist and orator; active
in U.S., though British born.]

1145. DARWENTWATER, Countess of
<u>see</u> RADCLIFFE, Amelia

1146. DARWENTWATER, John, Fourth
Earl of, co-author <u>see</u> RADCLIFFE,
Amelia

1147. DAVENPORT, Mrs. Malcolm <u>see</u>
DAVENPORT, N.

1148. DAVENPORT, N., Mrs. Malcolm
Davenport [Br. 19c]
Journal of a fourteen days' ride
through the bush from Quebec to
Lake St. John.
Quebec: pr. at the "Daily
Mercury" office, 1872. 35p. NUC
BL

1149. DAVEY, Mary [Br. 19c]
Icnusa, or pleasant reminiscences
of a two years' residence in the
island of Sardinia.
Bath: Binns & Goodwin; L: E.
Marlborough, 1860. 325p. NUC BL
[Also pub as: Sardinia]

1150. DAVID, Caroline Martha,
Lady [Br. b. 1857] ALT: David,
Mrs. T. W. Edgeworth
Funafuti; or, three months on a
coral island: an unscientific
account of a scientific
expedition.
L: J. Murray, 1899. 318p. NUC BL
OCLC

1151. DAVID, Mrs. T. W. Edgeworth
<u>see</u> DAVID, Caroline Martha, Lady

1152. DAVIDSON, Margaret [Br.
18c]
The extraordinary life and
Christian experience of Margaret
Davidson, as dictated by herself.
... To which are added some of
her letters and hymns. By the
Rev. Edward Smyth.
Dublin: pr. for the ed., 1782.
164p. BL

1153. DAVIDSON, Margaret Miller
[Am. 1823-1838]
Biography and poetical remains of
the late Margaret Miller
Davidson. Ed. Washington Irving.
Philadelphia: Lea & Blanchard,
1841. 359p. NUC BL OCLC
[Also includes tales. Younger
sister of author Lucretia Maria
Davidson.]

1154. DAVIDSON, Margaret (Miller)
[Am. 1787-1844]

Selections from the writings of
Mrs. Margaret M. Davidson, the
mother of Lucretia Maria and
Margaret M. Davidson.
Philadelphia: Lea & Blanchard,
1843. 272p. NUC BL OCLC
[Includes poetry]

1155. DAVIDSON, Mary, ed. <u>see</u>
CHARLES, Elizabeth (Rundle)

1156. DAVIE, Mrs. C. Ferguson-,
ed. <u>see</u> ALICE MAUD MARY

1157. DAVIES, Arabella, Mrs. E.
Davies [Br. 18c]
The diary of Mrs. Arabella
Davies, late wife of the Rev. E.
Davies.
L: Buckland, 1788. 258p. NUC BL

1158. DAVIES, Bessie (Williams),
Mrs. Russell Davies [Br. 19c]
ALT: Fitzgerald, Bessie;
Williams, Bessie
The clairvoyance of Bessie
Williams ... related by herself.
Ed. Florence Marryat [Church
Lean].
L: Bliss, Sands & Foster, 1893.
270p. NUC BL OCLC

1159. DAVIES, Catherine [Br. 19c]
Eleven years' residence in the
family of Murat, King of Naples,
by Catherine Davies.
L: How & Parsons, 1841. 92p. NUC
BL MB OCLC
[Experiences as governess]

1160. DAVIES, Christian
Cavenaugh, Mrs. [Br. 1667-1739]
ALT: Davies, Christine; Ross,
Mother
The life and adventures of Mrs.
Christine Davies, commonly called
Mother Ross. Taken from her own
mouth.
L: R. Montagu, 1740. 2pts. NUC BL
OCLC
[Fictionalized account of woman
who joined army as a man for 12
yrs., had 3 husbands & 4
children.]

1161. DAVIES, Christine <u>see</u>
DAVIES, Christian Cavenaugh

1162. DAVIES, Mrs. E. see DAVIES, Arabella

1163. DAVIES, Eliza, Mrs. [Br. 19c]
The story of an earnest life: a woman's adventures in Australia, and in two voyages around the world.
Cincinnati, OH: Central book concern, 1881. 570p. NUC K OCLC
[Scottish Baptist missionary]

1164. DAVIES, George Christopher, co-author see BROUGHALL, Mary

1165. DAVIES, Jane Miles Ennis [Am. 19c] PSEUD: Mountain Queen, The
A birdseye view of the rebellion, by the Mountain Queen.
San Francisco: n.p., 1865. 16p. NUC OCLC
[Personal narrative: Civil War]

1166. DAVIES, Lady Lucy Clementina (Drummond) [Br. 1795-1879]
Recollections of society in France and England.
L: Hurst & Blackett, 1872. 2v. NUC BL MB OCLC

1167. DAVIES, Mrs. Russell see DAVIES, Bessie (Williams)

1168. DAVIS, Elizabeth (Cadwaladyr) [Br. 19c]
The autobiography of Elizabeth Davis, a Balaclava nurse, daughter of Dafydd Cadwaladyr.
Ed. Jane Williams.
L: Hurst & Blackett, 1857. 2v. NUC BL MB OCLC
[Includes travel: W. Indies, U.S., Australia, Africa, Crimean War: personal narrative.]

1169. DAVIS, Jane [Br. 18/19c] PSEUD: Inhabitant of Congleton, An
Letters from a mother to her son, on his going to sea: and a letter to Capt. S. By an inhabitant of Congleton.
2d ed. Stockport: J. Clarke, 1799. 70p. BL OCLC

1170. -----Letters from a mother to her son: written upon his return from his first voyage at sea.
Stockport: J. Clarke, 1801. 64p. BL

1171. DAVIS, Phebe B. [Am. 19c]
The travels and experiences of Miss Phebe B. Davis of Barnard, Windsor County, VT.
Syracuse, NY: J. G. K. Truair & co., pr., 1860. 127p. NUC BL OCLC

1172. -----Two years and three months in the New York lunatic asylum at Utica together with the outlines of twenty years' perigrinations in Syracuse.
Syracuse, NY: the author, 1855. 87p. NUC BL

1173. DAVIS, Sally [Am. 19c]
The loss of the Barber, and the preservation of life, composed by the captain's wife, Mrs. Sally Davis.
Bridgport, CT: n.p., 1851. 2p. NUC

1174. DAVIS, Sarah Matilda Henry, Mrs. [Am. 19c]
Norway nights and Russian days.
NY: Fords, Howard & Hulbert, 1887. 325p. NUC OCLC

1175. DAWSON, Jane (Flower) [Br. 1760-1825]
The life and writings of Mrs. Dawson, of Lancaster.
n.p.: Kirkby Lonsdale, Arthur Foster, 1828. 187p. NUC BL

1176. DAY, Martha [Am. 1813-1833]
The literary remains of Martha Day.
New Haven, CT: pr. Hezekiah Howe & co., 1834. 121p. NUC BL OCLC

1177. DAY, Mary L. see ARMS, Mary L. (Day)

1178. DAY, Susan de Forest [19c]
The cruise of the Scythian in the West Indies.
L & NY: F. T. Neely, 1899. 297p. NUC OCLC

1179. DEAN, ANNA, MISS, pseud.
see MORRIS, Anna

1180. DEAN, Teresa H. [Am. d.
1935]
White City chips.
Chicago: Warren Pub. co., 1895.
425p. NUC
[Journal; Chicago World's
Columbian Exposition]

1181. DEANE, A., Mrs. [Br. 19c]
A tour through the upper
provinces of Hindostan ...
between the years 1804 and 1814.
L: C. & J. Rivington, 1823. 291p.
NUC BL OCLC

1182. DEANE, MARGERY, pseud. see
PITMAN, Marie J. (Davis)

1183. DEANE, Miranda A., Mrs.
[Am. 19c]
Out of darkness into light; from
the journal of a bereaved mother.
Shelbyville, IL: J. L. Douthet &
son, 1891. 185p. NUC OCLC

1184. DEANS, Charlotte (Lowes)
[Br. b. 1768]
Memoirs of the life of Mrs.
Charlotte Deans; ... being a
journal ... arranged by herself.
Wigton: H. Hoodless, 1837. 111p.
NUC OCLC

1185. DE BURGH, Emma Maria (Hunt)
[Br. 19c]
The voice of many waters. A
selection from the compositions,
in prose and verse, of the late
... Emma Maria De Burgh. Ed. her
sister, Miss C[aroline] Hunt.
L: J. F. Shaw, 1858. 90p. NUC BL

1186. DE CAMP, Maria [Am. 1789-
1808]
A short account of the life and
triumphant death of Maria DeCamp,
daughter of John and Susanna
DeCamp ... who departed ... aged
nineteen years. [Comp.] Susanna
DeCamp.
Philadelphia: Solomon Wiatt,
1809. 36p. NUC

1187. DE CAMP, Susanna, comp. see
DE CAMP, Maria

1188. DEERING, Mabel Clare
(Craft) [Am. b. 1872]
Hawaii nei.
NY: G. A. S. Wisner's; San
Francisco: W. Doxey, 1899. 197p.
NUC OCLC

1189. DE FONBLANQUE, Caroline
Alicia [Br. 19c]
Five weeks in Iceland.
L: R. Bentley & son, 1880. 180p.
NUC BL OCLC

1190. DE KROYFT, Helen (Aldrich)
[Am. 1818-1915] ALT: DeKroyft,
Sarah; DeKroyft, Susan Helen
A place in thy memory.
NY: J. F. Trow, 1850. 191p. NUC
BL OCLC
[Letters to her friends.]

1191. DE KROYFT, Sarah see DE
KROYFT, Helen (Aldrich)

1192. DE KROYFT, Susan Helen see
DE KROYFT, Helen (Aldrich)

1193. DELAND, Margaret Wade
(Campbell) [Am. 1857-1945]
Florida Days.
Boston: Little, Brown & co.; L &
Cambridge, MA: Longmans, Green &
co., 1889. 200p. NUC BL OCLC

1194. DELANEY, Lucy Ann Berry
[Am. b. 1828?]
From the darkness cometh the
light, or struggles for freedom.
St. Louis, MO: J. T. Smith, 189-
?. 64p. NUC OCLC
[Autobiography. Memories of
slavery; active in civic life in
St. Louis. Personal narrative.]

1195. DELANEY, Theresa (Fulford),
co-author see GOWANLOCK, Theresa

1196. DELANY, Mary Granville
Pendarves [Br. 1700-1788] ALT:
Pendarves, Mary Granville
The autobiography and
correspondence of Mary Granville,
Mrs. Delany. Ed. Lady Llanover.
L: Richard Bentley, 1861. 3v. NUC
BL MB OCLC

1197. -----Letters from Mrs.
Delany ... to Mrs. Frances
Hamilton form 1779-1788.
L. Longman, Hurst, Rees, Orme &
Brown, 1820. 106p. NUC BL OCLC

1198. DE LA WARR, Constance Mary
Elizabeth (Cochrane-Baillie)
Sackville, Countess [Br. b. 1846]
ALT: Sackville, Constance Mary
Elizabeth (Cochrane-Baillie),
Countess De La Warr
An Eastern cruise in the
"Edeline".
Edinburgh: Blackwood & sons,
1883. 119p. NUC BL OCLC
[Mediterranean]

1199. DE LESDERNIER, Emily
Pierpoint, Mme. [Am. 19c]
Headland home; or, a soul's
pilgrimage. By Madame De
Lesdernier.
NY: James Miller, 1868. 346p. NUC
BL OCLC
[Autobiography]

1200. DELMARD, Sophie Duberly
[Br. 19c]
Village life in Switzerland.
L: Longman, Green, Longman,
Roberts & Green, 1865. 323p. NUC
BL

1201. DE MORGAN, Augustus, co-
author <u>see</u> DE MORGAN, Sophia
Elizabeth (Frend)

1202. DE MORGAN, Mrs. Augustus
<u>see</u> De MORGAN, Sophia Elizabeth
(Frend)

1203. DE MORGAN, Mary Augusta,
ed. <u>see</u> De MORGAN, Sophia
Elizabeth (Frend)

1204. DE MORGAN, Sophia Elizabeth
(Frend), Mrs. Augustus De Morgan
[Br. 1809-1892] PSEUD: D., C.
From matter to spirit. The result
of ten years' experience in
spirit manifestations. By C. D.
L: Longman, Green, Longman,
Roberts & Green, 1863. 388p. NUC
BL OCLC

1205. -----Threescore years and
ten. Reminiscences of the late
Sophia Elizabeth De Morgan. To
which are added letters to and
from her husband, the late
Augustus De Morgan ... and
others. Ed. her daughter, Mary
Augusta De Morgan.
L: Richard Bentley & son, 1895.
259p. NUC BL MB OCLC

1206. DEMPSTER, Charlotte Louisa
Hawkins [Br. 1835-1913]
The maritime Alps and their
seaboard.
L: Longmans, Green & co., 1885.
384p.; Leipzig: B. Tauchnitz,
1885. 2v. NUC BL OCLC

1207. DE NAVARRO, Mrs. Antonio F.
<u>see</u> De Navarro, Mary (Anderson)

1208. DE NAVARRO, Mary
(Anderson), Mrs. Antonio F. De
Navarro [Am. 1859-1940] ALT:
Anderson, Mary
A few memories.
L: Osgood, McIlvaine & co.; NY:
Harper, 1896. 266p. NUC BL OCLC

1209. ---Girlhood of an
actress.
L. Osgood, McIlvaine & co., 1895.
105p. NUC BL

1210. DENISON, Grace E. [19c]
A happy holiday.
Toronto: n.p., 1890. NUC
[Travel: Europe]

1211. DENNEY, Elizabeth Reid
(Cotton), Hope [Br. 19c] ALT:
Cotton, Elizabeth Reid; Hope,
Elizabeth Reid (Cotton), Lady
Sunny footsteps; or, when I was a
child.
L: James Nisbet & co., 1879. BL
MB
[Her childhood in India. Told for
children.]

1212. DENNY, Lydia B. (Kinney)
[Am. 19c]
Letters.
Boston: n.p., 1863. 24p. NUC
[On confinement in McLean Asylum]

1213. DENT, Amelia Jane [Br. 19c]
Ceylon. A descriptive poem, with
notes.
L: Kegan, Paul & co., 1886. 32p.
BL

1214. DENT, Caroline, ed. see
ROLLESTON, Frances

1215. DERGAN, Bridget [Am. 1843-
1867]
The life and confession of
Bridget Dergan, who murdered Mrs.
Ellen Coriell.
Philadelphia: Barclay, 1867. 45p.
K

1216. DERING, Edward Henage, ed.
see CHATTERTON, Henrietta
Georgiana Marcia Lascelles
(Iremonger), Lady

1217. DESPENSER, BARONESS, pseud.
see LEE, Rachel Fanny Antonina

1218. DE VERE, Clara [Am. 19c]
PSEUD: Vassar Graduate, A
The exposition sketch book. Notes
of the Cincinnati exposition of
1881, by a Vassar graduate.
Cincinnati, OH: E. W. Weisbrodt &
co., 1881. 32p. NUC OCLC

1219. DEVEREUX, ROY, pseud. see
PEMBER-DEVEREUX, Margaret Rose
Roy (McAdam)

1220. DEVEY, Louisa, ed. see
LYTTON, Rosina Anne Doyle
(Wheeler) Bulwer-Lytton, Baroness

1221. DEVONSHIRE, Elizabeth
Christiana (Hervey) Foster
Cavendish, Duchess of [Br. 1757-
1824] ALT: Cavendish, Elizabeth
Christiana (Hervey) Foster,
Duchess of Devonshire
Anecdotes and biographical
sketches.
L: priv. pr., 1863. 137p. NUC BL
OCLC

1222. DEVONSHIRE, Elizabeth
Christiana (Hervey) Cavendish,
co-author see DEVONSHIRE,
Georgiana (Spencer) Cavendish,
Duchess of

1223. DEVONSHIRE, Georgiana
(Spencer) Cavendish, Duchess of
[Br. 1758-1806] ALT: Cavendish,
Georgiana (Spencer), Duchess of
Devonshire
The two duchesses, Georgiana,
Duchess of Devonshire, Elizabeth,
Duchess of Devonshire. Family
correspondence. Ed. Vere H. L.
Foster.
L: Blackie & son, 1898. 497p. NUC
BL OCLC

1224. DEWEY, Mary E., comp. see
LANE, Caroline E. (Lamson)

1225. DEWEY, Mary Elizabeth, ed.
see SEDGWICK, Catherine Maria

1226. DE WINDT, Caroline Abigail
(Adams), ed. see SMITH, Abigail
(Adams)

1227. DEXTER, Annie B. [Am. 19c]
Selections from the
correspondence of Annie B.
Dexter, 1856-58.
Utica, NY: Curtiss & Childs,
1868. 101p. NUC

1228. DEXTER, A. H., co-author
see GODMAN, Inez A.

1229. DEXTER, Mrs. Elijah see
DEXTER, Mary (Morton)

1230. DEXTER, Mary (Morton), Mrs.
Elijah Dexter [Am. 1785-1822]
Memoirs and letters of Mrs. Mary
Dexter, late consort of Rev.
Elijah Dexter.
Plymouth, MA: A. Danforth, 1823.
260p. NUC

1231. DEXTER, Sarah E., comp. see
CHICKERING, Hannah

1232. DICKERMAN, Elizabeth
Mansfield (Street), comp. see
STREET, Elizabeth Mansfield

1233. DICKEY, Laura (Anderson)
[Am. b. 1811]
Autobiography of Mrs. Laura
Dickey and choice miscellaneous
selections.
Chicago: n.p., 1892. 80p. NUC

1234. DICKINS, Marguerite [Am. 19c]
Along shore with a man-of-war.
Boston: Arena pub. co., 1893. 242p. NUC BL OCLC
[Letters of a Navy wife, describing S. America & its culture.]

1235. DICKINSON, Anna Elizabeth [Am. b. 1842]
A ragged register of people, places, and opinions.
NY: Harper & bros., 1879. 286p. NUC BL OCLC
[Travel: California, Washington, D. C. Adventures of a public orator on train tour through the West.]

1236. DICKINSON, Emily Elizabeth [Am. 1830-1886]
Letters of Emily Dickinson. Ed. Mabel Loomis Todd.
Boston: Roberts bros., 1894. 2v. NUC BL OCLC

1237. DICKSON, Maria Frances [Br. 19c] ALT: D., M. F.; Smith, Maria Frances (Dickson)
Norway and the Vöring-Fos. By M. F. D.
Dublin: McGlasham & Gill, 1870. 2v. BL

1238. -----Scenes on the shores of the Atlantic.
L: T. C. Newby, 1845. 2v. NUC OCLC

1239. -----Souvenirs of a summer in Germany in 1836. By M. F. Dickson.
L: H. Colburn, 1837. 2v. NUC BL OCLC

1240. DIGGES, West, co-author see WARD, Sarah

1241. DILLINGHAM, Emma Louise Smith [Am. 1844-1920]
Diamond Head.
Honolulu, HI: n.p., 1891. 12 l. NUC OCLC

1242. DIVEN, C. L., Mrs. [Am. 19c]
A Rocky mountain sketch.

Boston: S. Usher, 1898. 29p. NUC OCLC
[Frontier & pioneer life. Rocky Mt. region]

1243. DIVERS, Vivia H. [Am. 19c]
The 'Black hole'; or, the missionary experiences of a girl in the slums of Chicago, 1891-2.
St. Louis, MO: n.p., 1893. 192p. NUC OCLC

1244. DIX, Emily Woolsey (Soutter) [Am. 19c]
Reminiscences of the Knox and Soutter families of Virginia.
NY: De Vinne press, 1895. 107p. NUC OCLC
[Incl. 18th century family letters and the author's autobiography and travel journals]

1245. DIXIE, Lady Florence Caroline (Douglas) [Br. 1857-1905] ALT: Douglas, Lady Florence Caroline
Across Patagonia.
NY: Worthington; L: R. Bentley & son, 1880. 251p. NUC BL OCLC

1246. -----A defense of Zululand and its king: echoes from the blue books.
L: Chatto and Windus, 1882. 129p. NUC BL

1247. -----In the land of misfortune.
L: R. Bentley & son, 1882. 434p. NUC BL OCLC
[Travel: South Africa]

1248. DIXON, Sophie [Br. 19c]
A journal of ten days' excursion on the western and northern borders of Dartmoor.
Plymouth: n.p., 1830. BL MBD

1249. DOBBS, Hannah [Br. 19c]
The Euston Square mystery; extraordinary statement made by Hannah Dobbs.
L: G. Purkess, 1879?. 16p. NUC
[Dobbs accused and acquitted of a murder at Euston Square, London, 1877. Trial and original statement dated 1879.]

1250. DOD, Samuel Bayard, ed. see
BAYARD, Martha Pintard

1251. DODD, Anna Bowman (Blake)
[Am. 1855-1929]
Cathedral days. A tour through
southern England.
Boston: Roberts bros.; L: Ward &
Downey, 1887. 390p. NUC BL OCLC

1252. -----In and out of three
Normandy inns.
NY: Lovell, Corvell & co., 1891.
394p. NUC BL OCLC

1253. DODGE, Ellen Ada Phelps,
Mrs. [Am. 19c]
Poems and letters.
NY: pr. for the family, 1894.
127p. NUC OCLC

1254. DODGE, Emily Pomeroy [Am.
19c]
Anniversary memorial [of the
family of Lemuel Pomeroy of
Pittsfield, Mass].
L: Chambers, 1859. 29p. NUC
[Letter to her brothers recalling
a family reunion, 2 other
letters.]

1255. DODGE, Mary Abigail [Am.
1833-1896] PSEUD: Hamilton, Gail
A battle of the books. Ed. & pub.
by Gail Hamilton.
Cambridge, MA: Riverside Press,
1870. 288p. NUC BL OCLC
[Account of her dealings with her
publishers.]

1256. DODSHON, Frances (Henshaw)
Paxton [Br. 1714-1793]
Some account of the convincement
and religious experience of
Frances Dodshon, late of
Macclesfield.
Warrington: W. Leicester, 1803.
53p. NUC BL

1257. DOEBNER, Dr. Richard, ed.
see MARY II, Queen of Great
Britain

1258. DOHERTY, Sarah [Br. 19c]
ALT: D., S.
A narrative of the conversion and
sufferings of S. D.: illustrative
of Popery in Ireland.

Edinburgh: A. Jack & co., 1835?.
222p. NUC BL
[May contain personal material.]

1259. DONALDSON, Madelaine H.
(Everett) [Am. b. 1841] ALT:
Everett, Madelaine H.
The thrilling narrative and
extraordinary adventures of Miss
Madelaine H. Everett.
Philadelphia: Barclay & co.,
1859. 40p. NUC OCLC

1260. DONELLAN, Mary Anne
(Faulkner) [Br. 18c] ALT:
Faulkner, Mary Anne
The genuine memoirs of Miss
Faulkner, otherwise Mrs. D***l**n
or, Countess of H****** [Halifax]
in expectancy. Containing the
amours and intrigues of several
persons of ... distinction.
L: pr. for W. Bingley, 1770.
338p. NUC BL OCLC
[Possibly fiction]

1261. DONNER, Mrs. Josef
Alexander [Br. 19c]
Down the Danube in an open boat.
L: James Blackwood & co., 1895.
145p. NUC BL

1262. DOOLITTLE, Mary Antoinette
[Am. 1810-1886]
Autobiography of M. A. Doolittle,
containing a brief history of
early life, also an outline of
life ... among the Shakers.
Mt. Lebanon, NY: n.p., 1880. 48p.
NUC BL K OCLC

1263. DORAN, John, comp. see
MONTAGU, Elizabeth (Robinson)

1264. DORNFORD, Eleanor, Mrs.
[Br. 18c] ALT: D., E., Mrs.
Some memoirs of the life and
death of Mrs. E. D.
L: Andrews & sons, 1790. 101p. BL
OCLC
[Includes journal & poems.]

1265. DORR, Julia Caroline
(Ripley) [Am. 1825-1913]
Bermuda ... . An idyll of the
summer islands.
NY: C. Scribner's sons, 1884.
148p. NUC BL OCLC

1266. -----A cathedral
pilgrimage.
L & NY: Macmillan & co., 1896.
277p. NUC BL OCLC

1267. -----The flower of
England's face. Sketches of
English travel.
L & NY: Macmillan & co., 1895.
259p. NUC BL OCLC

1268. DOUGLAS, Lady Florence
Caroline see DIXIE, Lady Floroance
Caroline (Douglas)

1269. DOUGLAs, Lady Jane [Br.
1698-1753] ALT: Stewart, Lady
Jane (Douglas)
Letters from Lady Jane Douglas,
found in Lord Milton's
repositories.
[Edinburgh: n.p., 1767]. 7p. NUC
[Relates to the Douglas cause.]

1270. -----Letters of the Right
Honorable Lady Jane Douglas; to
her husband Sir John Stewart,
bart. Ed. James Boswell.
Dublin: pr. J. Exshaw, 1768.
203p. NUC OCLC

1271. -----Letters, with several
other important pieces of private
correspondence ... to which are
subjoined the dying declarations
of Lady Jane Douglas, Sir John
Stewart, and their attendant,
Helen Hewit.
L: pr. for J. Wilkie, 1767. 160p.
NUC BL OCLC
[Includes letters to her husband
in 1752-3.]

1272. DOUGLAS, Lucretia J. [Am.
b. 1830]
Grace for every trial, containing
sketches of the author's life and
family and her wonderful
religious experience, with
original poems and letters.
Dublin, GA: K. H. Walker, 1893.
258p. NUC OCLC

1273. DOUGLAS, M. Mrs. [Br. 18c]
ALT: D., M.
Notes of a journey from Berne to
England, through France. Made in
the year 1796. By M. D.
L: n.p., 1797. 56p. BL

1274. DOUTNEY, Harriet G.
(Storer), Mrs. T. Narcisse
Doutney [Am. 1822-1907] PSEUD:
B., R. L.
An autobiography.
Cambridge, MA: n.p., 1871. 240p.
NUC K OCLC
[Also pub. as: "I told you so"
and "Marrying a moustache"]

1275. DOUTNEY, Mrs. T. Narcisse
see DOUTNEY, Harriet G. (Storer)

1276. DOW, Ann Eliza see ALBY.
Ann Eliza (Dow)

1277. DOW, Mrs. Lorenzo see DOW,
Peggy

1278. DOW, Peggy, Mrs. Lorenzo
Dow [Am. 1780-1820] ALT: D., P.
Vicissitudes exemplied; or, the
journey of life.
NY: J. C. Totten, 1814. 124p. NUC
BL MAd OCLC

1279. DOWNING, Lucy [Am. 17c]
Letters of Mrs. Lucy Downing,
1626-1674.
Boston: J. Wilson, 1871. 63p. NUC

1280. DOYLE, Dr., co-author see
ANDERSON, Bessie

1281. DOYLE, John Andrew, ed. see
FERRIER, Susan Edmonstone

1282. DOYLE, Mary Aloysius,
Sister of Mercy [Br. 19c] ALT:
Sister Mary Aloysius
Memories of the Crimea.
L: Burns & Oates, 1897. 128p. NUC
BL OCLC

1283. DREW, Mrs. John see DREW,
Louise (Lane)

1284. DREW, Louisa (Lane), Mrs.
John Drew [Br. 1820-1897]
Autobiographical sketch of Mrs.
John Drew.
NY: Scribner & sons, 1899. 199p.
NUC BL K MB OCLC
[Actress, emigree to U.S.]

1285. DRINKER, Elizabeth
(Sandwith) [Am. 1734-1807]

Extracts from the journal of
Elizabeth Drinker, from 1759 to
1807. Ed. Henry D. Biddle.
Philadelphia: J. B. Lippincott,
1889. 423p. NUC MAD OCLC
[Diary of Philadelphia resident.]

1286. DRINKWATER, Anne T., comp.
see PORTER, Deborah H. (Cushing)

1287. DRUMGOOLD, Kate [Am. 19c]
A slave girl's story; being an
autobiography of Kate Drumgoold.
Brooklyn, NY: priv. pr., 1898.
62p. NUC OCLC

1288. DUANE, Harriet Constable
[Am. 1794-1860]
Recollections of an old-fashioned
lady, recorded by her eldest for
her youngest daughter. By Mary
Ann (Duane) Lowell.
Newark, NJ: L. J. Hardham, 1884.
71p. NUC
[Written in first person by
Lowell. Authentic recollections
of her mother; Duane's childhood
in Canada.]

1289. DUANE, Mary Ann, comp. see
DUANE, Harriet Constable

1290. DUBERLY, Frances Isabella
(Locke), Mrs. Henry Duberly [Br.
1829-1903]
Campaigning experiences in
Rajpootana and Central India
during the suppression of the
mutiny 1857-1868.
L: London, Smith, Elder & co.,
1859. 254p. NUC BL MB

1291. -----Journal kept during
the Russian War from the
departure of the army from
England in April 1854 to the fall
of Sebastopol.
L: Longman, Brown, Green &
Longmans, 1855. 311p. NUC BL MBD
OCLC

1292. DUBERLY, Mrs. Henry see
DUBERLY, Frances Isabella (Lock)

1293. DUDLEY, Charlotte, co-
author see DUDLEY, Elizabeth

1294. DUDLEY, Dorothy [Am. 18c]
Theatrum majorum. The Cambridge
of 1776 ... with which is
incorporated the diary of Dorothy
Dudley. Ed. Arthur Gilman.
2d ed. Cambridge, MA: Lockwood,
Brooks, c1875, 1876. BL MAD OCLC

1295. DUDLEY, Elizabeth [Br.
1779-1849]
Memoirs of E. D.; consisting
chiefly of selections from her
journal and correspondence.
Interspersed with extracts from
the diary and letters of her
sister, Charlotte Dudley. Ed.
Charles Tylor.
L: A. W. Bennett, 1861. 336p. NUC
BL MBD OCLC

1296. DUDLEY, Elizabeth, ed. see
DUDLEY, Mary

1297. DUDLEY, Hannah, co-author
see DUDLEY, Mary

1298. DUDLEY, Lady Jane (Grey)
[Br. 1538-1554] ALT: Grey; Lady
Jane
The life, death and actions of
... the Lady Jane Gray,
containing foure principall
discourses, written with her owne
hands.
L: G. Eld for I. Wright, 1615.
NUC BL OCLC

1299. -----The literay remains of
Lady Jane Grey.
L: Harding, Triphook & Lepard,
1825. 61p. NUC BL

1300. DUDLEY, Lucy Bronson [Am.
19c]
Letters to Ruth.
NY: pr. for priv. circ., 1896.
112p. NUC BL
[Travel: Europe]

1301. DUDLEY, Mary [Br. 1750-
1823]
The life of Mary Dudley,
including an account of her
religious engagements and
extracts from her letters. With
an appendix containing some

account of the illness and death
of her daughter, Hannah Dudley
[1784-1810]. Ed. Elizabeth
Dudley.
L: J. & A. Arch, 1825. 380p.;
Philadelphia: B. & T. Kite, 1825.
327p. NUC BL OCLC
[Society of Friends]

1302. DUFFERIN AND AVA, Hariot
Georgina (Hamilton) Hamilton-
Temple- Blackwood, Marchioness of
[Br. 1843-1936] ALT: Blackwood,
Hariot Georgina
My Canadian journal, 1872-8.
L: John Murray, 1891. 422p.; NY:
D. Appleton & co., 1891. 456p.
NUC BL MB OCLC
[1872-77 travel & official life.]

1303. -----Our viceregal life in
India; selections from my
journal, 1884-88.
L: John Murray, 1889. 2v. NUC BL
MB OCLC

1304. -----Unprotected females in
Sicily, Calabria, and on the top
of Mount Aetna ... .
L: Routledge, Warnes, &
Routledge, 1859. 32p. OCLC

1305. DUFF GORDON, Lucie (Austin)
see GORDON, Lucie (Austin) Duff

1306. DUFFY, Susan Gavon [Br.
19c]
The English abroad.
L: T. Fisher Unwin, 1894. BL
[Travel: Italy, Germany; author
resident of Australia.]

1307. DUMOND, Annie (Hamilton)
Nelles [Am. b. 1837] ALT: Nelles,
Annie (Hamilton)
Annie Nelles; or, the life of a
book agent. An autobiography.
Cincinnati, OH: the author, 1868.
385p. NUC BL K OCLC

1308. DUNBAR, Margaret Juliana
Maria [Br. 19c] ALT: D., M. J. M.
Art and nature under an Italian
sky. By M. J. M. D.
Edinburgh: T. Constable & co.; L:
Hamilton, Adams & co., 1852.
301p. NUC BL OCLC

1309. DUNBAR, Sophia (Orred),
Lady [Br. 19c]
A family tour round the coasts of
Spain and Portugal, during the
winter of 1860-61.
Edinburgh & L: W. Blackwood &
sons, 1862. 184p. NUC BL OCLC

1310. DUNCAN, Mary Balfour Manson
[Br. 1835-1865] ALT: D., M. B. M.
Bible hours: being leaves from
the note-book of ... M. B. M. D.
Edinburgh: n.p., 1866. BL
[Includes poems]

1311. -----"Under the shadow"
being additional leaves from the
note-book of ... M. B. M. D.
Edinburgh: n.p., 1867. BL
[Religious meditations, personal
information, four poems]

1312. DUNCAN, Mary (Grey) Lundie
[Br. 19c] ALT: Lundie, Mrs. J. C.
America as I found it!.
L: J. Nisbet & co., 380p.; NY: R.
Carter & bros., 1852. 440p. NUC
BL OCLC

1313. DUNCAN, Mary (Grey) Lundie,
comp. see DUNCAN, Mary (Lundie)

1314. DUNCAN, Mary (Lundie), Mrs.
W. W. Duncan [Br. 1814-1840/41]
ALT: Lundie, Mary
Memoir of Mrs. W. W. Duncan,
being recollections of a
daughter. By her mother, Mrs. J.
C. Lundie [Mary (Grey) Lundie
Duncan].
Edinburgh: W. Oliphant, 1841.
308p. NUC BL MBD OCLC
[Numerous editions; includes
letters, diary & poems.]

1315. DUNCAN, Mrs. W. W. see
DUNCAN, Mary (Lundie)

1316. DUNIWAY, Abigail Jane
(Scott) [Am. 1834-1915]
Captain Gray's company.
Portland, OR: S. J. McCormick
pub., 1889. 342p. NUC
[Subtitle: Crossing the plains
and living in Oregon. A
fictionalized account of covered
wagon trip.]

1317. DUNLOP, Alison Hay [Br. 19c]
Anent old Edinburgh and some of the worthies who walked its streets, with other papers. Ed. her brothers.
Edinburgh: R. & H. Somerville, 1890. 191p. NUC OCLC
[Historical descriptions, short fiction and poetry]

1318. -----The book of old Edinburgh. With her brother, John Charles Dunlop.
Edinburgh: T. & A. Constable, 1886. 160p. NUC OCLC

1319. DUNLOP, Frances Anna (Wallace) [Br. 1730-1815]
Robert Burns and Mrs. Dunlop; correspondence now published in full for the first time. Ed. William Wallace.
NY: Dodd, Mead & co., 1898. 2v.; L: Hodder & Stoughton, 1898. 434p. NUC BL OCLC

1320. DUNLOP, John Charles, co-author see DUNLOP, Alison Hay

1321. DUNLOP, Madeline Anne (Wallace) [Br. 19c] ALT: Wallace, Madeline Anne
How we spent the autumn; or, wanderings in Brittany. With Rosalind Harriet Maria (Wallace) Inverarity.
L: Richard Bentley, 1860. 342p. NUC BL OCLC

1322. -----The timely retreat; or, a year in Bengal before the mutinies. By two sisters. With Rosalind Harriet Maria (Wallace) Inverarity.
L: Richard Bentley, 1858. 2v. NUC BL OCLC

1323. DUNN, Mrs. Archibald see DUNN, Sara H.

1324. DUNN, Sara H., Mrs. Archibald Dunn [Br. 19c]
Sunny memories of an Indian winter.
L: Walter Scott, ltd., 1898. 220p. NUC BL

1325. -----The world's highway with some impressions whilst journeying along it. By Mrs. Archibald Dunn.
L: Gay & Bird; Newcastle-on-Tyne: Mawson, Swan & Morgan, 1894. 376p. NUC BL OCLC
[Travel: Ceylon, China, Japan, Canada, U.S.]

1326. DUNRAVEN, Caroline (Wyndham), Countess of [Br. 1789/90-1870]
Memorials of Adare manor, by Caroline, Countess of Dunraven.
Oxford: pr. for priv. circ. by Messrs. Parker, 1865. 303p. NUC

1327. DURAND, Bessie, ed. see PARKER, Mary

1328. DURAND, Silas H., ed. see PARKER, Mary

1329. DUSTIN, Mrs. Caleb see DUSTIN, Mary

1330. DUSTIN, Mary, Mrs. Caleb Dustin [Am. 1784-1806]
Experiences of Mary Dustin ... written by herself.
Concord, NH: pr. by George Haugh, 1807. 30p. NUC OCLC

1331. DUTTON, Adelaide Rosalind (Kirchner) [Am. 19c] ALT: Kirchner, Adelaide Rosalind
A flag for Cuba. Pen sketches of a recent trip across the Gulf of Mexico to the island of Cuba.
Pub. as: Adelaide Rosalind Kirchner
NY: Mershon co., 1897. 177p. NUC OCLC

1332. DUTTON, Amy [Br. 19c] ALT: D., A.
The streets and lanes of a city: being the reminiscences of A. D.
L: Macmillan & co., 1871. 159p. NUC BL OCLC
[Experiences as a district visitor.]

1333. -----Homes and hospitals: or, two phases of woman's work, as exhibited in the labors of Amy Dutton and Agnes Elizabeth Jones.

Boston: Amer. Tract Soc.; NY:
Hurd & Houghton, 1873. 336p. NUC
OCLC
["Homes" first pub. as the
Streets and homes of a city.
"Hospitals" is a memoir about
Agnes E. Jones]

1334. DUTTON, Anne, Mrs. [Br.
1692-1765] ALT: D. A.
A brief account of the gracious
dealings of God with a poor,
sinful ... creature.
L: pr. J. Hart, 1850.
[Religious journal. Pt1, Pt2 L:
J. Hart, 1743; Pt3 L: J. Hart
1750. NUC BL]

1335. -----A discourse upon
walking with God ... also a brief
account of how the author was
brought into gospel liberty.
L: pr. for the author, 1735.
170p. NUC BL OCLC

1336. -----Letters on spiritual
subjects, and diverse occasions,
sent to relations and friends. By
one who has tasted that the Lord
is gracious.
L: n.p., 1748. 288p. BL

1337. DYER, Catherine Cornelia
(Joy) [Am. b. 1817]
A brief history of the Joy
family. By one of them.
NY: Thomas Whitaker, 1876. 37p.
NUC

1338. -----Sunny days abroad; or,
the old world seen with young
eyes.
NY: Thomas Whitaker, 1871. 262p.
NUC OCLC
[A travel journal: England,
France, Italy, Switzerland,
Germany & Belgium. Family went
there by steamer; Charles Dickens
was on board.]

1339. DYER, Mrs. D. B. [Am. 19c]
Fort Reno or picturesque Cheyenne
and Arrapahoe army life before
the opening of Oklahoma.
NY: G. W. Dillingham, 1896. 216p.
NUC BL K OCLC

1340. DYER, Frances J. [Am. 19c]
The Congregationalist and herald
of gospel liberty. New world
pilgrims at old world shrines:
the book of the pilgrimage.
Boston: The Congregationalist,
1896. 154p. NUC OCLC
[Record of pilgrimage to England
and Holland.]

1341. DYER, Lucile [Am. 19c]
Confidences ... containing
impressions of the world and its
people in general, and things
theatrical in particular; as seen
by an actress.
Kansas City, MO: Model Printing
co., 1899. 93p. NUC

1342. DYER, Mary M. see Marshall,
Mary M. Dyer

1343. DYMOND, Ann [Br. 1768-1816]
Some account of Ann Dymond, late
of Exeter.
York: pr. for W. Alexander, 1820.
124p. NUC BL MBD OCLC
[Member of Society of Friends;
includes diary, travel in S. W.
England.]

1344. DYMOND, Henry, ed. see
DYMOND, Mary

1345. DYMOND, Mary [Br. 1808-
1855]
Memoir of Mary Dymond, late of
Lewes, compiled chiefly from her
letters and memoranda. Ed. Henry
Dymond.
L: W. & F. G. Cash, 1857. 98p.
NUC BL MBD
[Member of Society of Friends:
diary, 1828-1837]

1346. DYOTT, Eleanor [Br. 19c]
Memoir of Mrs. D. under the
solemn form of an oath written by
herself.
L: W. Wright, 1821. BL
[Letters]

1347. DYSON, Mrs. Charles [Br.
19c]
Memorials of a departed friend.
Preface signed C. D. [i.e.
Charles Dyson].

L: Rivington, 1835. 328p. NUC BL
[Diary of reflections and
observations, chiefly religious]

1348. DYSON, Charles, comp. see
DYSON, Mrs. Charles

1349. DYSON, Julia A. (Parker)
[Am. 1818-1852]
Life and thought: or, cherished
memorials of the late Julia A.
Parker Dyson. Ed. Miss E.
Latimer.
Boston: Whittemore, Niles & Hall,
1856. 314p. NUC OCLC
[Includes letters, miscellanies,
poetry and essays]

1351. E., C. A. see EATON,
Charlotte Ann (Waldie)

1352. E., J. R. see EDKINS, Jane
Robotham (Stobbs)

1353. EAMES, Jane Anthony [Am.
1816-1894]
Another budget; or, things which
I saw in the East.
Boston: Ticknor & Fields, 1855.
481p. NUC OCLC
[Travel: Levant]

1354. -----The budget closed.
Boston: Ticknor & Fields, 1860.
368p. NUC OCLC
[Travel: Europe]

1355. -----A budget of letters,
or, things which I saw abroad.
Boston: W. D. Ticknor & co.,
1847. 470p. NUC OCLC
[Travel: Europe]

1356. -----Letters from Bermuda.
Concord, NH: Republican press
assoc., pr., 1875. 50p. NUC OCLC

1357. EARLE, Alice (Morse), ed.
see WINSLOW, Anna Green

1358. EASTLAKE, Elizabeth
(Rigby), Lady [Br. 1809-1893]
ALT: Rigby, Elizabeth
Fellowship: letters addressed to
my sister mourners.
NY: A. D. F. Randolph, 1868.
101p. NUC BL OCLC

1359. -----Journals and
correspondence of Lady Eastlake.
Ed. her nephew, Charles Eastlake
Smith.
L: J. Murray, 1895. 2v. NUC BL
OCLC

1360. -----A residence on the
shores of the Baltic, described
in a series of letters. Pub.
anon.
L: J. Murray, 1841. 2v. NUC BL
OCLC
[Also pub as: Letters from the
shores of the Baltic]

1361. EASTLICK, Lavina (Dat),
Mrs. [Am. 1833-1923]
Thrilling incidents of the Indian
war of 1862: being a personal
narrative of the outrages and
horrors witnessed ... in
Minnesota.
Lancaster, WI: Herald bk. & job
office, 1864. 32p. NUC
[Dakota Indians' Wars, 1862-1863]

1362. EASTMAN, Elaine (Goodale)
[Am. b. 1863] ALT: Goodale,
Elaine
Journal of a farmer's daughter.
By Elaine Goodale.
NY: G. P. Putnam's sons, 1881.
184p. NUC OCLC
[Farm life]

1363. EASTMAN, Mary (Henderson)
[Am. 1818-1890]
Dahcotah; or, life and legends of
the Sioux around Ft. Snelling.
NY: J. Wiley, 1849. 268p. NUC BL
OCLC
[Tells of her associations with
Indians.]

1364. EATON, Charlotte Ann
(Waldie) [Br. 1788-1859] ALT: E.,
C. A.; Waldie, Charlotte Ann
PSEUD: Englishwoman, An

The Battle of Waterloo, containing accounts published by authority, British and foreign, and other relative, with circumstantial details ... By a near observer. Ed. John Booth.
L: Booth T. Egerton, 1815. 116p. BL OCLC

1365. -----Narrative of a residence in Belgium, during the campaign of 1815, and of a visit to the field of Waterloo. By an Englishwoman.
L: John Murray, 1817. 351p. NUC BL OCLC
[NUC also attr. this to her sister, Jane (Waldie) Watts]

1366. -----Rome in the nineteenth century: containing a complete account of the ruins of the ancient city, the remains of the middle ages, and the monuments of modern times. With remarks on the fine arts, on the state of society, and on the religious ceremonies, manners, and customs of the modern Romans. In a series of letters, written during a residence at Rome in 1817 and 1818. Pub. anon.
Edinburgh: A. Constable, 1820. 3v. NUC BL OCLC

1367. ECKEL, L. St. John, Mrs. see HARPER, Lizzie (St. John)

1368. ECKLEY, Sophia May [Br. 19c]
The oldest of the Old World.
L: Bentley, 1883. 300p. NUC BL
[Travel: Levant & Egypt]

1369. EDEN, Hon. Eleanor, ed. see EDEN, Hon. Emily

1370. EDEN, Hon. Emily [Br. 1797-1869]
Letters from India. Ed. her niece, the Hon. Eleanor Eden.
L: Richard Bentley & son, 1872. 2v. NUC BL OCLC
[Sequel to "Up the country;" incl. letters by her sister, Hon. Frances Eden.]

1371. -----Portraits of the Princes and people of India.
L: J. Dickinson & son, 1843. 2pts. NUC BL OCLC

1372. -----"Up the country". Letters written to her sister from the upper provinces of India.
L: R. Bentley, 1866. 2v. NUC BL OCLC

1373. EDEN, Hon. Frances, co-author see EDEN, Hon. Emily

1374. EDEN, Lizzie Selina [Br. 19c]
A lady's glimpse of the late war in Bohemia.
L: n.p., 1867. 305p. NUC BL OCLC

1375. -----My holiday in Austria.
L: Hurst & Blackett, 1869. 300p. NUC BL

1376. EDGCUMBE, Lady Ernestine Emma Horatia [Br. b. 1843]
Four months' cruise in a sailing yacht. With Lady Mary Susan Felicie Wood.
L: Hurst & Blackett, 1888 [1883 OCLC]. 307p. NUC BL OCLC

1377. EDGEWORTH, Frances Anne (Beaufort), comp. see EDGEWORTH, Maria

1378. EDGEWORTH, Maria [Br. 1767-1849]
The life and letters of Maria Edgeworth. Ed. Augustus John Cuthbert Hare.
L: E. Arnold, 1894. 2v. NUC BL OCLC

1379. -----A memoir of Maria Edgeworth with selections from her letters by Frances Anne (Beaufort) Edgeworth. Ed. her children.
L: J. Masters & son, 1867. 3v. NUC BL OCLC

1380. EDKINS, Jane Rowbotham (Stobbs) [Br. 1838-1861] ALT: E., J. R.

Chinese scenes and people, with notices of Christian missions ... in a series of letters from various parts of China. By J. R. E. Ed. S. S. Stobbs.
L: J. Nisbet, 1863. 307p. NUC BL OCLC

1381. EDMONDS, Elizabeth Mayhew (Waller) [Br. 19c]
Fair Athens.
L: Remington & co., 1881. 320p. NUC BL OCLC

1382. EDMONDS, S. EMMA E., pseud.
see EDMUNDSON, Sarah Emma

1383. EDMUNDSON, Sarah Emma [Am. 1841-1898] PSEUD: Edmonds, S. Emma E.
Nurse and spy in the Union Army: comprising the adventures and experiences of a woman in hospitals, camps, and battlefields.
Hartford, CT: W. S. Williams & co., 1864. 384p. NUC BL K C OCLC
[Also pub. as: Unsexed, or the female soldier and as: The female spy in the Union Army.]

1384. EDWARD, Catherine Grant, Mrs. [Br. 19c]
Missionary life among the Jews in Moldavia, Galicia, and Silesia. Memoir and letters.
L: Hamilton, Adams & co., 1867. 320p. NUC BL

1385. EDWARD, Eliza [Br. 19c]
Diary of a quiet life.
L: Hatchards, 1887. 404p. BL MB
[Includes meditations, her reading, etc.]

1386. EDWARDES, E. C. Hope see EDWARDES, Ellen Charlotte Hope

1387. EDWARDES, Ellen Charlotte Hope [Br. b. 1837] ALT: Edwardes, E. C. Hope; Hope-Edwardes, Ellen Charlotte
Azahar. Extracts from a journal in Spain in 1881-2.
L: R. Bentley & son, 1883. 310p. NUC BL OCLC

1388. -----Eau-de-nil; a chronicle.
NY: G. Munro; L: R. Bentley & son, 1882. 32p. NUC BL
[Travel: Egypt]

1389. EDWARDS, Amelia Ann Blanford [Br. 1831-1892]
Egypt and its monuments: pharoahs, fellahs, and explorers.
NY: Harper & bros.; L: Osgood & McIlvaine, 1891. 325p. NUC BL OCLC
[Pub. in England as: Pharoahs, fellahs, and explorers]

1390. -----Sights and stories: being some account of a holiday tour through the north of Belgium.
L: n.p., 1862. BL

1391. -----A thousand miles up the Nile.
L: Longmans, Green & co., 1877. 732p. NUC BL OCLC

1392. -----Untrodden peaks and unfrequented valleys.
L: Longmans, Green & co., 1873. 385p. NUC BL OCLC
[Also pub. with subtitle: A midsummer ramble in the Dolomites]

1393. EDWARDS, Matilda Barbara Betham- [Br. 1836-1919] ALT: Betham-Edwards, Matilda Barbara
France of today, a survey comparative and retrospective.
L: Percival & co., 2v.; NY: Lovell, Coryell & co., 1892. 309p. NUC BL

1394. -----Friends over the water, a series of sketches of French life.
L: Houlston & sons, 1879. 140p. NUC BL

1395. -----Holiday letters from Athens, Cairo, and Weimar.
L: Strahan & co., 1873. 247p. NUC BL OCLC

1396. -----Holidays among the mountains; or, scenes and stories of Wales.
L: Griffith & Farran, 1861. 318p. NUC BL

1397. -----Holidays in eastern France.
NY: Harper, 1875. 239p. NUC BL OCLC

1398. -----Home life in France.
L: Methuen & co., 1879. 310p. BL

1399. -----Reminiscences.
L: G. Redway, 1898. 354p. NUC BL MB OCLC
[Her autobiography]

1400. -----The roof of France, or, the Causses of the Lozère.
L: Richard Bentley & son, 1889 NUC BL OCLC

1401. -----Through Spain to the Sahara.
L: Hurst & Blackett, 1868. 317p. NUC BL OCLC

1402. -----A winter with the swallows.
L: Hurst & Blackett, 1867. 286p. NUC BL OCLC
[Travel: Algeria]

1403. -----A year in western France.
L: Longmans, Green & co, 1877. NUC BL OCLC

1404. EELLS, Mrs. Cushing see EELLS, Myra Fairbanks

1405. EELLS, Myra Fairbanks, Mrs. Cushing Eells [Am. 19c]
Journal of Myra F. Eells, kept while passing through the United States. In: Oregon Pioneer Association Transactions.
n.p.: n.p., 1889. NUC BL
[First white woman in Oregon Territory; reached there on horseback to be missionary to Indians.]

1406. EGERTON, Hon. Eleanor see WESTMINSTER, Eleanor (Egerton) Grosvenor, Marchioness of

1407. EGERTON, Harriet Catherine (Greville) Leveson Gower, Countess of Ellesmere see ELLESMERE, Harriet Catherine (Greville) Leveson Gower Egerton, Countess of

1408. EGERTON OF TATTON, Alice Anne (Montgomery) Temple-Nugent Brydges-Chandos Grenville, Countess [Br. 19/20c] ALT: Buckingham and Chandos, Alice Anne (Montgomery) Temple-Nugent Brydges-Chandos, Duchess of; Grenville, Alice Anne (Montgomery) Temple-Nugent Brydges-Chandos, Countess Egerton of Tatton
Glimpses of four continents: letters written during a tour of Australia, New Zealand and North America, in 1893.
L: J. Murray, 1894. 291p. NUC BL OCLC

1409. EICKEMEYER, Carl, co-author see EICKEMEYER, Lilian Westcott

1410. EICKEMEYER, Lilian Westcott [Am. 19c]
Among the Pueblo Indians. With Carl Eickemeyer.
NY: Merriam & co., c1895. 195p. NUC OCLC
[Travel: New York to New Mexico]

1411. ELAW, Zilpha, Mrs. [Am. 19c]
Memoirs of the life, religious experience, ministerial travels and labours of Mrs. Zilpha Elaw, an American female of colour, together with some account of the great religious revival in America, written by herself.
L: the authoress, 1846. 172p. NUC BL K

1412. ELDRED, Ellen E. [Am. 19c]
Reminiscences of a lecture tour.
Laurens, NY: n.p., 1885?. 74p. NUC
[Temperance; in verse]

1413. ELDRIDGE, Elleanor [Am. b. 1785]
Elleanor's second book. [Comp.] Frances Harriet (Whipple) Greene McDougall.
Providence, RI: Albro, pr., 1839. K OCLC

1414. -----Memoirs of Elleanor Eldridge. [Comp.] Frances Harriet (Whipple) Greene McDougall.
Providence, RI: Albro, pr., 1838. 128p. NUC K OCLC

1415. ELIOT, GEORGE, pseud. see EVANS, Marian

1416. ELISABETH, Princess Palatine, Abbess of Herford [1618-1680]
Memoirs of the Princess Palatine, Princess of Bohemia; including her correspondence with the great men of her day ... . Ed. Marie Pauline Rose, Baroness Blaze de Bury.
L: Richard Bentley, 1853. 400p. NUC BL OCLC

1417. ELIZABETH [Am. 1765?-1866]
Elizabeth: a colored minister of the gospel born in slavery.
Philadelphia: Tract Assn. of Friends, 1889. 16p. NUC
[Recollections of slavery, ministry in U. S. and Canada]

1418. ELIZABETH [Br. 19c]
Poetry and prose. By Elizabeth. Including some original correspondence with distinguished literary characters.
Doncaster: C. & J. White, 1821. 137p. BL OCLC

1419. ELIZABETH OF ENGLAND, Consort of Friedrich V; Landgrave of Hesse-Homburg [Br. 1770-1840]
ALT: Elizabeth, Princess of Hesse-Homburg
Letters of Princess Elizabeth of England, daughter of George III, and Landgravine of Hesse-Homburg; written for the most part to Miss Louisa Swinburne.
L: T. F. Unwin, 1898. 360p. NUC BL OCLC

1420. ELIZABETH, Princess of Hesse-Homburg see ELIZABETH OF ENGLAND, Consort of Friedrich V

1421. ELIZABETH, Queen of England [Br. 1533-1603]
Letters of Queen Elizabeth and King James VI of Scotland. Ed. John Bruce.
L: pr. for the Camden society, 1849. NUC OCLC

1422. -----Letters to the Argyll family, from Elizabeth Queen of England, Mary Queen of Scots, ... and others.
Edinburgh: pr., T. Constable, 1839. NUC OCLC

1423. ELLA [Br. 19c]
Roman fragments.
L: Waters, Westbourne Grove, 1885. 16p. BL
[Travel: Rome in 1862-63]

1424. ELLERSLIE, Alma [Br. 19c]
PSEUD: Actress, An
Diary of an actress, or, realities of stage life. Ed. Henry Cary Shuttleworth.
L: Griffith, Farran & co., 1885. 160p. BL MB
[Travels and experiences of a British actress in the 1880s.]

1425. ELLESMERE, Harriet Catherine (Greville) Leveson Gower Egerton, Countess of [Br. 1800-1866] ALT: Egerton, Harriet Catherine (Greville) Leveson Gower, Countess of Ellesmere; Gower, Lady Francis Leveson
Journal of a tour in the J Land in May and June 184C
L: Harrison & co., 1841. NUC BL OCLC

1426. ELLET, Elizabeth Fries (Lummis), Mrs. William Henry Ellet [Am. 1818-1877]
Summer rambles in the West.
NY: J. C. Riker, 1853. 268p. NUC BL OCLC
[Old Northwest, Michigan, Illinois, Minnesota]

1427. -----Rambles about the country.
Boston: Marsh, Capen, Lyon & Webb, 1840. 257p. NUC BL OCLC
[Travel: U. S.]

1428. ELLET, Mrs. William Henry see ELLET, Elizabeth Fries (Lummis)

1429. ELLIOTT, Charlotte [Br. 1789-1871]
Leaves from the unpublished journals, letters and poems of Charlotte Elliott.
L: Religious Tract Society, 1874. 256p. NUC BL OCLC

1430. ELLIOTT, Eleanor (Weatherall) [Br. 1813-1882]
Manx recollections. Memorials of Eleanor Elliott. By Katherine A. Forrest.
L: J. Nisbet & co.; Douglas, Isle of Man: James Brown & son, 1894. 241p. NUC BL OCLC
[Patient suffering of her blindness; includes letters and diary.]

1431. ELLIOT, Frances Minto (Dickinson), Mrs. Gilbert Elliot [Br. 1820-1898]
Diary of an idle woman in Constantinople.
L: John Murray, 1892. 425p. BL OCLC
[Travel: Orient Express and steamboat.]

1432. -----Diary of an idle woman in Italy.
L: Chapman & Hall, 1871. 2v. BL

1433. -----Diary of an idle woman in Sicily.
L: R. Bentley & son, 1881. 2v. BL

1434. -----Diary of an idle woman in Spain.
L: F. V. White & co., 1884. 2v. BL

1435. -----Pictures of old Rome.
New ed. L: Chapman & Hall, 1872. 316p. BL OCLC

1436. -----Roman gossip.
L: Murray, 1894. 362p. BL OCLC

1437. ELLIOT, Mrs. Gilbert see ELLIOT, Frances Minto (Dickinson)

1438. ELLIOTT, Grace (Dalrymple) [Br. d. 1823]
Journal of my life through the French revolution.
L: R. Bentley, 1859. 206p. NUC BL MB OCLC

1439. ELLIOTT, Jane [Br. 1840-1861]
Memoir of a beloved niece. Comp. Jane Walker.
Oxford: n.p., 1862. 23p. BL
[Includes extracts of letters.]

1440. ELLIS, Annie Raine, ed. see ARBLAY, Frances (Burney) d'

1441. ELLIS, Beth see ELLIS, Elizabeth

1442. ELLIS, Mrs. Charles [Br. 19c]
A summer in Normandy with my children.
L: n.p.; NY: G. Routledge, 1878. 195p. BL OCLC

1443. ELLIS, Elizabeth [Br. 19/20c] ALT: Ellis, Beth
An English girl's first impressions of Burmah.
Wigan: R. Platt, 1899. 248p. NUC BL

1444. ELLIS, Elizabeth Furss [Br. 19c] PSEUD: Cornishwoman, A
"Evenings with grandmama" [i.e. Rebecca Forfar]. Recollections of the Scilly Islands. By a Cornishwoman.
Truro: Netherton & Worth, 1896. 31p. BL

1445. ELLIS, Grace A., comp. see BARBAULD, Anna Letitia (Aikin)

1446. ELLIS, Sarah (Stickney) [Br. 1812-1872] ALT: Stickney, Sarah
Summer and winter in the Pyrenees.
2d ed. L: Fisher, son & co., 1841. 393p. NUC BL OCLC

1447. ELLSWORTH, Helen Yale
(Smith) [Am. 19c]
Some letters from abroad.
n.p.: n.p., 187-. 38p. NUC
[Whimsical letters from travels
in 1873 & 1874 to Germany, Norway
and Finland.]

1448. ELSSLER, Fanny [Am. 1810-
1884]
The letters and journal of Fanny
Elssler, written before and after
her operatic campaign in the
United States.
NY: H. G. Daggers, 1845. 65p. NUC
OCLC

1449. ELWOOD, Anne Katherine
(Curteis) [Br. 19c]
Narrative of a journey overland
from England, by the continent of
Europe, Egypt and the Red Sea to
India including a residence
there, and voyage home, in the
years 1825, 26, 27, and 28.
L: H. Colburn & R. Bentley, 1830.
2v. NUC BL OCLC

1450. ELY, Adelia (Miner) [Am.
1855-1925]
Reminiscences of pioneer days on
the Illinois prairie.
Winona Lake, IN: Alma Ely Porter,
n.d. 46p. NUC OCLC

1451. ELY, Caroline T. (Holmes),
comp. see HOLMES, Harriet Ann

1452. ELY, Jane (Hope-Vere)
Loftus, Marchioness of [Br. 1821-
1890] ALT: Loftus, Jane (Hope-
Vere), Marchioness of Ely
Mafeesh, or, nothing new; the
journal of a tour in Greece,
Turkey, Egypt, the Sinai-Desert,
Petra, Palestine, Syria and
Russia.
L: Pr. by W. Clowes & sons, 1870.
2v. NUC BL OCLC

1453. EMBE, pseud. see BURGESS,
Marianna

1454. EMERSON, Eleanor (Read)
[Am. 1777-1808]
Account of Mrs. Emerson. Written
by herself.
Andover, MA: New England Tract
Soc., 1823. 24p. NUC OCLC

1455. ---Memoirs of Mrs. Eleanor
Emerson; ... with some of her
writings.
Boston: Lincoln & Edmands, 1809.
96p. NUC

1456. -----Memoirs of the life,
conversion, and happy death of
Mrs. Eleanor Emerson.
NY: C. Dodge, 1817. 49p. NUC
[Extracts from her letters and
journal. May be a later version
of preceding entry.]

1457. EMERSON, Jesse Milton [Am.
1818-1898]
European glimpses and glances.
NY: Cassell & co., 1889. 221p.
NUC OCLC

1458. -----New York to the
Orient. A series of letters.
NY: E. R. Pelton & co., 1886.
218p. NUC OCLC
[Travel: Levant, Italy, France,
England]

1459. EMERSON, Joseph, ed. see
WOODBURY, Fanny

1460. EMERSON, Sarah Hopper, ed.
see GIBBONS, Abby (Hopper)

1461. EMERY, Sarah Anna, ed. see
EMERY, Sarah (Smith)

1462. EMERY, Sarah (Smith) [Am.
1787-1879]
Reminiscences of a nonagenerian.
Ed. Sarah Anna Emery.
Newburyport, MA: W. H. Huse &
co., pr., 1879. 336p. NUC BL OCLC

1463. EM'LY, pseud. see WOLF,
Annie S.

1464. EMMOTT, Elizabeth
(Braithwaite), comp. see
BRAITHWAITE, Martha

1465. EMRA, Lucy see CROGGON,
Lucy (Emra)

1466. ENFIELD, Mary, comp. see
NEEDHAM, Hester

1467. ENGLISH GOVERNESS, pseud.
see CHENNELLS, Ellen

1468. ENGLISH LADY, AN, pseud.
<u>see</u> BAYMAN, A. Phelps

1469. ENGLISH LADY, AN, pseud.
<u>see</u> SMITH, Mary Ann Pellew

1470. ENGLISH, Mary Katharine
(Jackson) [Am. 19c]
Prairie sketches, or fugitive
recollections of an army girl of
1899.
n.p.: n.p., 1899?. 76p. NUC OCLC

1471. ENGLISH VISITOR, AN, pseud.
<u>see</u> LONGWORTH, Maria Theresa

1472. ENGLISH WOMAN, AN, pseud.
<u>see</u> MILLER, Anna (Riggs), Lady

1473. ENGLISHWOMAN, AN, pseud.
<u>see</u> D'ARUSMONT, Frances (Wright)

1474. ENGLISHWOMAN, AN, pseud.
<u>see</u> EATON, Charlotte Ann
(Waldie)

1475. ENGLISHWOMAN, AN, pseud.
<u>see</u> WARD, Emma Georgina
Elizabeth

1476. ESCOMBE, Edith [Br. 19c]
PSEUD: Grown-up, A
Bits I remember. By A Grown-Up.
L: Eden, Remington & co., 1892.
94p. BL
[Anecdotes of her childhood]

1477. ESPINASSE, Francis, ed. <u>see</u>
FLETCHER, Maria Jane (Jewsbury)

1478. EUDORA <u>see</u> SOUTH, Eudora
Lindsay

1479. EVANGELINE, pseud. <u>see</u>
NEWMAN, A. E., Mrs.

1480. EVANS, H. Lloyd, Mrs. [Br.
19c]
Last winter in Algeria.
L: Chapman & Hall, 1868. 343p.
NUC BL

1481. EVANS, Rev. John <u>see</u>
BROOKE, C., Mrs.

1482. EVANS, Katharine [Br. d.
1692]

This is a short relation of some
of the cruel sufferings of
Katharine Evans and Sarah
Cheevers in the Inquisition in
the isle of Malta. Ed. D. Baker.
L: pr. for Robert Wilson, 1662.
104p. NUC OCLC
[Quaker women; includes their
letters to friends and family.]

1483. EVANS, Marian [Br. 1819-
1880] ALT: Cross, Marian (Evans);
Evans, Mary Ann PSEUD: Eliot,
George
George Eliot's life, as related
in her letters and journals. Ed.
her husband, John Walter Cross.
Edinburgh & L: William Blackwood
& sons; NY: Harper & bros., 1881.
3v.   NUC BL OCLC PD
[Extracts of letters beg. 1855
(diary beg. 1849); journal of her
literary efforts, reading,
travel.]

1484. EVANS, Mary Ann <u>see</u> EVANS,
Marian

1485. EVANS, Mary L. (Smith) [Am.
1807-1887]
Glimpses by sea and land, during
a six months trip to Europe.
Philadelphia: W. H. Pile, 1870.
361p. NUC OCLC

1486. EVANS, Rachel [Br. 19c]
Home scenes; or, Tavistock and
its vicinity.
L: Simpkin & Marshall; Tavistock:
J. L. Commins, 1846. 258p.   NUC BL

1487. EVANS, Rebekah, Mrs. [Br.
19c]
Memoirs of Mrs. R. Evans.
Boston: n.p., 1836. BL
[May contain personal material.]

1488. EVE, Sarah [Am. 18c]
Extracts from the journal of Miss
Sarah Eve. Written while living
near the city of Philadelphia in
1772-73.
Philadelphia: Collins, 1881. 32p.
NUC OCLC

1489. EVELYN, John <u>see</u> GODOLPHIN,
Margaret Blagge

1490. EVENS, Tillie [Am. 19c]
From darkness to light. The life
story of Gypsy Tillie Evens
together with songs used at her
meetings.
NY; Chicago: Fleming H. Revell
co., 1893. 60p. NUC

1491. EVERARD, Margaret [Br. 17c]
An epistle of Margaret Everard.
L: n.p., 1699. NUC
[Member of Society of Friends]

1492. EVERETT, Anne Gorham [Am.
1823-1843]
Memoir of Anne Gorham Everett,
with extracts from her
correspondence and journal. Comp.
Philippa Call Bush.
Boston: priv. pr., 1857. 320p.
NUC OCLC

1493. EVERETT, Madelaine H.
DONALDSON, Madelaine H. (Everett)

1494. EVERETT, Seraphina (Haynes)
[Am. 1823-1871 OCLC: 1823-1854]
The missionary sisters: a
memorial of Mrs. Seraphina Haynes
Everett and Mrs. Harriet Martha
(Lovell) Hamlin, [Am. d. 1857]
late missionaries of the A. B. C.
F. M. at Constantinople. [Ed.]
Mary Gladding (Wheeler) Benjamin.
Boston: American Tract Soc.,
c1860. 335p. NUC OCLC
[Letters quoted extensively.]

1495. EVERSHAW, Mary [Br. 19c]
Five years in Pennsylvania.
L: W. Strange, 1840. 227p. NUC OCLC

1496. EWBANKS, Lucinda [Am. 19c]
Statement of Lucinda Ewbanks,
giving an account of her
captivity among the Indians.
Denver, CO: n.p., 1865?. NUC

1497. EWING, Barbara (Maxwell)
[Br. 19c]
Letters to a friend.
Glasgow: G. Gallie, 1835. 16p. NUC

1498. -----A memoir of Barbara
Ewing. By Greville Ewing.
2d ed. Glasgow: G. Gallie, 1819.
249p. BL
[May contain personal material.]

1499. EWING, Greville, comp. see
EWING, Barbara

1500. EYRE, Mary [Br. 19c]
A lady's walks in the south of
France in 1863.
L: R. Bentley, 1865. 436p. NUC BL
OCLC

1501. -----Over the Pyrenees into
Spain.
L: R. Bentley, 1865. 361p. NUC BL
OCLC

1502. F., A. see FREEMAN, Ann

1503. F., A., ed. see THAXTER,
Celia (Leighton)

1504. F., M. see FRY, Marie

1505. FAHYS, Maria (L'Hommedieu)
[Am. 19c]
Around the world.
NY?: n.p., 1893?. 99p. NUC
[Voyage around the world, 1892-93]

1506. FAIRCHILD, Ashbel Green,
comp. see LOWRIE, Louisa Ann
(Wilson)

1507. FAIRFIELD, Jane (Frazer),
Mrs. Sumner Lincoln Fairfield
[Am. b. 1810]
The autobiography of Jane
Fairfield.
Boston: Bazin & Ellsworth, 1860.
328p. NUC BL K OCLC

1508. FAIRFIELD, Mrs. Sumner
Lincoln see FAIRFIELD, Jane
(Frazer)

1509. FAITHFULL, Emily, Miss [Br.
1835-1895]
Three visits to America.
Edinburgh: D. Douglas, 1884.
377p. NUC BL N OCLC

1510. FALCONBRIDGE, Anna Maria
[Br. 18c]
Narrative of two voyages to the
river Sierra Leone, during the
years 1791-2-3, in a series of
letters.
L: n.p., 1794; L: J. I. Higham,
1802. 287p. NUC BL OCLC

1511. FALKLAND, Amelia
(Fitzclarence) Carey, Viscountess
[Br. 1803-1858] ALT: Carey,
Amelia (Fitzclarence),
Viscountess Falkland
Chow-chow: being selections from
a journal kept in India, Egypt
and Syria.
L: Hurst & Blackett, 1857. 2v.
NUC BL OCLC

1512. FALLS, Alicia Maria
[19/20c]
Foreign courts and foreign homes.
L: Longmans, Green & co., 1898.
320p. NUC BL OCLC
[Travel: Europe]

1513. FANE, Priscilla Ann
(Wellesley-Pole), Countess of
Westmorland see WESTMORLAND,
Priscilla Ann (Wellesley-Pole)
Fane, Countess of

1514. FANSHAWE, Anne [NUC: Ann]
(Harrison), Lady [Br. 1625-1680]
Memoirs of Lady Fanshawe ...
written by herself. Ed. Sir
Nicholas Harris Nicholas.
L: H. Colburn, 1829. 395p. NUC BL
MB OCLC
[Wife of the Right Hon. Sir
Richard Fanshawe, bart;
Ambassador from Charles II to
Spanish court in 1665. Includes
extracts of his correspondence.
Memoir written in 1676.]

1515. FANSHAWE, Sir Richard,
bart., co-author see FANSHAWE,
Anne

1516. FARNHAM, Eliza Woodson [Am.
1815-1864]
California, in-doors and out; or,
how we farm, mine, and live
generally in the golden state.
NY: Dix, Edwards & co., 1856.
508p. NUC BL K OCLC

1517. -----Life in prairie land.
NY: Harper & bros., 1846. 408p.
NUC BL OCLC

1518. FARRAND, Eliza see FARRAND,
Rebecca

1519. FARRAND, Rebecca [Br. 1821-
1836]
A sister's memorial, or, a little
account of R. Farrand. Also drawn
up by her, a brief sketch of an
elder sister [Eliza (Farrand)
Taylor; 1815-1844]. By Sarah Ann
Farrand.
L: W. & F. G. Cash, 1857. 142p.
NUC BL MBD
[Members of Society of Friends;
includes Rebecca's diary, travel
to New York State.]

1520. FARRAND, Sarah Ann, comp.
see FARRAND, Rebecca

1521. FARRAR, Eliza Ware (Rotch),
Mrs. John Farrar [Am. 1791-1870]
Recollections of seventy years.
Boston: Ticknor & Fields, 1865.
331p. NUC BL OCLC

1522. FARRAR, Mrs. John see
FARRAR, Eliza Ware (Rotch)

1523. FARRAR, Maria Marcia Fanny
(Trench) see TRENCH, Maria Marcia
Fanny

1524. FARRER, Mary (Goldsmith)
[Br. 18c]
The appeal of an injured wife
against a cruel husband. Written
by Mrs. Farrer.
L: pr. for the author, 1788. 66p.
NUC BL OCLC

1525. FAULKNER, Mary Anne see
DONELLAN, Mary Anne (Faulkner)

1526. FAWCETT, W., comp. see
SHIRREFF, Mary (Russel)

1527. FAY, Amy [Am. 1844-1928]
Music study in Germany. From the
home correspondence of Amy Fay.
NY: Macmillan & co., c1880.
352p.; Chicago: Jansen, McClurg &
co., 1881. 348p. NUC BL OCLC

1528. FAY, Eliza, Mrs. [Br. 19c]
Original letters from India;
containing a narrative of a
journey through Egypt, and the
author's imprisonment at Calicut
by Hyder Ally. To which is added
an abstract of three subsequent
voyages to India.
Calcutta: n.p., 1821. BL

1529. FEATHERSTONHAUGH, Lady [Br.
18c]
Memorials personal and historical
of Admiral Lord Gambier. [Comp.]
Henrietta Georgiana Marcia
Laselles (Iremonger), Lady
Chatterton.
L: Hurst & Blackett, 1861. 2v.
NUC BL MBD OCLC
[Her travel diary, 1748-1753, in
France, Switzerland, Italy,
Germany in Vol. II.]

1530. FEILDEN, Eliza Whigham [Br.
19c]
My African home; or, bush life in
Natal when a young colony, 1852-
7.
L: S. Low, Marston, Searle, &
Rivington, 1887. 304p. NUC BL OCLC

1531. FELL, Margaret (Askew) see
FOX, Margaret (Askew) Fell

1532. FELLOWS, Sarah A. W., Mrs.
[Br. 19c]
Thirty years' experience.
L: Eliot Stock, 1874. 30p. BL
[Spiritual autobiography]

1533. FELTON, Mrs. [Br. 19c]
Life in America. A narrative of
two years' city and country
residence in the United States.
Hull: J. Hutchinson, 1838. 120p.
NUC BL N OCLC
[New York]

1534. FEMALE TEACHER, A, pseud.
[Br. 19c]
My Sunday scholars; or, a female
teacher's recollections of her
class.
L: n.p., 1844. BL

1535. FENNING, Elizabeth [Br.
1793-1815]

The genuine trial and affecting
case of Eliza Fenning who was
convicted ... of attempting to
poison the family of Mr. Turner
... correct copies of the whole
of the numerous and affecting
letters, written by her to her
parents, her lover, etc.
L: Hay & Turner, 1815?. 24p. NUC
BL OCLC
[8th ed. with add. letters, also
pub. 1815]

1536. FERGUSON, Alexander, ed.
see CALDERWOOD, Margaret
(Stewart)

1537. FERGUSON-DAVIE, Charlotte
Elizabeth, comp. see ALICE MAUD
MARY, Consort of Louis IV, Grand
Duke of Hesse Darmstadt

1538. FERRIER, John, comp. see
FERRIER, Susan Edmonstone

1539. FERRIER, Susan Edmonstone
[Br. 1782-1854]
Memoir and correspondence of
Susan Ferrier 1782-1854. Based on
her private correspondence.
Collected by her grandnephew,
John Ferrier. Ed. John Andrew
Doyle.
L: J. Murray, 1898. 349p. NUC BL
OCLC

1540. FERRIS, Mrs. Benjamin G.
[Am. 19c]
The Mormons at home; with some
incidents of travel from Missouri
to California, 1852-3. In a
series of letters.
NY: Dix & Edwards, 1856. 299p.
NUC BL OCLC
[BL attr. to her husband.]

1541. FERRYBRIDGE, Mrs. Henry
Nelson [Br. 19c]
Naples and Sicily under the
Bourbons. A series of sketches.
L: T. C. Newby, 1867. 324p. NUC
BL OCLC

1542. FEUDGE, Fannie Roper [Am.
19c]
Eastern side; or, missionary life
in Siam.
Philadelphia: Bible & pub. soc.,
1871. 364p. NUC OCLC

1543. -----India.
Boston: D. Lothrop & co., 1880.
640p. NUC OCLC

1544. -----Many lands and many
people.
Philadelphia: J. B. Lippincott &
co., 1875. 256p. NUC OCLC
[Travel: Peru, Athens, China,
Japan, Constantinople, Palestine,
California]

1545. -----A queer people.
Boston: D. Lothrop & co., 1878.
59p. NUC OCLC
[Japan]

1546. FIELD, Adele Marion see
FIELDE, Adele Marion

1547. FIELD, Henriette (Deluzy-
Desportes), Mrs. Henry Martyn
Field [Am. d. 1875]
Home sketches in France, and
other papers. Ed. Henry Martyn
Field.
NY: G. P. Putnam's sons, 1875.
256p. NUC BL

1548. FIELD, Henry Martyn, ed.
see FIELD, Henriette (Deluzy-
Desportes)

1549. FIELD, Mrs. Henry Martyn
see FIELD, Henriette (Deluzy-
Desportes)

1550. FIELD, Kate see FIELD, Mary
Katherine Keemle

1551. FIELD, Mary Katherine
Keemle [Am. 1838-1896] ALT:
Field, Kate
Hap-hazard.
Boston: J. R. Osgood & co., 1873.
253p. NUC OCLC
[Collection of short pieces,
including travel in England and
Europe.]

1552. -----Ten days in Spain.
Boston: J. R. Osgood & co., 1875.
NUC BL OCLC

1553. FIELDE, Adele Marion [Am.
1839-1916] ALT: Field, Adele
Marion
Pagoda shadows, studies from life
in China.

Boston: W. G. Corthell, 1885.
285p. NUC OCLC
[Christian missionary; chronicles
her observations of Chinese
customs concerning women.]

1554. FIELDS, Annie (Adams), Mrs.
James T. Fields [Am. 1834-1915]
Authors and friends.
Boston & NY: Houghton Mifflin; L:
T. F. Unwin, 1896. 355p. NUC BL
OCLC

1555. FIELDS, Annie (Adams), ed.
see THAXTER, Celia (Leighton)

1556. FIELDS, Mrs. James T. see
FIELDS, Annie (Adams)

1557. FIENNES, Celia [Br. 1662-
1741]
Through England on a side saddle
in the time of William and Mary,
being the diary of Celia Fiennes.
Ed. Robert Willis Blencowe.
L: Field & Tuer; NY: Scribner &
Welford, 1888. 336p. NUC BL MBD
OCLC

1558. FINCH, Lady Louisa
Elizabeth (Somerset), comp. see
BEAUFORT, Charlotte Sophie
(Leveson Gower) Somerset, Duchess
of

1559. FINCH, Marianne [Br. 19c]
An Englishwoman's experience in
America.
L: R. Bentley, 1853. 380p. NUC BL N

1560. FINN, Elizabeth Anne
(MacCaul) [Br. 1825-1921] ALT:
MacCaul, Elizabeth Anne
Home in the Holy Land. A tale
illustrating customs and
incidents in modern Jerusalem.
L: Nisbet, 1866. NUC BL

1561. -----Sunrise over
Jerusalem, with other pen and
pencil sketches.
L: n.p., 1873. BL

1562. -----A third year in
Jerusalem: a tale illustrating
customs and incidents of modern
Jerusalem.
L: n.p., 1869. BL

1563. FISH, Angelina [Am. 19c]
Pencilings abroad.
Rochester, NY: Rodell bros., pr.,
1890. 338p. NUC
[Travel: Europe]

1564. FISH, Henry, comp. see
COOPER, Mary Sarson (Winfield)

1565. FISHER, Elizabeth (Munro)
[Am. b. 1759]
Memoirs ... written by herself.
NY: the author, 1810. 48p. NUC K
OCLC
[Domestic tribulations, six
years' imprisonment]

1566. FISHER, Fanny E. [Br. 19c]
Poems and notes descriptive of
Killarney.
L: T. Fisher Unwin, 1890. 68p.
NUC BL

1567. FISHER, Lydia Jane
Leadbeater, Mrs. [19c]
Letters from the kingdom of
Kerry, in the year 1845.
Dublin: Webb & Chapman, 1847.
98p. NUC

1568. FITTON, Anne see NEWDIGATE,
Anne (Fitton), Lady

1569. FITTON, Mary, co-author see
NEWDIGATE, Anne (Fitton), Lady

1570. FITZATHERLEY, Mrs. see
ADDERLEY, C. F.

1571. FITZGERALD, Bessie see
DAVIES, Bessie (Williams)

1572. FITZGERALD, Mary [Br. 19c]
A child of the Sacred Heart.
L: n.p., 1868. BL
[A religious of the Sacred Heart;
may be autobiographical.]

1573. FITZGIBBON, Mary Agnes [Br.
1851-1915]
A trip to Manitoba.
L: R. Bentley & son, 1880. 248p.
NUC BL MC OCLC
[Year and a half in Manitoba.]

1574. FITZ-JAMES, Zilla [Am. b.
1827]
Zilla Fitz-James, the female
bandit of the Southwest ... an
autobiographical narrative. Ed.
Rev. A. Richards.
Little Rock, AR: A. B. Orton,
1852. 31p. NUC K

1575. FITZMAURICE, F. M., Mrs.
[Br. 19c]
Recollections of a rifleman's
wife at home and abroad.
L: Hope, 1851. 215p. NUC BL

1576. FLANNIGAN, Mrs. [Br. 19c]
Antigua and the Antiguans: a full
account of the colony and its
inhabitants. Interspersed with
anecdotes and legends. Also an
impartial view of slavery and the
free labour system: the
statistics of the island and
biographical notices.
L: Saunders & Otley, 1844. 2v.
NUC BL OCLC
[Halkett & Laing, Cushing ascribe
to Mrs. Flannigan. V. L. Oliver
attributes to "Mrs. Lanaghan."]

1577. FLETCHER, A., Miss [Am.
19c]
Within Fort Sumter; or, a view of
Major Anderson's garrison family
for one hundred and ten days.
Pub. anon.
NY: N. Tibbals & co., 1861. 72p.
NUC OCLC

1578. FLETCHER, Eliza (Dawson)
[Br. 1770-1858]
Autobiography of Mrs. Fletcher of
Edinburgh, with selections from
her letters and other family
memorials. Comp. and arr. by M.
R. [Mary (Fletcher), Lady
Richardson].
Carlisle: Thurnam, 1874. 337p.
NUC BL MB OCLC

1579. FLETCHER, Isabel, Mrs. [Br.
17c]
The Embassadour of Peace: being a
wonderful, but true relation of a
white dove seated on a rainbow
that appears to several persons,
in the parish of Peter's Carlile;

particularly to Mrs. Isabel
Fletcher ... to whom it relates
strange and wonderful things ...
asserting universal peace and
plenty ... the ensuing year 1697.
L: J. Bradford, 1696. 8p. BL

1580. FLETCHER, Mrs. John William
see FLETCHER, Mary (Bosanquet)

1581. FLETCHER, Margaret [Br.
19/20c]
Sketches of life and character in
Hungary.
L: S. Sonnenschein & co.; NY:
Macmillan & co., 1892. 248p. NUC
BL OCLC

1582. FLETCHER, Maria Jane
(Jewsbury) [Br. 1800-1833] ALT:
Jewsbury, Maria Jane
Lancashire worthies. [By] Francis
Espinasse.
2d series. L: Simpkin, Marshall &
co., 1877. 494p. NUC BL MB OCLC
[Travel in India; extracts of
diary and autobiography.]

1583. FLETCHER, Mary (Bosanquet),
Mrs. John William Fletcher [Br.
1739-1814] ALT: Bosanquet, Mary;
La Fléchère, Mme. Jean Guillaume;
La Fléchère, Mary (Bosanquet)
An aunt's advice to a niece, in a
letter to Miss Mary Gausson.
3d ed. Madeley: pr. J. Edmunds,
1795. 76p. NUC

1584. -----A letter to the Rev.
Mr. Wesley on the death of the
Rev. Mr. Fletcher ... .
Shropshire; Falmouth: pr., P.
Elliot, 1788. 16p. NUC

1585. -----A letter written to
Elizabeth A--ws on her removal
from England.
Leads: J. Bowling, 1770. 24p. NUC

1586. -----The life of Mrs. Mary
Fletcher, consort and relict of
the Rev. John Fletcher... .
Compiled from her journal and
other authentic documents. By
Henry Moore.
L: Thomas Cordeaux; Birmingham:
J. Pearl & son, 1817,18. 2v. NUC
BL MBD OCLC
[Contains letters & diary.]

1587. FLETCHER, Mrs. [Br. 19c]
A letter to the loving and
beloved people of the parish of
Madeley, and its vicinity, who
have lost a friend to piety in
the death of Mrs. Fletcher ... .
By Mary Tooth.
Ironbridge: W. Smith, 1816. 59p.
NUC BL

1588. FOGGITT, W. Smith, ed. see
SCHIMMELMANN, Adeline, Countess

1589. FOLEY, Julia A. [Am. 19c]
Two deaf girls, a few extracts
from the diary of J. A. Foley.
Mt. Airey [sic], PA: Pennsylvania
Institution, pr., 1896. 15p. NUC
OCLC

1590. FOLLOWS, Ruth Adcock [Br.
1719?-1809]
Memoirs of Ruth Follows ... for
sixty years a minister in the
Society of Friends: with extracts
from her letters. Ed. S.
Stansfield.
Liverpool: C. Bentham & co.,
1829. 156p. NUC BL MB OCLC

1591. FOOTE, Mrs. Henry Grant
[Br. 19c]
Recollections of Central America
and the west coast of Africa.
L: T. C. Newby, 1869. 221p. NUC
BL OCLC

1592. FOOTE, Julia A. J. [Am.
1823-1900]
A brand plucked from the fire. An
autobiographical sketch.
Cleveland, OH: pr. for the author
by W. F. Schneider, 1879. 124p.
NUC OCLC
[Black evangelist]

1593. FORBES, Annabella (Keith)
[Br. d. 1922]
Insulinde: experiences of a
naturalist's wife in the Eastern
Archipelago.
Edinburgh & L: W. Blackwood &
sons, 1887. NUC OCLC
[Travel: Malay Peninsula]

1594. FORBES, E. A., Mrs. see
FORBES, Elizabeth A.

1595. FORBES, Elizabeth A., Mrs.
[Am. 19c] ALT: Forbes, E. A.,
Mrs.
A woman's first impression of
Europe. Being wayside sketches
made during a short tour in 1863.
NY: Derby & Miller, 1865. 355p.
NUC BL OCLC

1596. FORBES, Margaret (Perkins)
[Am. d. 1856]
Voyage of the Midas. Ed. her son,
Robert Bennet Forbes.
Boston: n.p., 188-?. 44p. NUC
[Extracts from letters written to
her sister, Mrs. Mary Abbot of
Exeter.]

1597. FORBES, Robert Bennet, ed.
see FORBES, Margaret (Perkins)

1598. FORD, Anne see THICKNESSE,
Anne (Ford)

1599. FORD, Helen Cordelia [Br.
19c]
Notes of a tour in India and
Ceylon during the winter of 1888-
89.
L: Women's printing society,
1889. 180p. NUC BL OCLC

1600. FORDE, Gertrude [Br. 19c]
A lady's tour in Corsica.
L: R. Bentley & son, 1880. 2v.
NUC BL OCLC

1601. FORDYCE, Henrietta, Mrs.
James Fordyce [Br. 19c]
Memoir of the late Mrs. H. F.,
relict of James Fordyce, D. D.
containing original letters,
anecdotes, and pieces of poetry.
L: n.p., 1823. NUC BL

1602. FORDYCE, Mrs. James see
FORDYCE, Henrietta

1603. FORESTER, FANNY, pseud.,
comp. see JUDSON, Sarah (Hall)
Boardman

1604. FORFAR, Rebecca see ELLIS,
Elizabeth Furss

1605. FORMBY, Catherine [Br. 19c]
Formby Reminiscences.
n.p.: n.p., 1897. MB
[Includes travel to France]

1606. FORREST, Katherine A.,
comp. see ELLIOTT, Eleanor
(Weatherall)

1607. FOSTER, Amy, Mrs. Arnold
Foster [Br. 19/20c]
In the valley of the Yangtse.
L: London missionary society,
1899. 216p. NUC BL OCLC

1608. FOSTER, Mrs. Arnold see
FOSTER, Amy

1609. FOSTER, Lillian [Am. 19c]
Way-side glimpses, north and
south.
NY: Rudd & Carleton, 1860. 250p.
NUC OCLC
[Travel: USA]

1610. FOSTER, Lydia W. [Am. d.
1861]
Diary of Lydia W. Foster.
Westerly, RI: G. B. & J. H.
Utter, steam pr., 1872. 70p. NUC
OCLC
[Society of Friends]

1611. FOSTER, Vere H. L., ed. see
DEVONSHIRE, Georgiana (Spencer)
Duchess of

1612. FOUCHÉ, Catherina Therése
Lovisa Fredrika Elisabeth (von
Stedingk) Grey, Duchesse
d'Otranto [Br. 1837-1901] ALT:
Grey, Hon. Therése; Grey, Hon.
Mrs. William
Journal of a visit to Egypt,
Constantinople, the Crimea,
Greece, etc; in the suite of the
Prince and Princess of Wales.
L: Smith, Elder & co., 1869.
203p. NUC BL MBD OCLC
[MBD ascribes to Maria Georgina
(Shirreff) Grey, Mrs. William
Grey]

1613. FOULKE, Hugh, ed. see
PRICE, Rebecca

1614. FOWLER, Rachel, Mrs. [Br.
19c]
A short memoir of R. F. with
extracts from her memoranda.
Norwich: J. Fletcher, pr., 1838.
126p. NUC BL

1615. FOX, Bitha <u>see</u> LLOYD, Bitha (Fox)

1616. FOX, Caroline [Br. 1819-1871]
Memories of old friends, from journals and letters ... from 1835-1871. Ed. Horace Noble Pym. L: Smith, Elder & co.; NY: G. Munro, 1881. 355p. NUC BL MBD OCLC PD
[Literary activities, travel in Spain.]

1617. FOX, Eliza, Mrs. W. J. Fox [Br. 19c]
Memoir of Mrs. E. F. To which extracts are added from the journals and letters of her husband, the late W. J. Fox. Ed. Franklin Fox.
L: n.p., 1869. BL MB

1618. FOX, Franklin, ed. <u>see</u> FOX, Eliza

1619. FOX, Mrs. George <u>see</u> FOX, Margaret (Askew) Fell

1620. FOX, Jane Gurney, ed. <u>see</u> BACKHOUSE, Hannah Chapman (Gurney)

1621. FOX, Margaret <u>see</u> KANE, Margaret (Fox)

1622. FOX, Margaret (Askew) Fell, Mrs. George Fox [Br. 1614-1702]
ALT: Fell, Margaret (Askew)
A brief collection of remarkable passages and occurences relating to the birth, education, life, etc. of that ancient, eminant and faithful servant of the Lord, M. F.
L: J. Sowles, 1710. 535p. NUC BL OCLC
[Includes correspondence]

1623. FOX, Maria (Middleton) [Br. 1793-1844]
Memoirs of Maria Fox, late of Tottenham, consisting chiefly of extracts from her journal and correspondence. Ed. Samuel Fox.
L: C. Gilpin, etc., 1846. 493p. NUC BL MBD OCLC

[Member of Society of Friends; diary, travel in England, Holland, Germany]

1624. FOX, Samuel, ed. <u>see</u> FOX, Maria (Middleton)

1625. FOX, Mrs. W. J. <u>see</u> FOX, Eliza

1626. FRAME, Elizabeth [1820-1913] PSEUD: Nova Scotian, A
Descriptive sketches of Nova Scotia, in prose and verse, by a Nova Scotian.
Halifax: A. & W. Mackinlay, 1864. 242p. BL

1627. FRAMPTON, Mary [Br. 1773-1846]
The journal of Mary Frampton, from the year 1779, until the year 1846. Including various interesting and curious letters, anecdotes, etc., relating to events which occured during that period. Ed. her niece, Harriot Georgiana (Frampton) Mundy.
L: S. Low, Marston, Searle, & Rivington, 1885. 425p. NUC BL MBD OCLC
[Country diary, visits to London, etc.]

1628. FRANCES, May [Br. 19c]
Beyond the Argentine: or, letters from Brazil.
L: W. H. Allen, 1890. 148p. NUC BL OCLC

1629. FRANCESCA <u>see</u> ALEXANDER, Esther Frances

1630. FRANCIS, Beata, ed. <u>see</u> BARNWELL, Anne

1631. FRANCIS, Harriet Elizabeth (Tucker) [Am. 1828-1889]
Across the meridians, and fragmentary letters.
NY: The DeVinne press, 1887. 300p. NUC OCLC

1632. -----By land and sea; incidents of travel, with chats about history and legends.
Troy, NY: Nims & Knight, 1891. 198p. NUC OCLC

1633. FRANCIS, Lydia Maria see CHILD, Lydia Maria (Francis)

1634. FRANKLIN, Eliza see LESLIE, Eliza (Franklin)

1635. FRASER, Agnes [b. 1859] PSEUD: Francis Macnab British Columbia for settlers. By Francis Macnab. L: Chapman & Hall, ltd., 1898. 369p. NUC BL OCLC

1636. -----On veldt and farm in Bechuanaland--Cape Colony--the Transvaal--and Natal, by Francis Macnab. L & NY: E. Arnold, 1897. 320p. NUC BL OCLC

1637. FRASER, Eliza Anne [Am. 19c] Narrative of the capture, sufferings, and miraculous escape of Mrs. Eliza Fraser. NY: C. S. Webb, 1837. 24p. NUC

1638. FRASER, Mrs. Hugh see FRASER, Mary (Crawford)

1639. FRASER, Marie [19c] In Stevenson's Samoa. L: Smith, Elder & co.; NY: Macmillan, 1895. 190p. NUC BL OCLC [Travel: Samoan Islands]

1640. FRASER, Mary (Crawford), Mrs. Hugh Fraser [Br. 1851-1922] A diplomatist's wife in Japan. Letters from home to home. L: Hutchinson & co., 1899. 2v. NUC BL MB OCLC

1641. FRAZAR, Mae Douglas (Durell) [Am. 19c] Ten days in Switzerland. By Mrs. M. D. Frazar. Boston: J. A. Cummings, 1891. 37p. NUC OCLC

1642. FRAZIER, R., Mrs. [Am. 19c] Reminiscences of travel from 1855 to 1867. San Francisco: n.p., 1868. 156p. NUC OCLC [Travel: western USA]

1643. FREEMAN, Ann [Br. 1797-1826] ALT: F., A. A memoir of the life and ministry of A. F., written by herself and an account of her death by ... Henry Freeman. L: n.p.; Exeter, NH: N. Toole, 1826. 216p. NUC BL MB MBD OCLC [Quaker ministry; travel in England and Ireland]

1644. FREEMAN, Ellen (Coates) [1818-1851] ALT: Coates, Ellen Memorials of the mind and heart of Ellen Freeman. L: Waterlow & sons, 1853. 273p. NUC BL

1645. FREEMAN, Henry, ed. see FREEMAN, Ann

1646. FREEMAN, Julia Susan (Wheelock) [Am. 1833-1900] ALT: Wheelock, Julia Susan The boys in white; the experience of a hospital agent in and around Washington. NY: Lange & Hillman, 1870. 268p. NUC K C OCLC [Civil War nurse]

1647. FRÉMONT, Jessie Benton [Am. 1824-1902] Far West sketches. Boston: D. Lothrop & co., 1890. NUC OCLC [Travel: California & Arizona]

1648. -----Souvenirs of my time. Boston: D. Lothrop & co., 1887. NUC BL OCLC [Washington D. C. public life.]

1649. -----The story of the guard: a chronicle of the war. Boston: Ticknor & Fields, 1863. 227p.; NY: Harper & bros, 1863. NUC BL OCLC

1650. -----A year of American travel. NY: Harper & bros., 1878. 190p. NUC OCLC

1651. FRENCH, Maria [19c] Under the shadow of St. Peter. L: Spottiswoode & co., 1884. 22p. NUC

1652. FRENCH, Mathilda [Am. 19c]
Thrilling narrative of Matilda
French and brother, who were
shipwrecked.
Philadelphia: n.p., 1848. 24p. NUC

1653. FRERE, Alice M. see CLERK,
Alice M. (Frere)

1654. FRESHFIELD, Mrs. Henry see
FRESHFIELD, Jane Quintin (Crawford)

1655. FRESHFIELD, Jane Quintin
(Crawford), Mrs. Henry Freshfield
[Br. d. 1901]
Alpine byways; or, light leaves
gathered in 1859 and 1860.
L: Longman, Green, Longman &
Roberts, 1861. 232p. NUC BL OCLC

1656. -----A summer tour in the
Grisons and Italian valleys of
the Bernina.
L: Longman, Green, Longman &
Roberts, 1862. 292p. NUC BL OCLC

1657. FRIEND, A, pseud., comp.
see ADAMS, Hannah

1658. FRIEND, A., pseud., comp.
see BROOKHOUSE, Ann

1659. FRIEND, Sarah E. [Am. 19c]
A mother's bequest: poems,
essays, extracts from the diary
and religious experience.
Keyser, WV: Mountain Echo water
power printing house, 1894. 199p.
NUC OCLC

1660. FRINK, Margaret Ann (Alsip)
[Am. 19c]
Journal of the adventures of a
party of California goldseekers.
Oakland, CA: n.p., 1897. 131p.
NUC MAD OCLC
[Repr. of priv. pr. ed. 1850]

1661. FROST, Sarah (Scofield)
[19c]
Kingston and the loyalists ... to
which is appended a diary written
by Sarah Frost on her voyage to
St. John, N.B., with the
loyalists of 1783. Ed. Walter
Bates.
St. John, New Brunswick: Barnes &
co., 1889. NUC

1662. FROUDE, James Anthony, ed.
see CARLYLE, Jane Baillie (Welsh)

1663. FRY, Caroline see WILSON,
Caroline (Fry)

1664. FRY, Elizabeth (Gurney)
[Br. 1780-1845]
Life and labors of the eminent
philanthropist, preacher, and
prison reformer. Comp. from her
journal and other sources by
Edward Ryder.
NY: E. Walker's son, 1884. 381p.
NUC MBD OCLC

1665. -----Life of Elizabeth Fry.
Compiled from her journal, as ed.
by her daughters, and from
various other sources. Ed.
Susanna Corder.
Philadelphia: H. Longstreth; L:
W. & F. G. Cush, 1853. 627p. NUC
BL OCLC

1666. -----Memoir of the life of
Elizabeth Fry, with extracts from
her journal and letters. Ed. by
two of her daughters [Katherine
Fry and Rachel Elizabeth (Fry)
Cresswell].
L: C. Gilpin, J. Hatchard & co.,
1847. 2v. NUC BL MBD OCLC PD
[Member of Society of Friends]

1667. -----Memories of her mother
in a letter to her sisters. By
Rachel Elizabeth (Fry) Cresswell,
Mrs. Francis Cresswell.
L: pr. for priv. circ., 1845.
86p. NUC BL

1668. FRY, Katherine, ed. see
FRY, Elizabeth (Gurney)

1669. FRY, Marie [Br. 19c] ALT:
F., M.
Selections from the
correspondence of ... M. F. ... .
With a ... biographical notice.
Ed. Mrs. H. G. Guinness.
L: n.p., 1874. BL

1670. FULLER, Arthur B., ed. see
OSSOLI, Sarah Margaret (Fuller),
Marchesa di

1671. FULLER, Berenice Morrison
[Am. 19c]
Plantation life in Missouri.
n.p.: n.p., 18--. 34p. NUC OCLC
[Autobiography]

1672. FULLER, Emeline L., Mrs.
[Am. b. 1847]
Left by the Indians. Story of my
life.
Mt. Vernon, IA: Hawk-eye steam
pr., 1892. 40p. NUC OCLC
[Overland journey to the Pacific]

1673. FULLER, Margaret see
OSSOLI, Sarah Margaret (Fuller),
Marchesa di

1674. FULLERTON, Amy Fullerton
[Br. 19c]
A lady's ride through Palestine
and Syria, with notices of Egypt
and the canal of Suez.
L: S. W. Partridge & co., 1872.
349p. NUC BL

1675. FULLERTON, Lady Georgiana
Charlotte (Leveson-Gower) [Br.
1812-1885]
The inner life of Lady Georgiana
Fullerton. With notes of retreat
and diary. By Fanny Margaret
Taylor.
L: Burns & Oates, 1899. 399p. NUC
BL MB

1676. FULTON, Frances I. Sims
[Am. 19c] PSEUD: Pennsylvania
Girl, A
To and through Nebraska. By a
Pennsylvania girl.
Lincoln, NB: Journal co., 1884.
273p. NUC BL OCLC

1677. FURLEY, E. M., Miss [Br.
19c]
From Mombasa to Mengo, being an
account of the journey of the
first party of lady missionaries
to Uganda, from the journals of
Miss E. M. Furley.
L: Church Missionary Society,
1896. 47p. BL

1678. G., Miss see GRANE, Miss

1679. G., A. E. see GUILD, Anne
Eliza (Gore)

1680. G., A. M. see GASCOYNE,
Annie M.

1681. G., C. see GEIER, Christeen

1682. G., C. H. see GILMAN,
Caroline (Howard)

1683. G., E. see GOW, Elizabeth

1684. G., E. L., ed. see LINDSAY,
Sarah

1685. G., H. see GROTE, Harriet
(Lewin)

1686. G., J. T., comp. see GRANT,
Emily Fredericka

1687. G., M. see GRAHAM, Margaret

1688. G., M. A. see GILPIN, Mary
Ann

1689. G., M. R. see GOODWIN, Mary
R.

1690. G., Margaret Day, Mrs. [Br.
1814-1851]
A sister's memorial. Ed. Amelia
T.
Brighton: n.p., 1851. BL
[Includes extracts from her
diary: primarily religious]

1691. G., Marie L. [Br. 19c]
The female Jesuit; or, the spy in
the family. An account of Marie
L-G- a pretended convert. With a
portrait and an autobiography.
Comp. Jemima (Thompson) Luke.
L: n.p., 1851. 3pt.; NY: M. W.
Dodd, 1851. 353p. BL OCLC

1692. GALINDO, Catherine, co-
author see SIDDON, Mrs.

1693. GALLETTI DI CADHILAC, Hon.
Margaret Isabella (Collier),
Countess [Br. 1846-1928] ALT:
Cadhilac, Margaret Isabella
(Collier) Galleti d', Countess
Our home by the Adriatic.

L: Richard Bentley & son, 1886.
250p. NUC BL OCLC
[Twelve years residence in
Italy.]

1694. GALLOWAY, Rev. J. C., comp.
see GIFFEN, Mary E. (Galloway)

1695. GALPIN, Barbara (Johnson)
[Am. b. 1856]
In foreign lands.
Boston: New England pub. co.,
1892. 156p. NUC OCLC
[Travel in Europe]

1696. GALT, J., ed. see PIGOTT,
Harriet

1697. GALTON, Gwendolen Douglas
see TRENCH GASCOIGNE, Laura
Gwendolen Douglas (Galton)

1698. GAMBIER, Admiral Lord, co-
author see FEATHERSTONHAUGH, Lady

1699. GAMEWELL, Mary Louise
(Ninde) [Am. 1858-1947]
We two alone in Europe.
8th ed. Chicago: A. C. McClurg,
1885. 348p. NUC OCLC

1700. GANNETT, Deborah (Sampson)
[Am. 1760-1827] ALT: Sampson,
Deborah
An address delivered with
applause at the Federal Street
Theatre, Boston, four successive
nights ... beginning March 22,
1802; and after, at other
principal towns ... by Deborah
Gannett.
Dedham, MA: pr. H. Mann, 1802.
24p. NUC BL OCLC
[Personal narrative; served 3
years in American army disguised
as man.]

1701. -----The female review: or,
memoirs of an American young lady
(Deborah Sampson), whose life and
character are peculiarly distinguished, being a continental
soldier for nearly three years,
in the late American War ... .
Dedham, MA: n.p., 1797. BL

1702. GARDINER, Everilla Anne,
comp. see GARDINER, Jane (Arden)

1703. GARDINER, Jane [Br. 19c]
An excursion from London to
Dover ... .
L: Longman, Hurst, Rees, & Orme,
etc., 1806. 2v. NUC

1704. GARDINER, Jane (Arden) [Br.
1758-1840]
Recollections of a beloved
mother. Comp. Everilla Anne
Gardiner.
L: W. M'Dowall, 1842. BL
[Contains letters and diary]

1705. GARDINER, Marguerite
(Power) Farmer see BLESSINGTON,
Marguerite (Power) Farmer
Gardiner, Countess of

1706. GARDINER, Marilla (Dunton),
comp. see BOWEN, Harriet M.
(Gardiner)

1707. GARDINER, Mrs. William,
comp. see BOWEN, Harriet M.
(Gardiner)

1708. GARDNER, Hon. Mrs. Alan see
GARDNER, Nora Beatrice (Blyth)

1709. GARDNER, H. C., Mrs. [Am.
19c]
Glimpses of our Lake Region in
1863, and other papers.
NY: Nelson & Phillips;
Cincinnati, OH: Hitchcock &
Walden, 1874. 420p. NUC BL OCLC
[OCLC: Irish in Massachusetts]

1710. GARDNER, Mary Crilley [Am.
b. 1796]
The useful disciple; or, a
narrative of Mrs. Mary Gardner.
[By] Phoebe (Worrell) Palmer.
Cincinnati, OH: Swormstedt &
Bower, 1851. 175p. NUC BL
[BL: 1st British ed., 1857.
"Sketched as taken from the lips
of Mrs. G. by Mrs. L. A. Baily.]

1711. GARDNER, Nora Beatrice
(Blyth), Hon. Mrs. Alan Gardner
[Br. 19c]
Rifle and spear with the
Rajpootes: being the narrative of
a winter's travel and sport in
Northern India. By Mrs. Alan
Gardner.
L: Chatto & Windus, 1895. 336p.
NUC BL OCLC

1712. GARLAND, Bessie (Ford) [Br. 19c]
The old man's darling; a series of character sketches.
Toronto: pr. for authoress, 1881. 157p. NUC MC
[Autobiography of childhood in Ireland and life as emigrant in Canada.]

1713. GARLAND, Jessie [Am. 19c]
My book.
Washington, D.C.: Gray & Clarkson, 1885. 151p. NUC
[New Englander married to southern gentleman, describes her life on a plantation, pre-Civil War.]

1714. GARNETT, Sarah Ann (Tompkins) [Am. b. 1809]
Cursory family sketches.
Albany, NY: John Munsell, 1870. 140p. NUC K OCLC
[Tompkins family and autobiography]

1715. GARRARD, Lewis Hector, comp. see RISKE, Charlotte (Chambers) Ludlow

1716. GASCOIGNE, Gwendolen (Galton) Trench see TRENCH GASCOIGNE, Laura Gwendolen Douglas (Galton)

1717. GASCOYNE, Annie M. [Br. 19c] ALT: G., A. M.
Sunbeams from a western hemisphere. By A. M. G.
Dublin: McGlashan & Gill, 1874. 117p. NUC BL OCLC
[Travel: U.S.]

1718. GASKELL, Charles Milnes, ed. see LUMB, Anne (Milnes)

1719. GASKIN, John, ed. see BUDGETT, Sarah

1720. GATTY, Mrs. Alfred see GATTY, Margaret (Scott)

1721. GATTY, Margaret (Scott), Mrs. Alfred Gatty [Br. 1809-1875]
The old folks from home; or, a holiday in Ireland in 1861.
L: Bell & Daldy, 1862. 256p. NUC BL OCLC

1722. GAY, Rev. Bunker, comp. see HOWE, Jemima (Sartwell)

1723. GAY, Mary Ann Harris [Am. b. 1827]
Life in Dixie during the war. 1863-64-65.
Atlanta, GA: Constitution job office, 1892. 255p. NUC OCLC
[1894 ed. adds 1861-1862]

1724. GAYLE, Sarah (Haynesworth) [Am. 1804-1835]
Extracts from the journal of Sarah Haynesworth Gayle.
New Rochelle, NY: The Knickerbocker press, 1895. 50p. NUC OCLC

1725. GEARY, Caroline [Br. 19/20c]
In other lands.
L: Digby & Long; Watford: G. W. Lea, 1889. BL
[Travel: Spain, Italy & Austria]

1726. -----Rural life: its humour and its pathos.
L: J. Long, 1899. 259p. BL OCLC
[Prose sketches, observations of country life in other lands.]

1727. GEBBIE, Mary [Br. 19c]
Sketches of the town of Strathavon and parish of Avondale.
Edinburgh: J. Menzies & co., 1880. 224p. NUC OCLC

1728. GEIER, Christeen [Am. 19c]
ALT: Christeen; G., C.; Grier, Christeen
An adopted daughter; or, the white slave. By C. G.
Evansville, IN: I. Esslinger, pr., 1878. 103p. NUC OCLC
[Autobiography of German-American servant girl.]

1729. -----Forty years of life; or, gladness out of gloom. By Christeen.
Evansville, IN: Keller pr. co., 1891. 573p. NUC OCLC
[Extension of autobiography, including travel to California.]

1730. GEMMILL, Jane Wilson [Am. 19c]

Notes on Washington, or, six years at the national capital.
Washington: Brentano bros., c1883; Philadelphia: E. Claxton & co., 1894. 316p. NUC BL OCLC

1731. GENUNG, Hattie E. [Am. 19c]
A trip to Alaska.
Boston: United Society of Christian Endeavor, c1894. 16p. NUC

1732. GEORGE, Elizabeth [Br. 1831-1856]
Memoir of Elizabeth George. By Henry James Piggott.
L: n.p., 1858. BL MBD
[Includes religious diary, 1851-1856]

1733. GERMAN PRINCESS, THE see CARLETON, Mary (Moders)

1734. GERMON, Maria Vincent, Mrs. R. C. Germon [Br. 19c]
A diary kept by Mrs. R. C. Germon at Lucknow, between the months of May and December 1857.
L: Waterlow & son, 1870. 142p. BL MB

1735. GERMON, Mrs. R. C. see GERMON, Maria Vincent

1736. GETHIN, Grace (Norton), Lady [Br. 1676-1696]
Misery's virtues whet-stone. Reliquiae Gethinianae, or, some remains of the most ingenious and excellent lady, the Lady Grace Gethin ... being a collection of choice discourses, pleasant apothegemes, and witty sentences, etc.
L: D. Edwards for the author, 1699. 90p. NUC BL OCLC
[Mostly essays]

1737. GIBBONS, Abby (Hopper) [Am. 1801-1893]
Life of Abby Hopper Gibbons, told chiefly through her correspondence. Ed. her daughter, Sarah Hopper Emerson.
NY: G. P. Putnam's sons, 1896-97. 2v. NUC BL OCLC

1738. GIBBONS, Hannah (Pusey) [Am. 1771-1868]
Memoir of Hannah Gibbons.

Philadelphia: W. H. Pile, pr., 1873. 220p. NUC OCLC
[Memoranda kept by author, 1796-1864, brought up to April, 1868 by members of her family.]

1739. GIBSON, (Cogan) [Br. 19c]
Recollections of my youth, written at the request of my daughter.
Tunbridge Wells: L. Hepworth, 188-?. 14p. NUC

1740. GIBSON, Jane [Br. 19c]
Memoirs of ... Jane Gibson ... including selections from her correspondence. [Comp.] Francis Athon Wells.
L: n.p., 1837. BL

1741. GIBSON, Margaret Dunlop (Smith), ed. see LEWIS, Agnes (Smith)

1742. GIBSON, Mary Ann Metcalfe [Br. 19c]
Family notes and reminiscences.
Kendal: T. Wilson, pr., 1899. 187p. BL

1743. GIDDINGS, Sarah (Powell) [Am. b. 1847]
In the enemies' land; a personal experience.
Chicago: Regan pr. house, c1899. 259p. NUC K OCLC
[Autobiography of southern woman's life in the north, post Civil War]

1744. GIFFEN, Mary E. (Galloway) [Am. 1842-1881]
Life and letters of Mrs. Mary Galloway Giffen. Comp. Rev. J. C. Galloway.
Louisville, GA: n.p., 1882. 294p. NUC

1745. GILBERT, Anne (Taylor) [Br. 1782-1866] ALT: Taylor, Anne
Autobiography and other memorials of Mrs. Gilbert, formerly Ann Taylor. Ed. Josiah Gilbert.
L: H. D. King & co., 1874. 2v. NUC BL MB OCLC
[Autobiography to 1813]

1746. GILBERT, Mrs. H. A., comp. & ed. see JUKES, Harriet Maria (Hole)

1747. GILBERT, Josiah, ed. see GILBERT, Ann (Taylor)

1748. GILBERT, Linda [Am. 1847-1895]
Sketch of the life and work of Linda Gilbert, with statistical reports and engraving of herself.
NY: pr., Industrial School of the Hebrew Orphan Asylum, 1876. 99p. NUC OCLC

1749. GILBERT, Mary [Br. 1751-1768]
An extract of Miss M. Gilbert's journal, with some account of the Lady Elizabeth Hastings, etc.
L: n.p., 1763. 66p. NUC BL MBD OCLC
[Diary 1765-1768; chiefly religious]

1750. GILCHRIST, Anne (Burrows) [Br. 1828-1885]
Anne Gilchrist, her life and writings. Ed. H. H. Gilchrist. 2d ed. L: T. F. Unwin, 1887. 368p. NUC BL OCLC
[Contains essays, sketches, and religious writings. Biog. incl. letters of Mrs. Gilchrist and her friends, the Rossettis, Carlyles, and others.]

1751. GILCHRIST, H. H., ed. see GILCHRIST, Anne (Burrows)

1752. GILES, Susan R. H., Mrs. [Am. 19c]
Memories and hopes.
Boston: The Fourth Bapt. Church, 1887. 12p. NUC OCLC
[Unrhymed poem detailing history of the Fourth Baptist Church in Boston.]

1753. GILL, Isobel (Black), Lady [Br. 19c]
Six months in Ascension. An unscientific account of a scientific expedition.
L: J. Murray, 1878. 285p. NUC BL OCLC
[Astronomy: Opposition of Mars in 1877]

1754. GILMAN, Arthur, ed. see DUDLEY, Dorothy

1755. GILMAN, Caroline (Howard), Mrs. Samuel Gilman [Am. 1794-1888] ALT: G., C. H.
The poetry of travelling in the United States: with additional sketches by a few friends, and a week among autographs by Samuel Gilman.
NY: S. Colman, 1838. 430p. NUC BL OCLC

1756. -----Recollections of the private centenniel celebration of the overthrow of the tea.
Cambridge, MA: Press of J. Wilson & son, 1874. 51p. NUC OCLC

1757. GILMAN, Caroline (Howard), ed. see WILKINSON, Eliza (Yonge)

1758. GILMAN, Emily Serena, comp. and ed. see COIT, Mehetabel (Chandler)

1759. GILMAN, Emily Serena, comp. see GREENE, Martha (Coit) Hubbard

1760. GILMAN, Marie Petit, comp. and ed. see COIT, Mehetabel (Chandler)

1761. GILMAN, Marie Petit, comp. see GREENE, Martha (Coit) Hubbard

1762. GILMAN, Samuel, co-author see GILMAN, Caroline (Howard)

1763. GILMAN, Mrs. Samuel see GILMAN, Caroline (Howard)

1764. GILPIN, Mary Ann [Br. 1813-1838] ALT: G., M. A.
Memoir of M. A. G. ... consisting chiefly of extracts from her diary and letters.
L: Fry, 1840. 236p. NUC BL MB MBD OCLC
[Quaker; diary 1829-1838]

1765. GLADDING, E. N., Mrs. [Am. 19c]
Leaves from an invalid's journal, and poems.
Providence, RI: George H. Whitney, 1858. 235p. NUC OCLC
[Includes journal, two short stories, and poems.]

1766. GLENORCHY, Willielma
(Maxwell) Campbell, Viscountess
[Br. 1741-1786] ALT: Campbell,
Willielma (Maxwell), Viscountess
Glenorchy
The life of the right Honourable
Willielma, Viscountess Glenorchy,
containing extracts from her
diary and correspondence. By
Thomas Snell Jones.
Edinburgh: William Whyte & co.;
L: Longman, Rees, Orme & Brown,
1822. NUC BL OCLC

1767. -----Memorials of the
Clayton Family. With ...
correspondence of ... Lady
Glenorchy. Ed. Thomas W. B.
Aveling.
L: Jackson, Walford & Hodder,
1867. 516p. NUC BL OCLC

1768. GODDARD, Sarah Madeline
(Vinton) see DAHLGREN, Sarah
Madeline (Vinton) Goddard

1769. GODFREY, Miss [19c] PSEUD:
Viola
Sketches from life; or, leaves
from a clairvoyant's note-book.
Signed: Viola.
L: J. Burns, 18??. 3p. NUC

1770. GODMAN, Inez A. [Am. 19c]
Gilbert Academy and Agricultural
College, Winstead, LA: Sketches
and incidents: selections from
journal. With William Davis
Godman and A. H. Dexter.
NY: pr., Hunt & Eaton, 1893.
307p. NUC OCLC

1771. GODMAN, William Davis, co-
author see GODMAN, Inez A.

1772. GODOLOPHIN, Margaret Blagge
[Br. 1652-1678]
The life of Mrs. Godolphin. By
John Evelyn ... Now first pub. &
ed. by Samuel, Lord Bishop of
Oxford.
L: William Pickering, 1847.
265p.; NY: D. Appleton & co.,
1847. 147p. BL OCLC
[Contains excerpts of letters.]

1773. GODWIN, Mary
(Wollstonecraft) see
WOLLSTONECRAFT, Mary

1774. GODWIN, William, ed. see
WOLLSTONECRAFT, Mary

1775. GODWIN, Mrs. William see
WOLLSTONECRAFT, Mary

1776. GOFF, Dinah Wilson [Br.
1784-1858]
Divine protection through
extraordinary dangers;
experienced by Jacob and
Elizabeth Goff and their family,
during the Irish rebellion in
1798.
Philadelphia: The Tract
Association of Friends, 1857.
41p.; 2d ed. L: M. & F. G. Cash,
1857. 45p. NUC BL
[Goff's daughter's recollections
of her Quaker family's
experiences.]

1777. GOLLOCK, Georgina Anne [Br.
1861-1940]
A winter's mails from Ceylon,
India and Egypt; being journal
letters written home by G. A.
Gollock.
L: Church Missionary Society,
1895. 189p. NUC BL

1778. GOOCH, Elizabeth Sarah
(Villa-Real) [Br. b. 1754] ALT:
Gooch, Mrs. Villa-Real
An appeal to the public on the
conduct of Mrs. Gooch, written by
herself.
L: G. Kearsley, pr., 1788. NUC BL

1779. -----[MB: Entradas] The
life of Mrs. Gooch, written by
herself.
L: C. & G. Kearsley, 1792. 3v.
NUC BL MB OCLC
[Written in prison, on her
divorce]

1780. GOOCH, Fanny (Chambers) see
INGLEHART, Fanny (Chambers) Gooch

1781. GOOCH, Mrs. Villa-Real see
GOOCH, Elizabeth Sarah (Villa-
Real)

1782. GOOD, D. R., comp. see
RANKIN, Mary

1783. GOODAL, Mrs. [Br. 19c]
Memoir. Written by herself. In:

Select biographies. Comp. William King Tweedie.
Edinburgh: pr. for the Wodrow society, 1845-47. 2v. NUC BL OCLC

1784. GOODALE, Anna [Am. 19c]
Memoir of Miss Anna Goodale, with a collection of familiar letters, in a course of correspondence with Christian friends. Ed. Joanna (Graham) Bethune.
Worcester, MA: Dorr, Howland & co., 1834. 120p. NUC

1785. GOODALE, Elaine see
EASTMAN, Elaine (Goodale)

1786. GOODENOUGH, Mary [Br. d. 1692]
Fair warning to murderers of infants: being an account of the tryal codemnation [!] and execution of Mary Goodenough. Together with the advice sent by her to her children, 1692, in a letter signed by her own hand the night before she was executed.
L: pr. for Jonathan Robinson, 1692. 14p. NUC BL

1787. GOODHUE, Mrs. Joseph see
GOODHUE, Sarah (Whipple)

1788. GOODHUE, Sarah (Whipple), Mrs. Joseph Goodhue [Am. 1641-1681]
The copy of a valedictory and monitory writing, left by Sarah Goodhue, the wife of Joseph Goodhue, of Ipswich, in N.E. and found after her decease.
Cambridge, MA: n.p., 1681; Salem, MA: Samuel Hall, 1770. 13p. NUC BL OCLC

1789. GOODMAN, Margaret [Br. 19c]
Experiences of an English Sister of Mercy.
L: Smith, Elder & co., 1862. 234p. NUC BL MB OCLC
[On her social and charitable work]

1790. GOODRICH, Abigail (Spencer), Mrs. George Goodrich [Am. 1801-1828]
Memoir of Mrs. Abigail Goodrich, late of Winchester, CT. Comp. George Goodrich.

Hartford, CT: J. Russell, 1829. 36p. NUC
[Includes letters and misc. writings]

1791. GOODRICH, George, comp. see
GOODRICH, Abigail (Spencer)

1792. GOODRICH, Mrs. George
GOODRICH, Abigail (Spencer)

1793. GOODWIN, Ellen (King) [Br. 19c]
Memorials of my mother [Catherine King] and my home.
L: n.p., 1889. NUC

1794. GOODWIN, Mary R. [Am. 19c]
ALT: G., M. R.
The passion play of 1890.
Boston: J. G. Cupples, 1890. 12p. NUC
[Describes author's visit to Oberammergau and the play.]

1795. GORDON, Elizabeth Anne [BL: Anna], Mrs. [Br. 19/20c]
"Clear Round!" or, seeds of a story from other countries.
L: Sampson, Low, Marston & co., 1893. 442p. NUC BL
[Travel: Canada, Japan, China, India & Egypt.]

1796. GORDON, Elizabeth (Brodie) Gordon, Duchess of [Br. 1794-1864]
Life and letters of Elisabeth, last Duchess of Gordon. By Rev. A. Moody Stuart.
2d ed. L: J. Nisbet & co., 1865. 396p.

1797. GORDON, F. E., Mrs. see
BROWN, Jane

1798. GORDON, Ishbel Maria (Marjoribanks), Marchioness of Aberdeen and Temair see ABERDEEN AND TEMAIR, Ishbel Maria (Marjoribanks) Gordon, Marchioness of

1799. GORDON, Jane, Duchess of [Br. 19c]
An autobiographical chapter in the life of Jane, Duchess of Gordon. Ed. J. W. Guild.
Glasgow: priv. pr., 1864. 19p. BL
[Letters to F. Farquherson.]

1800. GORDON, Janet Hamilton,
Mrs. [Br. d. 1696] ALT: Hamilton,
Janet
An account of the particular
soliloquies and covenant
engagements (with God), past
betwixt Mrs. Janet Hamilton ...
upon the several diets, and at
the several places underwritten,
which were found in her cabinet
... after her death ... 1696. In:
Select biographies. Comp. William
King Tweedie.
Edinburgh: pr. for the Wodrow
Society, 1845-47. 2v. NUC BL OCLC

1801. GORDON, Julia [Br. b. 1827]
Awful disclosures of Miss Julia
Gordon, the white nun, or female
spy.
L: G. Abington, 1858. 16p. NUC

1802. GORDON, Lina Duff see
WATERFIELD, Lina (Duff Gordon)

1803. GORDON, Lucie (Austin)
Duff, Lady [Br. 1821-1869] ALT:
Duff Gordon, Lucie (Austin), Lady
Last letters from Egypt. To which
are added letters from the Cape.
[Comp.] her daughter, Janet Ann
(Duff Gordon) Ross.
L: Macmillan & co., 1875. 346p.
NUC BL OCLC

1804. -----Letters from Egypt,
1863-65. Ed. Sarah (Taylor)
Austin.
L: n.p., 1865. NUC BL

1805. GORDON, Lucie (Austin)
Duff, Lady, co-author see TAYLOR,
Susannah (Cook)

1806. GORDON, Lucy Amelia [Br.
19c]
The life and extraordinary
adventures of Lucy Amelia Gordon,
who was well known some years
since as the handsome servant
maid of Grosvenor Square. A true
narrative, written by herself.
L: pr. for J. Ker, M'Gowen &
others, 1807. 38p. NUC

1807. GORDON, Margaret Maria
(Brewster) [Br. b. 1823] ALT:
Brewster, Margaret Maria
Letters from Cannes and Nice.
Edinburgh: T. Constable, 1857.
253p. NUC BL OCLC

1808. GORDON, S. Anna [Am. 19c]
Camping in Colorado, with
suggestions to gold seekers,
tourists and invalids.
NY: the author's pub. co., 1879.
201p. NUC OCLC

1809. GORDON-CUMMING, Constance
Frederica [Br. 1837-1924] ALT:
Cumming, Constance Frederica
Gordon
At home in Fiji.
L & Edinburgh: W. Blackwood &
sons, 1881. 2v. NUC BL OCLC

1810. -----Fire fountains: the
kingdom of Hawaii, its volcanoes,
and the history of its missions.
Edinburgh: W. Blackwood, 1893.
2v. NUC OCLC

1811. -----From the Hebrides to
the Himalayas. A sketch of
eighteen months' wanderings in
western isles and eastern
highlands.
L: S. Low, Marston, Searle &
Rivington, 1876. 2v. NUC BL OCLC

1812. -----In the Hebrides. Vol 1.
New ed. L: Chatto & Windus, 1883.
431p. NUC OCLC

1813. -----In the Himalayas and
on the Indian plains. Vol 2.
L: Chatto & Windus, 1884. 608p.
NUC OCLC

1814. -----Granite Crags.
Edinburgh & L: W. Blackwood &
sons, 1884. 384p. NUC BL OCLC
[Travel: California]

1815. -----A Lady's cruise in a
French man-of-war.
Edinburgh & L: W. Blackwood &
sons, 1882. 2v. NUC BL OCLC
[Oceanica and Polynesia]

1816. -----Two happy years in
Ceylon.
Edinburgh & L: W. Blackwood &
sons; NY: Charles Scribner's
sons, 1892. 2v. NUC OCLC

1817. -----Via Cornwall to Egypt.
L: Chatto & Windus, 1885. 361p.
NUC OCLC

1818. -----Wanderings in China.
Edinburgh & L: W. Blackwood &
sons, 1886. 2v. NUC BL OCLC

1819. GOSSE, Emily [Br. 19c]
Sea-side pleasures. With Philip
Henry Gosse.
L: Society for the Promotion of
Christian Knowledge, 1853. 85p.
BL
[Naturalist's observations and
personal experiences]

1820. GOSSE, Philip Henry, co-
author see GOSSE, Emily

1821. GOTHERSON, Dorothea (Scott)
see HOGBEN, Dorothea (Scott)
Gotherson

1822. GOVION BROGLIO SOLARI,
Catherine (Hyde), Marchioness
[Br. 1755/6-1844]
Letters of the Marchioness
Broglio Solari ... containing a
sketch of her life and
recollections of celebrated
characters, with notes.
L: W. Pickering, 1845. 142p. NUC
BL OCLC

1823. -----Private anecdotes of
foreign courts.
L: H. Colburn, 1827. 2v. NUC BL
OCLC
[Court gossip heard by traveling
author.]

1824. GOW, Elizabeth [Br. 19c]
ALT: G., E.
The faithful servant, an
authentic memoir of Elizabeth
Gow, as written by herself.
Edinburgh: J. Gall & son, 1825.
150p. NUC
[Later pub. as: A hidden one
brought to light; or, memoir of
E. G., written by herself. Ed. J.
J. Bonar. Glasgow: C. Glass &
co., 1880. 159p. BL]

1825. GOWANLOCK, Theresa [Am.
19c]
Two months in the camp of Big
Bear. The life and adventures of
Theresa Gowanlock and Therese
(Fulford) Delaney.
Parkdale: Times Office, 1885.
141p. NUC OCLC

[Indian captivity narrative; Part
2 by Mrs. Delaney.]

1826. GOWER, Hon. [Edward]
F[rederick] Leveson, ed. see
GRANVILLE, Harriet Elizabeth
(Cavendish) Leveson Gower, Countess

1827. GOWER, Hon. F. Leveson, ed.
see GRANVILLE, Harriet Elizabeth
(Cavendish) Leveson Gower,
Countess

1828. GOWER, Lady Francis Leveson
see ELLESMERE, Harriet Catherine
(Greville) Leveson Gower Egerton,
Countess of

1829. GOWER, Harriet Elizabeth
Georgiana Leveson, Duchess of
Sutherland see SUTHERLAND,
Harriet Elizabeth Georgiana
Leveson Gower, Duchess of

1830. GOWER, Henrietta Elizabeth
(Cavendish) Leveson, Countess
Granville see GRANVILLE, Harriet
Elizabeth (Cavendish) Leveson
Gower, Countess

1831. GOWER, Millicent Fanny (St.
Clair Erskine) Sutherland Leveson
see SUTHERLAND, Millicent Fanny
(St. Clair Erskine) Sutherland
Leveson Gower, Duchess of

1832. GOWER, Lord Ronald Charles
Sutherland Leveson, ed. see
SUTHERLAND, Harriet Elizabeth
Georgiana Leveson Gower, Duchess
of

1833. GRACE, Mrs. John see GRACE,
Mary

1834. GRACE, Mary, Mrs. John
Grace [Br. 19c]
Recollections of John Grace ...
together with ... letters by his
first wife (Mary Grace). Comp. N.
B. H.
L: Houlston & sons, 1893. 448p.
BL OCLC

1835. GRAHAM, Isabella (Marshall)
[Br. 1742-1814]
Letters of the late Mrs. Isabella
Graham ... in connection with
leading events of her life. Ed.
Rev. James Marshall.

Edinburgh: n.p., 1839. BL
[Contains letters previously pub.
by Joanna (Graham) Bethune;
family letters are added.]

1836. -----The power of faith:
exemplified in the life and
writings of Isabella Graham of
New York. [Comp.] Divie Bethune.
NY: J. Seymour, 1816. 411p. NUC
BL OCLC
[Includes devotional exercises,
poetry, letters, and addresses.
All religious in tone.]

1837. -----The unpublished
letters and correspondence of
Mrs. Isabella Graham, from the
year 1767 to 1814; exhibiting her
religious character in the
different relations of life.
Selected and arranged by her
daughter, Joanna (Graham)
Bethune.
NY: J. S. Taylor, 1838. 314p. NUC

1838. GRAHAM, Margaret [Br. 19c]
ALT: G., M.
An offering from St. Nicholas;
or, letters from abroad. By a
young lady. Ed. St. Nicholas.
L: n.p., 1834. BL
[Letters to "Anna" from M. G. who
is living in Germany.]

1839. GRAHAM, Maria (Dundas) see
CALLCOTT, Maria (Dundas) Graham,
Lady

1840. GRAHAM, Martha Morgan [Am.
b. 1825] ALT: Graham, Martha M.
Stout Morgan
An interesting life history of
Mrs. Martha M. Graham.
San Francisco: Women's
Cooperative Printing Union, 1875.
67p. NUC K OCLC
[Autobiography]

1841. GRAHAM, Martha M. Stout
Morgan see GRAHAM, Martha Morgan

1842. GRAHAM, Mary Jane [Br.
1803-1830]
Life and works of Miss Mary Jane
Graham, late of Stoke Fleming,
Devon. Ed. Rev. Charles Bridges.
NY: Robert Carter & bros., 1849.
326p. NUC OCLC
[Letters and religious essays.
From the 6th London edition.]

1843. -----A memoir of Miss Mary
Jane Graham, late of Stoke
Fleming, Devon. By Charles
Bridges.
Boston: Crocker & Brewster, 1834.
344p. NUC BL OCLC
[Extensive copies of her letters,
all on religion.]

1844. GRANE, Miss [Br. 19c] ALT:
G., Miss
Memoirs of Miss Grane, late of
Heathcote Street, Mecklenburgh
Square, illustrative of the
nature and effects of Christian
principles, compiled principally
from her own papers.
L: John Hatchard & son, 1819.
183p. BL

1845. GRANT, Anne (MacVicar) [Am.
1755-1838]
Letters from the mountains, being
the real correspondence of a lady
between the years 1773 and 1803.
L: Longman, Hurst, Rees & Orme,
1806. 3v. NUC BL
[Highlands of Scotland]

1846. -----Memoir and
correspondence of Mrs. Grant of
Laggan .... Ed. her son, J. P.
Grant, Esq.
L: Longman, Brown, Green &
Longman, 1844. 3v. NUC BL OCLC
[Letters, 1803-1838, written
during residence in Edinburgh.]

1847. -----Memoirs of an American
lady [Catalina E. Schuyler]: with
sketches of manners and scenery
in America, as they existed
previous to the revolution.
L: Longman, Hurst, Rees & Orme,
1808. 2v. NUC BL OCLC

1848. GRANT, Elizabeth see SMITH,
Elizabeth (Grant)

1849. GRANT, Emily Fredrica [Br.
19c]
"Looking unto Jesus"; a narrative
of the brief race of a young
disciple. By her mother, J. T. G.
[Judith Towers Grant].
L: J. Nisbet & co., 1865. 138p.
NUC BL
[Contains poetry and misc. prose.]

1850. GRANT, Genevieve Grahame (Jones), Mrs. George Rowswell Grant [Am. d. 1874]
Genevieve Grahame Grant.
Chicago: priv. pr. at the Lakeside press, 1895. 138p. NUC
[Travel essays describing Paris, Venice, Rome and Florence and social events.]

1851. GRANT, Mrs. George Rowswell Grant <u>see</u> GRANT, Genevieve Grahame

1852. GRANT, J. P. Esq., ed. <u>see</u> GRANT, Anne (MacVicar)

1853. GRANT, Jeannette A. [Am. 19c]
Miss Gray's girls; or, summer days in the Scottish Highlands.
Boston: J. Knight co., 1894; L: C. Page & co., c1893. 260p. NUC OCLC

1854. -----Through Evangeline's country.
Boston: Joseph Knight co., 1894. 100p. NUC OCLC
[Travel: Nova Scotia]

1855. GRANT, Judith Towers, comp. <u>see</u> GRANT, Emily Fredrica

1856. GRANT, L. Mrs., [Br. 19c]
Reminiscences of my tract district: a faithful account of four years' labour amongst brick-makers.
L: S. W. Partridge, 1863. 144p. BL

1857. GRANT, Mary Ann, Mrs. [19c]
Sketches of life and manners, with delineation of scenery in England, Scotland, and Ireland ... in original letters.
L: Cox, son, and Baylis, 1810. 2v. NUC OCLC

1858. GRANT, Minnie Caroline (Robinson), Mrs. W. Forsyth Grant [19c]
Scenes in Hawaii; or, life in the Sandwich Islands.
Toronto: Hart & co., 1888. 203p. NUC OCLC

1859. GRANT, Mrs. W. Forsyth <u>see</u> GRANT, Minnie Caroline (Robinson)

1860. GRANVILLE, Harriet Elizabeth (Cavendish) Leveson Gower, Countess [Br. 1785-1862]
ALT: Gower, Henrietta Elizabeth (Cavendish) Leveson, Countess Granville
Letters of Harriet Countess Granville, 1810-1845. Ed. her son, the Hon. [Edward] F[rederick] Leveson Gower.
L: Longmans & co., 1894. 2v. NUC BL OCLC

1861. GRASSIE, Olive L. [Am. b. 1827] PSEUD: Lewise
The city of the lakes: one woman's protest.
Chicago: Lakeside pr. & pub. co., 1821. 181p. NUC
[Guidebook to Madison, WI, character sketches of state leaders and personal opinions.]

1862. GRATIOT, Adèle Maria Antoinette (de Pedreauville) [Am. 1802-1873]
Mrs. Adèle P. Gratiot's narrative. Report and collections ... 1883-1885.
Madison, WI: Wisconsin State Historical Society, 1888. NUC
[Frontier life]

1863. GRAY, Edna, Mrs. [Am. 19c]
One woman's life. The steppings of faith, Edna Gray's story.
Atlanta, GA: The Franklin pr. & pub. co., 1898. 335p. NUC OCLC

1864. -----Thoughts when a sightless invalid: a story in verse of an eventful life.
Atlanta, GA: Mutual, 1898. 24p. NUC

1865. GRAY, Elizabeth Caroline (Johnstone) [Br. 1800-1887]
Tour to the sepulchres of Etruria, in 1839.
L: J. Hatchard & son, 1840. 507p. NUC BL OCLC

1866. GRAY, Fannie Barbour, Mrs. [Am. 19c]
Day in and day out; or, leaves from the record of 1877.
Louisville, KY: S. L. Ewing & co., 1879. 296p. NUC OCLC
[Diary]

1867. GRAY, Jonathan, comp. <u>see</u> GRAY, Margaret

1868. GRAY, Margaret [Br. 19c]
Some account of the personal
religion of M. Gray. Comp.
Jonathan Gray.
York: priv. pr., 1826. 112p. BL
[Letters and diary]

1869. GREATOREX, Eliza (Pratt),
Mrs. H. W. Greatorex [Am. 1819-
1897]
The homes of Ober-Ammergau. A
series of twenty etchings ...
together with notes from a diary
kept during a three months'
residence in Ober-Ammergau.
Munich: J. Albert, 1872. 44p. NUC
[Author's family lived with
German family.]

1870. -----Summer etchings in
Colorado.
NY: G. P. Putnam's sons, 1873.
96p. NUC BL

1871. GREATOREX, Mrs. H. W. see
GREATOREX, Eliza (Pratt)

1872. GREEN, Annie Maria V., Mrs.
[Am. 1835-1913]
Sixteen years on the great
American desert; or, the trials
and triumphs of a frontier life.
Titusville, PA: Frank W.
Truesdell, pr., 1887. 84p. NUC K
OCLC

1873. GREEN, Charles Ransley,
comp. see STONEBREAKER, Julia
(Peaslee)

1874. GREEN, Henrietta [Br. 1851-
1890]
A memoir. Printed for private
circulation.
Ashford, Kent: H. D. & B.
Headley, 1891. 237p. NUC OCLC
[Quaker missionary to China.
Excerpts from her letters
included.]

1875. GREEN, Lenamay [Am. 1869-
1952]
A girl's journey through Europe,
Egypt and the Holy Land.
Nashville, TN: pr. for the
author, Pub. House of the M. E.
Church South, 1889. 400p. NUC OCLC

1876. GREEN, Mary Anne Everett,
ed. see HENRIETTA MARIA, Queen
consort of Charles I

1877. GREEN, Rachel W. (Cope)
[Am. d. 1859]
Grace filling an earthen vessel
with glory; or, letters of Rachel
W. Green. Ed. W. R. Carroll.
Philadelphia: Protestant
Episcopal Book Society, 1860.
190p. NUC

1878. GREENE, Sister Mary Ignatia
[Am. 1821-1852]
Letters from Sister Mary Ignatia
to her own mother.
Boston: Peabody; Damrell & Moore,
1853. 83p. NUC OCLC

1879. GREENE, Martha (Coit)
Hubbard [Am. 1706-1784] ALT:
Coit, Martha
Martha, daughter of Mehetabel
Chandler Coit 1706-1784. By Marie
Petit Gilman, Emily Serena
Gilman, and L. G. Lane.
Norwich, CT: Bulletin Pr., 1895.
33p. NUC OCLC
[Contains letters between mother
and daughter.]

1880. GREENFIELD, M. Rose [Br. 19c]
Five years in Ludhiana; or, work
amongst our Indian sisters.
L: S. W. Partridge & co.;
Edinburgh: Religious Tract & Book
Society, 1886. 128p. NUC BL MB
OCLC
[Missionary work in Punjab]

1881. GREENHOW, Rose (O'Neal)
[Am. 1814-1864]
My imprisonment and the first
year of abolition rule at
Washington.
L: Richard Bentley, 1863. 352p.
NUC BL K OCLC

1882. GREENLEAF, Jane, Mrs. [Am.
1764-1851]
Memoir of Mrs. Jane Greenleaf, of
Newburyport, Mass. [Comp. her
daughter, Mary Coombs Greenleaf.]
Newburyport, MA: Moses. H.
Sargent, 1851. 177p. NUC OCLC
[2d ed. 1853, adds extensive
excerpts from her journals of
fifty years.]

1883. GREENLEAF, Mary Coombs,
Miss [Am. 1800-1857]
Life and letters of Miss Mary C.
Greenleaf, missionary to the
Chickasaw Indians....
Boston: Sabbath school society,
1858. 466p. NUC MAD OCLC
[Religious diary 1819-1837]

1884. GREENLEAF, Mary Coombs,
comp. see GREENLEAF, Jane

1885. GREENWELL, Dora see
GREENWELL, Dorothy

1886. GREENWELL, Dorothy [Br.
1821-1882] ALT: Greenwell, Dora
Colloquia Crucis. By Dora
Greenwell.
L: Strahan & co., 1871. 162p. NUC
OCLC
[A sequel to "Two friends".
Religious conversations with a
friend, Phillip]

1887. -----The soul's legend.
L: n.p., 1873. BL

1888. GREENWOOD, GRACE, pseud.
see LIPPINCOTT, Sara Jane
(Clarke)

1889. GREENWOOD, Mary [Br. 19c]
Passing strange.
n.p.: n.p., 1899. MB
[Member of Society of Friends;
mission work with sailors,
soldiers, dock workers.]

1890. GREER, Elizabeth [Br. 19c]
A selection from the memoranda
and letters of ... E. Greer.
Dublin: R. Chapman, 1872. 77p. BL
OCLC

1891. GREER, Sarah D. [Br. 19c]
Quakerism; or, the story of my
life.
Dublin: S. B. Oldham, 1851. 400p.
NUC BL MB OCLC

1892. GREGG, Mary (Kirby) [Br.
1817-1893] ALT: Kirby, Mary
"Leaflets from my life;" a
narrative autobiography.
L: Simpkin & Marshall, 1887.
244p. NUC BL MB OCLC

1893. GREGORY, Almira [Am. 19c]
Phases of the interior life! or,
a story of the heart, an
autobiography.
Ithaca, NY: Andrus, Gauntlett &
co., 1856. 192p. NUC OCLC

1894. GREGORY, Lucy [Br. 1803-
1876]
Leaning on her beloved, S. S.
viii.5; extracts from the diary
of Lucy Gregory.
Leominster: Orphans' Printing
Press, 1877. 101p. NUC MBD
[Quaker diary, 1829-1876]

1895. GREGORY, Hon. Victoria
Alexandrina Maria Louisa (Stuart
Wortley) Welby, Lady see WELBY-
GREGORY, Hon. Victoria
Alexandrina Maria Louisa (Stuart
Wortley), Lady

1896. GREGSON, Fanny see
LIESCHING, Fanny (Gregson)

1897. GREIG, John, ed. see
CAIRNS, Elizabeth

1898. GRENFELL, Lydia [Br. 19c]
Extracts from the religious diary
of Miss L. Grenfell. Ed. H. M.
Jeffery.
Falmouth: Lake & co., 1890. 142p.
BL MBD [Diary 1801-1821]

1899. GRENVILLE, Alice Anne
(Montgomery) Temple-Nugent
Brydges-Chandos, Countess Egerton
of Tatton see EGERTON OF TATTON,
Alice Anne (Montgomery) Temple-
Nugent Brydges-Chandos Grenville,
Countess

1900. GRETTON, G., Mrs. [Br. 19c]
The Englishwoman in Italy:
impressions of life in the Roman
states and Sardinia, during a ten
years' residence.
L: Hurst & Blackett, 1860. 2v. BL
NUC OCLC

1901. GREW, Harriet Catherine
[Am. 19c]
Memorials of a young Christian.
Philadelphia: pr. Merrihew &
Gunn, 1837. 106p. NUC OCLC
[Extracts from author's journal,
letters, and miscellanies.
Chiefly poetry.]

1902. GREY, Henry, co-author see
GREY, Mrs. Henry

1903. GREY, Mrs. Henry [Br. 19c]
Thoughts in the evening of life.
A sketch of the life of Rev.
Henry Grey, D.D., and passages
from the diary of Mrs. Grey. Ed.
The Rev. Charles Morton Birrell.
L: Religious Tract Society, 1871.
152p. NUC BL

1904. GREY, Lady Jane see DUDLEY,
Lady Jane (Grey)

1905. GREY, Maria Georgina
(Shirreff), comp. see SHIRREFF,
Emily Anne Eliza

1906. GREY, Maria Georgina
(Shirreff) see FOUCHÉ, Catherina
Therése Lovisa Fredrika Elisabeth
(von Stedingk) Grey, Duchesse
d'Otranto

1907. GREY, Mrs. William, comp.
see SHIRREFF, Emily Anne Eliza

1908. GREY, Hon. Mrs. William see
FOUCHÉ, Catherina Therése Lovisa
Fredrika Elisabeth (von Stedingk)
Grey, Duchesse d'Otranto

1909. GREY, Hon. Therése see
FOUCHÉ, Catherina Therése Lovisa
Fredrika Elisabeth (von Stedingk)
Grey, Duchesse d'Otranto

1910. GRIER, Christeen see GEIER,
Christeen

1911. GRIFFIN, Mary (Sands) [Am.
b. 1804] PSEUD: American Lady, An
Art Student; a narrative sketch
of old Nuremberg.
Dresden: n.p., 1870. NUC

1912. -----Impressions of
Germany, by an American lady ...
Dresden: B. G. Teubner, c1866.
451p. NUC

1913. -----Old facts and modern
incidents, supplementary to
impressions of Germany ... .
Dresden: C. Heinrich, 1868. 291p.
NUC OCLC

1914. -----Vagaries from the old
notebook of an American lady ...

Dresden: C. Heinrick, 1867. 292p.
NUC
[Account of residence in France
at Pau]

1915. GRIFFING, Jane R. [Am. 19c]
Letters from Florida on the
scenery, climate, social and
material conditions, and
practical advantages of the "Land
of flowers".
Lancaster, NH: Republican office,
1883. 122p. NUC BL OCLC

1916. GRIFFITH, Elizabeth
(Griffith) [Br. 1720?-1793]
A series of genuine letters
between Henry and Frances [i.e.
between Richard and Elizabeth
Griffith].
L: W. Johnston, 1757. 2v. NUC BL
OCLC
[Both a novel and selections from
correspondence.]

1917. GRIFFITH, Mrs. George Darby
see GRIFFITH, Lucinda Darby

1918. GRIFFITH, Lucinda Darby,
Mrs. George Darby Griffith [Br.
19c]
A journey across the desert, from
Ceylon to Marseilles, comprising
sketches of Aden, the Red Sea,
Lower Egypt, Malta, Sicily and
Italy.
L: H. Colburn, 1845. 2v. NUC BL
OCLC
[Illustrated by her husband,
Major G. D. Griffith]

1919. GRIFFITH, Mary, (Mrs.) [Am.
d. 1877]
Camperdown; or, news from our
neighborhood: being sketches.
Philadelphia: Carey, Lea &
Blanchard, 1836. 300p. NUC OCLC
[OCLC says Science fiction,
American]

1920. -----Our neighbourhood, or
letters on horticulture and
natural phenomena: interspersed
with opinions on domestic and
moral economy.
NY: E. Bliss, 1831. 332p. NUC OCLC

1921. GRIFFITH, Mattie [Am. 19c]
Autobiography of a female slave.
NY: NY Universities press, 1857.
401p. OCLC
[Slavery, personal narrative.]

1922. GRIFFITH, Richard, co-
author see GRIFFITH, Elizabeth
(Griffith)

1923. GRIFFITHS, Lydia [Br. 19c]
Lydia Griffiths and some
reminiscences of missionary life
in India. By a missionary's wife.
L: Hodder & Stoughton, 1885. 62p.
BL

1924. GRIMKÉ, Angelina Emily,
Mrs. Theodore Dwight Weld see
WELD, Angelina Emily (Grimké)

1925. GRIMKÉ, Sarah Moore see
WELD, Angelina Emily (Grimké)

1926. GRIMSTON, Dame Margaret
Shafto [Br. 1849-1935] ALT:
Kendal, Dame Madge
Dramatic opinions.
Boston: Little, Brown & co.,
1890. 180p. NUC MB OCLC
[BL has ed., 1925; contains
letters, reminiscences of
theatrical life.]

1927. GRIMWOOD, Ethel St. Clair
[Br. 19c]
My three years in Manipur, and
escape from the recent mutiny.
L: Bentley & son; Leipzig: B.
Tauchnitz, 1891. 278p. NUC BL MB
OCLC

1928. GRINDER, Martha [Am. 1832-
1866]
The life and confessions of
Martha Grinder, the poisoner.
Pittsburgh, PA: n.p., 1866. 23p.
NUC

1929. GRINNELL, Natalie B. [Am. 19c]
A Japanese journey.
NY: United States Book co., 1895.
112p. NUC OCLC

1930. GRISWOLD, Louise M.
(Roope), Mrs. Stephen M. Griswold
[Am. 19c]
A woman's pilgrimage to the Holy
Land; or, pleasant days abroad,
being notes of a tour through
Europe and the East.
Hartford, CT: J. B. Burr & Hyde,
1871. 423p. NUC OCLC

1931. GRISWOLD, Mrs. Stephen M.
see GRISWOLD, Louise M. (Roope)

1932. GROSE, Caroline Earle [Am.
19c]
Letters, miscellaneous pieces and
European journal.
Boston: George H. Ellis, 1888.
349p. NUC OCLC
[Contains some poetry. Travel:
Italy, 1861]

1933. GROSVENOR, Elizabeth Mary
(Leveson Gower), Marchioness of
Westminster see WESTMINSTER,
Elizabeth Mary (Leveson Gower)
Grosvenor, Marchioness of

1934. GROSVENOR, H. S., Mrs. [Am.
19c]
A sabbath in my early home.
Boston: n.p., 1850. 36p. NUC
[CHILDHOOD REMINISCENCES]

1935. GROSVENOR, Henrietta
(Vernon) Grosvenor, Countess [Br.
d. 1828] ALT: Porter, Henrietta
(Vernon) Grosvenor, Baroness de
Hochepied
The genuine ... letters which
passed between [Henry Frederick]
the Duke of Cumberland and Lady
Grosvenor.
L: n.p., 1770. NUC BL
[Evidence in a criminal
conversation action.]

1936. GROSVENOR, Lady Theodora
see GUEST, Lady Theodora (Grosvenor)

1937. GROTE, Harriet (Lewin) [Br.
1792-1878] ALT: G., H.
Some account of the hamlet of
East Burnham by a late resident.
L: pr. Savill & Edwards, 1858.
NUC BL

1938. GROTE, Mrs. Joseph, ed. see
GROTE, S. M., Mrs.

1939. GROTE, S. M., Mrs. [Br. 19c]
Letters from the late Mrs. G. ...
to her fourth son. Ed. Mrs.
Joseph Grote.
L: n.p., 1877. BL

1940. GROVE, Florence Craufurd [Br. d. 1902]
The frosty Caucasus: an account of a walk through part of the range and of an ascent of Elbruz in the summer of 1874.
L: Longmans, Green & co., 1875. 341p. NUC BL OCLC

1941. GROWN-UP, A, pseud. see ESCOMBE, Edith

1942. GRUBB, H., ed. see GRUBB, Sarah (Lynes)

1943. GRUBB, J., ed. see GRUBB, Sarah (Lynes)

1944. GRUBB, Sarah (Lynes) [Br. 1773-1842] ALT: Lynes, Sarah
Letters ... of Sarah (Lynes) Grubb. Ed. H. Grubb.
L: A. W. Bennett, 1864. 107p. NUC BL
[A selection from 1848 volume with a few unpublished letters added.]

1945. -----A selection from the letters of the late Sarah Grubb, formerly Sarah Lynes. Ed. J. & H. Grubb.
Sudbury: J. Wright, 1848. 451p. NUC BL

1946. GRUBB, Sarah (Tuke) [Am. 1756-1790]
Some account of the life and religious labors of Sarah Grubb, with an appendix continuing an account of and extracts from many of her letters.
Dublin: R. Jackson, 1792. 435p. NUC BL OCLC
[Minister of the Society of Friends]

1947. GUEDALLA, Hayyim, Mrs. [Br. 19c]
Diary of a tour to Jerusalem and Alexandria in 1855, with Sir Moses and Lady Montefiore.
L: Darling, 1890. 73p. NUC MBD

1948. GUERIN, Elsa Jane [Am. 19c]
Mountain Charley; or, the adventures of Mrs. E. J. Guerin, who was thirteen years in male attire.
Dubuque, IA: pub. for the author, 1861. 45p. NUC OCLC
[Autobiography]

1949. GUEST, Lady Theodora (Grosvenor) [Br. b. 1840] ALT: Grosvenor, Lady Theodora
A round trip in North America.
L: Edward Stanford, 1895. 270p. NUC BL OCLC

1950. GUILD, Anne Eliza (Gore), Mrs. James Guild [Am. 1826-1868] ALT: G., A. E.
A. E. G.
Cambridge, MA: n.p., 1869. 138p. NUC OCLC
[Contains excerpts of her letters and poetry.]

1951. GUILD, J. W., ed. see GORDON, Jane, Duchess of

1952. GUILD, Mrs. James see GUILD, Anne Eliza (Gore)

1953. GUINNESS, Geraldine see TAYLOR, Mary Geraldine (Taylor)

1954. GUINNESS, H. G., Mrs., ed. see FRY, Marie

1955. GUINNESS, Lucy Evangeline see KUMM, Lucy Evangeline (Guinness)

1956. GUINNESS, Lucy Evangeline, ed. see TAYLOR, Mary Geraldine (Guinness)

1957. GUNDRY, Maria [Br. 1814-1844]
Extracts from the letters and memoranda of Maria Gundry: with a short notice of a beloved elder sister [Martha Gundry, 1801-1846].
n.p.: pr. for priv. circ. by Cochrane, 1847. 74p. NUC BL OCLC

1958. GUNDRY, Martha see GUNDRY, Maria

1959. GUNN, Harriett (Turner) [Br. 1806-1869]
Letters written during a four-days tour in Holland, in the summer of 1834. Ed. Dawson Turner.
L: n.p., 1834.; Yarmouth?: priv. pr., 1834. 127p. NUC BL

1960. GUNNING, Susannah (Minifie)
[Br. 1740?-1800] ALT: Minifie,
Susannah
A letter from Mrs. Gunning,
addressed to His Grace the Duke
of Argyll.
Dublin: P. Wagan, 1791. 143p. NUC
OCLC
[Letter concerning the author's
daughter, Elizabeth (Gunning)
Plunkett [1769-1823], and the
letters supposedly written by
her, which the author claims were
actually forged by Captain and
Mrs. Bowen.]

1961. GURNEY, Eliza Paul
(Kirkbride) [Am. 1801-1881]
Memoir and correspondence of
Eliza P. Gurney. Ed. Richard F.
Mott.
Philadelphia: J. B. Lippincott &
co., 1884. 377p. NUC BL OCLC

1962. GURNEY, Mary (Gurney) [Am.
19c]
Mrs. Gurney's apology. In
justification of Mrs. ---'s
friendship.
Philadelphia: W. Brotherhead,
1860. 51p. NUC
[This is her explanation to her
childhood friend of elopement
with stable groom while married
to first cousin.]

1963. GURNEY, Priscilla Hannah
[Br. 1757-1828]
Memoir of the life and religious
experience of Priscilla Hannah
Gurney. Written by herself.
Bristol: J. Chilcott, 1834. 186p.
NUC MB
[Member of Society of Friends]

1964. GUTHRIE, Ellen Emma [Br.
1892-1888]
Retrospection. An exile's
memories of Skye.
Edinburgh: n.p., 1876. BL MB
[Memories in verse.]

1965. GUTHRIE, Kate see GUTHRIE,
Katherine Blanche

1966. GUTHRIE, Katherine Blanche,
Mrs. [Br. 19c] ALT: Guthrie, Kate
Life in western India.
L: Hurst & Blackett, 1881. 2v.
NUC BL MB OCLC

1967. -----My year in an Indian
fort.
L: Hurst & Blackett, 1877. 2v.
NUC BL MB OCLC

1968. -----Through Russia from
St. Petersburg to Astrakhan and
the Crimea.
L: Hurst & Blackett, 1874. 2v.
NUC BL OCLC

1969. GWATHMEY, Emmy Hendren [Am.
19c]
Unto two flags true: glimpses of
a child's experience during the
Civil War.
Norfolk, VA: Nusbaum book & news
co., 1899. 33p. NUC OCLC
[Memories of a Confederate girl
of the waning days of Richmond.]

1970. GWINNET, Richard, co-author
see THOMAS, Elizabeth

1971. H., A. M. see HOPTON, Anna
Maria

1972. H., C. see HART, Christian,
Mrs.

1973. H., E. see HUTCHINSON,
Elizabeth

1974. H., E. S. J. see HUNT,
Ellen Saint John

1975. H., H. see JACKSON, Helen
Maria (Fiske) Hunt

1976. H., L. see HILLS, Lydia

1977. H., M. see HAMILTON, Maria

1978. H., M. see HARRISS, Matilda

1979. H., M. W. see HOWIE, Mary
Wright

1980. H., R. F. see HILL, Rosa F.

1981. HAGERTY, Josephine, comp.
see COMERFORD, Rev. Mother Mary
Teresa

1982. HAGGER, Mary (Knight) [Br.
c1758-1840]
Extracts from the memoranda of
Mary Hagger, Ashford, Kent.
L: Harvey & Darton, 1841. 108p.
NUC BL MBD OCLC
[Member of Society of Friends;
diary 1814-1839]

1983. HAGUE, Parthenia Antoinette
(Vardaman) [Am. b. 1838]
A blockaded family: life in
southern Alabama during the Civil
War.
Boston & NY: Houghton, Mifflin,
1888. 176p. NUC BL K

1984. HAIGHT, Sarah (Rogers) [Am.
19c] PSEUD: Lady of New York, A
Letters from the old world. By a
lady of New York.
NY: Harper & bros, 1840. 2v. NUC
BL OCLC
[Travel: Levant]

1985. -----Over the ocean; or,
glimpses of travel in many lands.
NY: Paine & Burgess, 1846. 238p.
NUC BL OCLC

1986. HAINES, L. (Brown) [Am. b.
1824]
Life sketches and poems.
Minneapolis, MN: n.p., 1894.
235p. NUC OCLC
[Daughter of Maine sea captain,
autobiography and poetry.]

1987. HALDANE, Julia [Br. 19c]
The story of our escape from
Delhi, in 1857.
Agra: S. Brown & sons, 1888. 26p.
BL

1988. HALE, Rev. Edward Everett,
co-author see HALE, Susan

1989. HALE, Susan [Am. 1833-1910]
A family flight around home. With
Rev. Edward Everett Hale.
Boston: D. Lothrop & co., 1884.
NUC OCLC

1990. -----A family flight over
Egypt and Syria. With Rev. Edward
Everett Hale.
Boston: D. Lothrop & co., 1882.
387p. NUC OCLC

1991. -----A family flight
through France, Germany, Norway
and Switzerland. With Rev. Edward
Everett Hale.
Boston: D. Lothrop & co., 1881.
NUC OCLC

1992. -----A family flight
through Mexico. With Rev. Edward
Everett Hale.
Boston: D. Lothrop & co., 1886.
301p. NUC BL OCLC

1993. -----A family flight
through Spain.
Boston: D. Lothrop & co., [1883].
360p. NUC OCLC

1994. HALKETT, Anna see HALKETT,
Anne (Murray)

1995. HALKETT, Anne [BL: Anna]
(Murray), Lady [Br. 1632-1699]
The autobiography of Anne, Lady
Halkett. Ed. John Gough Nichols.
L: Camden Society, 1875. 118p.
NUC BL MB OCLC

1996. HALL, Adelaide Susan, Mrs.
[Am. b. 1857]
Two women abroad. What they saw
and how they lived while
travelling among the semi-
civilized people of Morocco, the
peasants of Italy and France, as
well as the educated classes of
Spain, Greece and other
countries.
Philadelphia; Chicago: Monarch
book co., 1897. 510p. NUC OCLC
[Also pub. as: Two travelers in
Europe]

1997. HALL, ALMIRA, pseud., co-
author see MUNSON, Rachel (Hall)

1998. HALL, Anna Maria
(Fielding), Mrs. Samuel Carter
Hall [Br. 1800-1881]
Ireland: its scenery, character,
etc. With Samuel Carter Hall.
L: How & Parsons, 1841-43. 3v.
NUC BL OCLC

1999. -----Pilgrimages to English
shrines.
L: A. Hall, Virtue & co., 1850.
294p. NUC BL OCLC
[A "2d series" appeared in 1853.]

2000. -----Tenby. With Samuel
Carter Hall.
Tenby: n.p., 1860. BL

2001. -----A week at Killarney.
With Samuel Carter Hall.
L: J. How, 1843. 208p. BL OCLC

2002. HALL, Arethusa [Am. 1802-
1891]
Arethusa Hall. A memorial ....
Ed. Frances E. Abbott.
Cambridge, MA: J. Wilson & son,
1892. 167p. NUC K OCLC
[Includes autobiography, excerpts
from notebooks, journals, letters]

2003. HALL, B. S., Mrs., comp.
see WILDER, Lucy

2004. HALL, Mrs. Cecil see HALL,
Mary Georgina Caroline

2005. HALL, Charlotte (Gordon),
Mrs. Newman Hall [Br. 19c]
Through the Tyrol to Venice.
L: J. Nisbet & co., 1860. 388p. NUC

2006. HALL, Mrs. E. B. see HALL,
Louisa Jane (Park)

2007. HALL, Elizabeth (Smith)
[Am. 19c]
Family reminiscences for private
circulation.
Ravenna, OH: pr. for the author,
1874. 30p. NUC

2008. HALL, Fanny W. [Am. 19c]
Rambles in Europe: or, a tour
through France, Italy,
Switzerland, Great Britain and
Ireland in 1836.
NY: E. French, 1839. 2v. NUC OCLC

2009. HALL, FRANCES, pseud. see
MUNSON, Rachel (Hall)

2010. HALL, Frances, Mrs. [Am.
19c]
Major Hall's wife.
Syracuse, NY: Weed & co., 1884.
47p. NUC
[Personal account of Civil War]

2011. HALL, Harrison, ed. see
HALL, Sarah (Ewing)

2012. HALL, Henrietta see SHUCK,
Henrietta (Hall)

2013. HALL, Louisa Jane (Park),
Mrs. E. B. Hall [Am. 1802-1892]
ALT: Park, Louisa Jane
My thimbles: a story from the
"Child's friend".
Boston: Crosby, Nichols, & co.,
1852. 35p. NUC BL
[Recollections of charitable
work.]

2014. HALL, Mary Georgina
Caroline, Mrs. Cecil Hall [Br.
19c]
A lady's life on a farm in
Manitoba.
L: W. H. Allen & co., 1884. 171p.
NUC BL MC OCLC

2015. HALL, Mrs. Newman see HALL,
Charlotte (Gordon)

2016. HALL, Samuel Carter, co-
author see HALL, Anna Maria
(Fielding)

2017. HALL, Mrs. Samuel Carter
see HALL, Anna Maria (Fielding)

2018. HALL, Sarah (Ewing) [Am.
1761-1830]
Selections from the writings of
Mrs. Sarah Hall, with a memoir of
her life. Ed. her son, Harrison
Hall.
Philadelphia: H. Hall, 1833. NUC
BL OCLC
[Poetry & prose.]

2019. HALLETT, Emma V., Miss [Am.
19c] PSEUD: Vale, Ferna
Tuckernuck. A story of Nantucket
and the Coffin family.
Hartford, CT: Plimpton pr., 1882.
28p. NUC
[Romanticized family history]

2020. HALLIDAY, Anna R. [Am. 19c]
Golden wedding, 1819 and 1869.
Syracuse, NY: n.p., 1869. 27p. NUC
[May contain personal material.]

2021. HALLOWELL, Anna Davis, ed.
see MOTT, Lucretia (Coffin)

2022. HALSEY, Calista (Patchin)
[Am. 19c]
Two of us.
NY: Carleton, 1879. 217p. NUC
[Fictionalized, but appears based
on personal experiences.]

2023. HAMER, Margaret see
Andrewes, Margaret (Hamer)

2024. HAMER, Sarah Sharp (Heaton)
[Br. 1839-1927] PSEUD: Patch,
Olive
Sunny Spain: its people and
places, with glimpses of its
history. Pub. as: Olive Patch
L & NY: Cassell & co., 1884.
316p. NUC BL

2025. HAMILTON, Lady Anne [Br.
1766-1846]
Private memoirs of the reigns of
George III and IV.
L: J. Phillips, 1832. NUC
[NUC: listed under title, attr.
to Lady Anne Hamilton. About
American Revolution.]

2026. HAMILTON, Mrs. Cospatrick
Baillie [Br. 19c]
Views in the Mediterranean,
Grecian archipelago, Bosphorus,
Black Sea, etc.
L: Day & son, 1857. 12p. NUC

2027. HAMILTON, Elizabeth [Br.
1758-1816]
Memoirs of the late Mrs.
Elizabeth Hamilton, with a
selection from her correspondence
and other unpublished writings.
Ed. Elizabeth Ogilvy Benger.
L: Longmans & co., 1818. 2v. NUC
BL OCLC

2028. HAMILTON, Emma (Lyon), Lady
[Br. 1761-1815]
Memoirs of Lady Hamilton.
L: Henry Colburn, 1815. 399p.;
Philadelphia: Moses Thomas, J.
Maxwell, pr., 1815. 194p. NUC BL
OCLC

2029. HAMILTON, GAIL, pseud. see
DODGE, Mary Abigail

2030. HAMILTON, James, comp. see
COLQUHOUN, Janet Sinclair, Lady

2031. HAMILTON, Janet see GORDON,
Janet Hamilton

2032. HAMILTON, Lady Margaret
(Cuninghame) see MAXWELL, Lady
Margaret (Cuninghame) Hamilton

2033. HAMILTON, Maria [Br. 19c]
ALT: H., M.
Narrative of the life of M. H.
Bristol: n.p., 1833. BL MB

2034. HAMILTON, Sarah, Miss [Br.
19c] PSEUD: Resident of Sherwood
Forest, A
Sonnets, tour to Matlock,
recollections of Scotland, and
other poems. By a resident of
Sherwood Forest.
L: J. Mawman, 1825. 260p. BL

2035. HAMILTON, Sarah Beckhouse
[Am. 1745-1806]
A narrative of the life of Mrs.
Hamilton. Written by herself.
Boston: E. Lincoln, 1803. 12p.
NUC BL K OCLC

2036. HAMILTON, Mrs. William
Meadows see ROMER, Isabella Frances

2037. HAMLIN, Harriet Martha
(Lovell), co-author see EVERETT,
Seraphina Haynes

2038. HAMLIN, Henriette Anne
Louise (Jackson) [Am. 1811-1858]
Light on the dark river; or,
memorials of Mrs. H. A. L.
Hamlin, missionary in Turkey. By
Margarette Oliver (Woods)
Lawrence.
Boston: Ticknor, Reed & Fields,
1854. 321p. NUC BL OCLC
[Biog. with many quoted letters.]

2039. HAMLINE, Melinda, Mrs., ed.
see SEARS, Angeline (Brooks)

2040. HAMM, Margherita Arlina
[Am. 1871-1907]
America's new possessions and
spheres of influence.
L: F. T. Neely, 1890. 280p. NUC
OCLC
[Based on her travel, largely
descriptive.]

2041. -----Manila and the
Philippines.
L & NY: F. Tennyson Neely, 1898.
218p. NUC OCLC

2042. -----Porto Rico and the
West Indies.
L & NY: F. T. Neely, 1899. 230p.
NUC BL OCLC

2043. HAMMOND, Mrs. John Hays see HAMMOND, Natalie (Harris)

2044. HAMMOND, Louisa, comp. see PARRY, Catherine Edwards

2045. HAMMOND, Mary Crowninshield (Warren), Mrs. Samuel Hammond [Am. 19c]
Letters from a little girl in Paris, written in 1852.
Boston: priv. pr., 1892. 75p. NUC OCLC
[Includes poetry]

2046. HAMMOND, Natalie (Harris), Mrs. John Hays Hammond [Br. d. 1931]
A woman's part in a revolution.
NY & L: Longmans Green & co., 1897. 159p. NUC BL OCLC
[Diary 1895-1896 dealing chiefly with the Jameson raids in Johannesburg, 1896]

2047. HAMMOND, Mrs. P., comp. see PARRY, Catherine Edwards

2048. HAMMOND, Phebe Parsons [Am. 1817-1829]
Memoir of Phebe P. Hammond, a pupil in the American Asylum at Hartford. [By] Lydia Howard (Huntley) Sigourney.
Hartford, CT: D. F. Robinson, 1833. 126p.; NY: Sleight & Van Norden, pr., 1833. 20p. NUC

2049. HAMMOND, Mrs. Samuel see HAMMOND, Mary Crowninshield (Warren)

2050. HANAFORD, Phebe Ann (Coffin) [Am. 19c]
The heart of Siasconset.
New Haven, CT: Hoggson & Robinson, pr., 1890. 180p. NUC
[Nantucket]

2051. HANKIN, Christine C., ed. see SCHIMMELPENNICK, Mary Anne (Galton)

2052. HANNAH, Rev. John, ed. see HILL, Sarah

2053. HANSON, Elizabeth, Mrs. John Hanson [Am. fl. 1703-1741]
God's mercy surmounting man's cruelty, exemplified in the captivity and redemption of Elizabeth Hanson, wife of John Hanson, of Knoxmarsh at Keacheachy, in Dover township, who was taken captive with her children and maid-servant, by the Indians in New England, in the year 1724.
NY: Keimer & Heurtin, 1728. 40p. NUC OCLC
[Account dictated to Samuel C. Bownas.]

2054. HANSON, Emma (Cole) [Am. 19c] ALT: Cole, Emma
The life and sufferings of Miss Emma Cole, being a faithful narrative of her life. Written by herself.
Boston: M. Aurelius, 1844. 36p. NUC BL K OCLC

2055. HANSON, Mrs. John see HANSON, Elizabeth

2056. HANWAY, Mary Anne [Br. 18/19c] PSEUD: Lady, A
A journey to the Highlands of Scotland with occasional remarks on Dr. Johnson's tour: by a lady.
L: Fielding & Walker, 1776. 163p. NUC BL OCLC
[Letters to various persons. Pub. anon.]

2057. HAPGOOD, Isabel Florence [Am. 1850-1928]
Russian rambles.
Boston & NY: Houghton, Mifflin & co.,; L: Longmans & co., 1895. 369p. NUC BL OCLC

2058. HARBISON, Mrs. J. see HARBISON, Massy (White)

2059. HARBISON, Massy (White), Mrs. J. Harbison [Am. b. 1770]
A narrative of sufferings of Mary Harbison from Indian barbarity, communicated by herself. Ed. J. Winter.
Pittsburgh, PA: E. Engles, 1825. 66p. NUC BL OCLC
[Captive in Allegheny River area, 1790-94]

2060. HARCOURT, Anne, Lady [Br. 1603?-1642]
The Harcourt Papers. Ed. Edward W. Harcourt.

Oxford: For priv. circ. by J.
Parker & co., 1880. MBD OCLC
[Extracts of her diary, 1649-1661
are included in v. I.]

2061. HARCOURT, Edward, ed. see
HARCOURT, Anne, Lady

2062. HARCOURT, Elizabeth
Harcourt, Countess [Br. 18c]
Harcourt's diary of the court of
King George III.
Biographical and historical
miscellanies. Vol. 13.
L: Philobiblian Society, 1871-72.
57p. BL

2063. HARCOURT, HELEN, pseud. see
WARNER, Helen Garvie

2064. HARD, Julia Taylor, comp.
see SEYMOUR, Juno (Waller)

2065. HARDCASTLE, Mrs., comp. see
HARDCASTLE, Eliza Mary

2066. HARDCASTLE, Eliza Mary [Br.
19c]
Memoir of a beloved daughter. By
a mother, [Mrs. Hardcastle].
Leeds: pr. for the author, 1834.
144p. BL
[Contains hymns and poems.]

2067. HARDIN, Charles Henry, co-
author see HARDIN, Mary Barr
(Jenkins)

2068. HARDIN, Mrs. Charles Henry
see HARDIN, Mary Barr (Jenkins)

2069. HARDIN, Mary Barr
(Jenkins), Mrs. Charles Henry
Hardin [Am. b. 1824]
Life and writings of Governor
Charles Henry Hardin. By his
wife. A life sketch of Mrs. C. H.
Hardin by Wiley J. Patrick.
St. Louis, MO: Buschart bros.,
pr., 1896. 316p. NUC OCLC
[Includes 2 poems and 1 letter by
her.]

2070. HARDINGE, Belle (Boyd) see
BOYD, Belle

2071. HARDWICKE, Susan (Liddell)
Yorke, Countess of, co-author see
NORMANBY, Maria (Liddell) Phipps,
Marchioness of

2072. HARDY, Iza Duffus [Br.
19/20c]
Between two oceans; or, sketches
of American travel.
L: Chapman and Hall, 1873. 2v.
NUC BL OCLC

2073. -----Oranges and
alligators: sketches of south
Florida life.
L: Ward & Downey, 1886. 240p. NUC
BL OCLC

2074. HARDY, Mary Anne (McDowell)
Duffus, Lady [Br. 1825?-1891]
Down south.
L: Chapman & Hall, 1883. 276p.
NUC BL N OCLC [Travel: U.S.]

2075. -----Through cities and
prairie lands, sketches of an
American tour.
NY: R. Worthington, 1881. 338p.
L: Chapman & Hall, 1881. 320p.
NUC BL N OCLC
[Travel: U.S. & Canada]

2076. HARE, Augustus John
Cuthbert, comp. see BUNSEN,
Frances (Waddington) von,
Baroness

2077. HARE, Augustus John
Cuthbert, comp. see EDGEWORTH,
Maria

2078. HARE, Augustus John
Cuthbert, ed. see EDGEWORTH, Maria

2079. HARE, C., comp. see
COMSTOCK, Elizabeth L. (Rous)
Wright

2080. HARLAND, MARION, pseud. see
TERHUNE, Mary Virginia (Hawes)

2081. HARLEY, Lady Brilliana
(Conway) [Br. 1600?-1643]
Letters of the Lady Brilliana
Harley.
L: Camden Society, 1854. 275p.
NUC BL OCLC

2082. HARMON, Marion Flower Hicks
[Am. 19c]
One woman wandering; or, Europe
on limited means.
Cincinnati, OH: The Editor pub.
co., 1899. 333p. NUC OCLC

2083. HARNESS, William, comp. see
MITFORD, Mary Russell

2084. HARPER, Elizabeth (Tuck)
[Br. 1734-1768]
An extract from the journal of
Elizabeth Harper.
L: n.p., 1769. 47p. NUC BL MBD
[Methodist]

2085. HARPER, Harriet [Am. 19c]
Letters from California.
Portland, ME: Press of B.
Thurston & co., 1888. 104p. NUC

2086. HARPER, Lizzie (St. John)
[Br. 1837-1916-17] ALT: Eckel, L.
St. John, Mrs.
Maria Monk's daughter; an
autobiography. By Mrs. L. St.
John Eckel.
NY: pub. for author by U.S. pub.
co., 1874. 604p. NUC
[Fictionalized account of her
mother, Maria Monk [d. c1850].
Roman Catholic apologia.]

2087. HARRINGTON, Adelaide L.
[Am. 19c]
The afterglow of European travel.
Boston: D. Lothrop, 1882. 295p.
NUC OCLC

2088. HARRIS, Mrs. see HORN,
Sarah Ann

2089. HARRIS, Caroline, Mrs.
Richard Harris [Am. 19c]
History of the captivity and
providential release therefrom of
Mrs. Caroline Harris, wife of the
late Mr. Richard Harris, of
Franklin Co., state of N. York,
who, with Mrs. Clarissa Plummer,
wife of Mr. James Plummer, were,
in the spring of 1835, (with
their unfortunate husbands,)
taken prisoners by the Comanche
tribe of Indians.
NY: G. Cunningham, 1838. 23p. NUC
OCLC

2090. HARRIS, Emily Marion see
ALLAN-OLNEY, Mary

2091. HARRIS, G., Mrs. James P.
Harris [Br. 19c]
A lady's diary of the siege of
Lucknow.
L: J. Murray, 1858. 208p. NUC BL
MB OCLC

2092. HARRIS, Helen (Balkwill)
[Br. 19c]
Letters from the scenes of the
recent massacres in Armenia. With
James Rendel Harris.
NY & Chicago: Fleming R. Revell
co.; L: James Nisbet & co., 1897.
254p. NUC BL OCLC
[Christian missionaries]

2093. -----Pictures of the East:
sketches of biblical scenes in
Palestine and Greece.
L: J. Nisbet & co., 1897. 77p.
NUC BL OCLC

2094. HARRIS, Isabella (Tindall)
[Br. 1791-1868]
Family memorials: chiefly the
memoranda left by Isabella
Harris. With some extracts from
the journal of her mother,
[Isabella (Mackiver) Tindall,
1761-1836], etc. Ed. M. A. Harris.
Leighton Buzzard: priv. pr.; L:
pr., R. Barrett & sons, 1869.
291p. NUC MBD
[Religious Society of Friends;
diary 1808-1868]

2095. HARRIS, Mrs. James P. see
HARRIS, G.

2096. HARRIS, James Rendel, co-
author see HARRIS, Helen
(Balkwill)

2097. HARRIS, Louisa, Mrs. [Am.
19c]
Behind the scenes; or, nine years
at the four courts of Saint
Louis. By Mrs. Louisa Harris,
police matron. Ed. Major C. A.
Bateman.
St. Louis, MO: A. R. Fleming,
1893. 220p. NUC K OCLC

2098. HARRIS, Lucy Hamilton [Am.
19c]
Each day's doings; or, a trip to
Europe in the summer of 1875.
Albany, NY: Weed, Parsons & co.,
1875?. 123p. NUC

2099. HARRIS, M. A., ed. see
HARRIS, Isabella (Tindall)

2100. HARRIS, Maria Welch [Am.
1833-1905]

United States girls across the
Atlantic.
Homer, NY: n.p., 1876. 204p. NUC
OCLC

2101. HARRIS, Miriam (Coles),
Mrs. Sidney S. Harris [Am. 1834-
1925]
A corner of Spain.
Boston & NY: Houghton, Mifflin &
co., 1898. 195p. NUC OCLC

2102. HARRIS, Mrs. Richard <u>see</u>
HARRIS, Caroline

2103. HARRIS, Mrs. Sidney S. <u>see</u>
HARRIS, Miriam (Coles)

2104. HARRISON, Alexina (Mackay)
<u>see</u> RUTHQUIST, Alexina (Mackay)

2105. HARRISON, Ann [Br. 19c]
Memoranda of the late Ann
Harrison, of Weston.
Sheffield: priv. pr., 1859. BL

2106. HARRISON, Mrs. J. W., ed.
<u>see</u> RUTHQUIST, Alexina (Mackay)

2107. HARRISS, Matilda, Miss [Br.
19c] ALT: H., M.
A glimpse of glory, being an
account of a remarkable vision,
by Miss M. H. ... with a sketch
of her life.
L: n.p., 1872. BL

2108. HART, Miss [Am. 19c]
Letters from the Bahama Islands.
Written in 1823-4. Pub. anon.
Philadelphia: H. C. Carey & I.
Lea, 1827. 207p. NUC BL OCLC

2109. HART, Mrs. Alfred <u>see</u> HART,
Dora

2110. HART, Alice Marion
(Rowlands), Mrs. Ernest Hart
[19c]
Picturesque Burma, past &
present. 1897.
L & Philadelphia: J. M. Dent,
1897. 400p. NUC BL OCLC

2111. HART, Christian, Mrs. [Br.
18c] ALT: H., C.
A letter from Mrs. C- H- to Mrs.
Margaret Caroline Rudd
elucidating several circumstances
which did not appear on the
trial, refuting particular
falsities ... asserted by that
... lady, and relating ... her
transactions during the time Mrs.
H. lived servant with her.
L: J. Williams, 1776. 70p. NUC BL

2112. HART, Dora, Mrs. Alfred
Hart [Br. 19c]
Tahiti, the garden of the
Pacific.
L: T. F. Unwin, 1891. 352p. NUC
BL OCLC

2113. -----Via Nicaragua. A
sketch of travel. By Mrs. Alfred
Hart.
L: Remington & co., 1887. 267p.
NUC BL OCLC
[Travel: California and Nicaragua]

2114. HART, Mrs. Ernest <u>see</u> HART,
Alice Marion (Rowland)

2115. HARVARD, Elizabeth, Mrs.
William Martin Harvard [19c]
Memoirs of Mrs. Elizabeth
Harvard, late of the Wesleyan
Mission to Ceylon and India; with
extracts from her diary and
correspondence. Comp. William
Martin Harvard.
2d ed. L: the author, 1825. 135p.
NUC BL

2116. HARVARD, William Martin,
comp. <u>see</u> HARVARD, Elizabeth

2117. HARVARD, Mrs. William
Martin <u>see</u> HARVARD, Elizabeth

2118. HARVEY, Annie Jane
(Tennant) [Br. d. 1898]
Cositas españoles; or, everyday
life in Spain.
L: Hurst & Blackett, 1875. NUC BL

2119. -----Our cruise in the
Claymore, with a visit to
Damascus and the Lebanon.
L: Chapman & Hall, 1861. 309p.
NUC BL OCLC

2120. -----Turkish harems and
Circassian homes.
L: Hurst & Blackett, 1871. 307p.
NUC BL OCLC
[Travel: Russia, the Crimea]

2121. HARVEY, Jane [Br. 18/19c]
A sentimental tour through
Newcastle, by a young lady.
Newcastle: pr., D. Akenhead,
1794. NUC BL

2122. HARVEY, Jane [Br. 19c]
Memoirs of an author.
Gainsborough: Henry Mozley, 1812.
3v. NUC
[May be fictional.]

2123. HASAN, Ali, Mir., Mrs. [Br.
19c]
Observations on the Mussulmauns
of India: descriptive of their
manners, customs, habits, and
religious opinions. Made during a
twelve years' residence in their
immediate society.
L: Parbury, Allen & co., 1832.
2v. BL OCLC

2124. HASKELL, Rebecca M., comp.
see MAC LELLAN, Frances E. H.

2125. HASLEHURST, May A. [Am.
19c]
Days forever flown.
NY: priv. pr., 1892. 401p. NUC
OCLC
[Travel: U.S., Alaska]

2126. HASLEWOOD, Frances C. [Br.
19c]
Poetry and fragments of
correspondence.
L: W. Skeffington & son, 1878.
71p. NUC BL

2127. -----Two letters on serious
subjects.
L: n.p., 1879. 18p. NUC

2128. HASSAL, Mary [Am. 19c]
Secret history; or, the horrors
of St. Domingo, in a series of
letters written by a lady at Cape
Francois, to Colonel Burr, late
Vice-President of the United
States, principally during the
command of General Rochambeau.
Philadelphia: Bradford & Inskeep,
1808. 255p. NUC OCLC
[Eye witness account of massacre
of whites by black revolutionists
in Haiti, 1791-1804.
Traditionally attr. Hassal, but
OCLC attr. Leonora Sansay.]

2129. HASTINGS, Clara L. [Am. 19c]
Notes from my diary.
San Francisco: Towne & Bacon,
pr., 1868. 72p. NUC OCLC
[Travel: Europe]

2130. HASTINGS, Lady Elizabeth
see GILBERT, Mary

2131. HASTINGS, Lady Flora
Elizabeth Rawdon [Br. 1806-1839]
The victim of scandal. Memoir of
Lady Flora Hastings, with the
statement of the Marquess of
Hastings, entire correspondence,
and a portrait.
Glasgow: D. Campbell, 1839. 47p.
NUC BL

2132. HASTINGS, George Augustus
Rawdon-Hastings, Marquis of, co-
author see HASTINGS, Lady Flora
Elizabeth Rawdon

2133. HASTINGS, Rosetta (Butler)
[Am. 1844-1934]
Personal recollections of Pardee
Butler, with reminiscences by his
daughter.
Cincinnati, OH: Standard pub.
co., 1889. NUC BL OCLC
[Kansas history]

2134. HASTINGS, Sally see
HASTINGS, Sarah (Anderson)

2135. HASTINGS, Sarah (Anderson)
[Am. 1773-1812] ALT: Hastings,
Sally
Poems on different subjects. To
which is added a descriptive
account of a family tour to the
West, in the year 1800, in a
letter to a lady. By Sally
Hastings.
Lancaster, PA: W. Dickson for the
authoress, 1808. 220p. NUC OCLC
[Travel: Pennsylvania]

2136. HASTINGS, Susannah
(Willard) Johnson [Am. 1730-1810]
ALT: Johnson, Susanna (Willard)
A narrative of the captivity of
Mrs. Johnson ... during four
years with the Indians and
French.
Walpole, NH: D. Carlisle, 1796.
144p. NUC BL OCLC

2137. HATFIELD, S., Miss [Br. 19c]
The terra incognita of
Lincolnshire; with observations,
moral, descriptive and historical
in original letters written ...
1815.
L: pr. for G. of S. Robinson, &
Gale & Fenner, 1816. 144p. NUC BL

2138. HATHAWAY, Edwin L., co-
author see HATHAWAY, Lucretia L.
(Russell)

2139. HATHAWAY, Mrs. Edwin L. see
HATHAWAY, Lucretia A. (Russell)

2140. HATHAWAY, Lucretia A.
(Russell), Mrs. Edwin L. Hathaway
[Am. b. 1816] ALT: Russell,
Lucretia A.
An interesting narrative of
facts; or, a correspondence of
three years ... between Edwin L.
Hathaway ... and Lucretia A.
Russell.
Cleveland, OH: the author, 1841.
NUC

2141. HATHAWAY, Mary Botsford see
HATHAWAY, Mrs. William, Jr.

2142. HATHAWAY, Thomas see
HATHAWAY, Mrs. William, Jr.

2143. HATHAWAY, Mrs. Williams,
Jr. [Am. 19c]
A narrative of Thomas Hathaway
and his family, ... with
incidents in the life of Jemina
Wilkinson [Quaker evangelists,
1752-1819], and the times in
which they lived.
New Bedford, MA: E. Anthony &
sons, pr., 1869. 43p. NUC
[Incl. recollections of Mary
Botsford Hathaway, 1772-1866,
pioneer in upstate New York.]

2144. HATTON, Augusta, Miss [Br.
19c]
Early piety, illustrated in the
brief memoir and journal of a
youthful member of the
congregation of St. James's
Chapel, Edinburgh. Ed. Daniel
Bagot.
Edinburgh: n.p., 1840. BL

2145. HAUSER, Mrs. I. L. see
HAUSER, Jeanette L.

2146. HAUSER, Jeanette L., Mrs.
I. L. Hauser [Am. 19c]
The Orient and its people.
Milwaukee, WI: I. L. Hauser &
co., 1876. 335p. NUC BL OCLC
[Travel: India and China]

2147. HAVERGAL, Frances Ridley
[Br. 1836-1879]
Letters by the late F. R.
Havergal. Ed. her sister, Maria
Vernon Graham Havergal.
L: J. Nisbet & co.; NY: A. D. F.
Randolph & co., 1885. 348p. NUC
BL OCLC

2148. -----Memorials of Frances
Ridley Havergal. By her sister,
Maria Vernon Graham Havergal.
L: J. Nisbet & co., 1880. 391p.
NUC BL MB OCLC
[Includes autobiography; life in
Germany. Taken mostly from her
letters.]

2149. -----Swiss letters and
Alpine poems. Ed. her sister,
Jane Miriam (Havergal) Crane.
L: J. Nisbet & co., 1881. 356p.
NUC BL OCLC

2150. HAVERGAL, Maria Vernon
Graham [Br. 1821-1887]
The autobiography of Maria Vernon
Graham Havergal, with journals
and letters. Ed. Jane Miriam
(Havergal) Crane.
L: J. Nisbet & co., 236p.; NY: A.
D. F. Randolph, 1887. 336p. NUC
BL MB OCLC

2151. HAVERGAL, Maria Vernon
Graham, ed. see HAVERGAL, Frances
Ridley

2152. HAVERGAL, Maria Vernon
Graham, ed. see SHAW, Ellen
Prestage (Havergal)

2153. HAVILAND, Laura (Smith)
[Am. 1808-1898]
A woman's life work: including
thirty years' service on the
underground railroad and in the
war.
5th ed. Grand Rapids, MI: S. B.
Shaw, 1881. 624p. NUC BL K
[Date of 1st ed. unknown; K lists
3d ed. as 1887; BL has 1882 ed.]

2154. HAWES, A. H., Mrs., comp.
see HAWES, Angelica Irene

2155. HAWES, Angelica Irene [Am.
1844-1851]
The grafted bud; a memoir of
Angelica Irene Hawes. By Mrs. A.
H. Hawes.
NY: Redfield, 1853. 102p. NUC BL
OCLC

2156. HAWES, Mrs. Joel, comp. see
VAN LENNEP, Mary Elizabeth (Hawes)

2157. HAWES, Louise (Fisher),
comp. see VAN LENNEP, Mary
Elizabeth (Hawes)

2158. HAWES, Lucy (Williams) [Am.
19c]
Buffalo fifty years ago. A paper
read before the Buffalo hist.
soc. April 27, 1886.
Buffalo, NY: The Courier co.,
pr., 1886. 10p. NUC BL
[Reminiscences of events, social
conditions, etc.]

2159. -----Lewiston: past,
present, and future.
Lewiston, ME: n.p., 1887. 15p.
NUC BL

2160. HAWKES, Sarah (Eden) [Br.
1759-1832]
Memoirs of Mrs. Hawkes ...
including remarks on
conversations and extracts from
sermons and letters of the late
Rev. Richard Cecil. Ed. Catherine
Cecil.
2d ed. L: R. B. Seeley & W.
Burnside, 1838. 679p. NUC BL OCLC
[Includes extracts from her diary
and letters.]

2161. HAWKEY, Charlotte, Mrs.
[Br. 19c]
Neota.
Taunton: priv. pr., 1871. 256p. BL
[Miscellaneous pieces in verse
with personal and family
memoirs.]

2162. HAWKINS, Laetitia Matilda
[Br. 1760-1835]
Anecdotes, biographical sketches
and memoirs.
L: F. C. & J. Rivington, 1822.
NUC BL

2163. -----Letters on the female
mind, its powers and pursuits;
addressed to Miss H. M. Williams,
with particular reference to her
letters from France.
L: Hookham & Carpenter, 1793. 2v.
NUC

2164. -----Memoirs, anecdotes,
facts, and opinions, collected
and preserved by L. M. H.
L: n.p., 1824. 2v. NUC BL OCLC
[Continuation of Anecdotes.]

2165. HAWKINS, Mary, comp. see
STANLEY, Lura A.

2166. HAWKSLEY, Cordelia J. [Br.
19c]
Eleven letters from the East to
my Bible class.
L: Hatchards, 1888. 73p. BL

2167. HAWLEY, Zerah [Am. 1781-1856]
A journal of a tour through
Connecticut, Massachusetts, New
York, the north part of
Pennsylvania and Ohio, including
a year's residence in that part
of the state of Ohio styled New
Connecticut, or Western Reserve.
New Haven, CT: pr., S. Converse,
1822. 158p. NUC BL OCLC

2168. HAWTHORNE, Sophia Amelia
(Peabody), Mrs. Nathaniel
Hawthorne [Am. 1811-1871]
Memories of [Nathaniel]
Hawthorne. [Comp.] Their
daughter, Rose (Hawthorne)
Lathrop. [Mother Mary Alphonse
Lathrop].
Boston & NY: Houghton Mifflin &
co.; L: Kegan Paul & co., 1897.
480p. NUC BL
[Primarily excerpts of letters
from Sophia to Nathaniel,
including courtship period.]

2169. -----Notes in England and
Italy.
NY: G. P. Putnam & son, 1869.
549p. NUC BL MBD OCLC
[Travel diary]

2170. HAWTHORNE, Mrs. Nathaniel
see HAWTHORNE, Sophia Amelia
(Peabody)

2171. HAYES, Alice M. [Br. 19/20c]
My leper friends; an account of personal work among lepers, and of their daily life in India.
L: W. Thacker & co., 1891. 127p. NUC BL OCLC

2172. HAYES, Alice (Smith) [Br. 1657-1720]
A legacy, or widow's mite; left by Alice Hayes to her children and others.
L: J. Sowle, 1723. 85p. NUC BL MB OCLC
[Quaker autobiography]

2173. HAYGOOD, Laura Askew [Am. 1845-1900]
A message from China to the Woman's Missionary Society of the Methodist Episcopal Church, South.
Shanghai: n.p., 1885. NUC OCLC

2174. HAYWARD, Abraham, ed. see PIOZZI, Hester Lynch (Salusbury) Thrale

2175. HAYWARD, Abraham, ed. see WYNN, Frances Williams

2176. HAYWARD, Harriet Cornelia [Am. 19c]
From Finland to Greece: or, three seasons in eastern Europe.
NY: John B. Alden, 1892. 327p. NUC OCLC

2177. HAYWARD, Jane Mary [Br. 1825-1894]
Bird notes. Ed. Emma Hubbard.
L & NY: Longmans, Green, & co., 1895. 181p. NUC BL OCLC
[Diary of a bird watcher; includes poems.]

2178. HAYWARD, Mrs. Joshua see HAYWARD, Lydia

2179. HAYWARD, Lydia, Mrs. Joshua Hayward [Am. 19c]
Narrative of Mrs. Lydia Hayward, including the life, experience, call to the ministry and extensive travels of her husband, the late Elder Joshua Hayward.
Union Mills, NY: W. Clarke, 1846. 93p. NUC

2180. HEATH, Betsey [Am. 1769-1853]
The Crafts family. By James Monroe Crafts & William F. Crafts.
Northampton, MA: Gazette pr. co., 1893. 803p. NUC MAD OCLC
[Diary extracts]

2181. HECKER, I. T., Rev., ed. see BARLOW, Debbie

2182. HECKFORD, Sarah, Mrs. [Br. 19c]
A lady trader in the Transvaal.
L: S. Low, Marston, Searle & Rivington, 1882. 412p. NUC BL OCLC

2183. HECKLEY, Elizabeth see KECKLEY, Elizabeth

2184. HEGGIE, Cora M. A. [Am. b. 1861]
The life and trials of a young lady convert.
Kansas City, MO: Palmer & son, 1880. 51p. NUC

2185. HELM, Mary (Sherwood) Wightman [Am. b. 1807]
Scraps of early Texas history.
Austin, TX: pr. for the author, 1884. 198p. NUC BL K OCLC

2186. HELPS, Arthur, ed. see VICTORIA, Queen of Great Britain and Ireland

2187. HEMANS, Felicia Dorothea (Browne) [Br. 1793-1835] ALT: Browne, Felicia Dorothea
The works of Mrs. Hemans; with a memoir of her life by her sister [Mrs. Harriet Hughes].
Edinburgh: W. Blackwood & sons; L: Thomas Cadell, 1839. 7v. BL NUC OCLC
[Vol. 2 pub. NY and L, all other data same.]

2188. -----Life of Mrs. Hemans, with illustration of her literary character, from her private correspondence. By Henry F. Chorley.
L: Saunders & Otley, 1836?. 2v. NUC BL

2189. HEMENWAY, Abby Maria [Am. 1828-1890]
Clarke papers. Mrs. Meech and her family. Home letters, familiar incidents and narrations linked for preservation.
Burlington, VT: pub. by Miss Hemenway, 1878. NUC OCLC

2190. HENDERSON, Alice Palmer [Am. 19c]
The rainbow's end: Alaska.
Chicago & NY: H. S. Stone & co., 1898. 296p. NUC OCLC

2191. HENDERSON, Mary Anne (Leslie), Mrs. Thomas Henderson [Br. 1820-1853]
The missionary's wife: a memoir of Mrs. M. A. Henderson, of Demerara. By her husband, [Thomas Henderson].
L: John Snow, 1855. 114p. NUC BL
[Missionary in British Guiana. Includes excerpts from her journals.]

2192. HENDERSON, Mrs. Thomas see HENDERSON, Mary Anne (Leslie)

2193. HENDERSON, Thomas, comp. see HENDERSON, Mary Anne (Leslie)

2194. HENRIETTA MARIA, Queen Consort of Charles I, King of Great Britain [Br. 1609-1669]
Letters of Queen Henrietta Maria, including her private correspondence with Charles the First. Ed. Mary Anne Everett Green.
L: R. Bentley, 1857 [1856]. NUC BL

2195. HENRY, Matthew, comp. see SAVAGE, Sarah (Henry)

2196. HERBERT, Amabel (Aston), Lady, co-author see RUSSELL, Rachel (Wriothesley) Vaughan, Baroness Russell

2197. HERBERT, Jemima (Taylor) [Br. 1798-1866]
The family pen. Memorials biographical and literary, of the Taylor family of Ongar. Ed. Rev. Isaac Taylor.
L: Jackson, Walford & Hodder, 1867. 2v. NUC OCLC

2198. HERBERT, Mary Elizabeth (A'Court), Baroness Herbert of Lea [Br. 1822-1911]
Cradle lands.
L: R. Bentley, 1867. 330p. NUC BL OCLC
[Travel: Egypt & Holy Land]

2199. -----Impressions of Spain in 1866.
L: R. Bentley, 1867. 280p. NUC BL OCLC

2200. -----A search after sunshine; or, Algeria in 1871.
L: Richard Bentley & son, 1872. 265p. NUC BL OCLC

2201. HERRITT, Sarah D. (Hall) [Am. b. 1815]
A keepsake: dedicated to my friends.
Cincinnati, OH: Elm Street prtg. co., 1876. 158p. NUC OCLC
[Missionary life in Illinois; includes poems.]

2202. HERSCHEL, Caroline Lucretia [Br. 1750-1848]
Memoir and correspondence of Caroline Herschel. Ed. Mary Cornwallis Herschel.
L: J. Murray, 1876. 355p. NUC BL

2203. HERSCHEL, Mary Cornwallis, ed. see HERSCHEL, Caroline Lucretia

2204. HERSCHELL, Helen S., Mrs. [Br. 19c]
"Far above Rubies." Memoirs of H. S. H. by her daughter. Ed. R. H. Herschell.
L: n.p., 1854. BL
[Includes The Bystander by Mrs. Herschell.]

2205. HERSCHELL, R. H., ed. see HERSCHELL, Helen S.

2206. HERTFORD, Frances, Countess of see SOMERSET, Frances (Thynne) Seymour, Duchess of

2207. HERVEY, Eleanora Louisa (Montagu), Mrs. Thomas Kibble Hervey [Br. 1811-1903] ALT: Montagu, Eleanora Louisa
The adventures of a lady in Tartary, Thibet, China, and

Kashmir ... with an account of the journey from the Punjab to Bombay overland ... also an account of the Mahableshwur and Neilgherry Mountains.
L: Hope & co., 1853. 3v. NUC BL MB OCLC

2208. HERVEY, Elizabeth Chudleigh [Br. 1720-1788] ALT: Bristol, Elizabeth Chudleigh Hervey, Countess of; Chudleigh, Elizabeth; Kingston, Elizabeth Chudleigh Hervey, Duchess of
The life and memoirs of Elizabeth Chudleigh.
L: R. Randall, 1788. 36p. NUC BL

2209. HERVEY, Hetta M. [Am. 19c]
Glimpses of Norseland.
Boston: J. G. Cupples for the author, 1889. 242p. NUC OCLC
[Travel: Norway]

2210. HERVEY, Mary (Lepell) Hervey, Baroness [Br. 1700?-1768]
Letters of Mary Lepel, Lady Hervey. Ed. the Right Hon. John Wilson Croker.
L: J. Murray, 1821. 332p. NUC BL OCLC

2211. HERVEY, Mrs. Thomas Kibble see HERVEY, Eleanora Louisa (Montagu)

2212. HESKETH, Harriet (Cowper) Lady [Br. 1733-1807]
Letters of Lady Hesketh to the Rev. John Johnson, L. L. D., concerning their kinsman, William Cowper, the poet. Ed. Catharine Bodham (Donne) Johnson.
L: Jarrold & sons, 188-?[BL: 1901]. 128p. NUC BL

2213. -----Poems, the early productions of William Cowper, with anecdotes ... collected from letters of Lady Hesketh written during her residence at Olney.
Ed. James Croft.
L: Baldwin, Cradock & Joy, 1825. 75p. BL

2214. HICKS, DORCAS, pseud. see PERKINS, Mary H.

2215. HICKS, Rachel (Seaman) [Am. 1789-1878]

Memoir of Rachel Hicks (written by herself) late of Westbury, Long Island, a minister in the Society of Friends; together with some letters and a memorial of Westbury Monthly Meeting.
NY: Putnam, 1880. 287p. NUC K

2216. HIELD, Mary [Br. 19c]
Glimpses of South America; or, the land of the pampas.
L & NY: Cassell; Peter Galpin, 1882. 222p. NUC BL OCLC

2217. -----The land of temples; or, sketches from our Indian Empire.
L & NY: Cassell, 1882. 212p. NUC

2218. HIGGINSON, Ella (Rhoads) [Am. b. 1862]
The snow pearls; a poem.
Seattle, WA: Lowman & Hanford stationery & pr. co., 1897. 10 l. NUC
[Travel: Puget Sound]

2219. HIGGINSON, Mary Potter (Thacher) [Am. 1844-1941] ALT: Thacher, Mary P.
Seashore and prairie.
Boston: J. R. Osgood & co., 1877. 239p. NUC BL OCLC
[Essays and short prose descriptions of personal experiences]

2220. HIGGINSON, Sarah Jane (Hatfield) [Am. 1840-1916]
Java, the pearl of the East.
Boston & NY: Houghton, Mifflin & co., c1890. 204p. NUC OCLC

2221. HILL, Elizabeth (Freeman) [Am. 19c]
The widow's offering: an authentic narrative of the parentage, life, trials and travels of Mrs. Elizabeth Hill. Written by herself.
New London, CT: D. S. Ruddock, pr., 1852. 179p. NUC K OCLC

2222. HILL, Elisabeth Lord (Chase) [Am. 19c]
Gleanings: girlhood and womanhood.
Concord, NH: Republican press assoc., 1887. 76p. NUC
[Memorial volume of poetry and prose]

2223. HILL, Florence Davenport, co-author see HILL, Rosamond Davenport

2224. HILL, Hannah [Am. 1703-1714]
A legacy for children, being some of the last expressions, and dying sayings of Hannah Hill. Of the city of Philadelphia, in the province of Pennsylvania, in America, aged eleven years and near three months.
Dublin: n.p., 1719. 29p. NUC

2225. HILL, Laura C., Mrs. [Am. 19c]
Laure; history of a blasted life.
Philadelphia: Claxton, Remsen & Haffelfinger, 1872. 371p. K

2226. HILL, Lucy Ann [Am. b. 1831]
Rhine roamings.
Boston: Lee & Shepard, 1880. 267p. NUC OCLC

2227. HILL, Marie (Carroll) [Am. 19c]
A real story, affectionately dedicated to my dear dad by me.
Chicago: Corbitt & Birnham, 1897. 210p. NUC
[Autobiography; Phildelphia Irish Catholic family. Includes travel in Canada, Mexico, Florida and California.]

2228. HILL, Mary Sophia [Br. b. 1819]
A British subject's recollections of the Confederacy while a visitor and attendant in its hospitals and camps.
Baltimore, MD: Turnbull bros., 1875. 114p. NUC OCLC

2229. HILL, Minerva Lucretia [Am. 1812-1844]
Some of the most peculiar words which my holy Savior has said to me from time to time.
Harvard, MA: n.p., n.d. NUC

2230. HILL, Phillipina (Burton) [Br. 18c] ALT: Burton, Philippina
Mrs. Hill's apology for having been induced to appear in the character of Scrub, Beaux Stratagem, ... at Brighthelmstone last year, 1786. Also some of Mrs. Hill's letters to HRH, the Prince of Wales, Mrs. Fitzherbert [Maria Anne Smythe Fitzherbert], and others.
L: printed for the authoress, 1787. 51p. NUC BL OCLC

2231. HILL, Rosa F. [Br. 19c]
ALT: H., R. F.
To, at and from Berlin. By R. F. H.
L: Wyman & sons, 1871. 155p. BL
[Journey to Berlin to see return of German troops from Franco-Prussian War]

2232. HILL, Rosamond Davenport [Br. 1825-1902]
What we saw in Australia. With Florence Davenport-Hill.
L: Macmillan & co., 1875. 438p. NUC BL

2233. HILL, Sarah [Br. 19c]
Memoir of Mrs. Sarah Hill, of Liverpool. With extracts from her correspondence. By the Rev. John Hannah.
L: James Nichols, pr. for priv. circ., 1851. 46p. BL

2234. HILL, Sarah Anne Curties, Mrs. [Br. 19c]
Some account of the life ... of S. A. C. H. ... with extracts from her diary.
Woodbridge: n.p., 1821. BL

2235. HILLS, Caroline Parker [Am. 19c]
A Nantucket hermitage and other poems.
Washington, D.C.: Byron S. Adams, 1895. 64p. NUC OCLC

2236. HILLS, Lydia [Br. 17c] ALT: H., L.
A relation of the miraculous cure of Mrs. L. H. of a lameness of eighteen years continuance ... the 17th of November, 1694. With her deposition of the same before the Lord Mayor, etc. Pub. as: H., L.
L: n.p., 1695. NUC BL
[Expanded edition L: W. Wilde, 1896]

2237. HILLS, Marilla Marks
(Hutchins) [Am. 1807-1901]
Reminiscences. A brief history of
the Free Baptist India mission.
Dover, NH: Free Baptist Woman's
Missionary Society, 1885. 336p.
NUC OCLC

2238. HILLS, Mrs. Nathan Cushman
see HILLS, Sabrina Ann (Loomis)

2239. HILLS, Sabrina Ann
(Loomis), Mrs. Nathan Cushman
Hills [Am. b. 1811]
Memories, by Mrs. Nathan Cushman
Hills.
Cleveland, OH: pr. for priv.
circ., 1899. 57p. NUC K OCLC

2240. HINDERER, Anna (Martin)
[Br. 1827-1870]
Seventeen years in the Yoruba
Country. Memorials of A. H. ...
gathered from her journals and
letters.
L: Seeley, Jackson & Halliday,
1852 [BL: 1872]. 342p. NUC BL MB
OCLC

2241. HINKSON, Mrs. H. A. see
HINKSON, Katherine (Tynan)

2242. HINKSON, Katherine (Tynan),
Mrs. H. A. Hinkson [Br. 1861-
1931] ALT: Tynan, Katherine
A cluster of nuts: being sketches
among my own people.
L: Lawrence & Bullen, 1894. 242p.
NUC BL OCLC
[Sketches of Irish characters met
during the author's travels.]

2243. HINSDALE, Laura (Fenling)
[Am. 19c]
Legends and lyrics of the Gulf
coast.
Biloxi, MS: Herald Press, 1896.
40p. NUC OCLC

2244. HIRST, Joseph, comp. see
ARUNDELL, Mary Ann

2245. HITCHCOCK, Edward, comp.
see LYON, Mary

2246. HITCHCOCK, Mary E., Mrs. R.
D. Hitchcock [Am. 1837-1874]
Two women in the Klondike; the
story of a journey to the gold-
fields of Alaska.

NY & L: G. P. Putnam's sons,
1899. 485p. NUC BL OCLC

2247. HITCHCOCK, Mrs. R. D. see
HITCHCOCK, Mary E.

2248. HITCHENS, Mrs. Kate [Am. b.
1862]
Christian castle building; or,
lessons learned in suffering.
McKeesport, PA: Daily news pub.
house, 1890. 256p. NUC
[Autobiography]

2249. HOARE, Angelina Margaret
[Br. 19c]
The life of Angelina Margaret
Hoare, by her sisters [Caroline
Charlotte and Katherine Hoare]
and [Jessie (Robertson) Hoare]
Mrs. Walter M. Hoare.
L: W. Gardner, Darton & co.,
1894. NUC
[May contain personal material.]

2250. HOARE, Caroline Charlotte
see HOARE, Angelina Margaret

2251. HOARE, Jessie (Robertson)
see HOARE, Angelina Margaret

2252. HOARE, Katherine see HOARE,
Angelina Margaret

2253. HOARE, Rachel (Newenham)
[Br. 1775?-1850]
Christian experience: a memoir of
Mrs. Hoare, with extracts from
her correspondence. Ed. her son,
W. W. Hoare.
L: W. H. Dalton, 1852. 430p. NUC
BL

2254. HOARE, Mrs. Walter M. see
HOARE, Angelina Margaret

2255. HOARE, W. W., ed. see
HOARE, Rachel (Newenham)

2256. HOBBIE, Hannah [Am. 1806-
1831]
Memoir of Hannah Hobbie; or,
Christian activity and triumph in
suffering. By Robert G. Armstrong.
NY: American Tract Society,
1837?. 255p. NUC MAD
[Includes extracts of religious
journal]

2257. HODGES, A., Mrs., ed. <u>see</u>
WOODMAN, Fanny (Crosskey)

2258. HODGES, Ellen G. [Am. 19c]
Surprise land, a girl's letters
from the West.
Boston: Cupples, Upham, 1887.
121p. NUC

2259. HODGETS, John, ed. <u>see</u>
LUXBOROUGH, Henrietta (Saint-
John) Knight, Baroness

2260. HODGKIN, Elizabeth
(Howard), Mrs. J. Hodgkin, Jr.
[Br. 1803-1836]
Extracts from the familiar
letters of the late Elizabeth
Hodgkin, ... interspersed with a
few memoranda. Collected and
arranged by her husband.
L: Harvey & Darton, 1842. 225p.
NUC BL OCLC

2261. HODGKIN, Jr., J., comp. <u>see</u>
HODGKIN, Elizabeth (Howard)

2262. HODGKIN, Jr., Mrs. J. <u>see</u>
HODGKIN, Elizabeth (Howard)

2263. HODGKIN, Lucy Violet [Br.
b. 1869] ALT: Holdsworth, Lucy
Violet (Hodgkin)
Pilgrims in Palestine.
L: G. P. Putnam's sons;
Newcastle-on-Tyne: Mawson, Swan &
Morgan, 1891. 259p. NUC

2264. HODGSON, Christopher
Pemberton, co-author <u>see</u> HODGSON,
Mrs. Christopher Pemberton

2265. HODGSON, Mrs. Christopher
Pemberton [Br. 19c]
A residence at Nagasaki in 1859-
1860 ... . By C. P. Hodgson. With
a series of letters on Japan, by
his wife.
L: R. Bentley, 1861. 350p. NUC BL

2266. HODING, Sarah [Br. 19c]
The land log-book; a compilation
of anecdotes and occurrences
extracted from the journal kept
by the author, during a residence
of several years in the U.S. of
A.
L: Simpkin, Marshall & co., 1836.
278p. NUC BL OCLC

2267. HODSON, Henrietta [Br. 19c]
A letter from Miss Henrietta
Hodson, an actress, to the
members of the dramatic
profession, being a relation of
the persecutions which she has
suffered from Mr. William
Schwenck Gilbert, a dramatic
author.
L: n.p., 1877. 22p. NUC BL

2268. HOFFMAN, Virginia Hale <u>see</u>
HOFFMAN, Virginia Haviside

2269. HOFFMAN, Virginia Haviside,
Mrs. [Am. 1832-1855] ALT:
Hoffman, Virginia Hale
Life of Mrs. Virginia Hale
Hoffman, late of the Protestant
Episcopal Mission to western
Africa. By George David Cummins.
Philadelphia: Lindsay &
Blakiston, 1859. 256p. NUC BL MAD
OCLC
[Missionary journal, 1847-1855.]

2270. HOFLAND, Barbara (Wreaks)
Hoole [Br. 1770-1844] ALT: HOOLE,
Barbara (Wreaks)
Africa described, in its ancient
and present state.
L: Longman, Rees, Orme, Brown &
Green, 1828. 291p. NUC BL OCLC

2271. -----Richmond, and its
surrounding scenery.
L: W. B. Cooke, 1832. 74p. NUC BL
OCLC

2272. HOGBEN, Dorothea (Scott)
Gotherson [Br. 1611-1680] ALT:
Gotherson, Dorothea (Scott);
Scott, Dorothea
Dorothea Scott, otherwise
Gotherson and Hogben, of Egerton
House, Kent, 1611-1680. A new and
enlarged edition. [Comp] G. D.
Scull.
Oxford: pr. for priv. circ. by
Parker & co., 1883. 222p. NUC BL
OCLC
[Collection of her letters and
other writings.]

2273. HOLBROOK, Ann Catherine
(Jackson) [Br. 1780-1837]
The dramatist; or, memoirs of the
stage. With the life of the
authoress, prefixed, and

interspersed with, a variety of anecdotes, humorous and pathetic.
Birmingham: pr., Martin & Hunter, 1809. 68p. NUC BL MB OCLC

2274. -----Memoirs of an actress.
Manchester: J. Harrop, 1807. 35p. BL

2275. HOLBROOK, Mary H. [Am. 19c]
Jottings by the way.
Portland, OR: n.p., 1892?. 21p. NUC
[Travel: British Columbia]

2276. -----Souvenir commemorating the exodus of the Couch and Holbrook pilgrims from Boston to Portland, Oregon in 1852.
Portland, OR: Baltes, 1899. 27p. NUC

2277. HOLBROOK, H. P. see PINCKNEY, Eliza (Lucas)

2278. HOLCOMB, Mrs. Rev. Frederick see HOLCOMB, Nancy (Merriam)

2279. HOLCOMB, Helen Harriet Howe, Mrs. [Am. b. 1836]
Bits about India.
Philadelphia,: Pres. board of publication, 1888. 272p. NUC OCLC

2280. HOLCOMB, Nancy (Merriam), Mrs. Frederick Holcomb [Am. b. 1796]
Watertown reminiscences; read at the centennial of Watertown, June 17th, 1880; also continued reminiscences, written for the amusement of the writer; and thirdly, family reminiscences, written expressly for the family relatives.
Waterbury, CT: Press of F. P. Steele, 1880. 32p. NUC

2281. HOLDERNESS, Mary, Mrs. [Br. 19c]
New Russia. Journey from Riga to the Crimea, by way of Kiev. ...
With some account of the manners and customs of the colonists of New Russia to which are added notes relating to the Crim Tatars.
L: Sherwood Jones & co., 1823. 316p. NUC BL OCLC

2282. -----Notes relating to the manners and customs of the Crim Tatars, written during a four years' residence among that people.
L: J. Warren, 1821. 168p. NUC BL OCLC

2283. HOLDICHE, Mrs. L. A., comp. see HUBER, Mary Elizabeth

2284. HOLDING, Nannie Emory [Am. 19c]
A decade of mission life in Mexican mission homes.
Nashville, TN: Publishing House M. E. Church, South, 1895. 275p. NUC OCLC

2285. HOLDSWORTH, Lucy Violet (Hodgkin) see HODGKIN, Lucy Violet

2286. HOLLAND, Bernard, ed. see HOLLAND, Mary Sibylla (Lyall)

2287. HOLLAND, E. J. see HOLLOND, Ellen Julia (Teed)

2288. HOLLAND, Emma,, comp. see LOWDELL, Mary Caroline

2289. HOLLAND, Mary Sibylla (Lyall) [Br. 1836-1891]
Letters of Mary Sibylla Holland.
Ed. her son, Bernard Holland.
L: E. Arnold, 1898. 303p. NUC BL OCLC

2290. HOLLEY, Mary (Austin) [Am. 1784-1846]
Texas, observations, historical, geographical and descriptive, in a series of letters written during a visit to Austin's colony in 1831.
Baltimore, MD: Armstrong & Plaskitt, 1833. 167p. NUC BL OCLC
[First book on Texas published in English.]

2291. -----Texas.
Lexington, KY: J. Clarke & Co., 1836. 410p. NUC BL
[Greatly enlarged edition of previous entry.]

2292. HOLLEY, Sallie [Am. 1818-1893]
A life for liberty; anti-slavery and other letters of Sallie

Holley. Ed. John White Chadwick.
NY & L: G. P. Putnam's sons,
1899. 292p. NUC BL

2293. HOLLOND, Ellen Julia
(Teed), Mrs. Robert Hollond [Br.
1822-1884] ALT: Hollond, E. J.
A lady's journal of her travels
in Egypt and Nubia (1858-9). By
E. J. Hollond.
L: E. Faithfull, 1864. 218p. NUC

2294. HOLLOND, Mrs. Robert see
HOLLOND, Ellen Julia (Teed)

2295. HOLLOWAY, Elvira Haskins
[Am. 19c]
Gleanings from the golden state.
San Francisco: n.p., 1893. 48p. NUC

2296. HOLME, Mary [Br. 19c]
Recollections of a residence in
Fairfield Sister's House ... In a
series of letters addressed to
the present inhabitants.
L: priv. pr., 1876. 92p. BL

2297. HOLMES, Augusta
(Macgregor), Mrs. Dalkeith Holmes
[Br. d. 1857] PSEUD: Lady, A
A ride on horseback to Florence
through France and Switzerland.
Described in a series of letters
by a lady.
L: J. Murray, 1842. 2v. NUC BL

2298. HOLMES, Mrs. Dalkeith see
HOLMES, Augusta (Macgregor)

2299. HOLMES, Elizabeth (Emra),
Mrs. Marcus H. Holmes [Br. 1804-
1843]
A sister's record, or memoir of
Mrs. Marcus H. Holmes.
L: Hamilton, Adams & co., 1844.
176p. BL
[Includes letters, poems, one
short story]

2300. HOLMES, Georgiana (Klingle)
[Am. 19c] PSEUD: Kingle, George
Bethlehem to Jerusalem; a new
poem. Pub. as: George Klingle.
NY: F. A. Stokes & bro., 1888.
NUC
[Travel: Palestine; in verse]

2301. HOLMES, Harriet Ann [Am.
1816-1841]

Memoir of Harriet Ann Holmes, by
her sister, Mrs. Caroline T.
(Holmes) Ely.
Philadelphia: Perkins & Purves,
1844. 108p. NUC
[Extracts from her diary; chiefly
religious.]

2302. HOLMES, Jessie [Br. 19c]
The private nurse. Some
reminiscences of eight years'
private nursing.
L: T. F. Unwin, 1899. 113p. BL MB

2303. HOLMES, Mrs. Marcus H. see
HOLMES, Elizabeth (Emra)

2304. HOLSTEIN, Anna Morris
(Ellis), Mrs. William H. Holstein
[Am. 1824-1901]
Three years in field hospitals of
the Army of the Potomac.
Philadelphia,: J. B. Lippincott &
co., 1867. 131p. NUC BL K

2305. HOLSTEIN, Mrs. William H.
see HOLSTEIN, Anna Morris (Ellis)

2306. HOLT, Miss C. E. [Am. 19c]
An autobiographical sketch of a
teacher's life including a
residence in the northern and
southern states, California, Cuba
and Peru.
Quebec: pr. by J. Carrel, 1875.
104p. NUC K

2307. HOLWORTHY, Sophia Matilda
[Br. 19c]
Alpine scrambles and classic
rambles: a gipsy tour in search
of summer snow and winter sun.
L: James Nisbet & co., 1885.
114p. BL
[Switzerland, France and Italy]

2308. HOLYOKE, Maria (Ballard)
[Am. b. 1833]
Golden memoirs of Old World
lands, or what I saw in Europe,
Egypt, Palestine and Greece.
Chicago,: Charles H. Kerr, 1893.
542p. NUC OCLC

2309. HOME, Hon. J. A., ed. see
COKE, Lady Mary

2310. HOME, Hon. James Archibald,
ed. see STUART, Lady Louisa

2311. HONEY, Laura Bell [Br.
1816?-1843]
The annals of the green room, and
biography of the stage!
Comprising the lives of the most
eminent London performers.
L: Smith, 1842. 24p. NUC
[Part I: Memoirs of Mrs. Honey]

2312. HOOD, Isabel [Br. 19c]
Memoirs and manuscript of Isabel
Hood. [Comp.] Rev. John
MacDonald.
2d ed. Edinburgh: n.p., 1844. BL

2313. HOOD, Jessie, comp. see
Lyall, Isabella D.

2314. HOOKER, Isabella (Beecher),
comp. see STOWE, Harriet
Elizabeth (Beecher)

2315. HOOLE, Barbara (Wreaks) see
HOFLAND, Barbara (Wreaks) Hoole

2316. HOOPES, Elizabeth Walter
[Am. 1818?-1882]
Extracts from the memoranda of
Elizabeth W. Hoopes from 1873 to
1881.
Philadelphia: W. H. Pile, pr.,
1882. 47p. NUC OCLC
[Society of Friends]

2317. -----A remarkable instance
of divine favour, exemplified in
the life of a pious blind woman.
West Chester, PA: F. S. Hickman,
1874. 12p.
[May contain personal material.]

2318. HOPE, Elizabeth Reid
(Cotton), Lady see DENNEY,
Elizabeth Reid (Cotton) Hope

2319. HOPE-EDWARDES, Ellen
Charlotte see EDWARDES, Ellen
Charlotte Hope

2320. HOPKINS, Louisa (Payson),
co-author see PRENTISS, Elizabeth

2321. HOPKINS, Salem Armstrong
see HOPKINS, Saleni (Armstrong)

2322. HOPKINS, Saleni
(Armstrong), M.D. [Am. b. 1855]
ALT: Hopkins, Salem Armstrong
Within the purdah; also, In the
zenana homes of Indian princes,
and Heroes and heroines of Zion;
being the personal observations
of a medical missionary in India.
NY: Eaton & Mains; Cincinnati,
OH: Curts & Jennings, 1898. 248p.
NUC BL OCLC
[Describes customs and condition
of women in purdah; includes
poems and letters.]

2323. HOPKINS, Samuel, comp. see
ANTHONY, Susanna

2324. HOPKINS, Samuel, D. D.,
comp. see OSBORN, Sarah (Haggar)

2325. HOPKINS, Sarah Winnemucca,
Mrs. [Am. 1844?-1891]
Life among the Piutes, their
wrongs and claims. Ed. Mary Tyler
(Peabody) Mann, Mrs. Horace Mann.
Boston & NY: G. B. Putnam's,
1883. 263p. NUC K OCLC
[Autobiography]

2326. HOPLEY, Catherine Cooper
[Br. 19c]
Life in the South; from the
commencement of the war. By a
blockaded British subject.
L: Chapman & Hall, 1863. 2v. NUC
BL C
[Coulter also lists Sarah L.
Jones, but attr. this work to
Hopley.]

2327. -----Rambles and adventures
in the wilds of the West.
L: Religious Tract Society, 1870.
126p. NUC BL

2328. HOPTON, Anna Maria [Br. d.
1857] ALT: H., A. M.
A brief memoir and extracts from
the letters of A. M. H.
L: Emily Faithful, pr., 1858?.
165p. BL
[Journals, travel]

2329. HOPWOOD, D. Caroline
(Skene) [Br. fl. 1788]
An account of the life and
religious experiences of D.
Caroline Hopwood, of Leeds,
deceased ... to which is added, a
collection of pieces in prose and
poetry, on various subjects,
written by the same author.
Leeds: E. Baines, 1801. 64p. NUC
BL

2330. HORE, Annie Boyle [Br. b. 1853]
To Lake Tanganyika in a bath chair.
L: Sampson Low, Marston, Searle & Rivington, 1886. 217p. NUC BL OCLC

2331. HORN, Sarah Ann [Am. 19c]
A narrative of the captivity of Mrs. Horn, and her two children, with Mrs. Harris, by the Camanche [sic] Indians, after they had murdered their husbands and travelling companions.
St. Louis, MO: C. Keemble, pr., 1839. 60p. NUC OCLC
[Told by Sarah Ann Horn to E. House]

2332. HORN, Sylvia (Hall), co-author see MUNSON, Rachel (Hall)

2333. HORNBY, Mrs. Edmund see HORNBY, Emelia Bithynia (Maceroni), Lady

2334. HORNBY, Emelia Bithynia (Maceroni), Lady [Br. d. 1866]
ALT: Hornby, Mrs. Edmund
In and around Stamboul.
L: R. Bentley, 2v.; Philadelphia: J. Challen & son, 1858. 499p. NUC BL
[Also pub. as: Constantinople during the Crimean War]

2335. HORNER, Ann Susan [Br. d. 1900] ALT: Horner, Susan
Walks in Florence. With Joanna B. Horner.
L: Strahan & co., 1873. 2v. NUC BL OCLC

2336. HORNER, Hattie [Am. 19c]
Not at home.
NY: J. B. Alden, 1889. 307p. NUC OCLC
[Travel: southern U. S.]

2337. HORNER, Joanna B., co-author see HORNER, Ann Susan

2338. HORNER, Susan see HORNER, Ann Susan

2339. HOSKENS, Jane (Fenn) [Br. b. 1694]
The life and spiritual sufferings of that faithful servant of Christ, Jane Hoskens, a public preacher among the people called Quakers.
Philadelphia: William Evitty; Manchester: Manchester & Stockport Tract Depository, 1771. 31p. NUC BL MB

2340. HOSMER, Harriet Goodhue [Am. 1830-1908]
Boston and Boston people, in 1850.
Boston: n.p., 1850. NUC
[Account of a stroll through Boston, sights and characters, in rhymed verse.]

2341. HOSNER, Miss, co-author see MENDELL, Miss

2342. HOTCHKISS, Fanny Winchester, comp. see MATTEINI, Harriette

2343. HOUGHTON, Georgiana [Br. b. 1814]
Evenings at home in spiritual séance, prefaced and welded together by a species of autobiography.
L: Trübner & co., 1881. NUC BL MB OCLC
[Experiences as a medium]

2344. HOUSE, Abigail (Clark) [Am. 1790-1861]
Memoirs of the religious experience and life of Abigail House. Ed. Josiah Atkins.
Jefferson, OH: Ashtabula Sentinel steam press, 1861. 264p. NUC K OCLC

2345. HOUSE, E., comp. see HORN, Sarah Ann

2346. HOUSER, Julia Crouse [Am. 19c]
Letters from Japan, written by an American girl traveling in the Far East to her friends at home.
NY: William Edwin Rudge, 189-?. 115p. NUC

2347. HOUSMAN, H., Mrs [Br. d. 1735]
The power and pleasure of the divine life; exemplify'd in the late Mrs. Housman, as extracted from her own papers. Ed. R. Pearsall.

L & Boston: n.p., 1744. NUC BL MBD
[Religious diary, 1711-1732]

2348. HOUSTOUN, Matilda Charlotte
(Jesse) Fraser [Br. 1815?-1892]
Hesperos: or, travels in the West.
L: J. W. Parker, 1850. 2v. NUC BL
OCLC
[Travel: Western U. S.]

2349. -----Texas and the Gulf of
Mexico: or, yachting in the New
World.
L: J. Murray, 1844. 2v. NUC BL
OCLC

2350. -----Twenty years in the
wild West; or, life in Connaught.
L: J. Murray, 1879. 288p. NUC BL
MB OCLC [autobiography]

2351. -----A woman's memories of
well-known men.
L: F. V. White, 1883. 2v. NUC BL
OCLC

2352. HOW, Mary Jane (Gordon)
[Am. 1816-1847]
Life and confession ... by John
S. Calhoun.
August, ME: the author, 1847.
32p. NUC K OCLC
[Murderer]

2353. HOWARD, Catherine Mary
(Neave) [Br. d. 1849]
Reminiscences for my children.
Carlisle: pr. for the author by
C. Thurman, 1836. 4v. NUC BL MB

2354. HOWARD, Eliot, ed. see
WESTON, Mary (Pace)

2355. HOWARD, Henrietta (Hobart),
Countess of Suffolk see SUFFOLK.
Henrietta (Hobart), Howard,
Countess of

2356. HOWARD, Luke, ed. see
HOWARD, Rachel

2357. HOWARD, Rachel [Br. 1804-
1837]
Memoranda of Rachel Howard. Ed.
Luke Howard.
L: Simpkin & Marshall, 1839.
342p. NUC BL MBD OCLC
[Contains Quaker diary and
letters.]

2358. HOWARD OF GLOSSOP, Winifred
Mary (DeLisle) Howard, Baroness
[Br. d. 1909]
Journal of a tour in the United
States, Canada and Mexico.
L: S. Low, Marston & co., 1897.
355p. NUC BL MC OCLC

2359. HOWARD-VYSE, L., Mrs. [Br.
19c] ALT: Vyse, L. Howard, Mrs.
A winter in Tangier, and home
through Spain.
L: Hatchards, 1882. 276p. NUC BL
OCLC

2360. HOWE, Jemima (Sartwell)
[Am. 1713?-1805]
A genuine and correct account of
the captivity, sufferings and
deliverance of Mrs. Jemima Howe,
of Hinsdale, in New Hampshire.
Taken from her own mouth, and
written, by the Rev. Bunker Gay.
Boston: pr. at Apollo press by
Belknap & Young, 1792. 20p. NUC
OCLC
[Reissue of Jeremy Belknap's
History of New Hampshire. v.3,
1792. Capture of Pequot Indian
fort in 1637.]

2361. HOWE, John Moffatt, comp.
see HOWE, Mary Mason

2362. HOWE, Mrs. John Moffatt see
HOWE, Mary Mason

2363. HOWE, Julia (Ward) [Am.
1819-1910]
From the oak to the olive: a
plain record of a pleasant journey.
Boston: Lee & Shepard, 1868.
304p. NUC BL OCLC
[Travel: Europe and England]

2364. -----Reminiscences, 1819-
1899.
Boston & NY: Houghton Mifflin &
co., 1899. 465p. NUC BL K OCLC

2365. -----A trip to Cuba.
Boston: Ticknor & Fields, 1860.
251p. NUC BL

2366. HOWE, Mary Mason, Mrs. John
Moffatt Howe [Am. 1794-1841]
Memoir of Mrs. Mary Howe ...
containing selections from her
letters and diary. [Ed.] her
husband, John Moffat Howe.

NY: G. Lane & P. P. Sandford, 1843. 282p. OCLC

2367. HOWEL, Martha [Am. 19c]
Narrative of the remarkable restoration of Martha Howel.
NY: n.p., 1807. NUC

2368. HOWIE, Mary Wright [Br. 19c] ALT: H., M. W.
Memorial of a beloved daughter. A selection from the poetical remains of M. W. H.
Edinburgh: priv. pr., 1870. 112p. BL

2369. HOWITT, Anna Mary see WATTS, Anna Mary (Howitt)

2370. HOWITT, Margaret [Br. b. 1839]
Twelve months with Fredrika Bremer in Sweden.
L: Jackson, Walford, & Hodder, 1866. 2v. NUC BL OCLC

2371. HOWITT, Margaret, ed. see HOWITT, Mary (Botham)

2372. HOWITT, Mary (Botham) [Br. 1799-1888]
Mary Howitt: an autobiography.
Ed. her daughter, Margaret Howitt.
L: W. Isbister, ltd., 1891. 356p. NUC BL MB

2373. HOWLAND, Eliza Newton (Woolsey), co-author and jt. ed.
see BACON, Georgeanna Muirson (Woolsey)

2374. HOWLAND, Sarah (Hazard) [Am. 1784-1847]
Extracts from the journal of Sarah Howland, and some of the poetry, letters, and other papers preserved by her.... Comp. Howland Pell.
NY: priv. pr., 1890. 122p. NUC BL OCLC

2375. HOYT, Dolly Eunice [Am. 1797-1820]
Memoirs of Dolly E. Hoyt, a member of the Union missionary family: who died on the Arkansas river, while ascending the same, on her passage to the Osage nation, the place of her destination, aged 23.

Danbury, CT: Osborn, 1828. 107p. NUC OCLC
[Preface signed: Comfort Hoyt]

2376. HUBBARD, Bela [Am. 1814-1896]
Memorials of a half-century.
NY & L: G. P. Putnam's sons, 1887. 581p. NUC OCLC
[Her life in Michigan]

2377. HUBBARD, Emma, ed. see HAYWARD, Jane Mary

2378. HUBBELL, Martha (Stone), comp. see HUBBELL, Mary E.

2379. HUBBELL, Mary E. [Am. 1833-1854]
The memorial; or, the life and writings of an only daughter. By her mother [Martha (Stone) Hubbell].
Boston: J. P. Jewett; Cleveland, OH: H. P. B. Jewett, 1857. 384p. NUC BL OCLC
[Includes letters, poems, fiction and essays.]

2380. HUBER, Mary Elizabeth [Am. 19c]
The cross and the crown. A memorial of Mary Elizabeth Huber.
Comp. Mrs. L. A. Holdiche.
NY: pr. F. Somers, 1864. 68p. NUC
[Includes letters and journal]

2381. HUDDLESTON, Lady Diana De Vere (Beauclerk) [Br. b. 1840]
ALT: Beauclerk, Lady Diana de Vere
A summer and winter in Norway. By Lady Di Beauclerk.
L: J. Murray, 1868. 148p. NUC BL OCLC

2382. HUDSON, Gertrude [Br. 19c]
PSEUD: Israfel
Ivory, apes and peacocks. Pub. as: Israfel
L: At the sign of the Unicorn; NY: M. P. Mansfield & A. Wassels, 1899. 274p. NUC BL OCLC
[Travel: India]

2383. HUDSON, Mary E. (Clemmer) Ames see AMES, Mary E. (Clemmer)

2384. HUGGAN, Nancy (McClure) [Am. b. 1836] ALT: McClure, Nancy
The story of Nancy McClure:

captivity among the Sioux.
Minn. Hist. Soc. Collections,
v.6. St. Paul, MN: Minnesota
hist. soc., 1894. NUC OCLC

2385. HUGHES, C., ed. see HUGHES,
Margaret Smith

2386. HUGHES, Mrs. H., comp. see
HEMANS, Felicia Dorothea (Browne)

2387. HUGHES, Harriet, comp. see
HEMANS, Felicia Dorothea (Browne)

2388. HUGHES, Margaret Smith [Am.
19c]
Letter ... to her father,
narrating the loss of the packet
ship Poland, on her way from New
York to Haore, 16 May, 1840. With
other correspondence. Ed. C.
Hughes.
Baltimore, MD: J. O. Troy, 1845.
34p. NUC BL

2389. HULL, Carrie E., Mrs. [Am.
19c]
The Hull baby; or, a mother's
wrongs; being a complete account
of the celebrated case pending in
the courts of Kansas.
St. Louis, MO: The author, 1878.
145p. NUC OCLC
[Fictionalized account of a
mother whose baby was kidnapped
by the father and kept from her.]

2390. HULTON, Anne (Henry), co-
author see SAVAGE, Sarah (Henry)

2391. HUMBERT, Mabel [Br. 19c]
Continental chit-chat.
L: F. V. White & co., 1897. BL
OCLC
[Travel: Germany & France]

2392. HUME, Sophia [Am. 1701-
1774]
An exhortation to the inhabitants
of South Carolina ... to which is
inserted, some account of the
author's experience.
Philadelphia,: pr. William
Bradford, 1747. 158p. NUC BL K
OCLC
[Society of Friends doctrine plus
account of Charleston hurricane,
Sept. 19, 1752]

2393. HUMPHREY, Mrs. E. J. [Am.
19c]
Six years in India; or, sketches
of India and its people, as seen
by a lady missionary.
NY: Carlton & Porter, 1866. 286p.
NUC BL

2394. HUNT, Ann [Br. 1810-1897]
Memorials and letters of Ann
Hunt. Comp. Matilda Sturge.
L: Headley bros., 1898. 187p. BL
OCLC
[Society of Friends, England]

2395. HUNT, Caroline, ed. see DE
BURGH, Emma Maria (Hunt)

2396. HUNT, Ellen Saint John [Br.
1837-1863] ALT: H., E. S. S.
Thoughts of sunshine in sorrow,
and pilgrim thoughts.
First series. L: James Nisbet &
sons, 1862. 134p. NUC BL

2397. -----Thoughts of sunshine
in sorrow.
Second series. L & Norwich: Henry
Fogg, 1866. NUC BL
[Memoirs of an invalid; includes
poetry]

2398. HUNT, Harriot Kesia, M. D.
[Am. 1805-1875]
Glances and glimpses; or, fifty
years social, including twenty
years professional life.
Boston: John P. Jewett; NY:
Sheldon, Lamport, & Blakeman,
1856. 418p. NUC BL K OCLC

2399. HUNT, Helen Maria (Fiske)
see JACKSON, Helen Maria (Fiske)
Hunt

2400. HUNT, Louise Livingston,
comp. see LIVINGSTON, Louise
(Davecac) Moreau

2401. HUNT, Marion Edith (Waugh)
Holman, Mrs. William Holman Hunt
[Br. 19c]
Children at Jerusalem: a sketch
of modern life in Syria.
L: Ward, Lock & co., 1881. 189p.
NUC

2402. HUNT, Sarah (Morey) [Am.
1797-1889]

Journal of the life and religious labors of Sarah Hunt (late of West Grove, Chester County, PA). Philadelphia: Friends book assoc., 1892. 262p. NUC OCLC

2403. HUNT, Mrs. William Holman see HUNT, Marion Edith (Waugh) Holman

2404. HUNTER, Ella [Br. 19c] A lady's drive from Florence to Cherbourg; or, Santo, Lucia, and co., where they stayed, and what they paid. Edinburgh: W. Blackwood & sons, 1883. 123p. NUC BL

2405. -----Santo, Lucia, and co. in Austria ... where they've been ... and what they paid. Edinburgh & L: W. Blackwood & sons, 1883. 161p. BL

2406. HUNTER, Grace [Br. 19c] Witnessing and working: memoir of G. Hunter ... chiefly written by herself. [Ed.] Rev. G. Alley. Belfast: J. Adams, 1896. 249p. BL

2407. HUNTER, Jean (Dickson) lady [Br. 1775-1844] The journal of Gen. Sir Martin Hunter and some letters of his wife, Lady Hunter. Edinburgh: The Edinburgh press, 1894. NUC BL

2408. HUNTER, General Sir Martin, co-author see HUNTER, Jean (Dickson)

2409. HUNTINGTON, Anne (Huntington), Mrs. Benjamin Huntington [b. 1740?] The Huntington letters, in the possession of Julia Chester Wells. Ed. D. William McCracken. NY: The Appleton press, 1897. 220p. NUC [First period (1761-1792) mainly letters between Benjamin and Anne Huntington. Second period (1796-1798) mainly letters by Rachel (Huntington) Tracy to her sisters, Lucy and Anne.]

2410. HUNTINGTON, Arria Sargent see PHELPS, Elizabeth

2411. HUNTINGTON, Benjamin, co-author see HUNTINGTON, Anne (Huntington)

2412. HUNTINGTON, Mrs. Benjamin see HUNTINGTON, Anne (Huntington)

2413. HUNTINGTON, Rachel, co-author see HUNTINGTON, Anne (Huntington)

2414. HUNTINGTON, Susan (Mansfield) [Am. 1791-1823] Memoirs of the late Mrs. Susan Huntington: consisting principally of extracts from her journals and letters. Ed. Benjamin B. Wisner. Boston: Crocker & Brewster, 1826. 408p.; L: Scott, Webster, 18--. 431p. NUC BL MAD OCLC

2415. HUNTLEY, Lydia Howard see SIGOURNEY, Lydia Howard (Huntley)

2416. HURD, Fanny see HURD, Mary Fanny (Bickford)

2417. HURD, Mrs. Henry see HURD, Mary Fanny (Bickford)

2418. HURD, Mary Fanny (Bickford), Mrs. Henry Hurd [Br. 19c] ALT: Hurd, Fanny Fanny Hurd; or, the story of a West Indian missionary's daughter. Ed. Nehemiah Curnock. L: J. Woolner, 1886. 50p. BL

2419. HURLL, Mary [Br. 18c] An account of the remarkable conversion and Christian experience ... [with meditations on some passages of the Scriptures,] as taken from her own mouth. 2d ed. L: n.p., 1708. NUC BL

2420. HURST, Lulu see ATKINSON, Lulu (Hurst)

2421. HUSTON, Isabella Pennock (Lukens) [Am. 1822?-1889] Superficial glimpses of travel. Philadelphia: Porter & Coates, 1888. 256p. NUC OCLC [Travel: Europe]

2422. HUSTON, Mary E. [Am. 19c]
PSEUD: Cousin Mary
A summer journey in Europe. Pub.
as: Cousin Mary
Cincinnati, OH: Robert Clarke,
1881. 274p. NUC BL OCLC

2423. HUTCHEON, Mrs. John [Br. 19c]
Glimpses of India, and of mission
life.
L: Wesleyan Conference office,
1878. 200p. NUC BL

2424. -----Leaves from a mission
house in India.
L: Wesleyan Methodist mission
house, 1871. 64p. NUC BL

2425. HUTCHINSON, Elizabeth [Br.
19c] ALT: H., E.
A sermon occasioned by the death
of ... Miss E. H. with an
appendix containing a short
memoir of her life, etc. Together
with letters written by the
deceased. By Edward Burn.
Birmingham: Grafton & Reddell,
1800. 62p. BL

2426. HUTCHINSON, Louisa [Br.
19c]
In tents in the Transvaal.
L: Richard Bentley & son, 1879.
225p. NUC BL OCLC
[Travel: South Africa]

2427. HUTCHINSON, Lucy (Apsley)
[Br. 1620-1671]
Memoirs of the life of Colonel
Hutchinson, Governor of
Nottingham Castle and town. ...
to which is prefixed the life of
Mrs. Hutchinson, written by
herself, a fragment.
L: n.p., 1806. 446p. NUC BL MB
OCLC

2428. HUTSON, Mary, Mrs. [Am.
18c]
Living Christianity delineated,
in the diaries and letters of two
eminently pious persons lately
deceased; viz., Mr. Hugh Bryan,
and Mrs. Mary Hutson, both of
South Carolina.
L: J. Buckland, 1760. NUC BL

2429. HUTTON, Catherine [Br.
1756-1846]
Catherine Hutton and her friends.

Ed. Mrs. Catherine Hutton Beale.
Birmingham: Cornish bros., 1895.
264p. NUC BL OCLC
[Letters. OCLC dates 1865]

2430. -----Reminiscences of a
gentlewoman of the last century:
letters of Catherine Hutton. Ed.
her cousin, Mrs. Catherine Hutton
Beale.
Birmingham: Cornish bros., 1891.
250p. NUC BL

2431. HYDE, Nancy Maria [Am.
1792-1816]
The writings of Nancy Maria Hyde,
of Norwich, Conn., connected with
a sketch of her life. Ed. Lydia
Howard (Huntley) Sigourney.
Norwich CT: Russell Hubbard,
1816. 252p. NUC BL MAD
[Diary of a teacher, includes
many original verses.]

2432. I., M. see INNES, Martha

2433. I. M., pseud. see IRBY,
Adeline Paulina

2434. IMMEN, Loraine (Pratt) [Am.
b. 1840]
Letters of travel in California
in the winter and spring of 1896.
Grand Rapids, MI: n.p., 1896?.
54p. NUC OCLC

2435. INCHBALD, Elizabeth
(Simpson) [Br. 1753-1821]
Memoirs of Mrs. I.: including her
familiar correspondence with the
most distinguished persons of her
times. Ed. James Boaden.
L: R. Bentley, 1833. 2v. NUC BL

2436. INGALLS, Marilla Baker,
Mrs. [Am. 1828-1902]
Ocean sketches of life in Burmah.
Philadelphia: American Baptist
Publication Society, 1857?. 318p.
NUC OCLC

2437. INGLEBY, KATE, pseud. see
LELAND, Hattie M. (Perkins)

2438. INGLEHART, Fanny (Chambers)
Gooch [Am. 1842/1849?-1913] ALT:
Chambers, Fanny; Gooch, Fanny
(Chambers)
Face to face with the Mexicans.
Pub. as: Fanny Chambers
NY: Fords, Howard & Hubbard,
1887. 584p. NUC BL
[Anecdotes of seven years in
Mexico and notes on customs.]

2439. INGLIS, Julia Selina
(Thesiger), Lady [Br. 1833-1904]
Letter containing extracts from a
journal kept by Lady Inglis
during the siege of Lucknow.
L: pr. for priv. circ., 1858.
31p. NUC BL

2440. -----The siege of Lucknow.
A diary.
L: J. R. Osgood, McIlvaine & co.;
NY: C. Scribner's sons, 1892.
240p. NUC BL

2441. INGRAM, Helen K., Mrs. [Am.
19c]
Three on a tour.
Detroit, MI: J. Barnman & son,
1895. 120p. NUC OCLC
[Mackinac Island]

2442. -----Tourists' and
settlers' guide to Florida.
Jacksonville, FL: DaCosta, 1895.
135p. NUC OCLC

2443. INHABITANT OF CONGLETON,
AN, pseud. see DAVIS, Jane

2444. INNES, Emily [Br. 19c]
The Chersonese with the gilding
off.
L: R. Bentley & son, 1885. 2v.
NUC BL OCLC
[Travel: Malay Peninsula]

2445. INNES, Martha, Mrs. William
Innes [Br. 19c] ALT: I., M.
Memoir of Mrs. M. I.; with
extracts from her diary and
letters. Comp. & ed. her husband,
Rev. William Innes.
L: n.p., 1844. BL

2446. INNES, Mrs. William see
INNES, Martha

2447. INNES, Rev. William, comp.
& ed. see INNES, Martha

2448. INVERARITY, Rosalind
Harriet Maria (Wallace), co-
author see DUNLOP, Madeline Anne
(Wallace)

2449. IRBY, Adeline Paulina [Br.
1833-1911] PSEUD: M., I. [With
Georgina Mary Muir (Mackenzie)
Sebright, Lady, Br. d. 1874]
Across the Carpathians. By I. M.
[Irby and Sebright].
Cambridge & L: Macmillan & co.,
1862. 299p. NUC BL OCLC

2450. -----Notes on the south
Slavonic countries in Austria and
Turkey in Europe. By I. M. [Irby
& Sebright].
Edinburgh: W. Blackwood & sons,
1865. 66p. NUC

2451. -----Travels in the
Slavonic provinces of Turkey-in-
Europe. By I. M. [Irby and
Sebright].
L & NY: A. Strahan, 1866. 687p.
NUC BL OCLC
[Also pub. as: The Turks, the
Greeks, and the Slavons. Travels
in the Slavonic provinces]

2452. IRELAND, Mrs. Alexander see
IRELAND, Annie Elizabeth
(Nicholson)

2453. IRELAND, Mrs. Alexander,
ed. see JEWSBURY, Geraldine
Endsor

2454. IRELAND, Annie Elizabeth
(Nicholson), Mrs. Alexander
Ireland [Br. d. 1893]
Longer flights: recollections and
studies.
L: Digby Long & co., 1898. 257p.
NUC BL MB
[Travel and memoirs]

2455. IRELAND, Annie Elizabeth
(Nicholson), ed. see JEWSBURY,
Geraldine Endsor

2456. IRVING, Washington, ed. see
DAVIDSON, Margaret Miller

2457. ISRAFEL, pseud. see HUDSON,
Gertrude

2458. J., C., Mrs. see JEMMAT, Catherine (Yeo)

2459. JACKSON, Anne [Br. 17c]
An account of Anne Jackson.
n.p.: n.p., 1832. MB
[Spiritual autobiography]

2460. JACKSON, Charles, ed. see THORNTON, Alice (Wanderford)

2461. JACKSON, Helen Maria (Fiske) Hunt [Am. 1831-1885] ALT: H., H.; Hunt, Helen Maria (Fiske)
Bits of travel. By H. H.
Boston: J. R. Osgood & co., 1872. 304p. NUC

2462. -----Bits of travel at home. By H. H.
Boston: Roberts bros., 1878. 413p. NUC
[Ten chapters repr. as: Colorado Springs, with cover title: Pike's Peak profiles.]

2463. -----Glimpses of California and the missions.
Boston: Little, Brown & co., 1885. 202p. NUC

2464. -----Glimpses of three coasts. By Helen Jackson (H. H.).
Boston: Roberts bros., 1886. 418p. NUC
[California, Scotland, England, Norway, Denmark, Germany]

2465. JACKSON, Julia (Newell) [Am. 19c]
A winter holiday in summer lands.
Chicago: A. C. McClurg & co., 1890. 221p. NUC
[Travel: Cuba and Mexico]

2466. JACKSON, Margaret, Miss [Br. d. 1822]
Extracts from letters and other pieces written by M. Jackson, during her last illness.
Dublin: Bentham & Gardiner, 1824. 89p. NUC BL

2467. JACKSON, Mary [Br. 19c]
Rambles in the United States.
Liverpool: J. Looney, 1855. 61p. NUC

2468. JACKSON, Mary Catherine [Br. 19c]

Word-sketches in the sweet South.
L: R. Bentley & son, 1873. 301p. NUC BL
[Travel: Southern Europe]

2469. JACKSON, Mattie Jane [Am. b. 1845]
The story of Mattie J. Jackson, her parentage--experience of ... slavery. Written by Dr. L. S. Thompson ... as given by Mattie.
Lawrence, MA: pr. at Sentinel office, 1866. 34p. NUC K OCLC

2470. JACKSON, Rachel Maria [Br. 1755-1836]
Memoranda of Rachel Maria Jackson; with extracts from some of her letters. Comp. Martha Wright.
Dublin: pr. Robert Chapman, 1854. 198p. NUC
[Chiefly religious]

2471. JACOBS, Annie, co-author see JACOBS, Sarah Sprague

2472. JACOBS, Esther [Am. 19c]
Love and law. A story of joy and woe in a singer's life.
NY: G. W. Dillingham, 1895. NUC
[May be fictional.]

2473. JACOBS, Harriet (Brent) [Am. 1818-1896] ALT: Brent, Linda
Incidents in the life of a slave girl, written by herself. Ed. L[ydia] Maria (Francis) Child.
Boston: pub. for the author, 1860. 306p. NUC K OCLC
[Linda was her slave name; escaped north at 21 years.]

2474. JACOBS, Sarah Sprague [Am. b. 1813]
Journal of Sarah Sprague Jacobs and Annie Jacobs, sisters, of Cambridge, Mass.
Providence, RI: n.p., 1864?. 90p. NUC
[Written on visit to Rhode Island in 1864; first half by S. J., second by A. J.]

2475. JACOBY, Teresa [Br. 19c]
Angelic revelations concerning the origin ... of the human spirit. Illustrated by the experiences in earth and spirit life of Teresa Jacoby, now known

as the Angel Purity (and other angels).
Manchester: pr. for priv. circ., 1875-85. 5v. BL

2476. JAMES, Alice [Am. 1848-1892]
The diary of Alice James.
Cambridge, MA: John Wilson & son, 1894. 280p. NUC
[4 copies printed]

2477. JAMES I, King of Great Britain and Ireland, co-author see ELIZABETH, Queen of England

2478. JAMES I, King of Great Britain and Ireland, co-author see MARY II, Queen of Great Britain and Ireland

2479. JAMES VI, King of Scotland, co-author see ELIZABETH, Queen of England

2480. JAMESON, Anna Brownell (Murphy) [Br. 1794-1859/60]
A lady's diary.
Paris: Baudry's European library; L: H. Colburn, 1826. 354p. NUC BL MB OCLC
[Contains "The diary of an Ennuyé" and "The diary of a Désennuyée" under which titles the work was also pub. Travel: Northern Europe]

2481. -----Memoirs of the life of Anna Jameson ... by her niece, Geraldine (Bate) Macpherson.
L: Longmans, Green & co., 1878.; Boston: Roberts bros., 1878. 362p. NUC BL OCLC

2482. -----Visits and sketches at home and abroad.
L: Saunders & Otley, 1834. 4v. NUC BL OCLC
[Collection of her travel writings, tales and sketches; Germany, Belgium, France]

2483. -----Winter studies and summer rambles in Canada.
L: Saunders & Otley, 1838. 3v. NUC BL
[Shortened version pub as: Sketches in Canada and rambles among the red men.]

2484. JANEWAY, Catherine [Br. 19c]

Glimpses at Greece, today and before yesterday.
L: K. Paul, Trench, Trübner & co., 1897. 148p. NUC BL

2485. -----Ten weeks in Egypt and Palestine.
L: Kegan, Paul & co., 1894. 158p. BL

2486. JANET, pseud. see COLLINS, N. J. H., Mrs.

2487. JAQUES, Mary J. [Br. 19c]
Texan ranch life: with three months through Mexico in a "Prairie Schooner".
L: Horace Cox, 1894. 363p. NUC BL K OCLC

2488. JARDINE, H., Mrs. [Br. 19c]
A voyage in the S. S. Oceanic.
Manchester: J. E. Cornish, pr., 1882. 92p. NUC BL

2489. JAY, MRS. W. M. L., pseud. see WOODRUFF, Julia Louisa Matilda (Curtiss)

2490. JEBB, Ann (Torkington) [Br. 1735-1812]
Memoirs of Mrs. Jebb. Ed. George Wilson Meadly.
L: T. Davison, 1812?. 62p. NUC BL
[Wrote on political and church issues as Priscilla.]

2491. JEFFERY, H. M., ed. see GRENFELL, Lydia

2492. JEFFREYS, Mrs. Keturah [Br. 19c]
The widowed missionary's journal, containing some account of Madagascar... .
Southampton: pr. for the author, 1827. 216p. NUC MB OCLC

2493. JEMMAT, Catherine (Yeo) [Br. 1752-1771] ALT: J., C., Mrs.
Memoirs of Mrs. Catherine Jemmat, daughter of the late Admiral Yeo of Plymouth ... written by herself.
L: n.p., 1771. 2v. NUC BL MB

2494. JENKIN, Prudence [Br. 19c]
The triumphs of Grace exemplified, in the diary, correspondence, experience, and

happy deaths of Prudence and Mary
Jenkin. Comp. their surviving
sister.
L: n.p., 1836. BL

2495. JENKIN, Mary, co-author <u>see</u>
JENKIN, Prudence

2496. JENKINS, Howard M., comp.
<u>see</u> WISTER, Sarah

2497. JENKINS, Sarah, Miss [1808-
1827]
Memoirs of Miss Sarah Jenkins. By
Miss [Mary] Tooth of Madeley.
NY: Emory & Waugh, 1831. 78p. NUC
OCLC
[NUC notes Eliza Talitha Tooth as
supposed author, but entry is
under Mary Tooth]

2498. JENNER, Mrs. Henry <u>see</u>
JENNER, Katherine Lee (Rawlings)

2499. JENNER, Katherine Lee
(Rawlings), Mrs. Henry Jenner
[Br. 19c] ALT: Lee, Katherine
In the Alsatian mountains: a
narrative of a tour in the
Vosges. Pub. as: Katherine Lee.
L: R. Bentley & son, 1883. 282p.
NUC BL OCLC

2500. JENNESS, Caroline Elizabeth
[Am. 1824-1857]
Writings of Caroline Elizabeth
Jenness. With a memoir.
Boston: pr. J. Wilson & son,
1858. 275p. NUC OCLC

2501. JEPHSON, Harriet Julia
(Campbell), Lady [Br. 19/20C]
A Canadian scrapbook.
L: Marshall & Russell, 1897. NUC
BL

2502. JERNINGHAM, Hon. Frances
(Dillon), Lady [Br. d. 1825]
The Jerningham letters (1780-
1843). Being excerpts from the
correspondence and diaries of
Lady Jerningham and of her
daughter, [Charlotte], Lady
Bedingfield [d. 1854]. Ed.
Egerton Castle.
L: R. Bentley & son, 1896. 2v.
NUC BL MBD OCLC

2503. JESSUP, Mrs. Henry Harris
[Am. 19c]

The holy land. Extracts from the
journal of Mrs. Henry H. Jessup.
n.p.: n.p., 1885?. 31p. NUC

2504. JESUP, Lucy [Br. 19c]
Extracts from the papers and
letters of Lucy Jesup.
Sudbury: Wright & Gilbert, 1858.
57p. NUC BL

2505. JESUP, Maria [BL: Mary]
(King) [Br. 1799-1837]
Extracts from the memoranda and
letters of Maria Jesup. ... Also
a few extracts from the papers of
her younger sister, Marianne King
[1804?-1818].
York: W. Alexander & co., 1840?.
96p. NUC BL

2506. JESUP, Martha <u>see</u> JESUP,
Mary Brown

2507. JESUP, Mary <u>see</u> JESUP,
Maria (King)

2508. JESUP, Mary Brown [Br.
1770-1835]
Selections from the writings of
Mary Jesup: late of Halstead,
Essex: with some account of two
of her children [Martha Jesup,
1809-1830; Priscilla Jesup, d.
1829].
L: Harvey & Darton, 1842. 124p.
NUC MBD OCLC
[Member of Society of Friends.
Diary 1787-1835]

2509. JESUP, Priscilla <u>see</u> JESUP,
Mary Brown

2510. JETER, J. B., comp. <u>see</u>
SHUCK, Henrietta (Hall)

2511. JEWEL, Adele M., Mrs. [Am.
b. 1834]
A brief narrative of the life of
Mrs. Adele M. Jewel, being deaf
and dumb.
Ann Arbor, MI: Chase's steam pr.
house, 1869. 24p. NUC K

2512. JEWSBURY, Geraldine Endsor
[Br. 1812-1880]
Selections from the letters of
Geraldine Endsor Jewsbury to Jane
Welsh Carlyle. Ed. Mrs. Alexander
[Annie Elizabeth (Nicholson)]
Ireland.

L: Longmans, Green & co., 1892.
443p. NUC BL OCLC

2513. JEWSBURY, Maria Jane see
FLETCHER, Maria Jane (Jewsbury)

2514. JOCELIN, Elizabeth (Brooke)
see JOCELINE, Elizabeth (Brooke)

2515. JOCELINE, Elizabeth
(Brooke) [Br. 1596-1622] ALT:
Jocelin, Elizabeth (Brooke)
The mothers legacie to her unborn
childe.
L: John Haviland for W. Barrett,
1624. 114p. NUC BL
[Written during pregnancy; her
fears of death, advice on
upbringing.]

2516. JOHNSON, Anna Cummings,
Miss [Am. 1818-1892] PSEUD: Lady,
A
The cottages of the Alps. By A
Lady.
NY: Charles Scribner, 1860.
422p.; L: Sampson, Low son & co.,
1860. 2v. NUC BL OCLC

2517. -----Peasant life in
Germany.
NY: Charles Scribner, 1858. 430p.
NUC BL

2518. JOHNSON, Catherine Bodham
(Donne), ed. see HESKETH, Harriet
(Cowper), Lady

2519. JOHNSON, Elizabeth Jackson,
Mrs. [Br. 1721-1798]
An account of Mrs. Elizabeth
Johnson, well known in the city
of Bristol for more than half a
century, for her eminent piety
and benevolence. To which is
added, an extract from her diary.
Bristol: pr., W. Pine & son;
Dublin: B. Dugdale, 1799. 46p. BL
MBD OCLC [Methodist]

2520. -----Some account of the
experience of E. J.
L: pr., G. Paramore, 1792. 11p.
OCLC

2521. JOHNSON, Rev. Grant see
BELL, Frances Augusta

2522. JOHNSON, Jane [Br. 19c]
The life of Jane Johnson, the

champion drunkard of the world,
captured by the Salvation Army,
as related by herself.
Leeds: Pinder & Howes, 1883. 18p.
BL

2523. JOHNSON, Laura (Winthrop),
Mrs. William Templeton Johnson
[Am. 1825-1889]
Eight hundred miles in an
ambulance.
Philadelphia: J. B. Lippincott,
1889. 131p. NUC BL OCLC
[First printed in Lippincott's
Magazine]

2524. JOHNSON, Samuel, co-author
see PIOZZI, Hester Lynch
(Salusbury) Thrale

2525. JOHNSON, Sarah (Barclay)
[Am. 1837-1885]
Hadji in Syria; or, three years
in Jerusalem.
Philadelphia: J. Challen & sons,
1858. 303p. NUC OCLC

2526. JOHNSON, Sophia [Am. b.
1798]
The friendless orphan. An
affecting narrative of the trials
and afflictions of Sophia
Johnson, the early victim of a
cruel step-mother.
NY: S. Johnson, 1841. 24p. NUC BL
[Served in American Army, 1812]

2527. JOHNSON, Susan Griffith
(Colpoys) [Br. 19c]
Adventures of a lady in the war
of independence in America.
Wokington: P. D. Lambe, pr.,
1874. 57p. NUC

2528. JOHNSON, Susanna (Willard)
see HASTINGS, Susanna (Willard)
Johnson

2529. JOHNSON, Virginia Wales
[Am. 1849-1916]
The lily of the Arno, or Florence
past and present.
Boston: Estes & Lauriat; L: Gay &
Bird, 1891. 354p. NUC BL
[Also pub. as: Florence]

2530. -----Genoa the superb, the
city of Columbus.
Boston: Gates & Lauriat; L: Gay &
Bird, 1892. 288p. NUC BL

2531. JOHNSON, Mrs. William
Templeton see JOHNSON, Laura
(Winthrop)

2532. JOHNSTON, Elizabeth [Br.
19c]
The rose and the lotus; or, home
in England and home in India. By
the wife of a Bengal civilian.
L: n.p., 1859. BL

2533. JOHNSTON, Elizabeth Bryant
[Am. 1833-1907]
Christmas in Kentucky, 1862.
Washington, D.C.: Gibson bros.,
pr., 1892. 24p. NUC OCLC
[How slaves received the
Emancipation Proclamation.]

2534. JOHNSTON, Ellen [Br. 19c]
Autobiography. Poems and songs.
Glasgow: W. Love, 1867. 232p. NUC
BL MB
[Cover title: Factory girl's
poems]

2535. JOHNSTON, R. L. N., ed. see
MORTIMER, Madge

2536. JOHNSTONE, Catherine Laura
[Br. 1838-1923]
Winter and summer excursions in
Canada.
L: Digby, Long & co., 1894. 213p.
NUC BL OCLC

2537. JOHNSTONE, Julia [Br. 19c]
Confessions of Julia Johnstone
written by herself, ... in
contradiction to the fables of
Harriette Wilson.
L: Benbow, 1825. 354p. NUC BL MB

2538. JOHNSTON, Priscilla
(Buxton) [Br. 1808-1852]
Extracts from Priscilla
Johnston's journal [and letters].
Comp. her daughter, E. MacInnes.
Carlisle: Charles Thurman & sons,
1860. 203p. NUC BL MBD OCLC

2539. JONES, Agnes Elizabeth [Br.
1832-1868]
Memorials of Agnes Elizabeth
Jones, by her sister, Miss J.
Jones.
L: Strahan & co., 1871. 486p. NUC
BL MBD OCLC

[Nurse; includes excerpts of
diary. Pub. in U.S. as: Una and
her paupers.]

2540. JONES, Agnes Elizabeth, co-
author see DUTTON, Amy

2541. JONES, Eliza (Grew) [Am.
1803-1838]
The Burman village in Siam. A
missionary narrative.
Philadelphia: American Baptist
pub. society, n.d. 25p. NUC

2542. -----Memoir of Mrs. Eliza
G. Jones, missionary to Burmah
and Siam.
Philadelphia: American Baptist
pub.& Sunday school society,
1842. 172p. NUC
[Contains poems]

2543. JONES, Elizabeth [Br. 19c]
Educational reminiscences.
L: n.p., 1839. BL

2544. JONES, Henrietta (Spink)
Clark [Am. b. 1818]
Sketches from real life.
Watertown, NY: D. E. Hungerford,
1898. 239p. NUC OCLC
[Autobiography]

2545. JONES, Miss J., comp. see
JONES, Agnes Elizabeth

2546. JONES, Sarah, Mrs. [Am.
1754?-1794]
Devout letters: or, letters
spiritual and friendly.
Alexandria, VA: Samuel Snowden,
1804. 154p. NUC OCLC

2547. JONES, Sibella [Br. 19c]
Mountains and cities; or the home
of our princess.
L: n.p., 1858. BL
[Travel: Europe]

2548. JONES, Thomas Snell, comp.
see GLENORCHY, Willielma
(Maxwell) Campbell, Viscountess

2549. JORDAN, Dorothy (Bland)
[Br. 1761-1816]
The life of Mrs. Jordan,
including original private
correspondence, and numerous
anecdotes of her contemporaries.

Ed. James Boaden.
L: E. Bull, 1831. 2v. NUC BL OCLC

2550. JOSS, Catherine (Smith)
[Am. b. 1820]
Autobiography of Catherine Joss,
born in Philadelphia, Pa.,
October 7, 1820. Daughter of
Christian Smith, who moved his
family to Payne tp., Holmes co.,
O., in May, 1829, and laid out
and established the village of
Weinsburg.
Cleveland, OH: n.p., 1891. 464p.
NUC K OCLC

2551. JOWITT, Jane [Br. b. 1770]
Memoirs of Jane Jowitt, the poor
poetess: aged 74 years ...
written by herself.
Sheffield: J. Pearce jun., 1844.
BL MB OCLC
[Includes poetry]

2552. JUDD, Laura Fish [Am. 1804-
1872]
Honolulu. Sketches of life,
social, political and religious
in the Hawaiian Islands from 1828
to 1861.
NY: A. D. F. Randolph & co.,
1880. 258p. NUC BL OCLC

2553. JUDSON, Ann (Hasseltine)
[Am. 1789-1826]
An account of the American
Baptist Mission to the Burman
Empire.
L: J. Butterworth, 1823. 334p.
NUC BL OCLC
[Correspondence]

2554. -----American biography:
or, memoirs of Mrs. A. Judson and
Mrs. M. L. Ramsay.
Edinburgh: n.p., 1831. BL

2555. JUDSON, Emily E. (Chubbuck)
[Am. 1817-1854] ALT: Chubbuck,
Emily
The life and letters of Mrs.
Emily C. Judson. Comp. Asahel C.
Kendrick.
NY: Sheldon & co.; Boston: Gould
& Lincoln, 1860. 426p. NUC BL MAD
OCLC
[Autobiography; diaries;
missionary life in Burma]

2556. JUDSON, Emily E.
(Chubbuck), comp. see CHUBBUCK,
Harriet

2557. JUDSON, Emily E.
(Chubbuck), comp. see JUDSON,
Sarah (Hall) Boardman

2558. JUDSON, Sarah (Hall)
Boardman [Am. 1803-1845]
[BL: Missionary Biography] The
memoir of Sarah B. Judson, member
of the American Mission to
Burmah. By Fanny Forester [Emily
E. (Chubbuck) Judson].
Cincinnati, OH: N. Anderson; NY:
Sheldon; L. Colby & co., 250p.;
L: Aylott & Jones, 1848. 180p.
NUC BL OCLC
[Contains letters and a few poems.]

2559. JUKES, Harriet Maria
(Hole), Mrs. M. R. Jukes [Br.
1817-1854]
The earnest Christian: memoir,
letters and journals of Harriet
Maria, wife of M. R. Jukes. Comp.
& ed. Mrs. H. A. Gilbert.
NY: R. Carter, 1859. 314p. NUC BL
MB

2560. JUKES, Mrs. M. R. see
JUKES, Harriet Maria (Hole)

2561. JUSTICE, Elizabeth (Surby)
[Br. 18C]
A voyage to Russia, to which is
added, translated from the
Spanish, a curious account of the
relicks ... in the Cathedral of
Oviedo.
York: pr., Thomas Gent, 1739.
59p. NUC BL [Governess]

2562. K., A. see KEARY, Annie

2563. K., F. E., Mrs. see KING,
Frances Elizabeth

2564. K., M. see KERR, M., Mrs.

2565. K., M. A. see KELTY, Mary
Ann

2566. K., S. R. <u>see</u> KAY, Sarah R.

2567. KANE, Elisha Kent, co-author <u>see</u> KANE, Margaret (Fox)

2568. KANE, Mrs. Elisha Kent <u>see</u> KANE, Margaret (Fox)

2569. KANE, Margaret (Fox), Mrs. Elisha Kent Kane [1833-1893] ALT: Fox, Margaret
The love-life of Dr. [Elisha Kent] Kane; containing the correspondence, and a history of the acquaintance, engagement, and secret marriage between E. K. Kane and M. Fox.
NY: Carleton, 1866. 288p. BL OCLC

2570. KAUTZ, Augusta [Am. 19/20c]
Straggling thoughts among homely duties.
San Francisco: n.p., 1898. 80p. NUC
[May contain personal material.]

2571. -----A world my own.
San Francisco: H. S. Crocker, 1896. 56p. NUC
[May contain personal material]

2572. KAVANAGH, Julia [Br. 1824-1877]
A summer and winter in the two Sicilies.
L: Hurst & Blackett, 1858. 2v. NUC BL OCLC

2573. KAY, Sarah R., Mrs. [Am. 19c] ALT: K., S. R.
Twelve states and a kingdom. By S. R. K.
Watseka, IL: Iroquois county times, pr., 1878. 96p. NUC
[Travel: USA]

2574. KAYE, Sir J. W., ed. <u>see</u> KNIGHT, Ellis Cornelia

2575. KEARY, Annie [Br. 1825-1879] ALT: K., A.
Letters of Annie Keary.
L: Christian Knowledge Society, 1883. 86p. NUC BL

2576. KECKLEY [BL: Heckley], Elizabeth (Hobbs) [Am. 1824-1907]
Behind the scenes; or, thirty years a slave, and four years in the White House. By Elizabeth Keckley, formerly a slave, but more recently modiste, and friend to Mrs. Lincoln.
NY: G. W. Carleton, 1868. 371p. NUC BL K OCLC
[Worked for Mary Todd Lincoln. Reminiscences of slavery; includes some letters from Mrs. Lincoln.]

2577. KEESE, Catherine (Robinson) [Am. 1806-1860]
A memoir of Catherine R. Keese, late of Peru, N.Y. Comprising extracts from her letters and other sketches. Ed. Samuel Keese.
NY: J. Egbert, pr., 1866. 76p. NUC OCLC

2578. KEESE, Samuel, ed. <u>see</u> KEESE, Catherine (Robinson)

2579. KEITH, Caroline Phebe (Tenney) [Am. 1821-1862]
The conflict and the victory of life. Memoir of Mrs. Caroline P. Keith, missionary of the Protestant Episcopal Church to China. Ed. her brother, William C. Tenney.
NY: D. Appleton & co., 1864. 392p. NUC OCLC

2580. KELLY, Fanny (Wiggins) [Am. b. 1845]
Narrative of my captivity among the Sioux Indians.
Cincinnati, OH: Wilstach, Baldwin & co.; Hartford, CT: Mutual pub. co., 1871. 285p. NUC BL OCLC

2581. KELLY, Mary (Spence) [Br. 19c] ALT: Spence, Mary
A glimpse of Norway.
Manchester: pr. certified industrial schools, Ardwick Green, 1868. 82p. NUC BL

2582. KELLY, Sophia (Sherwood), ed. <u>see</u> SHERWOOD, Mary Martha (Butt)

2583. KELTY, Mary Ann [Br. 1789-1873] ALT: K., M. A.
Loneliness and leisure, a record of the thoughts and feelings of advanced life. By M. A. K.
L: Adams & co, 1867. NUC BL MB
[Possibly fiction]

2584. -----Reminiscences of thought and feeling. By M. A. K. L: W. Pickering, 1852. 290p. NUC BL MB OCLC [Possibly fiction]

2585. -----Visiting my relations, and its results; a series of small episodes in the life of a recluse. L: W. Pickering, 1851. 337p. NUC OCLC [Possibly fiction]

2586. KEMBLE, Fanny see KEMBLE, Frances Anne

2587. KEMBLE, Frances Anne [Br. 1809-1893] ALT: Butler, Frances Anne (Kemble); Kemble, Fanny Journal of a residence in America. By Frances Anne Butler (Miss Fanny Kemble). Paris: A & W Galinani, 326p.; L: J. Murray; Philadelphia: Carey, Lea & Blanchard; Brussels: A. Wahlen, 1835. 2v. NUC BL MAD N PD OCLC

2588. -----Journal of a residence on a Georgian plantation in 1838-1839. By Frances Anne Kemble. L: Longmans, Green, Roberts & Green, 434p.; NY: Harper & bros., 1863. 337p. NUC BL MAD N PD OCLC

2589. -----Record of a girlhood. By Frances Ann Kemble. L: R. Bentley & son, 1878. 3v. NUC BL MBD OCLC

2590. -----Records of later life. L: R. Bentley & sons, 3v.; NY: H. Holt, 1882. 676p. NUC BL K MB OCLC

2591. -----Further records, 1848-1883. A series of letters... . L: R. Bentley & son, 1890. 2v. NUC BL K MB OCLC

2592. -----A year of consolation. By Mrs. Butler, late Fanny Kemble. L: E. Moxon, 2v.; NY: Wiley & Putnam, 1847. 2v. in 1. NUC BL OCLC [Travel: Italy]

2593. KEMPE, John A., ed. see BRAY, Anna Eliza (Kempe) Stothard

2594. KEMPE, Margery (Burnham) [Br. b. c1373] A short treatyse of contemplacyon taught by our lorde Ihesu Cryste, or taken out of the boke of Margerie Kempe of Lynn. L: Wynkyn de Worde, c1501. NUC BL [Only one copy survives; many later editions and transcriptions.]

2595. KENDAL, Dame Madge see GRIMSTON, Dame Margaret Shafto

2596. KENDALL, Catherine see WOODS, Catherine (Kendall)

2597. KENDALL, Phebe Mitchell, comp. see MITCHELL, Maria

2598. KENDRICK, Asahel C., comp. see JUDSON, Emily E. (Chubbuck)

2599. KENNEDY, Lady Margaret see BURNET, Lady Margaret (Kennedy)

2600. KENNING, Elizabeth [Br. 19c] Some account of the life of Elizabeth Kenning, chiefly drawn up by herself. Bradford: n.p., 1829. BL

2601. KENNY, May [Am. 19c] Well trodden paths; a diary.... Atlanta, GA: Autocrat pub. co., 1896. 270p. NUC OCLC [Travel: Europe]

2602. KENT, E. C., Mrs. [Am. 19c] "Four years in Secessia". Buffalo, NY: Franklin pr. house, 1865. 35p. NUC C K OCLC [Life in the South; escape from Richmond.]

2603. -----Life sketches. San Antonio, TX: n.p., 1884. 64p. K [Schoolteacher in Texas]

2604. KENYON, Frederick G., ed. see BROWNING, Elizabeth (Barrett)

2605. KERR, M., Mrs. [Br. 19c] ALT: K., M. Memorials of a departed friend; consisting of selections from her letters. Ed. Stewart Kerr. n.p.: n.p., 1847. 171p. BL [Earlier letters signed M. D., later ones signed M. K.]

2606. KERR, Stewart, ed see KERR, M., Mrs.

2607. KETTLE, Mary Rosa Stuart, ed. see MITFORD, Mary Rosa

2608. KILHAM, Hannah (Spurr) [Br. 1774-1832]
Extracts from the letters of Hannah Kilham, now at Sierra Leone. Reprinted from the Friends' Magazine.
L: n.p., 1831. BL

2609. -----Memoir of the late Hannah Kilham; chiefly comp. from her journal, and ed. by her daughter-in-law, Sarah Biller.
L: Darton & Harvey, 1837. 506p. NUC BL MBD
[Work in Sierra Leone; religious and social life]

2610. KINDERSLEY, Jemima, Mrs. Nathaniel Edward Kindersley [Br. 19c]
Letters from the Island of Teneriffe, Brazil, the Cape of Good Hope and the East Indies.
L: T. Nourse, 1777. 301p. NUC BL OCLC

2611. KINDERSLEY, Mrs. Nathaniel Edward see KINDERSLEY, Jemima

2612. KING, Annie (Liddon) [Br. 19c]
Dr. Liddon's tour in Egypt and Palestine in 1866: being letters descriptive of the tour, written by his sister, Mrs. King.
L & NY: Longmans, Green & co., 1891. 213p. NUC BL OCLC

2613. KING, Catherine see GOODWIN, Ellen King

2614. KING, E. Augusta, Mrs. Robert Moss King [Br. 19c]
The diary of a civilian's wife in India, 1877-1882.
L: R. Bentley & son, 1884. 2v. NUC BL MB OCLC

2615. -----Italian highways.
L: R. Bentley & son, 1896. 435p. NUC BL OCLC

2616. KING, Elizabeth (Taber) [Am. 1820-1856]

Memoir of Elizabeth Taber King. With extracts from her letters and journals.
Baltimore, MD: Armstrong & Berry, 1859. 128p. NUC BL OCLC

2617. KING, Frances Elizabeth, Mrs. Richard King [Br. 1757-1821]
ALT: K., F. E., Mrs.
A tour in France in 1802. Pub. as: Mrs. F. E. K.
L: J. Barfield for J. Booth, 1808. 91p. NUC BL

2618. KING, Marianne, co-author see JESUP, Maria (King)

2619. KING, Mary B. (Allen) [Am. 19c]
Looking backward; or, memories of the past.
NY: Anson D. F. Randolph & co., c1870. 455p. NUC K OCLC
[Memoirs; travel in Europe]

2620. KING, Mrs. Richard see KING, Frances Elizabeth

2621. KING, Mrs. Robert Moss see KING, E. Augusta

2622. KINGSFORD, Anna (Bonus) [Br. 1846-1888]
Anna Kingsford, her life, letters, diary and work. [Comp.] Edward Maitland.
L: n.p. [2d ed.: G. Redway], 1896. 2v. NUC BL MBD OCLC
[Theosophist; religious diary, 1881-1887]

2623. KINGSLEY, Charles, ed. see KINGSLEY, Rose Georgina

2624. KINGSLEY, Mary Henrietta [Br. 1862-1900]
The story of West Africa.
L: H. Marshall & son, 1899. 169p. NUC BL OCLC

2625. -----Travels in West Africa, Congo Francais, Corisco and Cameroons.
L & NY: MacMillan, 1897. 743p. NUC BL OCLC

2626. -----West African studies.
L & NY: Macmillan, 1899. 639p. NUC BL OCLC

2627. KINGSLEY, Rose Georgina
[Br. b. 1845]
South by west; or, winter in the
Rocky Mountains and spring in
Mexico. Ed. Rev. Charles
Kingsley.
L: W. Isbister & co., 1874. 411p.
NUC OCLC

2628. KINGSTON, Elizabeth
Chudleigh Hervey, Duchess of see
HERVEY, Elizabeth Chudleigh

2629. KINNAN, Mary (Lewis) [Am.
1763-1848]
A true narrative of the
sufferings of Mary Kinnan, who
was taken prisoner by the Shawnee
nation of Indians on the
thirteenth day of May, 1791 and
remained with them till the
sixteenth of August, 1794.
Elizabethtown: S. Kollock, 1795.
15p. NUC BL

2630. KINNEY, Hannah (Hanson)
[Am. 19c]
A review of the principal events
of the last ten years in the life
of Mrs. Hannah Kinney, together
with some comments on the late
trial. Written by herself.
Boston: J. N. Bradley, 1841. 87p.
NUC BL K OCLC
[Tried for murder of her husband]

2631. KINZIE, Mrs. John H. see
KINZIE, Juliette Augusta (Magill)

2632. KINZIE, Juliette Augusta
(Magill), Mrs. John H. Kinzie
[Am. 1806-1870]
Wau-Bun, the "early days" in the
North-west.
NY: Derby & Jackson; Cincinnati,
OH: H. W. Derby & co., 1856.
498p. NUC BL OCLC
[Travel in Wisconsin & Illinois;
life at Ft. Winnebago, WI, 1830-
1833; Chicago in 1831; Chicago
massacre of 1812.]

2633. KIRBY, Augusta (Klein) see
KLEIN, Augusta

2634. KIRBY, Georgiana (Bruce)
[Am. b. 1818]
My first visit to Brook Farm.
San Francisco: n.p., 1870. 19p.
NUC BL

2635. -----Years of experience:
an autobiographical narrative.
L & NY: G. P. Putnam's sons,
1887. 315p. NUC BL K

2636. KIRBY, Mary see GREGG, Mary
(Kirby)

2637. KIRCHNER, Adelaide Rosalind
see DUTTON, Adelaide Rosalind
(Kirchner)

2638. KIRKLAND, Caroline Matilda
(Stansbury) [Am. 1801-1864]
PSEUD: Clavers, Mary, Mrs.
Holidays abroad; or Europe from
the west.
NY: Baker & Scribner, 1849. 2v.
NUC BL OCLC

2639. -----A new home--who'll
follow? or, glimpses of western
life. By Mrs. Mary Clavers.
NY: C. S. Francis; Boston: J. H.
Francis, 1839. 317p. NUC BL K
OCLC
[Based on pioneer life in
Michigan. Later published as:
Montecute; and as: Our new home
in the West.]

2640. -----Western clearings.
NY: Wiley & Putnam, 1845. 238p.
NUC BL OCLC
[Tales and essays illustrating
pioneer life around Chicago and
Milwaukee in the 1830s.]

2641. KLEIN, Augusta [Br. 19/20c]
ALT: Kirby, Augusta (Klein)
Among the gods. Scenes of India;
with legends by the way.
Edinburgh & L: W. Blackwood &
sons, 1895. 355p. NUC BL OCLC

2642. KLINGLE, GEORGE, pseud. see
HOLMES, Georgiana (Klingle)

2643. KLOCK, Annie Marie
(Brengle) [Am. 19c] ALT: Brengle,
Annie Marie
Some reminiscences of a life of
struggle. Pub. as: Annie M.
Brengle
Chattanooga, TN: n.p., c1889.
22p. NUC K

2644. KNIGHT, Cornelia see
KNIGHT, Ellis Cornelia

2645. KNIGHT, Elleanor (Warner)
[Am. b. 1799]
A narrative of the Christian
experience, life and adventures,
trials and labours of Elleanor
Knight, written by herself. To
which is added a few remarks and
verses.
Providence, RI: n.p., 1839. 126p.
NUC

2646. KNIGHT, Ellis Cornelia [Br.
1757-1837] ALT: Knight, Cornelia
Autobiography of Miss Cornelia
Knight, lady companion to the
Princess Charlotte of Wales. With
extracts from her journals and
anecdote books. Ed. Sir J. W. Kaye.
L: W. H. Allen & co., 1861. 2v.
NUC BL MB MBD
[Court life; travel in Italy and
France]

2647. KNIGHT, Helen (Cross),
comp. see TAYLOR, Jane

2648. KNIGHT, Henrietta (Saint-
John), Baroness Luxborough see
LUXBOROUGH, Henrietta (Saint-
John) Knight, Baroness

2649. KNIGHT, Jane D. [Am. 19c]
Brief narrative of events
touching various reforms. By Jane
D. Knight, who was reared in the
Society of Friends, and united
with the Shakers at Mt. Lebanon,
Columbia co., N.Y., in the year
1826, in the twenty-second year
of her age.
Albany, NY: Weed, Parsons & co.,
1880. 29p. NUC K OCLC

2650. KNIGHT, Sarah (Jessup),
Mrs. Thomas Knight [Am. 1798-
1828]
Memoir of Sarah Knight, wife of
Thomas Knight, of Colchester, who
died on the 28th of the fifth
month, 1828.
Philadelphia: T. Kite, 1829. NUC
[Member of Society of Friends;
includes letters]

2651. KNIGHT, Sarah (Kemble) [Am.
1666-1727]
The journals of Madam Knight, and
Rev. Mr. Buckingham, from the
original manuscripts, written
1704 and 1710.

NY: Wilder & Campbell, 1825.
129p. NUC MAD OCLC
[Travel: New England: Boston to
NY in 1704.]

2652. KNIGHT, Mrs. Thomas see
KNIGHT, Sarah (Jessup)

2653. KNIGHT, William, ed. see
WORDSWORTH, Dorothy

2654. KNOTT, Mary John, comp. see
SMITH, Eliza

2655. KNOTT, Mary John [Br. 19c]
Two months at Kilkee, ... in the
county of Clare, near the mouth
of the Shannon, with an account
of a voyage down that river from
Limerick to Kilrush.
Dublin: William Curry, Jr. & co.
and Richard N. Tims, 1836. 255p.
NUC BL OCLC

2656. KNOX, Adeline (Trafton)
[Am. b. 1845]
An American girl abroad.
Boston: Lee & Shepard, 1872.
245p. NUC OCLC
[Travel: Europe]

2657. KRAFT, Kate, Miss [Am. 19c]
The nilometer and the sacred
soil; a diary of a tour through
Egypt, Palestine, and Syria.
NY: G. W. Carleton, 1869. 316p.
NUC OCLC

2658. KREMER, Anna M. [Am. b.
1841]
The life and adventures of Mrs.
Anna M. Kremer, written by herself.
Ionia, MI: Sentinel book & job
pr.estab., 1875. 121p. NUC OCLC

2659. KRIDER, Agnes (Thornton)
[Am. 19c]
The stolen child; or, Mrs.
Krider's narrative of how her
little daughter Katie was stolen
from her by a woman, who, having
been disappointed in obtaining
Mr. Krider for her husband, thus
took revenge on Mrs. Krider after
the death of the latter.
Philadelphia: C. W. Alexander,
1869. 48p. NUC

2660. KROUT, Mary Hannah [Am.
1857-1927]

Alice's visit to the Hawaiian islands.
NY: n.p., c1899. 208p. NUC

2661. -----Hawaii and a revolution; the personal experiences of a newspaper correspondent in the Sandwich islands during the crisis of 1893 and subsequently.
L: J. Murray; NY: Dodd, Mead, 1898. 330p. NUC BL K OCLC

2662. -----A looker on in London.
NY: Dodd, Mead, 1899. 352p. NUC BL K OCLC

2663. KUMM, Mrs. Karl see KUMM, Lucy Evangeline (Guinness)

2664. KUMM, Mrs. Karl, ed. see TAYLOR, Mary Geraldine (Guinness)

2665. KUMM, Lucy Evangeline (Guinness), Mrs. Karl Kumm [Br. 1865-1906] ALT: Guinness, Lucy Evangeline
Across India at the dawn of the twentieth century.
L: Religious Tract Society, 1898. 260p. NUC BL OCLC

2666. KUMM, Lucy Evangeline (Guinness), ed. see TAYLOR, Mary Geraldine (Guinness)

2667. KYME, Anne (Askewe) see ASKEWE, Anne

2668. L*** see LEFEVRE, Mrs.

2669. L----RE, Mrs. see LEFEVRE, Mrs.

2670. L., C., co-author see LAMBERT, S.

2671. L., H. see LLOYD, Harriette

2672. L., K. R. see LEDOUX, Kate Reid

2673. L., R., ed. see THAXTER, Celia (Leighton)

2674. L., R. C., ed. see LEHMANN, Nina Chambers

2675. L., S. see LAMBERT, S.

2676. L., Sarah, co-author see CARR, Mary Frances

2677. LL., H. see LLOYD, Harriette

2678. LACY, Mary [Am. 19c]
The female shipwright, or life and extraordinary adventures of Mary Lacy, giving an account of her leaving her parents disguised as a man, serving four years at sea, etc. Written by herself.
NY: printed for George Sinclair by J. C. Totten, 1807. 35p. NUC OCLC

2679. LADD, Elizabeth, comp. see CARDWELL, Lucy

2680. LADY, A, ed. see ALLEN, Rose

2681. LADY, A, comp. see BARLOW, Debbie

2682. LADY, A, pseud. see BARTRAM, Lady Alfred

2683. LADY, A, pseud. see CARTER, Agnes

2684. LADY, A, pseud. see HANWAY, Mary Anne

2685. LADY, A, pseud. see HOLMES, Augusta (Macgregor)

2686. LADY, A, pseud. see JOHNSON, Anna Cummings

2687. LADY, A, pseud. see LOUGHBOROUGH, Mary Ann (Webster)

2688. LADY, A, pseud. see MAC PHERSON, A., Mrs.

2689. LADY, A, pseud. see M'TAGGART, Anne (Hamilton)

2690. LADY, A, pseud. see MAITLAND, Julia Charlotte (Barrett)

2691. LADY, A, pseud. <u>see</u>
MELVILLE, Elizabeth

2692. LADY, A, pseud. <u>see</u> NICOL,
Martha

2693. LADY, A, pseud. <u>see</u> RITSON,
Anne, Mrs.

2694. LADY, A, pseud. <u>see</u> ROPES,
Hannah Anderson

2695. LADY, A, pseud. <u>see</u> WALLIS,
Mary Davis (Cook)

2696. LADY, A, pseud. [Br. 19c]
Educational outlines, and other
letters on practical duties. To
which is added a journal of a
summer's excursion made by the
author and her pupils.
L: T. Harrold; Groombridge &
sons, 1850. 116p. NUC BL OCLC

2697. LADY, A, pseud. [Am. 19c]
A trip to the Virginia Springs,
or the belles and beaux of 1835.
Lexington, VA: R. Glass, pr.,
1843. NUC

2698. LADY "FELON", A, pseud. <u>see</u>
SINCLAIR, Mrs.

2699. LADY OF BOSTON, A, pseud.,
comp. <u>see</u> SPEARE, Chloe

2700. LADY OF MASSACHUSETTS, A,
pseud. <u>see</u> RICHARDS, Anna Matlock

2701. LADY OF NEW YORK, A, pseud.
<u>see</u> HAIGHT, Sarah (Rogers)

2702. LADY OF OHIO, A, pseud. <u>see</u>
MERWIN, Loretta L. Wood

2703. LADY OF VIRGINIA, A, pseud.
<u>see</u> McGUIRE, Judith White
(Brockenbough)

2704. LADY OF VIRGINIA, A, pseud.
<u>see</u> RIVES, Judith Page (Walker)

2705. LADY RESIDENT NEAR THE
ALMA, A, pseud. <u>see</u> NEILSON, Mrs.
Andrew

2706. LADY VOLUNTEER, A, pseud.
<u>see</u> TAYLOR, Fanny Margaret

2707. LA FLÉCHÉRE, Mme. Jean
Guillaume <u>see</u> FLETCHER, Mary
(Bosanquet)

2708. LA FLÉCHÉRE, Mary de <u>see</u>
FLETCHER, Mary (Bosanquet)

2709. LAIRD, Elizabeth [Br. 19c]
ALT: Laird, Lizzie
Lizzie Laird.
Glasgow: Bryce & son, 1882. 18p.
BL
[May contain personal material.]

2710. LAIRD, Lizzie <u>see</u> LAIRD,
Elizabeth

2711. LAIRD, Marion [Br. 18c]
Memoirs of the life and
experiences of M. Laird .... To
which is subjoined a collection
of ... letters ... . With a
preface containing some farther
account of her life and death.
Glasgow: W. Smith, 1775. 254p. BL

2712. LAMB, Lady Caroline
(Ponsonby) [Br. 1785-1828]
Fugitive pieces and reminiscences
of Lord Byron ... also some
original poetry, letters, and
recollections of Lady Caroline
Lamb. By Isaac Nathan.
L: Whittaker, Treacher & co.,
1829. 196p. BL OCLC

2713. LAMB, Rose, ed. <u>see</u>
THAXTER, Celia (Leighton)

2714. LAMBERT, Charles J., co-
author <u>see</u> LAMBERT, S.

2715. LAMBERT, Charles J., Mrs.
<u>see</u> LAMBERT, S.

2716. LAMBERT, S., Mrs. Charles
J. Lambert [Br. 19c]
The voyage of the "Wanderer."
From the journals of C. and S. L.
Ed. Gerald Young.
L: Macmillan & co., 1883. 335p.
NUC BL OCLC

2717. LAMONT, Martha MacDonald
[Br. 19c]
Impressions, thoughts, and
sketches, during two years in
France and Switzerland.
L: Edward Moxon, 1844. 343p.

NUC BL OCLC
[School life in Paris; travel in
France, Belgium, Germany,
Switzerland]

2718. LANAGHAN, Mrs. see
FLANNIGAN, Mrs.

2719. LANCASTER, Rev. John, comp.
see MAXWELL, Darcy (Brisbane),
Lady

2720. LANCASTER, Lydia [Br. 19c]
Extracts from the letters of
Lydia Lancaster.
L: G. Luxford & co., 1840. 38p.
BL

2721. LANE, Amelia [Br. 19c]
Reminiscences of the Coronation,
and other historical tales.
L: C. T. Moon, 1844. 344p. BL
[May be fiction]

2722. LANE, Caroline E. (Lamson),
Mrs. David Lane [Am. 1816-1882]
In memoriam. Two sketches of Mrs.
David Lane by Mary E. Dewey and
Louisa L. Schuyler.
NY: n.p., 1882?. 16p. NUC
[May contain personal material]

2723. LANE, Mrs. David see LANE,
Caroline E. (Lamson)

2724. LANE, E. W., co-author see
POOLE, Sophia (Lane)

2725. LANE, Mrs. Levi C. see
LANE, P.

2726. LANE, L. G., comp. & ed.
see COIT, Mehetabel (Chandler)

2727. LANE, L. G. see GREENE,
Martha (Coit) Hubbard

2728. LANE, Lydia Spencer
(Blaney) [Am. 19c]
I married a soldier; or, old days
in the old army.
Philadelphia: J. B. Lippincott
co., 1893. 214p. NUC K OCLC
[Autobiography of wife of a
cavalry officer in Texas and New
Mexico.]

2729. LANE, P., Mrs. Levi C. Lane
[Am. 19c]
Letters of travel.
San Francisco: A. L. Bancroft &
co., 1886. 440p. NUC OCLC
[Travel: Great Britain,
Switzerland, Germany, Russia,
Egypt]

2730. LANGDON, M., Mrs. [Br. 19c]
Treasure trove in Ceylon.
L: C. H. Kelly, 1897. 32p. BL

2731. LANGTON, Anne [Br. d. 1893]
The story of our family.
Manchester: T. Sowler & co., pr.,
1881. 204p. NUC MC
[Life in England and Europe;
settlement in Canada]

2732. LANMAN, Adeline (Dodge),
Mrs. Charles Lanman [Am. 19c]
A tour down the river, St.
Lawrence.
Washington, D.C.: Pr. for the
amusement of a few friends, 1852.
37p. NUC

2733. LANMAN, Mrs. Charles see
LANMAN, Adeline (Dodge)

2734. LARCOM, Lucy [Am. 1824-1893]
Lucy Larcom: life, letters, and
diary. Ed. Daniel D. Addison.
Boston & NY: Houghton, Mifflin &
co., 1894. 295p. NUC BL MAD OCLC
[Diaries 1846-1891; travel; work
as a teacher]

2735. -----A New England
girlhood, outlined from memory.
Boston & NY: Houghton, Mifflin &
co., 1889. 274p. NUC BL K OCLC
[No. 8 of the "Riverside Library
for young people"]

2736. LARIMER, Sarah Luse, Mrs.
[Am. 19c]
The capture and escape; or, life
among the Sioux.
Philadelphia: Claxton, Remsen &
Haffelfinger, 1870. 252p. NUC
OCLC [Autobiographical account]

2737. LARKIN, Elizabeth T., ed.
see RICHARDSON, Mary (Walsham)
Few

2738. LASCELLES, Ann (Catley) see
CATLEY, Ann

2739. LATHROP, Clarissa Caldwell
[Am. 1847-1892]
A secret institution.
NY: Bryant pub. co., 1890. 329p.
NUC BL K
[Autobiographical account of
confinement in NY state lunatic
asylum]

2740. LATHROP, Mother Mary
Alphonse, comp. see HAWTHORNE,
Sophia (Peabody)

2741. LATHROP, Rose (Hawthorne),
comp. see HAWTHORNE, Sophia
(Peabody)

2742. LATIMER, E., Miss see
DYSON, Julia A. (Parker)

2743. LATTER, Mary, Mrs. [Br.
1725-1777]
The miscellaneous works in prose
and verse.
Reading: n.p., 1759. 3 pt. BL
[Includes "Epistolary
Correspondence"]

2744. LAUDER, Maria Elise Turner,
Mrs. [19c] ALT: Lauder, Toofie
Evergreen leaves: being notes
from my travel book.
Toronto: Rose pub. co., 1877.
384p. NUC
[Travel: Great Britain]

2745. -----Legends and tales of
the Harz Mountains. By Toofie
Lauder.
L: Hodder & Stoughton, 1881.
259p. NUC OCLC
[Travel: Germany]

2746. LAUDER, Toofie see LAUDER,
Maria Elise Turner

2747. LAUDERDALE, John, Duke of,
co-author see BURNET, Lady
Margaret (Kennedy)

2748. LAURIE, Catherine Ann, Mrs.
Simon Somerville Laurie [Br. d.
1895]
In memory of Catherine Ann
Laurie, Nairne Lodge,
Duddingston, Midlothian, who
departed this life on the 31st
July, 1895. Ed. Simon Somerville
Laurie.
Edinburgh: priv. pr. by Mrs. R.

F. Hamilton Bruce, 1896. 145p.
NUC
[Includes poetry and
miscellaneous writings]

2749. LAURIE, Simon Somerville,
ed. see LAURIE, Catherine Ann

2750. LAURIE, Mrs. Simon
Somerville see LAURIE, Catherine
Ann

2751. LAW, S. C., Mrs. see LAW,
Sallie Chapman (Gordon)

2752. LAW, Sallie Chapman
(Gordon) [Am. 19c] ALT: Law, S.
C., Mrs.
Reminiscences of the war of the
sixties between the North and
South.
Memphis, TN: Memphis pr. co.,
1892. 16p. NUC

2753. LAWRENCE, Caroline Wallace,
comp. see WHITALL, Alice B.

2754. LAWRENCE, Catherine Remsen
[Am. 1805-1875]
Family reminiscences.
n.p.: n.p., 18?. 9p. NUC
[Memoirs of her family.]

2755. LAWRENCE, Catherine S. [Am.
19c]
Autobiography. Sketch of life and
labors of Miss Catherine S.
Lawrence, who in early life
distinguished herself as a bitter
opponent of slavery and
intemperance.
Albany, NY: Amasa J. Parker,
1893. 174p. NUC OCLC

2756. LAWRENCE, Margarette Oliver
(Woods) see HAMLIN, Henriette
Anne Louise (Jackson)

2757. LAYARD, Gertrude, Mrs.
Granville Layard [BR. 19c] ALT:
Layard, Mrs. J. Granville
Through the West Indies.
L: S. Low, Marston, Searle &
Rivington, 1887. 168p. NUC BL OCLC

2758. LAYARD, Mrs. Granville see
LAYARD, Gertrude

2759. LAYARD, Mrs. J. Granville
see LAYARD, Gertrude

2760. LEADBEATER, Mary
(Shackleton) [Br. 1758-1826]
The Leadbeater papers. The annals
of Ballitore, by M. Leadbeater,
with a memoir of the author. ...
and the correspondence of Mrs. R.
[C.] Trench [Melesina (Chenevix)
St. George Trench; Br. 1768-1827].
L: Bell & Daldy, 1862. 2v. NUC BL

2761. LEADBEATER, Mary
(Shackleton), comp. see
SHACKLETON, Elizabeth (Carleton)

2762. LEAK, Ann E. [19c]
The autobiography of Miss Ann E.
Leak, born without arms;
containing an interesting account
of her early life and subsequent
travels in the United States and
Australia.
Melbourne: Azzoppardi, Hildreth &
co., 1867. 47p. NUC

2763. LEAKEY, Caroline Woolmer
[Br. 1827-1881]
Clear shining light: a memoir of
C. W. Leakey. By [her sister]
Emily P. Leakey.
L: J. F. Shaw & co., 1882. 142p. BL
[May contain personal material.]

2764. LEAKEY, Emily P., comp. see
LEAKEY, Caroline Woolmer

2765. LEAN, Florence (Marryat)
Church, Mrs. Francis Lean [Br.
1837-1899] ALT: Church, Mrs.
Ross; Marryat, Florence
"Gup." Sketches of Anglo-Indian
life and character. Pub. as: Mrs.
Ross Church
L: Richard Bentley, 1868. 284p.
NUC BL OCLC
[Seven years' experiences as Army
wife]

2766. -----Tom Tiddler's ground.
L: S. Sonnenschein, Lowrey & co.,
1886. 212p. NUC BL OCLC
[Travel: U. S. & Canada]

2767. LEAN, Florence (Marryat)
Church, ed. see DAVIES, Bessie
(Williams)

2768. LEAN, Mrs. Francis see
LEAN, Florence (Marryat) Church

2769. LE BLOND, Mrs. Aubrey see
LE BLOND, Elizabeth Alice Frances
(Hawkins-Whitsted) Burnaby Main

2770. LE BLOND, Elizabeth Alice
Frances (Hawkins-Whitshed)
Burnaby Main, Mrs. Aubrey Le
Blond [Br. 19/20c] ALT: Burnaby,
Elizabeth Alice Frances (Hawkins-
Whitshed); Burnaby, Mrs.
Frederick Gustavus; Main,
Elizabeth Alice Frances (Hawkins-
Whitshed) Burnaby
The high Alps in winter; or,
mountaineering in search of
health. By Mrs. Fred Burnaby.
L: Sampson Low, Marston, Searle &
Rivington, 1883. 204p. NUC BL OCLC

2771. -----High life and towers
of silence.
L: Sampson Low, Marston, Searle &
Rivington, 1886. 145p. NUC BL OCLC

2772. -----My home in the Alps.
L: Sampson Low, Marston & co.,
1892. 131p. NUC BL OCLC

2773. LE BRETON, Anna Laetitia
(Aikin) [Br. 1808-1885]
Memories of seventy years. By one
of a literary family. Ed. [and in
part written] by Mrs. Herbert
[Mary Emma (Le Breton)] Martin.
L: Griffith & Farran; NY: Dutton,
1883. 198p. NUC BL MB OCLC

2774. LE BRETON, Anna Letita
(Aikin), ed. see AIKIN, Lucy

2775. LE BRETON, Anna Letitia
(Aikin), comp. see BARBAULD, Anna
Letitia (Aikin)

2776. LE BRETON, Philip Hemery,
ed. see AIKIN, Lucy

2777. LECK, Jane [Br. 19c]
Iberian sketches; travels in
Portugal and the northwest of
Spain.
Glasgow: Wilson & McCormick,
1884. 166p. NUC BL

2778. LEDOUX, Kate Reid, Mrs.
[Am. 19c] ALT: L., K. R.
Ocean notes and foreign travel
for ladies. Pub. as: K. R. L.
NY: Cook, son & Jenkins, 1878.
64p. NUC

2779. LEE, Alfred, comp. see
ALLIBONE, Susan

2780. LEE, Eliza (Buckminster)
[Am. 1794-1864]
Sketches of a New England
village, in the last century.
Boston: J. Munroe & co., 1838.
110p. NUC K OCLC
[NUC lists as fiction; K as
autobiography.]

2781. LEE, Elizabeth (Scrope)
[Br. 1716?-1751] ALT: SCROPE,
Eliza
Miss Scrope's answer to Mr.
[Thomas Estcourt] Cresswell's
narrative.
L: pr. for R. Baldwin, 1749.
232p. NUC BL OCLC [Three letters]

2782. LEE, Hannah Farnham
(Sawyer), comp. see ADAMS, Hannah

2783. LEE, Jarena, Mrs. [Am. b.
1783]
The life and religious experience
of Jarena Lee, a coloured lady,
giving an account of her call to
preach the gospel. Rev. and cor.
from the original manuscript,
written by herself.
Philadelphia: pub. for the
author, 1836. 24p. NUC K OCLC

2784. LEE, Katherine see JENNER,
Katherine Lee (Rawlings)

2785. LEE, L. P., comp. see
SHARP, Abigail (Gardner)

2786. LEE, Rachel Fanny Antonia,
Mrs. [Br. 1774?-1829] ALT: R. F.
A. PSEUD: Despenser, Baroness
Memoirs of R. F. A.
L: James Gillet, 1812?. 105p. BL
MB

2787. -----A vindication of Mrs.
Lee's conduct towards the
Gordons. Written by herself.
L: Greenland & Norris, 1807. 66p.
NUC BL

2788. LEE, Mrs. Robert see LEE,
Sarah (Wallis) Bowdich

2789. LEE, S. M., Mrs. [Am. 19c]
Glimpses of Mexico and California.

Boston: G. H. Ellis, 1887. 124p.
NUC

2790. LEE, Sarah (Wallis)
Bowdich, Mrs. Robert Lee [Br.
1791-1856] ALT: Bowdich, Mrs.
Thomas Edward
Excursions in Madeira and Porto
Santo. Pub. as: Mrs. Thomas
Edward Bowdich. With Thomas
Edward Bowdich.
L: G. B. Whittaker, 1825. 278p.
NUC BL
[Completed her husband's work
after his death. Three chapters
are hers.]

2791. LEE, VERNON, pseud. see
PAGET, Violet

2792. LEES, Maria Charlotte
(Sullivan), Lady [Br. d. 1881]
A few days in Belgium and
Holland. An idle book for an idle
hour.
L: E. Stanford, 1872. 148p. NUC BL

2793. LEESON, Margaret, Mrs. [Br.
18c]
Memoirs of Mrs. Margaret Leeson,
written by herself, in which are
given anecdotes, sketches of the
lives and bon mots of some of the
most celebrated characters in
Great Britain and Ireland ...
which have usually frequented her
Citherean temple for these thirty
years past.
Dublin: n.p., 1797. 3v. BL MB

2794. LEFANU, Alicia, Miss, comp.
see SHERIDAN, Frances
(Chamberlaine)

2795. LEFEVRE, Mrs. [Br. d. 1756]
ALT: L***, Mrs.; L----re, Mrs.
An extract of letters by Mrs.
L***. Ed. John Wesley.
L: n.p., 1769.; L: G. Paramore,
1792. 106p. NUC BL OCLC
[Chiefly religious]

2796. -----Extracts of letters;
chiefly on religious subjects.
With meditations on some select
passages of scripture. By Mrs. L-
---re.
Edinburgh: n.p., 1800. 112p.;
Edinburgh: W. Whyte & co., 1819.
113p. NUC BL

2797. LEGARD, F. D., ed. see
SIMPSON, Mary Emily

2798. LEGGE, Alfred Owen, comp.
see LEGGE, Mary

2799. LEGGE, Mary, Mrs. [Br. 19c]
A life of consecration. Memorials
of Mrs. M. Legge. By one of her
sons, Alfred Owen Legge.
L: J. Nisbet & co., 1883. 439p.
NUC BL

2800. LEHMAN, Emma A. [Am. b.1841]
Sketches of European travel.
Winston, NC: Republican Steam
print., 1890. 115p. NUC OCLC

2801. LEHMANN, Nina Chambers [19c]
Familiar letters N. L. to F. L.
1864-1867. Sel. & arr. R. C.
L[ehmann].
Edinburgh: Ballantyne, Hanson &
co., 1892. NUC

2802. LEHMANN, R. C., ed. see
LEHMANN, Nina Chambers

2803. LEIGH, Elizabeth Medora
[Br. 1814-1849] ALT: Leigh, Medora
Medora Leigh: a history and an
autobiography. Ed. Charles
Mackay.
L: R. Bentley, 1869. 280p. NUC BL
MB OCLC
[Her life as Byron's daughter.]

2804. LEIGH, Frances (Butler),
Hon. Mrs. James Wentworth Leigh
[Br. 1838-1910]
Ten years on a Georgia plantation
since the war.
L: R. Bentley & sons, 1883. 347p.
NUC BL OCLC
[Daughter of Fannie Kemble]

2805. LEIGH, Hon. Mrs. James
Wentworth see LEIGH, Frances
(Butler)

2806. LEIGH, Marian [Am. 19c]
My own story.
NY: G. P. Putnam, 1865. 414p. NUC
BL [May be fiction.]

2807. LEIGH, Medora see LEIGH,
Elizabeth Medora

2808. LEIGHTON, Caroline C. [Am.
19c]

Life at Puget Sound, with
sketches of travel in Washington
territory, British Columbia,
Oregon, and California, 1865- 1881.
Boston: Lee & Shepard; NY: C. T.
Dillingham, 1883. 258p. NUC BL MC
OCLC

2809. LEININGER, Barbara [Am. 18c]
The narrative of Marie Le Roy and
Barbara Leininger, who spent
three and one-half years as
prisoners among the Indians and
arrived safely in this city on
the sixth of May. Written and
printed as dictated by them. 1759.
Philadelphia: German pr. off.,
1759. NUC

2810. LEITCH, Margaret W., co-
author see LEITCH, Mary

2811. LEITCH, Mary [Br. 19c]
Seven years in Ceylon. Stories of
mission life. With Margaret W.
Leitch.
NY: American Tract Society; L: S.
W. Partridge, 1890. 170p. NUC BL
MB OCLC
[Experiences as medical
missionaries]

2812. LEITH, Mrs. Disney see
LEITH, Mary Charlotte Julia
(Gordon)

2813. LEITH, Mary Charlotte Julia
(Gordon), Mrs. Disney Leith [Br.
19/20c]
Three visits to Iceland, being
notes taken at sea and on land;
comprising a pilgrimage to
Skalholt, and visits to Geysir
and the Njala district.
L: J. Masters & co., 1897. 218p.
NUC BL OCLC

2814. LELAND, Frank, comp. see
LELAND, Hattie M. (Perkins)

2815. LELAND, Mrs. Frank see
LELAND, Hattie M. (Perkins)

2816. LELAND, Hattie M.
(Perkins), Mrs. Frank Leland [Am.
1833?-1884] PSEUD: Ingleby, Kate
Affection's offering by Mrs.
Frank Leland. Comp. Frank Leland.
Madison, WI: n.p., 1882. 230p.
NUC OCLC

[Poems, 2 short prose pieces. Based on personal experiences with notes describing the circumstances.]

2817. -----Golden thoughts at Ingleside; gleaned from the life thoughts of Mrs. Frank Leland ("Kate Ingleby") with a sketch of her life. Comp. Frank Leland. Elkhorn, WI: n.p., 1887. NUC OCLC [Contains poetry]

2818. LELAND, Lillian [Am. 19c] Traveling alone. A woman's journey around the world. NY: American News co., 1890. 358p. NUC OCLC

2819. LE MESURIER, Henrietta see NICOL, Martha

2820. L'ENGLE, Susan [Am. 19c] Notes of my family and recollections of my early life. NY: Knickerbocker press, 1888. 67p. NUC OCLC

2821. LENNOX, Anne (Paton), Lady William Lennox [Br. 1802-1864] The highly interesting life of Lady William Lennox, formerly Miss Anne Paton. L: W. Lowe, 1830?. 8p. BL OCLC [May contain personal material.]

2822. LENNOX, Lady William see LENNOX, Anne (Paton)

2823. LEONOWENS, Anna Harriette Crawford, Mrs. [Br. 1834-1914] The English governess at the Siamese court: being recollections of six years in the royal palace at Bangkok. L: Trubner & co.; Boston: Fields Osgood & co., 1870. 321p. NUC BL MB OCLC

2824. -----Life and travel in India: being recollections of a journey before the days of railroads. Philadelphia: Porter & Coates, 1884. 325p. NUC BL MB

2825. -----Our Asiatic cousins. Boston: D. Lothrop co., 1889. 367p. NUC OCLC

2826. -----The romance of the harem.

L. Trubner: Boston: J.R. Osgood, 1873, 227p. NUC BL OCLC [Also pub. as: The romance of Siamese harem life.]

2827. LE PLONGEON, Alice (Dixon) [Am. b. 1851] Here and there in Yucatan. Miscellanies. N.Y: J.W. Bouton, 1886. 146p. NUC BL

2828. LE ROY, Marie, co-author see LEININGER, Barbara

2829. LE ROY, Virginia [Am. 19c] Three months in Europe; a journal of travel in England, France, Switzerland, Germany, Italy, Belgium. and Scotland. Streator, IL: LeRoy Printing House. 1896. 113p. NUC

2830. LESLEY, Susan Inches (Lyman, comp. see LYMAN, Anne Jean (Robbins)

2831. LESLIE, AMY, pseud. see BUCK, Lillie Brown (West) Jean (Robbins)

2831. LESLIE, AMY, pseud. see BUCK, Little Brown (West)

2832. LESLIE, Andrew, comp. see LESLIE, Eliza (Franklin)

2833. LESLIE, Eliza (Franklin) [Br. 1787-1858] ALT: Franklin, Eliza The vision of the heavenly world; to which is prefixed a memoir of Mrs. E. Leslie ... with extracts from her correspondence. By Andrew Leslie. L: Wightman & Cramp, 1828. 111p. BL

2834. LESLIE, Mrs. Frank see LESLIE, Miriam Florence (Following) Squier

2835. LESLIE, Miriam Florance (Follins) Squire, Mrs. Frank Leslie [Am. 1836-1914] ALT: Squire, Miriam F. California. A pleasure trip from, Gotham to the Golden Gate (April, May, June, 1877). NY: G.W. Carleton & co. L: S. Low, son & co., 1877. 286p. NUC BL OCLC

2836. LESTER, Mary [Br. 19c]
PSEUD: Soltera, Maria
A lady's ride across Spanish
Honduras. By Marie Soltera.
Edinburgh & L: W. Blackwood &
sons, 1884. 319p. NUC BL OCLC
[Pub. in Britain as: "Ride across
Spanish Honduras"]

2837. L'ESTRANGE, Rev. A. G., ed.
see MITFORD, Mary Russell

2838. L'ESTRANGE, M., Miss [Br.
19c]
Heligoland: or, reminiscences of
childhood; a genuine narrative of
facts. [Ed. Mrs. C. W.]
4th ed. L: J. W. Parker, 1851.
66p. NUC BL
[Chiefly religious; autobiography]

2839. LEVERING, Sarah R., comp.
see BLAKE, Margaret Jane

2840. LE VERT, Octavia Celeste
(Walton), Mme. [Am. 1810?-1877]
Souvenirs of travel.
Mobile, AL; NY: S. H. Goetzel &
co., 1857. 2v. NUC BL OCLC
[Travel: Cuba, Europe]

2841. LEVICK, Elizabeth Wetherill
[Am. 1789-1886]
Recollections of her early
days... .
Philadelphia: priv. pr., 1881.
117p. K OCLC
[Member of Society of Friends]

2842. LEWIS, Agnes (Smith) [Br.
1843-1926] ALT: Smith, Agnes
Eastern pilgrims: the travels of
three ladies.
L: Hurst & Blackett, 1870. NUC BL
[Travels to the Holy Land in 1868.]

2843. -----Glimpses of Greek life
and scenery.
L: Hurst & Blackett, 1884. 352p.
NUC BL OCLC

2844. How the Codex was found. A
narrative of two visits to Sinai,
from Mrs. Lewis's journals 1892-
1893. Ed. Margaret Dunlop (Smith)
Gibson.
Cambridge, MA: Macmillan & Bowes,
1893. 141p. NUC BL

2845. -----In the shadow of
Sinai: a story of travel and
research from 1895 to 1897.
Cambridge, MA: Macmillan & Bowes,
1898. 261p. NUC BL OCLC

2846. -----Through Cyprus.
L: Hurst & Blackett, 1887. 351p.
NUC BL

2847. LEWIS, Elizabeth Alicia
Maria, Mrs. [Br. 19c]
A lady's impressions of Cyprus in
1893; by Mrs. Lewis.
L & Sydney: Remington & co.,
1894. 346p. NUC OCLC

2848. LEWIS, Hannah, Mrs. [Am. 19c]
Narrative of the captivity and
sufferings of Mrs. Hannah Lewis,
and her three children, who were
taken prisoners by the Indians,
near St. Louis, on the 25th May,
1815, and among whom they
experienced all the cruel
treatment which savage brutality
could inflict--Mrs. Lewis and her
eldest son fortunately escaped on
the 3d April last, leaving her
two youngest children in the
hands of the unmerciful
barbarians.
2d ed. Boston: H. Trumbull, 1817.
24p. NUC OCLC
[Hannah called both Jane and
Harriot in reprints.]

2849. LEWIS, Harriot see LEWIS,
Hannah

2850. LEWIS, Jane see LEWIS,
Hannah

2851. LEWIS, Lady Maria Theresa
(Villiers) Lister, ed. see BERRY,
Mary

2852. LEWIS, Lady Theresa, ed.
see BERRY, Mary

2853. LEWISE, pseud. see GRASSIE,
Olive L.

2854. LIDDELL, Hon. Frances Jane,
co-author see NORMANBY, Maria
(Liddell) Phipps, Marchioness of

2855. LIESCHING, Mrs. Arthur see
LIESCHING, Fanny (Gregson)

2856. LIESCHING, Fanny (Gregson), Mrs. Arthur Liesching [Br. 1865-1893] ALT: Gregson, Fanny
Letters from Ceylon, by Fanny Gregson.
L: Marshall bros, 1893. 208p. NUC BL [Missionary experiences]

2857. LIGHT, Bianca [Br. 19c]
PSEUD: Vera
Our American cousins at home. By Vera.
L: S. Low, Marston, Low, & Searle, 1873. 268p. NUC BL OCLC

2858. LIKINS, J. W., Mrs [Am. 19c]
Six years experience as a book agent in California, including my trip from New York to San Francisco via Nicaragua.
San Francisco: Women's Union printing office, 1874. 168p. NUC OCLC

2859. LILIUOKALANI, Queen of Hawaii [Am. 1838-1917]
Hawaii's story by Hawaii's queen, Liliuokalani.
Boston: Lee & Shepard, 1898. 409p. NUC BL K OCLC

2860. LILLIE, R. Shepard, co-author see LILLIE, Mrs. R. Shepherd

2861. LILLIE, Mrs. R. Shepard [Am. 19c]
Two chapters from the book of my life, with poems by R. Shepard Lillie.
Boston: J. Wilson, 1889. 229p. NUC K OCLC
[On spiritualism]

2862. LINCOLN, Elizabeth (Knevitt) Clinton, Countess of [Br. 17c] ALT: Clinton, Elizabeth (Knevitt), Countess of Lincoln
The Countess of Lincoln's nurserie.
Oxford: J. Lichfield & J. Short, 1622. 21p. NUC BL
[Advice to her daughter-in-law.]

2863. LINCOLN, Martha D., Mrs. [Am. b. 1838]
Over the lawn to the White House.
Washington, D.C.: M. D. Lincoln & E. Maynicke, 1893. 20p. NUC BL
[[In verse]

2864. LINCOLN, Mary (Todd), co-author see KECKLEY, Elizabeth Hobbs

2865. LINDESAY, Harriott Hester (Williams-Wynn), ed. see WYNN, Charlotte Williams

2866. LINDSAY, Alexander William Crawford, Earl of Crawford and Balcasses, comp. see BARNARD, Lady Anne (Lindsay)

2867. LINDSAY, Lady Anne see BARNARD, Lady Anne (Lindsay)

2868. LINDSEY, Robert, co-author see LINDSEY, Sarah

2869. LINDSEY, Mrs. Robert see LINDSEY, Sarah

2870. LINDSEY, Sarah (Crosland), Mrs. Robert Lindsey [Am. 1804-1876]
Travels of Robert and Sarah Lindsey. Ed., one of their daughters (E. L. G.).
L: Samuel Harris, 1886. 189p. NUC BL MAD OCLC
[Members of Society of Friends; voyage to Panama, California & Hawaii]

2871. LINTON, Elizabeth (Lynn) [Br. 1822-1898] ALT: Linton, Eliza Lynn; Lynn, Elizabeth
My literary life.
L: Hodder & Stoughton, 1899. 103p. NUC BL MB

2872. LINTON, Eliza Lynn see LINTON, Elizabeth (Lynn)

2873. LIPPINCOTT, Mary Shoemaker (Hallowell) [Am. 1801-1888]
Life and letters of Mary S. Lippincott, late of Camden, New Jersey, a minister in the Society of Friends.
Philadelphia: W. H. Pile's sons, prs., 1893. 284p. NUC OCLC

2874. LIPPINCOTT, Sara Jane (Clarke) [Am. 1823-1904] ALT: Clarke, Sara Jane PSEUD: Greenwood, Grace
Europe: its people and princes--its pleasures and palaces. A graphic and interesting narrative

of a distinguished American
woman's tour of one year among
the leading attractions of
Europe, sketching her visits to
various homes and royal palaces.
By Grace Greenwood.
Philadelphia: Hubbard bros, 1888.
437p. NUC OCLC

2875. -----Greenwood leaves: a
collection of sketches and
letters.
1st Series Boston: Ticknor, Reed
& Fields. 1849.; 2d Series
Boston: Ticknor, Reed & Fields,
1853. 382p. BL
[First series: 20 sketches or
short stories, 26 letters. Second
series: 13 sketches, 1 poem, 39
letters, 2 editorials.]

2876. -----Haps and mishaps of a
tour in Europe. By Grace
Greenwood.
Boston: Ticknor, Reed, & Fields,
1854. 437p.; L: R. Bentley, 1854.
372p. NUC BL OCLC

2877. -----Merrie England.
Travels, descriptions, mixed
tales and historical sketches. By
Grace Greenwood.
Boston: Ticknor, Reed & Fields,
1855. 261p. NUC OCLC

2878. -----New life in new lands:
notes of travel. By Grace
Greenwood.
NY: J. B. Ford & co., 1872. 413p.
NUC
[Coll. of articles on travel to
Colorado, Utah, Nevada, and
California]

2879. ----Records of five years.
By Grace Greenwood.
Boston: Ticknor & Fields, 1867.
222p. NUC OCLC
[Essays containing personal
observation of the Civil War
times, 1861-1864, including a
visit to a Union camp in
Virginia.]

2880. -----Stories and sights of
France and Italy. By Grace
Greenwood.
Boston: Ticknor & Fields, 1867.
291p. NUC OCLC
[Also pub. as: A year abroad]

2881. LISLE, Mary [Br. 19c]
"Long, Long Ago:" an
autobiography.
L: J. & C. Mozley, 1856. 325p.
NUC BL MB

2882. LITTELL, Mary V. [Am. 19c]
From pot-closet to Palais Royal:
or, how a tired house-keeper went
to Europe.
NY: J. S. Ogilvie, 1899. 119p.
NUC
[Travel: Germany, Switzerland,
Belgium, Holland, & London]

2883. LITTLE, Alice E. Neva
(Bewicke) see LITTLE, Alice Helen
Neva (Bewicke)

2884. LITTLE, Alice Helen [BL:E.]
Neva (Bewicke), Mrs. Archibald J.
Little [Br. d. 1726] ALT:
Bewicke, Alice E. Neva
Intimate China. The Chinese as I
have seen them.
L: Hutchinson & co., 1899. 615p.
NUC BL OCLC

2885. -----My diary in a Chinese
farm.
Shanghai: Kelly & Walsh, 1894
[NUC]; 1898 [BL]. 74p. NUC BL MB
OCLC

2886. LITTLE, Mrs. Amos see
LITTLE, Anna P.

2887. LITTLE, Anna P., Mrs. Amos
R. Little [Am. 19c]
The world as we saw it.
Boston: Cupples & co., 1887.
476p. NUC OCLC
[Voyage around the world]

2888. LITTLE, Mrs. Archibald see
LITTLE, Alice Helen Neva
(Bewicke)

2889. LITTLE, Elisabeth N.[Am.19c]
Nor'east by east.
Newton, MA: n.p., 1885. 13p. NUC
[Visit to seashore around York,
Maine]

2890. LITTLE, Laura Jane (Roys)
[Am. 19c]
A mother's peace offering to
American houses; or, The martyr
of the nineteenth century.

NY: pr. J. A. Grays, 1861. 109p.
NUC
[Experiences of the writer in New England; also about slavery.]

2891. LITTLEBOY, Sarah (Edes)
[Br. 1795-1870]
Memoranda relating to the late Sarah Littleboy, of Boxwells, Great Berkhampstead. With selections from her poetry and manuscripts.
L: pr. for priv. circ., 1873. 194p. BL
[Includes an essay on decline of Quakerism]

2892. LIVERMORE, Harriet [Am. 1788-1868]
A narration of religious experiences. In twelve letters....
Concord, NH: pr. by Jacob B. Moore, for the author, 1826. 282p. NUC K OCLC
[Preacher in NY and New England]

2893. LIVERMORE, Mary Ashton (Rice) [Am. 1820-1905]
My story of the war: a woman's narrative of four years' personal experience as a nurse in the Union Army.
Hartford, CT: A. D. Worthington, 1887. 700p. NUC BL C K OCLC

2894. -----The story of my life; or, the sunshine and shadow of seventy years, with hitherto unrecorded incidents and recollections of three years' experience as an army nurse in the great civil war, and reminiscences of twenty-five years' experience on the lecture platform, ... to which is added six of her most popular lectures.
Hartford, CT: A. D. Worthington, c1897. 730p. NUC BL OCLC
[New, expanded version of My story of the war]

2895. LIVINGSTON, Mrs. Edward see LIVINGSTON, Louise (Davezac) Moreau

2896. LIVINGSTON, Louise (Davezac) Moreau, Mrs. Edward Livingston [Am. 1786-1860]
Memoir of Mrs. Edward Livingston, with letters hitherto unpublished. Comp. Louise Livingston Hunt.
NY: Harper & bros, 1886. 182p. NUC BL OCLC

2897. LLANOVER, Lady, ed. see DELANEY, Mary Granville Pendarves

2898. LLOYD, Bitha (Fox) [Br. 1811-1894] ALT: Fox, Bitha
How to see the English Lakes.
L: Religious Tract Society, 1858. 110p. BL

2899. LLOYD, Harriette [Br. 19c]
ALT: L., H.; Ll., H.
Hindu women: with glimpses into their life and zenanas.
L: J. Nisbet & co., 1882. 143p. NUC BL OCLC

2900. LLOYD, Marietta [Am. 19c]
A trip to Ireland, giving an account of the voyage scenes and incidents on landing. Sketch of the Round towers of Ireland. Also a graphic description of travel and sightseeing in Ireland, interspersed with historical legends and stories of her remarkable antiquities, including a romantic tour on the lakes of Killarney.
Chicago: Donohue & Hennaberry, 1893. 193p. NUC OCLC

2901. LLOYD, Susette Harriet see SMITH, Susette Harriet (Lloyd)

2902. LOBDELL, Lucy Ann [Am. b. 1824]
Narrative of Lucy Ann Lobdell, the female hunter of Delaware and Sullivan counties, N.Y.
NY: The authoress, 1855. 47p. NUC K

2903. LOBINGIER, Elizabeth Erwin (Miller) [Am. b. 1889] ALT: Miller, Elizabeth Erwin
Foreign experiences of an American girl.
Meadville, PA: the author, Messenger pr., 1895. 148p. NUC OCLC

2904. LOCKHART, Agnes Helen [Am. 19/20c]
Gems from Scotia's crown.

Boston: American pr. & engraving co., c1867. 47p. NUC OCLC
[Travel: Nova Scotia]

2905. LOCKIE, Katherine F. [Br. 19c]
Picturesque Edinburgh.
Edinburgh: John Lockie, 1899. 437p. NUC BL OCLC

2906. LOFTUS, Jane (Hope-Vere), Marchioness of Ely see ELY, Jane (Hope-Vere) Loftus, Marchioness of

2907. LOGAN, Deborah (Norris), Mrs. George Logan [Am. 1761-1839]
The Norris house.
Philadelphia: Fair-Hill press, 1867. 12p. NUC K OCLC

2908. LOGAN, Mrs. George see LOGAN, Deborah (Norris)

2909. LOGAN, Olive (Logan) [Am. 1839-1909] ALT: Sikes, Olive (Logan) Logan PSEUD: Chroniqueuse
The American abroad. By Olive Logan. n.p., 1882. 16p. NUC OCLC
[Travel: Europe]

2910. -----Apropos of women and theatres. With a paper or two on Parisian topics. By Olive Logan.
NY: Carleton; L: S. Low, son, & co., 1869. 240p. NUC BL OCLC
[Recollections of her life and acquaintances as an actress.]

2911. -----Before the footlights and behind the scenes: a book about "the show business" in all its branches: from puppet shows to grand opera; from mountebanks to menageries; from learned pigs to lecturers; from burlesque blondes to actors and actresses: with some observations and reflections (original and reflected) on morality and immorality in amusements: thus exhibiting the "show world" as seen from within, through the eyes of the former actress, as well as from without, through the eyes of the present lecturer and author.
Philadelphia: Parmelee; San Francisco: H. H. Bancroft, 1870. 612p. NUC K OCLC
[Correspondence, reminiscences]

2912. -----Photographs of Paris life; a record of the politics, art, fashion, and anecdote of Paris, during the past eighteen months. By Chroniqueuse.
L: William Tinsley, 1861. 344p. NUC BL OCLC

2913. LOMAX, Mattie Virginia Sarah Lindsay [Am. b. 1831] ALT: Lomax, Virginia
The old capitol and its inmates. By a lady, who enjoyed the hospitalities of the government for a "season".
NY: n.p., 1867. 226p.
[Detained on suspicion of conspiracy aftr Lincoln's assassination]

2914. LOMAX, Virginia see LOMAX, Mattie Virginia Sarah Lindsay

2915. LONDONDERRY, Frances Anne Emily (Vane-Tempest) Stewart Vane, Marchioness of [Br. 1800-1865] ALT: Stewart, Frances Anne Emily (Vane-Tempest) Vane, Marchioness of Londonberry; Vane, Frances Anne Emily (Vane-Tempest) Stewart, Marchioness of Londonberry
A journal of a three months' tour in Portugal, Spain, Africa, etc. by the Marchioness of Londonderry.
L: J. Mitchell & co., n.d. 94p. NUC BL OCLC

2916. -----Narrative of a visit to the courts of Vienna, Constantinople, Athens, Naples, etc.
L: H. Colburn, n.d. 342p. NUC OCLC

2917. LONG, Mrs. Walter H. C. [Br. 19c]
Peace and war in the Transvaal. An account of the defence of Fort Mary, Lydenberg.
L: Sampson Low & co., 1882. 118p. BL

2918. LONGSTRETH, Mary Anna [Am. 1811-1884]
Memoir of Mary Anna Longstreth. By an old pupil, Margaret Newlin.
Philadelphia: J. B. Lippincott co., 1886. 224p. NUC BL OCLC
[Includes excerpts from journals; trip to Europe in 1853]

2919. LONGWORTH, Maria Theresa
[Br. 1832?-1881] ALT: Avonmore,
Maria Theresa (Longworth)
Yelverton, Viscountess;
Yelverton, Hon. Theresa PSEUD:
Teresina; English Visitor, An
Saint Augustine, Florida.
Sketches of its history, objects
of interest, and advantages as a
resort for health and recreation.
By an English visitor. With notes
for northern tourists on St.
John's River, etc.
St. Augustine, FL: E. S. Carr;
NY: G. P. Putnam & son, 1869.
62p.   NUC OCLC

2920. -----Teresina in America.
[By Térèse Yelverton (Viscountess
Avonmore)]
L: Richard Bentley, 1875. 2v. NUC
BL N OCLC
[Travel: coast to coast]

2921. -----Teresina Peregrina;
or, fifty thousand miles of
travel round the world. [By
Thérèse Yelverton (Viscountess
Avonmore)]
L: Richard Bentley & son, 1874.
2v. NUC BL OCLC
[Vol. 1: Synopsis of trip to
U.S.-- Salt Lake City, Yosemite,
and Sandwich Islands. Travel in
Asia; Vol. 2: India, Ceylon, Spain]

2922. -----The Yelverton
correspondence, with introduction
and connecting narrative. Pub.
as: Hon. Teresa Yelverton,
Viscountess Avonmore
Edinburgh: Thomas Laurie, 1863.
208p. BL OCLC
[Published after her claim of
marriage to William C. Yelverton
was rejected in court.]

2923. LOOKER, Edith C.
(Phillips), Mrs. Horace R. Looker
[Br. 19/20c] ALT: Phillips, E.
C.; Phillips, Eliza Caroline
All the Russias. By E. C.
Phillips.
L, NY: Cassell & co., 1884. 224p.
NUC BL

2924. -----Peeps into China; or,
the missionary's children.
L & NY: Cassell, 1882. 224p. NUC
BL OCLC

2925. LOOKER, Mrs. Horace R. see
LOOKER, Edith C. Phillips

2926. LOOMER, Mrs. B. T. [Am. 19c]
Reminiscences of early times in
Douglas, Wisconsin. Also, behind
the door, a true story.
Montello, WI: The Express steam
pr., 1893. 45p. NUC
[May contain personal material.]

2927. LOPE, M. E. C. see LOPE,
Mary E. Clary

2928. LOPE, Mary E. Clary [Am.
19c] ALT: Lope, M. E. C.
Life, reminiscences and travels
of M. E. C. Lope.
Maysville, KY: F. W. Bauer, pr.,
c1889. 58p. NUC K OCLC
[Burning of the steamboat
Bostana.]

2929. LOSEE, Almira [Am. b. 1825]
Life sketches: being narrations
of scenes occurring in the
labours of Almira Losee. Written
by herself.
NY: pr. for the author by Nelson
& Phillips, 1877. 229p. NUC K
OCLC
[Methodist]

2930. LOTHROP, Harriet Mulford
(Stone) [Am. 1844-1924] PSEUD:
Sidney, Margaret
The golden West as seen by the
Ridgway Club. By Margaret Sidney.
Boston: D. Lothrop & co., c1886.
388p. NUC OCLC
[Travel: California]

2931. LOTT, Emmeline [Br. 19c]
The English governess in Egypt;
harem life in Egypt and
Constantinople.
L: R. Bentley, 1865. 2v. NUC BL
OCLC
[Also pub. as: The governess in
Egypt]

2932. -----The grand pacha's
cruise on the Nile in the Viceroy
of Egypt's yacht.
L: T. C. Newby, 1869. 2v. NUC BL
OCLC

2933. -----The Mohaddetyn in the
palace. Nights in the harem; or,
the Mohaddetyn in the Palace of
Ghezire.

L: Chapman & Hall, 1867. 2v. NUC
BL

2934. LOUGHBOROUGH, Mary Ann
(Webster) [Am. 1836-1887] PSEUD:
Lady, A
My cave life in Vicksburg. With
letters of trial and travel. Pub.
as: A Lady
NY: D. Appleton & co., 1864.
196p. NUC BL OCLC
[Experiences during siege of
Vicksburg, 1863.]

2935. LOUGHERY, Mrs. E. M. [Am.
19c]
A pen picture of the city of
Nacogdoches and Nacogdoches
County, their present and future.
An invitation to immigration,
capital and enterprise. Cities,
like men, shape their own
destiny.
Nacogdoches, TX: Spradley & Huff,
1895. 32p. NUC

2936. LOUTHAN, Hattie (Horner)
[Am. b. 1865]
"Not at home".
NY: J. B. Alden, 1889. 307p. NUC
[Travel: U.S.]

2937. LOVE, Christopher, co-
author see LOVE, Mary (Stone)

2938. LOVE, Mrs. Christopher see
LOVE, Mary (Stone)

2939. LOVE, Mary (Stone), Mrs.
Christopher Love [Br. 17c]
Love's name lives; or, a
publication of divers petitions
presented by Mistris Love to the
Parliament, in behalf of her
husband. With several letters
that interchangeably passed
between them a little before his
death.
L: n.p., 1651. 15p. NUC BL

2940. -----The strange and
wonderful predictions of Mr.
Christopher Love, minister of the
gospel... . who was beheaded on
Tower-Hill on account of his
religion. ... To which are added
two letters from his wife to him,
a little before his death, with
his answers to her again.
Carlisle: G. Kline, n.d. NUC BL

2941. LOWDELL, Mary Caroline [Br.
19c]
Loving and beloved, a memorial
sketch of Mary Caroline Lowdell.
[Comp.] Emma Holland.
Brighton: D. B. Friend, 1883.
103p. BL
[May contain original material]

2942. LOWE, Ann [Am. 19c]
Autobiography. Ed. Rev. George
Coles.
NY: n.p., 1846. NUC

2943. -----LOWE, Clara M. S. [Br.
19C]
Punrooty: or, the gospel winning
its way among the women of India.
L: Morgan & Scott, 1880. 142p.
NUC BL

2944. LOWE, Clara M. S., comp.
see MAC PHERSON, Annie

2945. LOWE, Emily [Br. 19c]
Unprotected females in Norway.
L & NY: G. Routledge, 1857. 295p.
NUC BL OCLC

2946. -----Unprotected females in
Sicily, Calabria, and on the top
of Mount Aetna.
L & NY: Routledge, Warnes &
Routledge, 1859. 265p. NUC BL
OCLC
[Travel with Helen Lowe; advice
for unescorted women travelers]

2947. LOWE, Helen, co-author see
LOWE, Emily

2948. LOWE, Louisa [Br. 19c]
My story, exemplifying the
injurious working of the lunacy
laws and the undue influence
possessed by lunacy experts.
L: Lunacy Law Reform office,
1878. 24p. NUC

2949. LOWELL, Mary Ann (Duane)
see DUANE, Harriet Constable

2950. LOWRIE, Mrs. John C. see
LOWRIE, Louisa Ann (Wilson)

2951. LOWRIE, Louisa Ann
(Wilson), Mrs. John C. Lowrie
[Br. 1809-1833]
Memoirs of Mrs. Louisa A. Lowrie,
wife of the Rev. John C. Lowrie,

missionary to northern India: who died at Calcutta, Nov. 21, 1833, aged 24 years. Compiled from her letters and private papers. By Ashbel Green Fairchild.
Pittsburg, PA: Luke Loomis, c1835. 162p. BL OCLC

2952. LOWRY, Jean [Am. 18c]
A journal of the captivity of Jean Lowry and her children, giving an account of her being taken by the Indians, the first of April, 1756, from William McCord's in Rocky Spring Settlement in Pennsylvania.
Philadelphia: William Bradford, 1760. 31p. NUC MAD

2953. LUCAS, Eliza see PINCKNEY, Eliza (Lucas)

2954. LUCAS, Margaret (Brindley) [Br. 1701-1769]
Account of the convincement and call to the ministry of Margaret Lucas, who died at Seek, in Staffordshire, the 24th of the sixth month, 1769.
2d ed. L: Darton and Harvey, 1797. 142p. NUC BL MB

2955. LUCAS, Rachel (Hinman) [Am. b. 1774]
Remarkable account of Mrs. Rachel Lucas, daughter of Mr. James Hinman, of Durham (Conn.) as written by herself and attested by her family and acquaintance.
Middletown, CT: pr. by T. & J. B. Dunning, 1805. 15p. NUC K OCLC [Account of illness and remarkable healing.]

2956. LUCAS, Sarah, co-author see CARR, Mary Frances

2957. LUCE, Mrs. Joel see LUCE, Phebe

2958. LUCE, Phebe, Mrs. Joel Luce [Am. 19c]
Maternal admonition, or the orphan's manual: by Mrs. Phebe Luce, to her children, supplementary to a work, entitled Vicissitudes of life; or the history of Mrs. Phebe Luce.
Cooperstown, NY: pr. for the author by H. & F. Phinney, 1819. 96p. NUC [Contains poems]

2959. LUCY, Mary Elizabeth [Br. 19c]
Biography of the Lucy family, of Charlecote Park, in the county of Warwick.
L: priv. pr. E. Faithful & co., 1862. 208p. BL

2960. -----The private journal of a tour on the Continent in the years 1841-1843.
L: C. Whittingham, 1845. 130p. NUC BL

2961. LUKE, Jemima (Thompson), comp. see G., Marie K.

2962. LUKENS, Matilda Barns, Mrs. [Am. 19c]
The inland passage. A journal of a trip to Alaska.
n.p.: n.p., 1889. 84p. NUC OCLC

2963. LUMB, Anne (Milnes) [Br. 18c]
Diaries of Mrs. Anne Lumb of Silcoates, near Wakefield, in 1755 and 1757. Ed. Charles Milnes Gaskell.
L: pr. Strangeways & sons, 1884. 40p. NUC MBD OCLC

2964. LUNDIE, Mrs. J. C. see DUNCAN, Mary (Grey) Lundie

2965. LUNDIE, Mrs. J. C., comp. see DUNCAN, Mary (Lundie)

2966. LUNDIE, Mary see DUNCAN, Mary (Lundie)

2967. LUNDIE, Mary (Grey) see DUNCAN, Mary (Grey) Lundie

2968. LUNDIE, Mary (Grey), comp. see DUNCAN, Mary Lundie

2969. LUSCOMBE, Ellen, Mrs. [Br. 19c]
Myrtles and aloes; or, our Salcombe sketch book. By Ellen Luscombe. With some addenda in the shape of a discursive gossip about Kingsbridge. By Francis Young.
Kingsbridge: G. P. Friend; L: Hamilton, Adams, 1861. 152p. NUC BL

2970. LUSHINGTON, Mrs. Charles see LUSHINGTON, Sarah (Gascoyne)

2971. LUSHINGTON, Henrietta (Prescott), Lady [Br. d. 1875]
Almeria's castle: or, my early life in India and in England.
L: Griffith, Farran, 1866. BL

2972. LUSHINGTON, Sarah (Gascoyne), Mrs. Charles Lushington [Br. d. 1839]
Narrative of a journey from Calcutta to Europe, by way of Egypt, in the years 1827-28.
2d ed. L: J. Murray, 1829. 280p. NUC BL OCLC

2973. LUTTON, Anne [Br. 1791-1881]
Light on the Christian's daily path. Compiled from the unpublished letters of A. L. Ed. A. S. Webb.
L: Nisbet & co., 1886. 87p. NUC BL

2974. -----Memorials of a consecrated life, compiled from the autobiography, letters and diaries of Anne Lutton. By J. H. W.
L: T. Woolmer, 1882. 523p. NUC BL MB OCLC

2975. LUTTRELL, Hope [Br. 19c]
Prince Hassan's carpet.
L: T. Cautley Newby, 1864. BL
[Travel: Corfu, Greece, France, Italy, Scotland]

2976. LUTTS, Lucia B., ed. see MADISON, Dorothy (Payne) Todd

2977. LUXBOROUGH, Henrietta (Saint-John) Knight, Baroness [Br. d. 1756] ALT: Knight, Henrietta (Saint-John), Baroness Luxborough
Letters ... to W. Shenstone, Esq. Ed. John Hodgetts.
L: J. Dodsley, 1775. 416p. NUC BL OCLC   [Letters from 1739 to 1756.]

2978. LYALL, Isabella D. [Br. d. 1891]
Nwan Ima: the woman of love. Memorial sketch of Isabella D. Lyall. Comp. Jessie Hood.
Edinburgh: Robert R. Sutherland, 1893. 81p. BL OCLC
[Presbyterian Missionary in Nigeria.]

2979. LYELL, Catharine [Br. 18c]
A tour to Sweden in the year 1767, printed from the manuscript journal of Miss Catharine Lyell.
L: J. Seally, 1770. 27p. NUC

2980. LYMAN, Anne Jean (Robbins) [Am. 1789-1867]
Memoir of the life of Mrs. Anne Jean Lyman. By Susan Inches (Lyman) Lesley.
Cambridge, MA: priv. pr. by J. Wilson & son, 1876. 543p. NUC BL OCLC
[Reprinted as: Recollections of my mother]

2981. LYMAN, Eliza B., comp. see WANTON, Mary

2982. LYMAN, Julie E. [Am. b 181?] ALT: A Lady
Doing and believing: the Christian experience of a lady.
Hartford, CT: Case, Lockwood & Brainard, 1873. 113p. NUC
[Spiritual autobiography of Baptist convert.]

2983. LYNCH, Anne Charlotte see BOTTA, Anne Charlotte, (Lynch)

2984. LYNCH, Hannah [Br. d. 1904]
Autobiography of a child.
NY: Dodd, Mead & co., 1899. 270p. NUC BL MB OCLC
[NUC and BL class as fiction; MB as autobiographical.]

2985. LYNCH, Mrs. Henry see LYNCH, Theodora Elizabeth (Foulks)

2986. LYNCH, Theodora Elizabeth (Foulks), Mrs. Henry Lynch [Br. 1812-1885]
The wonders of the West Indies.
L: Seeley, Jackson & Halliday, 1856. 315p. NUC BL

2987. LYNES, Sarah see GRUBB, Sarah (Lynes)

2988. LYNN, Elizabeth see LINTON, Elizabeth (Lynn)

2989. LYNN, Susanna [Br. (1785-1807)]
Extracts, &c. &c. from the journals of the late Miss Susanna Lynn, Esq. who died, February 3, 1807 aged twenty-one years and three months.

Dublin: J. Jones for Methodist book-room, 1814. 64p. NUC

2990. LYON, Mary [Am. 19c]
Memoirs of Mary Lyon of New Haven.
New Haven, CT: n.p., 1837. 25p. NUC

2991. LYON, Mary [Am. 1797-1849]
The power of Christian benevolence illustrated in the life and labors of Mary Lyon. Comp. Edward Hitchcok with the assistance of others.
Northampton, MA: Hopkins, Bridgman & co.; Philadelphia: Thomas, Cowperthwait & co., 1851. 486p. NUC BL OCLC
[Includes letters. Founder of Mt. Holyoke.]

2992. -----Recollections of Mary Lyon, with selections from her instructions to the pupils in Mt. Holyoke Female Seminary.
Boston: Amer. Tract Soc., [1866]. 333p. BL OCLC

2993. LYTTON, Edith Villiers Bulwer-Lytton, Countess [Br. 1841-1936] India, 1876-1880.
n.p.: Priv. pr. at the Chiswick Press, 1899. 259p. NUC

2994. LYTTON, Edward George Earle Bulwer-Lytton, Baron, co-author see LYTTON, Rosina Anne Doyle (Wheeler) Bulwer-Lytton, Baroness

2995. LYTTON, Rosina Anne Doyle (Wheeler) Bulwer-Lytton, Baroness [Br. 1802-1882] ALT: Bulwer, Rosina Doyle (Wheeler), Baroness Lytton
Letters of the late Edward Bulwer, Lord Lytton, to his wife. With extracts from her ms. "Autobiography, and other documents" published in vindication of her memory ... .
By Louisa Devey.
L: W. Swan Sonnenschein & co., 1884. 325p. BL OCLC

2996. -----Life of Rosina, Lady Lytton, with numerous extracts from her ms. autobiography and other original documents, published in vindication of her memory. By Louisa Devey.

L: Swan Sonnenschein, Lowrey & co., 1887. 432p. NUC BL MB

2997. MC ALLISTER, Agnes [Am. 19c]
A lone woman in Africa; six years on the Kroo Coast.
Cincinnati, OH: Cranston & Curtis; NY: Hunt & Eaton, 1896. 295p. NUC BL K OCLC
[Travel as a missionary in Nigeria]

2998. M'ALLISTER, M. E., Mrs. [Am. b. 1844]
Sunshine among the clouds; or, extracts from experience.
Cincinnati, OH: Hitchcock & Walden, 1873. 243p. NUC K OCLC
[Spiritual autobiography]

2999. MAC CARTHY, Florence see REAGH, Florence MacCarthy

3000. MC CARTHY, Rev. Florence [Am. b. 1838]
The cruel wrong done at the Fourth Baptist Church, in Chicago, to Florence McCarthy in the year 1874.
Chicago: The author, 1891. NUC

3001. -----The Fourth Baptist souvenir, being a narrative of the great mob at the Fourth Baptist Church in Chicago, in 1874, by the victim, Florence McCarthy.
Chicago: n.p., 1897?. NUC

3002. MAC CASKILL, A., Lady [Br. 19c]
Twelve days in Skye.
2d ed., L: Seeleys, 1852. 41p. BL

3003. MAC CAUL, Elizabeth Anne see FINN, Elizabeth Anne (MacCaul)

3004. MACAULEY, Elizabeth Wright [Br. 1785?-1837]
Autobiographical memoirs.
L: pr. for the author, 1834. 16p. BL

3005. -----Facts against falsehood being a brief statement of Miss Macauley's engagements at the winter theatres, etc.
L: Duncombe, 1824. 16p. NUC BL OCLC

3006. M'CLEERY, Anna see M'CRACKEN, Mary A.

3007. MAC CLELLAN, Kate [Br. 19c]
In memoriam: K. M. [i.e. Kate M'Clellan].
Brooklyn, NY: n.p., 1870?. 79p. NUC
[Includes selections from her writings, in prose and poetry.]

3008. -----Memories of a consecrated life; or, a memorial sketch of K. M'Clellan.
NY: n.p., 1869. BL

3009. MC CLELLAN, Katherine Elizabeth [Am. 19c]
Keene Valley. "In the heart of the mountains".
Saranac Lake, NY: pub. by author, 1898. 26p. NUC

3010. MC CLINTOCK, Eva (White), ed. see WILLARD, Caroline McCoy (White)

3011. MC CLURE, Nancy see HUGGAN, Nancy (McCLure)

3012. MC CLURG, Mary V. D. see MC CLURG, Virginia (Donaghé)

3013. MC CLURG, Virginia (Donaghé) [Am. 1858-1931] ALT: McClurg, Mary V. D.
Picturesque Utah.
Denver, CO: F. S. Thayer, 1888. 33p. NUC OCLC [Travel]

3014. MAC CONKEY, Harriet E. (Bishop) see BISHOP, Harriet E.

3015. MC CORMICK, Fannie [Am. 19c]
A Kansas farm; or, the promised land.
NY: J. B. Alden, 1892. 163p. NUC OCLC

3016. M'CRACKEN, Mary A. [Br. 1770-1866]
Historical notices of old

Belfast. By Robert Magill Young.
Belfast: M. Ward & co., 1896. NUC BL OCLC
[Biography of Mary A. M'Cracken by her grandniece, Anna M'Cleery. Incl. some of her letters about the Irish Rebellion.]

3017. MC CRACKEN, William D., ed. see HUNTINGTON, Anne (Huntington)

3018. MC CRACKIN, Josephine (Woempner) Clifford [Am. b. 1838]
Pen pictures of Ventura County, California; its beauties, resources, and capacities.
San Buenaventura, CA: Free printing office, 1880. 26p. NUC

3019. MACDONALD, Flora (Macdonald) [Br. 1722-1790]
The autobiography of Flora Macdonald, being the home of a heroine. Ed. her grand-daughter [Flora Frances (Macdonald) Wylde].
Edinburgh: W. P. Nimmo, 1870. 2v. NUC BL OCLC
[Most probably fiction]

3020. MAC DONALD, Rev. John, comp. see HOOD, Isabel

3021. M'DONNELL, Emily Fanny Dorothy (Osborn), ed. see OSBORN, Sarah (Byng)

3022. MC DOUGALD, Elizabeth, Mrs. [Am. b. 1796]
The life, travels, and extraordinary adventures of Elizabeth McDougald, who, attired as a man, travelled over the principal part of the United States and the Canadas between the years 1826 and 1834, in pursuit of her husband, for the avowed purpose of revenge and assassination, and who, during her travels, served two years in the army of the United States, without having her sex detected. Written by and pub. with her direction.
Providence, RI: S. S. Southworth, 1834. 24p. NUC

3023. MC DOUGALL, Frances Harriet (Whipple) Greene, comp. see ELDRIDGE, Elleanor

3024. MC DOUGALL, Francis Thomas, co-author <u>see</u> MC DOUGALL, Harriette (Bunyon)

3025. MC DOUGALL, Mrs. Francis Thomas <u>see</u> MC DOUGALL, Harriette (Bunyon)

3026. MC DOUGALL, Harriette (Bunyon), Mrs. Francis Thomas McDougall [Br. 1816/17-1886]
Letters from Sarawak; addressed to a child. Embracing an account of the manners, customs, and religion of the inhabitants of Borneo; the progress of the church mission and incidents of missionary life among the natives.
L: Grant & Griffith, 1854. 190p.
NUC MB

3027. -----Sketches of our life at Sarawak.
L: Society for Promoting Christian Knowledge, 1880?. 250p.
NUC OCLC

3028. -----Memoirs of Francis Thomas McDougal ... and of Harriette, his wife .... [Ed.] Charles John Bunyon.
L: Longmans & co., 1889. 368p. BL

3029. MC ELVAINE, Harriet Emily [Am. 19c]
Reminiscences; or, thirty years ago.
Columbus, OH: n.p., 1890. 71p.
NUC
[Orig. pub. in Indianapolis in a family religious paper.]

3030. MACFARLAN, D., comp. <u>see</u> MUIR, Martha

3031. MC GOODWIN, Bessie (Ware) [Am. b. 1851]
War-time memories of the Southland.
n.p.: n.p., 1890. NUC
[Resident of Selma, AL describes life during and after the Civil War.]

3032. MC GUIRE, Mrs. John P. <u>see</u> MC GUIRE, Judith White (Brockenbrough)

3033. MC GUIRE, Judith White (Brockenbrough), Mrs. John P.

McGuire [Am. 19c] PSEUD: Lady of Virginia, A
Diary of a southern refugee, during the war. By a lady of Virginia.
NY: E. J. Hale & son, 1867. 360p.
NUC BL C OCLC

3034. MACHARDY, Elizabeth A. [Br. 19c] Iona.
Edinburgh: D. Douglas, 1891. 46p.
NUC

3035. MAC INNES, E., comp. <u>see</u> JOHNSTON, Priscilla (Buxton)

3036. MAC KAY, Alexina <u>see</u> RUTHQUIST, Alexina (MacKAY)

3037. MAC KAY, Charles, ed. <u>see</u> LEIGH, Elizabeth Medora

3038. MAC KENZIE, Anne [Br. 19c] ALT: M., A.
Seeing and hearing; or three years experience in Natal. By A. M.
Edinburgh: n.p., 1857. BL

3039. -----Charlie Douglas's visit to a mission station: being recollections of mission work in Natal. By a sister of the late Bishop MacKenzie.
L: Christian Knowledge Society, 1869. BL

3040. MAC KENZIE, Anne, ed. <u>see</u> ROBERTSON, Henrietta (Woodrow)

3041. MAC KENZIE, Christina [Am. 19c]
Life's battle; facts and incidents.
Montgomery, AL: Barrett & Wimbish, 1859. 263p. NUC
[May contain personal material]

3042. MACKENZIE, Mrs. Colin <u>see</u> MACKENZIE, Helen (Douglas)

3043. MACKENZIE, Georgina Mary Muir, co-author <u>see</u> IRBY, Adeline Paulina

3044. MACKENZIE, Helen (Douglas), Mrs. Colin Mackenzie [Br. 19c]
Life in the mission, the camp, and the zenáná; or, six years in India.

L: R. Bentley, 1853. 3v. NUC BL
MB OCLC
[Contains diary, 1846-1851]

3045. MACKIN, Mrs. James see
MACKIN, Sarah Maria Aloisa
(Britton) Spottiswood

3046. MACKIN, Sally Britton
Spottiswood see MACKIN, Sarah
Maria Aloisa (Britton) Spottiswood

3047. MACKIN, Sarah Maria Aloisa
(Britton) Spottiswood), Mrs.
James Mackin [Am. 19c] ALT:
Mackin, Sally Britton Spottiswood
A society woman on two
continents, by Sally Britton
Spottiswood Mackin, a daughter of
the American revolution.
NY & L: Transatlantic, 1896.
327p. NUC K OCLC

3048. MC KINNON, Mary Narcissa
[Am. 19c]
Parsifal; a day at the Wagner-
Bayreuth festival.
Raleigh, NC: Edwards & Broughton,
1898. NUC

3049. MACKINTOSH, Mrs. [Br. 19c]
Damascus and its people: sketches
of modern life in Syria.
L: Seeley, Jackson, & Halliday,
1883. 296p. NUC BL OCLC

3050. MC LAREN, Valerie (Lamar)
[Am. 19c]
Scenes and dreams in other lands.
NY: Chambers pr. co., 1897. 290p.
NUC [Travel: Europe]

3051. MAC LAUGHLIN, Louisa
Elizabeth, co-author see PEARSON,
Emma Maria

3052. MAC LEAN, Jean [Br. d.
1897]
God my exceeding joy. A sketch of
the trials, labours, and triumphs
of the late Miss Jean McLean by
her twin sister, Margaret.
2d ed. L: Passmore & Alabaster,
1899. 233p. BL
[From her letters & diaries,
includes poems.]

3053. MAC LEAN, Margaret [Br. 19c]
Echoes from Japan.

L: Passmore & Alabaster, 1889.
315p. BL OCLC

3054. -----Seafarers from the
land of the rising sun in London.
L: Passmore & Alabaster, 1896.
56p. BL
[Mission work among Japanese
sailors.]

3055. MAC LEAN, Margaret, comp.
see MAC LEAN, Jean

3056. M'LEHOSE, Agnes (Craig)
[Br. 1759-1841] PSEUD: Clarinda
The correspondence between
[Robert] Burns and Clarinda. With
a memoir of Mrs. M'Lehose--
Clarinda. Arr. & ed. her
grandson, W. C. M'Lehose.
Edinburgh: William Tait, n.d.
297p.; NY: R. P. Bixby & co.,
1843. 600p. NUC BL OCLC

3057. -----Letters addressed to
Clarinda. ... Never before
published. By Robert Burns.
Glasgow: T. Stewart, 1802. 48p.
BL OCLC
[Letters published without Mrs.
M'Lehose's permission.]

3058. M'LEHOSE, W. C., ed. see
M'LEHOSE, Agnes (Craig) Maclellan
Frances

3059. MAC LELLAN, Frances E. H.
[Am. 1833-1852]
Memoir of Frances E. H. M'Lellan,
with a selection from her
letters, by her cousin Rebecca M.
Haskell.
NY: M. W. Dodd, 1856. 182p. NUC
OCLC

3060. MACLELLAN, Frances, Mrs.
[Br. 19c]
Evenings abroad.
L: Smith, Elder, 1836. 332p. NUC
BL OCLC

3061. -----Sketches of Corfu,
historical and domestic ...
interspersed with legends and
traditions.
L: Smith, Elder & co., 1835.
445p. BL

3062. MACLEOD, Anne Campbell see
WILSON, Anne Campbell (Macleod),
Lady

3063. MC LOUGHLIN, Emma V., co-author see WILSON, Lucy Langdon (Williams)

3064. MC MURPHY, Mary L., Mrs.
[Am. 19c]
Only glimpses.
Racine, WI: Advocate steam print., 1887. 148p. NUC OCLC
[Travel: Italy, France]

3065. MACNAB, FRANCES, pseud. see FRASER, Agnes

3066. MAC NAUGHT, Mrs. [Br. 19c]
Through distant lands. Diary of a tour round the world in 1886-7.
L?: for priv. circ., 1887?. 224p.
NUC OCLC

3067. MC NAUGHTON, Margaret [19c]
Overland to Cariboo; an eventful journey of Canadian pioneers to the gold-fields of British Columbia in 1862.
Toronto: William Briggs, 1896.
176p. NUC BL OCLC

3068. M'OWAN, Peter, ed. see PICKFORD, Elizabeth

3069. MC PHELEMY, May Kenny, Mrs.
[Am. 19c]
Well trodden paths, a diary.
Atlanta, GA: The Autocrat pub. co., 1896. 270p. NUC
[Travel: Europe]

3070. MAC PHERSON, A., Mrs. [Br. 19c] PSEUD: Lady, A.
My experiences in Australia.
Being recollections of a visit to the Australian colonies in 1856-7. Pub. as: A Lady
L: J. F. Hope, 1860. 367p. NUC

3071. MAC PHERSON, Annie, Miss
[Br. 19c]
God's answers: a record of Miss A[nnie] MacPherson's work at the Home of Industry, Spitalfields, London, and in Canada. [Comp.]
Clara M. S. Lowe.
L: James Nisbet, 1882. 212p. NUC BL

3072. MACPHERSON, Gerardine (Bate), comp. see JAMESON, Anna (Brownell)

3073. MACQUOID, Gilbert S., co-author see MACQUOID, Katherine Sarah (Gadsden)

3074. MACQUOID, Katherine Sarah (Gadsden) [Br. 1824-1917]
About Yorkshire. With Thomas Robert Macquoid.
L: Chatto & Windus, 1883. 357p.
BL OCLC

3075. -----In the Ardennes.
L: Chatto & Windus, 1881. 251p.
NUC BL OCLC

3076. -----In the volcanic Eifel; a holiday ramble. With Gilbert S. Macquoid.
L: Hutchinson & co., 1896. 342p.
NUC BL OCLC

3077. -----Pictures and legends from Normandy and Brittany. With Thomas Robert Macquoid.
L: Chatto & Windus, 1879; NY: G. P. Putnam's sons, 1881. NUC BL OCLC

3078. -----Through Brittany.
L: Chatto & Windus, 1877. 325p.
NUC BL OCLC

3079. -----Through Normandy.
L: Chatto & Windus, 1874. 556p.
NUC BL OCLC

3080. MACQUOID, Thomas Robert, co-author see MACQUOID, Katherine Sarah (Gadsden)

3081. MACRAE, Barbara Jane (Matlock) [Am. 1859-1943]
Trek across the plains by the Preston Hale Matlock family; from Missouri (1874) to Washington Territory (1875).
n.p.: n.p., n.d., 20 l. NUC

3082. M'TAGGART, Anne (Hamilton) [Br. 1753?-1834] PSEUD: Lady, A
Memoirs of a gentlewoman of the old school. By a lady.
L: Hurst, Chance & co., 1830. 2v.
NUC BL MB OCLC
[Autobiography; includes travel in France just before the Revolution, also Switzerland & Holland]

3083. M., A. see MAC KENZIE, Annie

3084. M., A., ed. see ROBERTSON, Henrietta (Woodrow)

3085. M., C. F. see MAITLAND, Hon. Caroline Fuller

3086. M., C. M. see MINER, Clara M.

3087. M., E. H. see MAIR, Elizabeth Harriet (Siddons)

3088. M., E. P. see MAUNY, E. P., Mrs.

3089. M., I., pseud. see IRBY, Adeline Paulina

3090. M., M. M. C., comp. see ANDERSON, Bessie

3091. M., S. see MARTIN, Selina

3092. MADISON, Dolly see MADISON, Dorothy (Payne) Todd

3093. MADISON, Dorothy (Payne) Todd, Mrs. James Madison [Am. 1768-1849] ALT: Madison, Dolly
Memoirs and letters of Dorothy Madison, wife of James Madison, President of the United States. Ed. her grand-niece [Lucia Beverly Cutts].
Boston: Houghton, Mifflin & co., 1886. 210p. NUC BL OCLC

3094. MADISON, Mrs. James see MADISON, Dorothy (Payne) Todd

3095. MAEDER, Clara (Fisher) [Am. 1811-1898]
Autobiography of Clara Fisher Maeder. Ed. Douglas Taylor.
NY: The Dunlap Society, 1897. 138p. NUC K OCLC

3096. MAGDALENE ADELAIDE, Sister see SHEPHERD, Margaret Lisle

3097. MAIN, Elizabeth Alice Frances (Hawkins-Whitshed) Burnaby see LE BLOND, Elizabeth Alice Frances (Hawkins-Whitshed) Burnaby Main

3098. MAINS, Lura A. [Am. b. 1847]
Mizpah: autobiographical sketches.
Grand Rapids, MI: Hensen & Reynders, 1892. 107p. K OCLC

3099. MAIR, Elizabeth Harriet (Siddons) [Br. d. 1876/7] ALT: M., E. H.
Recollections of the past, a series of letters.
Edinburgh: priv. pr. by R. & R. Clark, 1877. 102p. NUC BL MB OCLC
[Contains some poems. Reminiscences of Mrs. Siddons, the Kembles, and others.]

3100. MAITLAND, Hon. Caroline Fuller [Br. 19c] ALT: M., C. F.
How we went to Rome in 1857. By C. F. M.
L: pr. for priv. circ., 1892. 103p. BL

3101. MAITLAND, Edward, comp. see KINGSFORD, Anna (Bonus)

3102. MAITLAND, Julia Charlotte (Barrett) [Br. d. 1864] PSEUD: Lady, A
Letters from Madras, during the years 1836-1839, by a lady.
L: J. Murray, 1843. 300p. NUC BL OCLC

3103. MAITLAND, MARIA, pseud. see PHILLIPS, Phebe

3104. MAJOLIER, Christine R. see ALSOP, Christine R. (Majolier)

3105. MALCOLM, Clementina (Elphinstone), Lady [Br. d. 1830]
A diary of St. Helena, 1816, 1817. The journal of Lady Malcolm, containing the conversations of Napoleon with Sir Pulteney Malcolm. Ed. Sir Arthur Wilson.
L: A. D. Innes & co., 1899. 168p. NUC BL MBD OCLC

3106. MALLABONE, Mary Ann [Br. 1802-1822]
Memoirs of Mr. James Mallabone late of Nuneaton Fields, Warwicksh. and his daughter ... M. A. Mallabone, with extracts from her diary and letters. By R. M. Miller.
L: n.p., 1823. BL MBD
[MBD attr. to R. M. Mallabone.]

3107. MALLABONE, R. M. see MALLABONE, Mary Ann

3108. MANN, Agnes [Br. 19c]
Christ realized.
Torquay: n.p., 1871. 45p. BL
[Spiritual autobiography]

3109. MANN, Alice [Br. 19c]
Emigrant's guide to Port Stephens
(New South Wales).
L: W. Strange, 1850. NUC

3110. -----Mann's emigrant's
complete guide to the United
States of America.
Leeds: Alice Mann; 4th ed. L: Wm.
Strange, 1850. NUC

3111. MANN, Mrs. Horace, ed. see
HOPKINS, Sarah Winnemucca

3112. MANN, Mary Tyler (Peabody),
ed. see HOPKINS, Sarah Winnemucca

3113. MANNERS, Catherine
(Pollok), ed. see RUSSELL, Rachel
(Wriothesley) Vaughan, Baroness
Russell

3114. MANNERS, Janetta (Hughan),
Duchess of Rutland see RUTLAND,
Janetta (Hughan) Manners, Duchess
of

3115. MARCH, ANNE, pseud. see
WOOLSON, Constance Fenimore

3116. MARIS, Ann [Am. b. 1714]
Journal of Ann Maris. Some
remarks on a religious education
and the advantages thereof;
likewise, some observations on
the condescending goodness of a
merciful creator in visiting
mankind even in their tender
years, transmitted to posterity
in the life and memoirs of A. M.
Supposed to have been written in
or about the year 1772.
Philadelphia: Henry B. Ashmead,
1869. 76p. NUC OCLC

3117. MARIS, Eleanor (Wood) [Am.
1835-1871]
Selections from memoranda of
Eleanor W. Maris, with brief
notices of her life by her husband.
Philadelphia: pr. for priv.
circ., 1872. 20p. NUC

3118. MARISHALL, Jean [Br. 1765-
1788] ALT: Marshall, Jane

A series of letters.
Edinburgh: pr. for author by
Francis Noble, 1788. 2v. NUC BL

3119. MARKHAM, Pauline [19c]
Life of Pauline Markham. Written
by herself.
NY: n.p., 1871. 31p. NUC K OCLC
[English actress who appeared in
U. S. Doubtful attribution to
Richard Grant White.]

3120. MARRYAT, Florence see LEAN,
Florence (Marryat) Church

3121. MARRYAT, Florence, ed. see
DAVIES, Bessie (Williams)

3122. MARSDEN, Kate [Br. 1859-1931]
On sledge and horseback to
outcast Siberian lepers.
L: Record press, 1892. 243p.; NY:
Cassell pub. co., 1892. 291p. NUC
BL OCLC

3123. MARSHALL, Ann James [Am. b.
1813?]
The autobiography of Mrs. A. J.
Marshall, age 84 years.
Pine Bluff, AR: Adams-Wilson,
1897. 232p. NUC K OCLC
[Recollections of teacher &
minister's wife, 1846-1870.]

3124. MARSHALL, Elsie [Br. 1869-
1895]
"For his sake." A record of a
life consecrated to God and
devoted to Christ. Extracts from
the letters of Elsie Marshall,
martyred at Hwa-Sang, August 1,
1895.
L: Religious Tract Society; NY,
Chicago: F. H. Revell co., 1896.
223p. NUC BL OCLC
[Missionary work]

3125. MARSHALL, Florence A.
(Thomas), ed. see SHELLEY, Mary
Wollstonecraft (Godwin)

3126. MARSHALL, James, Rev., ed.
see GRAHAM, Isabella (Marshall)

3127. MARSHALL, Jane see
MARISHALL, Jean

3128. MARSHALL, Mrs. Julian, ed.
see SHELLEY, Mary Wollstonecraft
(Godwin)

3129. MARSHALL, Mary Louise, ed.
see CHAPIN, Elizabeth Leonard

3130. MARSHALL, Mary M. Dyer [Am.
b. 1780] ALT: Dyer, Mary M.
Shakerism exposed.
Hanover, NH: Dartmouth bros.,
1850?. 20p. BL

3131. MARSTON, Annie Westland see
MARSTON, Annie Wright

3132. MARSTON, Annie Wright [Br.
19/20c] ALT: Marston, Annie
Westland [NUC]
The great closed land. A plea for
Tibet.
L: S. W. Partridge & co., 1894.
112p. NUC BL OCLC
[Missionary work and travel]

3133. MARSTON, MRS. MILDRED,
pseud. see SCOTT, Anna (Kay)

3134. MARTIN, Annie [Br. 19c]
Home life on an ostrich farm.
L: George Philip, 1890. 288p. NUC
BL OCLC
[South Africa]

3135. MARTIN, Clara Barnes, Mrs.
[Am. d. 1886]
Mount Desert, on the coast of
Maine.
Portland, ME: Thurston & co.,
pr., 1867. 36p. NUC BL OCLC

3136. MARTIN, Cornelia (Williams)
[Am. 19c]
The old home [Pt. I] 1817-1850.
[Pt. II] 1850-1870.
n.p.: priv. pr., 1894. 49p. NUC
OCLC
[Pt. I: family history at New
York state homestead,
Willowbrook. Pt. II: personal
recollections.]

3137. MARTIN, Harriet Elizabeth
[Am. 1840-1860]
The joyful triumph. [Comp.] Mrs.
M. E. Whiting.
NY: A. D. F. Randolph, 1861. 44p.
NUC
[May contain personal material.]

3138. MARTIN, Mrs. Herbert, ed. &
co-author see LE BRETON, Anna
Laetitia (Aiken)

3139. MARTIN, Jane Ann [Am. 19c]
The bloody visions of my life are
ended, and the cruelty is
completed.
Plainfield, NJ: n.p., 1859. 63p.
NUC

3140. -----Credentials of J. A.
Martin; or, a narrative of her
religious experience.
NY: Piercy & Reed, 1846. 102p.
NUC OCLC

3141. -----The last month's
journal of the living martyr. A
wonder to the world.
NY: the author, 1854. 16p. NUC

3142. MARTIN, Maria, Mrs. [Am. b.
1779]
History of the captivity and
sufferings of Mrs. Maria Martin,
who was six years a slave in
Algiers: two of which she was
confined in a dark and dismal
dungeon, loaded with irons.
Written by herself. To which is
annexed a history of Algiers, a
description of the country, the
manners and customs of the
natives, their treatment of their
slaves, their laws and religion,
etc., etc.
Boston: W. Cleary, 180?. 40p. NUC
OCLC

3143. MARTIN, Mary Emma
(LeBreton), ed. & co-author see
LeBRETON, Anna Laetitia (Aiken)

3144. MARTIN, Mary (Parker), Lady
[Br. 19c]
Our Maoris.
L: Society for Promoting
Christian Knowledge, 1884. 220p.
NUC BL OCLC
[New Zealand missions]

3145. MARTIN, Sadie E., comp. see
ABBOTT, Emma

3146. MARTIN, Sarah [Br. 1791-
1843]
A brief sketch of the life of the
late Miss Sarah Martin of Great
Yarmouth, with ... her own prison
journal.
Yarmouth: n.p., 1844. NUC BL MB
OCLC
[Prison visitor]

3147. MARTIN, Selina [Br. 19c]
ALT: M., S.
Narrative of a three years'
residence in Italy, 1819-22, etc.
L: J. Murray, 1828. 355p. NUC BL
OCLC

3148. MARTIN, Violet Florence,
co-author <u>see</u> SOMERVILLE, Edith
Anna Oenone

3149. MARTINDELL, Anne, comp. <u>see</u>
CURWEN, Alice

3150. MARTINEAU, Harriet [Am.
1802-1876]
Autobiography. Ed. Maria Weston
Chapman.
L: Smith, Elder & co., 1877. 3v.;
Boston: J. R. Osgood, 1877. 2v.
NUC BL MB OCLC

3151. -----Eastern life, present
and past.
L: E. Moxon, 1848. 3v. NUC BL
OCLC [Travel: Levant]

3152. -----Letters from Ireland.
L: J. Chapman, 1852. 220p. NUC BL
OCLC

3153. -----Retrospect of Western
travel.
L: Saunders & Otley, 1838. 3v.
NUC BL N OCLC

3154. -----Society in America.
L & NY: Saunders & Otley, 1837.
3v. NUC BL N OCLC

3155. MARTYN, Caroline Eliza
Derecourt [Br. 1867-1896]
Life and letters of Caroline
Martyn. Ed. Lena Wallis.
L: Labour Leader pub. dept.,
1898. 93p. NUC OCLC

3156. MARY ALOYSIUS, Sister of
Mercy <u>see</u> DOYLE, Mary Aloysius,
Sister

3157. MARY II, Queen of Great
Britain [Br. 1662-1694]
"Memoirs of Mary, Queen of
England, 1689-1693," together
with her letters and those of
King James II and William III to
the Electress Sophia of Hanover.
Ed. Dr. Richard Doebner.
Leipzig: Veit & co.; L: David
Nutt, 1886. 115p. NUC BL MB OCLC

3158. MARY, Queen of Scots, co-
author <u>see</u> ELIZABETH, Queen of
England

3159. MASKELL, Eliza [Br. 19c]
The home traveller: thoughts on
London scenes and life.
L: n.p., 1856. BL

3160. MASON, Caroline [Br. 1810-
1850]
Extracts from the private diary
of Caroline Mason.
L: C. Gilpin, 1852. 24p. NUC

3161. MASON, Clara Stevens Arthur
[Am. 1844-1884]
Etchings from two lands.
Boston: D. Lothrop & co., 1886.
179p. NUC BL OCLC
[Travel: U. S. & Japan]

3162. MASON, Ellen (Huntly)
Bullard [Br. 19c]
Civilizing mountain men; or,
sketches of mission work around
the Karens. By Mrs. Mason of
Burmah. Ed. L. N. R[anyard].
L: James Nisbet & co., 1862.
384p. NUC BL OCLC
[Also pub. as: Great expectations
realized; or, civilizing mountain
men. Philadelphia: Am. Baptist
pub. soc.; NY: Blakeman & Mason,
1862. 480p.]

3163. MASON, Emily Virginia, ed.
<u>see</u> ORR, Lucinda (Lee)

3164. MASON, Rachel, comp. <u>see</u>
MASON, Susanna (Hopkins)

3165. MASON, Susanna (Hopkins)
[Am. 1749?-1805]
Selections from the letters and
manuscripts of the late S. Mason,
with a brief memoir of her life
by her daughter, Rachel.
Philadelphia: Rackliff & Jones,
1836. 312p. NUC BL OCLC
[Travel: Pennsylvania]

3166. MASSEY, Sarah [18c]
Minute to visit Great Britain and
Ireland.
n.p.: n.p., 1760. NUC

3167. MATHER, Rachel C., Mrs.
[Am. 19c]
The storm swept coast of South
Carolina.

Beaufort, SC: New South Publishing co., 1894. 95p.; Woonsocket, RI: C. E. Cook, pr., 1894. 116p. NUC OCLC
[On the hurricane of 1893]

3168. MATHEWS, Mrs. [19c]
Melancholy shipwreck and remarkable instance of the ... preservation of the lives of twelve unfortunate persons, who shipwrecked on the 3d of December last, (1833) on their passage from Portsmouth, (Eng.) to Bombay.
n.p.: n.p., 1834. 24p. NUC

3169. MATHEWS, Mary McNair, Mrs. [Am. 19c]
Ten years in Nevada: or, life on the Pacific Coast.
Buffalo, NY: Baker, Jones & co., prs., 1880. 343p. NUC BL OCLC

3170. MATTEINI, Harriette [Am. 19c]
Letters from Florence, Italy, in 1866. Pub. by her daughter, Fanny Winchester Hotchkiss.
New Haven, CT: n.p., 1893. 141p. NUC
[Also pub. as: Letters from Italy]

3171. MAUNY, E. P., Mrs. [Am. 19c] ALT: M., E. P.
The memories of a clergyman's wife. Written by herself.
Philadelphia: the author, 1876. 104p. NUC OCLC

3172. MAURICE, Colonel, ed. see SINCLAIR, Mrs.

3173. MAURY, Sarah Mytton (Hughes), Mrs. William Maury [Br. 1803-1849]
An Englishwoman in America.
L: T. Richardson & son, 1848. 204p. NUC BL N OCLC

3174. MAURY, Mrs. William see MAURY, Sarah Mytton (Hughes)

3175. MAW, Louisa [Br. 1806-1828]
A memoir of Louisa Maw. Comp. Lucy Maw, Mrs. Thomas Maw.
York: W. Alexander & son, 1828. 56p. NUC BL OCLC
[Contains excerpts from her papers]

3176. MAW, Lucy, comp. see MAW, Louisa

3177. MAW, Mrs. Thomas, comp. see MAW, Louisa

3178. MAWSON, Jane (Cameron) [Br. 1814-1844] ALT: Cameron, Jane
Memoir of Mrs. Jane Mawson, compiled from her diary and correspondence. Ed. an intimate friend.
Newcastle: priv. pr.; L: Chapman bros., 1846. 245p. NUC MBD PSI
[Primarily religious]

3179. MAXWELL, Darcy (Brisbane), Lady [Br. 1742-1810]
The life of Darcy, Lady Maxwell, of Pollock; late of Edinburgh: compiled from her voluminous diary and correspondence, and from other authentic documents. By the Rev. John Lancaster.
L: pr. by T. Cordeux for T. Blanshard, 1821. 2v. NUC BL MBD OCLC
[Methodist diary. 1768-1810]

3180. MAXWELL, Katherine [Br. 18c]
History of Miss Katty N *** containing a faithful and particular relation of her amours, adventures, and various turns of fortune, in Scotland, Ireland, Jamaica, and in England. Written by herself.
L: pr. for F. Noble & J. Noble, 1757. 225p. NUC BL MB
[May be fiction.]

3181. MAXWELL, Lady Margaret (Cuninghame) Hamilton [Br. d. 1622] ALT: Hamilton, Lady Margaret
A pairt of the life of Lady Margaret Cuninghame, daughter of the Earl of Glencairn, that she had with her first husband the Master of Evandale. Ed. Charles Kirkpatrick Sharpe.
Edinburgh: James Ballantyne & co., 1827. 30p. NUC BL MB OCLC
[Includes letters.]

3182. MAYER, S. R. T., ed. see BROWNING, Elizabeth (Barrett)

3183. MAYO, Amory Dwight, ed. see MAYO, Sarah Carter (Edgarton)

3184. MAYO, Mrs. Amory Dwight <u>see</u>
MAYO, Sarah Carter Edgarton

3185. MAYO, Sarah Carter
(Edgarton), Mrs. Amory Dwight
Mayo [Am. 1819-1848]
Selections from the writings of
Mrs. Sarah C. Edgarton Mayo: with
a memoir by her husband. Ed. A.
D. Mayo.
Boston: A. Tompkins, 1849. 432p.
NUC OCLC
[Excerpts of letters; poetry and
short fictional sketches.]

3186. MEAD, Ardelle Knapp [Am.
19c]
A trip from New York to Africa.
NY: n.p., 1899. 38p. NUC
[Missionary wife's diary,
returning to Africa after 15
years in America.]

3187. MEADE, Elizabeth, Countess
of Clanwilliam <u>see</u> MURRAY, Lady

3188. MEADLY, George Wilson, ed.
<u>see</u> JEBB, Ann (Torkington)

3189. MEADOWS, Mary Jane [18/19c]
Life, voyages, and surprising
adventures, of Mary Jane Meadows,
a woman of uncommon talents,
spirit, and resolution. Written
by her own hand.
L: pr. by J. Bonsor, for A.
Lemoine, 1802. 72p. NUC MB OCLC
[May be fiction; MB calls it
"Defoe like"; OCLC says Meadows a
pseud.]

3190. MEEKER, A. M., Mrs. [Am.
19c]
Eliza Ross; or, illustrated guide
of Lookout Mountain.
Atlanta, GA: Franklin Steam pr.
house, 1870. 36p. NUC OCLC

3191. MEIGS, Mary Noel (Bleecker)
Macdonald, comp. <u>see</u> BLEECKER,
Sophia

3192. MELVILL, Elizabeth <u>see</u>
COLVILLE, Elizabeth (Melvill),
Lady Colville of Culross

3193. MELVILLE, Elizabeth [Br.
19c] PSEUD: Lady, A.
A residence at Sierra Leone.
Described from a journal kept on
the spot and from letters written
to friends at home. By a lady.
Ed. the Hon. Mrs. [Caroline
Sheridan] Norton.
L: J. Murray, 1849. 335p. NUC MB
OCLC
[Diary 1841-1846]

3194. MENDELL, Miss [Am. 19c]
Notes of travel and life. By two
young ladies--Misses Mendell and
Hosmer.
NY: the authors, 1854. 288p. NUC
OCLC
[Travel: U. S.]

3195. MENDENHALL, Abby Grant
(Swift), Mrs. R. J. Mendenhall
[Am. 1832-1900]
Some extracts from the personal
diary of Mrs. R. J. Mendenhall;
also press notices, and some
early and later correspondence to
her, by her, etc.
Minneapolis, MN: n.p., 1900?.
542p. NUC OCLC

3196. MENDENHALL, Mrs. R. J. <u>see</u>
MENDENHALL, Abby Grant (Swift)

3197. MENZIES, J. M. <u>see</u> THACKER,
Anne

3198. MERCER, Margaret [Am. 1792-
1846]
Memoir of ... Margaret Mercer. By
Caspar Morris, M.D.
Philadelphia: n.p., 1847. NUC BL
OCLC
[Teacher & abolitionist; includes
letters]

3199. MEREDITH, Mrs. Charles <u>see</u>
MEREDITH, Louisa Anne (Twamley)

3200. MEREDITH, Louisa Anne
(Twamley), Mrs. Charles Meredith
[Br. 1812-1895] ALT: Twamley,
Louisa Anne
My home in Tasmania, during a
residence of nine years.
L: J. Murray, 1852. 2v. NUC BL
OCLC

3201. -----Notes and sketches of
New South Wales, during a
residence in that colony from
1839 to 1844.
L: J. Murray, 1844. 164p. NUC BL
OCLC

3202. -----Our island home, a
Tasmanian sketch book. L: Hobart
Town, J. Walch.; L: Marcus Ward,
1879. 43 l.   NUC BL

3203. -----Over the straits; a
visit to Victoria.
L: Chapman & Hall, 1861. 284p.
NUC MB OCLC

3204. MERING, Ann S. [Am. 19c]
Songs in the night, and musings
of an invalid.
Cincinnati, OH: pr. for the
author by William Doyle, 1855.
62p. NUC OCLC

3205. MERRIAM, Florence Augusta
see BAILEY, Florence Augusta
(Merriam)

3206. MERRIAM, George S., ed. see
BRIGGS, Caroline Clapp

3207. MERRITT, Rev. Timothy,
comp. see BUNTING, Hannah Syng

3208. MERRYWEATHER, Mary [Br. 19c]
Experience of factory life: being
a record of fourteen years' work
at Mr. Courtauld's silk mill at
Halstead, in Essex.
3d ed. L: E. Faithfull & co.,
1862. 79p. NUC BL
[Teacher in the factory school]

3209. MERWIN, Loretta L. Wood
[Am. 19c] PSEUD: Lady of Ohio, A
Three years in Chili. Pub. as: A
lady of Ohio
Columbus, OH: Follett, Foster,
1861. 158p. NUC BL OCLC
[Also pub. as: Chili, through
American spectacles]

3210. MERYON, Charles Louis,
comp. see STANHOPE, Lady Hester
Lucy

3211. METCALF, Ada [Am. 19c]
Lunatic asylums: and how I became
an inmate of one. Doctors,
incidents, humbuggery.
Chicago: Ottaway & Colbert, prs.,
1876. 75p. NUC K

3212. METHUEN, Louisa Mary, comp.
see METHUEN, Mary Matilda Cecilia

3213. METHUEN, Mary Matilda
Cecilia [Br. 1823-1853]
"The fountain sealed." A memoir
of M. M. C. Methuen. By her
mother [Louisa Mary Methuen].
Bath: Binns & Godwin, 1857. 318p.
BL
[Includes extracts from her
diary.]

3214. METHUEN, Mary Matilda
Cecilia, comp. see ANDERSON,
Bessie

3215. MEYERS, Mrs. George B.
Glenny see MEYERS, Myra
(Comstock) Glenny

3216. MEYERS, Myra (Comstock)
Glenny, Mrs. George B. Glenny
Meyers [Am. 19c]
Letters from Japan, China, India.
Buffalo, NY: Peter Paul & bro.,
1892?. 150p. NUC

3217. MICHENER, Amanda, comp. see
MICHENER, Frances Lavinia

3218. MICHENER, Fannie L. see
MICHENER, Frances Lavinia

3219. MICHENER, Frances Lavinia
[Am. 1866-1882] ALT: Michener,
Fannie L.
The prose and poetical works of
Fannie L. Michener. With a memoir
by Amanda Michener.
Philadelphia: J. B. Lippincott &
co., 1884. 386p. NUC OCLC

3220. "MIER PRISONER'S" WIDOW, A,
pseud. see WILSON, Mary A. C.

3221. MIFFLIN, Mildred [Am. 19c]
Out of darkness into light, from
the journal of a bereaved mother.
Shelbyville, IL: pr. at the
office of Our Best Words, 1888.
178p. NUC

3222. MILLARD, E. C., Mrs., ed.
see PHILLIPS, Minnie Mary
(Apperson)

3223. MILLER, Anna (Riggs), Lady
[Br. 1741-1781] PSEUD: English
woman, An
Letters from Italy, describing
the manners, customs,

antiquities, paintings, etc. of
that country in the years MDCCLXX
and MDCCLXXI, to a friend
residing in France, by an English
woman.
L: E. & C. Dilly, 1776. 3v. NUC
OCLC

3224. MILLER, Dora Richards [Am.
19c] PSEUD: Union Woman, A
A woman's diary of the siege of
Vicksburg [1863]; under fire from
the gunboats.
NY: n.p., 1885. NUC C OCLC
[Detached from Century magazine,
Sept., 1885, v. 30. Published in
1889 in G. W. Cable's Strange
true stories of Louisiana.]

3225. MILLER, Elizabeth E. [Am.
19c]
Foreign experiences of an
American girl.
Meadville, PA: the author,
Messenger print, 1895. 148p. NUC
OCLC

3226. MILLER, Elizabeth Erwin see
LOBINGER, Elizabeth Erwin (Miller)

3227. MILLER, Ellen Clare [Br.
19c] ALT: Pearson, Ellen Clare
(Miller)
Eastern sketches: notes of
scenery, schools, and tent life
in Syria and Palestine.
Edinburgh: Oliphant & co., 1871.
210p. NUC BL

3228. MILLER, Ellen E. [Br. 19c]
Alone through Syria.
L: K. Paul, Trench, Trübner &
co., 1891. 330p. NUC BL OCLC

3229. MILLER, Fannie de C. [Am.
19c]
Snap notes of an eastern trip,
from diary of Fannie de C.
Miller.
San Francisco: S. Carson co.,
1892. 162p. NUC OCLC [Travel: U.S.]

3230. MILLER, Lizzie E. [Am. 19c]
The true way. Life and
evangelical work of Lizzie E.
Miller (of Fairview, West Va.)
written by herself.
Los Angeles: pr. for the author,
1895. 320p. NUC K OCLC

3231. MILLER, Mary Christina [Am.
19c]
Judge Green's notebook.
Philadelphia: Presbyterian Board
of Publication, 1884. 311p. NUC
OCLC
[Travel: Europe, places important
to Protestant reformation]

3232. MILLER, R. M., comp. see
MALLABONE, Mary Ann

3233. MILLETT, Mrs. Edward [Br.
19c]
An Australian parsonage; or, the
settler and the savage in western
Australia.
L: E. Stanford, 1872. 418p. NUC
BL
[Five years' experience as
chaplain's wife; guide for
tourists and settlers.]

3234. MILN, Mrs. George Crichton
see MILN, Louise (Jordan)

3235. MILN, Louise (Jordan), Mrs.
George Crichton Miln [Br. 1864-
1933]
Quaint Korea.
L: Osgood and McIlvaine, 1895.
306p. NUC BL OCLC

3236. -----When we were strolling
players in the East.
L: Osgood and McIlvaine, 1894.
354p. NUC BL MB OCLC

3237. MILNER, Edith [Br. 19/20c]
Ober-Ammergau and back in ten
days.
L: Ben Johnson & co., 1890. 57p.
BL

3238. MINER, Clara M. [Am. 19c]
ALT: M., C. M.
Stray bits from the Orient.
Experiences of an American in
Hindostan. What she saw, heard
and learned.
Buffalo, NY: The Courier co.,
1892. 183p. NUC OCLC

3239. MINIFIE, Susannah see
GUNNING, Susannah (Minifie)

3240. MINTON, Emilie J. [Br. 19c]
Cemaes: as we saw it. With
Hampden A. Minton.
Manchester: J. Heywood, 1890. BL

3241. MINTON, Hampden A., co-author <u>see</u> MINTON, Emilie J.

3242. MISCA, Frederica E. [Am. 19c]
F. E. Misca's eight years' sufferings: humbly dedicated to his excellency, Governor Ritner, of Pennsylvania and her precious friends that have helped her in her difficulties.
n.p.: n.p., 1838. 12p. NUC

3243. MISSIONARY'S WIFE, A, pseud. <u>see</u> GRIFFITHS, Lydia

3244. MITCHELL, Amy Whitcomb [Am. 19c]
Extracts from western letters.
Milford, CT: n.p., 1893. 73p. NUC
[Travel: Chicago World's Fair, Michigan, Colorado]

3245. MITCHELL, Elizabeth Harcourt (Rolls) [Br. 19c]
Forty days in the Holy Land before and after.
L: K. Paul, Trench, Trübner & co., 1890. 207p. NUC BL OCLC

3246. MITCHELL, John Murray, ed. <u>see</u> MITCHELL, Maria Hay (Flyter)

3247. MITCHELL, Mrs. John Murray <u>see</u> MITCHELL, Maria Hay (Flyter)

3248. MITCHELL, Maria [Am. 1818-1889]
Maria Mitchell, life, letters and journals. Comp. Phebe Mitchell Kendall.
Boston: Lee & Shepard, 1896. 293p. NUC BL OCLC

3249. MITCHELL, Maria Hay (Flyter), Mrs. John Murray Mitchell [Br. d. 1907] ALT: Mitchell, Mrs. Murray
In India: sketches of Indian life and travel from letters and journals. Ed. John Murray Mitchell.
L & NY: T. Nelson & sons, 1876. 319p. NUC BL MB OCLC

3250. -----In southern India: a visit to some of the chief mission stations in the Madras presidency.
L: Religious Tract Society, 1885. 383p. NUC BL MB OCLC

[Also pub. as: Scenes in southern India]

3251. -----A missionary's wofe [sic] among the wild tribes of south Bengal. Extracts from the journal of Mrs. Murray Mitchell.
Edinburgh: John MacLaven, 1871. 70p. NUC BL MB

3252. -----The zenanas of Bengal.
Edinburgh: n.p., 1876. BL
[Repro. from " The family treasury"]

3253. MITCHELL, Mary (Callender) [Am. 1731-1810]
A short account of the early part of the life of Mary Mitchell, late of Nantucket, deceased, written by herself. With selections from some other of her writings and two testimonies of monthly meetings of Friends on Rhode Island and Nantucket concerning her.
New Bedford, MA: Abraham Shearman, Jr., 1812. 74p. NUC K OCLC

3254. MITCHELL, Mrs. Murray <u>see</u> MITCHELL, Maria Hay (Flyter)

3255. MITFORD, Mary Russell [Br. 1787-1855]
Recollections of a literary life; or, books, places, and people.
L: R. Bentley, 1852. 3v. NUC BL MB OCLC

3256. -----The life of Mary Russell Mitford ... related in a selection from her letters to her friends. 1st. series. Ed. Rev A. G. L'Estrange. By William Harness.
L: Richard Bentley; NY: Harper bros., 1870. 3v. NUC BL OCLC

3257. -----Memoirs and letters of Charles Boner ... with letters of Mary Russell Mitford to him during ten years. Ed. Mary Rosa Stuart Kettle.
L: R. Bentley & son, 1871. 2v. BL OCLC

3258. -----Letters of Mary Russell Mitford. 2d Series. Ed. Henry F. Chorley.
L: R. Bentley, 1872. 2v. NUC BL OCLC

3259. MIX, Mrs. Edward see MIX, Sarah A.

3260. MIX, Sarah A., Mrs. Edward [Am. 1832-1884]
In memory of departed worth. The life of Mrs. Edward Mix, written by herself in 1880.
Torrington, CT: Press of Register pr. co., 1884. 24p. NUC
[Black woman, chiefly religious.]

3261. MIXER, Elizabeth (Knowlton) [Am. 1827-1931] PSEUD: W. , M. E.
A reminiscence of Florida by M. E. W.
Buffalo, NY: The Peter Paul book co., 1899. 8p. NUC

3262. MODERS, Mary see CARLETON, Mary (Moders)

3263. MOIR, Ellen Beatrice (Pearson) [Br. 1875-1899]
In memoriam Ellen Beatrice Moir.
Glasgow: University press, 1899. 69p. NUC
[Contains her meditations and poems]

3264. MOIR, Mrs. Frederick L. M. see MOIR, Jane F. (Beith)

3265. MOIR, Jane F. (Beith), Mrs. Frederick L. M. Moir [Br. 19c]
A lady's letters from central Africa, a journey from Mandala, Shiré highlands, to Ujiji, Lake Tanganyika and back.
Glasgow: J. Maclehose & sons, 1891. 91p. NUC BL OCLC

3266. MOLLINEUX, Mary (Southworth) [Br. 1648-1695]
Fruits of retirement: or, Miscellaneous poems, moral and divine. Being some contemplations, letters, etc. written on variety of subjects and occasions. By Mary Mollineux, late of Leverpool, deceased. To which is prefixed, some account of the author.
n.p.: pr., T. Sowle, 1702. 174p. NUC BL OCLC

3267. MONCK, Frances Elizabeth Owen (Cole) [Br. d. 1919]
My Canadian leaves: an account of a visit to Canada in 1864-1865.
Dorchester: pr. at the "Dorset Country Express"; L: R. Bentley, 1891. 367p. NUC BL MC OCLC
[Travel diary May 1864-May 1865]

3268. MONCKTON, Rose C., Mrs. [Br. d. 1857]
Letters from Futtehgurh.
Clifton: n.p., 1858. BL
[Indian army wife, killed in mutiny]

3269. MONRO, Florence [Br. 19c]
Walking with God; or, early devotedness and early translation. Memorials of Florence, daughter of the late Rev. Robert Monro. Ed. her mother [Mrs. Robert Monro].
L: Wertheim, McIntosh & Hunt, 1862. 229p. BL
[Extracts from her journal and letters.]

3270. MONRO, Mrs. Robert, ed. see MONRO, Florence

3271. MONTAGU, Eleanora Louisa see HERVEY, Eleanora Louisa (Montagu)

3272. MONTAGU, Elizabeth (Robinson) [Br. 1720-1800]
A lady of the last century, illustrated by her unpublished letters. By John Doran.
L: n.p., 1873. BL OCLC
[Other letters appear in other collections of 18c letters]

3273. -----The letters of Mrs. E. Montagu, with some of the letters of her correspondents ... . pub. by Matthew Montagu, Baron Rokeby.
L: T. Cadell & W. Davies, 1809-13. 4v. NUC BL OCLC

3274. MONTAGU, Lady Mary (Pierrepont) Wortley [Br. 1689-1762]
The letters and works of Lady Mary Wortley Montagu. Ed. her great grandson, Lord Wharncliffe.
L: R. Bentley, 1837. 3v. NUC BL OCLC [3d ed., with additions, 1861]

3275. -----Letters of the Right Honourable Lady M--y W---y M---e: written, during her travels in Europe, Asia and Africa.

3d ed. L: T. Becket & P. A. De
Hondt, 1763. 3v. NUC BL OCLC
[New ed., with additions, 1816]

3276. MONTAGU, Matthew, Baron
Rokeby, comp. see MONTAGU,
Elizabeth (Robinson)

3277. MONTAUBAN, Mrs. Eliot [19c]
A year and a day in the East; or,
wanderings over land and sea.
L: Longmans, Brown, Green &
Longmans, 1846. 201p. NUC

3278. MONTEFIORE, Judith (Cohen),
Lady [Br. 1784-1862]
Diaries of Sir Moses and Lady
Montefiore. Ed. Sir Moses Haim
Montefiore, bart.
Chicago: Belford-Clarke co.,
1890. 2v. NUC OCLC

3279. -----Notes from a private
journal of a visit to Egypt and
Palestine, by way of Italy and
the Mediterranean.
L: pr., J. Rickerby, 1844. 410p.
NUC BL MBD OCLC [Not published]

3280. -----Private journal of a
visit to Egypt and Palestine.
L: pr., J. Rickerby, 1836. 320p.
NUC BL [Not published]

3281. MONTEFIORE, Sir Moses Haim,
bart., ed. and co-author see
MONTEFIORE, Judith (Cohen), Lady

3282. MONTGOMERY, Mrs. Alfred see
MONTGOMERY, Hon. Fanny Charlotte
(Wyndham)

3283. MONTGOMERY, CORA, pseud.
see CAZNEAU, Jane Maria (McManus)

3284. MONTGOMERY, CORINNE, pseud.
see CAZNEAU, Jane Maria (McManus)

3285. MONTGOMERY, Hon. Fanny
Charlotte (Wyndham), Mrs. Alfred
Montgomery [Br. 1820-1893] ALT:
Wyndham, Hon. Fanny Charlotte
On the wing. A southern flight.
L: Hurst & Blackett, 1875. 316p.
NUC BL [Travel: Italy]

3286. MONTROSE, Kate see BROWN,
Kate (Montrose) Eldon

3287. MOODIE, John Wedderburn
Dunbar, co-author see MOODIE,
Susannah (Strickland)

3288. MOODIE, Mrs. John
Wedderburn Dunbar see MOODIE,
Susannah (Strickland)

3289. MOODIE, Susanna see MOODIE,
Susannah (Strickland)

3290. MOODIE, Susannah
(Strickland), Mrs. John
Wedderburn Dunbar Moodie [Br.
1803-1885] ALT: Moodie, Susanna;
Strickland, Susannah
Life in the backwoods; a sequel
to roughing it in the bush.
NY: J. W. Lovell co., 1887. 224p.
NUC

3291. -----Life in the clearings
versus the bush.
L: R. Bentley, 1853. NUC BL MC
OCLC

3292. -----Roughing it in the
bush; or, life in Canada. With
John Wedderburn Dunbar Moodie.
L: R. Bentley; NY: G. P. Putnam,
1852. 2v. NUC BL MC OCLC

3293. -----Six years in the bush;
or, extracts from the journal of
a settler in upper Canada, 1832-
38.
L: Simpkin Marshall & co., 1838.
126p. NUC OCLC
[NUC lists her as supposed
author. Variously attributed to
T. Weed.]

3294. MOORE, Abbie Elizabeth
[19c]
Journal of Abbie Elizabeth Moore.
n.p.: n.p., 1888?. 50p. NUC OCLC

3295. MOORE, Althea [Am. 19c]
Diary of Althea Moore of Salem,
Oregon.
n.p.: n.p., 1877. NUC
[Miss Moore was about 18 years
old.]

3296. MOORE, Augusta S., ed. see
WADE, Alice Mary (Moore)

3297. MOORE, Henry, comp. see
FLETCHER, Mary (Bosanquet)

3298. MOORE, Jane Elizabeth
(Gobeil) [Br. b. 1738]
Genuine memoirs of Jane Elizabeth
Moore, late of Bermondsey, in the
county of Surry. Written by
herself: containing the singular
adventures of herself and family.
Her sentimental journey through
Great Britain; specifying the
various manufactures carried on
at each town.
L: Logographic press, 1785?. 3v.
NUC BL MB OCLC
[Autobiography & poems]

3299. MOORE, Madeline [Am. 19c]
The lady lieutenant. A wonderful
startling and thrilling narrative
of the adventures of Miss
Madeline Moore, who, in order to
be near her lover, joined the
army, was elected lieutenant and
fought in western Virginia.
Philadelphia: Barclay, 1862. BL K

3300. MOORE, Mary Ann [Am. 19c]
Musings of a blind and partially
deaf girl.
Philadelphia: J. B. Lippincott &
co., 1873. 144p. NUC OCLC
[Verse and prose]

3301. MOORE, Rachel Wilson
(Barker) [Am. 19c]
Journal of Rachel Wilson Moore,
kept during a tour to the West
Indies and South America, in
1863-64.
Philadelphia: T. E. Zell, 1867.
274p. NUC OCLC

3302. MOORE, Thomas, comp. see
PIGOT, Elizabeth Bridget

3303. MOORMAN, Mollie Claire,
Mrs. [Am. b. 1849]
An Iowa woman's vindication.
Chicago: pr. for the publisher,
1877. 116p. K
[Autobiography]

3304. MORDAUNT, Elizabeth
(Carey), Viscountess [Br. d.
1679]
Anecdotes, etc. of Elizabeth,
Viscountess Mordaunt, commencing
1656.
L: F. C. & J. Rivington, 1810.
137p. NUC BL OCLC PD

3305. -----The private diarie of
Elizabeth, Viscountess Mordaunt.
Duncairn: priv. press of Edmund
Macrory, 1856. 239p. NUC BL MBD

3306. MORDECAI, Margaret (Gregg),
Mrs. Randolph Mordecai [Am.
19/20c] PSEUD: Pennington, Mrs.
Clapham
A key to the orient. By Mrs.
Clapham Pennington.
Cambridge, MA: University press,
1897. 161p. NUC

3307. MORDECAI, Mrs. Randolph see
MORDECAI, Margaret (Gregg)

3308. MORE, Hannah [Br. 1745-1833]
The letters of Hannah More to
Zachary Macaulay, containing
notices of Lord Macaulay's youth.
Ed. Arthur Roberts.
L: J. Nisbet; NY: R. Carter &
bros., 1860. 215p. NUC BL OCLC

3309. -----Memoirs of the life
and correspondence of Mrs. Hannah
More. Ed. William Roberts.
L: R. B. Seeley & W. Burnside,
1834. 4v. NUC BL OCLC
[Shorter ed., 1856 pub as: The
life of H. M.]

3310. MORE, Martha [Br. 1746?-
1819]
Mendip annals; or, a narrative of
the charitable labours of Hannah
and Martha More. Being the
journal of Martha More in their
neighbourhood. Ed. Arthur
Roberts.
L: J. Nisbet & co., 1859. 254p.
NUC BL MB OCLC

3311. MORELAND, Eleanor [Br. 19c]
The life of Eleanor Moreland in a
letter of her niece.
Cambridge, MA: Hilliard and
Metcalf, 1822. 64p. NUC BL

3312. MORGAN, Elijah, comp. see
TIMMS, Mary

3313. MORGAN, Mrs. Irby see
MORGAN, Julia

3314. MORGAN, Julia, Mrs. Irby
Morgan [Am. 19c]
How it was; four years among the
Rebels.

Nashville, TN: Pr. for the author. Publishing house, Methodist Episcopal Church, South, 1892. 204p. NUC C OCLC

3315. MORGAN, Martha M., Mrs. [Am. 19c]
Journey across the plains in the year 1849, with notes of a voyage to California by way of Panama. Also, some spiritual songs, etc.
San Francisco: Pioneer Press, 1864. 31p. NUC OCLC
[Also pub. as: A trip across the plains]

3316. -----The polygamist's victim; or, the life experiences of the author during a six years' residence among the Mormon Saints, being a description of the massacres, struggles, dangers, toils and vicissitudes of border life, etc.
San Francisco: Women's union pr. office, 1872. 72p. NUC

3317. MORGAN, Martha M., comp.
see GRAHAM, Martha M.

3318. MORGAN, Mary, Mrs. [Br.18c]
A tour to Milford Haven, in the year 1791, by Mrs. Morgan.
L: J. Stockdale, 1795. 439p. NUC BL OCLC   [Wales]

3319. MORGAN, Sydney (Owenson) Lady [Br. 1783?-1859] ALT: O., S.; Owenson, Sydney France.
L: B. Clarke, pr.; H. Colburn, 1817. 2v. NUC BL OCLC

3320. -----France in 1829-30.
L: Saunders & Otley; NY: J. & J. Harper, 1830. 2v. NUC BL OCLC

3321. -----Italy.
L: H. Colburn & co.; NY: C. S. Van Winkle; Philadelphia: M. Carey & sons, 1821. 2v. NUC BL OCLC

3322. -----Lady Morgan's memoirs, autobiography, diaries and correspondence. Preface signed W. Hepworth Dixon.
L: William H. Allan & co., 1862. 2v. NUC BL OCLC

3323. -----An odd volume, extracted from an autobiography.
L: R. Bentley, 1859. NUC BL

3324. -----Passages from my autobiography.
L: R. Bentley, 1859. 339p.; NY: D. Appleton & co., 1859. 382p. NUC OCLC

3325. -----Patriotic sketches in Ireland, written in Connaught.
L: pr. for R. Phillips by T. Gillet, 1807. 2v. NUC BL OCLC

3326. MORRELL, Abby Jane (Wood) [Am. b. 1809]
Narrative of a voyage to the Ethiopic and South Atlantic Ocean, Indian Ocean, Chinese Sea, North and South Pacific Ocean in ... 1829-31.
NY: J. & J. Harper, 1833. 230p. NUC BL OCLC

3327. MORRILL, Sara [Am. 19c]
A life of service; or, woman's work in the church.
Milwaukee, WI: The young Churchman co., 1894. 303p. NUC
[Letters to a friend about church work.]

3328. MORRIS, Alice A. (Parmelee), Mrs. Robert C. Morris [Am. 19c]
Dragons and cherry blossoms.
NY: Dodd, Mead, & co., 1896. 266p. NUC OCLC [Travel: Japan]

3329. MORRIS, Anna [Am. 19c]
PSEUD: Dean, Anna, Miss
Drifted out. Pub. as: Miss Anna Dean
Columbus, OH: n.p., 1883. 184p. NUC K [Autobiography]

3330. MORRIS, Caspar, M. D., comp. see MERCER, Margaret

3331. MORRIS, Isabel [Br. 19c]
A summer in Kieff; or sunny days in southern Russia.
L: Ward & Downey, 1891. 205p. NUC BL OCLC

3332. MORRIS, Margaret (Hill) [Am. 1737?-1816]

Private journal, kept during a portion of the Revolutionary War, for the amusement of a sister. By Margaret Morris, of Burlington, NJ. Philadelphia: priv. pr, 1836. 31p. NUC BL OCLC
[Society of Friends' diary, Dec. 1776-June 1777 on the war.]

3333. MORRIS, Mrs. Robert C. see MORRIS, Alice A. (Parmelee)

3334. MORRIS, Sarah (Kane), Mrs. Thomas Morris [Am. b. 1778]
A letter from Mrs. Thomas Morris, to her nephew, the Hon. Judge John K. Kane, regarding the Kane and Kent families.
NY: n.p., 1889. 27p. NUC OCLC
[Recollections from childhood in Tory family who took refuge in Nova Scotia after the Revolution, but moved back to U.S.]

3335. MORRIS, Mrs. Thomas see MORRIS, Sarah (Kane)

3336. MORSE, Cora A. [Am. 19c]
Yosemite as I saw it.
Oakland, CA: The Outlook, 1896. 48p. NUC

3337. MORTIMER, Elizabeth (Ritchie) [Br. 1754-1835]
Memoirs of Mrs. Elizabeth Mortimer: with selections from her correspondence. [Ed.] Agnes (Collinson) Bulmer.
L: John Mason, 1836. 372p.; NY: T. Mason & G. Lane, for Methodist Episcopal Church, 1836. 287p. BL OCLC

3338. MORTIMER, Favell Lee (Bevan) [Br. 1802-1878]
Far off: or, Africa and America described.
L: T. Hatchard, 1854. 323p. NUC BL OCLC

3339. -----Far off; or, Asia and Australia described. With anecdotes and numerous illustrations.
NY: R. Carter, 1852. 327p. 2v. NUC BL
[Vol. II subtitled Australia, America, Africa described.]

3340. -----The countries of Europe described. With anecdotes and numerous illustrations.
Philadelphia: G. S. Appleton; NY: D. Appleton, 1849. 320p. NUC OCLC
[Also pub. as: Near home; or, the countries of Europe described.]

3341. MORTIMER, Madge [Am. 19c]
At the sign of the palm tree, a record of some idle hours in sunset land. By Madge Mortimer. Ed. R. L. N. Johnston.
L: T. F. Unwin, 1899. 152p. NUC OCLC [Travel: Morocco]

3342. MORTON, Harriet [Br. 19c]
Protestant vigils; or, evening records of a journey to Italy, in the years 1826 and 1827.
L: R. B. Seeley & W. Burnside, 1829. 2v. NUC BL OCLC

3343. MORTON, Sarah Wentworth (Apthorp) [Am. 1759-1846]
My mind and its thoughts, in sketches, fragments, and essays.
Boston: Wells & Lilly, 1823. 295p. NUC OCLC
[Verse and prose]

3344. MOTT, James, co-author see MOTT, Lucretia (Coffin)

3345. MOTT, Mrs. James see MOTT, Lucretia (Coffin)

3346. MOTT, Lucretia (Coffin), Mrs. James Mott [Am. 1793-1880]
James and Lucretia Mott: life and letters. Ed. their granddaughter, Anna Davis Hallowell.
Boston & NY: Houghton, Mifflin & co., 1884. 566p. NUC BL MAD MBD OCLC
[Contains diary of travel in Britain; members of Society of Friends.]

3347. MOTT, Richard F., ed. see Gurney, Eliza Paul (Kirkbride)

3348. MOULDING, Sarah, Mrs. [Br. d. 1871]
A brief sketch of the life of Mrs. Moulding. ... Chiefly derived from her own letters. [Comp.] Henry Smith.

L: W. Hunt & co., 1872. 78p. BL
[Spent last 16 years in St.
Alban's Union Workhouse; servant
& various clergy; includes poems.]

3349. MOULTON, Ellen Louise
(Chandler) [Am. 1835-1908] ALT:
Chandler, Ellen Louise; Moulton,
Louise (Chandler)
Lazy tours in Spain and
elsewhere.
Boston: Roberts bros.; L: Ward,
Lock & co., 1896. 377p. NUC BL
OCLC
[Health resorts in Europe]

3350. -----Random rambles.
Boston: Roberts bros., 1881.
282p. NUC BL OCLC [Travel: Europe]

3351. MOULTON, Louise (Chandler)
see MOULTON, Ellen Louise
(Chandler)

3352. MOUNTAIN QUEEN, THE, pseud.
see DAVIES, Jane Miles

3353. MOWATT, Anna Cora (Ogden)
see RITCHIE, Anna Cora (Ogden)
Mowatt

3354. MÜLLER, Georgina [BL:
Georgiana] Adelaide (Grenfell),
Mrs. Max Müller [19/20c]
Letters from Constantinople, by
Mrs. Max Müller.
L, NY: Longmans, Green & co.,
1897. 196p. NUC BL OCLC

3355. MÜLLER, Mrs. Max see
MÜLLER, Georgina Adelaide
(Grenfell)

3356. MUHR, Fannie [Am. 19c]
Fannie Muhr's reminiscences of
the Maccabean pilgrimage, April,
1897.
Philadelphia: Billstein co.,
1897. 19 1. NUC OCLC
[Travel: Palestine]

3357. MUIR, Jessie A. H. [Br. 19c]
Diary [by] J. A. H. M.
L: [Leaderhall pr.], 1886. 174p.
NUC BL [Travel: Japan]

3358. MUIR, Martha [Br. 1797-
1831]
Letters; with an introductory
memoir by ... D. Macfarlan.

Glasgow: Gallie, 1833. 204p. NUC
BL [Chiefly religious]

3359. MULGRAVE, Helen [Br. 19c]
Helen Mulgrave; or Jesuit
executorship: being passages in
the life of a seceder from
Romanism. An autobiography.
NY: DeWitt & Davenport, 1852?.
312p. NUC MB OCLC
[Possibly fiction: MB lists as
autobiographical.]

3360. MULHALL, Marion McMurrough,
Mrs. M. G. Mulhall [Br. 19/20C]
Between the Amazon and the Andes;
or, ten years of a lady's travels
in the pampas, Gran Chaco,
Paraguay and Matto Grosso.
L: E. Stanford, 1881. 340p. NUC
BL MB OCLC
[Missionary work & travel.]

3361. -----From Europe to
Paraguay and Matto Grosso.
L: E. Stanford, 1877. 115p. NUC
BL OCLC

3362. MULHALL, Mrs. M. G. see
MULHALL, Marion McMurrough

3363. MULOCK, Dinah Maria see
CRAIK, Dinah Maria (Mulock)

3364. MUNDY, Mrs. G. see MUNDY,
Louisa

3365. MUNDY, Rev. G., ed. see
MUNDY, Louisa

3366. MUNDY, Harriot Georgiana
(Frampton), ed. see Frampton,
Mary

3367. MUNDY, Louisa, Mrs. G.
Mundy [Br. d. 1842]
Memoir of Mrs. Mundy. Ed. The
Rev. G. Mundy.
L: J. Snow, 1845. 294p. NUC BL MB
[Letters & diary 1822-1842;
missionary life in India.]

3368. MUNROE, Bell, co-author see
BROOKE, Tina

3369. MUNSON, Rachel (Hall) [Am.
1816-1870] PSEUD: Hall, Frances
Narrative of the capture and
providential escape of Misses
Frances and Almira Hall [Sylvia

(Hall) Horn], two respectable young women (sisters) of the ages of 16 and 18, who were taken prisoners by the savages ... . NY: copyrighted by William P. Edwards, 1832. 24p. NUC OCLC

3370. MURPHY, Kate A. [Am. 19c] Trials and triumphs of a summer vacation. NY: M. Sullivan, 1886. 87p. NUC [Travel: Great Britain]

3371. MURPHY, Lady Blanche Elizabeth Mary Annunciata (Noel) [Br. 1845-1881] Down the Rhine. Cleveland, OH: Burrows bros. co., n.d.; Philadelphia: J. B. Lippincott, 75p. NUC OCLC

3372. MURRAY, Lady [Br. 19c] A journal of a tour in Italy. L: priv. pr., 1836?. 5v. NUC BL [Also attr. to Elizabeth Meade, Countess of Clanwilliam]

3373. MURRAY, Hon. Amelia Matilda [Br. 1795-1884] Letters from the United States, Cuba, and Canada. L: J. W. Parker & son, 1856. 2v.; NY: G. P. Putnam, 1856. 402p. NUC BL N OCLC

3374. -----Pictorial and descriptive sketches of the Odenwald: or, Forest of Oden. L: W. Robert & L. Dickinson, 1869. 2 pt. NUC BL OCLC [Mostly views]

3375. -----Recollections from 1803 to 1837. With a conclusion in 1868. L: Longmans, Green & co., 1868. 90p. NUC BL MB OCLC

3376. MURRAY, Elizabeth (Heaphy) [Br. d. 1882] Sixteen years of an artist's life in Morocco, Spain and the Canary Islands. L: Hurst & Blackett, 1859. 2v. NUC BL MB OCLC

3377. MURRAY, Frances Porter (Stoddard) [Br. 1843-1919] Summer in the Hebrides; sketches in Colonsay and Oronsay.

Glasgow: J. Maclehose & sons, 1887. 175p. NUC BL

3378. MURRAY, Grace, Mrs. see BENNET, Grace

3379. MURRAY, Lois Lovina (Abbott) [Am. b. 1826] Incidents of frontier life. In 2 parts. Containing religious incidents and moral comment, relating to various occurrences, evils of intemperance and historical and biographical sketches. Goshen, IN: Evangelical United Mennonite pub. house, 1880. 274p. NUC K OCLC [Kansas pioneer]

3380. MURRAY, Mary [Br. b. 1759] The Bagshawes of Ford, a biographical pedigree. By William Henry Greaves Bagshawe. L: Mitchell & Hughes, 1886. 610p. NUC BL MBD [Excerpts from diary Aug.-Oct. 1776]

3381. MURRAY, Sarah, Hon. Mrs. see AUST, Sarah (Maese) Murray

3382. MURRAY OF STANHOPE, Lady, comp. see BAILLIE, Lady Grisell (Hume)

3383. MURRAY-ANSLEY, Harriet Georgiana Maria (Manners-Sutton), Mrs. J. C. Murray-Ansley [Br. 1827?-1896 [NUC 1898] An account of a three months' tour from Simla through Bussahir, Kunówar and Spiti, to Lahoul. Calcutta: Thacker, Spink & co., 1882. 83p. NUC BL OCLC

3384. -----Our tour in southern India. L: F. N. White & co., 1883. NUC BL

3385. -----Our visit to Hindostán, Kashmir and Ladakh. L: Allen, 1879. 326p. NUC BL OCLC

3386. MURRAY-ANSLEY, Mrs. J. C. see MURRAY-ANSLEY, Harriet Georgiana Maria (Manners-Sutton)

3387. MUTER, Mrs. Dunbar Douglas see MUTER, Elizabeth (McMullin)

3388. MUTER, Elizabeth
(McMullin), Mrs. Dunbar Douglas
Muter [Br. 19/20c]
Travels and adventures of an
officer's wife in India, China
and New Zealand.
L: Hurst & Blackett, 1864. 2v.
NUC BL MB OCLC

3389. MYDDLETON, Frances Penelope
(Watson) [Br. 1798-1878]
Reminiscences of military life,
by a soldier's daughter.
Sleaford: W. Overton, 1879. 200p.
NUC

3390. MYHILL, Charlotte [Br. 19c]
How perversions are effected; or,
three years experience as a nun.
L: n.p., 1894. BL

3391. N., B. H., comp. see GRACE,
Mary

3392. N., H. see NOKES, Harriet

3393. NAIRNE, Carolina
(Oliphant), Baroness [Br. 1766-
1845] ALT: Oliphant, Carolina
Life and songs of the Baroness
Nairne, with a memoir and poems
of Caroline Oliphant the younger
[Br. 1807-1831]. Ed. the Rev.
Charles Rogers.
L: C. Griffin & co., 1869. 206p.;
Edinburgh: J. Grant, 1886. 303p.
NUC BL OCLC

3394. NATHAN, Isaac, comp. see
LAMB, Lady Caroline (Ponsonby)

3395. NEALE, Mary (Peisley) [Br.
1717-1757] ALT: Peisley, Mary
Some account of the life and
religious exercises of Mary
Neale, formerly Mary Peisley,
principally compiled from her own
writing. Ed. Samuel Neale.
Dublin: John Gough, 1795. 120p.
BL OCLC [Society of Friends]

3396. NEALE, Samuel, ed. see
NEALE, Mary (Peisley)

3397. NEALLY, Amy [Am. 19c]
To Nuremberg and back. A girl's
holiday.
NY: E. P. Dutton, 1892. 114p. NUC

3398. NEEDHAM, Hester [Br. 19c]
"God First;" or, Hester Needham's
work in Sumatra: her letters and
diaries. [Comp.] Mary Enfield.
L: Religious Tract Soc., 1899.
320p. NUC BL OCLC

3399. NEILSON, Mrs. Andrew [Br.
19c] PSEUD: Lady Resident Near
the Alma, A
The Crimea: its towns,
inhabitants and social customs.
By a lady, resident near the
Alma.
L: Partridge, Oakey, & co.;
Edinburgh: Shepherd & Elliott,
1855. 143p.   NUC BL OCLC

3400. NELLES, Annie (Hamilton)
see DUMOND, Annie (Hamilton)
Nelles

3401. NEVIUS, Helen Sanford
(Coan), Mrs. John Livingston
Nevius [Am. 1833-1910]
Our life in China.
NY: R. Canter & bros, 1869. 504p.
NUC K OCLC
[Missionary experiences]

3402. NEVIUS, Mrs. John
Livingston see NEVIUS, Helen
Sanford (Coan)

3403. NEWCASTLE, Margaret (Lucas)
Cavendish, Duchess of [Br. 1624?-
1674] ALT: Cavendish, Margaret
(Lucas), Duchess of Newcastle
A true relation of the birth,
breeding, and life of Margaret
Cavendish, Duchess of Newcastle.
Written by herself... . Ed. Sir
Egerton Brydges.
Kent: pr. Johnson & Warwick,
1814. 36p. NUC BL MB OCLC

3404. NEWCOMB, Mrs. H. A. W. see
NEWCOMB, Mary A.

3405. NEWCOMB, Mary A., Mrs. H.
A. W. Newcomb [Am. 1817-1893?]
Four years of personal
reminiscences of the war.
Chicago: H. S. Mills & co., 1893.
131p. NUC C K OCLC [Civil War]

3406. NEWDIGATE, Anne (Fitton), Lady [Br. 1574?-1618] ALT: Fitton, Anne
Gossip from a muniment room: being passages in the lives of Anne and Mary [1578?-1647] Fitton. Ed. Anne Emily (Garnier), Lady Newdigate-Newdegate.
L: D. Nutt, 1897. 160p. NUC BL
[Letters]

3407. NEWDIGATE, Hester Margaretta (Mundy), Lady [Br. d. 1800]
The Cheverals of Cheveral Manor [correspondence of Sir Roger and Lady Newdigate]. Ed. Anne Emily (Garnier) Newdigate-Newdegate, Lady.
L & NY: Longmans, Green & co., 1898. 231p. NUC BL

3408. NEWDIGATE-NEWDEGATE, Anne Emily (Garnier), Lady, ed. see NEWDIGATE, Anne (Fitton), Lady

3409. NEWDIGATE-NEWDEGATE, Anne Emily (Garnier), Lady see NEWDIGATE, Hester, Margaretta (Munday), Lady

3410. NEWELL, Fanny [Am. 1793-1824]
Diary of, with a sketch of her life.
4th ed. Boston: n.p., 1848. 252p. NUC
[Methodist]

3411. -----Memoirs of Fanny Newell, written by herself ....
Hallowell, ME: pr. Glazier & co., 1824. 267p. NUC OCLC

3412. NEWELL, Harriet (Atwood), Mrs. Samuel Newell [Am. 1793-1812]
The life and writings of Mrs. Harriet Newell.
Rev. ed. Philadelphia: Am. Sunday School Union, 1831. 267p. NUC BL OCLC

3413. -----Memoirs of Harriet Newell (late of America), wife of the Rev. S. Newell, American missionary to India, who died at the Isle of France, Nov. 30, 1812, aged 19 years.
L: Booth, 1815. 197p. NUC BL OCLC
[Includes letters]

3414. NEWELL, Mrs. Samuel see NEWELL, Harriet (Atwood)

3415. NEWLIN, Margaret, comp. see LONGSTRETH, Mary Anna

3416. NEWMAN, Mrs. A. E. [Am. 19c] PSEUD: Evangeline
European leaflets for young ladies. Pub. as: Evangeline
NY: J. F. Baldwin, 1861. 207p. NUC

3417. NEWMAN, Mrs. C. S. [Br. 19c]
Kuzularem; or, ten years' work amongst the girls of Constantinople.
L: Partridge & co., 1883. BL

3418. NEWTON, Margaret [Br. 19c]
Glimpses of life in Bermuda and the tropics.
L: Digby, Long & co., 1897. 256p. NUC BL OCLC

3419. NICHOLAS, Sir Nicholas Harris, ed. see FANSHAWE, Anne (Harrison)

3420. NICHOLL, Edith M. see BOWYER, Edith M. (Nicholl)

3421. NICHOLS, Alice S. [Am. 19c]
One night in a mountain camp. A sketch. With Charles W. Bacon.
Boston: S. E. Cassino, 1886. 22p. NUC OCLC
[White Hills of NH; climb of the highest mountain. Includes 3 poems]

3422. NICHOLS, Anne Susanna see NICHOLS, Ann Susannah

3423. NICHOLS, Ann Susannah [Br. 19c] ALT: Nichols, Anne Susanna
Journal of a very young lady's tour from Canonbury to Aldborough, through Chelmsford, Sudbury, and Ipswich; and back through Harwick, Colchester, etc. Sept. 13-21, 1804. Written hastily on the road, as circumstances arose.
L: Nichols, 1804. 16p. BL MBD OCLC [In verse]

3424. NICHOLS, John Gough, ed. see HALKETT, Anne (Massey), Lady

3425. NICHOLS, Laura D. [Am. 19c]
A Norway summer.
Boston: Roberts bros., 1897.
178p. NUC OCLC
[Told as epistolary novel, but
contains descriptive travel
material.]

3426. NICHOLSON, Asenath (Hatch)
[Am. 19c]
Ireland's welcome to the
stranger; or, an excursion
through Ireland in 1844 and 1845,
for the purpose of personally
investigating the condition of
the poor.
NY: Baker & Scribner, 1847.
456p.; L: C. Gilpin, 1847. 442p.
NUC BL OCLC

3427. -----Loose papers; or,
facts gathered during eight
years' residence in Ireland,
Scotland, England, France and
Germany.
NY: Sold at the anti-slavery
office, 1853. 311p. NUC OCLC

3428. NICOL, Martha [Br. 19c]
PSEUD: Lady, A
Ismeer; or Smyrna and its British
hospital in 1855. By a lady.
L: J. Madden, 1856. 350p. NUC BL
OCLC
[Attr. in OCLC to Henrietta Le
Mesurier. Experiences as a
volunteer.]

3429. NIEMEYER, Mary A. [Am. 19c]
Light in darkness. Autobiography
of Mary A. Niemeyer. Rev. Sarah
Sigourney Rice.
Baltimore, MD: J. Young;
Philadelphia: Lippincott, 1873.
223p. NUC K OCLC
[Autobiography of a blind woman]

3430. NIERIKER, Abigail May
(Alcott) [Am. 1840-1879]
Studying art abroad, and how to
do it cheaply.
Boston: Roberts bros., 1879. 87p.
NUC BL

3431. NIGHTINGALE, E., ed. see
COLLIER, Mrs.

3432. NIND, Mary C. [Am. 19c]
In journeyings oft. A sketch of
the life and travels of Mary C.
Nind. [Comp.] Georgiana Baucus.
Cincinnati, OH: Curts & Jennings,
1897. 334p. NUC BL OCLC
[Fictionalized account of her
Methodist missionary work, based
on conversations with Nind.]

3433. NIXON, Mary F. see ROULET,
Mary F. (Nixon)

3434. NOKES, Harriet [Br. 1830-
1895] ALT: N., H.
Twenty-three years in a House of
Mercy. Pub. as: H. N.
L: S. Sonenschein & co., 1886.
90p. NUC BL
[Church work with delinquent
girls at St. Mary's Home, Kent.]

3435. -----Thirty-two years in a
House of Mercy.
3d ed. L: Society for Promoting
Christian Knowledge, 1895. 96p.
NUC BL OCLC
[Reissue of above, with additions]

3436. NORMANBY, Maria (Liddell)
Phipps, Marchioness of [Br. 1798-
1882]
Extracts of letters from Maria,
Marchioness of Normanby; the Hon.
Frances Jane Liddell, [1799-
1823]; the Hon. Anne Elizabeth
Liddell, Lady Williamson [1801-
1878]; Jane Elizabeth Liddell
Keppel, Viscountess Barrington
[1804-1883]; the Hon. Elizabeth
Charlotte (Liddell) Villiers
[1807-1890]; Susan[(Liddell)
Yorke], Countess of Hardwicke
[1810-1886]; the Hon. Charlotte
Amelia (Liddell) Trotter [1819-
1883]. Ed. Georgiana (Liddell)
Bloomfield, Baroness Bloomfield.
Hertford: pr. Simson & co., 1892.
424p. NUC BL OCLC
[On cover: "My sisters."]

3437. NORTH, Marianne [Br. 1830-
1890]
Recollections of a happy life:
being the autobiography of
Marianne North. Ed. her sister,
Mrs. John Addington Symonds
[Janet Catherine (North)
Symonds].
NY & L: Macmillan & co., 1892.
2v. NUC BL OCLC

3438. -----Some further
recollections of a happy life.
Selected from the journals of
Marianne North. Ed. Mrs. J. A.
Symonds.
L & NY: Macmillan & co., 1893.
316p. NUC BL MB OCLC
[Includes travel: N. & S.
America, India, Asia, Australia &
S. Africa.]

3439. NORTH, Mary E. [Am. 19c]
Early crowned: a memoir of Mary
E. North. By Louisa J. Crouch.
NY: Carlton & Porter, 1866. 256p.
NUC BL OCLC
[Contains extensive excerpts from
her letters; religious]

3440. NORTHUMBERLAND, Elizabeth
(Seymour) Percy, Duchess of [Br.
1716-1776] ALT: Percy, Elizabeth
(Seymour), Duchess of
Northumberland
A short tour made in the year
1771.
L: n.p., 1775. 89p. NUC BL OCLC
[BL also ascribes this work to
Anne, Baroness Percy. Travel:
France, Holland, Belgium]

3441. NORTON, Hon. Mrs., ed. see
MELVILLE, Elizabeth

3442. NORTON, Caroline Elizabeth
Sarah (Sheridan), Hon. Mrs.
George Chapple Norton [Br. 1808-
1877] ALT: Stirling-Maxwell,
Caroline Elizabeth Sarah
(Sherridan) Norton, Lady
Letters, etc. Dated from June,
1836 to July, 1841.
3 pt. L: priv. pr., 1841?. NUC BL

3443. NORTON, Caroline
(Sheridan), Hon. Mrs., ed. see
MELVILLE, Elizabeth

3444. NORTON, Hon. Mrs. George
Chapple see NORTON, Caroline
Elizabeth Sarah (Sherridan)

3445. NORTON, Minerva (Brace)
[Am. b. 1837]
In and around Berlin.
Chicago: A. C. McClurg & co.,
1889. 268p. NUC OCLC

3446. NORTON, Sarah Goodsell
(Wolcott) [Am. 1790-1822?]

The two sisters' poems and
memoirs. With Eliza Wolcott
[1795-1832].
New Haven, CT: Baldwin &
Treadway, pr., 1830. NUC

3447. NOTLEW, FRANCES, pseud. see
WELTON, N. J., Mrs.

3448. NOVA SCOTIAN, A, pseud. see
FRAME, Elizabeth

3449. NOWELL, Nancy [Am. 19c]
Testimony of Nancy Nowell; a copy
of my journals commenced in
Lapeer, Michigan.
Salt Lake City, UT: G. Q. Cannon
& sons, 1892. 355p. NUC
[Mormon; spiritual autobiography]

3450. NOYES, Mrs. C. P. [Am. 19c]
Recollections of India: or,
reminiscences of a six years'
residence in Orissa.
Providence, RI: G. H. Whitney,
1852. 120p. NUC OCLC

3451. NUGENT, Hon. Ermengarda
Greville [Br. 19c]
A land of mosques and marabouts.
L: Chapman & Hall, 1894. 190p.
NUC BL OCLC
[Travel: Algiers & Tunis]

3452. NUGENT, Maria (Skinner),
Lady [Br. 1771?-1834]
A journal from the year 1811 till
the year 1815, including a voyage
to, and residence in, India, with
a tour to the north-western parts
of the British possessions in
that country, under the Bengal
government.
L: n.p., 1839. 2v. BL

3453. -----A journal of a voyage
to, and residence in, the island
of Jamaica, from 1801 to 1805,
and of subsequent events in
England from 1805 to 1811.
L: T. & W. Boone, 1839. 2v. NUC
BL OCLC

3454. NYE-STARR, Kate [Am. b.
1838]
A self-sustaining woman; or, the
experience of seventy-two years.
Chicago: Illinois printing &
binding co., 1888. 161p. NUC K
OCLC [Autobiography]

3455. O., S. see MORGAN, Sydney (Owenson), Lady

3456. OBER, Corolyn Faville, Mrs. [Am. 19c]
Manhattan: historic and artistic; a six day tour of New York City. With Cynthia May (Westover) Alden [Am b. 1862].
NY: Lovell, Coryell & co., 1892. 232p. NUC OCLC
[1897 pub. as: The greater New York guide book.]

3457. O'BRIEN, Attie see O'BRIEN, Frances Marcella

3458. O'BRIEN, Frances Marcella [Br. 1840-1883] ALT: O'Brien, Attie
Glimpses of a hidden life: memories of Attie O'Brien. Gathered by Mrs. Morgan John [Mary Anne (Bianconi)] O'Connell.
Dublin: M. H. Gill, 1887. 272p. NUC
[May include personal material]

3459. O'CONNELL, Catherine M. [Br. 19c]
Excursions in Ireland during 1844 and 1850. With a visit to the late Daniel O'Connell, MP.
L: R. Bentley, 1852. 295p. NUC BL OCLC

3460. O'CONNELL, Mary Anne (Bianconi), comp. see O'BRIEN, Frances Marcella

3461. O'CONNELL, Mrs. Morgan John, comp. see O'BRIEN, Frances Marcella

3462. OGDEN, Antoinette [Am. 19c]
"A drive through the Black Hills" ... presented to the traveling public, with the compliments of the "North Western line".
Battle Creek, MI: W. C. Gage & sons, co, 1892. 96p. NUC OCLC
[Also pub. as: "The wonderful Black Hills." S. Dakota & Wyoming]

3463. OGILVIE, Alice [Br. 19c]
A visit to the summer home in the Saetersdal and southern Norway.
Edinburgh: Macniven and Wallace, 1891. 104p. BL

3464. O'GORMAN, Edith [Am. b. 1842] ALT: Auffray, Edith (O'Gorman); Chantal, Sister Teresa de
Convent life unveiled: or, six years a nun; trials and persecutions of Miss Edith O'Gormon, otherwise Sister Teresa de Chantal.
Hartford, CT: Connecticut pub. co., 1871. 264p. NUC BL K
[Also pub. as: Trials and persecutions ...]

3465. OLIPHANT, Carolina see NAIRNE, Carolina (Oliphant), Baroness

3466. OLIPHANT, Caroline, the younger, co-author see NAIRNE, Carolina (Oliphant), Baroness

3467. OLIPHANT, Margaret Oliphant (Wilson) [Br. 1828-1897]
Autobiography and letters of Mrs. Margaret Oliphant Wilson Oliphant. Ed. Mrs. Harry Coghill.
L & Edinburgh: W. Blackwood & sons, 1899. 451p. NUC BL MB

3468. OPIE, Amelia (Alderson) [Br. 1769-1853]
Memorials of the life of Amelia Opie; selected and arranged from her letters, diaries and other manuscripts. Ed. Cecelia Lucy Brightwell.
Norwich: Fletcher & Alexander, 1854. 409p. NUC BL MBD

3469. ORINDA, pseud. see Philips, Katherine (Fowler)

3470. ORR, Lucinda (Lee) [Am. 18c]
Journal of a young lady of Virginia, 1782. Ed. Emily Virginia Mason.
Baltimore, MD: L. Murphy & co., 1871. 56p. NUC MAD
[Personal allusions in the journal indicate that it was dated 1787.]

3471. OSBORN, Emily F. D., ed. see OSBORN, Hon. Sarah (Byng)

3472. OSBORN, Lucy Reed (Drake) [Am. b. 1844]
Heavenly pearls set in a life; a

record of experiences and labors in America, India and Australia. NY & Chicago: Fleming H. Revell, 1893. 364p. NUC K OCLC

3473. OSBORN, Sarah (Byng), Hon. Mrs. [Br. 1693-1775] Political and social letters of a lady of the eighteenth century, 1721-1777. Ed. [Hon. Mrs.] Emily F[anny] D[orothy] (Osborn) [M'Donnell]. L: Griffith Farran & co., 1890. 190p. NUC BL

3474. OSBORN, Sarah (Haggar) [Am. 1714-1796] Familiar letters, written by Mrs. Sarah Osborn and Miss Susanna Anthony, late of Newport, R.I. Newport, RI: pr. at the office of the Newport Mercury, 1807. 170p. NUC BL OCLC

3475. -----Memoirs of the life of Mrs. Sarah Osborn who died at Newport, Rhode Island, on the second day of August, 1796. In the eighty-third year of her age. By Samuel Hopkins, D. D..... Worcester, MA: Leonard Worcester, 1799. 380p. NUC BL [Includes excerpts from diary; chiefly religious]

3476. OSBORNE, Mrs., ed. see OSBORNE, Catherine Rebecca (Smith), Lady

3477. OSBORNE, Catherine Isabella, Mrs. [Br. 19c] A few pages from real life; or, a guide book from notes of impressions received from well-known places. L: n.p., 1874. 2v. BL

3478. -----Last year and now ... . Dublin: Hodges, Foster & co., 1870. 31p. NUC BL [Travel: France]

3479. OSBORNE, Catherine Isabella, comp. see OSBORNE, Catherine Smith

3480. OSBORNE, Catherine Rebecca (Smith), Lady [Br. 1795-1856] Memorials of the life and

character of Lady Osborne and some of her friends. Ed. her daughter, Mrs. Catherine Isabella Osborne. Dublin: Hodges, Foster & co., 1870. 2v. NUC BL OCLC

3481. OSBORNE, Dorothy see TEMPLE, Dorothy (Osborne)

3482. OSBORNE, Edith [Br. 19c] ALT: Blake, Edith (Osborne) Twelve months in southern Europe. L: Chapman & Hall, 1876. 341p. BL OCLC

3483. OSSOLI, Sarah Margaret (Fuller), Marchesa d' [Am. 1810-1850] ALT: Fuller, Margaret At home and abroad, or, things and thoughts in America and Europe. Ed. her brother, Arthur B. Fuller. Boston: Crosby, Nichols & co., 1856. 466p. NUC BL OCLC [Great Lakes, Europe, Rome]

3484. -----Memoirs of Margaret Fuller Ossoli. Boston: Phillips, Sampson & co., 1851. 2v. NUC BL K OCLC

3485. -----Summer on the Lakes, in 1843. Boston: Charles C. Little & James Brown; NY: C. S. Francis & co., 1844. 256p. NUC BL OCLC [Repr. in "At Home..."; Great Lakes]

3486. OSWALD, Elizabeth Jane [Br. 19c] By fell and fjord; or, scenes and studies in Iceland. L & Edinburgh: W. Blackwood & sons, 1882. 282p. NUC BL OCLC

3487. OSWALD, Margaret [Br. 18/19c] A sketch of the most remarkable scenery near Callender of Manteith, particularly the Trosachs. Stirling: C. Randall, 1800. 24p. BL

3488. OTHEMAN, Edward, comp. see PICKARD, Hannah Maynard (Thompson)

3489. OTIS, Harriet [Am. 19c]
Cary letters. Ed. Caroline
Gardiner (Cary) Curtis.
Cambridge, MA: Riverside Press,
1891. 335p. NUC MAD OCLC
[Diary of a trip to Saratoga,
1819, included in this
collection.]

3490. OUVRY, Mrs. M. H. [Br. 19c]
A lady's diary before and during
the Indian mutiny.
Lymington: C. T. King, 1892.
166p. NUC BL MB

3491. OWEN, Mrs. A. L. see OWEN,
Nellie (Huggins)

3492. OWEN, Caroline, Mrs. [Br.
d. 1873]
The life of Richard Owen. By his
grandson, Rev. Richard Startin
Owen.
NY: D. Appleton; L: J. Murray,
1894. 2v. NUC BL MB OCLC
[Her diary 1834-1873 excerpted.]

3493. OWEN, Nellie (Huggins),
Mrs. A. L. Owen [Am. 1854-1916]
"Elmwood" ... During the war, and
my old battered canteen.
(Dedicated to the Reunion of the
United Confederate Veterans at
Richmond, VA June 30, July 1 & 2,
1896).
Richmond, VA: Southern Eng. co.,
1896?. 15p. NUC OCLC
[One family's life in Richmond
during the Civil War. OCLC says
fiction.]

3494. OWEN, Richard Startin,
comp. see OWEN, Caroline

3495. OWENSON, Sydney see MORGAN,
Sydney (Owenson), Lady

3496. OXFORD, Samuel, Lord Bishop
of, ed. see GODOLPHIN, Margaret
Blagge

3497. P., F. E. F. see PENNY,
Fanny Emily (Farr)

3498. P., M. E. see PEARSON, Emma
Maria

3499. PACE, Mary see WESTON, Mary
(Pace)

3500. PACKARD, Elizabeth Parsons
(Ware) [Am. 1816-1895]
The exposure on board the
Atlantic- and Pacific-car of
emancipation for the slaves of
old Columbia; ... or,
Christianity and Calvanism
compared with an appeal ... to
emancipate the slaves of the
marriage union... .   V. 1 Ed. a
Slave, now imprisoned in
Jacksonville insane asylum.
Chicago: The authoress, 1864.
158p. NUC OCLC

3501. -----Great disclosure of
spiritual wickedness!! in high
places. ...
Boston: The authoress, 1865.
158p. NUC
[Concerns marriage, trial, etc.]

3502. -----The great drama: or,
the millennial harbinger. Written
1862.
Hartford, CT: The Case, Lockwood
& Brainard co., 1878. NUC OCLC

3503. -----Marital power
exemplified in Mrs. Packard's
trial, and self-defense from the
charge of insanity; or, three
years' imprisonment for religious
belief, by the arbitrary will of
a husband ... .
Hartford, CT: the Authoress,
1866. 137p. NUC OCLC

3504. PACKER, Jane B. (Knight)
[Am. b. 1824]
Life and spiritual experiences of
Mrs. Dr. Jane B. Packer,
clairvoyant physician.
Taunton, MA: Sweet, 1892. 80p.
NUC K

3505. PAGE, Mary Ann (Reynolds)
[Am. 1828-1872]
Memoir of Mrs. Mary Reynolds
Page. Ed. Aaron Gaylord Pease.
Cambridge, MA: Riverside, 1873.
183p. NUC OCLC
[Includes journal of a trip to
Britain and France.]

3506. PAGE, Priscilla Sewall
(Webster) [Am. 1823-1899?]
Personal reminiscences ... 1885-
86.
NY: J. J. Little, pr., 1886.
160p. NUC K OCLC

3507. PAGET, Georgiana Theodosia
(Fitzmoor-Halsey), Mrs. Leopold
Grimston Paget [Br. d. 1919]
Camp and cantonment: a journal of
life in India in 1857-1859, with
some account of the way thither.
L: Longman, Green, Longman,
Roberts & Green, 1865. 469p. NUC
BL MB OCLC

3508. PAGET, Mrs. Leopold
Grimston see PAGET, Georgiana
Theodosia (Fitzmoor-Halsey)

3509. PAGET, Violet [Br. 1856-
1935] PSEUD: Lee, Vernon
Genius loci: notes on places. By
Vernon Lee.
L: G. Richards, 1899. 211p. NUC
BL OCLC
[Travel: Italy, France & Germany]

3510. PAINE, Caroline [Am. 19c]
Tent and harem: notes of an
oriental trip.
NY: D. Appleton & co., 1859.
300p. NUC BL OCLC

3511. PAINE, Susanna [Am. 19c]
Roses and thorns; or,
recollections of an artist; a
tale of truth for the grave and
gay.
Providence, RI: B. T. Albro, pr.,
1854. 204p. NUC K OCLC
[May be fiction; K lists as
autobiography.]

3512. PAKENHAM, Frances Julia,
Mrs. [Br. 19c]
Life lines; or, God's work in a
human being.
L: n.p., 1862. BL
[Spiritual autobiography]

3513. PALLISER, Fanny (Marryat)
Bury, Mrs. [Br. 1805-1878] ALT:
Bury Paliser, Mrs.
Brittany and its byways; some
account of its inhabitants and
its antiquities; during a
residence in that country.
L: J. Murray, 1869. 314p. NUC BL

3514. PALMER, Ann [Br. 1800/1806-
1834]
Extracts from the diary of Ann
Palmer ... a Christian in humble
life ... With a short memoir by
G. P. Richards.
3d ed. Exeter: n.p., 1838. BL MBD
[Mainly spiritual autobiography;
letters and poems.]

3515. PALMER, Mrs. H. R. see
PALMER, Lucia A. (Chapman)

3516. PALMER, Lucia A.
(Champman), Mrs. H. R. Palmer
[Am. 19c]
Grecian days.
NY & Chicago: Fleming H. Revell
co., 1896. 92p. NUC OCLC

3517. -----Oriental days.
NY: The Baker & Taylor co., 1897.
252p. NUC OCLC

3518. PALMER, Mary [Am. 1775-
1800]
Miscellaneous writings on
religious subjects: together with
some extracts from a diary. ...
The whole written during six
years of lingering sickness.
Windsor, VT: pr., A. Spooner,
1807. 119p. NUC
[Includes poems.]

3519. PALMER, Phoebe (Worrell),
Mrs. Walter Charles Palmer [Am.
1807-1874]
Four years in the old world;
comprising the travels and
evangelistic labours ... of Dr.
and Mrs. Palmer in England,
Ireland, Scotland and Wales. With
Walter Charles Palmer.
3d ed. NY: York, Foster and
Palmer Jr., 1866. 700p. NUC
[Methodist Church, Gt. Britain]

3520. PALMER, Phoebe (Worrell),
comp. see COX, Lydia (Noyes)

3521. PALMER, Phoebe (Worrell),
ed. see GARDNER, Mary Crilley

3522. PALMER, S. A. see PALMER,
Sarah A.

3523. PALMER, Sarah A., Mrs. [Am.
19c] ALT: Palmer, S. A. PSEUD:
Aunt Becky

The story of Aunt Becky's army
life. By S. A. Palmer.
NY: John F. Trow & co., 1867.
215p. NUC C
[Hospital work with Union
soldiers in Virginia]

3524. PALMER, Sarah L. [Am. 19c]
Six months among the
secessionists. A reliable and
thrilling narrative of the
sufferings and trials of Miss
Sarah L. Palmer, a native of
Pennsylvania, who, at the opening
of the great southern rebellion,
was teaching school in Knoxville,
the home of Parson Brownlow.
Philadelphia: Barclay & co.,
1862. 40p. NUC BL OCLC
[Some eds. say native of
Massachusetts; possibly fiction.]

3525. PALMER, Walter Charles, co-
author see PALMER, Phoebe
(Worrell)

3526. PALMER, Mrs. Walter Charles
see PALMER, Phoebe (Worrell)

3527. PALMER, William, ed. see
CARTER, Anna Maria

3528. PALMERTON, Ann [Am. b.
1800]
The alarming state of the world.
Rochester, NY: pr. for the
author, 1859. 302p. NUC OCLC
[Primarily religious; includes
poems.]

3529. PAPENDIEK, Charlotte Louise
Henrietta (Albert) [Br. 1765-
1839]
Court and private life in the
time of Queen Charlotte: being
the journals of Mrs. Papendiek,
assistant keeper of the wardrobe
and reader, to Her Majesty. Ed.
her grandaughter, Mrs. Vernon
Delves Broughton.
L: Bentley & son, 1887. 2v. NUC
BL MB OCLC

3530. PARDOE, Julia S. H. [Br.
1806-1862]
The beauties of the Bosphorus.
L: George Virtue, 1838. 164p. NUC
BL OCLC
[Travel: Constantinople]

3531. -----The city of the
Magyar, or Hungary and her
institutions in 1839-40.
L: George Virtue, 1840. 3v. NUC
BL OCLC

3532. -----The city of the
Sultan, and, domestic manners of
the Turks in 1836.
L: H. Colburn; Philadelphia:
Carey, Lea & Blanchard, 1837. 2v.
NUC BL OCLC

3533. -----Pilgrimages in Paris.
L: W. Lay, 1855. 376p. NUC BL

3534. -----The river and the
desart, or recollections of the
Rhône and the Chartreuse.
L: H. Colburn; Philadelphia: E.
L. Carey & A. Hart, 1838. 2v. NUC
BL OCLC

3535. -----Traits and traditions
of Portugal collected during a
residence in that country.
L: Saunders & Otley, 1833. 2v.
NUC BL OCLC

3536. PARHAM, Helena Beatrice
Richenda, Mrs. [Br. 19c] ALT:
Parham, H. B. Richenda, Mrs.
PSEUD: Ultra Marine
The contents of a Madeira mail-
bag; or, island etchings. By
Ultra Marine.
L: Moran & co., c1885. 129p. BL
[Letters of a stay in Madeira;
includes poetry.]

3537. PARHAM, H. B. Richenda see
PARHAM, Helena Beatrice Richenda

3538. PARK, Louisa Jane see HALL,
Louisa Jane (Park)

3539. PARKER, Adaline Rice [Am.
19c]
Letters. Ed. W. Salter.
Boston: Crosby & Nichols, 1863.
302p. NUC BL OCLC

3540. PARKER, Agnes, comp. see
POLLARD, Madeline Valeria

3541. PARKER, Elizabeth Maria
Bonney Wills, Mrs. [Am. 19c]
The Sandwich Islands as they are,
not as they should be.

San Francisco: Burgess, Gilbert &
Still, 1852. 18p. NUC OCLC

3542. PARKER, Mrs. John see
PARKER, Mary Ann

3543. PARKER, Lucretia [19c]
Piratical barbarity; or, the
female captive. Comprising the
particulars of the capture of the
English sloop Eliza-Ann on her
passage from St. Johns to Antigua
and the horrid massacre of the
unfortunate crew by the pirates,
March 12, 1825. And of the
unparalleled sufferings of Miss
Lucretia Parker, a passenger on
board said sloop--who after being
retained a prisoner 11 days by
the pirates, was miraculously
delivered from their cruel hands.
Providence, RI: W. Avery; NY: G.
G. Parker, 1825. 36p. NUC OCLC
[Autobiography]

3544. PARKER, Margaret E., Mrs.
[Br. 19c]
Six happy weeks among the
Americans.
Glasgow: H. Nisbet, 1876?. 128p.
NUC

3545. PARKER, Mary [Am. b. 1848]
Reminiscences and letters. Ed.
Silas H. Durand & Bessie Durand.
Philadelphia: G. H. Buchanan,
1891. 303p. NUC K OCLC

3546. PARKER, Mary Ann, Mrs. John
Parker [Br. 19c]
A voyage around the world, in the
Gorgon man of war; captain, John
Parker. Performed and written by
his widow.
L: pr. J. Nichols, 1795. 149p.
NUC BL
[Voyage to Cape Town and New
South Wales.]

3547. PARKER, W., Mrs. [Am. 19c]
PSEUD: Philadelphia Lady, A
Wandering thoughts and wandering
steps. Pub. as: A Philadelphia
Lady
Philadelphia: J. B. Lippincott &
co., 1880. 323p. NUC
[Travel: Europe]

3548. PARKES, Bessie Rayner see
BELLOC, Bessie Rayner (Parkes)

3549. PARKINSON, Richard, ed. see
BYROM, Elizabeth

3550. PARKS, Fanny see PARLBY,
Fanny (Parks)

3551. PARLBY, Fanny (Parks) [Br.
19c] ALT: Parks, Fanny
Wanderings of a pilgrim in search
of the picturesque, during four-
and-twenty years in the East;
with revelations of life in the
zenana.
L: Pelham Richardson, 1850. 2v.
NUC BL MB

3552. PARR, Catharine see
CATHARINE, Queen of England

3553. PARRIS, Miss, comp. see
PARRIS, Mary

3554. PARRIS, Miss, comp. see
PARRIS, Miriam

3555. PARRIS, Hephzibah, co-
author see PARRIS, Mary

3556. PARRIS, Mary [Br. 1825-
1846]
Memoirs of Mary and Hephzibah
[1833-1850] Parris, and a brief
memoir of Miriam Parris. By their
sister [Miss Parris].
L: n.p., 1858. BL
[Includes letters and poems by
Hephzibah.]

3557. PARRIS, Miriam [Br. 1813-
1825]
Brief memoir of Miss Miriam
Parris whose death was occasioned
by her clothes catching fire. By
Miss Parris.
L: F. Westley, 1825. 32p. BL

3558. PARRY, Catherine Edwards
[Br. 19c]
Catherine Edwards Parry: a record
of her life, told chiefly in
letters. Comp. her daughter
[Louisa (Parry) Hammond], Mrs. P.
Hammond.
Norwich: pr. for priv. circ.,
1898. 557p. BL

3559. PARRY, Edward Abbot, ed.
see TEMPLE, Dorothy (Osborne)

3560. PARRY, Emma Louise [Am. 19/20c]
Life among the Germans.
Boston: D. Lothrop & co., 1887.
340p. NUC BL

3561. PARRY, Fannie [Am. 1840-1860]
Wayside gleanings. A collection of the miscellaneous writings of Fannie Parry.
Providence, RI: H. L. Hastings, 1861. 163p. NUC
[Includes letters and poems]

3562. PARSONS, Emily Elizabeth [Am. 1824-1880]
Memoir of Emily Elizabeth Parsons.
Boston: Little, Brown & co., 1880. 159p. NUC [Chiefly letters]

3563. PATCH, OLIVE, pseud. see HAMER, Sarah Sharp (Heaton)

3564. PATON, Jan., B. A., ed. see PATON, Margaret (Whitecross)

3565. PATON, Maggie (Whitecross) see PATON, Margaret (Whitecross)

3566. PATON, Margaret (Whitecross) [Br. 19/20c] ALT: Paton, Maggie (Whitecross)
Letters and sketches from the New Hebrides. Ed. James Paton.
L: Hodder & Stoughton, 1894. 382p. NUC BL OCLC

3567. PATRICK, Wiley J., comp. see HARDIN, Mary Barr (Jenkins)

3568. PATTEN, Ruth (Wheelock), Mrs. William Patten [Am. 1740/44-1831]
Interesting family letters, of the late Mrs. Ruth Patten, of Hartford, Conn.
Hartford, CT: D. B. Moseley, 1845. 306p. NUC OCLC

3569. -----Memoirs of Mrs. Ruth Patten, of Hartford, Conn. With letters and incidental subjects. By William Patten, D.D.
Hartford, CT: pr., P. Canfield, 1834. 148p. BL OCLC

3570. PATTEN, William, D. D., comp. see PATTEN, Ruth (Wheelock)

3571. PATTEN, Mrs. William see PATTEN, Ruth (Wheelock)

3572. PAUL, Almira, Mrs. [Am. b. 1790]
The surprising adventures of Almira Paul, a young woman, who, garbed as a male, has ... actually served as a common sailor, on board of English and American vessels without a discovery of her sex being made.
Boston: pr. for N. Coverly, Jr., 1816. 24p. NUC K

3573. PAUL, Almira see STEPHENS, Ellen

3574. PAWSON, Frances (Mortimer), Mrs. John Pawson [Br. 1736-1809]
The experience of the late Mrs. Frances Pawson, wife of the late Rev. John Pawson, who was about 44 years an itinerant preacher in the Methodist connexion. Ed. Joseph Sutcliffe.
2d ed. L: J. Nichols, 1821. 114p. NUC OCLC
[Based on her memoirs.]

3575. PAWSON, Mrs. John see PAWSON, Frances (Mortimer)

3576. PAXSON, Ann J. (Johnson) [Am. d. 1883]
Memoirs of the Johnson family: with an autobiography.
Philadelphia: pr., J. B. Lippincott & co., 1885. 258p. NUC OCLC

3577. PEAKE, Elizabeth [Am. 19c]
Pen pictures of Europe.
Philadelphia: J. B. Lippincott & co., c1873. 599p. NUC BL OCLC

3578. PEARSALL, R., comp. see HOUSMAN, H., Mrs.

3579. PEARSON, Ellen Clare (Miller) see MILLER, Ellen Clare

3580. PEARSON, Emma Maria [Br. 1828-1893] ALT: P., M. E.
From Rome to Metana.
L: Saunders, Otley & co., 1868. 308p. NUC BL B OCLC

3581. -----Our adventures during the war of 1870. With Louisa

Elizabeth MacLaughlin.
L: Bentley, 1871. 2v. NUC BL

3582. -----Service in Servia
under the Red Cross. With Louisa
Elizabeth MacLaughlin.
L: Tinsley bros., 1877. 367p. NUC
BL MB OCLC

3583. PEARSON, George, comp. <u>see</u>
PEARSON, Susannah

3584. PEARSON, Jane, Mrs. [Br.
c1735-1816]
Sketches of piety, in the life
and religious experiences of Jane
Pearson. Extracted from her own
memoir and manuscripts. Ed.
Thomas Wilkinson.
York: Wm. Alexander & co., 1817.
100p. NUC BL MBD
[Also pub. as: Memoir of the life
and religious experiences... .]

3585. PEARSON, Susannah, Mrs.
[Br. 1779-1820]
Memoirs of the life and character
of Susannah Pearson, with a
selection of letters from her
spiritual correspondence. By
George Pearson.
Ipswich: n.p., 1829. BL

3586. -----Essays and letters.
2d ed. Ipswich: n.p., 1827. BL

3587. PEARY, Josephine
(Diebitsch), Mrs. Robert Edwin
Peary [Am. 1863-1955]
My Arctic journal, a year among
ice-fields and Eskimos.
NY & Philadelphia: Contemporary
pub. co.; L: Longmans & co.,
1893. 240p. NUC BL OCLC
[Travel: Greenland]

3588. PEARY, Mrs. Robert Edwin
<u>see</u> PEARY, Josephine (Diebitsch)

3589. PEASE, Aaron Gaylord, ed.
<u>see</u> PAGE, Mary Ann (Reynolds)

3590. PEASE, Louisa [Br. 1833-
1861]
Selections from the private
memoranda of Louisa Pease.
L: E. Barrett, 1862. 75p. NUC MBD
[Member of Society of Friends;
diary 1854-1858]

3591. PEASE, Martha Lucy (Aggs)
[Br. 1824-1853]
A memoir of Martha Lucy Pease.
[Comp. her mother] Mary Aggs.
L: R. Barrett, 1859. 59p. NUC
[Chiefly letters]

3592. PEATTIE, Mrs. E. W. <u>see</u>
PEATTIE, Elia (Wilkinson)

3593. PEATTIE, Elia (Wilkinson)
[Am. b. 1862] ALT: Peattie, Mrs.
E. W.
A journey through wonderland; or,
the Pacific Northwest and Alaska,
with a description of the country
traversed by the Northern Pacific
railroad.
Chicago & St. Paul, MN: Rand
McNally & co., c1890. 94p. NUC
OCLC

3594. PECK, Minnie Hannah [Am.
19c]
The view of roses.
San Francisco: pr. for the
author, 1893. 154p. NUC K
[Spiritual autobiography]

3595. PEEL, Agnes Helen [Br. b.
1870]
Polar gleams. An account of a
voyage on the yacht "Blencathra".
Chicago: A. C. McClurg & co.; L:
E. Arnold, 1894. 211p. NUC BL
OCLC
[Four month trip up the Yanesei
River in Siberia]

3596. PEISLEY, Mary <u>see</u> NEALE,
Mary (Peisley)

3597. PELHAM, CORNELIA, pseud.
<u>see</u> TUTTLE, Sarah

3598. PELHAM, R. W., ed. <u>see</u>
CARR, Mary Frances

3599. PELL, Howland, comp. <u>see</u>
HOWLAND, Sarah (Hazard)

3600. PEMBER, Phoebe Yates, Mrs.
[Am. 1823-1913]
A southern woman's story.
NY: G. W. Carleton & co.; L: S.
Low, son & co., 1879. 192p. NUC
BL K OCLC
[Hospital work in Richmond during
the Civil War.]

3601. PEMBER-DEVEREUX, Margaret
Rose Roy (McAdam) [Br. b. 1877]
PSEUD: Devereux, Roy
Sidelights on South Africa. Pub.
as: Roy Devereux
L: Sampson, Low, Marston & co.,
1899. 273p. NUC BL OCLC

3602. PENDARVES, Mary Granville
see DELANEY, Mary Granville
Pendarves

3603. PENDER, Mary Rose (Gregge-
Hopwood), Lady [Br. 19c]
A lady's experiences in the wild
West in 1883.
L: G. Tucker, 1888. 80p. NUC OCLC

3604. -----No telegraph; or, a
trip to our unconnected colonies,
1878.
L: Gilbert & Rivington, 1879.
152p. NUC
[Travel: South Africa]

3605. PENN, Norman, ed. see
PENINGTON, Mary (Proude)
Springett

3606. PENINGTON, Mary (Proude)
Springett [Br. 1616/1624?-1682]
A brief account of my exercises
from my childhood. Left with my
dear daughter, Guilielma Maria
Penn.
Philadelphia: n.p., 1848. 39p.
NUC BL OCLC

3607. -----Experiences in the
life of Mary Penington (written
by herself). Ed. Norman Penn.
Philadelphia: Biddle press, 18--.
116p. NUC OCLC
[Society of Friends]

3608. -----Some account of
circumstances in the life of Mary
Pennington, from her manuscript,
left for her family.
L: Harvey & Darton, 1821. 103p.
NUC BL

3609. PENNELL, Elizabeth
(Robins), Mrs. Joseph Pennell
[Am. 1855-1936]
A Canterbury pilgrimage: ridden,
written, and illustrated. By
Joseph and Elizabeth Pennell.
L: Seeley & co., 1885. 78p. NUC
BL OCLC

3610. -----To gipsyland.
L: T. F. Unwin; NY: Century,
1893. 240p. NUC BL OCLC
[About Gipsies]

3611. -----An Italian pilgrimage.
By Joseph and Elizabeth Robins
Pennell.
L: Seeley & co., 1887. 228p. NUC
OCLC
[Pub. in USA as: Two pilgrims'
progress from fair Florence to
the eternal city of Rome.]

3612. -----Our journey to the
Hebrides. With Joseph Pennell.
NY: Harper & bros., 1889. 225p.
NUC BL OCLC

3613. -----Our sentimental
journey through France and Italy.
With Joseph Pennell.
L: T. F. Unwin, 255p.; NY:
Century co., 1893. 110p. NUC BL
OCLC

3614. -----Over the Alps on a
bicycle.
L: T. F. Unwin, 1898. 110p. NUC
BL OCLC

3615. -----Play in Provence:
being a series of sketches,
written and drawn. With Joseph
Pennell.
NY: Century, 1892. 202p. NUC BL
OCLC

3616. -----The stream of
pleasure. A narrative of a
journey on the Thames from Oxford
to London. With Joseph Pennell.
NY: Macmillan; L: T. F. Unwin,
1891. 159p. NUC OCLC

3617. -----A sylvan city: or,
quaint corner in Philadelphia.
Philadelphia: Our Continent pub.
co.; NY: Fords, Howard & Hulbert,
1883. 508p. NUC OCLC

3618. -----Tantallon Castle; the
story of the castle and the ship.
Edinburgh: T. & A. Constable,
1895. 37p. NUC BL OCLC

3619. PENNELL, Joseph, co-author
see PENNELL, Elizabeth (Robins)

3620. PENNELL, Mrs. Joseph see
PENNELL, Elizabeth (Robins)

3621. PENNELL, Lemira Clarissa, Mrs. [Am. 19c]
The memorial scrap book. A combination of precedents by Mrs. L. C. Pennell, whose novel experience almost exceeds belief.
Boston: n.p., 1883. 48p. NUC
[On her confinement in mental institutions.]

3622. PENNINGTON, MRS. CLAPHAM, pseud. see MORDECAI, Margaret (Gregg)

3623. PENNINGTON, Montagu, ed. see CARTER, Elizabeth

3624. PENNSYLVANIA GIRL, A, pseud. see FULTON, Frances I. Sims

3625. PENNY, Fanny Emily (Farr) [Br. d. 1939] ALT: P., F. E. F.
Fickle fortune in Ceylon.
Madras; L: Addison & co., 1887. 69p. NUC BL
[Life as planter's wife.]

3626. PENNYMAN, Lady Margaret (Anger) [Br. 1688-1733]
Miscellanies in prose and verse, by ... Lady Margaret Pennyman, containing, i. Her late journey to Paris ... ii. Poems on several occasions, with familiar letters to a friend. Published from her original manuscripts. To which are annexed, some other curious pieces ... .
L: pr. for E. Curll, 1740. 4pt. NUC BL OCLC

3627. PEPYS, Lady Charlotte Maria [Br. 1822-1889]
A journey on a plank from Kiev to Eaux-Bonnes, 1859. Verses and translations from Russian.
L: Hurst & Blackett, 1860. 2v. NUC BL OCLC
[Travels in invalid coach: Russia, Poland, Germany, France]

3628. PERCY, Anne, Baroness see NORTHUMBERLAND, Elizabeth (Seymour) Percy, Duchess of

3629. PERCY, Elizabeth (Seymour), Duchess of Northumberland see NORTHUMBERLAND, Elizabeth (Seymour) Percy, Duchess of

3630. PERDITA, pseud. see ROBINSON, MARY (DARBY)

3631. PERKINS, Eliza [Am. 1804-1822]
Memoirs and moral productions and selections of Miss Eliza Perkins.
NY: G. Hilton for W. Randall, 1823. 96p. NUC OCLC
[Primarily religious]

3632. PERKINS, Mary H. [Am. 19c]
PSEUD: Hicks, Dorcas
From my corner, looking at life in sunshine and shadow. By Mary H. Perkins, (Dorcas Hicks).
NY: A. D. F. Randolph, 1894. 206p. NUC OCLC
[Spiritual autobiography]

3633. -----Through my spectacles.
NY & Boston: T. Y. Crowell & co., 1898. 144p. NUC
[Spiritual autobiography]

3634. PERRIER, Amelia [Br. 19c]
A winter in Morocco.
L: H. S. King & co., 1873. 365p. NUC BL OCLC

3635. PERRY, Kate [Br. 19c]
Reminiscences of a London drawing room.
Chesham Place: priv. pr., 1849. 12p. NUC OCLC
[Journal of visits to Miss Berry's, where gossip is of celebrities: Mme. de Stael, Napoleon, etc.]

3636. PETHERICK, Kate Harriet see PETHERICK, Katherine Harriet (Edlman)

3637. PETHERICK, Katherine Harriet (Edlman), Mrs. John Petherick [Br. 1827-1877] ALT: Petherick, Kate Harriet
Travels in Central Africa, and explorations of the western Nile tributaries. With John Petherick.
L: Tinsley bros., 1869. 2v. NUC BL OCLC

3638. PETHERICK, John, co-author see PETHERICK, Katherine Harriet (Edlman)

3639. PETHERICK, Mrs. John see
PETHERICK, Katherine Harriet
(Edlman)

3640. PFEIFFER, Emily Jane
(Davis) [Br. 1827-1890]
Flying leaves from east and west.
L: Field & Tuer; NY: Scribner &
Welford, 1885. 302p. NUC BL

3641. PFIRSHING, Mena C. [Am. 19c]
Memories of Italian shores.
Chicago: Dial Press, 1895. 175p.
NUC

3642. PHELPS, Mrs. Albert H. [Am.
19c]
Gathering jewels, or, life and
labors of Mr. and Mrs. A. H.
Phelps in New Zealand, Norfolk
island and their native land.
Meriden, CT: Journal pub. co.,
1896. NUC OCLC
[Methodist missionary; includes
her journal.]

3643. PHELPS, Elizabeth (Porter)
[Am. 1747-1817]
Under a colonial roof-tree.
[Comp.] Arria Sargent Huntington.
Boston & NY: Houghton, Mifflin &
co., 1891. 133p. NUC MAD OCLC
[Includes extracts of diary,
1763-1812: Resident of Hadley, MA]

3644. PHELPS, Elizabeth Stuart
see WARD, Elizabeth Stuart
(Phelps)

3645. PHIBBS, Isabelle Mary [Br.
19c]
A visit to the Russians in
Central Asia.
L: K. Paul, Trench, Trübner &
co., 1899. 238p. NUC BL OCLC

3646. PHILADELPHIA LADY, A,
pseud. see PARKER, W., Mrs.

3647. PHILIP, Mrs. [Am. 19c]
Letters from Algiers: containing
a brief sketch of the city and
its neighborhood; religious
customs of its inhabitants, etc.
Edinburgh: W. Oliphant, 1853.
60p. NUC

3648. PHILIPS, Katherine (Fowler)
[Br. 1631-1664] PSEUD: Orinda
Familiar letters written by the
late [John Wilmot] Earl of
Rochester, ... with letters
written by ... Mrs. K. Philips.
Ed. T[homas] Brown.
L: Samuel Briscoe, 1697. 2v. BL
OCLC

3649. -----Letters from Orinda to
Poliarchus [Sir Charles
Cotterell].
L: W. B. for Bernard Lintott,
1705. 246p. NUC BL OCLC
[Enlarged ed., 1729]

3650. PHILLIPPS, Henrietta
Elizabeth Molyneux [Br. 19c]
Fragment of a tour [from Middle
Hill, Worcestershire, into South
Wales].
Middle Hill: n.p., 1835. 4p. BL

3651. PHILLIPS, Catherine
(Payton) [Br. 1727-1794]
Memoirs of the life of Catherine
Phillips: to which are added some
of her epistles.
L: J. Phillips & son, 1797. 382p.
NUC MAD MB OCLC

3652. PHILLIPS, Dorothea Sarah
Florence Alexandra (Ortlepp),
Lady [Br. 19/20c] ALT: Phillips,
Florence; Phillips, Mrs. Lionel
Some South African recollections.
L & NY: Longmans, Green & co.,
1899. 183p. NUC BL OCLC

3653. PHILLIPS, E. C. see LOOKER,
Edith C. (Phillips)

3654. PHILLIPS, Edith C. see
LOOKER, Edith C. (Phillips)

3655. PHILLIPS, Eliza Caroline
see LOOKER, Edith C. (Phillips)

3656. PHILLIPS, Florence, Lady
see PHILLIPS, Dorothea Sarah
Florence Alexandra (Ortlepp),
Lady

3657. PHILLIPS, Mrs. H. S. see
PHILLIPS, Minnie Mary (Apperson)

3658. PHILLIPS, Ida Orissa [Am.
19c]
The bright and dark sides of
girl-life in India.
Boston: Morning Star pub. house,
1891. 32p. NUC

3659. PHILLIPS, Mrs. Lionel see PHILLIPS, Dorothea Sarah Florence Alexandrea (Ortlepp), Lady

3660. PHILLIPS, Minnie Mary (Apperson), Mrs. H. S. Phillips [Br. 19c] ALT: Apperson, M. M. Victory. Being reminiscences of and letters from M. M. Apperson (late Mrs. H. S. Phillips). Ed. Mrs. E. C. Millard.
L: E. Marlborough & co., 1896. 213p. NUC BL

3661. PHILLIPS, Phebe [Br. 18/19c] PSEUD: Maitland, Maria The woman of the town; or, authentic memoirs of Maria Maitland; well known in the vicinity of Covent Garden. Written by herself.
L: T. Maiden for J. Roe & Ann Lemoine, 1810?. NUC BL MB OCLC
[Memoirs of a courtesan]

3662. PHILLIPS, Teresia Constantia [Br. 1709-1765] Apology for the conduct of Mrs. Teresea Constantia Phillips, more particularly that part of it which relates to her marriage with an eminent Dutch merchant.
L: pr. for the author, 1748-49. 3v. NUC MB OCLC

3663. PHILPOT, L. C., Miss, ed. see W., E. A., Miss

3664. PHIPPS, Elvira Anna [Br. 19c]
Memorials of Clutha; or, pencilings on the Clyde.
L: C. Armand for the author, 1841. 107p. NUC BL
[Travel narrative; includes poems]

3665. PIATT, Mrs. Donn see PIATT, Louise (Kirby)

3666. PIATT, Louise (Kirby), Mrs. Donn Piatt [Am. 1826-1864] Bell Smith abroad.
NY: J. C. Derby, 1855. 326p. NUC OCLC
[Letters from Paris to the Home Journal]

3667. PICKARD, Hannah Maynard (Thompson), Mrs. Humphrey Pickard [Am. 1812-1844]

Memoir and writings of Hannah Maynard Pickard, late wife of Rev. Humphrey Pickard. [Comp.] Edward Otheman.
Boston: David H. Ela, pr., 1845. 250p. NUC OCLC
[Includes letters, poems and prose sketches.]

3668. PICKARD, Mrs. Humphrey see PICKARD, Hannah Maynard (Thompson)

3669. PICKFORD, Elizabeth, Mrs. [Br. 1786-1855]
Love made perfect; illustrated in the life and diary of Mrs. Elizabeth Pickford, late of Salisbury. Ed. Peter M'Owan.
L: Hamilton, Adams, 1858. 314p. NUC BL MB
[Wife of sea captain; chiefly religious.]

3670. PIGGOTT, Harriet see PIGOTT, Harriet

3671. PIGGOTT, Henry James, ed. see GEORGE, Elizabeth

3672. PIGOT, Elizabeth Bridget [Br. 1783-1866]
Letters and journals of Lord Byron [George Gordon Noel Byron, Baron Byron]: with notices of his life by Thomas Moore.
L: John Murray, 1830. 2v. NUC BL
[Her correspondence with Byron is included.]

3673. PIGOTT, Blanche Anne Frances, ed. see PIGOTT, Emma (Upcher)

3674. PIGOTT, Emma (Upcher) [Br. 1812-1889]
Recollections of our Mother, Emma Pigott followed by "Mary's Annals," by Mary S. Pigott [d. 1826]. Ed. her daughter, Blanche Anne Frances Pigott.
L: James Nisbet & co., 1890. 419p. BL
[Autobiography of Emma to 1863]

3675. PIGOTT, Harriet [Br. 1766-1839] ALT: PIGGOTT, Harriet The private correspondence of a woman of fashion.
L: H. Colburn & R. Bentley, 1832.

2v. NUC BL MB OCLC
[Convert to Roman Catholicism, lived mainly in France.]

3676. -----Records of real life in the palace and the cottage. Rev. the late J. Galt.
L: Saunders & Otley, 1839. 3v. NUC BL MB
[Semi-autobiographical, includes letters]

3677. PIGOTT, Mary S., co-author see PIGOTT, Emma (Upcher)

3678. PILKINGTON, Laetitia (Van Lewen); Mrs. Matthew Pilkington [Br. 1712-1750]
A letter from Mrs. L--tia Pilk--ton to the celebrated Mrs. T--sia C--tia Ph--ps. [Teresia Constantia Phillips Muilman]. Containing many remarks and observations on that lady's apology for her conduct. Together with some curious anecdotes of her life.
L: H. Carpenter, 1748?. 45p. NUC OCLC

3679. -----Memoirs of Mrs. Laetitia Pilkington, wife to the Rev. Mr. Matthew Pilkington. Written by herself. Wherein are occasionally interspersed, all her poems; with anecdotes of several eminent persons, living and dead.
Dublin: pr. for author, 1748. 2v. NUC BL OCLC

3680. PILKINGTON, Mary (Hopkins) [Br. 1766-1839]
Margate!!! or, sketches descriptive of that celebrated place of resort, with its environs.
L: n.p., 1813. NUC

3681. -----Memoirs of Mrs. Pilkington.
L: n.p., 1812. BL
[From the "Lady's Monthly Museum"]

3682. PILKINGTON, Mrs. Matthew see PILKINGTON, Laetitia (Van Lewen)

3683. PINCKNEY, Mrs. Charles see PINCKNEY, Eliza (Lucas)

3684. PINCKNEY, Eliza (Lucas), Mrs. Charles Pinckney [Am. 1722-1793] ALT: Lucas, Eliza
Eliza Pinckney. By Harriott Horry (Rutledge) Ravenel.
NY: Charles Scribner's sons, 1896. 323p. NUC BL OCLC
[Based on her letters; wife of Chief Justice Charles Pinckney and mother of C. C. and Thomas Pinckney; South Carolina, colonial period.]

3685. -----Journal and letters of Eliza Lucas. Ed. H. P. Holbrook.
Wormsloe, GA: n.p., 1850. 30p.

3686. PIOZZI, Hester Lynch (Salusbury) Thrale [Br. 1741-1821] ALT: Thrale, Hester Lynch
Anecdotes of the late Samuel Johnson, L. L. D., during the last twenty years of his life.
L: T. Cadell; Dublin: Messrs. Moncrieffe et al, 1786. 306p. NUC BL OCLC

3687. -----Autobiography, letters and literary remains of Mrs. Piozzi (Thrale). Ed. Abraham Hayward.
Boston: Ticknor & Fields, 1861. 531p.; L: n.p., 1861. 2v. BL OCLC

3688. -----Letters to and from the late Samuel Johnson to which are added some poems never before printed.
L: pr. for A. Strahan, 1788. 2v. NUC OCLC

3689. -----Love letters of Mrs. Piozzi, written when she was eighty to William Augustus Conway.
L: J. R. Smith, 1843. 39p. NUC BL

3690. -----Observations and reflections made in the course of a journey through France, Italy and Germany.
L: pr. for A. Strahan & T. Cadell, 1789. 2v.; Dublin: pr. for H. Chamberlaine et al, 1789. 502p. NUC BL OCLC

3691. PITMAN, Emma Raymond [Br. b. 1841]
Central Africa, Japan and Fiji; a story of missionary enterprise, trials, and triumphs.

L: Hodder & Stoughton, 1882.
296p. NUC BL OCLC

3692. -----My governess life: or,
using my one talent.
L: Blackie & son, 1883. 307p. NUC
BL MB

3693. PITMAN, Emma Raymond, comp.
see BALDWIN, Mary Briscoe

3694. PITMAN, Marie J. (Davis)
[Am. 1850-1888] PSEUD: Deane,
Margery
European breezes. By Marie J.
Pitman (Margery Deane).
Boston: Lee & Shepard; NY: C. T.
Dillingham, 1882. 318p. NUC BL
OCLC

3695. PITTAR, Fanny Maria, Mrs.
[Am. 19c]
A Protestant converted to
Catholicism by her Bible and
prayer book.
Philadelphia: H. M'Grath, 1847.
154p. NUC BL [Autobiography]

3696. PLACE, Mrs. Perry [Am. 19c]
The affectionate son: for the use
of children. In 2 parts.
7th ed. Portland, OR: n.p., 1830.
36p. NUC
[Memoir of her son; account of
her life as poor clergyman's
wife.]

3697. -----The orphan; or, a
brief memoir of Mrs. Place.
Written by herself.
Philadelphia: Am. Sunday School
Union, 18--. 19p. NUC
[Recounts her suffering after her
father's death when she was 9;
religious in tone.]

3698. PLAIN WOMAN, A., pseud. see
BARTER, Charlotte

3699. PLATT, Miss [Br. 19c]
Journal of a tour [of H. Tattam
and Miss Platt] through Egypt,
the peninsula of Sinai and the
Holy Land in 1838, 1839.
L: pr. for priv. circ. by R.
Watts, 1841, 1842. 2v. BL OCLC
[OCLC enters under Mrs. Henry
Tattam.]

3700. PLATT, Cyrus, comp. see
PLATT, Jeanette Hulme

3701. PLATT, Jeanette Hulme, Mrs.
[Am. 1816-1877]
Life and letters of Mrs. Jeanette
H. Platt. Comp. Cyrus Platt.
Philadelphia: E. Claxton & co.,
1882. 363p. BL OCLC

3702. PLATT, Mrs. Lorin L. [Am.
19c]
Spiritual experience with
spiritual impressions annexed.
New Haven, CT: J. H. Benham,
1852. 40p. NUC OCLC
[Spiritual autobiography]

3703. PLUMLEY, Matilda [Br. 19c]
Days and nights in the East; from
the original notes of a recent
traveller through Egypt, Arabia,
Petra, Syria, Turkey, and Greece.
L: T. C. Newby, 1845. 287p. NUC
BL OCLC

3704. PLUMMER, Clarissa, co-
author see HARRIS, Caroline

3705. PLUMMER, Mrs. James, co-
author see HARRIS, Caroline

3706. PLUMPTRE, Anne [Br. 1760-
1818]
Narrative of a residence in
Ireland during the summer of 1814
and that of 1815.
L: H. Colburn, 1817. 398p. NUC BL
MB OCLC

3707. -----A narrative of three
years' residence in France,
principally in the southern
departments, from the year 1802
to 1805; including some authentic
particulars respecting the early
life of the French Emperor, and a
general inquiry into his
character.
L: J. Mawman, 1810. 3v. NUC BL MB
OCLC

3708. PLUNKETT, Elizabeth
(Gunning) see GUNNING, Susannah
(Minifie)

3709. PLUNKETT, Hon. Fredrica
Louisa Edith [Br. d. 1886]
Here and there among the Alps.

L: Longmans, Green & co., 1875. 195p. NUC

3710. POLEHAMPTON, Edward, ed. see POLEHAMPTON, Emily

3711. POLEHAMPTON, Emily, Mrs. Henry Stedman Polehampton [Br. 19c] Memoir, letters, and diary [of H. S. Polehampton]. Ed. Edward Polehampton and Thomas Stedman Polehampton. 2d ed. L: R. Bentley, 1858. 414p. NUC OCLC [Letters and diary. Personal narrative of Siege of Lucknow and Sepoy Rebellion, India, 1857-58.]

3712. POLEHAMPTON, Mrs. Henry Stedman see POLEHAMPTON, Emily

3713. POLEHAMPTON, Thomas Stedman, ed. see POLEHAMPTON, Emily

3714. POLIARCHUS, pseud. see PHILIPS, Katherine (Fowler)

3715. POLLARD, Madeline Valeria [Am. b. 1866] ALT: Pollard, Madeleine The real Madeleine Pollard. A diary of 10 weeks' association with the plaintiff in the famous Breckinridge-Pollard suit. An intimate study of character. By Agnes Parker. NY: G. W. Dillingham, 1894. 336p. NUC

3716. POMFRET, Henrietta Louisa, Countess of, co-author see SOMERSET, Frances (Thynne) Seymour, Duchess of

3717. POMROY, Rebecca Rossignol (Holliday) [Am. 1817-1884] Echoes from hospital and White House. A record of Mrs. Rebecca R. Pomroy's experience in war times. [Comp.] Anna L. Boyden. Boston: D. Lothrop & co., 1884. 250p. NUC BL OCLC

3718. POOLE, Annie Sampson [Br. 19c] PSEUD: Resident, A Mexicans at home in the interior. By a resident. L: Chapman & Hall, 1884. 183p. NUC BL OCLC

[Diary of 18 mos. residence in Guanaxuato by an English couple.]

3719. POOLE, Mrs. E. R. see POOLE, Sophia (Lane)

3720. POOLE, Reginald Stuart, co-author see POOLE, Sophia (Lorne)

3721. POOLE, Sophia (Lane), Mrs. E. R. Poole [Br. 1804-1891] The Englishwoman in Egypt: letters from Cairo written during a residence there in 1842, 3 and 4. 1st series. L: Charles Knight & co., 1844. 2v. NUC BL; 2d series. L: Charles Knight & co., 1846. 249p. NUC BL OCLC [Letters, 1845-6. With her brother, E. W. Lane.]

3722. -----The Englishwoman in Russia; impressions of the society and manners of the Russians at home. By a lady, ten years resident in that country. L: J. Murray, 1855. 350p.; NY: Charles Scribner, 1855. 316p. NUC OCLC

3723. -----Cairo, Sinai, and Jerusalem, and the pyramids of Egypt: a series of sixty photographic views by Francis Frith. With descriptions by Mrs. Poole and Reginald Stuart Poole. L: J. S. Virtue, 1860. 60p. NUC BL

3724. -----Egypt, Sinai and Jerusalem; a series of twenty photographic views by Francis Frith. With descriptions by Mrs. Poole and Reginald Stuart Poole. L: William Mackenzie, 1860. 1v. NUC BL OCLC

3725. POOLE, Stanley Lane, ed. see BLUNT, Fanny Janet (Sandison), Lady

3726. PORTARLENGTON, Caroline (Stuart) Dawson, Countess of, co-author see STUART, Lady Louisa

3727. PORTER, Deborah H. (Cushing), Mrs. C. G. Porter [Am. 1809-1847] Memoir of Mrs. Deborah H. Porter. [Comp.] Anne T. Drinkwater. Portland, ME: Sanborn & Carter,

1848. 269p. NUC MAD OCLC
[Includes journal; primarily
religious]

3728. PORTER, Mrs. G. C. <u>see</u>
PORTER, Deborah H. (Cushing)

3729. PORTER, Henrietta (Vernon)
Grosvenor, Baroness de Hochapied
<u>see</u> GROSVENOR, Henrietta
(Vernon) Grosvenor, Countess

3730. PORTER, M. E., Mrs. [Am. 19c]
Buckeye blossoms.
Cincinnati, OH: Pub. for the
author by the Elm Street pub.
co., 1871. 146p. NUC OCLC
[Travel: Ohio]

3731. PORTER, Maria S. (Alley)
[Am. 1832-1904]
Recollections of Louisa May
Alcott, John Greenleaf Whittier,
and Robert Browning, together
with several memorial poems.
Boston: pub. for the author by
the New England magazine corp.,
1893. 59p. NUC BL OCLC
[Personal recollections not
available elsewhere. Includes 3
memorial poems by Porter.]

3732. PORTER, Rose [Br. 1845-
1906]
Open windows: a heart-to-heart
diary.
NY: A. D. F. Randolph & co.,
c1890. 107p. NUC

3733. -----The years that are
told.
NY: A. D. F. Randolph & co.,
c1875. 233p. NUC BL MB OCLC
[May be fiction; MB says
autobiographical material.]

3734. POST, Loretta J., Mrs. [Am.
19c]
Scenes in Europe; or,
observations by an amateur
artist.
Cincinnati, OH: Hitchcock &
Walden; NY: Nelson & Phillips,
1874. 336p. NUC BL OCLC

3735. POSTANS, Mrs. Thomas <u>see</u>
YOUNG, Marianne (Postans)

3736. POTTER, Eliza [Am. 19c]
A hairdresser's experience in
high life.

Cincinnati, OH: pub. by the
author, 1859. 294p. NUC OCLC
[Autobiography of child's nurse
and servant in England, France
and U.S.]

3737. POTTER, Louisa, Mrs. [Br.
19c]
Lancashire memories.
L: Macmillan & co., 1879. 199p.
NUC BL MB

3738. POWER, Marguerite A. [Br.
1815-1867]
Arabian days and nights; or, rays
from the East.
L: S. Low & son co., 1863. 308p.
NUC BL   [Travel: Egypt]

3739. POWERS, Elvira J. [Am. 19c]
Hospital pencillings: being a
diary while in Jefferson General
Hospital, Jeffersonville, Ind.,
and others at Nashville,
Tennessee, as matron and visitor.
Boston: Edward L. Mitchell, 1866.
211p. NUC C OCLC

3740. POWERSCOURT, Theodosia A.
(Howard) Wingfield, Viscountess
[Br. d. 1836] ALT: Wingfield,
Theodosia A. (Howard),
Viscountess Powerscourt
Letters and papers by the late
Theodosia A., Viscountess
Powerscourt. Ed. Rev. Robert Daly.
Dublin: Curry, 1838. 307p.; L:
Hatchard & son, 1838. 316p. NUC
BL OCLC

3741. POWYS, Caroline (Girle),
Mrs. Philip Lybbe Powys [Br.
1738-1817]
Passages from the diaries of Mrs.
Philip Lybbe Powys, of Hardwick
House, Oxon., A. D. 1756 to 1808.
Ed. Emily Jane Climenson.
L, NY & Bombay: Longmans, Green &
co., 1899. 399p. NUC BL MBD

3742. POWYS, Mrs. Philip Lybbe
<u>see</u> POWYS, Caroline (Girle)

3743. PRENTISS, Elizabeth
(Payson), Mrs. George L. Prentiss
[Am. 1818-1878]
The life and letters of Elizabeth
Prentiss. [Comp.] Rev. George L.
Prentiss.
NY: A. D. F. Randolph & co.,

1882; L: Hodder & Stoughton, 1882. 573p. NUC BL MAD OCLC [Includes diaries, accounts of her literary endeavors; also contains extracts of diary of Louisa (Payson) Hopkins, Am. 1812-1862.]

3744. PRENTISS, Rev. George L., comp. <u>see</u> PRENTISS, Elizabeth (Payson)

3745. PRENTISS, Mrs. George L. <u>see</u> PRENTISS, Elizabeth (Payson)

3746. PRESCOTT, Anne M. [Am. d. 1923] Hawaii.
San Francisco: C. A. Murdock & co., 1891. 133p. NUC OCLC

3747. -----Makapala-by-the-sea, Hawaii.
Honolulu, HI: Hawaiian Gazette co.'s print., 1899. 1v. NUC OCLC

3748. PRESTON, Annie Turner [Am. 19c]
Short journeys on a long road.
Chicago & Milwaukee, WI: The Passenger Dept. of the Chicago Milwaukee & St. Paul Railway, 189?. 111p. NUC
[Rail journey: Chicago through upper Mid-West.]

3749. PRESTON, Margaret (Junkin) [Am. 1820-1897]
A handful of monographs, continental and English.
NY: A. D. F. Randolph, 1886. 229p. NUC OCLC [Travel: Europe]

3750. PRICE, Eleanor Catherine [Br. 19/20c]
May in Anjou, with other sketches and studies.
Edinburgh: David Douglas, 1889. 82p. BL OCLC
[Ten short pieces: two on Britain, others on France.]

3751. PRICE, Elizabeth <u>see</u> BANBURY, Elizabeth Price

3752. PRICE, Hannah Ann (Foulke) [Am. 1814-1887]
A memoir of Hannah A. Price, late of Fallston, Maryland.
Norristown, PA: Morgan R. Wills, 1889. 157p. NUC OCLC

[Contains her diary; Society of Friends, Pennsylvania]

3753. PRICE, Mary D., co-author <u>see</u> PRICE, Rebecca

3754. PRICE, Rebecca [Am. 19c]
Memoranda and reflections of Rebecca Price, a recorded minister belonging to Baltimore quarterly meeting of Friends. Ed. Hugh Foulke.
Philadelphia: W. H. Pile's sons, 1896. 193p. NUC OCLC
[Incl. memoranda of Mary D. Price.]

3755. PRICHARD, Helen M. [Br. 19c]
Friends and foes in the Transkei: an Englishwoman's experiences during the Cape frontier war of 1877-8.
L: S. Low, Marston, Searle & Rivington, 1880. 296p. NUC BL OCLC

3756. PRINCE, Nancy (Gardener) [Am. b. 1799]
A narrative of the life and travels of Mrs. Nancy Prince.
Boston: the author, 1850. 87p. NUC BL K OCLC
[Russia, West Indies. Black woman]

3757. PRINGLE, Mrs. Alexander <u>see</u> PRINGLE, M. A.

3758. PRINGLE, M. A., Mrs. Alexander Pringle [Br. 19c]
Towards the Mountains of the Moon. A journey in East Africa.
Edinburgh & L: W. Blackwood & sons, 1884. 386p. NUC BL OCLC

3759. PRIOR, Margaret (Barrett Allen) [Am. 1773-1842]
Walks of usefulness. Or, reminiscences of Mrs. Margaret Prior.
NY: Am. F. G. Society, 1843. 324p. NUC OCLC
[Extracts from her journal]

3760. PROCTOR, Edna Dean [Am. 1829-1923]
A Russian journey.
Boston: Houghton, Mifflin, 1871. 321p. NUC BL OCLC

3761. PRUYN, Mary, Mrs. [Am. 19c]
Grandmamma's letters from Japan.

Boston: James H. Earle, 1877.
219p. NUC OCLC

3762. PRYER, Ada, Mrs. [Br. 19c]
A decade in Borneo.
L: Hutchinson & co., 1894. 199p.
NUC BL OCLC

3763. PULLMAN, Rev. Joseph, ed.
see COOKE, Bella (Beeton)

3764. PUTNAM, Sallie A. (Brock)
[Am. b. 1845?] PSEUD: Richmond
Lady, A
Richmond during the war; four
years of personal observation. By
a Richmond lady.
NY: G. W. Carleton & co., 1867.
389p. NUC OCLC

3765. PYLADES, pseud., co-author
see THOMAS, Elizabeth

3766. PYM, Horace Noble, ed. see
FOX, Caroline

3767. QUILLINAN, Dorothy
(Wordsworth) [Br. 1804-1847] ALT:
Wordsworth, Dora
A journal of a few months'
residence in Portugal, and
glimpses of the south of Spain.
L: E. Moxon, 1847. 2v. NUC BL MBD
OCLC

3768. QUINCY, Eliza Susan, co-
author and comp. see QUINCY,
Eliza Susan (Morton)

3769. QUINCY, Eliza Susan
(Morton) [Am. 1773-1850]
Memoir of the life of Eliza S. M.
Quincy. [Comp. her daughter,
Eliza Susan Quincy, 1798-1884]
Boston: J. Wilson & son, 1861.
267p. NUC BL K
[Part I consists of a fragment of
autobiography, 1821; Part II,
continuation by the author's
daughter.]

3770. R., E. L. see ROBINSON, E.
L., Mrs.

3771. R., L. N., ed. see MASON,
Ellen (Huntley) Bullard

3772. R., L. N. R. see ROBINSON,
Lilias Napier Rose

3773. R., M., comp. see FLETCHER,
Eliza (Dawson)

3774. R. R., comp. see WRIGHT,
Hannah Mary

3775. RADCLIFFE, Amelia [Br. 19c]
ALT: Darwentwater, Countess of
Jottings of original matter from
the diary of Amelia, Countess and
heiress of Darwentwater, and from
the journal of ... John, Fourth
Earl of Darwentwater.
L: n.p., 1869. BL

3776. RADCLIFFE, Ann (Ward) [Br.
1764-1823]
Gaston de Blondeville, or the
Court of Henry III. Keeping
festival in Ardenne, a romance.
St. Alban's abbey, a metrical
tale; with some poetical pieces
... to which is prefixed a memoir
of the author, with extracts from
her journals.
L: H. Colburn, 1826. 4v. NUC BL
OCLC

3777. -----A journey made in the
summer of 1794, through Holland
and the western frontier of
Germany, with a return down the
Rhine, to which are added
observations during a tour to the
lakes of Lancashire, Westmoreland
and Cumberland.
Dublin: W. Porter for P. Wogan,
499p.; L: G. G. & J. Robinson,
1795. 500p. NUC BL OCLC

3778. RADCLIFFE, Mary Ann, Mrs.
[Br. 18/19c]
The memoirs of Mrs. Mary Ann
Radcliffe: in familiar letters to
her female friend.
Edinburgh: pr. for the author,
1810. 544p. NUC BL MB
[Includes poetry and The Female
Advocate]

3779. RADFORD, Eleanor (Henry), co-author see SAVAGE, Sarah (Henry)

3780. RAINS, Fanny L. [Br. 19c]
By land and ocean; or, the journal and letters of a young girl who went to South Australia with a lady friend, then alone to Victoria, New Zealand, Sydney, Singapore, China, Japan and across the continent of America home.
L: S. Low, Marston, Searle, & Rivington, 1878. 250p. NUC BL

3781. RAINY, C., Miss [Br. 19c]
A visit to our Indian mission field.
Paisley: n.p., 1887. 358p. NUC BL

3782. RAMSAY, Agnes Dick (Marshall), Lady [Br. 19/20c]
ALT: Mrs. W. M. Ramsay
Everyday life in Turkey.
L: Hodder & Stoughton, 1897. 303p. NUC BL OCLC

3783. RAMSAY, Claudia Hamilton, Mrs. [Br. 19c]
A summer in Spain.
L: Tinsley bros., 1874. 421p. NUC OCLC

3784. RAMSAY, David, comp. see RAMSAY, Martha (Laurens)

3785. RAMSAY, Mrs. M. L., co-author see JUDSON, Ann (Hasseltine)

3786. RAMSAY, Martha (Laurens) [Am. 1759-1811]
Memoirs of the life of Martha Laurens Ramsay, who died in Charleston, S. C. on the 10th of June, 1811 ... With an appendix, containing extracts from her diary, letters and other private papers.... By David Ramsay.
Philadelphia: James Maxwell, pr., 1811. 308p. NUC BL MAD OCLC

3787. RAMSAY, Mrs. W. M. see RAMSAY, Agnes Dick (Marshall)

3788. RAMSEY, Vienna G. (Morrell) [Am. b. 1817]
Evenings with the children; or, travels in South America.

Boston: D. Lothrop & co., 1871. 234p. NUC

3789. RAND, Olive [Am. 19c] ALT: Clarke, Olive (Rand)
A vacation excursion from Massachusetts Bay to Puget Sound.
Manchester, NH: Press of John B. Clarke, 1884. 203p. NUC OCLC

3790. RANDALL, Isabelle, Mrs. [Br. 19c]
A lady's ranch life in Montana.
L: W. H. Allen & co., 1887. 170p. NUC K OCLC

3791. RANKIN, Mary [Am. b. 1821]
The daughter of affliction. A memoir of the protracted sufferings and religious experience of Miss Mary Rankin; as communicated by her to her late attending physician, D. R. Good.
Dayton, OH: pr. at the United Brethren pr. estab., 1858. 253p. NUC K OCLC
[Contains autobiographical account]

3792. RANKIN, Melinda [Am. 19c]
Twenty years among the Mexicans.
St. Louis, MO: Christian pub. co.; Cincinnati, OH: Chase & Hall, 1875. 214p. NUC BL K OCLC
[Also pub. as: A narrative of missionary labor]

3793. RANYARD, L. N., ed. see MASON, Ellen (Huntley) Bullard

3794. RATCLIFF, Mildred (Morris) [Am. 1773-1847]
Memoranda and correspondence of Mildred Ratcliff.
Philadelphia: W. H. Pile's sons, pr., Friends' book store, 1890. 210p. NUC MAD
[Religious diary; travel in southern U.S.]

3795. RATHBONE, Mrs. Ambrose, ed. see COKE, Lady Jane (Wharton)

3796. RATHBONE, Florence A. Monica, ed. see COKE, Lady Jane (Wharton)

3797. RATTRAY, Harriet [Br. 19c]

Country life in Syria. Passages of letters written from Anti-Lebanon.
L: Seeley, Jackson & Halliday, 1876. 232p. NUC BL

3798. RAVENEL, Harriott Horry (Rutledge) <u>see</u> PINCKNEY, Eliza (Lucas)

3799. REAGH, Florence MacCarthy [Br. 19c] ALT: MacCarthy, Florence
The life and letters of Florence MacCarthy Reagh, Tanist of Carbery, MacCarthy Mor, with some portion of "The history of the ancient families of the south of Ireland," comp. solely from unpub. docs. in HM's State Paper Office.
Dublin: n.p., 1867. BL

3800. REDFORD, E. (Eustace) [Br. b. 1816]
The Banbury female martyr (composed by herself).
Banbury: n.p., 1864. BL
[Deathbed confession written down by her 9 year old daughter.]

3801. REED, Anna Stevens [Am. 19c]
Mount Holyoke days in war time.
Boston & Chicago: The Pilgrim press, 1899. 376p. NUC OCLC

3802. REED, Rebecca Theresa [Am. b. ca. 1813]
Six months in a convent ..., or, the narrative of Rebecca Theresa Reed, who was under the influence of the Roman Catholics about two years, and an inmate of the Ursuline convent on Mount Benedict, Charlestown, Mass., nearly six months, in the years 1831-2.
NY: Leavitt, Lord & co.; Boston: Russell, Odiorne & Metcalf, 1835. 192p. NUC BL OCLC
[Also pub. as: Narrative of six months' residence in a convent and as: The nun.]

3803. REEDPEN, PEREGRINE, pseud. <u>see</u> ADDERLEY, C. F.

3804. REES, Laura L., Miss [Am. 19c]
We four. Where we went and what

we saw in Europe.
Philadelphia: J. B. Lippincott & co., 1880. 304p. NUC OCLC

3805. REEVE, Barbara Jane [Br. 19c]
Chapters of the autobiography of a Fifeshire lady, by Barbara Jane Reeve, of Eden Park.
Edinburgh: pr. for priv. circ., 1874. 106p. NUC
[Relation of cruel treatment and disinheritance by mother and sister.]

3806. REEVE, S., Mrs. [Br. 19c]
The illegal arrest; or, twelve months of widowhood.
Horsham: J. Clarke, 1842. 57p. BL

3807. REID, Lottie [Am. 19c]
Narrative of a trip across the continent to attend the 20th national encampment of the G. A. R. and the fourth national convention of the W. R. C. held at San Francisco, Cal., Aug. 4, 1886.
Wooster, OH: n.p., 1886?. 17p. NUC

3808. RENNIE, Eliza [Br. 1828-1860] PSEUD: Contemporary, A
Traits of character; being twenty-five years' literary and personal recollections. By a contemporary.
L: Hurst & Blackett, 1860. 2v. BL OCLC

3809. RESIDENT, A, pseud. <u>see</u> POOLE, Annie Sampson

3810. RESIDENT OF SHERWOOD FOREST, A, pseud. <u>see</u> HAMILTON, Sarah

3811. REYNOLDS, Catherine [Am. 1810-1840/41?]
Memoirs of Miss Catherine Reynolds, of Poughkeepsie, NY: with selections from her diary and letters. Ed. Rev. George Coles.
NY: Methodist book room, 1844. 212p. NUC OCLC

3812. REYNOLDS, Lucy Brown [Am. 19c]
Drops of spray from southern seas.

Waterville, ME: Mail pub. co., 1896. 282p. NUC OCLC
[Voyage on her father's ship to South America and South Pacific.]

3813. RHODES, Mrs. Benjamin see RHODES, Elizabeth

3814. RHODES, Edith E. [Br. d. 1905]
The adventures of five spinsters in Norway.
L: J. & R. Maxwell, 1886. 127p. NUC BL OCLC

3815. RHODES, Elizabeth, Mrs. Benjamin Rhodes [Br. 19c]
Memoir of Mrs. Elizabeth Rhodes, widow of the late Rev. Benjamin Rhodes, who was an itinerant preacher in the Wesleyan connection for upwards of forty years, written by herself; ... appended an account of the life, sufferings, and triumphant death of Miss Hannah Rhodes, who died in consequence of an accident by fire....
L: J. Mason, 1829. 215p. NUC BL OCLC
[Methodist; may also contain personal material of Hannah Rhodes.]

3816. RHODES, Hannah, co-author see RHODES, Elizabeth

3817. RICE, Sarah Sigourney, ed. see NIEMEYER, Mary A.

3818. RICH, Mary (Boyle), Countess of Warwick see WARWICK, Mary (Boyle) Rich, Countess of

3819. RICHARDS, Rev. A., ed. see FITZ-JAMES, Zilla

3820. RICHARDS, Anna Matlock, Mrs. [Am. 19c] PSEUD: Lady of Massachusetts, A
Memories of a grandmother, by a lady of Massachusetts.
Boston: Gould & Lincoln, 1854. 141p. K

3821. RICHARDS, Elizabeth Barnes [Am. 19c]
The heart's streamlet; or, buds from memory's store house.
Worcester, MA: Hervey & co.,

1856. 168p. NUC
[43 pieces by Richards; 17 by others. Hers include poems & reminiscences.]

3822. RICHARDS, G. P., comp. see PALMER, Ann

3823. RICHARDS, Laura Elizabeth (Howe) [Am. 1850-1943]
When I was your age.
Boston: D. Estes; Page, 1893. 210p.   NUC K OCLC

3824. RICHARDS, Lucy [Am. 1792-1837]
Memoirs of the late Miss Lucy Richards, of Paris, Oneida County, N.Y. Written by herself. Ed. by another hand. Rev. by the editor.
NY: G. Lane & P. P. Sanford for the Methodist Episcopal Church, 1842. 272p. NUC K OCLC

3825. RICHARDSON, Eliza (Smith) [Br. 19c] ALT: Smith, Eliza
Five years a Catholic: with incidents of foreign convent life.
L: n.p., 1850. BL

3826. -----Personal experience of Roman Catholicism....
L: Walsall, 1864; Philadelphia: J. B. Lippincott & co., 1869. NUC BL MB
[Expanded eds. of "Five years" and "The progress"; religious autobiography.]

3827. -----The progress of beguilement to Romanism. A personal narrative.
L: n.p., 1850. BL

3828. RICHARDSON, Mary (Fletcher), Lady, comp. see FLETCHER, Eliza (Dawson)

3829. RICHARDSON, Mary (Walsham) Few [Am. b. 1821]
Scenes in the eventful life of Mary W. Few Richardson. Ed. Elizabeth T. Larkin.
Columbus, OH: W. G. Hubbard & co., 1894. 266p. NUC K OCLC
[Temperance worker]

3830. RICHARDSON, Samuel, co-author see CHAPONE, Hester (Mulso)

3831. RICHINGS, Emily A. [Br. 19c]
Pen and ink sketches from Naples
to the North Cape.
L: Digby & Long, 1890. 128p. BL
[Travel: Italy, Switzerland,
Denmark & Sweden]

3832. RICHMOND LADY, A, pseud.
see PUTNAM, Sallie A. (Brock)

3833. RICKMAN, Matilda [Am. 1800-
1882]
An account of some of the
experiences of Matilda Rickman.
Written by herself.
Newport, RI: J. E. Southall,
1882. 24p. NUC

3834. RIDDELL, Maria (Woodley)
[Br. 1772?-1808]
Voyages to the Madeira and
leeward Caribbean Isles, with
sketches of the natural history
of these islands.
Edinburgh: P. Hill, and T.
Cadell, 1792. 105p. NUC OCLC

3835. RIDEOUT, Mrs. Jacob
Barzilla [Am. 19c]
Camping out in California.
San Francisco: R. R. Patterson,
1889. 237p. NUC OCLC

3836. -----Six years on the
border; or, sketches of frontier
life.
Philadelphia: Presbyterian Board
of Publication, 1883. 221p. NUC
BL K OCLC

3837. RIGBY, Elizabeth see
EASTLAKE, Elizabeth (Rigby), Lady

3838. RIGDEN, Martha [Br. 19c]
Recollections of a winter in the
sunny South.
L: George Stoneman, 1888. 24p. BL
[Travel: France & Italy]

3839. RIPLEY, Dorothy [Br. b.
1767]
The bank of faith and works
united.
Philadelphia: J. H. Cunningham,
1819. 204p. NUC BL OCLC
[Member of Society of Friends;
letters describing her 1805
missionary travels.]

3840. -----The extraordinary
conversion and religious
experience of Dorothy Ripley,
with her first voyage and travels
in America.
NY: pr. by G. & R. Waite, 1810.
168p. NUC MB OCLC
[Society of Friends]

3841. RIPLEY, Eliza Moore (Chinn)
McHatton [Am. 1832-1912]
From flag to flag. A woman's
adventures and experiences in the
South during the war, in Mexico,
and in Cuba.
NY: D. Appleton & co., 1889.
296p. NUC BL C K OCLC

3842. RIPPON, Sarah [Am. b. 1714]
The true state of the case of
Sarah Rippon, widow. Written by
herself.
L: pr. for the author & sold by
S. Hooper, 1756. 30p. NUC

3843. RISKE, Charlotte (Chambers)
Ludlow [Am. d. 1821] ALT:
Chambers, Charlotte
Memoir of Charlotte Chambers. By
her grandson, Lewis Hector
Garrard.
Philadelphia: pr. for the author,
1856. 135p. NUC MAD OCLC
[Her letters 1797-1821 relating
to early settlement of Cincinnati
and NW Territory. Also diary
extracts Dec. 1796-Apr. 1821]

3844. RITCHIE, Anna Cora (Ogden)
Mowatt [Am. 1819-1870] ALT:
Mowatt, Anna Cora
Autobiography of an actress; or,
eight years on the stage.
Boston: Ticknor, Reed & Fields,
[1853]. 448p. NUC BL OCLC

3845. -----Italian life and
legends.
NY: Carleton, 1870. 299p. NUC
OCLC
[Sketches of travel, 1864-1865]

3846. RITCHIE, Anna Cora (Ogden)
Mowatt, ed. see ARBLAY, Frances
(Burney) d'

3847. RITCHIE, Anne Isabella
(Thackeray), Lady [Br. 1837-1919]
ALT: Ritchie, Mrs. Richmond;

Thackeray, Anne Isabella
Chapters from some memoirs.
L & NY: Macmillan & co.; NY:
Harper bros., 1894. 215p. NUC BL
MB OCLC
[Harper's Am. ed.: Chapters from
some unwritten memoirs]

3848. RITCHIE, David G., ed. <u>see</u>
CARLYLE, Jane Baillie (Welsh)

3849. RITCHIE, Mrs. Richmond <u>see</u>
RITCHIE, Anne Isabella (Thackeray)

3850. RITSON, Anne, Mrs. [Br.
19c] PSEUD: Lady, A
A poetical picture of America,
being observations made during a
residence of several years, at
Alexandria, and Norfolk, in
Virginia; illustrative of the
manners and customs of the
inhabitants and interspersed with
anecdotes, arising from a general
intercourse with society in that
country, from the year 1799 to
1807. By a lady.
L: pr. for author by W. Wilson,
1809. 177p. NUC OCLC

3851. RIVES, Judith Page (Walker)
[Am. 1802-1882] PSEUD: Lady of
Virginia, A
Tales and souvenirs of a
residence in Europe. By a lady of
Virginia.
Philadelphia: Lea & Blanchard,
1842. 301p. NUC OCLC

3852. ROBERTS, Arthur, ed. <u>see</u>
MORE, Hannah

3853. ROBERTS, Arthur, ed. <u>see</u>
MORE, Martha

3854. ROBERTS, Deborah S., co-
author <u>see</u> SEELY, Catherine

3855. ROBERTS, Emma [Br. 1794?-
1840]
The East India voyager, or ten
minutes advice.
L: J. Madden, 1839. 263p. NUC BL
OCLC

3856. -----Hindostan, its
landscapes, palaces, temples,
tombs; the shores of the Red Sea;
and the sublime and romantic
scenery of the Himalaya mountains.

L: Fisher, son & co., 1845-47.
2v. NUC BL
[Illustrations; commentary by
Roberts. Also pub. as: Views in
India, China and on the shores of
the Red Sea ... with descriptions
by E. Roberts. 1835.]

3857. -----Notes of an overland
journey through France and Egypt
to Bombay.
L: W. Allen, 1841. 333p. NUC BL

3858. -----Scenes and
characteristics of Hindostan,
with sketches of Anglo-Indian
society.
L: W. H. Allen & co., 1835. 3v.
NUC BL OCLC

3859. ROBERTS, Jane [Br. 19c]
Two years at sea: being the
narrative of a voyage to the Swan
River and Van Dieman's Land;
during the years 1829, 30, 31.
L: R. Bentley, 1834. 396p. NUC BL
OCLC

3860. ROBERTS, Mary Eleanor <u>see</u>
ANDERSON, Mary Eleanor (Roberts)

3861. ROBERTS, Mildred Crompton-,
co-author <u>see</u> ROBERTS, Violet
Crompton-

3862. ROBERTS, Violet Crompton-
[Br. 19c]
A jubilee jaunt to Norway.
By three girls [V. Crompton-
Roberts, Mildred Crompton-Roberts
and another]
L: Griffith,Farran, Okeden &
Welsh, 1888. 204p. BL OCLC

3863. ROBERTS, William, ed. <u>see</u>
MORE, Hannah

3864. ROBERTSON, Agnes Heatley
[Br. 1837-1886]
Extracts from the diary, letters,
and miscellaneous writings of
Agnes Heatley Robertson.
Glasgow: James Maclehose & sons,
1895. 377p. NUC

3865. ROBERTSON, Eliza Frances
[Br. 1771-1805]
Consolatory verses of the late E.
F. Robertson. With some account
of the life and character of the

author. To which are added
observations ... on her very
remarkable case.
L: James & Bumford, 1808. NUC BL
[Chiefly poetry; account of
imprisonment in the Fleet for
debt.]

3866. -----Dividends of immense
value; and my claim on others
evidenced, by indisputable
authorities. To which is added a
poetical epistle to a friend.
L: pr. for the author by J.
Cundee, 1801. 36p. BL OCLC

3867. -----Life and memoirs of
Miss Robertson of Blackheath.
Faithfully recorded by her to the
best of her knowledge and belief.
L: pr. by W. Burton for C.
Sharpe, 1802. 110p. NUC BL OCLC

3868. ROBERTSON, Hannah [Br. b.
1724]
The life of Mrs. Robertson ...
who, though a grand-daughter of
Charles II has been reduced ...
from splendid affluence to the
greatest poverty.
Derby: J. Drewry, 1791. 47p. NUC
BL MB OCLC
[Autobiography]

3869. ROBERTSON, Henrietta
(Woodrow), Mrs. R. Robertson [Br.
d. 1864]
Mission life among the Zulu-
Kafirs; memorials of Henrietta
Robertson, wife of the Rev. R.
Robertson. Compiled chiefly from
letters and journals written to
the late Bishop Mackenzie and his
sisters. Ed. Anne Mackenzie.
Cambridge: Deighton, Bells, 1866.
380p. NUC BL OCLC

3870. -----ROBERTSON, Janet [Br.
19c]
Lights and shades of a
traveller's path; or, scenes in
foreign lands.
L & Edinburgh: William & Norgate,
1851. 134p. BL

3871. ROBERTSON, Mrs. R. see
ROBERTSON, Henrietta (Woodrow)

3872. ROBINSON, E. L., Mrs. [Br.
19c] ALT: R., E. L.

Scenes among which we labour. By
the wife of a missionary in
Bengal (E. L. R.).
L: n.p., 1868. BL

3873. ROBINSON, Lilias Napier
Rose [Br. 19c] ALT: R., L. N. R.
Our trip to the Yosemite Valley
and Sierra Nevada range. By L. N.
R. R.
L: J. Martin & son, 1883. 37p.
NUC

3874. -----A short account of our
trip to the Sierra Nevada
Mountains. By L. N. R. R.
L: J. Martin & son, 1884. 49p. NUC

3875. ROBINSON, Louise B. [Am. 19c]
A bundle of letters from over the
sea.
Boston: J. G. Cupples, 1889.
294p. NUC OCLC

3876. ROBINSON, Mary (Darby) [Br.
1758-1800] PSEUD: Perdita
Memoirs of the late Mrs.
Robinson, written by herself.
With some posthumous pieces. [Ed.
her daughter, Mary Elizabeth
Robinson]
L: pr. by Wilkes & Taylor for R.
Phillips, 1801. 4v. NUC BL MB
OCLC

3877. -----The memoirs of Perdita.
L: G. Lister, 1784. 180p. BL
[NUC has 1894 ed.]

3878. ROBINSON, Mary Elizabeth,
ed. see ROBINSON, Mary (Darby)

3879. ROBINSON, Sarah [Br. 19/20c]
Life record.
n.p.: n.p., 1898. MB
[Missionary work with soldiers
and sailors.]

3880. ROBSON, Elizabeth J. J.
(Bayes) [Br. 1828-1859]
A memoir of Elizabeth J. J.
Robson, late of Saffron Walden,
who died 15th of 10th month,
1859.
L: A. W. Bennett, 1860. 44p. NUC
BL MBD OCLC
[Extracts from her diary 1840-
1859. Member of Society of
Friends.]

3881. ROCHE, Harriet A. [Br. 19c]
On trek in the Transvaal; or,
over berg and veldt in South
Africa.
L: S. Low, Marston, Searle &
Rivington, 1878. 367p. NUC BL
OCLC

3882. ROCHESTER, Earl of, co-
author see PHILIPS, Katherine
(Fowler)

3883. RODEN, Anne, Countess [Br.
18/19c]
The diary of Anne, Countess
Dowager of Roden, from 6th
August, 1797, to 11th April, 1802.
Dublin: R. T. White, pr., 1870.
181p. NUC OCLC

3884. ROE, Elizabeth A. (Lyon)
[Am. b. 1805]
Recollections of frontier life.
Rockford, IL: Gazette pub. house,
1885. 295p. NUC K OCLC
[Reminiscences of a young girl
converted by the Baptists, later
a Methodist; life as farm wife &
mother in West.]

3885. ROGERS, Aurelia (Spencer)
[Am. 1834-1922]
Life sketches of Orson Spencer
and others; and history of
primary work.
Salt Lake City, UT: pr. by George
Q. Cannon & sons, 1898. 333p. NUC
K OCLC
[Mormon]

3886. ROGERS, Rev. Charles, ed.
see NAIRNE, Carolina (Oliphant),
Baroness

3887. ROGERS, Ellen M., Mrs. G.
Albert Rogers [Br. 19c]
A winter in Algeria, 1863-64.
L: S. Low, son & Marston, 1865.
372p. NUC BL OCLC

3888. ROGERS, Mrs. G. Albert see
ROGERS, Ellen M.

3889. ROGERS, Hester Ann (Roe)
[Br. 1756-1794]
A short account of the experience
of Mrs. Hester A. Rogers, written
by herself; also, spiritual
letters.

L: n.p., 1802. 60p. NUC BL MB
OCLC
[Methodist. Numerous later eds.]

3890. ROGERS, Mary Eliza [Br.
19c]
Domestic life in Palestine.
L: Bell & Daldy, 1861. 422p. NUC
BL OCLC

3891. ROGERS, Thomas, comp. see
ULYATT, Elizabeth Ann

3892. ROKEBY, Matthew Montagu,
Baron see MONTAGU, Elizabeth
(Robinson)

3893. ROLLESTON, Frances [Br.
1781-1864]
Letters of Miss Frances
Rolleston, of Keswick. Ed.
Caroline Dent.
L: Rivingtons, 1867. 642p. NUC BL

3894. ROLLINS, Alice Marland
(Wellington) [Am. 1847-1897]
From palm to glacier; with an
interlude; Brazil, Bermuda, and
Alaska.
NY & L: G. P. Putnam's sons,
1889. 145p. NUC

3895. ROMER, Isabella Frances
[Br. d. 1852] ALT: Hamilton, Mrs.
William Meadows
A pilgrimage to the temples and
tombs of Egypt, Nubia and
Palestine in 1845-6.
L: R. Bentley, 1846. 2v. NUC BL
OCLC

3896. -----The Rhone, the Darro,
and the Guadalquivir; a summer
ramble in 1842.
L: R. Bentley, 1843. 2v. NUC BL
OCLC

3897. RONDEAU, Mrs. William see
VIGOR, (Ward) Rondeau

3898. ROPER, Charlotte [Br. 19c]
Zigzag travels.
L: T. F. Unwin, 1895. 3v. BL
[Three year journey: N. America,
Far East, Middle East]

3899. ROPES, Hannah Anderson [Am.
19c] PSEUD: Lady, A
Six months in Kansas. By a lady.
Boston: J. P. Jewett & co.; NY:

Sheldon, Blakeman & co., 1856.
231p.   NUC OCLC
[Letters to her mother on
settlement in Kansas]

3900. ROSS, Catherine Colace [Br.
18c]
Memoirs or spiritual exercises of
Mistress Ross. Written with her
own hand.
Edinburgh: n.p., 1735. BL

3901. ROSS, Janet Ann (Duff
Gordon) [Br. 1842-1927]
Early days recalled.
L: Chapman & Hall, 1891. 203p.
NUC BL OCLC
[Includes travel: Egypt, Turkey]

3902. -----Italian sketches.
L: K. Paul, Trench & co., 1887.
268p. NUC BL OCLC

3903. -----The land of Manfred,
prince of Tarentum and king of
Sicily. Rambles in remote parts
of southern Italy, with special
reference to their historical
associations.
L: J. Murray, 1889. 365p. NUC BL
OCLC

3904. ROSS, Janet Ann (Duff
Gordon), ed. see GORDON, Lucie
(Austin) Duff

3905. ROSS, Janet Ann (Duff
Gordon), ed. see TAYLOR, Susannah
(Cook)

3906. ROSS, Mrs. Malcolm [Br. 19c]
Scattered seeds; or, five years'
zenana work in Poona.
Edinburgh & L: Blackwood & sons,
1880. 158p. BL

3907. ROSS, MARTIN, pseud. see
SOMERVILLE, Edith Anna Oenone

3908. ROSS, Mother see DAVIES,
Mrs. Christian Cavenaugh

3909. ROULET, Mary F. (Nixon)
[Am. d. 1930] ALT: Nixon, Mary F.
With a pessimist in Spain.
Chicago: A. F. McClurg & co.,
1897. 360p. NUC BL OCLC

3910. ROUNDELL, Mrs. Charles see
ROUNDELL, Julia Anne Elizabeth
(Tollemache)

3911. ROUNDELL, Julia Anne
Elizabeth (Tollemache), Mrs.
Charles Roundell [Br. 19/20c]
A visit to the Azores. With a
chapter on Madeira.
L: Bickers & son, 1889. 197p. NUC
BL OCLC

3912. ROUTH, Martha (Winter) [Br.
1743-1817]
Memoir of the life, travels and
religious experience of Martha
Routh. Written by herself, or
compiled from her own narrative.
York: W. Alexander & son, 1822.
317p. NUC BL MB MBD OCLC
[Includes visit to U.S.; Society
of Friends]

3913. ROVER, RUTH, pseud. see
BAILEY, Margaret Jewett (Smith)

3914. ROWE, Elizabeth Singer [Br.
1674-1737]
The miscellaneous works, in prose
and verse of Mrs. Elizabeth Rowe.
Pub. by her order by Theophilus
Rowe.
L: pr. for J. Buckland, G. Keith,
W. Nicholl, G. Pearch, and H.
Gardner, 1772. 2v. NUC BL OCLC
[Includes letters]

3915. ROWLANDSON, Mary (White)
[Br. c1635-1678]
The soveraignty and goodness of
God together, with the
faithfulness of his promises
displayed; being a narrative of
the captivity and restauration of
Mrs. Mary Rowlandson. Commended
by her, to all that desires to
know the Lords doings to, and
dealings with her. Especially to
her dear children; relations, the
second addition corrected and
amended. Written by her own hand
for her private use; now made
publick at the earnest desire of
some friends and for the benefit
of the afflicted.
Cambridge, MA: pr., Samuel Green,
1682. 73p. NUC BL OCLC
[Indian captive; many later
versions of her story]

3916. ROYALL, Anne (Newport) [Am.
1769-1854] PSEUD: A Traveller
The black book; or, a
continuation of travels in the
United States.

Washington, D.C.: pr. for the author, 1828-29. 3v. NUC OCLC

3917. -----Letters from Alabama on various subjects; to which is added, an appendix, containing remarks on sundry members of the twentieth and twenty-first Congress, and other high characters, etc. at the seat of government. In one volume. Washington, D.C.: n.p., 1830. 232p. NUC BL OCLC

3918. -----Mrs. Royall's Pennsylvania, or, travels continued in the United States. Washington, D.C.: the author, 1829. NUC

3919. -----Mrs. Royall's southern tour, or, second series of the black book. Washington, D.C.: n.p., 1830-31. NUC BL OCLC

3920. -----Sketches of history, life, and manners, in the United States. By a traveller. New Haven, CT: pr. for the author, 1826. 392p. NUC BL OCLC

3921. RUDD, Margaret Caroline [Br. 18c] PSEUD: Stewart, Margaret Caroline Facts: or, a plain and explicit narrative of the case of Mrs. Rudd. Published from her own manuscript... . L: T. Bell, 1775. 90p. NUC OCLC

3922. -----Mrs. Stewart's case, written by herself, and respectfully submitted to the enlightened part of the publick: including her letter to Lord Rawdon. L: pr. Stafford & Davenport for J. Kerby; & Scatcherd & Whitaker, 1788. 27p. NUC BL

3923. RUNCIE, Constance Owen (Faunt LeRoy) [Am. 1836-1911] Divinely led; or, Robert Owen's granddaughter. NY: James Pott, 1880. 36p. NUC K OCLC [Conversion]

3924. RUSKIN, John, ed. see ALEXANDER, Esther Frances

3925. RUSSELL, Caroline [Br. 19c] The English captive. Lincoln: Bradbury & Dent, 1823. 112p. BL [Capture by French privateer, prison in Holland; includes poems.]

3926. RUSSELL, Florence, Mrs. [Am. 19c] Child life in Oregon. A true story. Boston: Ira Bradley & co.; H. Hoyt, 1866. 193p. NUC BL OCLC [Life in Cape Hancock lighthouse]

3927. RUSSELL, Lucretia A. see HATHAWAY, Lucretia A. (Russell)

3928. RUSSELL, Rachel (Wriothesley) Vaughn, Baroness Russell [Br. 1636-1723] Letters of Lady Rachel Russell from the manuscript in the library at Woburn Abbey. [Ed. T. Sellwood, Mrs.] L: E. & C. Dilly, 1773. 216p. NUC BL

3929. -----Memoirs of Lady Russell and Lady Herbert [Anabel (Aston) 17c], 1623-1723, compiled from original family documents by Catherine (Pollok) Manners [Lady Stepney]. L: A. & C. Black, 1898. 244p. NUC BL

3930. -----Some account of the life of Rachel Wriothesley, Lady Russell. ... Followed by a series of letters ... to her husband from 1672 to 1682. To which are added eleven letters from Dorothy Sidney, Countess of Sutherland to George Saville, Marquis of Halifax in the year 1680. [Comp.] Mary Berry. L: Longman, Hurst, Rees, Orme, & Brown, 1818. 387p. NUC BL

3931. RUTHQUIST, Alexina (MacKay) Harrison, Mrs. Johan Ruthquist [Br. 1848-1892] ALT: MacKay, Alexina A. MacKay Ruthquist; or, singing the gospel among the Hindus and Gonds. Comp. Mrs. J. W. Harrison [Alexina (MacKay) Harrison]. L: Hodder & Stoughton, 1893. NUC BL [Letters from India included]

3932. RUTHQUIST, Mrs. Johan <u>see</u>
RUTHQUIST, Alexina (Mackay)

3933. RUTLAND, Janetta (Hughan)
Manners, Duchess of [Br. d. 1899]
ALT: Manners, Janetta (Hughan),
Duchess of Rutland
Impressions of a visit to Bad-
Hamburg, comprising a short
account of the women's
associations of Germany under the
Red Cross.
Edinburgh: W. Blackwood & sons,
1882. 84p. NUC BL

3934. RUTLEDGE, Catherine [Am. b.
1833]
Twenty-five years fighting fate,
or thrilling reminiscences of the
travels of Samuel W. Shockey,
with supplementary experiences of
Catherine Rutledge, by Samuel W.
Shockey.
Boston: the author, 1892. 201p.
NUC K OCLC
[Methodist, spiritual
autobiography]

3935. RYDER, Hon. Anne, co-author
<u>see</u> RYDER, Hon. Elizabeth

3936. RYDER, Edward, comp. <u>see</u>
FRY, Elizabeth (Gurney)

3937. RYDER, Hon. Elizabeth [Br.
18c]
Journal for the year 1792.
n.p.: priv. pr., 1792. 69p. BL
[Part of the Ryder family papers]

3938. -----Letters between the
Hon. Elizabeth Ryder and her
brothers, 1780-1791. Together
with letters respecting her last
days ... and recollections of her
written by her nieces. Also
letters from the Hon. Anne Ryder
... and other family letters.
n.p.: priv. pr., 1891. 63p. BL
[Part of the Ryder family
papers.]

3939. S-, Elizabeth <u>see</u> SMITH,
Elizabeth

3940. S., M. <u>see</u> SMITH, Mary

3941. S., M. E. <u>see</u> SIMPSON, Mary
Emily

3942. S., M. F. <u>see</u> SEYMOUR, Mary
Seamer

3943. SABIN, Elijah R., comp. <u>see</u>
CUTLER, Esther

3944. SACKVILLE, Constance Mary
Elizabeth (Cochrane-Baillie),
Countess <u>see</u> DE LA WARR,
Constance Mary Elizabeth
(Cochrane-Baillie) Sackville,
Countess

3945. SAGATOO, Mary A.
(Henderson) Cabay [Am. 19c]
Wah sash kah moqua; or, thirty-
three years among the Indians.
Boston: C. A. White co., 1897. K
OCLC
[Chippewas]

3946. SAGE, L. A., Mrs. [Br. 18c]
A letter addressed to a female
friend, by Mrs. Sage, the first
English female aerial traveller,
describing the general appearance
and effects of her expedition
with Mr. Lunardi's balloon, which
ascended from St. George's fields
on Wednesday, 29th June, 1785,
accompanied by George Biggin, Esq.
2d ed. L: J. Bell, 1785. 32p. NUC
BL

3947. ST. GEORGE, Melesina
(Chenevix) <u>see</u> TRENCH, Melesina
(Chenevix) St. George

3948. ST. MAWR, Mrs. Algernon <u>see</u>
SOMERSET, Susan Margaret
(McKinnon) St. Mawr, Duchess of

3949. SALE, Lady Florentia
(Wynch) [Br. 1790-1853]
A journal of the disasters in
Affghanistan, 1841-2.
L: J. Murray, 1843. 451p. NUC BL
MB OCLC

3950. SALM-SALM, Agnes Elizabeth
Winona LeClerq (Joy), Prinzessin
zu [Am. 1844?-1912] ALT: Salm-
Salm, Princess Felix

Ten years of my life, by the
Princess Felix Salm-Salm.
L: R. Bentley, 1876. 2v. NUC BL K
OCLC

3951. SALM-SALM, Princess Felix
see SALM-SALM, Agnes Elizabeth
Winona LeClerq (Joy), Prinzessin
zu

3952. SALTER, W., ed. see PARKER,
Adaline Rice

3953. SAMPSON, Deborah see
GANNETT, Deborah (Sampson)

3954. SANBORN, Helen Josephine
[Am. 1857-1917]
A winter in Central America and
Mexico.
Boston: Lee & Shepard; NY: C. T.
Dillingham, 1886. 321p. NUC BL
OCLC

3955. SANBORN, Kate see SANBORN,
Katherine Abbott

3956. SANBORN, Katherine Abbott
[Am. 1839-1917] ALT: Sanborn,
Kate
A truthful woman in southern
California.
NY: D. Appleton & co.; L: Sampson
Low, 1893. 192p. BL NUC OCLC

3957. SANDEMAN, Mrs. Glas see
SANDEMAN, Margaret (Stewart)

3958. SANDEMAN, Margaret
(Stewart), Mrs. Glas Sandeman
[Br. 1803-1883] ALT: Sandeman,
Mrs. Stewart
Memoir of Mrs. Stewart Sandeman,
of Bonskeid and Springland, by
her daughter [Margaret Frazer
Barbour].
L: Nisbet & co., 1883. 272p. NUC
BL
[Contains extensive quotes from
her letters and journals.]

3959. SANDEMAN, Mrs. Stewart see
SANDEMAN, Margaret (Stewart)

3960. SANDERS, Sue A. (Pike) [Am.
1842-1931]
A journey to, on and from the
"golden shore".
Delavan, IL: Times printing
office, 1887. 118p. NUC OCLC
[Travel: California]

3961. SANDES, Elise [Br. 19c]
Enlisted; or, my story. Incidents
of life and work among soldiers
... reprinted from "Forward,"
1894-96, and edited by ... M. T.
Schofield.
Cork: Office of "Forward", 1896.
224p. BL MB

3962. SANSAY, Leonora see HASSAL,
Mary

3963. SANSOM, Oliver, ed. see
VOKINS, Joan

3964. SARGENT, Angelina M. [Am.
19c]
Notes of travel and mementos of
friendship.
Rochester, NY: E. R. Andrews,
pr., 1894. 130p. NUC OCLC
[Travel: U.S.]

3965. SARMIENTO, F. L., comp. see
CUSHMAN, Pauline

3966. SATCHELL, Agnes F. [Br.
19c]
Reminiscences of missionary life
in the Caribbean Islands.
Loughborough: n.p., 1858. BL

3967. SATTER, W., ed. see PARKER,
Adaline Rice

3968. SAUNDERS, Ann [19c]
Narrative of the shipwreck and
sufferings of Miss Ann Saunders,
who was a passenger on board the
ship Francis Mary, which
foundered at sea on the 5th Feb.
1826 on her passage from New
Brunswick to Liverpool ...
Written by herself ... Annexed is
a solemn address of Miss
Saunders.
Providence, RI: pr. for Z. S.
Crossman, 1827. 38p. NUC BL OCLC

3969. SAVAGE, Sarah (Henry) [Br.
1664-1752]
Memoirs of the life and character
of Mrs. Sarah Savage. [Comp.] Sir
John Bickerton Williams. To which
are added memoirs of Mrs. Anne
Hulton [1668-1697] and Mrs.
Eleanor Radford [1667-1697], by
their brother, Matthew Henry.
Philadelphia: Presbyterian Board
of Publication, 1818. 360p. NUC

BL MBD OCLC
[Includes excerpts of Savage's
religious diary.]

3970. SAVORY, Martha see
YEARDLEY, Martha (Savory)

3971. SAWYER, Mrs. C. M., comp.
see SCOTT, Julia H. (Kinney)

3972. SAWYER, Caroline Mehitabel
(Fisher), comp. see SCOTT, Julia
H. (Kinney)

3973. SAXBY, Jessie Margaret
(Edmondston) [Br. 1842-1940]
Auld Lerwick. A personal
reminiscence.
Edinburgh: pr. for the Lerwick
Church Improvement Scheme Bazaar,
1894. 64p. BL

3974. -----Coaching tours (round
Edinburgh), or romance of the
road.
Edinburgh: J. & H. Lindsay, 1896.
NUC

3975. -----West-Nor'-west.
L: J. Nisbet, 1890. 154p. NUC BL
[Travel: Canada]

3976. SAXBY, Mary (Holloway) [Br.
19c]
Memoirs of a female vagrant,
written by herself.
Dunstable: n.p., 1806. 82p. NUC
BL

3977. SAXON, ISABELLE, pseud. see
SUTHERLAND, Mrs. (Redding)

3978. SCHILLIO, Jane Harriet [Br.
19c]
Journal of a tour from Bath to
the lakes of Westmoreland,
Cumberland, Lancashire, etc.
L: J. Horne, 1836. 79p. BL

3979. SCHIMMELMANN, Adeline,
Countess [Br. b. 1854]
Adeline countess Schimmelmann:
glimpses of my life at the German
court, among Baltic fisherman and
Berlin socialists and in prison.
Ed. W. Smith Foggitt.
L: Hodder & Staughton, 1896.
210p. NUC BL OCLC

3980. SCHIMMELPENNICK, Mary Anne
(Galton) [Br. 1778-1856]

Life of Mary Anne
Schimmelpennick. Ed. her
relation, Christiane C. Hankin.
L: Longman, Brown, Green,
Longmans & Roberts, 1858. 2v. NUC
BL MB OCLC
[Contains autobiography &
letters]

3981. SCHUYLER, Louisa L., comp.
see LANE, Caroline E. (Lamson)

3982. SCIDMORE, Eliza Ruhamah
[Am. 1856-1928]
Alaska, its southern coast and
the Sitkan archipelago.
Boston: D. Lothrop & co., [1885].
333p. NUC OCLC
[Travel: Alaska]

3983. -----Java, the garden of
the East.
NY: The Century co., 1897. 339p.
NUC OCLC
[Travel: Java]

3984. -----Jinrikisha days in
Japan.
NY: Harper & bros., 1891. 385p.
NUC OCLC
[Travel: Japan]

3985. -----Westward to the Far
East, a guide to the principal
cities of China and Japan ... .
Montreal: Canadian Pacific
Railway co., 1891. 51p. NUC OCLC

3986. SCOFIELD, Hannah [Am. 1795-
1820]
Memoirs of Miss Hannah Scofield,
of Stamford.
New Haven, CT: pr., Nathan
Whiting, 1820. 123p. NUC

3987. SCOTT, Alicia E., Lady [Br.
19c]
A lady's narrative.
L: Webster and Larkin, 1874.
303p. NUC BL MB
[Life in India]

3988. SCOTT, Amey, Mrs. [Am. 19c]
Memoirs of Mrs. Amey Scott:
written by herself.
Lowell, MA: n.p., 1840. NUC

3989. SCOTT, Anna (Kay) [Am.
1838-1923] PSEUD: Marston, Mrs.
Mildred
Korno Siga, the mountain chief;
or, life in Assam. By Mrs.
Mildred Marston.
Philadelphia & NY: The American
Sunday School Union, 1889. 209p.
NUC OCLC
[Missionary]

3990. SCOTT, Anna M. (Steele),
Mrs. H. R. Scott [Am. 19c]
Glimpses of life in Africa. By
Mrs. Anna M. Scott, missionary of
the Protestant Episcopal Church
at Cape Palmas, West Africa.
NY: American Tract Society,
[1857]. 64p. NUC OCLC
[Grebo tribe]

3991. -----Rome as it is: being
reminiscences of a visit to the
"city of the Caesars". By Mrs. H.
R. Scott.
Philadelphia: J. B. Lippincott &
co., 1874. 291p. NUC OCLC

3992. SCOTT, Dorothea see HOGBEN,
Dorothea (Scott) Gotherson

3993. SCOTT, Mrs. H. R. see
SCOTT, Anna M. (Steele)

3994. SCOTT, Julia H. (Kinney)
[Am. 1809-1842]
Memoir of Mrs. Julia H. Scott;
with her poems and selections
from her prose. [Ed.] Caroline
Mehitabel (Fisher) Sawyer.
Boston: A. Tompkins, 1853. 432p.
NUC BL OCLC

3995. SCOTT, LEADER, pseud. see
Baxter, Lucy E. (Barnes)

3996. SCROPE, Eliza see LEE,
Elizabeth (Scrope)

3997. SCUDAMORE, Rebecca
(Thornhill) [Br. 1729-1790]
Some particulars relating to the
life and death of Rebecca
Scudamore, interspersed with
interesting reflexions; together
with extracts from divers of her
letters; collected by Sarah
Young. Including an account of
her own case.
Bristol: S. Bonner, 1790. 67p.
NUC BL OCLC

3998. SCULL, G. D., comp. see
HOGBEN, Dorothea (Scott) Gotherson

3999. SEAMAN, Elizabeth
(Cochrane) see COCHRANE, Elizabeth

4000. SEAMER, Mrs. F. see
SEYMOUR, Mary Seamer

4001. SEARING, Annie Eliza
(Pidgeon) [Am. b. 1857]
The land of Rip Van Winkle: a
tour through the romantic parts
of the Catskills; its legends and
traditions.
NY & L: G. P. Putnam's sons,
1884. 147p. NUC BL OCLC

4002. SEARLE, Elizabeth [Br. 19c]
The pathway of providence; or,
recollections of my pilgrimage.
L: Bonmahon, 1855. BL
[Spiritual autobiography]

4003. SEARS, Angeline (Brooks)
[Am. 1817-1848]
Memoirs of Mrs. Angeline B.
Sears, with extracts from her
correspondence. Ed. Mrs. Melinda
Hamline.
Cincinnati, OH: Swormstedt &
Power for the Methodist Episcopal
Church, 1850. 294p. NUC OCLC

4004. SEBRIGHT, Georgina Mary
Muir (Mackenzie), Lady, co-author
see IRBY, Adeline Paulina

4005. SEDGWICK, Catherine Maria
[Am. 1769-1867]
Letters from abroad to kindred at
home.
NY: Harper & bros.; L: Edward
Moxon, 1841. 2v. NUC BL K OCLC
[Travel: Belgium, Germany, Italy,
Switzerland]

4006. -----Life and letters of
Catherine M. Sedgwick. Ed. Mary
Elizabeth Dewey.
NY: Harper & bros., 1871. 446p.
NUC OCLC

4007. SEEBOHM, Benjamin, co-
author see SEEBOHM, Esther
(Wheeler)

4008. SEEBOHM, Mrs. Benjamin see
SEEBOHM, Esther (Wheeler)

4009. SEEBOHM, Esther (Wheeler), Mrs. Benjamin Seebohm [Br. 1798-1864]
Private memories of Benjamin and Esther Seebohm. Ed. their sons.
L: Provost, 1873. 443p. BL MB OCLC
[Members of Society of Friends; travel in Germany]

4010. SEELY, Catharine see SEELY, Catherine

4011. SEELY, Catherine [Am. 1799-1838] ALT: Seely, Catharine
Memoir of Catherine Seely, late of Darien, Conn.
NY: Collins, bros. & co., 1843. 140p. NUC OCLC
[Includes poetry]

4012. -----Memoirs of Catherine Seely, and Deborah S. Roberts [Am. 1802-1838].
2d ed. NY: D. Goodwin, 1844. 252p. NUC MAD OCLC
[Members of Society of Friends; religious journals]

4013. SELLWOOD, T., (Mrs.), ed. see RUSSELL, Rachel (Wriothesley) Vaughn, Baroness Russell

4014. SELWYN, Elizabeth, Mrs. [Br. 19c]
Continuation of journals in the years 1824, 25, 27, 28, 29.
Kensington: pr., W. Birch, 1830. 194p. NUC BL OCLC

4015. ---Journal of excursions through the most interesting parts of England, Wales, and Scotland ... 1819,1820,1821,1822 AND 1823.
L: pr., Plummer & Brewis, 1824?. 256p. NUC BL MBD OCLC

4016. SEMPLE, Emily Virginia [Am. b. 1829]
Reminiscences of my early life and relatives.
Montgomery, AL: Brown printing co., 1893?. 20p. NUC

4017. SENIOR, Mary Charlotte Mair see SIMPSON, Mary Charlotte Mair (Senior)

4018. SETON, Elizabeth Anne, Mother [Am. 1774-1821]
Memoir, letters and journal of Elizabeth Seton; convert to the Catholic faith, and Sister of Charity. Ed. Robert Seton.
NY: P. O'Shea, 1869. 2v. NUC BL OCLC

4019. SETON, Robert, ed. see SETON, Elizabeth Anne

4020. SEWALL, Georgiana [Am. 19c]
The Dutch East Indies; a narrative of a voyage to the Pacific and Indian Ocean.
Chicago: Kendall co., 1893. 67p. NUC

4021. SEWARD, Anna [Br. 1747-1809]
Letters (1782-1807). Ed. A. Constable.
Edinburgh: A. Constable & co., 1811. 6v. NUC BL OCLC

4022. SEWARD, Olive Risley [Am. d. 1908]
Around the world stories.
Boston: D. Lothrop co., 1889. 346p. NUC OCLC
[Voyage around the world by two young American girls: China, Java, India, Abyssinia, France, & England.]

4023. SEWELL, Elizabeth Missing [Br. 1815-1906]
Impressions of Rome, Florence, and Turin.
L: Longman, Green, Longman, & Roberts, 1862. 330p. NUC BL OCLC

4024. -----A journal kept during a summer tour for the children of a village school.
NY: D. Appleton & co., 1852. 3v. in 1. NUC BL OCLC
[Travel: Germany, Switzerland, Great Britain]

4025. SEWELL, Mary (Wright) [Br. 1797-1884]
The life and letters of Mrs. Sewell. By Mrs. [Mary] Bayly.
3d ed. L: J. Nisbet, 1899. 336p. NUC BL MB
[Member of Society of Friends; includes autobiography.]

4026. SEXTON, Lydia (Casad) Cox Moore [Am. 1799-1892?]
Autobiography of Lydia Sexton: ... over seventy-two years, from 1799 to 1872: ... as child, wife, mother, and widow, as minister of the gospel, as prison chaplain ... .
Dayton, OH: United Brethren pub. house, 1885. 655p. NUC K OCLC

4027. SEYMOUR, Frances (Thynne), Duchess of Somerset see SOMERSET, Frances (Thynne) Seymour, Duchess of

4028. SEYMOUR, Juno (Waller) [Am. 1790-1883]
Life of Maumer Juno of Charleston, S. C. A sketch of Juno (Waller) Seymour. [Comp.] Julia Taylor Hard and Ellen Ann Whilden.
Atlanta, GA: Foote & Davies, pr., 1892. 41p. NUC OCLC
[Slave; includes accounts of her conversations.]

4029. SEYMOUR, Mary Seamer [Br. 19c] ALT: S., M. F.; Seamer, Mrs. F.
My golden days. By M. F. S.
3d ser. L: R. Washbourne, 1872. BL
[Stories of her own childhood told for her daughter.]

4030. SHACKLETON, Elizabeth (Carleton), Mrs. Richard Shackleton [Br. 1726-1804]
Memoirs and letters of Richard and Elizabeth Shackleton, late of Ballitore, Ireland; compiled by their daughter, Mary Leadbeater.
L: Harvey & Darton, 1822. 221p. NUC BL OCLC

4031. SHACKLETON, Richard, co-author see SHACKLETON, Elizabeth (Carleton)

4032. SHACKLETON, Mrs. Richard see SHACKLETON, Elizabeth (Carleton)

4033. SHAFTOE, Frances [Br. 18c]
Mrs. Frances Shaftoe's narrative, containing an account of her being in Sir Theophilus Oglethorpe's family; where

hearing many treasonable things, and among others, that the pretended Prince of Wales was Sir Theophilus's son, she was tricked into France by Sir Theophilus's daughter and barbarously us'd to make her turn Papist and nun, in order to prevent a discovery; but at last made her escape to Swisserland, and from thence arriv'd in England in December, 1706.
L: n.p., 1707. 31p.; L: pr., H. Hills, 1708. 24p. NUC BL MB OCLC

4034. SHAIRP, John Campbell, ed. see WORDSWORTH, Dorothy

4035. SHARP, Abigail (Gardner) [Am. b. 1843]
History of the Spirit Lake massacre: 8th March, 1857, and of Miss Abigail Gardner's three month's captivity among the Indians according to her own account, as given to L. P. Lee.
New Britain, CT: L. P. Lee, pub., 1857. 47p. NUC OCLC

4036. SHARPE, Charles Kirkpatrick, ed. see MAXWELL, Lady Margaret (Cuninghame) Hamilton

4037. SHAW, Annie DeWitt [Am. 19c]
Will, Annie, and I, travellers in many lands.
NY: L. A. Skinner, 1898. 363p. NUC

4038. SHAW, Ellen Prestage (Havergal) [Br. 1823-1886]
Outlines of a gentle life. A memorial sketch of Ellen P. Shaw. Ed. her sister, Maria Vernon Graham Havergal.
L: J. Nisbet & co.; NY: A. D. F. Randolph & co., 1887. 183p. NUC BL
[Includes extracts from her letters.]

4039. SHAW, Marion [Br. 18c]
Elijah's mantle; or, the memoirs and spiritual exercises of Marion Shaw, ... written by her own hand. Whereunto is annexed a brief account of the latter part of the life ... of the author.
Glasgow: n.p., 1765. BL

4040. SHEIL, Mary Leonora
(Woulfe), Lady [Br. 19c]
Glimpses of life and manners in
Persia. By Lady Sheil. With notes
on Russia, Koords, Toorkomans,
Nestorians, Khiva and Persia.
L: J. Murray, 1856. 402p. NUC BL
OCLC

4041. SHELDON, Ann [Br. 18c] ALT:
Archer, Ann (Sheldon)
Authentic and interesting memoirs
of Miss Ann Sheldon; (now Mrs.
Archer:) A lady who figured,
during several years, in the
highest line of public life and
in whose history will be found,
all the vicissitudes, which so
constantly attend on women of her
description. Written by herself.
L: The authoress, 1787. 4v. NUC
BL MB

4042. SHELDON, Electa Maria
(Bronson) [Am. 1817-1902]
Childhood memories of life in
Detroit.
n.p.: n.p., [1896]. 12p.

4043. SHELDON, Grace Carew [Am.
1855-1921]
As we saw it in '90.
Buffalo, NY: The Woman's
Exchange, 1890. 248p. NUC BL OCLC
[Travel: Europe. Letters &
descriptions.]

4044. -----From Pluckemin to
Paris, by the way of Touraine,
the Midi, Provence, the Rhone and
eastern France.
Buffalo, NY: the author, 1898.
399p. NUC BL

4045. SHELDON, Louise (Vescelius)
[Am. 19c]
Yankee girls in Zulu land.
NY: Worthington co., 1888. 287p.
NUC BL OCLC
[Travel: South Africa. Also pub.
as: "Yankee girls in Oom Paul's
land"]

4046. SHELDON, Mary (French) [Am.
1847-1936]
Adventures in East Africa; or,
Sultan to Sultan. By M. French-
Sheldon.
Boston: Arena; Dana Estes; L:
Saxon & co., 1892. 435p. NUC BL
OCLC

[Also pub. as: "Sultan to Sultan.
Adventures among the Masai and
other tribes of East Africa"]

4047. SHELLEY, Harriet
(Westbrook) [Br. 1795-1816]
Harriet Shelley's letters to
Catherine Nugent.
L: priv. pr., 1889. 64p. NUC BL
OCLC

4048. SHELLEY, Mary
Wollstonecraft (Godwin), Mrs.
Percy Bysshe Shelley [Br. 1797-
1851]
History of a six weeks's tour
through a part of France,
Switzerland, Germany and Holland.
With Percy Bysshe Shelley.
L: T. Hookham & C. & J. Ollier,
1817. 183p. NUC BL MBD OCLC

4049. -----Life and letters of
Mary Wollstonecraft Shelley. Ed.
Mrs. Julian Marshall [Florence A.
(Thomas) Marshall].
L: R. Bentley & son, 1889. 2v.
NUC BL OCLC PD
[Diary covers 1814-1840.]

4050. -----Rambles in Germany and
Italy in 1840, 1842 and 1843.
L: E. Moxon, 1844. 2v. NUC BL
OCLC

4051. SHELLEY, Mrs. Percy Bysshe
see SHELLEY, Mary Wollstonecraft
(Godwin)

4052. SHELLEY, Percy Bysshe, co-
author see SHELLEY, Mary
Wollstonecraft (Godwin)

4053. SHELTON, Ada Stewart [Am.
19/20c]
Song of the Indian River.
Buffalo, NY: Matthew-Northrup
co., 1890. 12p. NUC OCLC
[Travel: Indian River, Florida.
Description in verse.]

4054. SHEPARD, Isabel Sharpe [Am.
b. 1861]
The cruise of the U. S. Steamer
"Rush" in Behring Sea, summer of
1889.
San Francisco: Bancroft co.,
1889. 257p. NUC OCLC
[Travel: Aleutian Islands]

4055. SHEPHERD, Margaret Lisle
[Am. b. 1859] ALT: Sister
Magdalene Adelaide
My life in the convent.
10th ed. Columbus, OH: n.p.,
1892. 408p. NUC OCLC
[Note in NUC: A fraud unmasked;
the career of Mrs. Margaret L.
Shepherd ... see under Brady, M.
J. Anti-Catholicism, U. S.]

4056. SHEPHERD, Maria [Br. 19c]
Leaves from a journal of prison
visits, torn out and tied
together.
L: n.p., 1857. BL
[May contain autobiographical
material.]

4057. SHERIDAN, Frances
(Chamberlaine), Mrs. Thomas
Sheridan [Br. 1724-1766]
Memoirs of the life and writings
of Mrs. F. Sheridan ... and
selections from the works of Mrs.
Sheridan, by her grand-daughter,
[Miss] Alicia Lefanu.
L: G. & W. B. Whittaker, 1824.
435p. NUC BL

4058. SHERIDAN, Mrs. Thomas see
SHERIDAN, Frances (Chamberlaine)

4059. SHERIFF, Miriam [Br. 1794-
1821]
The care of divine providence and
the comforts of true religion; as
exhibited in a narrative and
extracts from the journal of
Miriam Sheriff ... written by
herself.
5th ed. L: n.p., 1835. BL
[Spiritual autobiography;
servant]

4060. SHERWOOD, Henry, co-author
see SHERWOOD, Mary Martha (Butt)

4061. SHERWOOD, Mrs. Henry see
SHERWOOD, Mary Martha (Butt)

4062. SHERWOOD, Mrs. John see
SHERWOOD, Mary Elizabeth (Wilson)

4063. SHERWOOD, Mary Elizabeth
(Wilson), Mrs. John Sherwood [Am.
1830-1903]
An epistle to posterity, being
rambling recollections of many
years of my life.

NY: Harper & bros., 1897. 380p.
NUC K OCLC
[Mormon]

4064. -----Here and there and
everywhere; reminiscences.
Chicago: Herbert S. Stone & co.,
1898. 301p. NUC K OCLC
[Europe]

4065. SHERWOOD, Mary Martha
(Butt), Mrs. Henry Sherwood [Br.
1775-1851] ALT: Butt, Mary Martha
The life of Mrs. Sherwood,
chiefly autobiographical; with
extracts from Mr. [Henry]
Sherwood's journal. ... Ed. her
daughter, Sophia (Sherwood)
Kelly.
L: Darton & co., 1854. 600p. NUC
BL MB OCLC

4066. SHINDLER, Mrs. Mary Dana
see SHINDLER, Mary Stanley Bunce
(Palmer) Dana

4067. SHINDLER, Mary Stanley
Bunce (Palmer) Dana [Am. 1810-
1883] ALT: Shindler, Mrs. Mary
Dana; Dana, Mary S. B.
Letters to relatives and friends
in reply to arguments in support
of the doctrine of the Trinity.
Boston: J. Munroe, 1845. 318p.
NUC BL OCLC

4068. SHIPLEY, Mary Elizabeth
[Br. b. 1842]
Looking back; a memory of two
lives.
NY: Dutton & co., 1879. NUC BL MB

4069. SHIRREFF, Emily Anne Eliza
[Br. 1814-1897]
Memorials of Emily A. E.
Shirreff, with a sketch of her
life. By Maria Georgina
(Shirreff) Grey, Mrs. William
Grey.
L: n.p., 1897?. 83p. NUC BL

4070. SHIRREFF, Mary (Russel),
Mrs. William Shirreff [Br. 1784-
1860]
The hidden life. A memoir of Mary
Shirreff, wife of the Rev.
William Shirreff. Compiled
chiefly from her papers by W.
Fawcett.

Edinburgh: A. Elliot, 1868. 211p.
BL
[Chiefly religious; includes diary.]

4071. SHIRREFF, Mrs. William <u>see</u>
SHIRREFF, Mary (Russel)

4072. SHOCKLEY, Samuel W., co-author <u>see</u> RUTLEDGE, Catherine

4073. SHORE, Arabella <u>see</u> SHORE,
Margaret Emily

4074. SHORE, Emily, comp. <u>see</u>
SHORE, Margaret Emily

4075. SHORE, Louisa Catherine,
comp. <u>see</u> SHORE, Margaret Emily

4076. SHORE, Margaret Emily [Br.
1819-1839] ALT: Shore, Emily
Journal of Emily Shore. [Comp.]
her sisters, Louisa Catherine and
Arabella.
L: K. Paul, Trench, Trübner &
co., 1891. 373p. NUC BL MBD OCLC
PMD
[Selection from her journal which
begins when the writer was 11,
and ends in 1839.]

4077. SHUCK, Henrietta (Hall)
[Am. 1817-1844] ALT: Hall,
Henrietta
An American woman in China, and
her missionary work there. Comp.
J. B. Jeter.
Boston: n.p., 1874. BL
[Includes extracts from letters.]

4078. -----Scenes in China; or,
sketches of the country,
religion, and customs of the
Chinese.
Philadelphia: American Baptist
pub. soc., 1852. 252p. NUC BL
OCLC

4079. SHUTTLEWORTH, Henry Cary,
ed. <u>see</u> ELLERSLIE, Alma

4080. SIDDON, Mrs. [Br. 19c]
Mrs. Catherine Galindo's letter
to Mrs. Siddon, being a
circumstantial detail of Mrs.
Siddon's life for the last seven
years: with several of her
letters.
L: pr. for authoress, 1809. 80p.
NUC BL

4081. SIDDONS, Leonora [Am. 19c]
The female warrior; an
interesting narrative of the
sufferings and singular and
surprising adventures of Miss
Leonora Siddons, who, ... joined
the Texian Army under General
Houston.
NY: E. E. & G. Barclay, 1843.
23p. NUC K OCLC
[On captivity by Indians; OCLC
says fictional.]

4082. SIDNEY, MARGARET, pseud.
<u>see</u> LOTHROP, Harriet Mulford

4083. SIGOURNEY, Lydia Howard
(Huntley) [Br. 1791-1865] ALT:
Huntley, Lydia Howard
Letters to my pupils: with
narrative and biographical
sketches.
NY: R. Carter & bros., 1851.
341p. NUC BL OCLC
[Includes letters, essays,
sketches, childhood
autobiography, and poems.]

4084. -----Letters of life.
NY: D. Appleton & co., 1866.
414p. NUC BL K OCLC

4085. -----Pleasant memories of
pleasant lands.
Boston & Cambridge, MA: J. Munroe
& co., 1842. 368p. NUC BL OCLC
[Travel: Great Britain]

4086. -----Scenes in my native
land.
Boston: J. Munroe & co., 1845.
319p. NUC BL OCLC
[Prose and verse: Atlantic states]

4087. SIGOURNEY, Lydia Howard
(Huntley), comp. <u>see</u> HAMMOND,
Phebe Parsons

4088. SIGOURNEY, Lydia Howard
(Huntley), ed. <u>see</u> HYDE, Nancy
Maria

4089. SIKES, Olive (Logan) Logan
<u>see</u> LOGAN, Olive (Logan)

4090. SIMON, Lady Rachel [Br. b.
1824]
Records and reflections; selected
from her writings during half a
century.

L: Wertheimer, Lea & co., 1894.
130p. NUC BL MB

4091. SIMPSON, Elspeth <u>see</u>
BUCHAN, Elspeth (Simpson)

4092. SIMPSON, M., Mrs. [Br.
1787-1829]
Extracts from the diary of Mrs.
Simpson.
Glasgow: n.p., 1832. MBD
[Religious diary 1805-1821]

4093. SIMPSON, Mary Charlotte
Mair (Senior) [Br. 19c] ALT:
Senior, Mary Charlotte Mair
Many memories of many people.
L: Edward Arnold, 1898. 334p. NUC
BL MB OCLC

4094. SIMPSON, Mary Emily [Br.
19c] ALT: S., M. E. PSEUD:
Clergyman's daughter, A
Gleanings. Being a sequel to
"Ploughing and sowing." By a
Clergyman's daughter. Ed. F. D.
Legard.
L: J. & C. Mozley, 1876. BL
[Personal account of running a
village school; includes letters]

4095. -----Ploughing and sowing;
or, annals of an evening school
in a Yorkshire village and the
work that grew out of it. From
letters and private notes. By A
Clergyman's daughter. Ed. F. D.
Legard.
L: J. & C. Mozley, 1861. 267p. BL

4096. SINCLAIR, Mrs. [19c] PSEUD:
Lady "Felon", A
Letters from Donegal in 1886. By
a lady "Felon". Ed. Colonel
Maurice.
L & NY: Macmillan & co., 1886.
75p. NUC
[English maltreatment of Irish
landowners, the potato famine,
the Parnellites, etc.]

4097. SINCLAIR, Catherine [Br.
1800-1864]
Hill and valley, or hours in
England and Wales.
Edinburgh: William Whyte & co.;
NY: R. Carter, 1838. 454p. NUC BL
OCLC

4098. -----Scotland and the
Scotch; or, the western circuit.

Edinburgh: William Whyte & co.,
1840. 348p.; NY: D. Appleton &
co., 1840. 346p. NUC BL OCLC
[Also pub as: Sketches and
stories of ...]

4099. -----Sketches and stories
of Wales and the Welsh.
L: n.p., 1850. 409p. NUC BL

4100. SINCLAIR, Olivia [Br. 19c]
Across to Africa and back by
Spain.
Wick: John O'Groat Journal
office, 1874. 35p. BL

4101. -----From Cannes to
Constantinople and what we saw by
the way.
Wick: John O'Groat Journal
office, 1875. 27p. BL

4102. -----Impressions of Cairo,
Jerusalem and Damascus.
Wick: John O'Groat Journal
office, 1876. 24p. BL

4103. SKENE, Felicia Mary Frances
[Br. 1821-1899]
Wayfaring sketches among the
Greeks and the Turks and on the
shores of the Danube, by a seven
years' resident in Greece.
L: Chapman & Hill, 1847. 343p.
NUC BL OCLC

4104. SKINNER, Thomas H., comp.
<u>see</u> ANON.

4105. SLEEMAN, Lucy, co-author
<u>see</u> BLENNERHASSETT, Rose

4106. SLEEPER, Sarah, comp. <u>see</u>
SMITH, Martha Hazeltine

4107. SLOCUM, Phebe B. [Am. 19c]
Witnessing; a concise account of
a marvelous event with its happy
results.
Brattleboro, VT: E. L. Hildreth,
1899. 99p. NUC K OCLC
[Member of Society of Friends.]

4108. SMALLEY, Mrs. B. H., comp.
<u>see</u> BARLOW, Debbie

4109. SMALLEY, Julia C. (Marvin),
comp. <u>see</u> BARLOW, Debbie

4110. SMART, A., comp. <u>see</u>
ANDREW, Jane

4111. SMART, Mrs. Daniel, co-
author <u>see</u> ANDREW, Jane

4112. SMART, Jane, Mrs. [Br. 18c]
A letter from a lady at Madrass
to her friends in London: giving
an account of a visit, made by
the Governor of that place, with
his lady and other, to the Nabob
... and his lady ... with some
account of the manners and
customs of the Moors in general.
L: n.p., 1743. 8p. NUC BL

4113. SMITH, Abigail (Adams) [Am.
1765-1813] ALT: Adams, Abigail
Journal and correspondence of
Miss Adams, daughter of John
Adams, second president of the
United States. Written in France
and England 1785. Ed. her
daughter, [Caroline Abigail [ALT:
Amelia] Adams de Windt].
NY & L: Wiley & Putnam, 1841,42.
2v. NUC BL MAD OCLC
[Travel diary, 1784-1787]

4114. SMITH, Agnes <u>see</u> LEWIS,
Agnes (Smith)

4115. SMITH, Amanda (Berry) [Am.
1837-1914]
An autobiography; the story of
the Lord's dealings with Mrs.
Amanda Smith, the colored
evangelist.
Chicago: Meyer & bros.; Christian
Witness co., 1893. 506p. NUC BL
K OCLC
[Methodist; travels in
northeastern U. S., Great
Britain, India and Africa. Born
in slavery.]

4116. SMITH, Ann [Br. b. 1798]
A brief sketch of the life of Ann
Smith.
Ipswich: E. Hunt, 1826?. 36p. BL
[Autobiography: appeal for
financial aid]

4117. SMITH, Ann Eliza
(Brainerd), Mrs. J. Gregory Smith
[Am. 1818-1905]
Notes of travel in Mexico and
California.
St. Albans, VT: Messenger &
Advertiser office, 1886. 123p.
NUC OCLC

4118. SMITH, Anna C. [Am. b.
1825]
The orphan blind girl.
Baltimore, MD: J. W. Bond & co.,
1865. 166p. NUC OCLC
[Correspondence, reminiscences,
etc. of a blind musician.]

4119. SMITH, Charles Eastlake,
ed. <u>see</u> EASTLAKE, Elizabeth
(Rigby) Lady

4120. SMITH, Eliza, Mrs. [Br.
19c]
Memoir of Eliza Smith, who was
transported for shoplifting,
written by herself, with some
introductory remarks by [Mary
John Knott].
Dublin: n.p., 1839. 6p. BL
[Repentance tract and
autobiography]

4121. SMITH, Eliza <u>see</u>
RICHARDSON, Eliza (Smith)

4122. SMITH, Elizabeth [Br. 1776-
1806] ALT: S-, Elizabeth
Fragments in prose and verse. By
a young lady lately deceased. Ed.
Henrietta Maria Bowdler.
L: Richard Cruttwell; Dublin:
Graisberry & Campbell for W.
Watson, 1808. 232p. NUC BL OCLC
[Includes letters]

4123. SMITH, Elizabeth A. [Am.
19c]
A wanderer's journal.
NY: priv. pr., 1889. 107p. NUC
OCLC
[Travel: Atlantic states and
Washington, D.C.]

4124. SMITH, Elizabeth (Grant)
[Br. 1797-1885] ALT: Grant,
Elizabeth
Memoirs of a Highland lady. The
autobiography of Elizabeth Grant
of Rothiemurchus, afterwards Mrs.
Smith of Baltiboys, 1797-1830.
Ed. Jane Maria (Grant) Strachey,
Lady.
Edinburgh: R. & R. Clark, 1897.
484p.; L: John Murray, 1898.
425p. NUC BL OCLC
[Written for her children]

4125. SMITH, Emily Tennyson
(Bradley), ed. <u>see</u> STUART, Lady
Arabella

4126. SMITH, Ethan, ed. <u>see</u>
BAILEY, Abigail (Abbot)

4127. SMITH, Georgina [Br. 19c]
Among the high and lowly. Two
letters.
L: London Missionary Society,
1899. 31p. BL
[On experiences as missionary in
Peking]

4128. SMITH, Grace, Mrs. [Am.
18c]
The dying mother's legacy. On the
good and heavenly counsel of that
eminent and pious matron, Mrs.
Grace Smith, taken from her own
mouth a little before her death,
by the minister of that town
where she died.
Boston: Timothy Green, 1712. 12p.
NUC
[Includes poems]

4129. SMITH, Hannah Logan
(Fisher) [Am. 1777-1846]
Miscellanies.
Philadelphia: n.p., 1839. 326p.
NUC OCLC
[Member of Society of Friends;
includes accounts of visits from
European friends.]

4130. -----Sketches of the life
of Hannah Logan Smith.
Philadelphia: n.p., 1847. NUC

4131. SMITH, Hannah (Whiteall),
comp. <u>see</u> WHITALL, Ann

4132. SMITH, Hannah Whitall, ed.
<u>see</u> WHITALL, Alice B.

4133. SMITH, Henry, comp. <u>see</u>
MOULDING, Sarah

4134. SMITH, Mrs. J. Gregory <u>see</u>
SMITH, Ann Eliza (Brainerd)

4135. SMITH, Jennie [Am. 1842-
1924]
From Baca to Beulah.
Philadelphia: Garriques bros.,
1880. 358p. NUC OCLC

4136. -----Ramblings in Beulah
land. A continuation of
experiences in the life of Jennie
Smith.

Philadelphia: Garriques bros.,
1886-88. 2v. NUC OCLC

4137. -----Valley of Baca: a
record of suffering and triumph.
Cincinnati, OH: Hitchcock &
Walden, 1876. 288p. NUC OCLC
[Autobiographical accounts of her
evangelism]

4138. SMITH, Julia A. (Norcross)
Crafts [Am. 19c]
The reason why; or spiritual
experiences of Mrs. Julia Crafts
Smith, physician, assisted by her
spirit guides.
Boston: the author, 1881. 187p.
NUC K OCLC

4139. SMITH, Lydia Adeline
(Jackson) Button [Am. 19c]
Behind the scenes; or, life in an
insane asylum.
Chicago: pr. by Culver, Page,
Hoyne, c1879. 257p. NUC K OCLC

4140. SMITH, Maria Frances
(Dickson) <u>see</u> DICKSON, Maria
Frances

4141. SMITH, Martha [Am. 1787-
1841]
Letters of Martha Smith, with a
short memoir of her life,
prepared and published by a few
of her particular friends.
NY: Piercy & Reed, pr., 1844.
230p. NUC

4142. SMITH, Martha Hazeltine
[Am. 1808-1841]
Memoir of the late Martha
Hazeltine Smith. [Comp.] Sarah
Sleeper.
Boston: Joseph Smith, 1843. 294p.
NUC BL OCLC
[Includes letters; New Hampshire
Female Seminary]

4143. SMITH, Mary [Am. 1858-1879]
The diary and letters of Mary
Smith.
L: W. Wileman, 1879?. 104p. NUC

4144. SMITH, Mary [Br. 1822-1889]
ALT: S., M.
The autobiography of Mary Smith,
schoolmistress and non-
conformist. A fragment of a life.

With letters from Jane Welsh and
Thomas Carlyle.
L: Bemrose & sons, 1892. 2v. NUC
BL OCLC
[Vol. 2 contains her poems]

4145. SMITH, Mary Ann (Clarke),
comp. see CLARKE, Mary (Cooke)

4146. SMITH, Mary Ann Pellew [Br.
19c] PSEUD: English Lady, An
Six years' travel in Russia, by
an English lady.
L: Hurst & Blackett, 1859. 2v.
NUC BL OCLC

4147. SMITH, Mary Ettie V.
(Coray) [Am. b. 1829]
Fifteen years among the Mormons:
being the narrative of Mrs. M. E.
V. Smith ... a sister of one of
the Mormon high priests ... .
NY: C. Scribner; H. Dayton, 1858.
388p. NUC BL K OCLC
[First person narrative but
authorship is claimed by Nelson
Winch Green in NUC.]

4148. SMITH, Mary Stuart (White),
comp. see WHITE, Mary Abiah
(Dodge)

4149. SMITH, Mrs. Richard, comp.
see CLARKE, Mary (Cooke)

4150. SMITH, Sophia, Mrs. [Br.
1795-1824]
Letters written by Sophia Smith,
during her last illness.
L: J. S. Hughes, 1825. 71p. BL
[Primarily religious]

4151. SMITH, Susan E. D. [Am. b.
1817]
The soldier's friend; being a
thrilling narrative of Grandma
Smith's four years' experience
and observation, as a matron, in
the hospitals of the South,
during the late disastrous
conflict in America.
Memphis, TN: Bulletin pub. co.,
1867. 300p. NUC C K OCLC

4152. SMITH, Susette Harriet
(Lloyd) [Br. 19c] ALT: Lloyd,
Susette Harriet
Sketches of Bermuda. Pub. as:
Susette Harriet Lloyd
L: J. Cochrane & co., 1835. 258p.

BL OCLC
[Sights, people she met, etc. in
letters home.]

4153. SMITH, Susette Harriet
(Lloyd), comp. see Thompson,
Elizabeth Maria (Lloyd)

4154. SMOLLETT, Tobias, co-author
see VANE, Frances Anne,
Viscountess

4155. SMYTH, Agnes, Mrs. Edward
Smyth [Br. d. 1783]
The Christian's triumph over sin,
the devil, and the grave,
exemplified in the life, death
and spiritual experience of that
chosen vessel, Mrs. Agnes Smyth.
L: pr. for ed. by Frys &
Couchman. Sold by Mr. Atlay,
1783. 269p. NUC BL

4156. -----An extract of the
life, death and spiritual
experience of Mrs. A. Smyth
(Written by herself).
L: pr. for Rev. Edward Smyth,
1790. NUC BL
[Bound with next entry.]

4157. -----The religion of the
heart, delineated in a series of
letters written by ... A. Smyth.
L: pr. for the Rev. Edward Smyth,
1783. NUC BL

4158. SMYTH, Ann see CARSON, Ann
(Baker)

4159. SMYTH, Mrs. Edward see
SMYTH, Agnes

4160. SMYTH, Rev. Edward, ed. see
DAVIDSON, Margaret

4161. SMYTH, Florida (Watts) [Am.
19/20c]
The varied grace of nature's
face.
St. Lóuis, MO: E. E. Carreras,
pr., 1895. 119p. NUC OCLC
[Travel: Europe. In verse.]

4162. SMYTH, Georgiana Theophila
[Br. 19c]
Memorial of a beloved son;
containing extracts from a
mother's diary ... also, a few of
his own letters, journal.
Bristol: priv. pr., 1841. BL

4163. SMYTH, Mrs. Richard <u>see</u> CARSON, Ann (Baker)

4164. SMYTHE, Emily Anne (Beaufort) <u>see</u> STRANGFORD, Emily Anne (Beaufort) Smythe, Viscountess

4165. SMYTHE, Sarah Maria (Bland), Mrs. William James Smythe [Br. 19c]
Ten months in the Fiji Islands. Ed. William James Smythe.
Oxford: J. H. & J. Parker, 1864. 282p. NUC MB OCLC

4166. SMYTHE, William James, ed. <u>see</u> SMYTHE, Sarah Maria (Bland)

4167. SMYTHE, Mrs. William James <u>see</u> SMYTHE, Sarah Maria (Bland)

4168. SNEDEKER, Florence Watters [Am. 19c]
A family canoe trip.
NY: Harper, 1892. 137p. NUC OCLC
[Travel: N.Y. State, Lakes George and Champlain]

4169. SNELL, Hannah [Br. 1723-1792]
The female soldier; or, the surprising life and adventures of Hannah Snell ... who took upon herself the name of James Gray; and being deserted by her husband, put on mens apparel, and travelled to Coventry in quest of him, where she enlisted in Col. Guise's regiment of foot ... .
L: R. Walker, 1750. 187p. NUC BL MB OCLC
[Served in India and at Carlisle during Scottish rebellion.]

4170. SNELL, Mina Sloane, Miss [Am. b. 1841]
Essays, short stories and poems ... including a short sketch of the author's life.
Chatham: Banner steam pr., 1881. 162p. NUC BL
[May contain personal material]

4171. SOJOURNER, TRUTH <u>see</u> TRUTH, Sojourner

4172. SOLDENE, Emily [Br. 1844?-1912]

My theatrical and musical recollections.
L: Downey & co., 1897. 315p. NUC BL K MB OCLC
[Includes tour of U. S.]

4173. SOLTERA, MARIE, pseud. <u>see</u> LESTER, Mary

4174. SOMERSET, Charlotte Sophie (Leveson Gower), Duchess of Beaufort <u>see</u> BEAUFORT, Charlotte Sophie (Leveson Gower) Somerset, Duchess of

4175. SOMERSET, Frances (Thynne) Seymour, Duchess of [Br. 1699-1754] ALT: Hertford, Frances, Countess of; Seymour, Frances (Thynne), Duchess of Somerset
Correspondence between Frances, Countess of Hartford (afterwards Duchess of Somerset) and Henrietta Louisa, Countess of Pomfret, between the years 1738 and 1741. Ed. W. Bingley.
L: pr., I. Gold for Richard Phillips, 1805. 3v. NUC BL

4176. SOMERSET, Helen [Br. 19c]
Adventures of Mrs. Colonel Somerset in Caffraria, during the war.
L: J. F. Hope, 1858. 309p. NUC BL

4177. SOMERSET, Susan Margaret (McKinnon) St. Mawr, Duchess of [Br. 19/20c] ALT: St. Mawr, Mrs. Algernon
Impressions of a tenderfoot during a journey in search of sport in the far West.
L: J. Murray, 1890. 279p. NUC BL MC OCLC
[Travel: Canada]

4178. SOMERVILLE, Edith Anna Oenone [Br. 1858-1949] PSEUD: Ross, Martin [with her cousin Violet Florence Martin; Br. 1862-1915]
Beggars on horseback. A riding tour in North Wales.
L & Edinburgh: W. Blackwood & sons, 1895. 186p. NUC BL OCLC

4179. -----In the vine country. By Martin Ross. [Somerville and Martin]

L: W. H. Allen & co., 1893. 237p.
NUC BL OCLC
[Travel: France]

4180. -----Through Connemara in a
governess cart. By Martin Ross.
[Somerville and Martin]
L: W. H. Allen & co., 1893. 200p.
NUC BL OCLC

4181. SOMERVILLE, Martha, ed. <u>see</u>
SOMERVILLE, Mary (Fairfax)

4182. SOMERVILLE, Mary (Fairfax)
[Br. 1780-1872]
Personal recollections, from
early life to old age, of Mary
Somerville. With selections from
her correspondence. Ed. her
daughter, Martha Somerville.
L: J. Murray, 1873. 377p. NUC BL
MB OCLC

4183. SONO, Tel, Miss [Am. 19c]
Tel Sono, the Japanese reformer;
an autobiography.
NY: Hunt & Eaton, 1890. 66p. NUC
OCLC

4184. SOPER, Grace [Br. 1766-
1830]
Reminiscences of past
experiences. By the late Mrs. G.
Soper. Ed. one of her sons.
L: Darton & Clark, 1839. 204p.
NUC BL MB
[Letters, 1821-22 on her
conversion from Methodism to
Anglicanism]

4185. SOUTH, Eudora Lindsay, Mrs.
[Am. 19c] ALT: Eudora
Wayside notes and fireside
thoughts. By Eudora.
St. Louis, MO: J. Burns' pub.
co., 1884. 562p. NUC OCLC
[Travel: Europe]

4186. SOUTHALL, Eliza (Allen)
[Br. 1823-1851]
Portions of the diary, letters
and other remains of Eliza
Southall. Selected by William
Southall.
Birmingham: priv. pr. by White &
Pike, 1855. 141p. NUC BL MBD OCLC
[Member of Society of Friends;
includes poems]

4187. SOUTHALL, William, ed. <u>see</u>
SOUTHALL, Eliza (Allen)

4188. SOUTHERN LADY, A [Am. 19c]
Behind the scenes; or, southern
morals during the war, by a
southern lady.
NY: n.p., 1866.

4189. SOUTHEY, Caroline Anne
(Bowles), Mrs. Robert Southey
[Br. 1786-1854] ALT: Bowles,
Caroline
The correspondence of Robert
Southey with Caroline Bowles. Ed.
Edward Dowden.
Dublin: Hodges, Figgis & co.,
1881. 388p. NUC BL OCLC

4190. SOUTHEY, Robert, co-author
<u>see</u> SOUTHEY, Caroline Anne
(Bowles)

4191. SOUTHEY, Mrs. Robert <u>see</u>
SOUTHEY, Caroline Anne (Bowles)

4192. SOUTHWELL, Mary Elizabeth,
Baroness de Clifford [Br. 19c]
A short journal of a tour, made
through part of France,
Switzerland and the banks of the
Rhine, to Spa, Antwerp, Ghent, etc.
Richmond, Surrey: pr., F. H.
Wall, c1871. 134p. BL

4193. SOUTHWICK, Mary (Frank)
[Am. b. 1846]
History of the phantom lady, a
remarkable woman. Written by
herself.
NY: New York popular pub. co.,
c1881. 14p. NUC
[Autobiographical account of
woman who at age 35 weighed 50
pounds.]

4194. SOUTHWICK, Sarah H. [Am. b.
1821]
Reminiscences of early anti-
slavery days.
Cambridge, MA: priv. pr. at the
Riverside press, 1893. 39p. NUC
BL K OCLC

4195. SPAETH, Maria Dorothea
(Duncan) [Am. 1844-1878]
Maria Dorothea Duncan Spaeth.
Born in Edinburgh, Scotland,
February 12, 1844. Died in
Philadelphia, Penn'a, December
21, 1878. From her letters and
diaries.
Philadelphia: pr. for priv.
circ., 1879. 227p. NUC OCLC

4196. SPAULDING, E. A., Mrs. [Am. b. 1811]
Bric-a-brac: fugitive pieces.
Boston: pr. for author, 1886. 128p. NUC OCLC
[Includes autobiography, poems and essays.]

4197. SPEARE, Chloe, Mrs. [Am. 19c]
Memoir of Mrs. Chloe Speare, a native of Africa who was enslaved in childhood and died in Boston, Jan. 3, 1815. By a lady of Boston.
Boston: J. Louny, 1832. NUC

4198. SPEDDING, James, ed. see BACON, Anne (Coke)

4199. SPEEDY, Cornelia Mary, Mrs. [Br. 19c]
My wanderings in the Soudan.
L: R. Bentley, 1884. 2v. NUC BL OCLC

4200. SPEID, Mrs. John B. [Br. 19c]
Our last years in India.
L: Smith, Elder & co., 1862. 331p. NUC BL MB OCLC

4201. SPENCE, Elizabeth Isabella [Br. 1768-1832]
Letters from the north Highlands during the summer, 1816.
L: Longman, Hurst, Rees, Orme & Brown, 1817. 364p. NUC BL OCLC
[Travel diary & letters to Miss Porter]

4202. -----Sketches of the present manners, customs, and scenery of Scotland.
L: pr. for Longman, Hurst, Rees, Orme & Brown, 1811. 2v. NUC BL OCLC
[Letters to the Countess Winterton.]

4203. -----Summer excursions through parts of Oxfordshire, Gloucestershire, Warwickshire, Staffordshire, Herefordshire, Derbyshire, and South Wales.
L: Longman, Hurst, Rees, & Orme, 1809. 2v. NUC BL

4204. SPENCE, Mary see KELLY, Mary (Spence)

4205. SPENCER, Alla (Hubbard) [Am. 1860-1889]
A souvenir: posthumous writings of Alla Hubbard Spencer.
NY: J. B. Alden, 1890. 120p. NUC OCLC
[Includes poetry]

4206. SPENCER, Mrs. Canning [Br. 19c]
Early and late recollections.
L: n.p., 1853. BL
[Reminiscences, 65 p. of poems]

4207. SPENCER, Mrs. S. see WOODS, Catherine (Kendall)

4208. SPURGEON, Susanna (Thompson) [Br. 1832-1903]
Ten years of my life in the service of the book fund: being a grateful record of my experience of the Lord's ways, and work, and wages.
L: Passmore & Alabaster, 1886. 431p. NUC BL OCLC

4209. SQUIER, Mrs. Frank Leslie see LESLIE, Miriam Florence (Folline) Squier

4210. SQUIER, Louise Smith [Am. 19c]
Sketches of southern scenes.
NY: J. W. Pratt & son, 1885. 203p. NUC OCLC
[Travel: Virginia]

4211. SQUIER, Miriam F. see LESLIE, Miriam Florence (Folline) Squier

4212. SQUIRRELL, Elizabeth see SQUIRRELL, Mary Elizabeth

4213. SQUIRRELL, Mary Elizabeth [Br. b. 1838] ALT: Squirrell, Elizabeth
The autobiography of Elizabeth Squirrell of Shottishaur and selections from her writings.
L: Simpkin, Marshall, & co., 1858. 300p. NUC BL MB
[Deaf and blind woman.]

4214. STACY, Sarah Elizabeth [Br. 19c]
Memoir.
Norwich: n.p., 1849. MB
[Girlhood; religious life]

4215. STAFFORD, Millicent, Marchioness of see SUTHERLAND, Millicent Fanny (St. Clair Erskine) Sutherland Leveson Gower, Duchess of

4216. STANHOPE, Lady Hester Lucy [Br. 1776-1839]
Memoirs ... as related by herself in conversation with her physician [Charles Louis Meryon]. L: H. Colburn, 1845. 3v. NUC BL MB OCLC
[Levant]

4217. -----Travels of Lady Hester Stanhope, forming the completion of her memoirs narrated by her physician [Charles Louis Meryon]. L: H. Colburn, 1846. 3v. NUC BL MB
[Asia]

4218. STANLEY, Arthur Penrhyn, ed. see STANLEY, Catherine

4219. STANLEY, Catherine, Mrs. Edward Stanley [Br. 1791-1861]
Memoirs of Edward and Catherine Stanley. Ed. Arthur Penrhyn Stanley. L: John Murray, 1879. 337p. BL MBD OCLC
[Contains extracts of her letters and journal. Incl. life of Mary Stanley, 1813-1879]

4220. STANLEY, Edward, co-author see STANLEY, Catherine

4221. STANLEY, Mrs. Edward see STANLEY, Catherine

4222. STANLEY, Lura A. [Am. 1842-1870]
Memoir of Lura A. Stanley, or waiting at the golden gate. [Comp.] Mary Hawkins. Dayton, OH: Christian pub. ass'n., 1873. 125p. NUC OCLC
[Memoir written by her sister, includes quotations, letters, and journals.]

4223. STANLEY, Maria Josepha (Holroyd), Baroness Stanley of Alderley [Br. 1771-1863]
The early married life of Maria Josepha, Lady Stanley. Ed. Jane Henrietta Adeane.

L & NY: Longmans, Green & co., 1899. 461p. NUC BL MB OCLC
[Correspondence]

4224. -----The girlhood of Maria Josepha Holroyd, Lady Stanley of Alderley. Recorded in letters of a hundred years ago, from 1776 to 1796. Ed. Jane Henrietta Adeane. L & NY: Longmans, Green & co., 1896. 420p. NUC BL OCLC

4225. STANLEY, Mary see STANLEY, Catherine

4226. STANNARD, M. [Br. 19c]
Memoirs of a professional lady nurse. L: Simpkin, Marshall & co., 1873. 239p. NUC BL MB
[Includes travel to Canada]

4227. STANSFIELD, S., ed. see FOLLOWS, Ruth

4228. STANTON, Elizabeth (Cady) [Am. 1815-1902]
Eighty years and more, 1815-1897. Reminiscences of E. C. Stanton. NY: European pub. co.; L: T. F. Unwin, 1898. 474p. NUC BL OCLC

4229. STARKE, Mariana [Br. 1762?-1838]
Letters from Italy between the years 1792 and 1798, containing a view of the revolutions in that country from the capture of Nice by the French Republic to the expulsion of Pius VI from the ecclesiastical state. L: R. Phillips, 1800. 2v. NUC BL OCLC

4230. -----Travels in Europe between the years 1824 and 1828 ... comprising an historical account of Sicily, etc. L: John Murray, 1828. 615p. NUC BL OCLC

4231. -----Travels on the Continent: written for the use and particular information of travellers. L: John Murray, 1820. 545p. NUC BL OCLC

4232. STATHAM, John, comp. see STATHAM, Louisa Maria

4233. STATHAM, Louisa Maria [Br. 19c]
Memoir of L. M. Statham ... including extracts from her diary and correspondence ... . [Comp.] John Statham.
L: n.p., 1842. BL MB

4234. STAVER, Mary Wiley [Am. 19c]
Fifty years after; a schoolgirl abroad fifty years ago.
Bethlehem, PA: Moravian pub. concern, 1899. 222p. NUC OCLC

4235. STEADMAN, Mary (Moders) see CARLETON, Mary (Moders)

4236. STEARNS, Elizabeth Prescott [Am. 19c]
Autobiography ... with a brief sketch of Dr. Benjamin Franklin and Col. William Prescott.
Boston: n.p., 1887. 39p. NUC

4237. STEBBINS, Emma, ed. see CUSHMAN, Charlotte Saunders

4238. STEELE, Eliza R., Mrs. [Am. 19c]
A summer journey in the West.
NY: J. S. Taylor, 1841. 278p. NUC BL OCLC
[Travel: U.S.: NY state, Great Lakes, Ill. River, down Mississippi to Ohio River, up the Ohio and across Pennsylvania and Maryland.]

4239. STEELE, Elizabeth [Br. 18c]
The memoirs of Mrs. Sophia Baddeley, late of the Drury Lane Theatre.
L: pr. for the author at the Literary Press, Clerkenwall, 1787. 6v. NUC BL MB
[Experiences as companion to Baddeley. Also attr. to Alexander Bicknall.]

4240. STENHOUSE, Fanny, Mrs. T. B. H. Stenhouse [Br. b. 1829]
Exposé of polygamy in Utah. A lady's life among the Mormons. A record of personal experience as one of the wives of a Mormon elder during more than twenty years.
NY: Am. News co., 1872. 221p. NUC BL OCLC

4241. -----"Tell it all:" the story of a life's experience in Mormonism. An autobiography.
Hartford, CT: A. D. Worthington, 1874. 623p. NUC BL K MB OCLC
[Expanded ed. of above; also pub. as: "An English woman in Utah"]

4242. STENHOUSE, Mrs. T. B. H. see STENHOUSE, Fanny

4243. STEPHENS, Ellen, Mrs. [Am. 19c]
The cabin boy wife, or, singular and surprising adventures ... .
NY: C. E. Daniels, 1840. 24p. NUC BL K OCLC
[Surprising adventures of Almira Paul, p.13-23.]

4244. STEPHENSON, Eliza (Tabor) [Br. b. 1835] ALT: Tabor, Eliza
Diary of a novelist.
L: Hurst & Blackett, 1871. 317p. NUC BL
[Aug. 10, 1869-Aug. 3, 1870; personal reflections.]

4245. STEPHENSON, Sarah [Br. 1738-1802]
Memoirs of the life, and travels in the service of the gospel, of Sarah Stephenson.
Philadelphia: Kimber, Conrad & co.; L: Joseph Gurney Bevan, 1807. 233p. NUC BL MB OCLC
[Society of Friends]

4246. STEPNEY, Catherine (Pollok) Manners, Lady, ed. see RUSSELL, Rachel Wriothesley Vaughan, Baroness Russell

4247. STERNDALE, Mary, Mrs. [Br. 19c] ALT: Stockdale, Mary R.
Vignettes of Derbyshire. Description of places and character sketches of Duchess of Devonshire, Countess of Besborough and Miss Seward.
L: G & W. B. Whittaker, 1824. 135p. BL

4248. STEVENS, Maria, Mrs. [Br. 19c]
Letters to various friends. Ed. her sister.
L: Thomas Ditton, 1842. BL
[Chiefly religious]

4249. STEVENS, Mrs. Mark [Am. 19c]
Six months at the World's Fair.
Detroit, MI: Detroit Free Press
pr. co., 1875. 382p. OCLC
[World's Columbian Exposition:
Chicago, 1893]

4250. STEVENSON, Mrs. A. Scott-
see STEVENSON, Esmé Gwendoline
(Grogan) Scott-

4251. STEVENSON, Mary Esmé
Gwendoline (Grogan) Scott-, Mrs.
A. Scott-Stevenson [Br. 19c]
On summer seas.
L: Chapman & Hall, 1883. 408p.
NUC BL OCLC
[Mediterranean, Agean, Aionian,
Adriatic, Euxine, and a voyage
down the Danube.]

4252. -----Our home in Cyprus.
2d ed. L: Chapman & Hall, 1880.
332p. NUC BL MB OCLC

4253. -----Our ride through Asia
Minor.
L: Chapman & Hall, 1881. 400p.
NUC BL OCLC

4254. STEVENSON, Sara (Yorke)
[Am. 1847-1921]
Maximilian in Mexico. A woman's
reminiscences of the French
intervention 1862-1867.
NY: The Century co., 1899. 327p.
NUC BL OCLC

4255. STEWART, Christina Brooks
[Br. 19c]
The loiterer in Argyllshire; or,
a ramble during the summer of
1845.
Edinburgh: J. Johnstone, 1848.
143p. BL OCLC

4256. STEWART, Ellen (Brown) [Am.
19c]
Life of Mrs. Ellen Stewart,
together with biographical
sketches of other individuals.
Also, a discussion with two
clergymen, and arguments in favor
of women's rights, together with
letters on different subjects.
Written by herself.
Akron, OH: Beebe & Elkins, 1858.
243p. NUC OCLC

4257. STEWART, Eliza (Daniel)

[Am. 1816-1908] ALT: Stewart,
Mother
Memories of the crusade ... a
thrilling account of the great
uprising of the women of Ohio in
1873, against the liquor crime.
By Mother Stewart, the leader.
Columbus, OH: Wm. G. Hubbard,
1888. 535p. NUC K OCLC

4258. STEWART, Lady Jane
(Douglas) see DOUGLAS, Lady Jane

4259. STEWART, Frances Anne Emily
(Vane-Tempest) Vane, Marchioness
of Londonderry see LONDONDERRY,
Frances Anne Emily (Vane-Tempest)
Vane, Marchioness of

4260. STEWART, MARGARET CAROLINE,
pseud. see RUDD, Margaret
Caroline

4261. STEWART, Mother see
STEWART, Eliza (Daniel)

4262. STICKNEY, Sarah see ELLIS,
Sarah (Stickney)

4263. STIRLING-MAXWELL, Caroline
Elizabeth Sarah (Sherridan)
Norton, Lady see NORTON, Caroline
Elizabeth Sarah (Sherridan)

4264. STIRREDGE, Elizabeth [Br.
1634-1706]
The life and Christian testimony
of ... E. S. ... written by her
own hand.
Philadelphia: W. & T. Evans, The
Friends Library, 1837. BL MB

4265. -----Strength in weakness
manifest: in the life, various
trials, and Christian testimony
... of E. S. ... written by her
own hand.
L: n.p., 1711. 206p. NUC BL MB
OCLC
[Society of Friends]

4266. STISTED, Clotilda
Elizabeth, Mrs. Henry Stisted
[Br. 19c]
Letters from the bye-ways of
Italy.
L: J. Murray, 1845. 496p. NUC BL
OCLC

4267. STISTED, Mrs. Henry see
STISTED, Clotilda Elizabeth

4268. STOBBS, S. S., ed. <u>see</u>
EDKINS, Jane Rowbotham (Stobbs)

4269. STOCKDALE, Mary R. <u>see</u>
STERNDALE, Mary, Mrs.

4270. STONE, Letitia Willgoss
[Br. 19c] PSEUD: A., E. S.
The world in which I live, and my
place in it. By E. S. A. Ed. John
H. Broome.
L: Wertheim & Macintosh, 1856.
782p. BL

4271. STONE, Mary Amelia (Boomer)
[Am. b. 1823]
A summer in Scandinavia.
NY: A. D. F. Randolph & co.,
c1885. 204p. NUC OCLC

4272. STONE, Olivia M. [19c]
Norway in June.
L & NY: Marcus Ward, 1882. 448p.
NUC BL OCLC

4273. -----Tenerife and its six
satellites; or, the Canary
Islands past and present.
L: M. Ward & co., 1887. 2v. NUC
BL OCLC

4274. STONE, Timothy Dwight
Porter, ed. <u>see</u> WEBSTER, Rebecca
Gair (Russell)

4275. STONEBREAKER, Julia
(Peaslee) [Am. b. 1833]
Twice a pioneer ... . [Written
by] Charles Ransley Green.
Lyndon, KS: n.p., 1897. 12p. NUC
K OCLC
[Based on her own account; life
in Iowa and Kansas.]

4276. STONES, Elizabeth, Mrs.
William Stones [Br. 19c]
A memoir of ... E. Stones, wife
of W. Stones, ... compiled from
her diary and correspondence. By
her husband [William Stones].
L: n.p., 1825. BL
[Methodist]

4277. STONES, Robert, comp. <u>see</u>
CAMPBELL, Isabella

4278. STONES, William, comp. <u>see</u>
STONES, Elizabeth

4279. STONES, Mrs. William <u>see</u>
STONES, Elizabeth

4280. STORY, Agnes (Beaumont)
[Br. d. 1720] ALT: Beaumont, Agnes
Real religion: exemplified in the
singular experience and great
sufferings of Mrs. A. Beaumont
... as written by herself.
L: Hutton & son, 1801. 24p. BL
[Previously pub. with other
accounts of religious
persecution; events occurred in
1674.]

4281. STOTHARD, Anna Eliza
(Kempe) <u>see</u> BRAY, Anna Eliza
(Kempe) Stothard

4282. STOTHARD, Charles Alfred,
co-author <u>see</u> BRAY, Anna Eliza
(Kempe) Stothard

4283. STOTHARD, Mrs. Charles
Alfred <u>see</u> BRAY, Anna Eliza
(Kempe) Stothard

4284. STOTT, Grace (Ciggie) [Br.
19c]
Twenty-six years of missionary
work in China.
L: Hodder & Stoughton, 1897.
366p. NUC BL OCLC

4285. STOWE, Charles Edward,
comp. <u>see</u> STOWE, Harriet
Elizabeth (Beecher)

4286. STOWE, Harriet Elizabeth
(Beecher) [Am. 1811-1896]
A brief sketch of the life of
Harriet Beecher Stowe. By her
sister [Isabella (Beecher)
Hooker].
Hartford, CT: Plimpton Press,
1896. 16p. NUC OCLC

4287. -----Life and letters. Ed.
Annie (Adams) Fields.
Boston & NY: Houghton, Mifflin &
co., 1897. 406p. NUC BL OCLC

4288. -----Life of Harriet
Beecher Stowe, compiled from her
letters and journals by her son,
Charles Edward Stowe.
Boston & NY: Houghton, Mifflin &
co., 1889. 530p. NUC BL OCLC

4289. -----Palmetto leaves.
Boston: J. R. Osgood & co., 1873.
321p. NUC BL OCLC
[Florida]

4290. -----Sunny memories of foreign lands.
Boston: Phillips, Sampson, 1854. 2v. NUC BL OCLC
[Travel: Europe; several 1854 eds.]

4291. STRACHEY, Jane Maria (Grant), Lady, ed. see SMITH, Elizabeth (Grant)

4292. STRAHAN, Lisbeth Gooch (Séguin) [Br. d. 1890]
The Black Forest. Its people and legends.
L: Strahan co., 1878. 428p. NUC BL OCLC

4293. -----The country of the passion-play; the highlands and highlanders of Bavaria.
L: Strahan & co., c1880?. 361p. NUC BL OCLC

4294. -----A picturesque tour in picturesque lands.
L: Strahan & co., 1881. 312p. NUC BL OCLC
[Travel: European continent]

4295. -----Rural England. Loiterings along the lanes, the common-sides, and the meadow-paths, with peeps into the halls, farms and cottages.
L: Strahan & co., 1884. 280p. NUC BL OCLC

4296. STRANGFORD, Emily Anne (Beaufort) Smythe, Viscountess [Br. 1826-1887] ALT: Beaufort, Emily Anne; Smythe, Emily Anne (Beaufort)
The eastern shores of the Adriatic in 1863, with a visit to Montenegro with Viscount Strangford.
L: R. Bentley, 1864. 386p. NUC BL OCLC

4297. -----Egyptian sepulchres and Syrian shrines ... stay at Lebanon, Palmyra and in Turkey.
L: Longman, Green, Longman & Roberts, 1861. 2v. NUC BL OCLC

4298. STRANGFORD, Viscount, co-author see STRANGFORD, Emily Anne (Beaufort) Smythe, Viscountess

4299. STRATHMORE, Mary Eleanor Bowes Lyon, Countess of [Br. 1749-1800]
The confessions of the Countess of Strathmore; written by herself. Carefully copied from the original lodged in Doctor's Commons.
L: W. Locke, 1793. 100p. NUC BL MB OCLC
[From her deposition in divorce case.]

4300. STRAUB, Maria [Am. 19c]
The story of starved rock; or, the last of the Illinoisans.
Chicago: Straub & co., 1890. 23p. NUC
[Account of an excursion to Starved Rock in 1882, with sketch of its history.]

4301. STREET, Elizabeth Mansfield (Rutty) [Am. d. 1887]
A memorial of two lives: Owen Street [1816-1887] and Elizabeth Mansfield (Rutty) Street. By Elizabeth Mansfield (Street) Dickerman.
Amherst, MA: pr., J. E. Williams, 1888. 168p. NUC
[May contain personal material]

4302. STREET, Mary Evarts (Anderson) see ANDERSON, Mary Eleanor (Roberts)

4303. STREET, Owen, co-author see STREET, Elizabeth Mansfield (Rutty)

4304. STRICKLAND, Catherine Parr see TRAILL, Catherine Parr (Strickland)

4305. STRICKLAND, Susannah see MOODIE, Susannah (Strickland)

4306. STRONG, Helen P. [Am. 19c]
Chautauqua impressions.
NY: Photo engraving co., 1890. 31p. NUC
[Account of two weeks experience at Chautauqua summer school.]

4307. STRUTT, Elizabeth [Br. 19c]
Domestic residence in Switzerland.
L: T. C. Newby, 1842. 2v. NUC BL

4308. -----Six weeks on the Loire.
L: W. Simpkin & R. Marshall,
1833. 408p. NUC BL OCLC

4309. -----A spinster's tour in
France, the states of Genoa, &c.
during the year 1827.
L: Longmans & co., 1828. 427p. BL
OCLC

4310. STUART, Rev. A. Moody,
comp. see GORDON, Elizabeth
(Brodie) Gordon, Duchess of

4311. STUART, Lady Arabella [Br.
1575-1615]
The life and letters of Lady
Arabella Stuart. By Elizabeth
Cooper.
L: Hurst & Blackett, 1866. 2v.
NUC BL OCLC

4312. -----Life of Lady Arabella
Stuart. In two parts: containing
a biographical memoir, and a
collection of her letters, with
notes and documents from original
sources relating to her history.
Ed. Emily Tennyson (Bradley)
Smith.
L: R. Bentley & son, 1889. 2v.
NUC BL OCLC

4313. STUART, Lady Louisa [Br.
1757-1851]
Gleanings from an old portfolio
containing some correspondence
between Lady Louisa Stuart and
her sister, Caroline [(Stuart)
Dawson], Countess of
Portarlengton [d. 1813], and
other friends and relatives. Ed.
Alice Georgina Caroline (Strong)
Clark, Mrs. Godfrey Clark.
Edinburgh: priv. pr. for D.
Douglas, 1895-1898. 3v. NUC BL
OCLC

4314. -----Lady Louisa Stuart.
Selections from her manuscripts.
Ed. Hon. James Archibald Home.
Edinburgh: D. Douglas, 1894.
308p.; NY: Harper & bros., 1894.
310p. NUC BL OCLC

4315. STUART, Sophia Margaret
Juliana [Br. 19c]
Stuartiana; or, bubbles blown by
and to some of the family of
Stuart. [Comp. William Stuart]

Menabilly?: priv. pr. Jonathan
Rushleigh, 1857. NUC BL
[Includes her anecdotes.]

4316. STUART, William, comp. see
STUART, Sophia Margaret Juliana

4317. STUART-WORTLEY, Lady
Emmeline Charlotte Elizabeth
(Manners) [Br. 1806-1855] ALT:
Wortley, Lady Emmeline Charlotte
Elizabeth (Manners) Stuart
Impressions of Italy and other
poems.
L: Saunders, 1837. NUC BL

4318. -----The sweet South,
travel.
L: pr. for priv. circ. by G.
Barclay, 1856. 2v. NUC

4319. -----Travelling sketches in
rhyme.
L: n.p., 1835. 116p. NUC BL

4320. -----Travels in the United
States, etc., during 1849 and
1850.
L: R. Bentley, 1851. 3v.; L: T.
Bosworth, 1853. 450p. NUC BL N
OCLC

4321. -----A visit to Portugal
and Madeira.
L: Chapman and Hall, 1854. 483p.
NUC BL

4322. STURDY, Alice Bragg, comp.
see BENTON, Rhoda Angeline

4323. STURGE, Matilda, comp. see
HUNT, Ann

4324. STURGES, Mrs. Jonathan see
STURGES, Mary Pemberton (Cady)

4325. STURGES, Mary Pemberton
(Cady), Mrs. Jonathan Sturges
[Am. 1806-1894]
Reminiscences of a long life.
NY: F. E. Parrish & co., 1894.
245p. NUC K OCLC

4326. STURT, Anne (Barnard) [Br.
1793-1872]
Reminiscences of our mother.
L: pr. by Unwin bros. for priv.
circ., 1873. 284p. NUC BL OCLC
[Includes poetry, stories,
religious writings]

4327. SUFFOLK, Henrietta (Hobart) Howard, Countess of [Br. 1688?-1767] ALT: Berkeley, Mrs. George; Howard, Henrietta (Hobart), Countess of Suffolk
Letters to and from Henrietta, Countess of Suffolk and her second husband, the Hon. George Berkeley. From 1712 to 1767. Ed. John Wilson Croker.
L: J. Murray, 1824. 2v. NUC BL OCLC

4328. SULLIVAN, Margaret Frances (Buchanan), co-author see BLAKE, Mary Elizabeth (McGrath)

4329. SUMBEL, Leah (Davies) Wells see SUMBEL, Mary (Davies) Wells

4330. SUMBEL, Mary (Davies) Wells [Br. 1781-1826] ALT: Sumbel, Leah (Davies); Wells, Leah (Davies); Wells, Mary (Davies)
Memoirs of the life of Mrs. Sumbel, late Wells; of the Theatres-Royal ... written by herself including her correspondence with Major Topham, Mr. Reynolds, etc.
L: C. Chapple, 1811. 3v. NUC BL MB OCLC

4331. SUMMERS, Samuel, ed. see BARFIELD, Mary

4332. SUMNER, Rev. George Henry, ed. see SUMNER, Mary Elizabeth (Heywood)

4333. SUMNER, Mrs. George Henry see SUMNER, Mary Elizabeth (Heywood)

4334. SUMNER, Mary Elizabeth (Heywood), Mrs. George Henry Sumner [Br. 1828-1921]
Our holiday in the East. Ed. Rev. George Henry Sumner.
L: Hurst & Blackett, 1881. 342p. NUC BL OCLC
[Egypt, Lebanon, Palestine, Syria]

4335. SUNDAY SCHOOL TEACHER, A, comp. see BROWN, Sarah

4336. SUNSHINE, SILVIA, pseud. see BROOKS, Abbie M.

4337. SUTCLIFFE, Joseph, ed. see PAWSON, Frances (Mortimer)

4338. SUTHERLAND, Dorothy Sidney, Countess of see RUSSELL, Rachel (Wriothesley) Vaughn, Baroness Russell

4339. SUTHERLAND, Harriet Elizabeth Georgiana Leveson Gower, Duchess of [Br. 1806-1868] ALT: Gower, Harriet Elizabeth Georgiana Leveson, Duchess of Sutherland
Stafford house letters. Ed. Lord Ronald [Charles Sutherland Leveson] Gower.
n.p.: Trench, Trübner & co., 1891. 250p. NUC BL

4340. SUTHERLAND, Mrs. (Redding) [19c] PSEUD: Saxon, Isabelle
Five years within the golden gate. By Isabelle Saxon.
L: Chapman & Hall, 1868. 315p. NUC BL OCLC
[Includes California, Nevada, & Hawaiian Islands]

4341. SUTHERLAND, Millicent Fanny (St. Clair Erskine) Sutherland Leveson Gower, Duchess of [Br. b. 1867] ALT: Gower, Millicent Fanny (St. Clair Erskine) Sutherland Leveson, Duchess of Sutherland; Stafford, Millicent, Marchioness of
How I spent my twentieth year, being a short record of a tour round the world, 1886-87, by the Marchioness of Stafford.
Edinburgh & L: Wm. Blackwood & sons, 1889. 289p. NUC BL OCLC

4342. SWEAT, Margaret Jane (Murray) [Am. b. 1823]
A fortnight in St. Petersburg.
NY: n.p., 1899. 64p. NUC OCLC

4343. -----Highways of travel; or, a summer in Europe.
Boston: Walker, Wise & co., 1859. 364p. NUC OCLC

4344. SWEET BRIAR, pseud. see BASKIN, Mary

4345. SWINTON, Captain E., co-author see SWINTON, Jane

4346. SWINTON, Mrs. E. see SWINTON, Jane

4347. SWINTON, Jane, Mrs. E.
Swinton [Br. 19c]
Journal of a voyage with Coolie
emigrants, from Calcutta to
Trinidad ... . By Captain and
Mrs. Swinton. Ed. James Carlile.
L: Alfred W. Bennett, 1859. 16p.
BL

4348. SWISSHELM, Jane Grey
(Cannon) [Am. 1815-1884]
Half a century.
Chicago: J. G. Swisshelm, 1880.
363p. NUC BL K OCLC
[Recollections of an abolitionist
and advocate of women's rights.
Pioneer in Saint Cloud, Minnesota]

4349. SYKES, Ella Constance [Br.
d. 1939]
Through Persia on a side-saddle.
L: A. D. Innes & co., 1898. 362p.
NUC BL OCLC

4350. SYMMES, Lydia Fletcher see
CLARK, Lydia Fletcher (Symmes)

4351. SYMONDS, Mrs. J. A., ed.
see NORTH, Marianne

4352. SYMONDS, Janet Catherine
(North), ed. see NORTH, Marianne

4353. SYMONDS, Mrs. John
Addington, ed. see NORTH, Marianne

4354. SYMONDS, Margaret, co-
author see WATERFIELD, Lina (Duff
Gordon)

4355. SYNGE, Georgina M. [Br. 19c]
A ride through wonderland.
L: Sampson Low, Marston & co.,
1892. 166p. NUC BL OCLC
[Travel: Yellowstone Park]

4356. T., Amelia, ed. see G.,
Margaret Day, Mrs.

4357. T., F. M. see TRENCH, Maria
Marcia Fanny

4358. TABOR, Eliza see
STEPHENSON, Eliza (Tabor)

4359. TADLOCK, Clara Moyse, Mrs.
[Am. 19c]
Bohemian days.
NY: J. B. Alden, 1889. 519p. NUC
OCLC

4360. TAFT, Mary Barritt [Br.
1772-1851]
Memoirs of the life ... written
by herself.
L: J. Stevens, 1827. 2v. MB OCLC
[Methodist]

4361. TALBOT, Catherine, co-
author see CARTER, Elizabeth

4362. TANNER, Clara (Coulthard)
see COULTHARD, Clara

4363. TATHAM, Emma [Br. 1830-
1855]
Etchings and pearls: or, a flower
for the grave of Emma Tatham. By
Mrs. J. Cooke Westbrook.
2d ed. L: n.p., 1837. BL
[Religious biography, includes
some of her poems]

4364. TATNALL, Esther [Br. 19c]
A narrative of twenty-three
years' superintendence of the
women and boys' wards in the gaol
at Warwick. Ed. Sir E. Eardley
Wilmot.
L: James Moyes, 1836. 36p. BL

4365. TATTAM, Mrs. Henry see
PLATT, Miss

4366. TAYLOR, Ann (Martin) [Br.
1757-1830]
Correspondence between a mother
and her daughter [Jane Taylor] at
school.
L: Taylor & Hessey, 1817. 145p.
BL OCLC

4367. TAYLOR, Ann (Martin), co-
author see TAYLOR, Jane

4368. TAYLOR, Anne see GILBERT,
Anne (Taylor)

4369. TAYLOR, Annie R. [Br. b.
1855]
Pioneering in Tibet. The origin
and progress of "The Tibetan

pioneer mission" together with my experiences in Tibet....
L: Morgan and Scott, 1895. 78p.
NUC BL OCLC
[Also pub. as: Tibetan Pioneer Mission.]

4370. TAYLOR, Catharine [Br. 19c]
Letters from Italy to a younger sister.
L: J. Murray, 1840. 334p. NUC BL OCLC

4371. TAYLOR, Douglas, ed. see MAEDER, Clara (Fisher)

4372. TAYLOR, Eliza (Farrand) see FARRAND, Rebecca

4373. TAYLOR, Elizabeth, ed. see CLARKE, Mary Anne (Thompson)

4374. TAYLOR, Elizabeth [Br. d. 1879]
The Braemar Highlands: their tales, traditions, and history.
Edinburgh: William P. Nimmo, 1869. 343p. NUC BL OCLC

4375. TAYLOR, Elizabeth (Colpeper) [Br. 1749-1836]
Memoir of Mrs. Elizabeth Taylor, late of Saffron-Walden, by her daughter, Mrs. H. E. Webster, with many of her unpublished poems.
4th ed. L: n.p., 1849. BL

4376. TAYLOR, Ellen M. [Br. 19c]
Madeira: its scenery, and how to see it. With letters of a year's residence, and lists of the trees, flowers, ferns, and seaweeds.
L: E. Stanford, 1882. 261p. NUC BL OCLC

4377. TAYLOR, Emily [Br. 1795-1872]
The Irish tourist, or, the people and the provinces of Ireland.
L: Darton & Harvey, 1837. 271p. NUC BL OCLC

4378. TAYLOR, Fanny Margaret [Br. 19c] ALT: Taylor, Frances Magdalen PSEUD: Lady Volunteer, A
Eastern hospitals and English nurses; the narrative of twelve months' experience in the hospitals of Koulali and Scutari.

Pub. as: A Lady Volunteer
L: Hurst & Blackett, 1856. 2v.
NUC BL OCLC

4379. -----Irish homes and Irish hearts.
L: Longmans, Green & co.; Boston: Patrick Donahoe, 1867. 240p. NUC BL OCLC

4380. TAYLOR, Fanny Margaret, comp. see FULLERTON, Lady Georgiana Charlotte (Leveson Gower)

4381. TAYLOR, Frances Magdalen see TAYLOR, Fanny Margaret

4382. TAYLOR, Hannah (Harris) [Br. c1784-1812]
Memoir of Hannah Taylor, extracted from her own memorandums.
York: W. Alexander, 1870. 168p.
NUC BL MBD OCLC
[Includes poetry; member of Society of Friends]

4383. TAYLOR, Mrs. Howard see TAYLOR, Mary Geraldine (Guinness)

4384. TAYLOR, Rev. Isaac, comp. see HERBERT, Jemima (Taylor)

4385. TAYLOR, Rev. Isaac, comp. & ed. see TAYLOR, Jane

4386. TAYLOR, Jane [Br. 1783-1824]
The family pen. Memorials, biographical and literary of the Taylor family of Ongar. Ed. Isaac Taylor.
L: Jackson, Walford & Hodder, 1867. 2v. BL OCLC
[Prose & verse; incl. writings of Ann (Martin) Taylor.]

4387. -----Jane Taylor: her life and letters. By Helen (Cross) Knight.
L: Thomas Nelson & sons, 1880. 176p. NUC BL OCLC

4388. -----Memoirs and poetical remains of the late Jane Taylor with extracts from her correspondence. [Comp.] Isaac Taylor.
L: B. J. Holdsworth, 1825. 2v.
NUC BL OCLC

4389. TAYLOR, Jane, co-author <u>see</u> TAYLOR, Ann (Martin)

4390. TAYLOR, Mrs. John <u>see</u> TAYLOR, Susannah (Cook)

4391. TAYLOR, Maria [Br. 19c]
Some old letters from North Africa.
Rome: n.p., 1889. 135p. BL
[Travel: N. Africa]

4392. TAYLOR, Mary Geraldine (Guinness), Mrs. Howard Taylor [Br. 19c] ALT: Guinness, Geraldine
In the far East; letters from Geraldine Guinness in China. Ed. her sister, Lucy Evangeline Guinness Kumm, Mrs. Karl Kumm.
L: Morgan & Scott, 1889. 120p. NUC BL OCLC

4393. TAYLOR, Susannah Cook, Mrs. John Taylor [Br. 1755-1823]
Three generations of English women. Memoirs and correspondence of Mrs. John Taylor, Mrs. Sarah (Taylor) Austin [1793-1867], and Lady Duff Gordon [Lucie (Austin); 1821-1869]. Ed. Janet Ann (Duff Gordon) Ross.
L: J. Murray, 1888. 2v. BL OCLC

4394. TEMPLE, Dorothy (Osborne), Lady [Br. 1627-1694] ALT: Osborne, Dorothy
Letters from Dorothy Osborne to Sir William Temple, 1652-1654. Ed. Edward Abbott Parry.
L: Griffith, Farran, Okeder & Welsh; NY: Dodd, Mead & co., 1888. 332p. NUC BL OCLC

4395. -----Memoirs of the life, works, and correspondence of Sir William Temple, bart. [Comp.] Thomas Peregrine Courtenay.
L: Longman, Rees, Orme, Brown, Green & Longman, 1836. 2v. NUC BL OCLC
[Includes extracts of her letters]

4396. TEMPLE, Sir William, bart., co-author <u>see</u> TEMPLE, Dorothy (Osborne)

4397. TENDUCCI, Dora (Maunsell) [Br. 18c]

A true and genuine narrative of Mr. and Mrs. Tenducci. In a letter [from Mrs. Tenducci] to a friend at Bath.
L: J. Pridden, 1768. 68p. BL OCLC
[On their marriage and annulment in 1775]

4398. TENISON, Lady Louisa Mary Anne (Anson) [Br. d. 1882]
Castile and Andalucia.
L: R. Bentley, 1853. 488p. BL OCLC

4399. TENNANT, Margaret E. [Am. 19c]
The golden chord, a story of trial and conquest.
Almonte, Ontario: pr., McLeod & McEwen, 1899. 133p. NUC OCLC
[Includes poetry]

4400. TENNEY, William C., ed. <u>see</u> KEITH, Caroline Phebe (Tenney)

4401. TERESA DE CHANTAL, Sister <u>see</u> O'GORMON, Edith

4402. TERESINA, pseud. <u>see</u> LONGWORTH, Maria Theresa

4403. TERHUNE, Mary Virginia (Hawes) [Am. 1830-1922] PSEUD: Harland, Marion
The home of the Bible, a woman's vision of the Master's land. By Marion Harland.
1st ed, Chicago & Philadelphia: Monarch book co., 1895. 414p. NUC OCLC
[Travel: Palestine]

4404. -----Loiterings in pleasant paths. By Marion Harland.
NY: Charles Scribner's sons, 1880. 435p. NUC BL OCLC
[Travel: Europe]

4405. -----Under the flag of the Orient.
Philadelphia: Historical pub. co., 1895. 414p. NUC
[Travel: Palestine & the Levant]

4406. TEUFFEL, Blanche Willis (Howard) von [Am. 1847-1898] ALT: Von Teuffel, Blanche Willis (Howard)
One year abroad.
Boston: J. R. Osgood & co., 1877. 247p. NUC OCLC

4407. TEVIS, Julia Ann
(Hieronymus) [Am. b. 1799]
Sixty years in a schoolroom: an
autobiography of Mrs. Julia A.
Tevis.
Cincinnati, OH: Western Methodist
book concern, 1878. 489p. NUC K
OCLC

4408. THACHER, Mary P. see
HIGGINSON, Mary Potter (Thacher)

4409. THACKER, Anne [Br. 19c]
The narrative of my experiences
as a volunteer nurse in the
Franco-German War of 1870-1. By
A. Thacker. With a sketch of her
life by J. M. Menzies.
L: Abbot & Jones, 1897. 92p. BL

4410. THACKER, PAGE, pseud. see
BURWELL, Letitia M.

4411. THACKERAY, Anne Isabella
see RITCHIE, Anne Isabella
(Thackeray)

4412. THAXTER, Celia (Leighton)
[Am. 1835-1894]
Letters of Celia Thaxter. Ed. her
friends, A. F. [Annie (Adams)
Fields] and R. L. [Rose Lamb].
NY & Boston: Houghton, Mifflin &
co., 1895. 232p. NUC BL OCLC

4413. THICKNESSE, Anne [NUC: Ann]
(Ford) [Br. 1737-1824] ALT: Ford,
Anne
A letter from Miss F--d,
addressed to a person of
distinction with a new ballad to
an old tune. Sent to the author
by an unknown hand.
L: n.p., 1761. 47p. NUC BL OCLC
[Attr. to Thicknesse. Supposedly
addressed to William Villiers,
Earl of Jersey.]

4414. THOMAS, Elizabeth [Br.
1677-1731] PSEUD: Corinna
Pylades and Corinna; or, memoirs
of the life, amours, and writings
of Richard Gwinnet, Esq., and
Mrs. Elizabeth Thomas, junr.... .
To which is prefixed the Life of
Corinna, written by herself ...
to which is added, a collection
of familiar letters between
Corinna, etc. ... .
L: n.p., 1731,32. 2v. NUC BL OCLC

4415. THOMAS, Julia B., Mrs. [Am.
19/20c]
Letters from the South.
Centreville, MI: n.p., 1896. 25p.
NUC
[Travel: Southern states]

4416. -----Letters of a tourist.
Land of the midnight sun.
NY: n.p., 1894. 57p. NUC
[Travel: North Cape, Norway]

4417. THOMAS, Julia M. [Am. 19c]
Miscellaneous writings.
NY: John W. Lovell co., 1890. NUC
[Includes travel to Thousand
Islands, San Francisco, Salt Lake
City]

4418. THOMAS, Margaret [Am.
19/20c]
A scamper through Spain and
Tangier.
L: Hutchinson; NY: Dodd, Mead,
1892. 302p. NUC BL OCLC

4419. THOMPSON, Mrs. Bowen see
THOMPSON, Elizabeth Maria (Lloyd)

4420. THOMPSON, Mrs. E. H. [Am.
19c]
From the Thames to the Trosachs.
Impressions of travel in England
and Scotland.
NY: Hunt & Eaton; Cincinnati, OH:
Cranston & Stowe, 1890. 203p. NUC
OCLC

4421. THOMPSON, Elizabeth Maria
(Lloyd), Mrs. Bowen Thompson [Br.
d. 1839] ALT: Thompson, Mrs.
James Bowen
The daughters of Syria. A
narrative of efforts by the late
Mrs. Bowen Thompson for the
evangelization of the Syrian
females. [By Susette Harriet
(Lloyd) Smith] Ed. Rev. H. B.
Tristram.
L: Seeley, Jackson & Halliday,
1872. 348p. NUC BL OCLC
[Based on her letters]

4422. THOMPSON, Ella W., Mrs.
[Am. 19c]
Beaten paths; or, a woman's
vacation.
Boston: Lee & Shepard; NY: Lee,
Shepard & Dillingham, 1874. 274p.
NUC OCLC
[Travel: Europe]

4423. THOMPSON, Mrs. James Bowen
see THOMPSON, Elizabeth Maria
(Lloyd)

4424. THOMPSON, James O., ed. see
CALDWELL, Nancy

4425. THOMPSON, Jemima, comp. see
G., Marie L.

4426. THOMPSON, Julia Carrie [Am.
d. 1883]
Trye's year among the Hindoos.
Philadelphia: Presbyterian Board
of Publication, 1872. 329p. NUC
OCLC

4427. THOMPSON, Dr. L. S., comp.
see JACKSON, Mattie Jane

4428. THOMPSON, Samuel, comp. see
BROADBELT, Ann

4429. THOMSON, Mrs. Charles [Br.
19c]
Twelve years in Canterbury, New
Zealand, with visits to the other
provinces and reminiscences of
the route home through Australia.
L: S. Low, son & Marston, 1867.
226p. NUC BL

4430. THOMSON, Fanny Mary [Br.
19c]
Memoranda of a journey to Moscow
in the year 1856.
Liverpool: G. Smith, Watts & co.,
1859. 354p. NUC

4431. THORNTON, Alice
(Wandesford) [Br. 1627-1707]
The autobiography of Mrs. Alice
Thornton of East Newton, co.
York. Ed. Charles Jackson.
Durham: Surtees Soc., 1875. 373p.
NUC BL MB OCLC

4432. THORNTON, Anne Jane [Br.
19c]
Interesting life and wonderful
adventures of ... A. J. Thornton,
the female sailor ... written by
herself.
L: n.p., 1835. BL MB
[Written in third person about
her adventures]

4433. THOROLD, Mrs. Arthur [Br.
19c]
Letters from Brussels, in the
summer of 1835.

L: Longman, Rees, Orme, Brown,
Green & Longman, 1835. 287p. NUC
BL

4434. THRALE, Hester Lynch
(Salusbury) see PIOZZI, Hester
Lynch (Salusbury) Thrale

4435. THURSTON, Mrs. Asa see
THURSTON, Lucy (Goodale)

4436. THURSTON, Lucy (Goodale),
Mrs. Asa Thurston [Am. 1795-1876]
Life and times of Mrs. Lucy G.
Thurston, wife of Rev. Asa
Thurston, pioneer missionary to
the Sandwich Islands, gathered
from letters and journals
extending over a period of more
than fifty years. Sel. & arr. by
herself.
Ann Arbor, MI: S. C. Andrews,
c1882. 311p. NUC OCLC

4437. -----The missionary's
daughter, or, Memoir of Lucy
Goodale Thurston of the Sandwich
Islands.
NY: Dayton & Newman, 1842. 233p.
NUC OCLC

4438. THWING, Carrie Frances
(Butler) [Am. 1855-1898]
An appreciation by friends. With
extracts from her journal of a
tour in Europe.
Cleveland, OH: Helman-Taylor co.,
1899. 194p. NUC OCLC

4439. TIMMS, Mary [Br. 1808-1834]
Memoirs of ... M. Timms,
extracted from her diary and
letters. [Comp.] Elijah Morgan.
Watchat: n.p., 1835. BL MBD
[Methodist; diary 1818-1834]

4440. TINDALL, Isabella
(Mackiver), co-author see HARRIS,
Isabella (Tindall)

4441. TIRARD, Helen Mary (Beloe)
[Br. 19c]
Sketches from a Nile steamer for
the use of travellers in Egypt.
With Nestor Charles Isidore
Tirard, Jr.
L: Kegan Paul, Trench, Trübner,
1891. 275p. NUC BL OCLC

4442. TIRARD, Nestor Charles
Isidore, Jr., co-author see
TIRARD, Helen Mary (Beloe)

4443. TITHERTON, Mary [Br. 1770-
1817]
A short account of Miss Mary
Titherton.
York: n.p., 1819. MBD
[Methodist diary, 1799-1817]

4444. TOASE, Margaret de Jersey,
Mrs. William Toase [Br. 1791?-
1852]
Memoirs of Margaret de Jersey
Toase, wife of the Rev. William
Toase ... compiled from her diary
and correspondence, by her
daughter, R. Lavinia R. Toase.
L: John Mason, 1859. 179p. BL MBD

4445. TOASE, R. Lavinia R., comp.
see TOASE, Margaret de Jersey

4446. TOASE, William, comp. see
ARRIVÉ, Elizabeth

4447. TOASE, Mrs. William see
TOASE, Margaret de Jersey

4448. TOBIN, Catherine (Ellis),
Lady [Br. 19c]
The land of inheritance; or,
Bible scenes revisited.
L: B. Quaritch, 1863. 437p. NUC BL

4449. -----Shadows of the East;
or, slight sketches of scenery,
persons and customs, from
observations during a tour in
1853 and 1854, in Egypt,
Palestine, Syria, Turkey and
Greece.
L: Longman, Brown, Green &
Longmans, 1855. 256p. NUC BL

4450. TODD, Mabel Loomis, ed. see
DICKINSON, Emily Elizabeth

4451. TOLLEMACHE, Marguerite,
Mrs. W. A. Tollemache [Br. 19c]
Spanish towns and Spanish
pictures.
L: J. T. Hayes, 1870. 221p. NUC
BL OCLC

4452. TOLLEMACHE, Mrs. W. A. see
TOLLEMACHE, Marguerite

4453. TOLSON, Annie see AUTY, Annie

4454. TOMES, Ann [Br. 1812-1831]
Memoirs of Miss Ann Tomes.
[Comp.] Francis Augustus Cox.
L: Westley & Davis, 1832. 119p.
BL MBD
[Methodist; includes diary]

4455. TONKIN, Mary [Br. 18c]
Facts. The female spy; or, Mrs.
Tonkin's account of her journey
through France, in the war, ...
at the express order of the Rt.
Hon. C. J. Fox, Secretary of
State, for which she has been
refused any ... compensation.
L: the authoress, 1785. 47p. NUC
BL

4456. TONNA, Charlotte Elizabeth
(Browne) Phelan [Br. 1790-
1846/49] ALT: Charlotte Elizabeth
Chapters on flowers. By Charlotte
Elizabeth.
6th ed. L: Selleys, 1836. 303p.
NUC BL
[On memories and people
associated with certain flowers]

4457. -----Letters from Ireland.
L: R. B. Seeley & W. Burnside,
1837. 436p. NUC BL

4458. -----Personal
recollections. By Charlotte
Elizabeth.
NY: J. S. Taylor & co., 1842.
303p. NUC OCLC

4459. TOOTH, Eliza Talitha, ed.
see CAMPLIN, [Sarah], Mrs.

4460. TOOTH, Eliza Talitha see
JENKINS, Sarah, Miss

4461. TOOTH, Mary, ed. see
JENKINS, Sarah, Miss

4462. TORREY, Almira (Little),
Mrs. Joseph Torrey [Am. 1796-
1822]
Selections from the diary and
other writings of Mrs. Almira
Torrey, wife of Rev. Joseph
Torrey, who died at Hanson,
(Mass.) Feb. 14, 1822 ... . Ed.
Joseph Torrey.
Boston: pr. Lincoln & Edmands,
1823. 196p. NUC OCLC

4463. TORREY, Joseph, ed. see
TORREY, Almira (Little)

4464. TORREY, Mrs. Joseph see
TORREY, Almira (Little)

4465. TOULMIN, Camilla Dufour see
CROSLAND, Camilla Dufour
(Toulmin)

4466. TOWLE, Nancy [Am. b. 1796]
Vicissitudes illustrated, in the
experiences of Nancy Towle, in
Europe and America. Written by
herself. With an appendix of
letters, etc.
Charleston, SC: pr. for authoress
by J. L. Burges, 1832. 294p. NUC
BL K OCLC

4467. TRACY, Rachel (Huntington),
co-author see HUNTINGTON, Anne
(Huntington)

4468. TRAIL, Ann Agnes [Br. 19c]
ALT: Trail, Sister Agnes Xavier
Conversion of Miss Trail, a
Scotch Presbyterian. Written by
herself.
L: Catholic Truth Soc., 1897. BL

4469. -----History of St.
Margaret's Convent, Edinburgh;
... and, the autobiography of the
first religious, Sister Agnes
Xavier Trail.
Edinburgh: J. Chisholm, 1886.
OCLC

4470. TRAIL, Sister Agnes Xavier
see TRAIL, Ann Agnes

4471. TRAILL, C. P. see TRAILL,
Catherine Parr (Strickland)

4472. TRAILL, Catherine Parr
(Strickland) [Br. 1802-1899] ALT:
Strickland, Catherine Parr
The backwoods of Canada: being
letters from the wife of an
emigrant officer.
L: Nattali & Bond, 1835?. 351p.
NUC BL MC OCLC

4473. -----Pearls and pebbles, or
notes of an old naturalist. By C.
P. Traill.
Toronto: W. Briggs; L: Sampson,
Low, Marston & co., 1894. 241p.
NUC BL OCLC

4474. TRAVELLER, A, pseud. see
ROYALL, Anne (Newport)

4475. TRENCH, Maria Marcia Fanny
[Br. b. 1852] ALT: Farrar, Maria
Marcia Fanny (Trench): T., F. M.
A journal abroad in 1868 ... By
F. M. T.
L: n.p., 1868. BL MBD
[Travel June-Aug. 1868 to
Switzerland.]

4476. TRENCH, Melesina (Chenevix)
St. George, Mrs. Richard Trench
[Br. 1768-1827] ALT: St. George,
Melesina (Chenevix)
Journal kept during a visit to
Germany in 1799, 1800. Ed. the
Dean of Westminster [Richard
Chenevix Trench].
L: Savill & Edwards, pr., 1861.
97p. NUC BL MBD OCLC

4477. -----The remains of the
late Mrs. Richard Trench, being
selections from her journals,
letters, and other papers. Ed.
her son, the Dean of Westminster,
Richard Chenevix Trench.
L: Parker, son & Bourn, 1860.
525p. NUC BL MBD OCLC

4478. TRENCH, Melesina (Chenevix)
St. George, co-author see
LEADBEATER, Mary

4479. TRENCH, Mrs. R. C., co-390p.
author see LEADBEATER, Mary
Shackleton

4480. TRENCH, Mrs. Richard see
TRENCH, Melesina (Chenevix) St.
George

4481. TRENCH, Richard Chenevix,
Dean of Westminster, ed. see
TRENCH, Melesina (Chenevix) St.
George

4482. TRENCH GASCOIGNE, Gwendolen
(Galton) see TRENCH GASCOIGNE,
Laura Gwendolen Douglas (Galton)

4483. TRENCH GASCOIGNE, Laura
Gwendolen Douglas (Galton) [Br.
19c] ALT: GASCOIGNE, Gwendolen
(Galton) Trench; TRENCH
GASCOIGNE, Gwendolen (Galton)
Among pagodas and fair ladies. An
account of a tour through Burma.
L: A. D. Innes, 1896. 312p. NUC
BL OCLC

4484. TREVELYAN, Paulina
(Jermyn), Lady [Br. 1816-1866]
Selections from the literary and
artistic remains of Paulina
Jermyn Trevelyan, first wife of
Sir Walter Calverley Trevelyan
... . Ed. David Wooster.
L: Longmans, Green & co., 1879.
239p. NUC BL OCLC

4485. TRIMMER, Sarah (Kirby) [Br.
1741-1810]
Some account of the life and
writings of Mrs. Trimmer, with
original letters and meditations
and prayers, selected from her
journal.
L: F. C. & J. Rivington, 1814.
2v. NUC BL MBD OCLC

4486. TRISTRAM, Rev. H. B., ed.
see THOMPSON, Elizabeth Maria
(Lloyd)

4487. TROLLOPE, Frances Eleanor
(Ternan), Mrs. Thomas Adolphus
Trollope [Br. 1834-1913]
The homes and haunts of Italian
poets. With Thomas Adolphus
Trollope.
L: Chapman and Hall, 1881. 2v.
NUC BL OCLC

4488. TROLLOPE, Frances Eleanor
(Ternan), comp. see TROLLOPE,
Frances (Milton)

4489. TROLLOPE, Frances (Milton)
[Br. 1780-1863]
Belgium and West Germany in 1833,
including visits to Baden-Baden,
Wiesbaden, Cassel, Hanover, the
Harz Mts.,etc.
L: J. Murray, 1839. 2v. NUC BL
OCLC

4490. -----Domestic manners of
the Americans.
L: pr. for Whittaker, Treacher &
co., 1832. 2v. NUC BL N OCLC

4491. -----Frances Trollope. Her
life and literary work from
George III to Victoria. By her
daughter-in-law, Frances Eleanor
(Ternan) Trollope.
L: R. Bentley & son, 1895. 2v.
NUC BL OCLC

4492. -----Paris and the
Parisians in 1835.

L: R. Bentley, 2v.; NY: Harper,
1836. 410p. NUC BL OCLC

4493. -----Travels and
travellers. A series of sketches.
L: Henry Colburn, 1846. 2v. NUC
BL OCLC

4494. -----Vienna and the
Austrians, with some account of a
journey through Swabia, Bavaria,
the Tyrol, and the Salzbourg.
L: R. Bentley, 1838. 2v. NUC BL
OCLC

4495. -----A visit to Italy.
L: R. Bentley, 1892. 2v. NUC BL

4496. TROLLOPE, Thomas Adolphus,
co-author see TROLLOPE, Frances
Eleanor (Ternan)

4497. TROLLOPE, Mrs. Thomas
Adolphus see TROLLOPE, Frances
Eleanor (Ternan)

4498. TROTTER, Mrs. Alexander see
TROTTER, Isabella (Strange)

4499. TROTTER, Hon. Charlotte
Amelia (Liddell), co-author see
NORMANBY, Maria (Liddell) Phipps,
Marchioness of

4500. TROTTER, Isabella
(Strange), Mrs. Alexander Trotter
[Br. 1816-1878]
First impressions of the new
world on two travellers from the
old, in the autumn of 1858. Pub.
anon.
L: Longman, Brown, Green,
Longmans & Roberts, 1859. 308p.
NUC BL OCLC

4501. TRUTH, Sojourner [Am. 1883]
ALT: Sojourner Truth
Narrative of Sojourner Truth, a
northern slave ... .
Boston: pr. for author, 1850.
144p. NUC K OCLC

4502. TUCKER, Sarah (Fish) [Am.
1779-1840]
Memoirs of the life and religious
experience of Sarah Tucker.
Providence, RI: Moore & Choate,
pr., 1848. 204p. NUC
[A minister of the Society of
Friends]

4503. TUCKER, Susannah Humphrey (Clapp) [Am. 1802-1833]
The hidden life of a Christian exemplified in the character and writings of Mrs. Susannah Tucker, late of Milton, MA. Ed. John Codman.
Boston: Perkins, Marvin & co., 1835. 340p. NUC

4504. TUCKETT, Elizabeth, Miss [Br. 19c]
Beaten tracks; or, pen and pencil sketches in Italy.
L: Longmans, Green & co., 1866. 278p. NUC BL OCLC

4505. -----How we spent the summer; or, a voyage in zigzag in Switzerland and Tyrol with some members of the Alpine Club.
L & Bristol: n.p., 1864. NUC BL

4506. -----Pictures in Tyrol & elsewhere. From a family sketchbook.
L: Longmans, Green & co., 1867. 313p. NUC BL OCLC

4507. TULLY, Miss [Br. 19c]
Narrative of a ten years' residence at Tripoli in Africa; from the original in the possession of the family of the late Richard Tully, Esq., British Consul, etc.
L: H. Colburn, 1816. 370p. NUC BL OCLC
[Author is Richard Tully's sister.]

4508. TURNER, Dawson, ed. see GUNN, Harriett (Turner)

4509. TURNER, Jane, Mrs. John Turner [Br. 17c]
Choice experiences of the kind dealings of God before, in, and after conversion. ... By J. Turner, wife to Captain John Turner.
L: pr. H. Hils, 1653. 208p. NUC BL MB OCLC

4510. TURNER, Joanna, Mrs. [Br. 18c]
The triumph of faith over the world, the flesh and the devil; exemplified in the life ... of ... Mrs. Joanna Turner. By Mary Wells.

Bristol: pr. for T. Mills, 1787. 329p. NUC BL
[May contain personal material.]

4511. TURNER, Joanna [Br. 19c]
Memoir of Mrs. Joanna Turner, as exemplified in her life, death, and spiritual experience. By David Bogue.
L: J. Nisbet, 1820. 264p. NUC MB
[Methodist]

4512. TURNER, Mrs. John see TURNER, Jane

4513. TUTHILL, H. N., Mrs. [Am. b. 1814]
An interesting narrative of the life of Mrs. H. N. Tuthill.
Lawrence, MA: pr. by Robert Bower, 1874. K OCLC
[Suffragist]

4514. TUTTLE, Sarah [Am. 19c]
PSEUD: Pelham, Cornelia
Letters on the Chickasaw and Osage missions.
Rev. ed. Boston: pr. by T. R. Marvin for the MA Sabbath School Soc., 1831. 161p. NUC BL
[Letters signed Cornelia Pelham; she also wrote fictionalized accounts of other missions.]

4515. TWAMLEY, Louisa Anne see MEREDITH, Louisa Anne (Twamley)

4516. TWEEDIE, Mrs. Alec see TWEEDIE, Ethel Brilliana (Harley)

4517. TWEEDIE, Ethel Brilliana (Harley), Mrs. Alec Tweedie [Br. d. 1940]
A girl's ride in Iceland.
L: Griffith, Farran, Okeden & Welsh, 1889. 166p. NUC BL OCLC

4518. -----The Oberammergau passion play, 1890.
L: K. Paul, Trench, Trübner, & co., 1890. 118p. NUC OCLC

4519. -----Through Finland in carts.
L: A. & C. Black, 1897. 366p. NUC BL OCLC

4520. -----A winter jaunt to Norway.
2d ed. L: Bliss, Sands, & Foster, 1894. 316p. NUC BL OCLC

4521. TWEEDIE, William King, comp. <u>see</u> COLVILLE, Elizabeth (Melvill), Lady Colville of Culross

4522. TWEEDIE, William King, comp. <u>see</u> GOODAL, Mrs.

4523. TWEEDIE, William King, comp. <u>see</u> GORDON, Janet Hamilton

4524. TWINING, Louisa [Br. 1820-1912]
Recollections of life and work: being the autobiography of Louisa Twining.
L: E. Arnold, 1893. 291p. NUC BL MB OCLC

4525. -----Recollections of workhouse visiting and management during twenty-five years.
L: C. Kegan Paul & co., 1880. 217p. BL

4526. TYACKE, Mrs. Richard Humphrey [Br. 19c]
How I shot my bears; or, two years' tent life in Kullu and Lahoul.
L: S. Low, Marston & co., 1893. 318p. NUC BL MB OCLC
[Travel: India]

4527. TYLER, Josephine [Am. 19c]
Waymarks; or, solo in Europe.
NY & Chicago: Brentano bros., 1885. 82p. NUC

4528. TYLER, Katherine E. [Am. 19c]
The story of a Scandinavian summer.
NY: G. P. Putnam's sons, 1881. 394p. NUC BL OCLC
[Norway]

4529. TYLOR, Charles, ed. <u>see</u> DUDLEY, Elizabeth

4530. TYNAN, Katherine <u>see</u> HINKSON, Katherine (Tynan)

4531. TYNDALE, Mrs. T. G., ed. <u>see</u> BATES, Elizabeth Mary

4532. TYNDALL, Mary [Br. 19c]
The diary of Mary Tyndall, one of the early Quakers.
L: Hall & co., 1876. 174p. NUC BL OCLC

4533. ULTRA MARINE, pseud. <u>see</u> PARHAM, Helena Beatrice Richenda

4534. ULYAT, Elizabeth Ann [Br. 19c]
Memoirs of ... by Thomas Rogers.
Boston: n.p., 1823. MB
[Lincolnshire Baptist; includes diary and letters.]

4535. UNION WOMAN, A <u>see</u> pseud. MILLER, Dora Richards

4536. UPDIKE, Elisabeth Bigelow [Am. 1831-1896]
In the old days: a fragment.
Boston: Merrymount Press, 1896. 13p. NUC OCLC
[Reminiscence of the author's grandparents' house written for her own great-grandchildren.]

4537. UPHAM, Phoebe (Lord) [Am. 19c]
The crystal fountain; or, faith and life.
Philadelphia: J. B. Lippincott & co., 1877. 140p. NUC OCLC
[From personal notebook]

4538. UPTON, Catherine, Mrs. [Br. 18c]
The siege of Gibraltar from the 12th of April to the 27th of May 1781. To which is prefixed some account of the Blockade.
L: the authoress, 1781. 23p. NUC BL
[Includes poetry]

4539. URBINO, Levina (Buoncouré), Mrs. S. R. Urbino [Am. 19c]
An American woman in Europe. Journal of two years and a half sojourn in Germany, Switzerland, France, and Italy.
Boston: Lee & Shepard, 1869. 338p. NUC BL OCLC

4540. URBINO, Mrs. S. R. <u>see</u> URBINO, Levina (Buoncouré)

4541. URQUHART, Mrs. D. <u>see</u> URQUHART, Harriet Angelina (Fortesque)

4542. URQUHART, Harriet Angelina (Fortescue), Mrs. D. Urquhart [Br. 1825-1889]
Memoir of Mrs. Urquhart. By Maria Catherine Bishop.

L: K. Paul, Trench, Trübner & co., 1897. 404p. NUC BL OCLC
[Includes excerpts from her letters.]

4543. USSHER, Elizabeth [Br. 1772?-1796]
Extracts from the letters of Elizabeth, Lucy [1776?-1797], and Judith [1780-1798] Ussher. With a short account of Susanna Ussher, and extracts from her letters. [Comp. Elizabeth Ussher, the younger]
Dublin: pr. J. Jones, 1812. 160p. NUC BL OCLC
[Members of Society of Friends]

4544. USSHER, Elizabeth, the younger, comp. <u>see</u> USSHER, Elizabeth

4545. USSHER, Judith, co-author <u>see</u> USSHER, Elizabeth

4546. USSHER, Lucy, co-author <u>see</u> USSHER, Elizabeth

4547. USSHER, Margaret Lilias, Mrs. [Br. 1813-1892]
Memoir of the late Mrs. Margaret Lilias Ussher, 1813-1892.
Bristol: J. Wright & co., 1893. 47p. BL

4548. USSHER, Susanna, co-author <u>see</u> USSHER, Elizabeth

4549. VAIL, Mary C., Mrs. [Am. 19c]
"Both sides told," or, southern California as it is ... .
Pasadena, CA: West Coast pub. co., 1888. 23p. NUC

4550. VALE, FERNA, pseud. <u>see</u> HALLETT, Emma V.

4551. VAN BRUNT, Leonora L. (Bigelow) [Am. b. 1812]
Autobiography ... .

Westmoreland, KS: Alliance news plant, 1891. K

4552. VAN CLEVE, Charlotte Ouisconsin (Clark) [Am. 1819-1907]
"Three score years and ten," life-long memories of Fort Snelling, Minn. and other parts of the West.
Minneapolis, MN: Pr. house of Harrison & Smith, 1888. 176p. NUC BL K

4553. VAN COTT, Maggie (Newton) [Am. b. 1830]
The harvest and the reaper. Reminiscences of revival work.
NY: N. Tibbals, 1876. 360p. NUC BL K OCLC
[Dictated account]

4554. VAN DE VELDE, M. B. <u>see</u> VELDE, M. B. Van de, Mme.

4555. VANE, Frances Anne, Viscountess [Br. 1713-1788]
The adventures of Peregrine Pickle. In which are included the memoirs of a lady of quality. By Tobias Smollett.
L: pr. for the author, sold by D. Wilson, 1751. 4v. BL OCLC
[Memoirs by Vane, rev. by Smollett]

4556. VANE, Frances Anne (Vane-Tempest), Marchioness of Londonderry [Br. 1800-1865]
Narrative of a visit to the courts of Vienna, Constantinople, Athens, Naples, etc.
L: H. Colburn, 1844. 342p. BL OCLC

4557. VANE, Frances Anne Emily (Vane-Tempest) Stewart, Marchioness of Londonberry <u>see</u> LONDONBERRY, Frances Anne Emily (Vane-Tempest) Stewart Vane, Marchioness of

4558. VAN LENNEP, Mrs. Henry J. <u>see</u> VAN LENNEP, Mary Elizabeth (Hawes)

4559. VAN LENNEP, Mary Elizabeth (Hawes), Mrs. Henry J. Van Lennep [Am. 1821-1844]
Memoir of Mrs. Mary E. Van Lennep, only daughter of the Rev.

Joel Hawes, D. D. and wife of the Rev. Henry J. Van Lennep, missionary in Turkey ... by her mother, Louisa (Fisher) Hawes, Mrs. Joel Hawes.
Hartford, CT: Wm. Jas. Hamersley, 1850. 383p. NUC BL MAD OCLC
[Includes diaries]

4560. VASSAR GRADUATE, A, pseud.
see DE VERE, Clara

4561. VAUCHES, H. L., Mrs. [Br. d. 1864]
Notes from my diary, by a small dog.
L: Gilbert & Rivington, pr., 1864. 75p. NUC
[Travel notes, told as from her dog, Zitto]

4562. VAUGHAN, Margaret (Symonds), co-author see WATERFIELD, Lina (Duff Gordon)

4563. VAVASOUR, Anne, Lady [Br. 19c]
My last tour and first work; or, a visit to the baths of Wildbad and Rippoldsau.
L: H. Cunningham, 1842. 458p. NUC BL

4564. VEITCH, Marion (Fairly), Mrs. William Veitch [Br. d. 1722]
Memoirs of Mrs. William Veitch ... .
Edinburgh: Church of Scotland, 1846. 152p. NUC BL OCLC
[Autobiography]

4565. VEITCH, Mrs. William see VEITCH, Marion (Fairly)

4566. VELAZQUEZ, Loreta Janeta [Am. b. 1842]
The woman in battle; a narrative of the exploits, adventures and travels of Madame Loreta Janeta Velazquez, otherwise known as Lieutenant Harry T. Buford, Confederate States Army. Ed. C. J. Worthington.
Hartford, CT: T. Belknap, 1876. 606p. NUC BL K OCLC

4567. VELDE, M. B. Van de, Mme. [Br. 19c] ALT: Van de Velde, M. B., Mrs. PSEUD: A Cosmopolitan
Cosmopolitan recollections.
Lt. Ward & Downey, 1889. 2v. NUC BL OCLC

4568. -----Random recollections of courts and society. By A Cosmopolitan.
L: Ward & Downey, 1898. 288p. BL NUC

4569. VELNET, Mary, Mrs. Henri Velnet [Am. b. 1774]
An affecting history of the captivity and sufferings of Mrs. Mary Velnet ... written by herself.
1st Am. ed. Boston: William Crane, 1800?. 96p. NUC OCLC
[Kidnap from lame ship; slavery in Tripoli.]

4570. VELNET, Mrs. Henri see VELNET, Mary

4571. VENEY, Bethany [Am. 19c]
ALT: Aunt Betty
The narrative of Bethany Veney. A slave woman.
Worchester, MA: n.p., 1890. 47p. OCLC
[On cover, "Aunt Betty's story"]

4572. VERA, pseud. see LIGHT, Bianca

4573. VICKERS, Lizzie, Miss [Am. 19c]
Old Norway and its fjords, or a holiday in Norseland.
Lincoln, NE: Akrill, Ruddock & Keyworth, 1893. 142p. NUC OCLC

4574. VICTOR, Frances Auretta (Fuller) Barrett [Am. 1826-1902]
All over Oregon and Washington.
San Francisco, CA: pr. by J. H. Carmany & co., 1872. 368p. NUC OCLC

4575. -----Atlantis arisen; or, talks of a tourist about Oregon and Washington.
Philadelphia: J. B. Lippincott co., 1891. 412p. NUC BL OCLC

4576. VICTOR, Sara Maria, Mrs. [Am. b. 1827]
The life story of Sarah M. Victor, for sixty years. Convicted of murdering her brother ... . Told by herself. Ed. Harriet L. Adams.
Cleveland, OH: Williams pub. co., 1887. 431p. NUC K OCLC

4577. VICTORIA, Queen of Great Britain and Ireland [Br. 1819-1901]
Leaves from the journal of our life in the highlands, from 1848-1861. To which are prefixed and added, extracts from the same journal, giving an account of earlier visits to Scotland, and tours in England and Ireland, and yachting excursions. Ed. Arthur Helps.
L: Smith, Elder & co., 1868. 315p. NUC BL MBD OCLC

4578. -----More leaves from the journal of a life in the Highlands from 1862 to 1882.
L. Smith, Elder & co., 1884. 407p. NUC BL MBD OCLC
[At least seven editions of this appeared in 1884. Matthews says 1st pub. 1883.]

4579. VIELÉ, Teresa (Griffin) [Am. b. 1832]
"Following the drum": a glimpse of the frontier life.
NY: Rudd & Carlston, 1858. 256p. NUC BL K OCLC
[Author's husband was a lieutenant in the 1st U.S. infantry, stationed on the Texas frontier.]

4580. VIGOR, (Ward) Rondeau, Mrs. William Vigor [Br. 1699?-1783]
ALT: Rondeau, Mrs. Claudius; Ward, Miss
Letters from a lady who resided some years in Russia to her friend in England. With historical notes.
L: J. Dodsley, 1776, 207p. NUC BL
[2d ed., expanded, 1777]

4581. VIGOR, Mrs. William see VIGOR, (Ward) Roudeau

4582. VILLARI, Linda (White) Mazini, Mrs. P. Villari [Br. 1836-1915]
Here and there in Italy and over the border.
L: W. H. Allen & Co., 1893. 269p. NUC BL OCLC

4583. -----On Tuscan hills and Venetian waters.
L: T. Fisher Unwin, 1885. 280p. NUC BL OCLC

4584. VILLARI, Mrs. P. see VILLARI, Linda (White) Mazini

4585. VILLIERS, Hon. Elizabeth Charlotte (Liddell), co-author see NORMANBY, Maria (Liddell) Phipps, Marchioness of

4586. VINCENT, Colonel Sir Charles Edward Howard, co-author see VINCENT. Ethel Gwendoline (Moffatt), Lady

4587. VINCENT, Ethel Gwendoline (Moffatt), Lady [Br. b. 1861]
China to Peru, over the Andes: a journey through South America ...
L: S. Low, Marston & co., 1894. 333p. NUC BL OCLC

4588. -----Forty thousand miles over land and water. The journal of a tour through the British Empire and America.
2d ed. L: S. Low, Marston, Searle & Rivington, 1886. 2v. NUC BL OCLC

4589. -----Newfoundland to Cochin China. By the golden wave, new Nippon, and the Forbidden city .... With reports on British trade and interests in Canada, Japan and China by Colonel Sir Charles Edward Howard Vincent.
L: S. Low, Marston & co., 1892. 374p. NUC BL OCLC

4590. VINCENT, Colonel Howard, co-author see VINCENT, Ethel Gwendoline (Moffatt), Lady

4591. VIOLA, pseud. see GODFREY, Miss

4592. VOKINS, Joan (Br. d. 1690]
God's mighty power magnified; as manifested and revealed in his faithful handmaid, J. V. Ed. Oliver Sansom.
L: Thomas Northcott, 1691. 130p. NUC BL MB OCLC

4593. VON TEUFFEL, Blanche Willis (Howard) see TEUFFEL, Blanche Willis (Howard) Von

4594. VYSE, L. Howard, Mrs. <u>see</u>
HOWARD-VYSE, L., Mrs.

4595. W., A. <u>see</u> WARREN, Anne
(Williams)

4596. W., A. L. <u>see</u> WILSON, Alice
Louise

4597. W., A., Mrs. <u>see</u> WILSON,
Ann

4598. W., C., Mrs., ed. <u>see</u>
L'ESTRANGE, M.

4599. W., E. A., Miss [Br. 19c]
"Words heard in quiet."
Searchings "out of the book of
the Lord" and fragments of
letters and poems. Ed. Miss L. C.
Philpot.
L: n.p., 1870. BL

4600. W., E. H. <u>see</u> WATSON, Emily
H.

4601. W., H. M. <u>see</u> WILLIAMS,
Helen Maria

4602. W., J. <u>see</u> WATTS, Jane
(Waldie)

4603. W., J. H., comp. <u>see</u>
LUTTON, Anne

4604. W., M. B. <u>see</u> WATERMAN,
Mary Bissell

4605. W., M. D. <u>see</u> WALLIS, Mary
Davis (Cook)

4606. W., M. E., pseud. <u>see</u>
MIXER, Mary Elizabeth (Knowlton)

4607. W., S. <u>see</u> WATTS, Susannah

4608. WADDELL, Hope Masterton
[Br. b. 1804?]
Twenty-nine years in the West
Indies and Central Africa: a
review of missionary work and
adventure. 1829-1858.

L & NY: T. Nelson & sons, 1863.
681p. NUC BL K MB OCLC
[Woman minister in Jamaica and
Nigeria.]

4609. WADE, Alice Mary (Moore)
[Br. 1850-1871]
In memoriam. Ed. her mother,
Augusta S. Moore.
Edinburgh: Sanson & co., pr.,
1872. 184p. NUC BL
[A memoir with extracts from
diaries, letters, etc.]

4610. WAGENTREIBER, Miss [Br.
19c]
The story of our escape from
Delhi in May, 1857.
Delhi: Imperial Medical Hall
press, 1894. 39p. BL

4611. WAKEFIELD, Priscilla (Bell)
[Br. 1751?-1832]
Excursions in North America.
Described in letters from a
gentleman and his young companion
to their friends in England.
L: Darton & Harvey, 1806. 420p.
NUC BL N
[Fictitious letters, signed
Arthur Middleton and Henry
Franklin.]

4612. -----Family tour through
the British Empire... .
L: Darton & Harvey, 1804. 436p.
NUC BL OCLC

4613. -----Perambulations in
London and its environs.
L: Darton & Harvey, 1810. 510p.
NUC BL OCLC

4614. WAKEFIELD, Sarah F. [Am.
19c]
Six weeks in the Sioux teepees: a
narrative of Indian captivity.
Minneapolis, MN: Atlas pr. co.,
1863. 54p. NUC OCLC
[Pub. as: Six weeks in Little
Crow's camp. 1864]

4615. WALDEN-PELL, Orleana
Ellery, Mrs. [Am. 1810-1895] ALT:
Warden-Pell, Orleana Ellery
Recollections of a long life.
L: W. P. Griffith & son, 1896.
120p. NUC K OCLC
[Her childhood in New Orleans;
social life in N.Y. & Newport.]

4616. WALDIE, Charlotte Ann <u>see</u>
EATON, Charlotte Ann (Waldie)

4617. WALDIE, Jane <u>see</u> WATTS,
Jane (Waldie)

4618. WALE, Henrietta (Whatley),
comp. <u>see</u> WHATELEY, Elizabeth
Jane

4619. WALES, Charlotte Augusta,
Princess of <u>see</u> CHARLOTTE AUGUSTA
OF WALES, Consort of Prince
Leopold of Saxe-Coburg

4620. WALKER, Mrs. Anthony <u>see</u>
WALKER, Elizabeth (Sadler)

4621. WALKER, Rev. Anthony, ed.
<u>see</u> WALKER, Elizabeth (Sadler)

4622. WALKER, Rev. Anthony, comp.
<u>see</u> WARWICK, Mary (Boyle) Rich,
Countess of

4623. WALKER, Bettina [Br. d.
1893]
My musical experiences.
L: R. Bentley & son, 1890. 330p.
NUC BL MB OCLC
[As student and teacher.]

4624. WALKER, Eliza Ann, comp.
<u>see</u> COOKE, Sophia

4625. WALKER, Elizabeth (Sadler),
Mrs. Anthony Walker [Br. 1623-
1690]
The holy life of Mrs. E. Walker.
[Ed.] her husband, Rev. Anthony
Walker.
L: pr., John Leake, 1690. NUC BL
OCLC
[Includes deathbed advice to her
children and her papers and
letters.]

4626. WALKER, Jane, comp. <u>see</u>
ELLIOTT, Jane

4627. WALKER, Mary Adelaide
(Rogers) [Br. 1866-1950]
Eastern life and scenery, with
excursions in Asia Minor,
Mytilene, Crete & Roumania.
L: Chapman & Hall, 1886. 2v. NUC
BL OCLC

4628. -----Old tracks and new
landmarks; wayside sketches in
Crete, Macedonia, Mitylene, etc.

L: R. Bentley, 1897. 365p. NUC BL
OCLC

4629. -----Through Macedonia to
the Albanian lakes.
L: Chapman & Hall, 1864. 274p.
NUC BL OCLC

4630. -----Untrodden paths in
Roumania.
L: Chapman & Hall, 1888. 355p.
NUC BL OCLC

4631. WALLACE, Charles, comp. <u>see</u>
COLLINS, Elizabeth M. (Smith)

4632. WALLACE, E. D., Mrs. [Am.
19c]
A woman's experiences in Europe.
NY: D. Appleton & co., 1872.
315p. NUC BL OCLC
[England, France, Germany, Italy]

4633. WALLACE, Mrs. Lew <u>see</u>
WALLACE, Susan Arnold (Elston)

4634. WALLACE, Mrs. Lewis <u>see</u>
WALLACE, Susan Arnold (Elston)

4635. WALLACE, M. T., Mrs. [Br.
19c]
A tour in Italy 1873-1874; being
the substance of two letters
addressed to her father.
Edinburgh: W. Blackwood & sons,
1876. 31p. NUC

4636. WALLACE, Madeline Anne <u>see</u>
DUNLOP, Madeline Anne (Wallace)

4637. WALLACE, Rosalind Harriet
Maria, co-author <u>see</u> DUNLOP,
Madeline Anne (Wallace)

4638. WALLACE, Susan Arnold
(Elston), Mrs. Lewis Wallace [Am.
1830-1907] ALT: Wallace, Mrs. Lew
The land of the Pueblos.
NY: J. B. Alden, 1888. 285p. NUC
OCLC

4639. -----The repose in Egypt, a
medley, and Along the Bosphorus.
NY: J. B. Alden; G. D. Hurst,
1888. 391p. NUC BL OCLC
[BL has separate eds.of each]

4640. -----The storied sea.
Boston: J. R. Osgood & co., 1883.
233p. NUC BL OCLC

4641. WALLACE, William, ed. <u>see</u>
DUNLOP, Frances Anna (Wallace)

4642. WALLIS, Lena, comp. <u>see</u>
MARTYN, Caroline Eliza Derecourt

4643. WALLIS, Mary Davis (Cook)
[Am. 19c] ALT: W., M. D. PSEUD:
Lady, A
Life in Feejee: or five years
among the cannibals. By A lady
(M. D. W.).
Boston: W. Heath, 1851. 422p. NUC
BL MB OCLC
[Missionary]

4644. WALLIS, Nettie [Br. 19c]
A brief account of the Lord's
dealings with one of his
handmaidens in France and
Switzerland, 1883.
L: G. T. Horn, 1884. 16p. BL

4645. WALWORTH, Jeannette Ritchie
(Hadermann) [Am. 1837-1918]
Southern silhouettes.
NY: H. Holt & co., 1887. 376p.
NUC OCLC
[Southern life and customs]

4646. WANTON, Mrs. John <u>see</u>
WANTON, Mary

4647. WANTON, Mary, Mrs. John
Wanton [Am. 18c]
A reminiscence of Newport before
and during the revolutionary war.
By Eliza B. Lyman.
n.p.: priv. pr., 1869. 21p. NUC
[Author's recollections of her
grandmother, Mary Wanton, and her
life.]

4648. WARD, Miss <u>see</u> VIGOR,
(Ward) Rondeau

4649. WARD, Charlotte
(Bickersteth), comp. <u>see</u>
BICKERSTETH, Elizabeth

4650. WARD, Elizabeth Stuart
(Phelps) [Am. 1844-1911] ALT:
Phelps, Elizabeth Stuart
Chapters from a life.
Boston & NY: Houghton, Mifflin;
L: J. Clarke & co., 1897. 278p.
NUC BL K OCLC

4651. WARD, Emma Georgina
Elizabeth [Br. 19c] PSEUD:

Englishwoman, An
Outside Paris during the two
sieges. By an Englishwoman.
L: S. M. & A. Warren, 1871. 92p.
BL

4652. WARD, Harriet, Mrs. [Br. 19c]
The Cape and the Kaffirs: a diary
of five years residence in
Kaffirland: with a chapter of
advice to emigrants ... and the
most recent information
respecting the colony.
3d ed. L: H. G. Bohn, 1851. 238p.
NUC BL

4653. -----Five years in
Kaffirland: with sketches of the
late war in that country to the
conclusion of peace.
L: H. Colborn, 1848. 2v. NUC BL
OCLC

4654. WARD, Hetta Lord (Hayes)
[Am. 1815-1842]
Memoir of Mrs. Hetta L. Ward,
with selections from her
writings.
Boston: pr., T. R. Marvin for
priv. circ., 1843. 136p. NUC OCLC

4655. WARD, Maria N. [Am. 19/20c]
Female life among the Mormons: a
narrative of many years' personal
experience. By the wife of a
Mormon elder, recently from Utah.
L: L. G. Routledge, 1855. 247p.
NUC BL OCLC
[Later pub. as: The Mormon wife.
May be fictional.]

4656. WARD, Sarah, Mrs. [Br. d.
1780 or 1781]
Letters which passed between Mr.
West Digges, a comedian, and Mrs.
Sarah Ward, 1752-59.
Edinburgh: T. Stevenson, 1833.
NUC BL OCLC
[Actress; love letters to father
of her illegitimate children.]

4657. WARDEN-PELL, Orleana Ellery
<u>see</u> WALDEN-PELL, Orleana Ellery

4658. WARING, Mary [Br. 1760-1805]
A diary of the religious
experience of M. W. ... late of
Godalming.
L: W. Phillips, 1809. 259p. NUC
BL MBD OCLC

4659. WARNE, E. A. see WARNE, Emoline Ann

4660. WARNE, Emoline Ann [Br. b. 1850]
A brief narrative of the lives of Ephraim Angell and Emoline Ann Warne. By E. A. Warne.
Yeovil: "Western Gazette" Works, 1886. 54p. BL
[Account of a blind brother and sister, includes poems and hymns]

4661. WARNE, Ephraim Angell, co-author see WARNE, Emoline Ann

4662. WARNER, Helen Garnie [Am. b. 1846] PSEUD: Harcourt, Helen
Home life in Florida. By Helen Harcourt.
Louisville, KY: J. P. Morton & co., 1889. 433p. NUC BL OCLC

4663. WARREN, Anne (Williams) [Br. 1778-1823] ALT: W., A.
Memoirs and select letters of Mrs. A. W. Ed. Samuel Warren.
L: J. Stephens, 1827. 308p. NUC BL OCLC
[Methodist: includes biography of her parents by Samuel Warren, LLD.]

4664. WARREN, Mary Bowers [Am. 19c]
Little journeys abroad.
Boston: J. Knight co.; Page, c1894. 313p. NUC OCLC
[Travel: Europe]

4665. WARREN, Mercy (Otis) [Am. 1728-1814]
History of the rise, progress, and termination of the American Revolution; interspersed with biographical, political, and moral observations.
Boston: pr., Manning & Loring for E. Larkin, 1805. 3v. NUC BL OCLC

4666. WARREN, Samuel, ed. see WARREN, Anne (Williams)

4667. WARWICK, Mary (Boyle) Rich, Countess of [Br. 1625-1678] ALT: Rich, Mary (Boyle), Countess of Warwick
Autobiography. Ed. Thomas Crofton Croker.

L: pr. for the Percy Society by Richards, 1848. 50p. NUC BL MB OCLC

4668. -----Eureka, Eureka, the virtuous woman found, her loss bewayl'd, and character exemplified in a sermon preached ... at the funeral of ... Mary, Countess Dowager of Warwick ... to which are annexed some of her pious ... meditations. [By Rev. Anthony Walker]
L: n.p., 1678. 2pt. NUC BL OCLC

4669. -----Memoir of Lady Warwick; also her diary from 1666-1672 ... to which are added, extracts from her other writings.
L: Religious Tract Society, 1847. 320p. NUC BL MBD OCLC
[Abridgement of Eureka, Eureka.]

4670. WAST, Elizabeth [Br. 18c]
Memoirs: or, spiritual exercises of Elizabeth Wast, written by her own hand.
Edinburgh: pr., T. Lumisden & J. Robertson, 1733. 266p. NUC BL

4671. WATERBURY, Maria [Am. 19c]
Seven years among the freedmen.
Chicago: T. B. Arnold, 1890. 144p. NUC K OCLC

4672. WATERFIELD, Mrs. Aubrey see WATERFIELD, Lina (Duff Gordon)

4673. WATERFIELD, Lina (Duff Gordon), Mrs. Aubrey Waterfield [Br. b. 1874] ALT: Gordon, Lina Duff
The story of Perugia. With Margaret Symonds [Vaughn, 1869-1928/1925?].
L: J. M. Dent; NY: Dutton, 1898. NUC BL OCLC

4674. WATERMAN, Mary Bissell [Am. 1836-1889] ALT: W., M. B.
Life from a wheeled chair.
Utica, NY: D. Waterman, n.d. 28p. NUC
[Account of the author's rheumatism transforming her to an invalid.]

4675. WATERS, Clara (Erskine) Clement [Am. 1834-1916] ALT: Clement, Clara (Erskine)

Constantinople, the city of the Sultans. By Clara Erskine Clement. Boston: Estes & Lauriat, c1875. 309p. NUC BL

4676. -----Egypt. By Clara Erskine Clement. Boston: D. Lothrop & co., 1880. 476p. NUC BL OCLC

4677. -----Naples, the city of Parthenope and its environs. By Clara Erskine Clement. Cambridge, Boston: Estes & Lauriat; L: Gay & Bird, 1894. 340p. NUC BL

4678. -----The queen of the Adriatic; or, Venice, medieval and modern. By Clara Erskine Clement. Boston: Estes & Lauriat; L: Gay & Bird, 1893. 380p. NUC BL OCLC

4679. WATKINS, Ann [Br. 1813-1885] Extracts from the memoranda and letters of Ann Watkins. Ipswich: S. & W. J. King, 1888. 159p. NUC MBD OCLC [Member of Society of Friends. Diary and autobiography; travel: Belgium, Northamptonshire, Ireland]

4680. WATSON, Agnes H. [Br. 19c] Our trip to America; being a diary and letters written during a holiday tour in the autumn of 1889. Edinburgh: pr., Oliver & Boyd, 1890. 112p. NUC

4681. WATSON, Emily H. [Am. 19c] ALT: W., E. H. Child-life in Italy. A story of six years abroad. Pub. anon. Boston: J. E. Tilton & co., 1866. 363p. NUC OCLC [Travel: Italy & Switzerland]

4682. WATSON, Lily, Mrs. Sydney Watson [Br. 19/20c] A village maiden's career. Life story of Mrs. Sydney Watson, told by herself. L: S. W. Partridge & co., 1899. BL

4683. WATSON, Rachel, Mrs. [Am. 19c]

The life of my family; or, the log-house in the Wildemere. NY: the author, 1871. 93p. NUC K [Farm life in N.Y.]

4684. WATSON, Mrs. Sydney see WATSON, Lily

4685. WATT, Agnes Craig (Paterson) [Br. 1846-1894] Twenty-five years' mission life on Tanna, New Hebrides. Paisley: J. & R. Parlane, 1896. 385p. NUC BL MB OCLC

4686. WATT, Hannah (Allen) see ALLEN, Hannah

4687. WATTS, Anna Mary (Howitt) [Br. 1824-1884] ALT: Howitt, Anna Mary An art-student in Munich. L: Longman, Brown, Green and Longmans, 1853. 2v. NUC BL OCLC

4688. WATTS, Jane (Waldie) [Br. 1793-1826] ALT: W., J.; Waldie, Jane Sketches descriptive of Italy in 1816-17; with a brief account of travels in various parts of France and Switzerland. Pub. anon. L: J. Murray, 1820. 4v. NUC BL

4689. WATTS, Jane (Waldie) see EATON, Charlotte Anne (Waldie)

4690. WATTS, Susannah, Mrs. [Br. 19c] ALT: W., S. Hymns and poems of Mrs. S. W., ... with a few recollections of her life. Leicester: n.p., 1842. BL

4691. WAYLAND, Mrs., comp. see ANON.

4692. WEBB, A. S., ed. see LUTTON, Anne

4693. WEBB, Eliza (Bowen) see WEST, Lucy (Brewer)

4694. WEBB, Elizabeth [Br. 19c] A letter from Elizabeth Webb to Anthony William Boehm; containing some account of her religious experience, with his answer. Philadelphia; n.p., 1781.

Warrington: W. Leicester;
Philadelphia: Joseph Rakestraw,
1802. 48p. NUC BL OCLC

4695. -----Narrations of the
convincement and other religious
experience of ... E. W.
The Friends' Library, v.13.;
Philadelphia: W. & T. Evans,
1837. BL

4696. WEBSTER, Mrs. H. E., comp.
see Taylor, Elizabeth
(Colepepper)

4697. WEBSTER, Rebecca Gair
(Russell) [Am. 1814-1846]
Biography of Mrs. Rebecca Gair
Webster. By Timothy Dwight Porter
Stone.
Boston: Crocker & Brewster, 1848.
420p. NUC OCLC
[May contain personal material.]

4698. WEIGALL, Lady Rose Sophia
Mary (Fane), comp. see CHARLOTTE
AUGUSTA OF WALES, Consort of
Prince Leopold of Saxe-Coburg

4699. WEIGALL, Lady Rose Sophia
Mary (Fane), ed. see WESTMORLAND,
Priscilla Anne (Wellesley Pole)
Fane, Countess of

4700. WEITBRECHT, Mrs. John James
see WEITBRECHT, Mary (Edwards)

4701. WEITBRECHT, Mary (Edwards),
Mrs. John James Weitbrecht [Br.
19c]
Missionary sketches in North
India: with references to recent
events.
L: J. Nisbet, 1858. 186p. NUC BL
OCLC
[Sepoy Rebellion-1857,8]

4702. WELBY-GREGORY, Hon.
Victoria Alexandrina Maria Louisa
(Stuart Wortley), Lady [Br. 1837-
1912] ALT: Gregory, Hon. Victoria
Alexandrina Maria Louisa (Stuart
Wortley) Welby, Lady; Wortley,
Hon. Victoria Alexandrina Maria
Louisa Stuart
A young traveller's journal of a
tour in North and South America
during the year 1850.
L: T. Bosworth, 1852. 260p. NUC
BL MAD N OCLC

4703. WELCH, Lydia Stuart
(Edwards) [Am. d. 1882]
In memoriam. Lydia Stuart Welch,
died February 5, 1882.
Detroit, MI: n.p., 1882?. 199p.
NUC OCLC
[Contains articles and poems.]

4704. WELD, A. G. see WELD, Agnes
Grace

4705. WELD, Agnes Grace [Br. 19c]
ALT: Weld, A. G.
Sacred palmlands, or, the journal
of a spring tour.
L: Longmans & co., 1881. 307p.
NUC BL OCLC
[Travel: Near East]

4706. WELD, Angelina Emily
(Grimké), Mrs. Theodore Dwight
Weld [Am. 1805-1879] ALT: Grimké,
Angelina Emily
In memory. Angelina Grimké Weld.
By Theodore Dwight Weld.
Boston: George H. Ellis, 1880.
81p. NUC OCLC
[Abolitionist. Includes excerpts
of letters and memorial sketches
of her sister, Sarah Moore
Grimké, 1792-1873.]

4707. WELD, Theodore Dwight,
comp. see WELD, Angelina Emily
(Grimké)

4708. WELD, Mrs. Theodore Dwight
see WELD, Angelina Emily
(Grimké)

4709. WELDON, Georgina (Treherne)
[Br. 1837-1914]
The ghastly consequences of
living in Charles Dickens' house.
L: n.p., 1882. 16p. BL

4710. -----The history of my
orphanage: or, the outpourings of
an alleged lunatic.
L: Mrs. Weldon, 1878. 40p. NUC BL
[Singer and music teacher;
accounts of legal and personal
troubles.]

4711. -----How I escaped the mad
doctors.
L: Mrs. Weldon, 1882. NUC BL

4712. WELLESLEY, Lady Victoria
Tylney Long [Br. 1818-1897]

The Lady Victoria Tylney Long
Wellesley. A memoir. By her
eldest god-daughter, Octavia
Barry.
L: Skeffington & son, 1899. 194p.
NUC BL OCLC
[Includes letters.]

4713. WELLS, Ella Marie Wilson
[Am. 1866-1880]
Ella's life and poems.
Norfolk, VA: pr. W. N. Grubb,
1880. 48p. NUC OCLC

4714. WELLS, Elvenah C.
(Raymond), Mrs. G. C. Wells [Am.
1826-1869]
Lingering sounds from a broken
harp. Ed. her husband, Rev. G. C.
Wells.
Albany, NY: S. R. Gray, 1869.
254p. NUC OCLC
[Devotional literature]

4715. WELLS, Francis Athon, comp.
see GIBSON, Jane

4716. WELLS, Rev. G. C., ed. see
WELLS, Elvenah C. (Raymond)

4717. WELLS, Mrs. G. C. see
WELLS, Elvenah C. (Raymond)

4718. WELLS, Leah (Davies) see
SUMBEL, Mary (Davies) Wells

4719. WELLS, Mary, comp. see
TURNER, Joanna

4720. WELLS, Mary (Davies) see
SUMBEL, Mary (Davies) Wells

4721. WELLS, Sarah Furnas, Mrs.
[Am. 19c]
Mysteries of the harems and
zenanas; or, life of oriental
women.
Indianapolis, IN: Morning Star
pub. co., 1886. 62p. NUC

4722. -----Ten years' travel
around the world, or from land to
land, isle to isle and sea to sea.
West Milton, OH: Morning Star
pub. co., 1885. 653p. NUC OCLC

4723. WELTON, N. J., Mrs. [Am.
19c] PSEUD: Notlew, Frances
A new tread in an old track. Pub.
as: Frances Notlew

NY: E. P. Dutton & co., 1882.
378p. NUC
[Travel: Europe]

4724. WEPPNER, Margaretha [Br. 19c]
The North Star and the Southern
Cross: being the personal
experiences ... of M. W., in a
two years' journey round the world.
L: S. Low, Marston, Low, &
Searle, 1875. 2v. NUC BL OCLC

4725. WESLEY, John, ed. see
LEFEVRE, Mrs.

4726. WEST, Charlotte, Mrs. [Br.
19c]
A ten years' residence in France,
during the severest part of the
revolution; from ... 1787 to
1797, containing ... anecdotes of
some of the most remarkable
personages of that period.
L: W. Sams, 1821. 100p. NUC BL MB

4727. WEST, Elizabeth [Br. 18c]
Memoirs or spiritual exercises of
E. W. Written by her own hand.
Glasgow: n.p., 1766. NUC BL MB
OCLC
[Covers 1694-1708. New ed. pub.
in 1831 as The Christian
Servant.]

4728. WEST, Lucy (Brewer) [Am.
18/19c] ALT: Baker, Louise;
Brewer, Lucy; Webb, Eliza (Bowen)
The adventures of Lucy Brewer,
alias Louise Baker; being a
continuation of Miss Brewer's
adventures from the time of her
discharge to the present day.
Boston: N. Coverly, 1815. 36p.
NUC OCLC
[Also pub. as: The Female Marine,
1816]

4729. -----An affecting narrative
of Louisa Baker, a native of
Massachusetts, who, in early life
having been shamefully seduced,
deserted her parents and
enlisted, in disguise, on board
an American frigate, as a marine.
Boston: pr., Nathaniel Coverly,
1816. NUC
[K attributes this work to Eliza
(Bowen) Webb, b. 1790 and lists
Louisa Baker and Lucy (Brewer)
West as alternative names. K

indicates that this edition contains material which appeared separately under different titles.]

4730. -----The awful beacon, to the rising generation of both sexes. ... This part (which being the third and last,) will be found to be still more interesting to the public than the two preceding ones.
Boston: pr. for N. Coverly, Jr., 1816. 32p. NUC

4731. -----The female marine.
n.p.: pr. for author, 1816. 100p. NUC K
[1st complete ed.]

4732. WEST, Mrs. Frederick see WEST, Theresa Cornwallis J. (Whitby)

4733. WEST, Maria Abigail [Am. 1827-1894]
The romance of missions; or, inside views of life and labor, in the land of Ararat.
NY: A. D. F. Randolph, 1875. 710p. NUC BL K OCLC
[Missionary in Turkey]

4734. WEST, Theresa Cornwallis J. (Whitby), Mrs. Frederick West [Br. 1805?-1886]
A summer visit to Ireland in 1846.
L: R. Bentley, 1847. 302p. NUC BL OCLC

4735. WESTBROOK, Mrs. J. Cooke, comp. see TATHAM, Emma

4736. WESTMINSTER, Dean of, ed. see TRENCH, Melesina (Chenevix)

4737. WESTMINSTER, Eleanor (Egerton) Grosvenor, Marchioness of [Br. d. 1846] ALT: Egerton, Hon. Eleanor
Diary of the Honourable Miss Egerton ... 1787 and 1788, giving an account of a tour in France and the north of Italy.
L: H. Massey, 1855. 206p. NUC

4738. WESTMINSTER, Elizabeth Mary (Leveson Gower) Grosvenor, 2d Marchioness of [Br. 1797-1891]

ALT: Grosvenor, Elizabeth Mary (Leveson Gower), Marchioness of Westminster
Diary of a tour in Sweden, Norway and Russia in 1827, with letters.
L: Hurst & Blackett, 1879. 297p. NUC BL MBD OCLC

4739. -----Narrative of a yacht voyage in the Mediterranean, during 1840-41.
L: J. Murray, 1842. 2v. NUC BL OCLC

4740. WESTMORLAND, Priscilla Anne (Wellesley Pole) Fane, Countess of [Br. 1793-1879] ALT: Burghersh, Priscilla Anne (Wellesley Pole) Fane, Lady; Fane, Priscilla Anne (Wellesley Pole), Countess of Westmoreland
The letters of Lady Burghersh (afterwards Countess of Westmorland) from Germany and France during the campaign of 1813-1814. Ed. by her daughter, Lady Rose [Sophia Mary (Fane)] Weigall.
2d ed. L: J. Murray, 1893. 241p. NUC BL OCLC

4741. WESTON, Agnes Elizabeth [Br. 1840=1918]
Safe moorings.
L & Aylesbury: Hazell & co., 1890. 15p. BL
[Account of her homes for sailors.]

4742. WESTON, Ann, Mrs. [Br. 19c]
The Christian mother: as seen by extracts from the diary of Ann Weston, the mother of a large family. [Comp.] A clergyman.
Bath: Binns & Goodwin, 1852. 32p. BL

4743. WESTON, Maria, ed. see MARTINEAU, Harriet

4744. WESTON, Mary (Pace) [Br. 1712-1766] ALT: Pace, Mary
The Eliot papers. Comp. Eliot Howard.
Gloucester: John Bellows, 1893-94. 2v. BL MAD MB MBD OCLC
[Member of Society of Friends; travel in New England; journal, 1787-1752]

4745. WESTOVER, Cynthia May, co-author see OBER, Carolyn Faville

4746. WESTROPP, J. E., Mrs. [Br. 19c]
Summer experiences of Rome, Perugia, and Siena in 1854.
L: Skeffington, 1856. 311p. NUC BL

4747. WETMORE, Elizabeth (Bisland) [Am. 1861-1929] ALT: Bisland, Elizabeth
A flying trip around the world. In seven stages.
NY: Harper & bros., 1891. 204p. NUC BL OCLC

4748. WETMORE, Mary Buel [Am. d. 1920]
Sounds from home and echoes of a kindgom.
Cincinnati, OH: The Editor pub. co., 1898. 127p. NUC OCLC
[Travel: Hawaii]

4749. WHARNCLIFFE, Lord, comp. see MONTAGU, Lady Mary (Pierrepont) Wortley

4750. WHATELY, Elizabeth Jane [Br. 1822-1893]
Elizabeth Jane Whately. Reminiscenses of her life and work. By her sister [Henrietta (Whately) Wale].
L: Seeley & co., 1894. 146p. BL

4751. WHATELY, Elizabeth Jane, comp. see WHATELY, Mary Louisa

4752. WHATELY, Mary Louisa [Br. 1824-1889] ALT: Whatley, Mary Louisa
Among the huts in Egypt. Scenes from real life. By M. L. Whately.
NY: Dodd & Mead, 1860. 344p. NUC BL OCLC

4753. -----Behind the curtain. Scenes from life in Cairo.
L: Seeley, Jackson & Halliday, 1882. 293p. NUC BL

4754. -----Letters from Egypt to plain folks at home.
L & Aylbury: n.p., 1878. NUC BL

4755. -----Life and work of M. L. W., by E[lizabeth] J[ane] Whately.

L: Religious Tract Society, 1890. 159p. NUC. OCLC

4756. -----Lost in Egypt.
L: Religious Tract Society, 1881. 291p. BL

4757. -----More about ragged life in Egypt.
2d ed. L: n.p., 1864. BL

4758. -----Ragged life in Egypt, and more about ragged life in Egypt. By M. L. Whately.
L: Seeley, Jackson & Halliday, 1862. 208p. NUC BL OCLC

4759. WHATLEY, Mary Louisa see WHATELY, Mary Louisa

4760. WHEELOCK, Julia Susan see FREEMAN, Julia Susan (Wheelock)

4761. WHILDEN, Ellen Ann, comp. see SEYMOUR, Juno (Waller)

4762. WHITALL, Alice B. [Br. 1839-1868]
On the rock: a memoir of A. B. W. Comp. Caroline Wallace Lawrence. Ed. Hannah Whitall Smith.
Philadelphia: George Maclean, 1870. 312p. NUC OCLC
[On cover: My beloved is mine, and I am His.]

4763. WHITALL, Ann [Am. 1716-1797]
John M. Whitall, the story of his life written for his grandchildren by his daughter, Hannah (Whitall) Smith.
Philadelphia: n.p., 1879. NUC BL MAD OCLC
[Members of Society of Friends; includes extracts of Ann Whitall's diary and also diary of Hannah Whitall, d. 1848.]

4764. WHITALL, Hannah, co-author see WHITALL, Ann

4765. WHITALL, John M., co-author see WHITALL, Ann

4766. WHITE, Caroline (Earle) [Am. 1833-1916]
A holiday in Spain and Norway.
Philadelphia: J. B. Lippincott co., 1895. 120p. NUC OCLC

4767. WHITE, Elizabeth, Mrs. Thomas White [Br. d. 1669]
The experiences of God's gracious dealing with Mrs. Elizabeth White, late wife of Mr. Thomas White of Caldecot in the county of Bucks; as they were written under her own hand, and found in her closet after her decease: she dying in child-bed, December 5th, 1669.
Boston: S. Kneeland & T. Green, 1741. 21p. NUC K

4768. WHITE, Ellen Gould (Harmon) [Am. 1827-1915]
A sketch of the Christian experience and views ....
Battle Creek, MI: Review & Herald; Oakland, CA: Pacific Press, 1882. 40p. K OCLC
[Seventh Day Adventist; she also pub. autobiography in 1915]

4769. WHITE, K. [Am. b. 1772]
A narrative of the life, occurences, vicissitudes and present situation of K. White. Comp. & collated by herself, Feb., 1809.
Schenectady, NY: pr. for authoress, 1809. 127p. NUC K
[Author born in Scotland, came to New England as child. Work concerns marital difficulties, debts.]

4770. WHITE, Mary Abiah (Dodge) [Am. 1808-1857]
In memory of a mother's love. January 5, 1857. By Mary Stuart (White) Smith.
NY: n.p., 1859. 116p. NUC
[Includes excerpts of journals & letters.]

4771. WHITE, Richard Grant see MARKHAM, Pauline

4772. WHITE, Mrs. Thomas see WHITE, Elizabeth

4773. WHITEING, Helen [Br. 19c] PSEUD: Alb
Living Paris and France. A guide to manners, monuments, ... and the life of the people; and handbook for travellers. By Alb.
L: Ward & Downey, 1886. 464p. BL OCLC

4774. WHITING, Mrs. M. E., comp. see MARTIN, Harriet Elizabeth

4775. WHITING, Martha [Am. 1795-1853]
The teacher's last lesson: a memoir of Martha Whiting, late of the Charleston female seminary. Consisting chiefly of extracts from her journals, interspersed with reminiscences and suggestive reflections. Ed. Catherine Naomi Badger.
Boston: Gould & Lincoln; NY: Sheldon, Lamport & Blakeman, 1855. 284p. NUC BL OCLC
[Chiefly religious]

4776. WHITTEN, Mary Delano [Am. 19c]
Blossom of Rocky Nook; or, life and writings of Mary Delano Whitten, 1822-1841. Ed. Sara Hall Brown.
Boston: O. L. Perkins, 1850. 179p. NUC BL OCLC

4777. WHITTIER, John Greenleaf see CHILD, Lydia Maria (Francis)

4778. WHITTY, E., Mrs. [Br. 19c]
A mother's journal during the last illness of her daughter, S[arah] Chisman [1801-1814].
L: B. J. Holdsworth, 1820. 172p.; Boston: Armstrong, 1821. 156p. NUC BL

4779. WHITWELL, Mrs. Edward Robson [Br. 19c]
Spain: as we found it in 1891.
L & Sydney: Eden, Remington & co., 1892. 160p. NUC BL OCLC

4780. WIGHT, Sarah [Br. 17c]
A wonderful pleasant and profitable letter written by Mrs. S. W. to a friend, expressing the joy is to be had in God in great, deep, long and sore afflictions, occasioned by the death of her brother. Ed. R. B.
L: n.p., 1656. BL

4781. WILDE, Jane Francesca Speranza (Elgee), Lady [Br. 1826-1896]
Driftwood from Scandinavia. By Lady Wilde.
L: R. Bentley & son, 1884. 297p. NUC BL OCLC

4782. WILDER, Lucy [Am. 19c]
Sketch of the life of Mrs. Lucy
Wilder. By a friend, Mrs. B. S.
Hall.
Springfield, IL: n.p., 1854. 22p.
NUC
[May contain personal writing]

4783. WILKINS, W. H. see BURTON,
Isabel (Arndell), Lady

4784. WILKINSON, Annie Margaret
(Green) [Br. 19c]
A lady's life and travels in
Zululand and the Transvaal during
Cetewaya's reign.
L: J. T. Hayes, 1882. 264p. NUC
OCLC
[Includes letters & journals.]

4785. WILKINSON, Eliza (Yonge)
[Am. 18c]
Letters of Eliza Wilkinson,
During the invasion and
possession of Charlestown, S.C.,
by the British in the
Revolutionary War. Arranged from
the original manuscripts, by
Caroline (Howard) Gilman.
NY: Scribner; Samuel Colman,
1829. 108p. NUC BL OCLC

4786. WILKINSON, Jemina see
HATHAWAY, Mrs. William, Jr.

4787. WILKINSON, Susannah, Mrs.
[Br. 1778-1832]
Extracts from the diairy of ...
Mrs. S. W.
L: n.p., 1832. BL MBD
[Religious]

4788. WILKINSON, Thomas, ed. see
PEARSON, Jane

4789. WILLARD, Caroline McCoy
(White), Mrs. Eugene S. Willard
[Am. 1853-1915]
Life in Alaska. Letters of Mrs.
E. S. Willard. Ed. her sister,
Eva (White) McClintock.
Philadelphia: Presbyterian Board
of Publication, 1884. 384p. NUC BL

4790. WILLARD, Emma (Hart) [Am.
1787-1870]
Journal and letters from France
and Great Britain.
Troy, NY: N. Tuttle, pr., 1833.
391p. NUC BL MBD

4791. WILLARD, Mrs. Eugene S. see
WILLARD, Caroline McCoy (White)

4792. WILLARD, Mrs. F. J. [Am.
19c] PSEUD: American Lady, An
Pictures from Paris in war and
seige. By an American lady.
L: R. Bentley & son, 1871. 213p.
NUC

4793. WILLARD, Frances Elizabeth
[Am. 1839-1898]
Glimpses of fifty years; the
autobiography of an American
woman.
Chicago: Women's Temperance pub.
assoc.; Boston: G. M. Smith &
co., 1889. 698p. NUC K OCLC
[Temperance worker. Later pub.
as: My happy half-century; the
autobiography of an American
woman.]

4794. WILLARD, Frances Elizabeth,
comp. see WILLARD, Mary E.

4795. WILLARD, Mary E. [Am. d.
1862]
Nineteen beautiful years; or,
sketches of a girl's life. By her
sister, Frances Elizabeth
Willard.
L & NY: Harper & bros., 1864.
241p. NUC BL OCLC
[Preface says first published in
1851. Includes excerpts from
Mary's diaries.]

4796. WILLEY, Chloe, Mrs. [Am. b.
1760]
A short account of the life and
remarkable views of Mrs. Chloe
Willey of Goshen, N.H. Written by
herself.
Amherst, MA: pr., Joseph Cushing,
1897. 24p. NUC K
[Religious]

4797. WILLIAM III, King of Great
Britain, co-author see MARY II,
Queen of Great Britain

4798. WILLIAMS, Bessie see
DAVIES, Bessie (Williams)

4799. WILLIAMS, Mrs. H. Dwight
see WILLIAMS, Martha (Noyes)

4800. WILLIAMS, Helen Maria [Br.
1762-1827] ALT: W., H. M.
Sketches of the state of manners

and opinions in the French republic towards the close of the eighteenth century. In a series of letters.
L: G. G. & J. Robinson, 1801. 2v NUC BL OCLC
[Also pub. as: Memoirs of the reign of Robespierre]

4801. -----A tour in Switzerland; or, a view of the present state of ... those cantons, with comparative sketches of the present state of Paris.
Dublin: P. Wogan: L: G. G. & J. Robinson, 1798. 2v. NUC BL

4802. WILLIAMS, Jane, ed. see DAVIS, Elizabth (Cadwaladyr)

4803. WILLIAMS, Jenny Perkins [Am. 19c]
Scattered verses and letters gathered again.
NY: French & Wheat, pr., c1869. 64p. NUC

4804. WILLIAMS, Sir John Bickerton, comp. see SAVAGE, Sarah (Henry)

4805. WILLIAMS, Martha (Noyes), Mrs. H. Dwight Williams [Am. 19c]
A year in China; and a narrative of capture and imprisonment ... on board the revel pirate, Florida.
NY: Hurd & Houghton, 1864. 362p. NUC BL OCLC

4806. WILLIAMS, Rosa Carnegie, Mrs. [Br. 19c]
A year in the Andes; or, a lady's adventures in Bogota.
L: London Literary Society, 1884. 270p. NUC BL OCLC

4807. WILLIAMSON, Hon. Anne Elizabeth (Liddell), Lady, co-author see NORMANDY, Maria (Liddell) Phypps, Marchioness of

4808. WILLIAMSON, Isabelle, Mrs. [Am. 19c]
Old highways in China.
NY: American Tract Society; 1884. 293p.; L: Religious Tract Society, 1884. 227p. NUC BL OCLC

4809. WILLIAMS-WYNN, Charlotte see WYNN, Charlotte Williams

4810. WILLIAMS-WYNN, Frances see WYNN, Frances Williams

4811. WILLS, Mary H. [Am. 19c]
A summer in Europe.
Phladelphia: J. B. Lippincpott & co., 1876. 170p. NUC BL OCLC

4812. -----A winter in California.
Norristown, PA: M. R. Wills, 1889. 150p. NUC OCLC

4813. WILLSON, Ann [Am. 1797/8-1843]
Familiar letters of Ann Willson.
Philadelphia: W. D. Parrish & co., 1850. 270p. NUC OCLC

4814. WILMOT, Sir E. Eardley, ed. see TATNALL, Esther

4815. WILMOT, John, Earl of Rochester, co-author see PHILIPS, Katherine (Fowler)

4816. WILSON, Alice, Mrs. [Br. 19c]
A short memoir of the late Mrs. Alice Wilson of Cornholme near Todmorden. By Joshua H. Wilson.
Manchester: priv. pr., 1877. 40p. BL

4817. WILSON, Alice Louise [Am. 19c] ALT: W., A. L.
Notes of travel. By A. L. W.
n.p.: n.p., 189?. 57p. NUC [Europe]

4818. WILSON, Ann, Mrs. [Br. 18/19c] ALT: W., A., Mrs.
Teisa: a descriptive poem of the river Teese, its towns and antiquities.
Newcastle upon Tyne: n.p., 1778. BL

4819. WILSON, Anne Campbell (Macleod), Lady [Br. d. 1921] ALT: Macleod, Anne Campbell
After five years in India; or, life and work in a Punjab district.
L: Blackie & son; NY: Charles Scribner's sons, 1895. 312p. NUC BL OCLC

4820. WILSON, Sir Arthur, ed. see MALCOLM, Clementina (Elphinstone), Lady

4821. WILSON, Caroline (Fry) [Br. 1787-1846] ALT: Fry, Caroline
An autobiography; letters and remains of the author of "The listener," "Christ our law," etc.
L: Seeleys, 1848. 495p. NUC BL MB OCLC

4822. -----Christ our example, to which is prefixed an autobiography.
NY: Am. Tract Soc.; Philadelphia: George Latimer, 1839. 386p. NUC BL MB OCLC

4823. WILSON, Eliza, Mrs. Robert Wilson [Br. 19c]
In the land of the Tui, my journal in New Zealand. By Mrs. Robert Wilson.
L: S. Low, Marston & co., 1894. 322p. NUC BL OCLC

4824. WILSON, Francesca Henrietta [Br. 19c]
Rambles in northern India, with incidents and descriptions of many scenes of the mutiny, etc.
L: S. Low, Marston, Low & Searle, 1876. 86p. NUC BL

4825. WILSON, Harriette [Br. 1786-1846]
Memoirs of Harriette Wilson, written by herself.
L: W. Dugdale, 1825? 322p.; 2d ed. Ed. T. Little. L: J. J. Stockdale, 1825. 4v. NUC BL MB OCLC
[Courtesan; many editions of her work were pub.]

4826. WILSON, Jane Adeline [Am. b. 1837]
A thrilling narrative of the sufferings of Mrs. Jane Adeline Wilson, during her captivity among the Comanche Indians, September, 1853.
Rochester, NY: D. M. Dewey, 1853?. 23p. NUC

4827. WILSON, John, comp. see WILSON, Margaret

4828. WILSON, Joshua H., comp. see WILSON, Alice

4829. WILSON, Lucy Langdon (Williams) [Am. b. 1864]

A too short vacation. With Emma V. McLoughlin.
Philadelphia: J. B. Lippincott co., 1898. 264p. NUC
[Travel: Europe]

4830. WILSON, Margaret (Bayne) [Br. 1795-1835]
A memoir of Mrs. Margaret Wilson ... incl. extracts from her letters and journals. By John Wilson.
Edinburgh: John Johnstone, 1838. 636p. NUC BL MB OCLC
[Missionary in India; diary 1828-1835 included]

4831. WILSON, Mary A. C., Mrs. [Am. 19c] PSEUD: "Mier Prisoner's" Widow, A
Reminiscences of persons, events, records and documents of Texian! times. By a "Mier prisoner's" widow.
Austin, TX: E. W. Swindels, 1882. 13p. NUC

4832. WILSON, Rachel (Wilson) [Am. 1720-1775]
A discourse delivered ... August, 1769, at the Friends meeting-house ... . Taken in short hand from the mouth of the speaker, by one of the audience.
NY and Newport, RI: pr., Solomon Southwick, 1769. 24p. NUC

4833. WILSON, Mrs. Robert see WILSON, Eliza

4834. WINGFIELD, Theodosia A. (Howard), Viscountess Powerscourt see POWERSCOURT, Theodosia A. (Howard) Wingfield, Viscountess

4835. WINSLOW, Anna Green [Am. 1759-1779]
Diary of Anna Green Winslow, a Boston school girl of 1771. Ed. Alice (Morse) Earle.
Boston & NY: Houghton Mifflin & co., 1894. 121p. NUC BL MAD OCLC

4836. WINSLOW, Harriet Wadsworth (Lathrop) [Am. 1796-1833]
Memoir of Mrs. Harriet L. Winslow. By Miron Winslow.
NY: Leavitt, Lord, 1835. 408p. NUC BL MAD OCLC
[Missionary diary 1813-1832, travels to India & Ceylon.]

4837. WINSLOW, Mary (Forbes) [Br. 1774-1854]
Christian experience: or, words of loving counsel and sympathy. Ed. her son, Octavius Winslow.
L: W. Hunt, 1868. 256p. NUC BL

4838. -----Heaven opened. A selection from the correspondence of Mrs. Mary Winslow. Ed. her son, Octavius Winslow.
NY: R. Carter & bros., 1867. 344p. NUC BL

4839. WINSLOW, Miron, comp. see WINSLOW, Harriet Lathrop

4840. WINSLOW, Octavius, ed. see WINSLOW, Mary (Forbes)

4841. WINTER, Catherine (Maillard) [Br. 19c]
One of the O'Mailleys: or, sketches from the diary of a lady lawyer.
Dublin: Thomas Bowles, 1862. 68p. BL
[Account of her mistreatment in a property case.]

4842. WINTER, J., ed. see HARBISON, Massy (White)

4843. WISNER, Benjamin B., ed. see HUNTINGTON, Susan (Mansfield)

4844. WISTER, Sally see WISTER, Sarah

4845. WISTER, Sarah [Am. 1761-1804] ALT: Wister, Sally
Amusing scenes of the Revolution. Journal of a young lady ... . Together with a letter from Martha Washington. In: Historical collections relating to Gwynedd. Comp. Howard M. Jenkins.
Philadelphia: the author, 1897. 456p. NUC MAD OCLC
[Journal 1777-1779; includes poems]

4846. WITTENMYER, Annie (Turner) [Am. 1827-1900]
Under the guns; a woman's reminiscences of the Civil War.
Boston: E. B. Stillings & co., 1895. 272p. NUC BL OCLC

4847. WITTITTERLY, JOHN ALTRAYD, pseud. see CARNE, Elizabeth Catherine Thomas

4848. WIXON, Susan Helen [Am. b. 1847]
Summer days at Onset.
Boston: G. E. Crosby, 1887. 84p. NUC
[Travel: Onset Bay, MA]

4849. WOLCOTT, Eliza see NORTON, Sarah Goodsell (Wolcott)

4850. WOLF, Annie S. [Am. 19c]
PSEUD: Em'ly
Foreign travel.
Philadelphia: Claxton, 1888. NUC

4851. -----Pictures and portraits of foreign travel. By Em'ly.
Philadelphia: E. Claxton & co., 1880. 420p. NUC OCLC

4852. -----Ten pictures of London society. The impressions of one season. By Annie Wolf (Em'ly).
Philadelphia: Linea Weaver & Wallace, pr., 1891. 71p. NUC

4853. WOLLEY, Anna see WOOLEY, Hannah

4854. WOLLEY, Hannah see WOOLEY, Hannah

4855. WOLLSTONECRAFT, Mary [Br. 1759-1797] ALT: Godwin, Mary (Wollstonecraft), Mrs. William Godwin
Letters written during a short residence in Sweden, Norway and Denmark.
L: J. Johnson, 1796. 262p. NUC BL OCLC
[Letters written to Gilbert Imlay, her first husband.]

4856. -----Posthumous works of the author of A vindication of the rights of woman. Ed. William Godwin.
L: John Johnson, 1798. NUC BL OCLC
[Includes letters to Imlay.]

4857. WOOD, Carrie see WOOD, Caroline

4858. WOOD, Caroline [Am. 1838-1857] ALT: Wood, Carrie
Recollections of our dear Carrie, who went, October, 1857. [By] Juliana (Randolph) Wood.

Philadelphia: n.p., 1868. 297p.
NUC OCLC

4859. WOOD, Julia Amanda
(Sargeant) [Am. 1826-1903]
My northern travels. The results
of faith and prayer. With the
author's autobiography.
Ashland, OH: The Brethern pub.
house, 1887. 160p. NUC OCLC
[Tour of nine months through
Illinois, Indiana, Michigan, New
York, Ohio, Pennsylvania, and
Canada.]

4860. WOOD, Julianna (Randolph)
[Am. d. 1885]
Family sketches.
Philadelphia: n.p., 1870. NUC
OCLC

4861. WOOD, Juliana (Randolph),
comp. see WOOD, Caroline

4862. WOOD, Lady Mary Susan
Felicie, co-author see EDGCUMBE,
Lady Ernestine Emma Horatia

4863. WOODBURY, Fanny [Am. 1791-
1814]
The journal and writings of Miss
Fanny Woodbury, who died at
Beverly, Nov. 15, 1814, aged 23
years ... by a clergyman of the
Church of Scotland. Ed. Joseph
Emerson.
2d ed. Edinburgh: pr. for J. T.
Smith & co., 1818. 320p.; 2d ed.
Boston: Samuel T. Armstrong,
1815. 288p. NUC BL OCLC
[Includes letters. OCLC title:
Writings of ... . pub. 1815.]

4864. WOODBURY, Josephine Curtis
(Battles) [Am. d. 1930]
War in heaven. Sixteen year's
experience in Christian Science
mind-healing.
3d ed. Boston: Samuel Usher,
1897. 69p. NUC K OCLC

4865. WOODMAN, Abby (Johnson)
[Am. b. 1828]
Picturesque Alaska; a journal of
a tour among the mountains, seas
and islands of the Northwest,
from San Francisco to Sitka.
Boston & NY: Houghton, Mifflin &
co.; Cambridge, MA: Riverside
press, 1889. 212p. NUC OCLC

4866. WOODMAN, Fanny (Crosskey)
[Br. 1860-1895]
Love's victory: memoirs of F.
Woodman, 1888-95. Ed. her sister,
A. Hodges.
L: Marshall bros., 1899. 133p.
NUC BL OCLC
[Includes extracts of diaries &
misc. writings. Missionary in
China.]

4867. WOODRUFF, Julia Louisa
Matilda (Curtiss) [Am. 1833-1909]
PSEUD: Jay, Mrs. W. M. L.
My winter in Cuba. By Mrs. W. M.
L. Jay.
NY: E. P. Dutton & co.; Hartford,
CT: Church press, 1871. 296p.
NUC BL OCLC

4868. WOODS, Catherine (Kendall)
[Am. b. 1824] ALT: Kendall,
Catherine
The true history of Catherine
Kendall. Forty years in the
wilderness. [Comp.] Mrs. S.
Spencer.
Portland, ME: G. W. Fish & co.,
1875. 84p. NUC

4869. WOODS, Kate (Tannatt) [Am.
1838-1910]
Across the continent. How the
boys and girls went from Bunker
Hill to the Golden Gate.
Boston: Lothrop pub. co., c1897.
240p. NUC OCLC

4870. -----Out and about: or, the
Hudson's trip to the Pacific.
Boston: D. Lothrop & co., 1882.
259p. NUC OCLC

4871. WOODS, Margaret [Br. 1748-
1821]
Extracts from the journal of the
late M. W. from ... 1771 to 1821.
L: n.p. 1829; 3d ed.
Philadelphia: H. Longstreth,
1850. 378p. NUC BL MBD OCLC
[Member of Society of Friends]

4872. WOODWARD, Jane [Br. 19c]
Our summer holiday.
L: James Nisbet & co., 1870. BL
[Travel: Lake country]

4873. WOODWORTH-ETTER, Maria
Beulah [Am. b. 1844]
Life and experience of Maria B.

Woodworth, written by herself.
Dayton, OH: United Brethren pub.
house, 1885. 80p. NUC K OCLC
[Evangelist]

4874. WOOLEY, Hannah [Br. fl.
1670] ALT: Wolley, Hannah; ALT:
Wolley, Anna
The gentlewoman's companion ...
with letters and discourses upon
all occasions ... .
L: pr. A. Maxwell for Dorman
Newman, 1673. 262p. NUC BL OCLC
[Spiritual autobiographies]

4875. WOOLSEY, Jane Stuart [Am.
19c]
Hospital days.
NY: D. Van Nostrand, for priv.
use, 1868. 180p. NUC BL OCLC
[Personal account of Civil War]

4876. WOOLSON, Constance Fenimore
[Am. 1840-1894] PSEUD: March, Anne
Mentone, Cairo and Corfu.
NY: Harper & bros., 1896. 358p.
NUC OCLC

4877. -----The old stone house.
By Anne March.
Boston: D. Lothrop & co.; Dover,
NH: G. T. Day & co., 1873. 427p.
NUC OCLC
[Novelist tells of her early life
in Cleveland.]

4878. WOOLVEN, Mary [Br. 19c]
The utterance of the heart:
consisting of letters, poetry,
etc. Ed. J. Hallett.
L: n.p., 1842. BL

4879. WOOSTER, David, ed. see
TREVELYAN, Paulina Jermyn
(Jermyn), Lady

4880. WORDSWORTH, Dora see
QUILLINAN, Dorothy (Wordsworth)

4881. WORDSWORTH, Dorothy [Br.
1771-1855]
The journals of Dorothy
Wordsworth. Ed. William Knight.
L & NY: Macmillan & co., 1897.
2v. NUC BL PMD OCLC

4882. -----Recollections of a
tour made in Scotland, A. D.
1803. Ed. John Campbell Shairp.

Edinburgh: David Douglas, 1874.
316p. NUC BL OCLC

4883. WORKMAN, Fanny (Bullock),
Mrs. William Hunter Workman [Am.
1859-1925]
Algerian memories: a bicycle tour
over the Atlas to the Sahara.
With William Hunter Workman.
L: T. Fisher Unwin; NY: A. D. F.
Randolph, 1895. 216p. NUC BL
OCLC

4884. -----Sketches awheel in
fin-de-siècle Iberia. With
William Hunter Workman.
L: T. F. Unwin, 1897. 228p.; NY &
L: G. P. Putnam's sons, 1897.
242p. NUC BL OCLC
[Also pub. as: Sketches awheel in
modern Iberia]

4885. WORKMAN, William Hunter,
co-author see WORKMAN, Fanny
(Bullock)

4886. WORKMAN, Mrs. William
Hunter see WORKMAN, Fanny (Bullock)

4887. WORMELEY, Katharine
Prescott [Am. 1830-1908]
The other side of war; with the
Army of the Potomac. Letters from
the headquarters of the U. S.
Sanitary Commission during the
peninsular campaign in Virginia
in 1862.
Boston: Ticknor & co., 1889
[1888]. 210p. NUC BL OCLC
[Pub. in 1898 as: The cruel side
of war. Letters to author's
family and friends from the
hospital ships.]

4888. WORTLEY, Lady Emmeline
Charlotte Elizabeth (Manners)
Stuart- see STUART-WORTLEY, Lady
Emmeline Charlotte Elizabeth
(Manners)

4889. WORTLEY, Hon. Victoria
Alexandrina Maria Louisa Stuart
see WELBY-GREGORY, Hon. Victoria
Alexandrina Maria Louisa (Stuart-
Wortley), Lady

4890. WRENCH, Matilda [Br. d.1866?]
The highland glen; or, plenty and
famine: founded on facts.
3d ed. L: B. Wertheim, 1847. 68p.
BL OCLC

4891. WRIGHT, Mrs. Charles Henry
Hamilton [Br. 19c]
Sunbeams on my path.
n.p.: n.p., 1890. MB
[Missionary in Sweden,
Switzerland & the Crimea; life in
England, Germany, France and
Ireland.]

4892. WRIGHT, Eliza [Br. 19c]
The gathered rose. Memoir of
Eliza Wright. By her father,
Philip James Wright.
L: J. B. Cooke, 1858. 285p. BL
[Chiefly religious, includes
letters]

4893. WRIGHT, Emily [Am. 19c]
From the Lakes to the Gulf.
Chicago: R. R. Donnelly &
sons,pr., c1884. 124p. NUC OCLC
[Travel: Mississippi Valley]

4894. WRIGHT, Frances see
D'ARUSMONT, Frances (Wright)

4895. WRIGHT, Hannah Mary [Br.
1840-1872]
The Ruthwell cross and other
remains of the late Hannah Mary
Wright ... with brief memoir of
the author. [signed R. R.]
Edinburgh: J. Taylor, 1873. 160p.
NUC BL

4896. WRIGHT, Julia (MacNair)
[Am. 1840-1903]
Among the Alaskans.
Philadelphia: Presbyterian Board
of Publication, 1883. 351p. NUC
BL OCLC

4897. WRIGHT, Marie (Robinson)
[Am. 1866-1914]
Picturesque Mexico.
Philadelphia: J. B. Lippincott
co., c1897. 445p. NUC OCLC

4898. WRIGHT, Martha, comp. see
JACKSON, Rachel Maria

4899. WRIGHT, Philip James, ed.
see WRIGHT, Eliza

4900. WRIGHT, Sarah Ann, Mrs.
[Am. 19c]
The boys in blue; or, a soldier's
life.
NY: NY pub. co., c1869. 100p. NUC
OCLC

[Civil War, personal & historical]

4901. WYATT, Sophia Hayes, Mrs.
[Am. 19c]
The autobiography of a landlady
of the old school.
Boston: pub. for the author,
Wright & Hasty, pr., 1854. 284p.
NUC K OCLC
[Reminiscences of Dover, NH and
other places in New England.]

4902. WYLDE, Flora Frances
(MacDonald), ed. see MacDONALD,
Flora (MacDonald)

4903. WYNDHAM, Hon. Fanny
Charlotte see MONTGOMERY, Hon.
Fanny Charlotte (Wyndham)

4904. WYNN, Charlotte Williams
[Br. 1807-1869] ALT: Williams-
Wynn, Charlotte
Extracts from letters and diaries
of Charlotte Williams-Wynn. Ed.
her sister, Harriot Hester
(Williams-Wynn) Lindesay.
L: Trübner & co., 1871. 284p. NUC
BL
[t.p.: Priv. printed]

4905. -----Memorials of Charlotte
Williams-Wynn. Ed. her sister,
Harriot Hester (Williams-Wynn)
Lindesay.
L: Longmans, Green & co., 1877.
383p. NUC BL

4906. WYNN, Frances Williams [Br.
1773-1857] ALT: Williams-Wynn,
Frances
Diaries of a lady of quality from
1797 to 1844. Ed. Abraham
Hayward.
L: Longman, Green, Longman,
Roberts & Green, 1864. 359p. NUC
BL OCLC
[Culled from 10 vols. of her
memories of famous people.]

4907. YATES, Mrs. Ashton see
YATES, F. M. L.

4908. YATES, F. M. L., Mrs.
Ashton Yates [Br. 19c]
Letters written during a journey
to Switzerland in the autumn of
1841.
L: Duncan & Malcolm, 1843. 2v.
NUC BL OCLC

4909. -----A winter in Italy. In a series of letters to a friend. L: H. Colburn, 1844. 2v. NUC BL OCLC

4910. YEARDLEY, John, co-author see YEARDLEY, Martha Savory

4911. YEARDLEY, Mrs. John see YEARDLEY, Martha Savory

4912. YEARDLEY, Martha Savory, Mrs. John Yeardley [Br. 1781-1851] Extracts from the letters of John and Martha Yeardley, whilst on a religious visit to some parts of the continent of Europe, the Ionian Isles, etc. Lindfield: pr., W. Eade, 1835. 56p. NUC BL OCLC [Society of Friends]

4913. YELVERTON, Maria Theresa (Longworth), Viscountess Avonmore see LONGWORTH, Maria Theresa

4914. YELVERTON, Hon. Theresa see LONGWORTH, Maria Theresa

4915. YOUNG, Ann Eliza (Webb) [Am. b. 1844] Wife no. 19; or the story of a life in bondage, being a complete exposé of Mormonism. Hartford, CT: Dustin, Gilman & co., 1875. 600p. NUC BL K OCLC

4916. YOUNG, Elizabeth (Davis) [Br. 1765-1842] The Christian experience of Mrs. Elizabeth Young. Bristol & L: Harvey & Darton, 1843. 122p. NUC BL MB MBD [Member of Society of Friends; includes diary, 1791-1840]

4917. YOUNG, Frances, Mrs., co-author see LUSCOMBE, Ellen, Mrs.

4918. YOUNG, Gerald, ed. see LAMBERT, S.

4919. YOUNG, Marianne Postans [Br. 19c] ALT: Postans, Mrs. Thomas Aldershot, and all about it. L: Routledge, 1857. NUC BL

4920. -----Cutch; or, random sketches, taken during a residence in one of the northern provinces of western India: interspersed with legends and traditions. L: Smith Elder & co., 1839. 283p. NUC BL

4921. -----Facts and fictions, illustrative of oriental character. L: William H. Allen & co., 1844. 3v. NUC BL [Travel in India & Egypt, interspersed with stories.]

4922. -----Our camp in Turkey and the way to it. L: R. Bentley, 1854. 313p. NUC BL

4923. -----Western India in 1838. L: Saunders & Otley, 1839. 2v. NUC BL OCLC

4924. YOUNG, Robert. M see M'CRACKEN, Mary A.

4925. YOUNG, Sarah, ed. see SCUDAMORE, Rebecca (Thornhill)

APPENDIX

CHRONOLOGICAL LISTING

1475-1599

*Askewe

Catharine

*Dudley, J. G.

(Kempe)

1600-1699

Allen, H.

*Bacon, A. C.; *Bacon, J. M. C.; Banbury; Blaugdone; *Burnet

Carleton; Cellier; *Colville; Cook; Curwen

*Downing; (Dudley, J. G.)

*Elisabeth, P.S.; *Elizabeth, Queen; Evans, K.; Everard

*Fanshawe; Fletcher, I.

Gethin; *Godolphin; Goodenough; Goodhue; *Gordon, J. H.

*Halkett; *Harcourt, A.; *Harley; *Henrietta Maria; Hills, L.; *Hogben; *Hutchinson, L. A.

Joceline

Lincoln, E.; Love

*Mary II; *Maxwell, Lady M. C. H.; *Mollineux; Mordaunt

*Newcastle

*Newdigate, A. F.

*Penington; Philips

Rowlandson

*Stuart, Lady A.

*Temple; Turner, Jane

Vokins

Walker, E. S.; Warwick; *White, E.; Wight; Wooley

1700-1749

*Baillie, G. H.; *Bell, D.; Bowers; Brereton; Bury, E. L.;

*Cairns; Chandler; *Cowper, M. C.

*Dalrymple; Davies, C. C.; Dutton, Anne

*Fiennes; Fox, M. A. F.

Hanson, E.; Hayes, A. S.; Hill, H.; Housman; Hume; Hurll

Justice

*Knight, S. K.

Lee, E. S.

(Mollineux)

Pennyman; (Philips); Phillips, T.; Pilkington, L. V. L.

Ross, C. C.; *Rowe; *Russell, R. W. V.

Shaftoe; Smart; Smith, Grace; Stirredge; *Story

Thomas, E.

*Veitch

Wast; (White, E.)

1750-1799

Alley; Althans; Anthony; *Ashbridge; Atmore; Aust

Ball; *Bayard; (Bell, D.); Bellamy; Billington; Blandy; *Brayton; Brine; Brittle; Brookhouse; Buchan

(Cairns); *Calderwood; Carter, A. M.; *Cary, M.; Catley; Charke; Cish; Coghlan; *Coit; *Coke, J. W. H.; *Coningsby; Cooper, J.; Cooper, M. S.; Craven, E. B.; Crowley, A.

Davidson, M.; Davies, A.; Davis, J.; *Delany; *Dodshon; Donellan; Dornford; Douglas, J.; Douglas, M.; *Dudley, D.

*Eve

Falconbridge; Farrer; *Featherstonhaugh; Fletcher, M. B.;

Gannett; Gilbert, M.; *Glenorchy; Gooch; *Greene, M. C. H.; Griffith, E. G.; Grosvenor, H. V. G.; Grubb, S. T.; Gunning

Hanway; *Harcourt, E. H.; Harper, E. T.; Hart, C.; Harvey, J.; Hastings, S. W. J.; Hawkins; Hervey, E. C.; *Hervey, M. L. H.; Hill, P. B.; Hoskins; Howe, J. S.; *Huntington, A. H.; Hutson

Jemmat; Johnson, E. J.

Kindersley; Kinnan

Laird, M.; Latter; Lee, E. S.; Leeson; Lefevre; Leininger; Lowry; Lucas, M. B.; *Lumb; Luxborough; Lyell

*Macdonald; *Maris, A.; Marishall; Massey; Maxwell, K.; Miller, A. R.; Montagu, Lady M. P. W.; Moore, J. E. G.; Morgan, M.

Neale; Northumberland

*Osborn, S. B.; Osborn, S. H.

Parker, M. A.; Phillips, C.; *Pinckney; Piozzi

Radcliffe, A. W.; Riddell; Rippon; Robertson, H.; Robinson, M. D.; *Rogers, H. A. R.; (Rowe); Rudd; (Russell, R. W. V.); Ryder
Sage; *Savage; Scudamore; Shaw, M.; Sheldon, A.; *Sheridan; Smyth, A.; Snell, H.; *Somerset, F. T. S.; Steele, E.; Strathmore; *Suffolk

Tenducci; Thicknesse; Tonkin; Turner, Joanna

Upton; *Ussher, E.

Vane, F. A.; Vigor

*Ward, S.; Webb; West, E.; *Weston, M. P.; *Whitall, A.; Williams, H. M.; Wilson, Ann; Wilson, R. W.; *Winslow, A. G.; Wollstonecraft

1800-1825

*Abington; *Adams, A. S.; Alexander, M.; Allen, S.; Anon; Arrive, (Ashbridge); *Austen

*Bagshawe; Bailey, A. A.; Bailey, A.; (Baillie, G. H.); Baillie, M.; Barbauld; Barfield; *Barnard, A. L; Barnard, S.; Barns; Bartlett; Bennet; *Bingham; Blessington; Bond, E.; Boone; *Bowne; Bradley; Bray; (Brayton); Brooke, C.; Brooker; Brown, E. S.; Brown, S.; *Byrom

Callcott; Cappe; Cardwell; Carey; Carson; Carter, A.; Carter, E.; Cary, C. E.; Chapone; Charlotte Augusta; Charlton; Clarke, M. A. T.; Cobb, M. B.; *Coke, M.; Cole, R.; Cooper, M. H.; Cope; Craven, E. B.; Cutler, E

D., Mrs. A. G.; Dabney; D'Arusmont; Davis, J.; *Dawson; Deane, A.; De Camp; (Delany); *Devonshire, E. C. H. F. C.; *Devonshire, G. S. C.; Dexter, M. M.; (Dodshon); Dow; *Drinker; (Dudley, J. G.); Dudley, M.; Dustin; Dymond, A.; Dyott

Eaton; Elizabeth; Emerson, E. R.; Ewing

Fay, E.; Fenning; Fisher, E. M.; Fletcher, M. B.; Fletcher, Mrs.; Fordyce; *Frost

Gannett; Gardiner, J.; (Glenorchy); Gordon, L. A.; Gow; Graham, I. M.; Grane; Grant, A. M.; Grant, M. A.; Grassie

Hamilton, E.; Hamilton, E. L.; Hamilton, S.; Hamilton, S. B.; Harbison; Harvard; Harvey, J.; Hassal; Hastings, S. A.; Hatfield; *Hathaway, Mrs. W.; Hawkins; Hawley; (Hervey, M. L. H.) Hesketh; Hill, S. A. C.; Holbrook; A. C. J.; Holderness; Hopwood; Howel; *Hoyt; *Huntington, S. M. ; Hutchinson, E.; (Hutchinson, L. A.); Hyde

*Inchbald

Jackson, Margaret; Jebb; *Jerningham; Johnstone, J.; Jones, Sarah; Judson, A. H.

King, F. E.; (Knight, S. K.)

Lacy; Lee, R. F. A.; Lee, S. W. B.; (Lefevre); Lewis, H.; Lucas, R. H.; Luce; Lynn

Macauley; M'Lehose; Mallabone; Martin, M.; *Mason, S. H.; Maxwell, D. B.; (Maxwell, M. C. H.); Meadows; Mitchell, M. C.; Montagu, E. R.; (Mordaunt) *More, M.; Moreland; Morgan, S. O.; *Morris, M. H.; Morton, S. W. A.

(Newcastle); *Newdigate, H.; Newell, F.; Newell, H. A.; Nichols, Ann S.; *Norton, S. G. W.

(Osborn, S. H.); Oswald, M.

Palmer, M.; Parker, L.; Parris, Miriam; Paul; Pawson; Pearson, J.; *Pearson, S.; (Penington); Perkins, E.; *Phelps, E. P.; Phillips, P.

Pilkington, M. H.; Plumptre; *Powys

Radcliffe, M. A.; Ramsay, M. L.; Ripley, D.; *Riske; Ritson; Robertson, E. F.; Robinson, M. D.; (Rogers, H. A. R.); Routh; Russell, C.; (Russell, R. W. V.)

(Savage); Saxby, M. H.; Scofield; Selwyn; *Seton; Seward, A.; Shackleton; *Shelley, H. W.; Shelley, M. W. G.; (Sheridan); *Sheriff; Siddon; *Smith, A. A.; Smith, Elizabeth; Smith, S.; (Somerset, F. T. S.); Spence; Starke; Stephenson, S.; Sterndale; Stones; (Story); (Suffolk); Sumbel

Taylor, A. M.; *Taylor, H. H.; Taylor, J.; *Taylor, S. C.; Titharton; Torrey; Trimmer; Tully; Turner, Joanna

Ulyat; (Ussher, E.)

Velnet

Wakefield, P. B.; Waring; Warren, M. O.; Watts, J. W.; Webb; West, C.; West, L. B.; White, K.; Whitty; Willey; Williams, H. M.; Wilson, H.; *Wister; Woodbury, F.; *Woods, M.

1826-1850

Abell; (Adams, A. S.); Adams, H.;
Adderley; *Adelaide; Agnew, M.;
Aquilar; Alby; Allen, E.; Allen,
R.; Anon; Arblay; Ashford; Ashmore;
(Askewe); Aylmer

*Backhouse, A. G.; Backhouse, D.;
*Backhouse, H. C. G.; (Ball);
(Barnard, A. L.); Barrot; Bartram;
Beauchamp; Beavan; Bell, F. A.;
*Bethune; Bettle; Betts; Bickford;
(Bingham); Birch; Birt; Blaze de
Bury, Blessington; Boddington;
Bolaine; Bolton; Bourne; Boutelle;
Bray; Broadbelt; Brown, S.;
Budgett; *Bulfinch; Bulmer;
Bunbury; Bunting; Burke; Burlend;
(Burnet); Bury; C. S. M. C.; Byrd
Cahoone; Calderon de la Barca;
Campbell, I.; Camplin; Capper;
Carmichael; Carnes; Carson; Cary,
C. E.; Cazneau; (Charlotte
Augusta); Chatterton; Child, F.;
Child, L. M. F.; Church; *Clarke,
M. C.; Clemans; Clemons; Clough, M.
M.; Collins, E. B. M.; Colquhoun;
(Colville); (Coningsby); Cooke, E.
S.; Costello; Coulthard; Cox, L.
N.; Craven, E. B.; Creamer;
Crocker; Croggon; Crowley; Cryer;
Culbertson; Cushing

Dabney; Damer; *Darling, G. H.;
D'Arusmont; Davidson, M. M.;
Davidson, M. (M.); Davies, C.;
(Dawson); Day, M.; Deans; De
Kroyft; Dickson; Dixon; Doherty;
*Dudley, E.; Duncan, M. L.;
(Dutton, Anne); Dyson, Mrs. C.

Eames; Eastlake; Eastman, M. H.;
Eden, E.; *Edgeworth; Elaw;
Eldridge; *Elizabeth of England;
(Elizabeth, Queen); Ellesmere;
Ellet; Ellis, S. S.; Elssler;
Elwood; Evans, Rachel; Evans,
Rebecca; Evershaw; (Ewing)

(Fanshawe); Farnham; *Farrand;
Felton; Female Teacher; Fisher, L.
J. L.; Flannigan; *Fletcher, M. J.
J.; Follows; Fowler; Fox, M. M.;
Fraser, E. A.; Freeman, A.; French,
Matilda; Fry, E. G.

Gardiner, J. A.; Gibson, J.;
Gilman; Gilpin; (Godolphin);
Goodal; Goodale; Goodrich; (Gordon,

J. H.); Govion Broglio Solari;
(Graham, I. M.); Graham, M.;
Graham, M. J.; Grant, A. M.; Gray,
E. C. J.; Gray, M. ; Grew;
Griffith, L. D.; Griffith, Mary;
Grosvenor; H. S.; Grubb, S. L.;
Gundry; Gunn; Gurney, P. H.

Hagger; Haight; Hall, A. M. F.;
Hall, F. W.; Hall, S. E.; Hamilton,
A.; Hamilton, M.; Hammond, P. P.;
Hanson, E. C.; Hardcastle; Harris,
C.; Hart, Miss; Hasan; Hastings, F.
E. R.; Hathaway, L. A. R.; Hatton;
Hawkes; Hayward, L.; Hemans; Hill,
M. L.; *Hoare, R. N.; Hobbie;
Hodgkin, E. H.; Hoding; Hofland;
Holley, M. A.; Holmes, A. M.;
Holmes, E. E.; Holmes, H. A.;
Honey; Hood; Horn; Hosmer;
Houstoun; How; Howard, C. M. N.;
Howard, R.; Howe, M. M.; *Howland;
(Hoyt); Hughes; (Huntington, S.
M.); *Hutton

(Inchbald); Innes, M.

Jackson, A.; Jameson; Jeffreys;
Jenkin; Jenkins; Jesup, M.; Jesup,
M. B.; Johnson, S.; Jones, E. G.;
Jones, E.; Jordan; Jowitt; Judson,
A. H.; Judson, S. H. B.

Kemble; Kenning; Kerr; Kilham;
Kinney; Kirkland; Knight, E. W.;
*Knight, E. C.; Knight, S. J.;
Knott

Lady, A; Lady, A; Lamb; Lamont;
Lancaster; Lane, A.; *Leadbeater;
Lee, E. B.; Lee, J.; Lennox;
Leslie, E. F.; *Leigh, E. M.;
Livermore, H.; *Logan, D. N.; Lowe,
A.; Lowrie; Lucy; Lushington, S.
G.; Lyon, M.; *Lyon, M.

Macauley; McDougald; M'Lehose;
Maclellan, F.; M'Taggart; *Madison;
Maitland, J. E. B.; *Malcolm; Mann,
Alice; Marshall, M. M. D.; Martin,
J. A.; Martin, Sarah; Martin,
Selina; Martineau; *Mason, C.;
(Mason, S. H.); Mathews, Mrs.;
Maury; Maw; Mawson; (Maxwell, Lady
M. C. H.) Mayo; Melville, Mercer;
Meredith; Misca; Montauban;
Montefiore; Moodie, More, H.;
Morgan, S. O.; Morrell; (Morris, M.
H.); Mortimer, E. R.: Mortimer, F.
L. B.; Morton, H.; Muir, M.; Mundy;

Munson; Murray, Lady

*Nairne; (Newell, F.); (Newell, H. A.); Nicholson; Norton, C. E. S. S.; (Norton, S. G. W.); Nugent, M. S.

Ossoli

Palmer, A.; *Papendiek; Pardoe; Parlby; *Parris, Mary; Patten; (Pearson, S.); (Penington); Perry; Phillipps, H. E. M.; Phipps; Pickard; Pigot; Pigott, H.; (Pinckney); (Piozzi); Pittar; Place; Platt; Plumley; Poole, S. L.; Porter, D. H. C.; Powerscourt; Prince; Prior

Quillinan; *Quincy

(Radcliffe, A. W.); Reed, R. T.; Reeve, S.; Reynolds, C.; Rhodes, E.; Richards, L.; Richardson, E. S.; Rives; Roberts, E.; Roberts, J.; Romer; Royall

Sale; Saunders; Schillio; Scott, A.; *Scott, J. H. K.; Sears; Sedgwick; Sealy; Selwyn; Shelley, M. W. G.; (Sheriff); Shindler; *Shore; *Shuck; Siddons; Sigourney; Simpson, M.; Sinclair, C.; Skene; (Smith, A. A.); Smith, A.; Smith, Eliza; Smith, H. L. F.; Smith, Martha; Smith, M. H.; Smith, S. H. L.; Smyth, G. T.; Soper; Speare; Stacy; Stanhope; Starke; Statham; Steele, E. R.; Stephens; Stevens, M.; Stewart, C. B.; (Stirredge); Stisted; Strutt; Stuart-Wortley

Taft; Tatham; Tatnall; Taylor, C.; Taylor, E. C.; Taylor, Emily; (Temple); *Thompson, E. M. L.; Thornton, A. J.; Thorold; Thurston; Timms; Tomes; Tonna; Towle; Traill; *Trench, M. C. S. G.; Trollope, F. M.; Truth; Tucker, S. F.; Tucker, S. H. C.; Tuttle

Vane, F. A. V. T.; Van Lennep; Vavasour; (Veitch)

Ward, H.; Ward, H. L. H.; (Ward, S.); Warren, A. W.; (Warwick); Watts S.; Webb; Webster; West, T. C. J. W.; *Westminster, E. E. G.; Westminster, E. M. L. G. G.;

Whitten; Wilkinson, E. Y.; Wilkinson, S.; Willard, E. H.; Willson; Wilson, C. F.; Wilson, M. B.; Winslow, H. W. L.; (Woods, M.); Woolven; Wrench

Yates; Yeardley; Young, E. D.; Young, M. P.

1851-1875

Abbott, E. M.; Acklom; (Adams, A. S.); (Adelaide); Agassiz; Aikin; Aitken; Alcott; Alexander, P.; Alexander, S.; Alford; Allibone; Ames, M. E. C.; Anderson, B.; Anderson, M. E. R.; Andrew, A.; Armour; Arms; Arnold; Aspinall; Atkinson, L.; Auty

(Backhouse, A. G.); (Backhouse, H. C. G); (Bacon, A. C.); Bacon, G. M. W.; Bacon, L. B. S.; Bailey, M J. S.; Baillie, E. C. C.; Baker, G.; Balcomb; (Barbauld); Barber, A. S.; Barber, M.; Barber, M. A. S.; Barclay; Barlow; Barlow; A. F.; Barlow, D.; Barney; Barter; Bartrum; Baskin; Bassett; Bates, D. B.; Bates, E. M.; Bayman; Beaufort; Beck; Beecher, C. E.; Beke; Bellairs; Belloc; Bennett, S.; Benson, P.; Berry; Best; (Bethune); Bevan; Bickersteth, E.; Bishop, H. E.; Bishop, I. L. B.; Black; Blackwell, C. S.; Blackwood; Bland; Bleecker; (Blessington); Blundell; Bocking; Boulingny; Bowen; Bowman; Boyd, B.; Brassey; Bridgman; Brittan; Bromley; Brooke, T.; Broome; Brown, H. E.; Brown, J.; Brown, K.; Brown, K. M. E.; *Browning, E. B.; Brownlow; Bryan; Bryce; Bullard; Bunbury; Bunkley; Burton; Bush, E. C.; Bush, R. H.; *Buxton, H. G.; Byrne; (Byrom)

*Caldwell; Cameron; Campbell, H. A.; Campbell, I., Mrs.; Campbell, T. M. A. E.; *Carlyle; Carne; Carpenter, M; Carr, M. F.; Carrington; Carter, M.; Case; Catlow; Cazneau; Cedarholm; Challice; Channing; Charles; (Charlotte Augusta); Chester; Child, F.; Chubbuck; Churchill, C. M. N.; Clacy; Claflin; Claghorn; Clare; *Clark, L. F. S.; (Clarke, M. C.); Clarke, M. E. B.; Clemens;

Lanman; Larimer; Lawrence, C. R.;
(Leadbeater); Leak; Lean; Lees;
(Leigh, E. M.); Leigh, M.;
(Leonowens); L 'Estrange; Le Vert;
Lewis, A. S.; Light; Likins;
Lipincott, S. J. C.; Lisle; Little,
L. J.. R.; Littleboy; *Livingston;
Lloyd, B. F.; Lobdell; Lockhart;
(Logan, D. N.); Logan, O. L.;
Lomax; Londonderry; Longworth;
Lott; Loughborough; Lowe, E.; Lucy;
Luscombe; Lushington; H. P.;
Luttrell; *Lyman, A. J. R.; Lyman,
J. E.; Lynch, T. E. F.; (Lyon, M.)

M'Allister; MacCaskill; Mac
Clellan; *M'Cracken; (Macdonald);
McDougall; McGuire; MacKenzie, A.;
MacKenzie, C.; Mackenzie, H. D.;
MacLellan, F. E. H.; MacPherson,
A.; Macquoid; Macrae; Mann,
Agnes;(Maris, A.) Maris, E. W.;
Markham; Martin, C. B.; Martin, H.
E.; Martin, J. A.; Martineau;
Maskell; (Mason, C.); Mason, E.. H.
B.; Meeker; Mendell; Meredith;
Mering; Merryweather; Merwin;
Methuen; Miller, E. C.; Millett;
Mitchell, M. H. F.; Mitford;
Monckton; Monro; (Montagu, E. R.);
(Montagu, Lady M. P. W.);
*Montefiore; Montgomery; Moodie;
Moore, M.; Moore, M. A.; Moore, R.
W. B.; (Mordaunt); (More, H.);
(More, M.); Morgan, M. M.; Morgan,
S. O.; Mortimer, F. L. B.;
Moulding; Mulgrave; Murray, A. M.;
Murray, E. H.; Muter

(Nairne); Neilson; Nevius; Newman,
Mrs. A. E.; Nicholson; Nicol;
Niemeyer; North, M. E.; Noyes;
Nugent, E. G.

O'Connell; O'Gorman; Opie; (Orr);
Osborne, C. I.; Osborne, C. R. S.;
(Ossoli)

Packard; Page, M. A. R.; Paget, G.
T. F. H.; Paine, C.; Paine, S.;
Pakenham; Palliser; Palmer, P. W.;
Palmer, S. A.; Palmer, S. L.;
Palmerton; Pardoe; Parker, A. R.;
Parker, E. M. B. W.; (Parris,
Mary); Parry, F.; Peake; Pearson,
E. M.; Pease, L.; Pease, M. L. A.;
Pepys; Perrier; Petherick; Philip;
Piatt; Pickford; (Piozzi); Platt,
Mrs. L. L.; Plunkett; Polehampton;

Poole, S. L. ; Porter, M. E.;
Porter, R.; Post; Potter, E.;
Power; Powers; Proctor; Putnam

(Quincy)

Radcliffe, A.; Ramsay, C. H.;
Ramsey; Rankin, Mary; Rankin,
Marinda; Reagh; Redford; Reeve, B.
J.; Rennie; Richards, A. M.;
Richards, E. B.; Richardson, E. S.;
(Riske); Ritchie, A. C. O. M.;
Robertson, H. W.; Robertson, J.;
Robinson, E. L.; Robson; Roden;
Rogers, E. M.; Rogers, M. E.;
Rolleston; Ropes; Russell, F.

Satchell; Schimmelpennick; Scott,
A. E.; Scott, A. M. S.; (Scott, J.
H. K.); Searle; Sedgwick; Seebohm;
(Seton); Sewell, E. M.; Seymour, M.
S.; Sharp; Sheil; Shepherd, M.;
Sherwood, M. M. B.; Shirreff, M.
R.; Shuck; Sigourney; Simpson, M.
E.; Sinclair, O.; Smith, A. C.;
Smith, M. A. P.; Smith, M. E. V.
C.; Smith, S. E. D.; Smythe;
Somerset, H.; Somerville, M.F.;
Southall; Southern Lady; Southwell;
Speid; Spencer, Mrs. C.; Squirrell;
*Stanley, C.; Stanley, L. A.;
*Stanley, M. J. H.; Stannard, M.;
Stenhouse; Stephenson, E. T.;
Stewart, E. B.; Stone, L. W.;
Stowe; Strangford; (Stuart, Lady
A.); *Stuart, Lady L.; Stuart, S.
M. J.; Stuart-Wortley; Sturt;
*Sutherland, H. E. G. L. G.;
Sutherland, Mrs.; Sweat; Swinton
Taylor, Elizabeth; Taylor, F. M.;
(Taylor, H. H.); (Taylor, J.);
Tenison; (Thompson, E. M. L.);
Thompson, E. W.; Thompson, J. C.;
Thomson, C.; Thomson, F. M.;
Thornton, A.; Toase; Tobin;
Tollemache; Trench, M. M. F.;
(Trench, M. C. S. G); *Trevelyan;
Trotter; Tuckett; Tuthill

Urbino

Vauches; Victor, F. A. F. B.;
Victoria; Viele

W., E. A.; Waddell; Wade;
Wakefield, S. F.; Walker, M. A. R.;
Wallace, E. D.; Wallis, M. D. C.;
Wanton; Ward, E. G. E.; Ward, H.;
Ward, M. N.; Waters; Watson, E. H.;

Watson, R.; Watts, A. M. H.; Weitbrecht; Welby-Gregory; Wells, E. C. R.; Weppner; West, M. A.; (Westminster, E. E. G.); Weston, A.; Westropp; Whately, M. L.; Whitall, A. B.; White, M. A. D.; Whiting; Wilder; Willard, Mrs. F. J.; Willard, M. E.; Williams, J. P.; Williams, M. N.; Wilson, J. A.; Winslow, M. F.; Winter; Wood, C.; Wood, J. R.; Woodruff; Woods, C. K.; Woodward; Woolsey; Woolson; Wordsworth; Wright, Eliza; Wright, H. M.; Wright, S. A.; Wyatt; Wynn, C. W.; Wynn, F. W.

Young, A. E. W.; Young, M. P.

1876-1899

Abbott, E.; Abbott, K. M.; Aberdeen and Temair; (Abington); Ackerman; (Adams, A. S.); Adams, B. A. S.; Adams, E. H.; Adams, M. R. C.; Adams, M. S.; Agnew, A.; Aiken; Alcott; Aldrich; Alexander, Esther F.; Alexander, Evelyn E; Alice Maud Mary; Allan-Olney; Alleman; Allen, H. H. S.; Allen, H. T.; Allen, M. S.; Alsop; Ambrosi; Ames, J. A.; Andrew, J.; Andrewes; Ansell; Antin; (Arblay); Archer; Arms; Armstrong, C. C.; Armstrong, I. J.; Arrington; Arundell; Atkins; Atkinson, L. H.; (Austen); Austin, E. M.; Austin, J. G.; Avery

Bacon, G. M. W.; (Bagshawe); Bailey, F. A. M.; Bainbridge; Baird; Baker, C. A.; Baker, F. J.; Baker, H. N. W.; Baldwin; Balfour; Ballin; Bancroft; Banim; Banks; Barber, J. L.; Barkly; Barnwell; Bateham; Bates, E. K.; Bathgate; Baxter, K. S.; Baxter, L. E. B.; (Bayard); Bayley; Beamish; Beaumont; Beckett; Beecher, E. W. B; Beers; Beesley; Bell, G. M. L.; Bennett, A. R. G.; Bensly; Benson, M. E.; Bentley; Benton, L.; Benton, R. A.; Berger; Berlyn; Besant; Bianciardi; Bickerdyke; Bickersteth, M. J.; Bishop, I. L. B.; Bishop, S. O.; Bixby; Blackall; Blackford; Blackwell, E.; Blackwood; Blake, M. J.; Blake, M. E.; Blake, M. E. M.; Blakeney; Blankenship; Blennerhassett;

(Blessington); Bloomer; Bloomfield; Blunden; Blunt, A. I. N.; Blunt, F. J. S.; Bond, C.; Boobbyer; Booth; Bothmer; Botta; Bottome; (Bowne); Bowyer; Boyd, O. B.; Boykin; Brain; Braithwaite; Brandreth; Brassey; Bray; Bremner; Bridges; Briggs; Brittan; Brook; Brooks, A. M.; Brooks, S. M.; Broome; Broughall; Brown, Miss; Brown, L.; Brown, M.; (Browning, E. B.); Browning, H. E.; Bryce; Buck; Buckhout; Buckland; (Bulfinch); Bumpass; Bunsen; Burdette; Burgess, E.; Burgess, M.; Burnham; Burns; Burton; Burwell; Bussing; Butler, A. R.; Butler, J. H.; Butler, J. E. G.; Buxton, C. E.; (Buxton, H. G.); Byrne

Caddy; Cake; (Calderwood); (Caldwell); Campbell, G. E. B.; Canary; Carbutt; (Carlyle); Carpenter, M. T.; Carr, A. V. S.; Carrothers; Carter, M. B.; Cary, A. M.; (Cary, M.); Caswell; (Catley); Cazneau; Chace; Champney; Chapin; Chaplin; Chapman; Charles; Chase; Chatterton; Cheever; Chennells; Chickering; Child, L. M. F. Churchill, C. M. N.; Churchill, E. K.; Cisneros; Clapp; (Clark, L. F. S.); Clark, S. C.; Clarke, M. V. N. C.; Clarke, O. C.; Clarke, Mrs. S.; Clough, A. J.; Cobb, P. H. S.; Cobbe; Cochnower; Cochrane; (Coit); (Coke, J. W. H.); (Coke, M.); Coker; Colenso; Collier; Collins, E. M. S.; Collins, L. G.; Collins, N. J. H.; Collis; Colman; Colvile; Comerford; Comstock; Cone; Conner; Constaple; Conway; Cooke, B. B.; Cooke, S.; Cooper, A. J. H.; Corbet; Cornaby; Corner; Cort; Coston; Cotterell; Coulomb; Cowell, E. S.; Cowper, K. C. C.; Craik; Crane; Craven, P. M. A. A.; Crawford, C. H.; Crawford, I. A. H.; Crawford, L.; Crommelin; Crosby; Crosland; Crosse; Crowley, J. M. C.; Cumming; Cusack; Cushman, C. S.; Custer; Cuthell

Dahlgren; Dall; Daly, H. W.; Daly, M. A.; Darling, F. A.; (Darling, G. H.); David; Davies, B. W.; Davies, E.; Davis, S. M. H.; Day, S. D.; Dean; Deane; Dean, M. A.; Deering; De Fonblanque; Deland; Delaney; De La Warr; De Morgan; Dempster; De

Navarro; Denison; Denney; Dent; De Vere; (Devonshire, G. S. C.); Dickey; Dickins; Dickinson, A. E.; Dickinson, E. E.; Dillingham; Diven; Divers; Dix; Dixie; Dobbs; Dodd; Dodge, E. A. P.; Donner; Doolittle; Dorr; Douglas, L. J.; Doyle; Drew; (Drinker); Drumgoold; (Duane); Dudley, L. B.; Dufferin and Ava; Duffy; Duniway; Dunlop, A. H.; Dunlop, F. A. W.; Dunn; Dutton, A. R. K.; Dyer, C. C. J.; Dyer, Mrs. D. B.; Dyer, F. J.; Dyer, L.

Eastlake; Eastman, E. G.; Eckley; Edgcumbe; (Edgeworth); Edmonds; Edward, E.; Edwardes; Edwards, A. A. B.; Edwards, M. B. B-; Eells; Egerton of Tatton; Eickemeyer; Eldred; Elizabeth; (Elizabeth of England); Ella; Ellerslie; Elliott, E. W.; Elliott, F. M. D.; Ellis, Mrs. C.; Ellis, E.; Ellis, E. F.; Ely, A. M.; Emerson, J. M.; Emery; English; Escombe; Evans, M.; (Eve); Evens

Fahys; Faithfull; Falls; Fay, A.; Feilden; (Ferrier); Feudge; Fielde; Fields; (Fiennes); Fish; Fisher, F. E.; Fitzgibbon; Fletcher, M.; (Fletcher, M. J. J.); Foley; Foote, J. A. J.; Forbes, A. K.; Forbes, M. P.; Ford; Forde; Formby; Foster, A.; Fox, C.; (Frampton); Frances; Francis; Fraser, A.; Fraser, M.; Fraser, M. C.; Frazar; Fremont; French, Maria; Friend; Frink; (Frost); (Fry, E. G.); Fuller, E. L.; Fullerton, G. C. L.; Fulton; Furley

Galletti di Cadhilac; Galpin; Gamewell; Gardner, N. B. B.; Garland; B. F.; Garland, J.; Gay; Gayle; Geary; Gebbie; Geier; Gemmill; Genung; Gibbons, A. H.; Gibson, C.; Gibson, M. A. M.; Giddings; Giffen; Gilbert, L.; Gilchrist; Giles; Gill; Godman; Gollock; Goodwin, E. K.; Goodwin, M. R.; Gordon, E. A.; Gordon, S. A.; Gordon-Cumming; Gowanlock; Grace; Grant, G. G. J.; Grant, J. A.; Grant, M. C. R.; Granville; Gratiot; Gray, E.; Gray, F. B.; Green, A. M. V.; Green, H.; Green, L.; (Greene, M. C. H.); Greenfield; Greenwood; Gregg; Gregory, L.;

Grenfell; Griffing; Griffiths; Grimston; Grimwood; Grinnell; Grose; Grote, S. M.; Guedalla; Guest; Gurney, E. P. K.; Guthrie, E. E.; Guthrie, K. B.; Gwathmey

Hague; Haines; Haldane; Hale; Hall, A. S.; Hall, A.; Hall, F.; Hall, M. G. C.; Hallett; Halsey; Hamer; Hamm; Hammond, M. C. W.; Hammond, N. H.; Hanaford; Hapgood; (Harcourt, A.); Hardin; Hardy, I. D.; Hardy, M. A. M. D.; Harmon; Harper, H.; Harrington; Harris, H. B.; Harris, L.; Harris, M. W.; Harris, M. C.; Hart, A. M. R.; Hart, D.; Haslehurst; Haslewood; Hastings, R. B.; Hauser; Havergal, F. R.; Havergal, M. V. G.; Haviland; Hawes, L. W.; Hawksley; (Hawthorne); Hayes, A. M.; Haygood; Hayward, H. C.; Hayward, J. M.; (Heath); Heckford; Heggie; Helm; Hemenway; Henderson, A. P.; Herritt; Herschel; Hervey, H. M.; (Hesketh); Hicks; Hield; Higginson, E. R.; Higginson, M. P. T.; Higginson, S. J. H.; Hill, E. L. C.; Hill, M. C.; Hills, C. P.; Hills, M. M. H.; Hills, S. A. L.; Hinkson; Hinsdale; (Hitchcock); Hitchens; Hoare, A. M.; Hodges; Hodgkin, L. V.; Hodson; (Hogben); Holbrook, M. H.; Holcomb, H. H. H.; Holcomb, N. M.; Holding; Holland; Holley, S.; Holloway; Holme; Holmes, G. K.; Holmes, J.; Holworthy; Holyoke; Hoopes; Hopkins, S. A.; Hopkins, S. W.; Hore; Horner, H.; Houghton; Houser; Houstoun; Howard of Glossop; Howard-Vyse; Howe, J. W.; Howitt, M. B.; (Howland); Hubbard; Hudson; Huggan; Hull; Humbert; Hunt, A.; Hunt, M. E. W.; Hunt, S. M.; Hunter, E.; Hunter, G.; Hunter, J. D.; (Huntington, A. H.); Hurd; Huston, I. P. L.; Huston, M. E.; Hutcheon; Hutchinson, L.; (Hutton)

Immen; Inglehart; Inglis; Ingram; Innes, E.; Ireland

Jackson, H. M. F. H.; Jackson, J. N.; Jacobs, E.; Jacoby; James; (Jameson); Janeway; Jaques; Jardine; Jenner; Jephson; (Jerningham); Jessup; Jewsbury; Johnson, J.; Johnson, L. W.;

Johnson, V. W.; Johnston, E. B.; Johnstone, C. L.; Jones, H. S. C.; Joss; Judd

Kautz; Kay; Keary; Kemble; Kenny; Kent; King, A. L.; King, E. A.; Kingsford; Kingsley, M. H.; Kirby; Klein; Klock; Knight, J. D.; Krout; Kumm

Laird, E.; Lambert; Lane, C. E. L.; Lane, L. S. B.; Lane, P.; Langdon; Langton; Larcom; Lathrop; Lauder; Laurie; Law; Lawrence, C. S.; Layard; Leakey; Lean; Le Blond; Le Breton; Leck; Ledoux; Lee, S. M; (Lefevre); Leage; Lehman; Lehmann; Leigh, F. B.; Leighton; Leitch; Leith; Leland, H. M.; Leland, L.; L'Engle; Le Plongeon; Leonowens; Le Roy; Leslie, M. F. F. S.; Lester; Levick; Lewis, A. S.; Lewis, E. A. M.; Liesching; Liliuokalani; Lillie; Lincoln, M. D.; Lindsey; Linton; Lippincott, M. S. H.; Lippincott, S. J. C.; Littell; Little, A. H.; Little, A. P.; Little, E. N.; Livermore, M. A. R.; (Livingston); Lloyd,, H.; Lloyd, M.; Lobingier; Lockie; Logan, O. L.; Long; Longstreth; Looker; Loomer; Lope; Losee; Lothrop; Loughery; Louthan; Lowdell; Lowe, C. M. S.; Lowe, L.; Lukens; (Lumb); Lutton; Lyall; (Lyman, A. J. R.); Lynch, H.; Lytton, E. V. B. L.; Lytton, R. A. D. W. B. L

McAllister; McCarthy; McClellan; McClurg; McCormick; (M'Cracken); McCrackin; McDougall; McElvaine; McGoodwin; Machardy; Mackin; McKinnon; Mackintosh; McLaren; MacLean, J.; MacLean, M.; McMurphy; MacNaught; McNaughton; McPhelemy; MacPherson, Annie; MacQuoid; (Madison); Maeder; Mains; Mair; Maitland, C. F.; (Malcolm); Marsden; Marshall, A. J.; Marshall, E.; Marston; Martin, A.; Martin, C. W.; Martin, M. P.; Martineau; Martyn; (Mary II); Mason, C. S. A.; Mather; Mathews, M. M.; Matteini; Mauny; Mead; Mendenhall; Meredith; Metcalf; Meyers; Michener; Mifflin; Miller, D. R.; Miller, Elizabeth E.; Miller, Ellen E.; Miller, F. de. C.; Miller, L. E.; Miller, M. C.; Miln; Milner; Miner; Minton;

Mitchell; A. W.; Mitchell, E. H. L.; Mitchell, M.; Mitchell, M. H. F.; Mix; Mixer; Moir, E. B. P.; Moir, J. F. B.; Monck; (Montefiore); Moodie; Moore, A. E.; Moore, A.; Moorman; Mordecai; Morgan, J.; Morrill; Morris, A. A. P.; Morris, A.; Morris, I.; (Morris, S. K.); Morse; Mortimer, M.; Mott; Moulton; Muller; Muhr; Muir, J. A. H.; Mulhall; Murphy, K. A.; Murphy, B. E. M. A. N.; Murray, F. P. S.; Murray, L. L. A.; Murray, M.; Murray-Ansley; Myddleton; Myhill

Neally; Needham; Newcomb; (Newdigate, A. F.); (Newdigate, H.); Newman, Mrs. C. S.; Newton; Nichols, Alice S.; Nichols, L. D.; Nieriker; Nind; Nokes; Normanby; North, M.; Norton, M. B.; Nowell; Nye-Starr

Ober; O'Brien; Ogden; Ogilvie; Oliphant; (Osborn, L. R. D.; (Osborn, S. B.); Osborne, E.; Oswald, E. J.; Otis, H.; Ouvry; Owen, C.; Owen, N. H.

Packard; Packer; Page, P. S. W.; Paget, V.; Palmer, L. A. C.; (Papendiek); Parham; Parker, M E.; Parker, M.; Parker, W.; Parry, C. E.; Parry, E. L.; Parsons,; Paton; Paxson; Pearson, E. M.; Peary; Peattie; Peck; Peel; Pember; Pember-Devereux; Pender; Pennell, E. R.; Pennell, L. C.; Penny; Perkins, M. H.; Pfeiffer; Pfirshing; Phelps, Mrs. A. H.; (Phelps, E. P.); Phibbs; Phillips, D. S. F. A. O.; Phillips, I. O.; Phillips, M. M. A.; Pigott, E. U.; (Pinckney); Pitman, E. R.; Pitman, M. J. D.; Platt, J. H.; Pollard; Pomroy; Poole, A. S.; Porter, M. S. A.; Porter, R.; Potter, L.; (Powys); Prentiss; Prescott; Preston, A. T.; Preston, M. J.; Price, E. C.; Price, H. A. F.; Price, R.; Prichard; Pringle; Pruyn; Pryer

Rains; Rainy; Ramsay, A. D. M.; Rand; Randall; Ratcliff; Rattray; Reed, A. S.; Rees; Reid; Reynolds, L. B.; Rhodes, E. E.; Richards, L. E. H.; Richardson, M. W. F.;

Richings; Rickman; Rideout; Rigden; Ripley, E. M. C. M.; Ritchie, A. I. T.; Roberts, V. C.; Robertson, A. H.; Robinson, L. N. R.; Robinson, L. B.; Robinson, S.; Roche; Roe; Rogers, A. S.; Rollins; Roper; Ross, J. A. D. G.; Ross, Mrs. M.; Roulet; Roundell; Runcie; (Rusell, R. W. V.); Ruthquist; Rutland; Rutledge; (Ryder)

Sagatoo; Salm-Salm; Sanborn, H. J.; Sanborn, K. A.; Sandeman; Sanders; Sandes; Sargent; Saxby, J. M. E.; Schimmelmann; Scidmore; Scott, A. K.; Searing; Semple; Sewall; Seward, O. R.; Sewell, M. W.; Sexton; Seymour, J. W.; Shaw, A. D.; Shaw, E. P. H.; Sheldon, E. M. B.; Sheldon, G. C.; Sheldon, L. V.; Sheldon, M. F.; (Shelley, H. W.); (Shelley, M. W. G.); Shelton; Shepard; Shepherd, M. L.; Sherwood, M. E. W.; Shipley; Shirreff, E. A. E.; (Shore); Simon; Simpson, A. C. M. S.; Simpson, M. E.; Sinclair, Mrs.; Sinclair, O.; Slocum; Smith, A. B.; Smith, A. E. B.; Smith, E. A.; Smith, E. G.; Smith, Georgina; Smith, J.; Smith, J. A. N. C.; Smith, L. A. J. B.; Smith, M. [Am.]; Smith, M. [Br.]; Smyth, F. W.; Snedeker; Snell, M. S.; Soldene; Somerset, S. M. M. S. M.; Somerville, E. A. O.; Sono; South; Southey; Southwick, M. F.; Southwick, S. H.; Spaeth; Spaulding; Speedy; Spencer, A. H.; Spurgeon; Squier; (Stanley, C.); (Stanley, M. J. H.); Stanton; Staver; Stearns; Stevens, Mrs. M.; Stevenson, M. E. G. G. S.; Stevenson, S. Y.; Stewart, E. D.; Stone, M. A. B.; Stone, O. M.; Stonebreaker; Stott; Stowe; Strahan; Straub; Street; Strong; (Stuart, Lady A.); (Stuart, Lady L.); Sturges; Sumner; (Sutherland, H. E. G. L. G.); Sutherland, M. F. S. C. E. S. L. G.; Sweat; Swisshelm; Sykes; Synge

Tadlock; Taylor, A. R.; Taylor, E. M.; (Taylor, J.); Taylor, M.; Taylor, M. G. G.; (Taylor, S. C.);; (Temple); Tennant; Terhune; Teuffel; Tevis; Thacker; Thaxter; Thomas, J. B.; Thomas, J. M.; Thomas, M.; Thompson, Mrs. E. H.;

Thurston; Thwing; Tirard; Trail; Traill; Trench Gascoigne; (Trevelyan); Trollope, F. E. T.; (Trollope, F. M.); Tweedie; Twining; Tyacke; Tyler, J.; Tyler, K. E.; Tyndall

Updike; Upham; Urquhart; Ussher, M. L

Vail; Van Brunt; Van Cleve; Van Cott; Velazquez; Velde; Veney; Vickers; Victor, F. A. F. B.; Victor, S. M.; Villari; Vincent

Wagentreiber; Walden-Pell; Walker, B.; Walker, M. A. R.; Wallace, M. T.; Wallace, S. A. E.; Wallis, N.; Walworth; Ward, E. S. P.; Warne; Warner; Warren, M. B.; Waterbury; Waterfield; Waterman; Waters; Watkins; Watson, A. H.; Watson, L.; Watt, Welch; Weld, A. G.; Weld, A. E. G.; Weldon; Wellesley; Wells, E. M. W.; Wells, S. F.; Welton; Westminster, E. M. L. G. G.; Westmorland; Weston, A. E.; (Weston, M. P.); Wetmore, E. B.; Wetmore, M. B.; Whately, E. J.; Whately, M. L.; (Whitall, A.); White, C. E.; White, E. G. H.; Whiteing; Whitwell; Wilde; Wilkinson, A. M.. G.; Willard, C. M. W.; Willard, F. E.; Williams, R. C.; Williamson; Wills; Wilson, Alice; Wilson, A. L.; Wilson, A. C. M.; Wilson, E.; Wilson, F. H.; Wilson, L. L. W.; Wilson, M. A. C.; (Winslow, A. G.); (Wister); Wittenmyer; Wixon; Wolf; Wood, J. A. S.; Woodbury, J. C. B.; Woodman, A. J.; Woodman, F. C.; Woods, K. T.; Woodworth-Etter; Woolson; (Wordsworth); Workman; Wormeley; Wright, Mrs. C. H. H.; Wright, Emily; Wright, J. M.; Wright, M. R.; Wynn, C. W.

INDEX